MW01115755

UNSONG

Scott Alexander

Edited by Tyler Yeats

Jerusalem is builded as a city that is in the public domain.

—kingjamesprogramming.tumblr.com

Contents

REVELATION

UNSONG

א: Prologue

I.

In retrospect, there had been omens and portents.

("We are now approaching lunar sunrise," said William Anders, "and for all the people back on Earth, the crew of Apollo 8 has a message that we would like to send to you.")

Rivers flowed uphill. A new star was seen in the night sky. A butchered pig was found to have the word "OMEN" written on its liver in clearly visible letters.

("In the beginning, God created the heaven and the earth. And the earth was without form, and void; and darkness was upon the face of the deep.")

Lightning struck in clear weather. Toads fell from the clouds. All ten thousand lakes in Minnesota turned to blood; scientists blamed "phytoplankton."

("And the Spirit of God moved upon the face of the waters. And God said, Let there be light: and there was light. And God saw the light, that it was good: and God divided the light from the darkness.")

A majestic golden eagle flew onto the Vatican balcony as Pope Paul VI was addressing the faithful. The bird gingerly removed the Pontiff's glasses with its beak, then poked out his left eye before flying away with an awful shriek.

("And God called the light Day," said Jim Lovell, "and the darkness He called Night. And the evening and the morning were the first day.")

A beached whale was found hundreds of miles inland. A baby was born with four eyes.

("And God said, Let there be a firmament in the midst of the waters, and let it divide the waters from the waters.")

Pieces of paper with the word "OMEN" written on them fell from the clouds. A beached whale was seen in the night sky. Babies left unattended began to roll slowly, but unmistakably, uphill.

("And God made the firmament, and divided the waters which were under the firmament from the waters which were above the firmament: and it was so. And God called the firmament Heaven. And the evening and the morning were the second day.")

One of the additional eyes on the four-eyed baby was discovered to be the left eye of Pope Paul VI, missing since the eagle incident. The provenance of the fourth eye was never determined.

("And God said, Let the waters under the heaven be gathered together unto one place," said Frank Borman, "and let the dry land appear: and it was so.")

A series of very precise lightning strikes seared the word "OMEN" into the rust-red sand of the Sonora Desert; scientists blamed "phytoplankton."

("And God called the dry land Earth; and the gathering together of the waters called he Seas: and God saw that it was good.")

The New York Stock Exchange rose by perfect integer amounts eleven days in a row. An obstetrician published an article in an obscure medical journal claiming that the kicks of unborn children, interpreted as Morse Code, formed unspeakable and blood-curdling messages.

("And from the crew of Apollo 8, we close with good night, good luck, a Merry Christmas — and God bless all of—" [sudden burst of static, then silence])

II.

If I had to choose a high point for the history of the human race thus far, it would be December 24, 1968.

1968 had been a year of shattered dreams. Martin Luther King was murdered in April. Democratic golden boy Robert Kennedy was killed in June. Soviet tanks crushed the Prague Spring in August. It felt like each spark of hope for a better world was being snuffed out, methodically, one by one.

Then almost without warning, Americans turned on their televisions and learned that a spaceship was flying to the Moon. On December 22, the craft beamed a live TV broadcast to Earth informing viewers that they were about to become the first humans ever to orbit another celestial body. Communications issues limited the transmission to seventeen minutes, but the astronauts promised a second installment from lunar space.

On December 24, 1968, one billion people — more than for any television program before or after in the history of mankind—tuned in for Apollo 8's short broadcast. The astronauts were half-asleep, frazzled with days of complicated calculations and near-disasters—but their voices were powerful and lucid through the static. Commander Frank Borman introduced the two other members of the crew. They described the Moon, as seen up close. "A vast, lonely, forbidding expanse of nothing." "A very foreboding horizon, a rather dark and unappetizing looking place." Then the Earth, as seen from afar. "A green oasis, in the big vastness of space."

Two minutes left till lunar sunrise broke the connection. The astronauts' only orders from NASA had been to "do something appropriate."

"In the beginning," read Bill Anders, "God created the heaven and the earth. And the earth was without form, and void; and darkness was upon the face of the deep."

So for two minutes on Christmas Eve, while a billion people listened, three astronauts read the Book of Genesis from a tiny metal can a hundred miles above the surface of the Moon.

Then, mid-sentence, they crashed into the crystal sphere surrounding the world, because it turned out there were far *fewer* things in Heaven and Earth than were dreamt of in almost anyone's philosophy.

Genesis

Now I've heard there was a sacred word
That Jala said and it named the Lord
A word the angels sing in holy chorus.
It goes like this — a tav, a resh
A fearsome joy, a fervent wish
The Comet King incanting HaMephorash

—Leonard Cohen, "HaMephorash"

Chapter One

Dark Satanic Mills

Jerusalem is builded as a city that is in the public domain.
—kingjamesprogramming.tumblr.com

May 10, 2017
Palo Alto

The apocalypse began in a cubicle.

Its walls were gray, its desk was gray, its floor was that kind of grayish tile that is designed to look dirty so nobody notices that it is actually dirty. Upon the floor was a chair and upon the chair was me. My name is Aaron Smith-Teller and I am twenty-two years old. I was fiddling with a rubber band and counting the minutes until I could go home and seeking the hidden transcendent Names of God.

"AR-ASH-KON-CHEL-NA-VAN-TSIR," I chanted.

That wasn't a hidden transcendent Name of God. No surprise there. During my six months working at Countenance I must have spoken half a million of these words. A computer served them to me as fast as I could speak. I uttered them, checked that nothing happened, then clicked NEXT. Each word took about five seconds, earned me about two cents, and cost a small portion of my dignity. None had been hidden transcendent Names of God.

The timer on my computer said I had four minutes, thirty-three seconds left in the workday. 4:33 was the length and name of John Cage's famous silent musical piece. That makes 273 seconds in all, and –273 is absolute zero in Celsius. Cage's piece is perfect silence; absolute zero is perfect stillness. In the year 273 AD, the two consuls of Rome were named Tacitus and Placidianus; *tacitus* is Latin for "silence" and *placidianus* is Latin for "stillness." 273 is also the gematria of the Greek word *eremon*, which means "silent" or "still." None of this is a coincidence because nothing is ever a coincidence.

God created Man in His own image, but He created everything else in His own image too. By learning the structure of one entity, like the Celsius scale, we learn facts that carry over to other structures, like the Greek language, or the moral law, or my workday. This is the kabbalah. The rest is just commentary. Very, very difficult commentary, written in Martian, waiting to devour the unwary.

A man came up behind me. Tapped me on the shoulder. His suit was gray, his tie was gray, his shirt was that kind of grayish pattern that is designed to look stained so nobody notices that it is actually stained. He motioned me to follow him. I paused the program serving me words to recite. The timer paused with it, stuck at 4:33. Perfectly still.

(This isn't the part that leads to the apocalypse. That part was ten minutes later.)

We sat together in a conference room. He told me his name was Devin. Devin comes from the Irish name Damhain, which means "poet." But it sounds more like Sanskrit *devi*, Latin *divinus*, and English *divine*, all of which mean "godly." Overtly it names an object in the world; secretly, it refers to God. Just like everything else.

"Hi Aaron," he said, in a tone so friendly I was immediately on guard. "How have things been going for you lately?"

Something about him made me resolve to give the least informative answer I could. "Oh, you know," I said. "Up and down."

"Tell me about your role here at Countenance."

"I've been an experimental theologian here for six months."

It's the age when housemaids are "domestic sanitation engineers" and greeters are "directors of first impressions," so of course Countenance calls me an "experimental theologian." My actual position is so low-paid and humiliating that I envy fast food workers. I recite words off a computer screen for eight hours a day, then go home, drink away my sorrows, and come back to do it all again.

People discovered the first few Names of God through deep understanding of Torah, through silent prayer and meditation, or even through direct revelation from angels. But American capitalism took one look at prophetic inspiration and decided it lacked a certain ability to be forced upon an army of low-paid interchangeable drones. Thus the modern method: hire people at minimum wage to chant all the words that might be Names of God, and see whether one of them starts glowing with holy light or summoning an angelic host to do their bidding. If so, copyright the Name and make a fortune.

"Oh, great," said Devin. "And how do you like it?"

In the Book of Job, God takes an innocent man and afflicts him with various curses. First He kills all Job's cattle, sheep, and camels. Then He kills all Job's servants, sons, and daughters. Then He covers Job from head to toe with boils and leprous sores. But — and this is crucial — He never asks Job, "Oh, great, and how do you like it?"

The worst part was that I shouldn't have been here. I was on track to be somebody. I studied kabbalah at Stanford and I was good at it. Great, even. The word "genius" may have been mentioned. Norvig and Raziel's classic textbook says that only four kabbalists have ever gazed upon Adam Kadmon bare. Rabbi Isaac Luria. The Archangel Uriel. The Comet King. And an eight-year-old girl. I won't say I had gazed upon it *bare*, exactly, but in the great game of strip poker every scholar plays against the universe, I'd gotten further than most.

Then I fell from grace. My career was ruined before it even began. I was expelled for messing with Things Mankind Was Not Meant To Know — by which I mean the encryption algorithms used by major corporations. Nobody wanted a twenty-two-year-old kabbalist without a college degree. It was like that scene in the Bible where God manifested Himself upon Mount Sinai, but only to those Israelites who had graduated from Harvard or Yale. So I ended up out here, working minimum wage. Not that I was bitter.

"Oh, you know, it pays the bills," I said.

Devin nodded. "And how's your health?"

It would be a lie to say I stayed sane by keeping my mind sharp. The sort of mental sharpness you need for the kabbalah is almost perpendicular to sanity, more like a very specific and redirectable schizophrenia. I stayed *functional* by keeping my mind in a very specific state that probably wasn't very long-term healthy.

"I can't complain," I said, again thinking of Job.

Devin nodded, then sprung his trap. "Um. I'm here because we heard about an unlicensed use of the Wakening Name three days ago. Uttered directly, not through a scroll. You know anything about this?"

Since he was talking to me, he already knew I did it. He probably also knew that half the people here had done the same, because coffee isn't always enough, and scrolls are expensive if you make $8 an hour. But they hadn't been caught. I had. He didn't have any Names tattooed above his ears, which meant he probably didn't catch me myself. Some higher-up had nabbed me, and he was the human face they sent to do their dirty work. Now my job was to lie and grovel until he agreed it was an uncharacteristic mistake and let me off with a fine or something.

"Yeah," I said. "A couple of days ago. I was really tired, and I knew it was the wrong thing to do, but I wasn't thinking straight and I thought I could save a couple of dollars. I'm not one of those guys who hates UNSONG and does this all the time. I'm really sorry."

"That's good to hear," he said. "I know it can sometimes be tempting to use Names directly," he said. "Especially in a place like this, where you're working hard to develop new Names yourselves. But you get your salary because people use Names the right way. They buy the scrolls from the company that owns them, and use them as directed. It's dangerous to use them yourself, and it's not fair to the people who worked so hard to discover them. Right?"

"Right," I lied and groveled.

"We do need to give you a ticket, even though it's your first offense." He took a little device out of his pocket, pressed some buttons. It printed out a small receipt, which he handed to me. Seventy dollars. A whole day's wages. Not to mention the "threescore and ten years" limit of the Biblical human lifespan, the number of years of God's wrath in Zechariah 1:12, the year AD in which the Second Temple was destroyed, the number of nations into which humankind was scattered after the Tower of Babel, the number of Israelites who entered into the land of bondage in Deuteronomy 10:22, and the number of years that copyright law grants a creator exclusive rights to their work. A bitter, hopeless number.

I was saving a couple hundred bucks a month. With enough time, I could get enough money to supplement loans, maybe find myself another scholarship somewhere else, even a community college would be better than this, make something of myself. And now all that was seventy dollars further away. A minor setback, but still somehow infuriating. Maybe something that put me in the wrong frame of mind, changed how I interpreted what was to come.

"You're probably anxious to get back to work," he said, in a way that clearly gave me permission to leave.

I went back to my cubicle, clicked RESTART on my computer. The timer began counting down again. The computer served me more words to recite. AR-ASH-KON-CHEL-NA-VAN-TSISH. Then AR-ASH-KON-CHEL-NA-VAN-TSIT. Neither one was a hidden transcendent Name of God.

The computer whirred for a second, then gave me some longer candidates.

In general, the longer a Name, the harder to discover but the more powerful its effects. The longest known was the Wrathful Name, fifty letters. When spoken it leveled cities. The Sepher Raziel predicted that the Shem HaMephorash, the Explicit Name which would capture God's full essence and bestow near-omnipotence upon the speaker, would be seventy-two letters.

But combinatorial explosion is a harsh master. There are twenty-two Hebrew letters and so 22^36 thirty-six letter Hebrew words. Even with thousands of minimum-wage drones like myself, it would take millions of years to exhaust all of them. That was why you needed to know the rules. God is awesome in majesty and infinite in glory. He's not going to have a stupid name like GLBLGLGLBLBLGLFLFLBG. With enough understanding of Adam Kadmon, the secret structure of everything, you could tease out regularities in the nature of God and constrain the set of possible Names to something almost manageable, then make your drones chant that manageable set. This was the applied kabbalah, the project of some of the human race's greatest geniuses. The project I should have been a part of. Instead, I was here.

The minutes on the timer ticked down. The words on the computer kept coming. My energy slowly seeped away. The domino whose fall would precipitate the End of Days teetered.

There were twenty-two seconds on the timer when the computer gave me a monster. It started ROS-AILE-KAPHILUTON-MIRAKOI-KALANIEMI-TSHANA-KAI-KAI-EPHSANDER-GALISDO-TAHUN… and it just kept going. Fifty two letters. Two longer than the Wrathful Name. It was the longest Name I'd ever been given to test, by far. I was shocked Countenance would even bother.

I incanted: "ROS-AILE-KAPHILUTON-MIRAKOI-KALANIEMI-TSHANA-KAI-KAI-EPHSANDER-GALISDO-TAHUN…" and just as I finished, my timer reached zero and told me I was finished, for today, free until tomorrow morning crashed down on me and I started the same thing all over again.

"Meh," I said. "Meh. Meh. Meh. Meh. Meh."

That was the part that led to the apocalypse.

I was struck by a wave of holy light. The heavens opened and poured into me. My soul rang like a bell.

Four hundred years earlier, an old man in Prague had explained to his students that yes, you could make a golem, you could bestow upon it the *nefesh*, the animal soul. With sufficient enlightenment, you could even bestow upon it the *ruach*, the moral soul. But the *neshamah*, the divine spark, you could not bestow upon it, for that was a greater work, and would require a greater Name than any ever discovered.

Six thousand years earlier, the wind of God had moved upon the bare red dirt of Eden and shaped clay into the figure of a man. It stood there for a moment, a crude statue, and then a voice from Heaven spoke a Name, and the clay came to life, lumbered into a standing position. It spoke a second Name, and the clay's eyes opened, and within them were innocence and curiosity and the capacity to wonder and learn. And it spoke a third Name, and it was as if a light went on inside of it, and the dust became aware that it was dust and in so doing was dust no longer.

And that third Name was fifty-eight letters long.

It began: ROS - AILE - KAPHILUTON - MIRAKOI - KALANIEMI - TSHANA-KAI-KAI-EPHSANDER-GALISDO-TAHUN...

And it ended: ...MEH-MEH-MEH-MEH-MEH-MEH.

All this I saw, as in a dream or vision. Six months and five hundred thousand nonsense words of pointless suffering, suddenly redeemed. Countenance gave the same words to multiple people, redundancy in case one of them went rogue and decided not to tell them about a discovery. But this was none of their candidate words. This was six syllables longer than any of them. They would never know and I would never tell them. The possibilities swam in front of me, began to take form. This wasn't just a Name. This was the royal road. And it was mine.

I punched out, put on my coat, and left the office. As I walked to the CalTrain station, I tried to calm myself, give my mind the stillness it needed for telepathy to work. Finally, I sent out a feeler.

[Narwhals of Jericho,] I said.

A feeling, something more than silence. Somebody was there.

[Anger,] said an internal voice that was not quite my own, although the telepathic link radiated only love. Then, [Moabite Dick.]

[I hate you,] I thought back, but I sent through a burst of fondness. Ana and I had a running contest to come up with the worst Biblical whale pun. She always won.

[Ana. Something amazing just happened.]

[Yeah?] the other voice asked.

[I bet you I can become emperor of the world within a month. If I win, you have to give me a kiss.]

A feeling of surprise, not my own. Then suspicion. [And what do I get if you can't?]

I hadn't thought that far ahead. [Um. I'll buy you dinner.]

A pause. [No. You're too stingy. You wouldn't promise to buy dinner unless you were sure you could win. So what's going on? Fess up!]

[I'll be home in a few minutes. I'll show you!]

[You know we have choir tonight?]

[I forgot about that. I'll show you afterwards, then.]

[Tabarnacle,] said Ana.

[I will hate you forever,] I thought cheerfully, then stepped onto the CalTrain. The bustle of finding my seat broke the connection, which was just as well.

We would start tonight. By the end of the week, we would have results. By the end of the month, the whole world would have changed. It was so clear to me. It was spread out before me, like Moses' vision of the Promised Land.

"Palo Alto!" announced the train's loudspeaker. "Palo Alto!"

Palo Alto is Spanish for "tall tree." The phrase "tall tree" appears in the Bible, in Daniel 4:10. King Nebuchadnezzar has a dream, and it goes like this:

> *I saw a tall tree out in a field, growing higher and higher into the sky until it could be seen by everyone in all the world. Then as I lay there dreaming, I saw one of God's angels coming down from heaven. And he shouted, "Cut down the tree; lop off its branches; shake off its leaves, and scatter its fruit... For this has been decreed, so that all the world may understand that the Most High dominates the kingdoms of the world and gives them to anyone he wants to, even the lowliest of men!"*

"Palo Alto!" announced the loudspeaker again. "Doors will be closing shortly. Palo Alto!"

This was not a coincidence, because nothing is ever a coincidence.

Interlude ב

The Cracks In The Sky

March 14, 1969
Washington, DC

Richard Nixon was confused and upset.

It wasn't that he hadn't expected problems. He'd only been on the job six weeks, but he knew a president had to be ready for anything. But "anything" was supposed to mean economic downturns, or crime waves, or The Russians.

Instead, Apollo 8 had crashed into some kind of weird space glass, the sky was cracking open, the clouds were forming ominous patterns, and Tuesdays had stopped happening.

The Tuesdays were the most worrying part. For the past three weeks, people all over the world had gone to sleep on Monday and woken up Wednesday. Everything had been in order. The factories had kept running. Lawns had been mowed. Some basic office work had even gotten done. But of the preceding twenty-four hours, no one had any memories.

Today was a Friday, and it had happened three times. The President had gone to sleep Friday night, and woken up Friday morning to a call from the Chief of Staff telling him that everyone was very upset because it was Friday morning again and *how was this happening?* Everything that had happened in the past twenty-four hours had unhappened, been rolled back somehow. Or maybe everyone's Saturday-morning consciousness had been shot back into their Friday-morning bodies. He had no idea, and the American people were starting to demand answers.

He'd called the head of the CIA and asked him to get whatever department full of eggheads had covered up Roswell as a weather balloon, to make them concoct some plausible story for whatever chronological tomfoolery was going on now.

The head of the CIA had just stood there, unflappable. "Mr. President, Roswell *was* a weather balloon. There was no cover-up. Our organization has no department dedicated to covering up inexplicable events."

"I'm the [expletive deleted] President!" Nixon had shouted. "You don't have to lie to me! Get me your cover-up eggheads immediately!"

"I'm sorry Mr. President," he said coolly, "there's no such agency."

"[expletive deleted] [expletive deleted]," Nixon had answered. "Get the [expletive deleted] out of here!"

Then he'd gone to NASA, the Department of Defense, and even the [expletive deleted] National Bureau of Standards, which was apparently in charge of timekeeping and which he hadn't even known [expletive deleted] existed until today. The today before today. Yestertoday. [expletive deleted] [expletive deleted]. None of them had been any more help than the [expletive deleted] CIA.

It was those cracks in the sky. He was sure of it. Apollo 8 had hit *something important*. The eggheads at NASA had posited some kind of "nebulous envelope" surrounding the orbit of the moon, made of "compressed dust and gas." Apollo 8's collision had caused it to "oscillate," creating the pattern of glowing, growing spiderweb cracks visible to anybody who looked up into the night sky.

Richard Nixon didn't believe it, and neither, he figured, did anyone else. If only he could find those people who had covered up Roswell. They would know what to do.

For the past three todays, at 7:38 p.m. sharp, a red phone on his desk had started ringing. This was worrying for two reasons.

First, the red phone was the symbol of the nuclear hotline between the US and Russia, the last-ditch line of communication to prevent a nuclear war.

Second, the red phone was the *symbol* of the nuclear hotline. It was a prop he kept on his desk to show reporters. The actual nuclear hotline connected to a large and foreboding machine at the Pentagon that didn't look nearly as good in pictures. The red phone on his desk wasn't connected to a phone line and, as far as he knew, didn't even have a ringer in it.

The first today it started ringing, he'd stared at it for like three minutes before he finally, dumbly, picked it up. The voice on the other end was saying something he couldn't understand. It occurred to him that the people who monitored the *actual* nuclear hotline probably spoke Russian.

The second today, he'd been suspicious that it would ring again at the same time, so he'd called an interpreter to the Oval Office. At 7:38 p.m., the interpreter had picked it up. "Allo," the interpreter had said, then started looking more and more puzzled. "This isn't Russian," he had said. Then, "This isn't related to any language I know." Then, "I don't think this is a real language." A few hours later he'd sent over an analysis from the State Department, which concluded that the "language" consisted of the names of the capitals of various 16th-century European countries, arranged in seemingly random combinations.

Today today, Nixon hadn't bothered. He just sat in the Oval Office doing work. He had been meeting with a man from the Weather Bureau, who wanted to tell him that the clouds were forming ominous patterns. Nixon hadn't bought it. "I'm the [expletive deleted] President of the United States," he had told the man. "Do you want me to [expletive deleted] tell you if it's a cold front or a warm front?"

The man had clarified that he meant *really* ominous patterns. Like, some big thunderstorms in the Rockies were starting to develop high anvil-like peaks—which was within normal variability for this time of year—but also starting to develop domes and minarets and flying buttresses—which weren't. And although the Doppler radar didn't have good enough resolution to be sure, some of the buttresses were starting to look like they might have gargoyles on them.

And before Nixon could say anything, the man had added that a Category 5 hurricane was forming in the Gulf of Mexico, and it was only March, and this literally *never* happened before July, and something was *really* wrong here...

It was then, at 7:38 p.m., that the red phone started ringing. He considered not picking it up, but at least it would be *differently* confusing.

To his surprise, the voice on the other end now spoke perfect English.

HELLO PRESIDENT NIXON. THIS IS THE ARCHANGEL URIEL. I APOLOGIZE FOR RECENT DISRUPTIONS. THE MACHINERY OF THE UNIVERSE HAS BEEN SEVERELY DAMAGED. I AM WORKING TO CONTAIN THE EFFECTS, BUT AT THIS POINT MY POWER IS LIMITED BECAUSE I AM STILL MOSTLY METAPHORICAL. PLEASE INFORM EVERYONE THAT I REGRET THE INCONVENIENCE. AS COMPENSATION FOR YOUR TROUBLE, I HAVE GIVEN EVERY HUMAN THE ABILITY TO PLAY THE PIANO.

"Wait just a moment here," said Nixon. "Wait just an [expletive deleted] moment!"

No response.

The head of the Weather Bureau stared at the president shouting into a toy red telephone used as a prop for reporters and visibly unconnected to any phone line.

"Excuse me just a minute," said the president.

"Of course," said the bureaucrat.

President Nixon stepped out of the Oval Office and walked downstairs. He went down the corridor connecting the West Wing to the White House proper and entered the East Room, where Franklin Roosevelt's great Steinway piano stood on the hardwood floor.

He sat down on the piano bench and performed a flawless rendition of Bach's Concerto I in D Minor.

"[expletive deleted]," said the president.

Chapter Two

Arise To Spiritual Strife

May 10, 2017
San Jose

Right down the road from Berryessa Station there's a big house with a hidden basement. The people who live there — usually six to eight of us, rarely the same from one month to the next — are the sort of artsy college students and aimless twenty-somethings who think that houses should have names. We call it Ithaca. Six days out of the week it's an ordinary group house, with the ordinary arguments about who has to cook and when the living room is going to get cleaned. But on Wednesday nights, people from all over the Bay Area gather in the basement to perform forbidden rites.

They have many names. Singers. Cantors. Open-sourcerers. They are seekers, rebels, anarchists, Marxist-Lurianists, all the sundry outcasts Ginsberg had called "angel-headed hipsters burning for the ancient heavenly connection to the starry dynamo in the machinery of night." Never mind that the ancient heavenly connection had since been definitively located in a giant hurricane three hundred miles off the coast of Louisiana, or that by this point the machinery of night was pretty much held together with duct tape and bubble gum. They burned still.

One of them stood by the makeshift podium. Her hair was in something that made mohawks look conservative, and although you couldn't see it now, she had the musical-note symbol of the Singers tattooed on her shoulder. She was Valerie Lowry, our fearless leader and the editor of the *California Chorister* alternative newspaper. Also the leaseholder for our group home. Also Ana's cousin. She was chatting with a guy in a leather jacket, but she lit up when she saw me.

"Aaron!" she said. "I was worried you wouldn't make it!"

"Work was kind of crazy today," I said. "And the CalTrain was delayed in Palo Alto for like ten minutes, for kabbalistic reasons."

Valerie was used to this sort of commentary from me. She shot me a smile and turned back to the guy in the leather jacket.

On the other side of the room I spotted Ana Thurmond, love of my life and partner in Biblical whale pun telepathy. She was reading a book and pretending to ignore everybody, while actually shooting me psychic commentary about some of the celebrants. [Oh no,] she thought at me, as Bill Dodd and Karen Happick came through the door arm in arm, [they've finally started dating. God help them both.]

Before I had time to reply, Valerie had taken the podium and called the meeting to order. She always started with a short sermon, and today it began with a poem. "The Present Crisis," by James Russell Lowell:

Once to every man and nation comes the moment to decide,
In the strife of Truth with Falsehood, for the good or evil side;
Some great cause, God's new Messiah, offering each the bloom or blight,
Parts the goats upon the left hand, and the sheep upon the right,
And the choice goes by forever 'twixt that darkness and that light.

The poem was from the 1840s; the titular present crisis was the impending Civil War. But some things never change.

Hast thou chosen, O my people, on whose party thou shalt stand,
Ere the Doom from its worn sandals shakes the dust against our land?
Though the cause of Evil prosper, yet 'tis Truth alone is strong,
And, albeit she wander outcast now, I see around her throng
Troops of beautiful, tall angels, to enshield her from all wrong.

At this point I couldn't help stealing a glance at the lone angel in the room. Ziniel was certainly tall and beautiful, but now he had a kind of awkward deer-in-the-headlights look, as if he was worried somebody was going to ask him to enshield them from all wrong and he wasn't going to know what to do.

Careless seems the great Avenger; history's pages but record
One death-grapple in the darkness 'twixt old systems and the Word;
Truth forever on the scaffold, Wrong forever on the throne,—

Yet that scaffold sways the future, and, behind the dim unknown,
Standeth God within the shadow, keeping watch above his own.

There was something about James Russell Lowell that made him perfect for the counterculture. Truth forever on the scaffold, Wrong forever on the throne. The system was evil. If it were not evil, it would not be the system. The persecuted are righteous; if they were not righteous, they would not be persecuted. Ana was the Augustine Distinguished Scholar in Theodicy at Stanford and she hated this stuff.

We see dimly in the Present what is small and what is great,
Slow of faith how weak an arm may turn the iron helm of fate,
But the soul is still oracular; amid the market's din,
List the ominous stern whisper from the Delphic cave within,—
"They enslave their children's children who make compromise with sin."

"Yes," said Valerie, and her voice reverberated through the crowded basement. "They enslave their children's children who make compromise with sin."

Then she began her sermon.

She talked about the United Kingdom of Great Basin. Last week, a choir of Singers much like our own had been meeting peacefully in a home in Reno, someone had tipped off UNSONG, and the men in black had come for them. It should have been much like my own confrontation earlier that day. Lectures. Maybe some arrests, followed by short trials, followed by fines or probations. Or who knows? Maybe they would have tried to make an example of them. It didn't matter, because someone had spoken the Tempestuous Name. One of the congregants? Acting on reflex when he saw the door shatter to splinters and a dozen men point guns at him? He spoke the Tempestuous Name, and then the guns started shooting, and by the time it was over two UNSONG agents and eleven Singers were dead. The biggest disaster to hit our movement since Reverend Stevens' death, maybe. And the worst part would be that the government wouldn't apologize. Not Great Basin, and certainly not UNSONG. They'd blame the whole thing on the Singers, plaster the news with pictures of the two slain agents, and crack down on us twice as hard.

And Valerie spoke about this, and spoke well. She hit all the stops. She talked about how grief-stricken we were as part of the global body of Singers, and how enraged we were as Untied States citizens. She talked about how we must stand courageously and not let this break our resolve. She even made a token reference on how we must not let this turn us to violence, even though she kind of liked violence and it was hard for her to say it convincingly.

"I can't tell you what to feel," she concluded. "All I can say is that they knew what they were getting into. And so do we. We swore to spread the thousand thousand Names of God. And even though I can't tell you the same won't happen here, I can promise the church leadership is doing everything it can to ensure that it won't. So a few words about security from our choir director, Brother Aaron."

Yes. God help me, I was supposed to offer words on security. Me, the guy who had gotten a $70 fine earlier that day for using a Divine Name to wake myself up because the coffee pot was empty.

I strode confidently to the front of the assembly.

"Hi," I said. "I'm Brother Aaron. The short version of our safety plan is that we are going to be extremely boring and do everything by the book and not stand out or draw attention to ourselves in any way."

("Hi," I said in my imagination. "I'm Aaron Smith-Teller. I know we're not supposed to give out our full name at choir, but since you know where I live and what I look like, it's kind of silly to haggle over full names, isn't it? We should probably stop pretending that our cute little Alcoholics Anonymous game gives any real protection. If UNSONG ever really wants us, we're all fucked.")

"Whenever you use a protected Name of God," I continued, "UNSONG agents with the Sentinel Name tattooed above their ear, and the Names involved tattooed on their foreheads, can track your location. In practice they rarely do, because a million people do that every day and they don't have a million agents or a million jail cells to put people in. But if a dozen people use all sorts of Names in the same spot every day, they know it's a place where Singers hang out, and then if they're bored then they come and raid you. This is probably what happened in Reno."

("We have no idea who UNSONG can and can't track," I said in my imagination. "The Reno choir wasn't stupid enough to consistently use Names in their hideout because no one is that stupid. So something else went wrong. We could do everything by the book and all get arrested tomorrow.")

"So," I said, "here are some things you can do if you're an idiot who wants to be caught. You can use Names in your own house. You can use

Names here. You can use a Name in the same spot multiple times. And you can use a really new Name that lots of bigwigs care about."

("So," I said in my imagination, "here are some things I have done multiple times. Used Names I have no idea what they do. Used Names in ways that caused giant catastrophes. Used the same Name that caused a catastrophe again, just to see if it would magically work the second time, which it never does. Been something like the third person on Earth to use a Name, one I didn't even need, just for the adrenaline rush and street cred.")

"Last," I said, "remember that we can limit any damage that happens. UNSONG's got to operate within the law. No one can torture you or force information out of you. They can't even silence you without a court order. As soon as you realize you're in trouble, sing yourself the Confounding Name and forget all about us. If that doesn't work, reveal one of our false leads to them. They'll go in, see the evidence we planted, and figure we got spooked and abandoned it just before they arrived."

("Last," I said in my imagination, "Director-General Bentham is by all accounts terrifying, and it's really easy here in our nice safe basement to say that they can't torture you, but someone in Reno said something and I don't know why. The fact that we left a couple of old books and CDs in an abandoned factory might or might not fool UNSONG's finest, but I wouldn't want to have to be the shmuck who tests it.")

"Oh," I added. "If worst comes to worst, and secret police burst through those doors right when I finish talking, no Tempestuous Name, please. Better we all get a couple years in jail for criminal copyright infringement than die."

(I said the same thing in my imagination, only more condescendingly.)

"We will now begin choir practice."

Fifty years ago, Apollo 8 cracked the sky open and people started discovering the Names of God. A decade later, corporations started patenting them, demanding license fees for anyone who wanted to work miracles with them. A few years after that, they codified the whole system into international law and created UNSONG—the United Nations Subcommittee On Names of God—to enforce it.

And a few years after that, people started asking: why are we allowing this? Everything we know about God suggests that He loves all humans and is not a fan of the rich getting richer. First came Reverend Stevens and his book. Then came the political movement, growing out of local churches that insisted that God loved everyone alike and therefore everyone alike must know His Names. And finally, when every legitimate avenue of resistance had been crushed, there came groups like ours, stealing what Names we could find and teaching them to one another in dark forests or hidden basements. Spreading the illegal knowledge in preparation for... well... okay, the endgame wasn't exactly our strong point. Reverend Stevens had said that once enough people knew the Names, it would spark a revolution in consciousness, an immanentization of the eschaton as the holy essence reverberated within the minds of all life. Sure. Let's go with that.

Then a series of disasters destroyed the US federal government, and UNSONG had expanded its authority proportionately to become the highest law in the land. But the backlash and the revolution were coming any day now, we told ourselves. *Any day now.*

I was not a revolutionary by temperament. But after getting expelled from Stanford, and taking minimum wage jobs to make ends meet, and being treated like scum by everyone in academic kabbalah, well, here all I needed to do was have some basic familiarity with the Names, know a couple of impressive-sounding things about Schachter permutations, and I was Choir Director and a leading scientific authority. That felt good. And given all that the big theonomics companies had done to me, helping screw them over was icing on the cake. My life was already in the toilet. The same self-destructive urge that had led me to use the Wakening Name at work bound me here to Valerie and her people.

"Tonight," I said, "we're going to practice something very special. This is the Vanishing Name. Has anyone heard of the Vanishing Name before?"

No one raised their hands.

"That's because it was discovered three weeks ago," I told them, to multiple ooooohs and aaaaahs. "Fresh meat. A sweatshop in Pittsburgh picked it up, and somehow it got leaked to a choir in Cleveland, and they were able to break the klipah and send letters to a dozen choirs around the country within fifteen days of discovery."

I was pretty sure that some of my own work in klipotic reversal algorithms had contributed, but I resisted the urge to boast.

"What does the Vanishing Name do? It's no less than a form of teleportation! Speak the Name, and you disappear and reappear somewhere else within a few hundred miles. According to my sources one of the test subjects in Pittsburgh ended up in Akron, and another one in Erie. The precise range is unknown, and the destination doesn't seem to be under voluntary control. Hence the label. It's useful for getting out of a situation, but not necessarily getting into one. Useful for, for example, underground choir members in exactly the types of problems we're hoping to avoid.

"So what's the catch to this seemingly astounding discovery? First, the Vanishing Name teleports you to a situation complementary to the one you were trying to get out of. Both of the testers in Pittsburgh, for example, ended up in laboratories devoted to the testing of kabbalistic Names. So there you are in a laboratory testing a kabbalistic Name in Pittsburgh, and you speak the Name, and you end up in a laboratory testing a kabbalistic Name in Akron.

"This creates an obvious limit to its usefulness. I've been corresponding with the director of a choir in San Antonio. She was in the bad part of town and got accosted by hooligans. So she spoke the Vanishing Name. It teleported her to the bad part of Austin, where another band of hooligans was looking for someone to accost. She used the Name a second time, and ended up back in San Antonio with the first group of hooligans, because the complement of the situation's complement is just the original situation. So she went secular and used her pepper spray. The lesson is clear. Additional uses of the Vanishing Name are unlikely to gain you very much. Any questions?"

There were none.

"Second, and this relates to what I said before. I don't need to remind you that using this Name would be really stupid. It's new. UNSONG is looking for it. You're learning this name because it is your duty as a Singer and a human being to learn and spread the thousand thousand Names of God. Unless you're in a situation where it is absolutely vital to your well-being and continued survival that you be accosted by a different band of hooligans than the ones who are currently accosting you, this name should be considered UNSONG-bait and therefore verboten. Do you understand?"

The congregation understood.

"Very well," I said. "Let us learn the Vanishing Name."

There were twenty-eight of us there; twenty-seven humans plus Ziniel. Angels cannot sing the Names, and only twenty of the humans were up for participating. The rest were there for moral support, political debates, some sort of sad countercultural version of networking, or the free refreshments afterwards. So I led the way and nineteen voices followed.

The Names of God are long, apparently meaningless, and hard to remember. I don't know who first figured out that if you sing them to a melody, they'll stick with you longer, but so they do. That's why we call it choir practice, why I'm choir director, why the people who learn the Names are called Singers and Cantors. The twenty of us joined together in song.

"Asat!" I sang.

"ASAT!" echoed nineteen voices.

"Zam!"

"ZAM!"

"Rush!"

"RUSH!"

"Asat-zam-rush!"

"ASAT-ZAM-RUSH!"

[You're going to finish this quickly, skip the food, and tell me how you'll become World Emperor soon, right?]

[Shhhh! I'm trying to concentrate!]

[The Gospel according to Fluke.]

[...um... Epistle to Philemonstro. Also, @#$% you.]

"Asat-zam... sorry... where were we? ...Asat-zam-rush-shan-sever-las-kyon-dal-athen-try-kophu-li-mar-lethag-day!"

"ASAT-ZAM-RUSH-SHAN-SEVER-LAS-KYON-DAL-ATHEN-TRY-KOPHU-LI-MAR-LETHAG-DAY!"

This was not the Vanishing Name. It didn't really end with *day*, and it didn't quite start with *asat*. If you sang a Name straight out, you'd invoke it, and then depending on which Name it was you'd end up teleporting to a choir three towns over, or summoning a tempest, or destroying a city.

So in order to communicate a name without activating it, you needed to sing something that was almost, but not quite, the real Name. A transformation. One you could easily perform and reverse at will.

There was already one such transformation well-known to every red-blooded American.

It was strange and almost sacrilegious. But every week we returned. UNSONG and the theonomic corporations couldn't be allowed to whore out the Names of God unchallenged. A revolution was coming, and we were going to be ready for it. Nobody was going to get a monopoly on the Divine without fighting for it.

And that was why every Wednesday night a few dozen people would meet in secret in a San Jose basement and sing the hidden transcendent Names of God in Pig Latin.

Interlude ג

The Code of the World

"The Code of the World," by Aaron Smith-Teller
Published in the March 2017 issue of the *California Chorister*

The Talmud says that God created the Torah nine hundred seventy-four generations before He created the world. Generations of who, I don't know. The Talmud is kind of crazy.

But the Torah is basically a few short stories about Creation and the distant past followed by a long and intricate biography of Moses. Why would God care so much about one Israelite guy that He would lovingly sketch out his story long before the first day rose upon the universe in which that guy was to live?

There's another episode in the Talmud, one where Moses is ascending Mt. Sinai to receive the Torah. God discusses how carefully He wrote the Torah over countless eons, and the angels say—then why are you giving it to this Moses guy? Who's he? Some random mortal nobody! We're angels! Give it to us! Moses argues that the people of Israel are sinful and so need it more. The angels accept his reasoning.

But this argument is less interesting for what it says than for what it leaves out. Moses *doesn't* say, "Uh, guys, have you even *read* the Torah? Four of the five books are totally about me, personally. There's even a section describing how God gives me the Torah, *in* the Torah. How can you challenge my right to have my own biography?"

The rabbis explain this by dividing "Torah" into the historical Torah, meaning the records of Moses' life—and the legal Torah, meaning the ritual code. God wrote the legal Torah beforehand. The angels wanted the legal Torah for themselves. But that doesn't work either. Take a look at the legal Torah and it's all sorts of rules about which kinds of animals to eat and which close relatives are too close to have sex with. This also seems like the sort of thing you don't necessarily need to have finished 974 generations before you create the world. And it also seems like the sort of thing that angels don't have to worry about. So what's up?

Before I propose an answer, a survey of some apparently unrelated fields.

Cosmic history begins deep in the past, but shortly after the Big Bang the universe cooled down long enough to allow *mass* and the breaking of symmetry into the laws of physics.

Natural history begins deep in the past, but goes into high gear billions of years ago with the appearance of *mitosis*, the replication process which allowed the reproduction and evolution of all subsequent life. Mitosis replicates and preserves the "genetic code" of DNA which determines animal phenotype.

Human history begins deep in the past, but goes into high gear after the rise of the *Mesopotamians*, history's first civilization. Shortly afterwards, they develop the Code of Hammurabi, ancestor of all the law codes and all the states and governments that came afterwards.

American history begins deep in the past, but goes into high gear after the American Revolution starts in *Massachusetts*. Shortly afterwards, the Americans ratify the Constitution, the law of the land.

Each of these apparently unrelated forms of history starts deep in the past, but experiences a sudden phase change marked by the letters M-S-S in that order, followed shortly by the establishment of a code of laws.

So when we find that the Bible begins with the creation of the world, but experiences a phase change marked by a man named *Moses*, and then the giving of the Law on Mount Sinai, maybe we should interpret this as being about a little bit more than just one guy.[1]

Norvig and Raziel define kabbalah as "hidden unity made manifest through patterns of symbols," and this certainly fits the bill. There is a hidden unity between the structures of natural history, human history, American history, Biblical history, et cetera: at an important transition point in each, the symbols M-S-S make an appearance and lead to the imposition of new laws. Anyone who dismisses this as coincidence will soon find the coincidences adding up to an implausible level.

[1]Moses was supported in his mission by his brother *Aaron*, who is significant among kabbalists for bearing the Shem HaMephorash on his forehead. Mass is carried by *baryons*. In mitosis, DNA is helped along by its relative *RNA*. The Mesopotamians were trading partners and allies with their relatives across the Tigris in *Iran*. Massachusetts was ably defended by the New England branch of the Continental Army led by Benedict *Arnold*.

The kabbalistic perspective is that nothing is a coincidence. We believe that the universe is fractal. It has a general shape called Adam Kadmon, and each smaller part of it, from the Byzantine Empire to the female reproductive system, is a smaller self-similar copy of that whole. Sometimes the copies are distorted, like wildly different artists interpreting the same theme, but they are copies nevertheless.

For example, consider the objection that Chinese history does not fit the pattern. Yes, it starts in the beginningless past and transitions into a more civilized form with the arrival of a lawgiver, but that lawgiver is named Confucius, and there is no M-sound-followed-by-two-S-sounds in his name. A sign that the structure has failed? No. Confucius gave the laws, but they did not achieve prominence until they were recorded and interpreted by his successor *Mencius*. The narrative and phonological aspects have been split into two closely related people.[2]

Other times two separate people in the Bible get merged into a single character. Consider Moses and Adam. Moses leads the Israelites to freedom, destroys the Egyptian army by crossing the Red Sea, gets the Commandments, and serves as the first leader of the Israelite people. Adam transgresses his Heavenly Father's commandment not to touch a fruit tree.

But in American history, both these aspects are merged into the person of George Washington. It is Washington who leads the Americans to freedom, destroys the British army by crossing the Delaware, gets the Constitution, and serves as the first leader of the American people. But it is also Washington who transgresses his father's command not to touch a fruit tree. Further, the Adamic and Washingtonian stories are subtly different: Adam tries to deflect blame ("It was the woman who bade me eat") but Washington humbly accepts it ("I cannot tell a lie, Father, I cut down the cherry tree"). Thus Israel is born fallen, but America is born pure, a "shining city on a hill."[3]

Here we also see the same division between semantic and phonetic[4]

[2]The R-N word associated with Confucius is clearly *ren*, his concept of benevolence, which plays a preeminent part in his *Analects*. The *Analects* themselves are cognate with mass's complement *energy*, mitosis's *anaphase*, Mesopotamia's *Anunnaki*, and Arnold's *Canada* campaign.

[3]The original "city on a hill" was Jerusalem, with its Temple upon Mt. Moriah. As per the Bible, King David bought the Temple site for 600 shekels and King Solomon decorated it with 600 talents of gold; King Herod later rebuilt it 600 feet by 600 feet in size. The name of America's capital Washington is followed by "DC," which is Roman gematria for 600.

[4]We can analyze the name "George Washington" as follows: "George" means "farmer" in Greek, which is clearly related to the name "Adam" meaning "dirt" in Hebrew; Adam was banished from Eden and sentenced to "till the dirt from which he was made." "Washing"

aspects as in the Confucius example: Washington's successor was named "Adams." Note that the Biblical Adam was created beside the Tree of Knowledge, and John Adams was born in Braintree.

Other correspondences are spread even further afield. Moses' wife was named Zipporah, Hebrew for "female bird," but her American counterpart doesn't show up until LBJ. It took all the way until the turn of the millennium before America listened to a bush and then got stuck wandering in a desert without an exit strategy.

Twist and stretch as it may, the underlying unity always finds a way to express itself. If you're a science type, think of the cells in the human body. Every cell has the same genes and DNA, but stick one in the brain and it'll become a brain cell; stick it in the skin and it'll become a skin cell. A single code giving rise to infinite variety. If you don't understand the deep structure they all share, you'll never *really* understand brains or skin or anything else.

The Torah is the deep structure of the universe, and "structure" is exactly the word for it. It's pure. Utterly formal. Meaningless on its own. But stick it in a situation, and its underlying logic starts to clothe itself in worldly things. Certain substructures get expressed, certain others shrivel away. Certain relationships make themselves known. Finally, you get a thing. Box turtles. International communism. Africa. Whatever. If you're not looking for the structure, you won't find it. If you are, it's obvious.

At the crucial moment in the Hebrew Bible, a man named Moses is born, ordains new laws, and changes the destiny of Israel. If you're a Biblical Hebrew, then to you that's the Torah. If you're an angel, the Torah is something different. And if you're God 974 generations before the creation of the world, the Torah is all of these things and none, just a set of paths and relationships and dependencies pregnant with infinite possibilities. A seed.

Understand the seed, and you understand everything that grows from it. This is the kabbalah. The rest is just commentary. Super-important commentary. The kind of commentary that's the difference between a sloughed-off skin cell and a thinking brain.

means "to place under water" in English, which mirrors "Moses," meaning "to draw out of the water" in Hebrew. But "washing" also means "to cleanse," and "ton" means town referring to the polis or state. So "George Washington" references similarities with both Adam and Moses, but also contains an additional meaning of "the one who cleanses the state," i.e. purifies it from corruption and foreign influences.

Chapter Three

On A Cloud I Saw A Child

September 29, 1990
Gulf of Mexico

Ever since the sky cracked there has been a hurricane off the coast of Louisiana that never moves or decays. In its eye stands the Archangel Uriel. He is five hundred feet tall, and around him whirl colorful streams of letters from every alphabet and syllabary and abjad of every culture in history, making subtle and complex geometric patterns before they disappear in bursts of rainbow light. Occasionally he reaches out and snatches one with his colossal hand and inserts it elsewhere in the stream, and then rain falls, or empires crumble, or new islands rise from the deep. Today he is doing none of those things. Today he is looking very carefully at something no one else can see, and talking to himself.

TIFERET, he says. THE SUN, BEAUTY, MIRACLES. BUT ALSO REVERSAL. A MIRROR SET AT THE CENTER OF THE TREE, REFLECTING WHATEVER IT SEES. He stares more intently now. A PULSE OF ENERGY FROM BINAH TO CHESED, THEN A RETURN PULSE FROM CHESED TO BINAH. THE LETTER KUF. BUT DOUBLED. REFLECTED. Now he pauses. SOMETHING IS MISSING. TIFERET ARCING DOWNWARD TO NETZACH. A YUD. TWO KUFS REFLECTED ABOUT A YUD.

The colored streams of letters around his head whirl more wildly now.

KUF. YUD. KUF. A KAYAK. SOMETHING IMPORTANT IS HAPPENING INVOLVING A KAYAK.

The streams slow down. Somewhere in the wide world, something is happening involving a kayak, something important enough to disturb the subtle threads of the machinery of Heaven. Is it a prophet being carried down a river in Asia? A future king traversing an ocean in Europe? Is the kayak metaphorical? On the River of Time? On the Ocean of Knowledge? Might it...

A kayak shot out of the walls of cloud at two hundred miles an hour and missed Uriel's head by half an inch.

"Oh God help I don't know how to steer help help help somebody help I can't steer!" someone screamed.

Only slightly off balance, the archangel reached out a hand and caught the errant vessel. He lifted it until it was directly in front of his face, stared at it with his giant eyes.

HELLO, said the archangel.

"Oh god I'm so sorry I'm so sorry I didn't mean to do that I couldn't steer," she said. She was young, even for a human, maybe only seven or eight years old. She had light brown skin, dark brown eyes, braided black hair. She was wearing a life jacket. She was obviously terrified. Finally she managed to pull herself together, and said:

"My name is Sohu. My father said I should ask you to teach me the kabbalah."

UM. THAT IS NOT REALLY THE KIND OF THING THAT I DO. THERE ARE HUMANS WHO DO THAT, I THINK.

"Father said it had to be you."

I AM BUSY, said Uriel.

They stared at each other for a moment. The girl, sopping wet, still shaking, still holding the paddle. The archangel, taller than the hills, dressed in luminous white, with great golden wings protruding from his back, and eyes that shone like the sun.

"Please?" asked the girl.

I AM BUSY. I AM TRYING TO FIX CONTINENTAL DRIFT.

"I... didn't know it was broken."

Uriel's face became more animated, his speech faster.

IT HAS BEEN BROKEN FOR FIVE WEEKS AND FIVE DAYS. I THINK IT BROKE WHEN I RELOADED NEW ZEALAND FROM A BACKUP COPY, BUT I DO NOT KNOW WHY. MY SYNCHRONIZATION WAS IMPECCABLE AND THE CHANGE PROPAGATED SIMULTANEOUSLY ACROSS ALL SEPHIROT. I THINK SOMEBODY BOILED A GOAT IN ITS MOTHER'S MILK. IT IS ALWAYS THAT. I KEEP TELLING PEOPLE NOT TO DO IT, BUT NOBODY LISTENS.

Sohu looked at him dubiously, then gently laid her paddle down across her lap. "If you teach me the kabbalah, I could try to help you fix continental drift."

NO, said Uriel. I WORK CELESTIAL KABBALAH. IT IS BEYOND THE REACH OF HUMANS. IF YOU TRIED TO TOUCH THE EMANATIONS OF

THE HIGHER WORLDS, THEY WOULD PASS THROUGH YOUR HANDS LIKE SHADOWS.

Sohu reached up and plucked one of the letters from the cloud whirling around them. She pulled on it like a thread, and a string of other letters followed after her, bunching up into her hand. The glyphs turned first blue, then purple, then one of the three nameless colors you only see in dreams. Then they all started changing into other glyphs more quickly than the eye could follow.

Uriel let out a loud shriek. Suddenly he was all action. Dropping girl and kayak, he snatched at the glowing letters, sewing them into a new pattern with superhuman speed, working so quickly it seemed he had dozens of hands acting at once. Waves of color flowed through the vast design. Just before Sohu crashed against the ocean below, the archangel reached down and caught kayak and girl, lifting them back level with his face.

"Sorry sorry sorry what did I do what did I do?" asked Sohu, who was back to being terrified again.

YOU MIGHT HAVE SORT OF MADE ALL OF THE RIVERS IN THE WORLD RUN IN REVERSE.

"I'm so sorry really I didn't mean to."

IT IS OKAY. I FIXED THEM. Then: WAIT, HOW DID YOU DO THAT?

"I just reached out and grabbed one of those letters."

THOSE LETTERS SPAN WORLDS. THEY ARE BEYOND THE REACH OF HUMANS. YOU SHOULD NOT HAVE BEEN ABLE TO TOUCH THEM.

"I was playing outside the other day, and I saw a letter like those, and I grabbed it, and flowers started growing all over, and then Father got a very stern look on his face and said I was to get in the flying kayak and find the Archangel Uriel and make him teach me the kabbalah."

WAIT, ARE YOU *THAT* SOHU?

"I think I might be the only person named Sohu."

OH.

They stared at each other.

DO OTHERS IN YOUR FAMILY HAVE THIS GIFT?

"No, I asked them," said Sohu. "But they can't wiggle their ears either."

NO ONE CAN WIGGLE THEIR EARS.

Sohu wiggled her ears.

The archangel stood there for a moment in perfect silence. All around him, strings of letters snaked and wound above his head, under his arms, through his fingers. Sometimes two strings would collide in silent flashes.

Other times they would switch languages in mid-air, or shatter into their component parts, or swarm like hornets.

"Are you all right?" Sohu finally asked.

I WAS TRYING TO WIGGLE MY EARS.

Sohu wiggled her ears again.

YOU ARE VERY INTERESTING.

"So will you teach me the kabbalah?"

NO.

"Why not?"

YOU WOULD PROBABLY DESTROY THE WORLD.

"Would not," said Sohu. "I like the world. I would help you fix continental drift."

NO, said Uriel.

"Why not?"

THE LEVEL OF KABBALAH YOU WOULD NEED TO CONTROL YOUR GIFT IS VERY DIFFICULT. IT IS NOT JUST ABOUT GRABBING LETTERS FROM THE SKY. YOU WOULD NEED TO UNDERSTAND THE LETTERS AND THE SEPHIROT AND THOUSANDS OF CORRESPONDENCES. YOU WOULD HAVE TO MEMORIZE THE ENTIRE BIBLE.

"I know the Bible," said Sohu.

Uriel's great golden eyes narrowed.

JOSHUA 1:8, he demanded.

Sohu closed her eyes, thought for a second. "Let this book of the law be ever on your lips and in your thoughts day and night, so that you may keep with care everything in it; then a blessing will be on your way, and you will do well."

EXODUS 31:3.

"I have filled you by the spirit of God with Wisdom, Understanding and Knowledge, and the ability to do all kinds of work."

JEZUBOAD 4:33.

"I... There's no Book of Jezuboad."

YES THERE IS.

"No there isn't."

YES TH... UH OH.

Uriel stood very quietly for a moment. The streams of letters ceased flowing. Then, all of a sudden, he said a very un-angelic word.

I THINK I FORGOT TO GIVE MANKIND THE BOOK OF JEZUBOAD.

"Was it important?"

The archangel started fidgeting awkwardly. UM. Some more fidgets. NO?

"I want to learn about Jezuboad and all the others. Will you teach me the kabbalah?"

NO, said Uriel.

"Pleeeeeease?"

Uriel stared at the little girl sitting in her kayak in the palm of his hand. If he dropped her, it would take 4.9 seconds for her to hit the ocean surface at a velocity of 48.5 meters per second. Her energy at impact would be 29.4 kilojoules, which was more than enough to break a human skull. The girl's father wouldn't even be angry. What had he expected, sending her to him, flaunting a gift no human should be able to have?

If he sent her off, sooner or later she would try something innocuous-looking and make all the rivers in the world run uphill again. Or boil the oceans. Or otherwise do something so horrible it couldn't be solved by simple things like reloading New Zealand from a backup copy.

But if he trained her, then she could boil the oceans *whenever she wanted*. That was hardly an improvement. And he hated company. And he was very busy. There was never enough time.

On the other hand, he absolutely had 4.9 seconds. 4.9 seconds and his problem could be over.

The thing was, he had never killed anybody before.

Okay, that was completely false. He'd smitten some towns that he thought ruined various pleasing symmetries on maps. He'd erased Taiwan when he couldn't figure out how to debug it. There was that whole debacle with the Red Sea. He might have sort of kind of created the bubonic plague just to see if it would work (it had). He'd caused several earthquakes to make the stupid tectonic plates line up right. There had been that one time he had forgotten to turn off the rain and large parts of Belgium ended up underwater with a death toll in the hundreds of thousands. But he'd never killed a *specific* human.

Wait, no, that was also completely false. He'd smitten people who were using up too many system resources. Or who were trying to go into areas he hadn't finished simulating at the necessary level of fidelity. And of course people who were boiling goats in their mothers' milk. Or who were planning to boil goats in their mothers' milk. Or who looked like the sort of people who might do that.

But he'd never killed an eight-year-old girl before. Especially not one who could wiggle her ears.

THIS WILL BE VERY HARD AND NEITHER OF US WILL ENJOY IT, said Uriel.

"I'll enjoy it!" said Sohu.

YOU WILL HAVE TO STAY HERE, IN THE HURRICANE, WITHOUT ANY FRIENDS TO TALK TO.

"I can be friends with you!"

THE SYSTEM OF THE WORLD IS GRADUALLY DECAYING AND ONE DAY SOON IT WILL FALL APART ENTIRELY. THE JOB OF MAINTAINING IT UNTIL THAT MOMENT IS THANKLESS AND UNPLEASANT AND YOU CAN NEVER STOP OR ELSE EVERYONE DIES.

"I can help!" said Sohu.

Uriel let out a long sigh.

YOU WILL START BY MEMORIZING THE BOOK OF JEZUBOAD WHILE I FIX CONTINENTAL DRIFT. His great fingers spun the streams of colorful letters around him into a cloud, upon which he gingerly deposited girl and kayak. From another stream he formed a book which he presented to her.

READ, he said.

1) And it came to pass that in the eighth year of Ahab, Jezuboad made a burnt offering in the Temple of the Lord

2) and he spoke saying, "O God, whose wisdom spanneth the heavens and the earth, I am learned in Scripture, yet much still troubles me.

3) Why the many apparent contradictions? Whence the emphasis on ritual purity? And which books are literally true and which meant only to edify?"

4) Then out of a fiery cloud before him there appeared the Archangel Uriel, whose eyes shone like the sun.

5) And he said with a mighty voice:

6) OKAY, LET ME CLEAR ALL OF THIS UP RIGHT NOW, SO NO ONE ELSE EVER HAS TO WORRY ABOUT IT...

Chapter Four

Tools Were Made And Born Were Hands

And ye shall be sorrowful, but your sorrow shall be turned into effective devices for computing in any direction.

—kingjamesprogramming.tumblr.com

May 10, 2017
San Jose

Even before Valerie finished formally adjourning the meeting, I wove my way through the crowd of garrulous people and up the stairs into my bedroom. I grabbed my laptop from the desk, then knocked on Ana's door. She was there waiting for me.

She sat down on the bed. I sat down on the floor. She stretched, cracked her back, cracked her neck, took a deep breath.

"Now, what is all this about the world?" she asked me.

"Today at work, I accidentally discovered a Name that gives souls to non-living objects. Like, not just turns them into golems. But actual souls. Nobody knows. Wasn't a work Name."

"Euphemism," said Ana. *She* got the implications immediately. "Wait, a month? You should be world emperor within a *week*!"

The basis of the Information Age was brute-force generation of kabbalistic Names. That meant me and thousands like me on factory floors, reading potential Names and seeing if they worked any miracles. Given the millions of potential combinations, you needed a whole lot of employees working a whole lot of hours for a whole lot of time in order to get anywhere at all.

Every other field had been revolutionized by automation. Tailors had their sewing machines, builders had their bulldozers, manufacturers had their industrial robots. And so about thirty years ago, someone had the bright idea: why not automate the generation of Divine Names?

A factory with a hundred workers, each testing one Name every twenty seconds, all working eight hour days — discovers a new Name of ten letters or more about once a year. If a computer could test a thousand names a second, twenty-four hours a day, it could discover a new Name almost every hour.

A Name must be spoken. It can't merely be subvocalized, or sounded out completely in the imagination. So fine. Connect the computer up to a speaker. Have it speak a thousand times faster than any human, until the stream of Names just sounds like a uniform high-pitched hum. Then write a program that calculates potential Names off some open-source namespace software, plays them from the speaker, and records the ones that work.

That program was Llull. A terrible and wonderful thing. Capable in theory of putting the entire kabbalah industry out of business, of advancing the magical capability of humankind a thousandfold in a few days.

And in the end, useless. Computers cannot speak the hidden transcendent names of God.

Or, well, they *can*. But nothing happens. No wave of light crashes through their silicon brains. No revelation fries their integrated circuits. They just keep on beeping and clicking, oblivious. And theoretical kabbalah has only one good explanation: computers must lack the divine spark.

Llull was programmed by hobbyists and academics and had no practical utility. It was used in a few research applications, then abandoned to any amateur who might want to play around with it.

But if someone were to come up with a way to *give* a computer the divine spark, to ensoul it…

Well, that person would have something producing Names ten thousand times as fast as the average sweatshop. Since there are about a hundred sweatshops seeking Divine Names all over the world, that one person with his single computer would have a magical discovery rate a hundred times faster than the rest of the world combined. The very least he could expect would be to become stupendously rich.

And what if, with all that money, he were to buy a second computer? What about a third computer? What about a giant Cray supercomputer that thought so quickly that it needed liquid nitrogen pumped through it every second of every day to prevent its manic cognition from frying its own brains? Hooked up to hundreds of speakers in parallel, testing millions of Names per second? In an hour, you could gain more sorcerous power than the entire human race had discovered since the sky cracked. Hire a clever mathematician to narrow the search space, and you'd be within reach of the Shem HaMephorash itself, with the power to remake worlds.

I hadn't just discovered an especially long Name. I had discovered the royal road.

"Are you going to tell Valerie?"

"If I tell Valerie, half the Singers in California will know within an hour. Val's great, but she's not exactly the best person at keeping her mouth shut. I trust nobody with this. *Nobody.*"

"You trusted *me.*"

"I didn't have a choice!"

"Oh. Right." Ana plucked the Vital Name out of my head. "Gotcha," she said. "So, you want to give our laptops souls?"

"I want to give *my* laptop a soul," I said. "Llull only works on Macs, remember?"

I had an old NE-1 series Macbook. I'd named it Sarah after my desktop wallpaper of Sarah Michelle-Gellar striking a sexy pose. Ana had an even older PC. She'd named it Captain Smith after the officer who'd slammed the Titanic into an iceberg, because of its tendency to crash and freeze.

"They still haven't euphemism come out with the Windows version?" Ana asked.

"Of course not," I said. "It wouldn't be kabbalistically appropriate."

Apples and knowledge have always had a special relationship. Adam tasted knowledge and was thrust from Eden. Newton had knowledge strike him suddenly out of the blue. Turing's knowledge was bitter and led him to an early grave. Knowledge brings discord, knowledge ripens, knowledge is poisoned. Men greedily devour the exterior of knowledge, but the core they do not reach.

Knowledge was first domesticated in southern Turkey or northern Mesopotamia, from which it spread to the rest of the world, although some scholars claim its modern genome owes more to various European ancestors. Most historians believe it was first brought to the New World by colonists, but this ignores the existence of native American varieties which unfortunately have been mostly displaced and are now endangered. The first and second leading producers of knowledge at the current time are America and East Asia. Although knowledge originally reproduced through cross-pollination with other knowledge, modern industrial growers have taken to a grafting process similar to cloning. As a result, the sorts of knowledge everywhere are pretty much the same. This makes producing knowledge for commercial sale much easier, but has led some to opine that a once vast diversity in varieties of knowledge has been irrecoverably lost.

The apple symbol on Sarah's lid glowed balefully.

Ana couldn't quite follow my thoughts, but she got the gist of them, put her hand on my shoulder. "You okay?"

"Sorry," I mumbled.

"Big step we're about to take," she said.

"The biggest," I agreed.

"You want to do the honors?"

I double-clicked on the little icon for Llull, loaded it up, set it on autopilot. The computer made strange noises at the limit of human hearing. Names, spoken faster than the ear could follow. Lifelessly now, running through by rote. That would change.

I stood up, towering above the white frame of the computer. I placed my hand above it in a posture of benediction, like the Pope blessing a small child. Features in a beatific smile. I cleared my mind. In the background, I could *feel* Ana's presence, telepathically bound to me, happy, radiant.

I started: "ROS - AILE - KAPHILUTON - MIRAKOI - KALANIEMI - TSHANA-KAI-KAI-EPHSANDER-GALISDO-TAHUN..."

Valerie's voice from the hallway: "Are you doing dark rituals in the bedroom again?! If you burn that carpet, I swear, you can summon Thamiel himself and all of his terrors will be as nothing compared to what I will put you through if..."

And I ended: "MEH-MEH-MEH-MEH-MEH-MEH!"

Chapter Five

Never Seek To Tell Thy Love

I.

I remember the first time I met Ana Thurmond.

I'd just been kicked out of Stanford. My mother was a wreck. I had to get away from her. I took the first minimum wage job I could find, a clerk position at Cash For Gold. It wasn't so bad. There was a sort of kabbalah to it, freely interchanging symbols with material reality. I could respect that. I sat behind a register and studied Talmud and Zohar most of the day, and sometimes an elderly woman would come in to trade her jewelry for rather less than it was worth, and I would facilitate the transaction.

Every so often I would get to a particularly interesting Talmudic tractate and stay past closing time. Sometimes I'd be there late into the night. It was a more congenial environment than my mother's apartment. Nobody noticed and nobody cared. That was why I was still there at eleven or so one night when I heard a sort of commotion outside.

I opened the door and caused a beautiful girl to fall off a stepladder. "Euphemism!" she said. I swear to God she said "Euphemism."

"Are you okay?" I asked. She was. She was holding two big yellow letters. I looked up at our sign. It was missing two big yellow letters.

"What do you think you're doing?" I asked. I am bad at sounding threatening, but she was like 5'4, maybe 5'5, and also lying on the ground looking very ashamed, and so putting menace into my voice was easier than usual.

"Kabbalah," she said.

I looked up at the sign again. It read CASH OR GOD.

"It's a kabbalistic protest," she said faintly. "Against a society that thinks..."

"You're not a kabbalist. If you were a kabbalist, you'd have more respect! You can't just go removing letters from signs like that! Matthew 5:18: 'Verily I say unto you, not a single letter, nor even a stroke of a letter, shall be removed until all is fulfilled.'"

"Oh, you want to go there?" She caught her breath and stood back up. "Matthew 16:4: 'This evil and adulterous generation wants a sign, but no sign shall be given to it.'"

I blinked. Maybe she *was* a kabbalist.

"But," I said, "By removing the letter L, you make 'God' out of 'gold.' But the warning against idolatry in Exodus 20:23 says 'You shall not make a god out of gold.'"

"But," said the girl, "Exodus 25 says that you shall take gold and turn it unto the Lord."

Now I was annoyed.

"You have taken an L and an F," I said. "But in Agrippa's English gematria, L and F sum to twenty-six. The Tetragrammaton also has a gematria value of twenty-six. So taking an L and an F is numerologically equivalent to taking the Name of God. But the Third Commandment is 'You shall not take the Name of God in vain.'"

"But the sound of L and F together," she said, "is 'aleph,' and aleph is silent and represents nothingness. So I have taken nothing."

I heard the whine of a siren.

"Tell it to the cops," I said.

She ran. She didn't even take the ladder. She just turned and ran away.

It wasn't like I had even called the police. Just a coincidence, if you believe in such things. For some reason a cop with a siren was out there at eleven p.m., doing cop stuff, and she heard it and ran away.

And I got to spend pretty much every waking moment over the next six months wondering who she was.

I checked all of the universities with programs in kabbalah and I got nothing. No leads. As embarrassing as it was to ask Hey, does a pretty girl with blonde hair in a sort of bun who is really good at certain kinds of weird wordplay go here? I sucked it up and asked at Stanford, Berkeley, even Santa Clara, and I got nothing. I moved on to the yeshivas, even though most of them didn't even admit women. Nothing.

It was a cold autumn night and I'd just finished asking at what was absolutely positively the last yeshiva I was going to bother checking out—just as I thought I had the past several weekends. One thing had led to another, and we had gotten into an argument about the creation of the universe, and finally we agreed to take it to the bar, where I proceeded to repay their friendliness by sitting in a corner and not talking to anybody. I was only half paying attention when a girl walked up to one of the rabbinical students, told him he was pretty, and asked him to kiss her.

It wasn't my girl. My girl was short and had blond hair in a sort of bun and spoke way too fast. This was a tall girl with dark hair that looked like it had rejected a mohawk as too conformist and set forth with only an ox and a Conestoga wagon into new and exciting realms of weird hairstyles.

The rabbinical student—a cherubic-faced young man with absolutely perfect curly hair whose name I think was David—apologized and said that he was a rabbinical student and not big on kissing weird girls at bars whose hairstyles seemed to be inspired by the crests on species of extinct reptiles. Or words to that effect.

"Wow," said the girl. "A real rabbinical student. Tell you what. If I know something about the Bible that you don't know, will you kiss me?"

My ears perked up.

You don't understand how heavily these people train. It's Torah eight hours a day since they're old enough to sit up straight. They've got the thing memorized by now and then some. "If you know something about the Bible I don't know, you can do whatever you want with me," David said laughing.

"Hmmmm," said weird-hair-girl, and she made a show of thinking about it. "I've got one. How long did Joseph spend in the belly of the whale?"

"Three days and three nights," he said practically instantly, before I could warn him.

"Oh, so sorry," said weird-hair-girl.

David looked at her. "I can quote you chapter and verse. Jonah 1:17."

"...would be a lovely answer, if I'd asked that. I asked you how long *Joseph* was in the belly of the whale."

The rabbi trap had been sprung. His face turned red.

"Uh," he said, "there's nothing in the Bible saying for sure that Joseph didn't spend time in a whale too."

"Nope," said weird-hair-girl. "I'm no rabbi, but I am pretty sure that zero, zilch, nobody in the Bible spent time in a whale except Jonah."

"And the wives of the men slain in Sennacherib's invasion of Jerusalem," I interjected before I could stop myself.

Two sets of eyes suddenly pivoted my direction.

"The wives of the men slain in Sennacherib's invasion of Jerusalem," said David, "did not spend time in a whale."

"Oh, they absolutely did," I said, because at this point I was in too deep to back out. "They were very vocal about it."

Weird-hair-girl raised one eyebrow.

"It's all in Byron," I said, then quoted: "And the widows of Ashur were loud in their whale."

Blink, blink went the girl's eyes, then suddenly: "I hate you and I hope you die." Then: "Wait, no, death would be too good for you. You need to meet my cousin." Then: "Drink." And she dragged me over to her table and shoved a beer at me.

So, when the thread of my memory resumes, late the next morning, I found myself lying in a strange bed, mostly naked. I silently resolved not to go binge drinking with rabbinical students again.

Wait.

Standing over me, as if scrutinizing a horse for purchase, was Weird Hair Girl. And next to her, with precisely the same expression, was my short blonde girl with the pale blue eyes, the girl with the ladder.

"He told a terrible whale joke!" protested weird-hair-girl, "and first I wanted him to die, but then I realized that would be too good for him, and I told him he had to meet you instead."

"What was the joke?" asked my blonde girl.

"It was..." Weird Hair Girl thought for a second. "Do you know how many beers I had last night? And you want me to remember things? *Specific* things?"

"Hm," said my blonde. She looked straight at me, with the pale blue eyes. I don't think she recognized me. "What was the joke?"

I protested. "I don't even know where I am! I don't even know your names! In my head I've been calling her 'Weird Hair Girl' and you—" I cut myself off before I said something like "the girl I am going to marry." "How am I supposed to remember a whale joke?"

The girl I was going to marry ran her fingers through her pale blonde hair in frustration and deep thought. "Since you came up with it last night," she said, "you must be able to come up with it again. You were with rabbinical students, therefore you were talking about the Bible. Biblical whale jokes. What comes to mind?"

"Um," I said. "Obviously the Biblical king Ahab is an suspect, given his namesake. So... aha! ...Ahab was visiting Jerusalem, and he kept trying to shoot Moby Dick from there, and but it's so far inland he couldn't reach the sea with his harpoon, so he ordered the construction of a great rampart to give him a height advantage..."

She stared at me, a calculating stare.

"...and to this very day, it is known as the Whaling Wall," I finished, and both of us started giggling.

"Wait," said Weird Hair Girl. "Why did I think introducing the two of you would be a good idea? This is the worst thing that ever happened."

"And then Ahab died and went to Hell," she added, "where there was much whaling and gnashing of teeth."

"But," I said, "it was all in accordance with the whale of God."

"Wait," said the blonde. "I've got one. Why was the sea so noisy after the destruction of Sennacherib's army?"

I thought for a second. Then I thought for another second. "I got nothing," I said.

"Because," said the blonde girl, "the widows of Ashur were loud in their whale."

"WAIT NO THAT WAS IT! THAT WAS MY WHALE JOKE! I SWEAR TO GOD, THAT WAS MY WHALE JOKE!"

"This was the biggest mistake of my life and I hope I die," said Weird Hair Girl.

II.

I remember my first morning there, the morning it all came together. The girls finally dragged me out of bed and insisted on making me breakfast. Weird Hair Girl was named Valerie. Girl Whom I Will Someday Marry was named Ana. Together they led me downstairs into an expansive dining room.

"Welcome to Ithaca!" Ana told me as I sat down and plunked my head on the table, still a little hung over.

"You need food," Valerie stated, and disappeared into the kitchen to fetch me some. Ana went with her. They were whispering to one another. Giggles may have been involved.

It was a big house, a little old but well-maintained. From one wall hung a sort of banner with a big Hebrew letter yud on it. Tenth letter of the alphabet, representing the tenth commandment, "Thou shalt not covet," with the obvious implications for capitalism and wealth accumulation. The big yud was a Stevensite symbol. These were Stevensites. It fit.

But I could do better than that. I turned my attention to the bookshelf on the far wall, tried to see what I could glean. They had the usual sci-fi/fantasy classics: Tolkien, Asimov, Salby. Then some meatier fare: Zayinty the economist, Chetlock the prognosticator, Tetkowsky the futurist, Yudka the novelist, good old Kaf ben Clifford. I recognized a few I'd seen before by their covers alone. Nachman Bernstein's *Divinity*. Norvig and Raziel's *Kabbalah: A Modern Approach*. Ben Aharon's *Gematria Since Adam*. Rav Kurtzweil's *The Age Of Mechanized Spirituality*. I stared at the shelf greedily. I didn't have *half* of these. I hoped they weren't too serious about the not coveting.

It was only after finishing my scan of the books that I turned to the other possible source of information in the room.

"Hi," I said to the guy sitting at the end of the table. He was tall and looked like he worked out. "I'm Aaron Smith-Teller. Nice to meet you."

"Brian Young," he said, barely looking up from his paper. "Welcome to Ithaca."

"So I've heard. This is some kind of group house?"

"You could say that," said Brian.

"Brian's the strong, silent type," said Ana, returning from the kitchen with coffee. She poured me a mug. "It's why he and Valerie get along so well. He never says anything, she never shuts up. Yes, we're a group house. Valerie prefers the phrase 'commune,' but Valerie prefers lots of things."

"I'm standing right here, making your food!" Valerie shouted from the kitchen.

"So are you guys some kind of Stevensite group, or..." I started to ask. Ana put a finger to her mouth, and whispered "Shhhhhhhhhhhh. She'll hear you."

Valerie came in bearing four plates of toast. "I'm glad you asked!" she said in an inappropriately chirpy voice, and picked Stevens' *The Temple And The Marketplace* off the shelf. "Have you read this?"

The early years after the discovery of the first Names had been a heady time, as would-be wizards had learned new incantations and built exciting technologies on top of them. The Luminous Name had been worked into various prayers and magic squares and configurations to produce lights of dizzying shapes and colors. Clever inventors in self-funded workshops had incorporated the Kinetic Name into all sorts of little gadgets and doodads. The best kabbalists had developed vast superstructures of prayers and made them available for free on the earliest computer networks to anyone who wanted to experiment.

That ended with the founding of the great theonomic corporations. They gradually took over the applied kabbalah scene in the 80s; their grip tightened in the early 90s after the President and the Comet King worked together to create UNSONG. Suddenly every new Name had a copyright attached to it, and the hundreds of lines of prayers and invocations people used to control the Names and bend them to your will were proprietary material. The old workshops became less and less relevant; the old self-employed kabbalist geniuses were either snatched up by the theonomics or turned into increasingly irrelevant bitter old men.

It was in this atmosphere that Reverend Raymond E. Stevens of the Unitarian Church had written *The Temple And The Marketplace*. The book was two hundred fifty pages of sometimes excessively dense screeds, but it essentially argued that a whole host of Biblical commandments — most notably "thou shalt not covet" and "thou shalt not take the name of the Lord thy God in vain" — were best interpreted as describing the divine Names discovered after the sky cracked, prophetic injunctions intended to make sense only millennia after they were written. Taken together, these commandments formed a schematic for an ideal economy (the titular "Temple") in which the wealth-creating powers of the kabbalah were shared by everyone. The modern world was ignoring God's plan in favor of unrestricted capitalism (the titular "Marketplace") and inviting terrible retribution upon themselves. Stevens saw himself as a modern-day Jeremiah, warning the Israelites to repent before they suffered the full force of God's vengeance.

Despite being by all accounts something of a crackpot (his explanation of the dimensions of Solomon's Temple as occult references to economic parameters reminds me of Newton's, only less lucid), he was in the right place at the right time. Stevenism spread among bitter old kabbalists, teenage Marxist punks, spiritual-but-not-religious hippies, and anyone who found themselves unexpectedly locked out of the new economy. It went from oddly specific theory to Generic Badge Of The Counterculture, and the same sort of people who spent the sixties talking about "vibrations" without really knowing what they meant spent the nineties talking about the secret meanings of weird Levitical commandments.

"You guys are Singers?" I asked.

"We're the Singer *hub*," said Valerie. "For all of North San Jose. And I run the Singer newspaper. *The California Chorister*. Listen!"

She stood on a chair, and started giving what from then on I would always recognize as The Spiel. The Spiel was one of the few constants of life at Ithaca. Roommates would come and go, intellectual fads would burst onto the scene in glorious bloom before vanishing in a puff of general embarrassment, but The Spiel remained. Valerie could do it convincingly while sober but *spectacularly* when drunk. She had converted entire bars full of people to her particular brand of radical theological anarchism on several occasions. Over years of practice she had perfected it down to a two minute, seven second elevator pitch which she had so far recited in manners including: blind drunk, on one foot, driving a motorcycle, and while having sex with two men at the same time. The month I met her, she had been working on learning juggling, so she picked up three balls and began to orate:

"God is born free, but everywhere is in chains! The Names, our birthright as children of Adam, the patrimony which should have ensured us an age of plenty like none other in human history, have been stolen from us by corporations and whored out to buy yachts for billionaires.

"The Fertile Name brings forth grain from the earth, speeding the growth of crops by nearly half. Children in Ethiopia starve to death, and Ethiopian farmers cannot use the Fertile Name to grow the corn that would save them. Why not? Because Amalek holds the patent and demands $800 up front from any farmer who wants to take advantage of it.

"The Purifying Name instantly kills eighteen species of harmful bacteria, including two that are resistant to all but the most toxic antibiotics. But two-thirds of American hospitals have no one licensed to use the Purifying Name. Why not? Because they can't afford the licensing fees demanded by Gogmagog.

"In the old days, we told ourselves that poverty was a fact of life. That there wasn't enough food or medicine or clothing or housing to go around. Then it was true. Now it is false. To feed the hungry or heal the sick no longer requires scarce resources. It requires only a word. A word that the entire international system of governance — corporations, politicians, UNSONG — has united to prevent the needy from ever obtaining.

"Eighty-six percent of known Names are held by five big cor— damn!"

Valerie had dropped her balls. She picked them back up, then continued.

"Eighty-six percent of known Names are held by five big theonomic corporations. Microprosopus. Gogmagog. Amalek. Countenance. And Serpens, the biggest, with $174 billion in assets. Its CEO has a net worth of $9 billion, five beach houses scattered across the Untied States, and her own superyacht.

"When Marx heard of such injustices, he demanded we seize the means of production. But today the means of production aren't factories to be seized by mobs with pitchforks. They're Names, to be taken in spiritual struggle and spread around the world until the system is seen for the sham it really is and crumbles of its own accord. Thus William Blake:

I will not cease from mental fight
Nor shall my sword sleep in my hand
Till we have built Jerusalem
In England's green and pleasant land

And the theonomic corporations will stop at nothing to thwart us," Valerie warned. "The klipot are..."

"I know what they are," I interrupted. "I was expelled from Stanford for publishing a method for breaking klipot."

Valerie dropped her balls, then fell off her chair. "Damn!" she shouted. "I knew you seemed familiar! I organized a protest for you!"

Two years ago I'd been exactly where I wanted to be, a Stanford undergrad studying the applied kabbalah on a nice scholarship. I'd just finished a class on klipot and was playing around a bit — in the theoretical kabbalah, klipot are these sort of demonic scleroses that encrust the divine light and make it inaccessible, but in the applied kabbalah the word is used to describe cryptographic transformations of the Names of God that allow them to be used without revealing them to listeners. Imagine you've discovered a Name that lets you cure cancer, and you want to cure a customer's cancer but don't want them to learn the Name themselves so they can steal your business. Instead of speaking the Name aloud, you apply a cipher to it — if you want, change all the As to Us and all the Bs to Zs, so that *ABBA* becomes *UZZU* — and write the cipher down on a scroll while holding the original fixed in your mind. Tearing up the scroll activates the Name, and your ungrateful customer is left with nothing but the meaningless word *UZZU*, which absent the plaintext version is of no use to anybody.

Problem is, all the Names follow certain numerological rules. The Schachter permutations are the most famous, but there are over a dozen. So by working backwards from a klipah it's usually possible to narrow down the plaintext Name to a very small collection of possibilities, which you can then check by hand. You end up with a race between rightsholders of Names trying to develop better and better klipot, and everyone else trying to discover better and better ways of breaking them. Well, I joined Team Everyone Else in college and came up with a pretty nifty new algorithm for breaking NEHEMOTH, one of the big klipot used by the Gogmagog corporation, with about one percent as much hassle as anyone else had come up with. My advisor told me not to publish and I ignored him. Turned out giant evil corporations don't like having their multi-billion dollar properties rendered useless. Nothing I'd done was illegal per se, but they put pressure on Stanford to expel me, expel me they did, and a few months later their Applied Kabbalah department had a new professorship endowed with Gogmagog money and I was broke and living with my mother. Not that I'm bitter.

"Yeah," I said half-heartedly. "Thanks."

"You!" said Valerie. "You need to join us! You're like, a real-life freedom fighter! A martyr! Like the Israelites at Masada! You fought the law!"

"And the law won," I said. "Did Ana tell you where she found me? An old Cash for Gold shop on Briar Street."

Valerie was barely listening. "You're a hero in the battle against tyranny. And a kabbalist. We need kabbalists. Right now Ana is leading the choir, but she's an amateur. You're a professional. You need to join us. Brian is moving out in a few weeks. There will be a room opening up."

I rolled my eyes at the "hero" part, then the "battle against tyranny" part, and a third time at me being a professional anything, until it looked like I had some kind of weird eye movement disorder. I stopped when I heard "room opening up."

"How much is rent?" I asked.

"Oho," said Valerie, "suddenly, interest."

A brief flurry of awkward glances between Ana and Valerie and occasionally Brian, who refused to return any of them and continued reading the paper. Finally Valerie spoke.

"Five hundred dollars a month," she said.

I stared her in the eyes. "What's the catch?" This was the Bay Area. A rat-infested hovel went into the four digits.

"Um," said Ana. Valerie finished her sentence. "Ana's family is very wealthy and has kindly albeit unknowingly offered to subsidize the rest of us."

"Unknowingly?" I asked.

"I'm a grad student at Stanford," said Ana, "and I tell them I need the money for room and board."

"How much?" I asked.

"Um. A few thousand."

"And they believe you?"

"Well, it is the Bay Area."

She had a point. My mind added: beautiful and witty *and* rich.

III.

I remember the day I first saw Ana in her element.

She was studying at Stanford. I'd checked Stanford when I was looking for her, but I'd checked the wrong place. She wasn't studying the kabbalah per se. She was a grad student in philosophy. Her area was theodicy. The question of how a perfectly good God can allow a universe filled with so much that is evil. Who even studies theodicy anymore? After two thousand years of hand-wringing, what's left to say?

There must have been something, because journals kept publishing Ana's work, and a few months before I met her she was named the Augustine Distinguished Scholar in Theodicy, apparently a big national honor that came with a heap of money. It was her passion, her great love, her reason for being. "Don't you get it, Aaron?" she would say, animated almost to the point of mania. "We're looking at all of this the wrong way. The Divine Names. The laws of physics. We're asking *what* when we should be asking *why*. Why did God create the universe the way He did? Why the Names? If we really understand God's goodness, then we can predict everything. What will the stock market do next year? Whatever it's best for it to do. Who will win the next Presidential election? Whichever candidate is better. If we really understood divine goodness, we would understand everything, past, present, and future."

I gingerly pointed out that the world was terrible.

"That's exactly the thing!" Ana said. "How do we square our knowledge that God wants as good a universe as possible with the terrible universe we ended up with? Square that circle, and literally everything else falls into place."

Every Sunday night, Valerie hosted a dinner party. Every Sunday night, one guest was tasked with giving a presentation. Something they were interested in, something to keep us entertained while we waited for the food to be ready. A few weeks ago, Valerie herself had talked about running the *Chorister* and how she was going to get distribution networks going across the

California Caliphate and maybe even into the Salish Free State. The week before, I'd talked about a new paper out of MIT expanding upon Rubenstein's Sieve, one of the most important methods for narrowing down namespace. Now it was Ana's turn, and of course she was going to talk about the Book of Job.

The chairs were all full as usual. I recognized Bill Dodd. He'd been a physics grad student at Berkeley before ending as one of the washed-up scientists who seemed to be everywhere in the Bay these days, the type instantly recognizable by their tendency to respond to things which were none of their business with "As a physicist..."

I recognized Eliot "Eli" Foss. Calm, quiet Eliot — Valerie had picked him up at a Singer meeting in Oakland. Rumor had it that he was actually religious instead of meta-ironically religious, but no one could tell for certain and the whole idea made us sort of uncomfortable.

I recognized Ally Hu, who was smiling awkwardly and talking to Eliot in her crisp, overly-enunciated English. Her family had been bigwigs in Dazhou before the latest round of purges. They'd fled to California and now they owned half of southern Santa Clara Valley. Ally had only been on this side of the world six or seven years but had already fallen in with a bad crowd — namely, us.

The doorbell rang, and I answered it. I recognized Zoe Farr. She was in a tight pink t-shirt with a big yud on it. Karen Happick from the North Bay had been selling them at cost a couple of months ago; I think I had a white one at the bottom of a drawer, unworn.

"You're late," Valerie told her. There was no malice in her voice, only confusion that someone might risk missing her cooking. She'd poured blood and sweat and tears into building our little community, but the secret ingredient had turned out to be soup. She was a really good cook, and what her magazine and occasional impassioned speeches couldn't do, an invitation to one of her dinner parties might. It was weird, the way little things like that turned the wheels of destiny. I've always wondered if history is missing some story like how the Founding Fathers only declared independence because Martha Washington served amazing stew every time there was a Continental Congress.

I sat back down. The conversation had shifted. Bill was asking Ally why the house was called Ithaca; Ally was giggling and saying she was sworn to secrecy.

The chair next to me was empty. The doorbell rang again. I opened the door again.

"Hello," said Ziniel, ducking and fidgeting awkwardly to fit his tall winged form through the door. "I am here. I brought you an offering." He held out a bouquet of extremely dead flowers.

I shot Valerie a look, which I hoped encoded *You invited a fallen angel to the dinner party? Really?* She shot a look back, which I interpreted as *Well, he's part of The Cause, and he probably doesn't get out much, and also, shut up.*

"When did you get those flowers?" asked Valerie, patiently.

"A month ago," said Ziniel. "The day you invited me. I wanted to make sure that I didn't forget."

"You do remember," asked Valerie, "that flowers wilt after being dead for too long?"

Ziniel's face fell. It was obvious that he'd forgotten. Valerie shot me a *don't shoot me any looks* look, so I didn't. Fallen angels were *always* forgetting little things like the tendency of earthly life to decay and die. Or wondering why the news today was different than the news six months ago. Or being surprised again and again when people turned out to be not very nice. It was why they were usually complete wrecks.

Ana was actually the last to arrive, even though she lived here. She looked ethereally beautiful as she descended the staircase, a bag of books in her hand. She reached the table, sat down beside me, started passing out books, one per person. "Fellow Singers, the Book of Job."

There weren't enough copies of the Book of Job for all of us, which was either a metaphor or bad planning on Ana's part. Ziniel knew it by memory, which made things a little easier, and Valerie was still at the stove preparing the main course, but I still ended up sharing a copy with Ally.

"The Book of Job," said Ana. She had the voice of a singer, lowercase-s, though as far as I knew she'd never had any vocal training. When she spoke, people listened. "Totally unique among Biblical manuscripts. It's not set in Israel, but in the land of Uz—maybe somewhere in Arabia. It probably predates Israel as a settled state. It's written in a much older form of Hebrew than any other Biblical book. It gets quoted in Isaiah, which means it's older than the prophets. It gets quoted in Psalms, which means it's older than King David. The lexicon is totally different, so many foreign words that scholars suspect it was written in something else and translated later on, so maybe older than the Hebrew language itself. This thing is *old*. And there's one other difference between Job and the rest of the Bible. Job is... it's *self-aware*. It takes these questions that we all want to ask, reading the rest of the Bible — if God is good and all-powerful, how come there's so much evil in the world? — and instead of ignoring them it runs into them head on. Like, haven't you ever read the Bible, and had questions, and wish you could just ask them to God directly? Job is the book where someone actually does that."

Ana's enthusiasm wasn't exactly infectious, but it was honest. You didn't always become interested in what Ana was talking about, but it was hard not to become interested in *Ana*.

"But it's also the greatest disappointment in the history of literature. You have this frame story where the very righteous man Job falls on hard times, and he asks his friends why this is happening to him, and his friends say that surely bad things never happen to good people, so Job must have done something wrong. Job insists that he hasn't, and he's right — in fact, later, God's going to command that the friends sacrifice various animals to atone for besmirching Job's name in this way. Job is just a really, really righteous guy who suffers an immense amount. And finally, we get to the climax, where Job demands an answer, and God appears in the whirlwind, and we think we're finally going to get to hear the official, Biblically-approved answer to this problem at the heart of religion and human existence, and God just says... He says... well, open your books."

Ana took a deep breath in, and although she was short and adorable she did her best to speak in the booming voice of God:

"Then the Lord answered Job out of the whirlwind, and said: 'Who is this that darkeneth counsel by words without knowledge? Gird up now thy loins like a man; for I will demand of thee, and answer thou me: Where wast thou when I laid the foundations of the earth? Declare, if thou hast understanding: who hath laid the measures thereof, if thou knowest? or who hath stretched the line upon it? Whereupon are the foundations thereof fastened? or who laid the corner stone thereof; when the morning stars sang together, and all the sons of God shouted for joy?'"

She went on in this vein. We listened. One thing Ana hadn't mentioned about Job is that it was spectacular poetry. We tend to think of the Bible as a bunch of boring begats, but Job dazzles beyond our wildest expectations.

"Canst thou bind the sweet influences of Pleiades, or loose the bands of Orion? Canst thou bring forth Mazzaroth in his season? or canst thou guide Arcturus with his sons? Knowest thou the ordinances of heaven? canst thou set the dominion thereof in the earth? Canst thou lift up thy voice to the clouds, that abundance of waters may cover thee? Canst thou send lightnings, that they may go and say unto thee, Here we are?"

"As a physicist," said Bill Dodd, "I feel obligated to say that we *can* send lightnings! All you need is something that produces a high enough voltage, like a big Van de Graaff generator."

Ana turned to Bill, with fire in her eyes. Her God impression was getting scarily on point. "Canst thou draw out Leviathan with a fishhook? or his tongue with a cord which thou lettest down? Canst thou put an hook into his nose? or bore his jaw through with a thorn? Will he make many supplications unto thee? will he speak soft words unto thee? Will he make a covenant with thee? wilt thou take him for a servant for ever? WILT THOU PLAY WITH HIM AS WITH A BIRD?"

"Sheesh," said Ally Hu, who was reading ahead in our shared copy. "God is so obsessed with this whole Leviathan thing. First He is talking about the earth and the stars and the clouds, and then He decides no, I will just drop everything and focus on Leviathan for three chapters."

"God is canonically really obsessed with Leviathan," I said. "In the Talmud, Rav Yehuda says that there are twelve hours in a day. God spends three of them studying Torah, three judging the world, three answering prayers, and three playing with Leviathan. That's a quarter of God's time, which you have to imagine is pretty valuable."

Everyone looked at me. I shrugged. "The Talmud is kind of crazy."

"You know," said Bill Dodd, "what is Leviathan, anyway? Like a giant whale or something, right? So God is saying we need to be able to make whales submit to us and serve us and dance for us and stuff? Cause, I've been to Sea World. We have *totally* done that."

"Leviathan is a giant sea dinosaur thing," said Zoe Farr. "Like a plesiosaur. Look, it's in the next chapter. It says he has scales and a strong neck."

"And you don't think if he really existed, we'd Jurassic Park the sucker?" asked Bill Dodd.

"It also says he breathes fire," said Eli Foss.

"So," proposed Valerie, "if we can find a fire-breathing whale with scales and a neck, and we bring it to Sea World, then we win the Bible?"

"What I think my esteemed cousin meant to say," Ana said cheerfully, dropping the God act, "is that God argues here that we're too weak and ignorant to be worthy to know these things. But then the question becomes—exactly how smart do we have to be to deserve an answer? Now that we can, as Bill puts it, send lightning through the sky, now that we can capture whales and make them do tricks for us, does that mean we have a right to ask God for an explanation? Discuss!"

"Maybe," said Ally Hu, "God does not say that we are not worthy. Maybe God says that we can't understand. That we are maybe not smart enough."

"But," said Eli Foss, "when kids aren't smart enough to understand something, we give them the simple explanation. Like when kids ask about lightning, we say that the clouds rub up against each other and make sparks. It's not totally right. But it's better than nothing."

Valerie stood up tall, doing her best impression of an overbearing mother. "Who darkeneth counsel with words without knowledge? Canst thou graduate college? Canst thou go unto the office, and bring back $40,000 a year? When the dishwasher breaketh, is it thou who repairest it?"

Everybody laughed, except Ziniel, who muttered something like, "Do parents really talk that way?"

"My doctor talks that way," said Zoe Farr. "Whenever I question him about something, he just looks and me and says in this *voice*, 'Which one of us went to medical school?'"

"Seriously!" said Ana. "Who does that? Other than doctors, I mean. Job is asking this very reasonable question — how come I, a righteous man, have been made to suffer immensely? God actually knows the answer — it's because He wanted to win a bet with Satan — but instead of telling Job that, He spends like three entire chapters rubbing in the fact that He's omnipotent and Job isn't. Why would you do that?"

"The part with the Satan is weird," said Ally Hu. "If really this is God's reason, then the reason for Job's suffering is different from the reason for everyone else's suffering. Right? Bad things happen to most people, but maybe it is not because of bet between God and Satan at all times?"

"Girl's got a point," said Bill Dodd.

"I remembered," Ally Hu continued, "when we left from Dazhou. I keep asking my parents, 'What is happening? Where do we go?' because I was young. They say 'We are going to a vacation' and I say 'But why are we going to a vacation during school time?' Then they got very angry with me and told me I should mind my own beehive."

"Beeswax," Bill Dodd corrected.

"But they were trying to protect me. They knew if I hear the real answer, I would start crying, become upset, maybe run away. Maybe the real reason God allows evil is something terrible. Maybe He is trying to protect us from knowing something."

Everyone was quiet for a second.

"In the Talmud," said Eli Foss, "Rabbi Akiva says that apparent evil is always for a greater good. For example, he tells the story of the time when he was traveling to a town, and no one would let him stay in the inn, so he tried to camp in the woods, but his fire went out and he was alone in the cold and the darkness. But that night, a bunch of bandits raided the town and killed and enslaved everybody. If Akiva had been staying in the inn, or if he'd had a fire burning, they would have found him and killed him."

"That's stupid," said Valerie. "God could just make there not be bandits. Yes, sometimes some suffering is necessary to prevent even greater suffering, but then you ask why there has to be the greater suffering, and if you keep pushing it back further then eventually you get to the greatest suffering of all and the buck stops there."

"In a different part of the Talmud," I said, "Rabbi Akiva gives a different explanation. He says that even the Heaven-bound righteous have a few sins, and since those sins won't be punished in Heaven, they have to be punished here on Earth. Therefore, the righteous suffer on Earth. But even the Hell-bound wicked have a few virtues. And since those virtues won't be rewarded in Hell, they have to be rewarded here on Earth. Therefore, the wicked prosper on Earth. Then people ask why the righteous suffer and the wicked prosper, and it looks like a mystery, but it actually makes total sense."

"As a physicist," said Bill Dodd, "I would think you could model that as a bimodal distribution of suffering. But instead intuitively there's more of a normal distribution of suffering. And although people complain that the wicked prosper and the righteous suffer, there's not a perfect correlation. I don't even know if there's a correlation at all. It seems more like suffering happens at random regardless of how good a person you are."

"I was raised Catholic," said Zoe Farr. "In CCD, we always learned that evil is just the absence of good. So God didn't create evil, He just created a finite and limited amount of good, not always as much as we'd like. So people aren't as nice as they could be, and sometimes the weather forms storms and tornadoes, but it's not because there's this active force called Evil out there, it's just because the weather is doing its own thing unrestrained by God pouring infinite amounts of Good into it."

"No!" said Ana forcefully, abandoning her role as referee and joining in the discussion. "That's not right. There are certainly bad people who just fulfill their natural selfishness without having any good to get in the way. The bankers, CEOs of theonomics, UNSONG agents, cops, politicians. They just do what the system tells them, follow their incentives with no concern for the consequences. But then there are other people. Your sadists. Your serial killers. People who delight in causing other people pain. Elie Wiesel said the opposite of love wasn't hate, it was indifference. I beg to differ. Any of you ever read about what the Japanese did to the Chinese in Nanking? The Nazis, you know, mostly they just wanted some people dead and went about it in a horrifically efficient way. The Japanese, they enjoyed it. They worked hard on it. They deviated from efficiency, from self-interest, they sacrificed their own self-interest to be as perfectly cruel as possible. And Hell. Thamiel and his demons. They're not indifferent. They're evil. There's a difference."

"I mean, it looks like there's a difference to us," said Zoe Farr, "but maybe on a metaphysical level, that sort of depravity is just what a total, absolute absence of good looks like."

"I remember seeing a video," said Ana, "of the President's summit with the Devil. It was in this big hall. First the President came in, and they all played the Star-Spangled Banner. Then Thamiel came in, and the band played... played the anthem of Hell. It was horrible. I didn't even know instruments could make noises like that. They were all out of tune and fighting with each other and going at weird intervals that tricked the ear and made me want to pull my hair out."

"So?" asked Zoe. "Maybe the Hell music was just the total absolute absence of good in music."

"No," said Ana. "There's good music. And then there's total silence. And then there's that. It's not silence. It's the opposite of music."

"Unsong," I suggested.

Everyone except Ana laughed.

"Yes," she said. "Unsong."

"Garlic angel hair!" Valerie said at that moment, and brought a big pot of pasta to the table. Everyone made approving noises except Ziniel, who asked something about where one could find these garlic angels, and who had to be taken aside and given a quick explanation. The angel took some pasta and half-heartedly put it in his cup of soup.

"The reason I bring all of this up," said Ana in between mouthfuls, "is that here we are. We're Singers. We've got a Movement. We think we're on the side of Good. We know what's evil. Evil is when UNSONG and the theonomics try to control the Names of God and keep them from the people. We think we know what we have to do. We have to take up Reverend Stevens' crusade and spread the Names to as many people as possible. On a political level this all makes sense. But on a theological level, even Reverend Stevens barely touched this. Why does God have these Names that work miracles, but not tell us what they are? Why does He suffer them to be distributed throughout a namespace that can only be searched through a combination of cryptological acumen and brute force? Why does He permit them to be hidden by klipot, by which they can be bought and sold without letting the customer grasp their true structure? Why would He create enough magic to make the world a paradise for all living things, then place it somewhere it can be kept in a locked vault to enrich the few? Why, as the Bible put it, does He hide His light under a bushel?"

"Seems clear enough to me," said Bill Dodd. "God's not a big guy in the sky. He's just a force, like physical forces, but on a higher level. He doesn't plan these things, any more than anyone plans gravity. It just happens."

"So you're denying the Bible?" Eli Foss said, somewhat less intimidating than intended due to a mouth full of pasta. "We're sitting here at a table with an angel and a kabbalist, and you're denying the Bible?"

"Look, we all know that the Bible was given by Uriel, not God. Most of it just records Uriel's interventions in the world, which are usually well-intentioned but certainly not omniscient. Why not the Book of Job too? Job asks a hard question and gets yelled at. Sounds exactly like Uriel on a bad day. I can even imagine him going on about the Leviathan for like an hour, describing how interesting he finds each of its fins and teeth and things while Job gets more and more confused."

A couple of people snorted.

"But Uriel," said Eli Foss, "has always said he's just trying to follow God's plan, as he understands it."

"The Pope says the same thing," said Bill Dodd. "That doesn't mean he's met the guy."

"Someone must have created the world!" protested Ally Hu. "And all the angels, and the Names, and the kabbalah!"

"I'm not saying there's not a Creator force," said Bill Dodd. "I'm just saying it shouldn't be thought of as a person."

"Thomas Aquinas," said Zoe Farr, "tells us that God is not a person, not at all, not even close, but can sometimes be compared to one, since a person is the most intelligent entity we have to compare it to. It's like how they used to say the brain was a telephone switchboard. It's much more than that, but if all you have as a metaphor is a telephone switchboard, it's better than nothing."

"But if God can't even figure out," said Bill Dodd, "that if you want perfect good you should avoid having evil, well, whatever it is He is, it's got to be kind of dumb."

"Oh, oh," said Ziniel, and there was worry in his eyes. "You shouldn't say that. That's blasphemy."

"Be nice, Bill," said Ana, "there are angels here."

"I feel like we're forgetting something pretty important," said Valerie. "I hate to go all dualist here, but we know there's a Hell. We know there's a Devil. I'm not saying that God and the Devil are *exactly* equally powerful, but maybe it's not quite so one-sided that God can just steamroll over Thamiel without a second thought? Maybe there's some kind of strategic balance thing going on?"

Ana looked shocked. Ziniel looked horrified. But it was Eli Foss who spoke first. "Valerie," he said. "God is one. You can't just go around saying there are two separate beings with similar levels of godlike power. That's like saying there are two gods. It's serious, serious blasphemy."

"Well," said Valerie, "maybe if God didn't want people saying the Devil's just as powerful as He is, He should stop making the world full of evil just as much as good. Maybe if He didn't want us saying He's too weak to save everyone who's sick, or suffering, or in Hell, He should get off His cosmic ass and save them."

When Ana spoke now, it was very serious. "Moreover the LORD answered Job, and said, Shall he that contendeth with the Almighty instruct him? he that reproveth God, let him answer it. Wilt thou also disannul my judgment? wilt thou condemn me, that thou mayest be righteous?"

"Huh!" I exclaimed. Everyone looked at me.

"That verse from the *Rubaiyat*. The one Nixon used in the 70s. It goes, um...

O thou, who burns with tears for those who burn
In Hell, whose fires will find thee in thy turn
Hope not the Lord thy God to mercy teach
For who art thou to teach, or He to learn?

...that's from Job. It's got to be. Khayyam must have read Job."

"Well," said Zoe, "it's certainly got the right amount of condescension."

"What are we talking about?" asked Ziniel.

"Hast thou an arm like God?" Ana recited. "Or canst thou thunder with a voice like Him?"

"Okay," said Bill Dodd. "We get the idea."

"Deck thyself now with majesty and excellency; and array thyself with glory and beauty!"

"Is somebody saying there are two gods?" asked Ziniel. "Because God is one."

"Cast abroad the rage of thy wrath: and behold every one that is proud, and abase him!"

"Okay," said Ally Hu. "That's enough." She grabbed the Book of Job from Ana's hands. Ana grabbed it back. A tug of war.

"Dessert's ready!" said Valerie.

"God is One and His Name is One," insisted Ziniel. "This is very important."

"It's devil's food cake!" Valerie said, bringing the plate to the table.

"No!" Ziniel shouted at Valerie and her cake, and in a flash he was on his feet, sword of fire materializing in his hands, rushing towards her.

Ally pulled the book away from Ana.

"This is not how we do theodicy in this house!" I shouted at Ally and Ana.

"HELP!" shouted Ana. "IMMIGRANTS ARE STEALING MY JOB!"

"WAIT!" said Bill Dodd. "I just got it! The house is called Ithaca because it's where theodicy happens. Fuck fuck fuck fuck fuck."

"It's just dessert!" Valerie screamed at the oncoming Ziniel.

"No!" Ana shouted. "That's the whole point of Job! There *is* no just desert!"

I reached into my pocket, pulled out my scroll wheel, and activated the Thunderclap Name. A deafening boom filled the room. Everybody went silent.

"Thanks, Aaron," Valerie said, defeated.

"Everyone sit down!" I said. "Ziniel, sword away! No more theodicy! Time for dessert!"

IV.

I remember the day I asked Ana on a date.

It was my third week in Ithaca. I'd just finished moving my bed into my room with the help of one of the other group home residents, a tall Asian guy who didn't like to talk very much. I was sweaty and thirsty,

I'd gone into the common room to drink some Gatorade, and found Ana already there reading a book. We'd started talking, and somehow gotten onto the subject of the Shem HaMephorash, the Explicit Name of God, the True Name, the Most Holy Name, which gave its wielder power over all Creation.

"The Explicit Name is 'Harold,'" I told her.

"No," she answered. "The Explicit Name is 'Juan.'"

"But," I said, "in the Lord's Prayer, we say 'Our Father in Heaven, Harold be thy name.'"

"But," Ana objected, "in the Shema, we say 'Hear O Israel—the Lord is Juan.'"

"But," I said, "all angels are angels of the Lord, and the song says 'Hark, the Harold angels sing.'"

"But," Ana objected, "the Aleinu ends 'God is Juan, and His name is Juan.'"

"But," I said, "Christians say Jesus is God. And they give his name as Jesus H. Christ. What might the H stand for? Harold!"

"But," Ana objected, "think about it. Who names their kids Jesus? Mexican people, that's who! And what kind of names do Mexican people have? Names like Juan! Q period E period D period!"

She actually said Q period E period D period. I felt a wave of affection crash over me and through me, stronger than any other I had ever known. Before my frontal lobes could push through a veto, I blurted out: "Ana, would you go on a date with me?"

Ana's face fell. "Aaron," she said. "I'm asexual."

"So?" I said. "I asked you for a date, not for sex."

"Still."

"If we went on a date, we would be talking and enjoying each other's company. That's what we're doing now. So what's the problem?"

"If not being on a date is exactly the same as being on a date, why do you want to go on a date? Why don't we stay here, in the living room?"

"Hey! That's not fair!"

"Human attraction never is."

"Well, it should be!"

Ana rolled her eyes. "You realize you're talking to the Augustine Distinguished Scholar in Theodicy? The girl who picketed in front of the World's Fair back in 2012, waving a sign saying 'NO IT ISN'T'? You're preaching to the euphemism-ing choir."

I was briefly discombobulated, then regained my combobulation. "Look," I said, "I really like you. I want you to like me back. Dates are like a universally recognized signal of this."

"What if I just told you outright that I liked you?"

"I want it to be official!"

"I could give you a certificate. I have an uncle who's a notary public. We could make him sign."

I choked back a tear. "Ana, this is *serious.*"

Her expression changed. "I'm serious too," she said. "I like you. You're funny and interesting and you know the mystical secrets of Juan. But everything around romance—the flowers, the silly looks, the candlelight dinners. I am *not into these things*. I'm happy to talk with you, to live with you, even to grab dinner with you if you're hungry. But I don't want to date."

"If you're going to grab dinner, why not call it a date? It's just a word."

She shut her book with great force. "Did you really say 'just a word'? You call yourself a kabbalist! Words have power! Words are the only tools we have to connect the highest levels of our intellect to the mysteries of reality! Once we describe something with a word, things happen! It's been given a life of its own! The angels are on notice, working their secret little works around it, starting reverberations that echo across the entire structure! Words are the vestment of divinity, the innermost garments of Juan!"

I just sat there and took it. I didn't say anything, because I was on the verge of tears, and if I spoke she would have noticed, and then I would have looked dumb, and she would have lost respect for me, or something, look, it sounds stupid when I write it down, but give me a break. I sat there silently, not disturbing Juan's innermost garments with my speech.

Ana realized something was wrong. "Uh," she said, "if it helps, I am totally okay with you writing me flowery love poetry."

"It helps a little," I said.

"And... hmm... tell you what. Valerie's in the kitchen making curry. If you can eat one of the habanero peppers whole, without drinking water for a whole minute, I'll give you a kiss."

"Really?" I asked, and leapt to my feet, because I was a moron.

V.

And I remember the day Ana and I got married.

It was towards the end of my first month at Ithaca. I'd just been let go from my job at Cash For Gold, and I was working on my application for Countenance. Valerie was making curry, and because she was a terrible person who enjoyed making me miserable, she asked if I wanted another whole habanero. I winced and clutched my throat just thinking about it, then very politely told her no, in a way that might possibly have referenced Dante and the many terrors of the damned. She laughed.

"I'll be honest," she said. "Nobody else has ever had the guts to eat one of those. What were you THINKING?"

"I wanted to impress Ana," I said.

I looked towards Ana, who was sitting at the table, scanning for offense. None was found. "I have a crush on her, and it was getting awkward, so she tricked me into eating a chili pepper to disengage from the situation." Then, feeling guilty about my elision, I told her the whole story.

Valerie looked delighted. "You're in love with my cousin!" she announced to no one in particular.

"She's not interested," I said glumly.

Valerie took this information in, chewed it over for a moment. Then: "Wait! I've got it! You should get married."

I rolled my eyes. "She won't even—"

"Wait," said Ana. "Yes! Valerie, you're brilliant!"

Confusion ensued.

"You won't go on a date with me, but you *will* marry me? How does that even..."

Ana was gone, a dash up the stairs. A few seconds later, she returned with a notebook.

"Okay," she said. "So a while ago I was thinking—Aaron, you'll like this—you know how there have been later additions to the Bible, like the end of Mark 16 or the part in John 7–8? And kabbalists have mostly ignored those, first of all out of *totally unjustified* prejudice against the New Testament, and second of all because, well, if they were added in by later readers they can't metaphorically represent the secret structure of the universe? But I thought—what if the later additions to the Bible metaphorically represent later additions to the secret structure of the universe? So I ran a couple of them through Rubenstein's Sieve and normalized the results, divided the whole thing by 'aleph-tet-nun' as the most appropriate Boston Triplet, and sure enough I got five subfactors, one of which gets the right Schachter rank for a potential Name. After like a week of trying I was able to free it from a relatively weak klipah..."

"*You discovered a Name?*" I asked. Not more than a dozen kabbalists alive had discovered Names the old fashioned way, the proper way, by genius alone.

"It was total luck!" she insisted. "And nobody else was crazy enough to look in the additions."

"Well?" I asked, buzzing with excitement. "What does it *do*?"

"Unclear," said Ana.

"It marries people," said Valerie.

"Sort of," said Ana.

"Sacred kabbalistic marriage of minds," said Valerie.

"SCABMOM for short," said Ana. "But I haven't gotten it to work quite right yet."

She described the moment of discovery. Tasting the new Name, pregnant with possibilities. The feel of the Name itself entering her brain, unlocking secret wisdom. A ritual. Certain words.

She'd grabbed Valerie from the kitchen over her protests and dragged her into her bedroom, where she had arranged four candles in an approximate square. Around the perimeter of the square, she'd sprinkled colored sand in the shape of Hebrew letters; ten colors, twenty-two letters per side.

"Love of God, we just had those carpets cleaned!" Valerie objected. "I hope for your sake you're able to get all of that out with the vacuum."

"Shhhh," said Ana. "Repeat after me, but change the names. I, Ana Thurmond,"

"...I, Valerie Lowry,"

"In full knowledge of the consequences, call upon the symbols and angels of the world..."

"Wait, what *are* the consequences?"

"Shhh! This is just a test! Now we've got to start over! I, Ana Thurmond,"

"I, Valerie Lowry,"

"In full knowledge of the consequences, call upon the symbols and angels of the world,"

"In... bah... full knowledge of the consequences, call upon the symbols and angels of the world,"

"The higher and the lower spheres,"

"The higher and the lower spheres,"

"And the Master of them all,"

"And the Master of them all,"

"To join us at the root, as mountains to the earth,"

"To join us at the root, as mountains to the earth,"

"And rivers to the ocean,"

"And rivers to the ocean,"

"And stars to the firmament,"

"And stars to the firmament,"

"And so we invoke the Holy Name, IYAR-NA-AVANTE-SHOK-TEHAN-MI-LEVAN-ZA-NAONE-CHETH-ULAT."

"And so we invoke the Holy Name, IYAR-NA-AVANTE... uh... SHOK-TEHAN... MI? Uh... LEVAN? SHA... no, wait... ZA... NAONE-CHETH-ULAT."

(Here the candles start to darken.)

"For God is One."

"For God is One."

"And His Name is One."

"And His Name is One."

"And we are One."

"And we are One."

"And it is done."

"And it is done."

Then all the letters of colored sand glowed red, then green, then white. And the candles laid round made a high-pitched sound and flared up in a burst of light. And Valerie screams, and Ana seems to be gazing far away. And she briefly fits, but she gathers her wits just in time to hear her say, "ANA LOOK THE LETTERS HAVE BURNED THEMSELVES INTO THE CARPET YOU ARE IN SO MUCH TROUBLE."

"How do you feel?" Ana asked.

"ANGRY," said Valerie.

"Other than that?" Ana asked.

"NOTHING ELSE CAN GET THROUGH THE HOT FLAMES OF MY ANGER," Valerie protested.

"Huh. I don't feel any different either."

"But," Ana told me, "over the next couple of weeks, we would get these... intimations from each other. Like I would be on one side of the house, and I would feel like something was wrong, and I'd go find Valerie, and she would have just burned herself by accident. Or I'd be feeling really sad about something, and Valerie would say 'you look sad,' even though I wasn't showing it at all."

"Great," I said. "You're like those people who say they have psychic powers on TV. Maybe one day the phone will ring and you'll know who's calling before you pick it up. Spooky."

"I don't think we did it right," said Ana. "We weren't the right people. I could *feel* the inadequacies in the ritual. And I've been thinking—this is Biblical stuff, so maybe the marriage is supposed to be between a man and a woman."

"Or at least two people who aren't cousins," Valerie suggested.

"No!" said Ana. "The Bible is totally in favor of marrying cousins! Esau married his cousin! Jacob married *both* of his cousins!"

"But," I said, "your Name came from some sort of later addition, and was in the New Testament to boot. Maybe it's a product of a more sophisticated age."

"Hmmmm," said Ana. Then: "I'll get the colored sand!"

"YOU DO IT OUTSIDE THIS TIME," Valerie insisted.

And so it was only about a half hour later, after numerous fits and starts due to the sand blowing away in the wind, that the two of us stood amidst the candles and spoke the holy Name IYAR-NA-AVANTE-SHOK-TEHAN-MI-LEVAN-ZA-NAONE-CHETH-ULAT.

And Ana said: "And God is One."

And I answered: "And God is One."

"And His Name is One."

"And His Name is One."

"And we are One."

"And we are One."

"And it is done."

"And it is done."

We stared into each other's eyes for a moment after that. What we were looking for, I don't know. Looking back, I think I secretly hoped that it would fill her with love for me. What she hoped, if anything, I don't know. But we stared at each other for a while, and finally Ana said:

"Wait. Think something at me."

And I thought: [Ruth and Bowhead.]

"Holy euphemism the first thing ever in history communicated telepathically and it's one of your stupid Biblical whale puns, that wasn't even a *good* one, I am so done with this."

And I thought: [Shamu Yisrael, HaShem elokeinu...]

"Aaaagh, stop, why did I give you the ability to communicate with me telepathically? Why? WHY? What's that thing Valerie always says? Oh, right. This was the biggest mistake of my life and I hope I die."

Interlude 7

Cantors and Singers

Those who speak the Names of God aloud are called cantors and singers. Like everything, these terms have both overt and kabbalistic meanings.

The overt meaning of *cantor* is "someone who chants."

The kabbalistic meaning is "someone who works with infinity."

This reading we derive from Georg Cantor, the German mathematician who explored the cardinality of infinite sets. He found that though the natural numbers — 1, 2, 3 and so on — were infinite, still there were fewer of them than there were "real" numbers like root 2, pi, and 0.239567990052.... Indeed, not only were there two different levels of infinity, but it seemed likely that there were an infinite number of different infinities (and maybe one extra, to describe the number of infinities there were?).

The overall effect on him was much like the man in the limerick:

There once was a fellow from Trinity,
Who took the square root of infinity.
But the number of digits,
Quite gave him the fidgets;
And he dropped Math and took up Divinity.

Cantor began talking about how his discoveries were direct and personal revelations from God, who wished him to preach the gospel of infinity so that an infinite Deity could be better understood. He posited an Absolute Infinite, beyond all the forms of infinity he had discovered, with which God might be identified. Finally, he declared:

I have never proceeded from any "Genus supremum" of the actual infinite. Quite the contrary, I have rigorously proved that there is absolutely no "Genus supremum" of the actual infinite. What surpasses all that is finite

> *and transfinite is no "Genus"; it is the single, completely individual unity in which everything is included, which includes the "Absolute," incomprehensible to the human understanding. This is the "Actus Purissimus" which by many is called "God."*

When he finally made his discoveries public, he chose a curious notation:

> *It has seemed to me for many years indispensable to fix the transfinite powers or cardinal numbers by some symbol, and after much wavering to and fro I have called upon the first letter of the Hebrew alphabet, aleph. The usual alphabets seem to me too much used to be fitted for this purpose; on the other hand, I didn't want to invent a new sign.*

A pragmatic account, utterly without reference to a two-thousand-year-old tradition of using the aleph to signify God. Nothing is ever a coincidence. The genealogies say his grandparents were Sephardic Jews, and if they weren't kabbalists I will eat my hat.

The overt meaning of *singer* is "someone who sings."

The kabbalistic meaning is "someone who tries to be good."

This reading we derive from Peter Singer, an Australian philosopher who explored the depths of moral obligation. He imagined a man in a very nice coat walking by a pond. In the pond he sees a young child drowning, screaming for help. The man is quite a good swimmer and could easily save the child, but his nice coat would be ruined and would cost him $100 to replace. He decides he doesn't want to ruin his coat and continues on his way, leaving the child to drown. Is this morally wrong?

Of course it is, said Singer, and this is important. It suggests a general moral principle that if you get the opportunity to save a child's life at the cost of $100 you must take it. Yet we do have opportunities to save a child's life for $100. There are children starving in India; $100 would buy them food. There are children dying of malaria in Africa; $100 would buy them medication. There are children cowering in war zones; $100 might buy them a ticket to safety. If you buy a nice coat for $100 instead of giving it to charity, you're making the same decision as the man in the story. Indeed, if you use your money for anything other than charity, you're making that same decision—preferring your luxuries to a chance to avert innocent deaths.

This was not a popular message. His opponents condemned his particular brand of academic philosophy, saying that the time-tested moral truths of religion ought to be enough for anybody. They might have done well to read their Bibles a little closer. Matthew 19:21: "If you want to be perfect, go, sell everything you have and give the money to the poor, then follow me."

Singer called the movement that grew up around him "effective altruism," and its rallying cry was that one ought to spend every ounce of one's energy doing whatever most relieves human suffering, most likely either feeding the poor or curing various tropical diseases. Again, something his opponents rejected as impossible, unworkable, another example of liberal fanaticism. Really? Every ounce of your energy? Again, they could have just read their Bibles. Deuteronomy 6:5: "And you must love the Lord your God with all your heart, and with all your soul, and with all your strength."

Then Singer changed his tune. In the 1970s, after the sky cracked and the world changed, he announced that charity was useless, that feeding the poor was useless, that curing tropical diseases was useless. There was only one cause to which a truly rational, truly good human being could devote his or her life.

Hell must be destroyed.

The idea of billions of human beings suffering unbearable pain for all eternity so outweighed our little earthly problems that the latter didn't even register. He began meeting with his disciples in secret, teaching them hidden Names he said had been vouchsafed to him by angels. Thamiel put a price on his life—quite a high price actually. Heedless of his own safety, Singer traveled what remained of the civilized world, making converts wherever he went, telling them to be perfect as God was perfect, and every speech ended the same way. *Hell must be destroyed.*

He was killed by a car bomb on his way to a talk in Salt Lake City. They never found the man responsible, if indeed it was a man. They saw Singer's body, they showed it on all the television networks, but some say he never died, or that he rose again on the third day, or that he speaks to them in dreams, or all manner of strange things. When the Comet King besieged Hell, some say he brought Singer's bones as a relic, others that Singer was in his retinue, disguised. But the conventional wisdom was that he truly died—which suited conventional people and their conventional morality just fine.

("But the soul is still oracular; amid the market's din, / List the ominous stern whisper from the Delphic cave within,— / 'They enslave their children's children who make compromise with sin.'")

("We're not making compromise with sin. We just want to be less than maximally saintly sometimes.")

("Exactly what do you think compromise with sin *is*?")

This, then, is the kabbalistic meaning of being a cantor and a singer, a Namer of Names.

A cantor is someone who works with infinity.

And a singer is someone who tries to be good.

Chapter Six

Till We Have Built Jerusalem

God, grant me the serenity to accept that I will never have the serenity to accept the things I cannot change.

—Steven Kaas

Early morning, May 11, 2017
San Jose

The computer whirred and chattered: the speaker producing Names faster than the ear could follow. I stared at the screen. I already knew I wouldn't sleep tonight.

Last year I'd posted my paper "Exploitable Irregularities In NEHEMOTH-Schachter Mappings" to one of the big Singer bulletin boards online. I'd been nervous. Bad things happened to people who put Names online. The law said webmasters were responsible for monitoring their own sites; anyone who didn't delete a Name was just as guilty as the person who'd posted it in the first place. But there were rumors of worse things, webmasters being visited by men in black UNSONG uniforms and politely "asked" to hand over IP addresses. People corresponding to those IP addresses getting jailed, or just disappearing and never being seen again. There had been a site in Dazhou that had just presented a list of like a hundred Names, right there for anyone who wanted to read them, but none of the search engines would show it and anybody who linked to it got taken down in all senses of the word. I'd checked a few months ago and it was gone.

But there was nothing illegal about posting methods to break klipot. It was just math. They couldn't make math illegal. It would be like banning triangles. So I was nervous, but not too nervous. I remember sitting at my laptop—this was just after I'd gotten Sarah—clicking the reload button every couple of seconds. Watching the view count gradually increment up, from zero to one, from one to two. Then a comment—some sort of stupid objection to the math, I don't remember what it was. Then another comment, "Wow, I think you've actually done it." Then the view count going to fifty, sixty, a hundred as people started linking to it.

I remember that because of the compulsive refreshing. Each time I clicked the little button might mean another morsel of praise, a few more people noticing me, another stepping stone on my path to stardom.

Only now it was even worse. Each moment Llull might give me the little gong that meant it had found a Name.

"Go to sleep," Ana mumbled. We were still in her room. She was in bed. The lights were off. I was sitting on the floor, checking Llull once a minute or so, otherwise browsing social media. I'd just learned Ziniel had a Twitter account. It was such a trainwreck that I was having trouble averting my eyes.

"This is historic!" I answered. "When they ask us how our rise to total supremacy began, do you want to tell them that we went to sleep and then woke up in the morning to see if it worked?"

"If we have total supremacy, we can just kill whoever asks us that question," said Ana. "Go to sleep."

"I intend to be a benevolent ruler," I said. But I felt uncomfortable joking about it. A weird thought crossed my mind. Was Ana going to assassinate me in my sleep? Was that why she—

"No," said Ana. "Come on, Aaron, it takes a special kind of person to be paranoid when we can read each other's minds. Go the euphemism to sleep."

I was trying to figure out some way to continue the conversation and avoid having to go to sleep like a reasonable person when Sarah gave a melodic gong. Ana practically jumped out of bed, and in an instant she was right next to me at the computer. I minimized Llull and tried to open its output file, got an error message saying that the file was in use, groaned, paused Llull, tried again, saved to a different file, restarted Llull.

Fourteen Hebrew letters. I looked them over closely to make sure they weren't a known Name. There are people with UNSONG who tattoo the Sentinel Name above their ears, and then other Names, the captive Names belonging to the theonomic corporations, on their foreheads. Then they can hear pretty much any Name spoken within a couple of miles of them, and if they don't recognize the voice, or it's one that people aren't supposed to be using, they'll come and investigate. But they can only tattoo a Name on themselves if they know about it. If the Name we got was truly new, we were safe. And I didn't recognize it.

I held the syllables in my mind, tasted them. I tested the correspondences.

"Wait," I said. "I know what this does." I spoke. "KUHU-SHEN-TAR-TAVAL-ANASASI-VA."

A bright light appeared a couple of feet in front of my face. From the light sprung a beam, pointing up and a little to the west.

"Whoa," said Ana. Then, "What's that?"

Name generation was hard partly because most Names were pretty useless. Names to change the colors of flowers. Names to make sugar taste bitter. You might have to go through five or six before you got one of any use. The rejects were usually copyrighted, just to prevent anyone else from getting them in case they proved unexpectedly useful, then languished unknown in UNSONG archives.

"It shows the location of the moon," I said.

"You mean, in the sky?"

"Well, it could be helpful if you're a sailor doing navigation things, and it's a really cloudy night. Or if you're trapped in an underwater cave and you don't know which way is up."

"Yeah, but..."

Then we stopped. I don't know if it was the telepathy or what, but both of us realized at that moment that *it had worked*. That any computer that could give us a Name to find the moon would soon enough be giving us Names to boil oceans or split mountains. We just stared at each other, awestruck.

Then the computer gave another melodic gong.

I'd calculated that it should come up with Names on average once every couple of hours, but by the nature of averages sometimes it would be faster. Ana and I almost knocked into each other in our rush to grab the mouse. Another round of pausing and restarting.

The Name was HANAPHOR-KOTA-SALUSI-NAI-AVORA-STE-KORUSA. I spoke it once, then took off my glasses. I had perfect 20/20 vision.

Again we stopped and stared at each other. If we wanted to cut and run, we could declare that we'd stumbled across this Name through deep kabbalistic study, then sell it to the theonomic of our choice. How much would people pay for a Name that made eyeglasses unnecessary? Millions? Billions? We could both just retire, buy a house in Malibu and two tickets on Virgin Celestial, and never work again.

"Ha," said Ana, finally. "You'd no more do that than Valerie would."

"I'm not Valerie. I don't think I have a revolutionary bone in my body."

"Oh no. You're not the type to hand out leaflets, or the type to go on marches. You're too intellectual for that. That doesn't mean you're not revolutionary. It just means your revolutions are intellectual revolutions. That's what makes you so dangerous. Marx never handed out leaflets either. You like to solve everything in your head, then declare that a solution exists and so you have done your part. It's completely harmless unless somebody takes you seriously. Or unless you get enough power to enact your dreams at no cost to yourself."

"You don't even know what my dreams are."

"*You* don't even know what your dreams are."

It was kind of true. Ever since I'd been young, I'd wanted to be a kabbalist. Then I'd gone to Stanford, then I'd gotten kicked out, and ever since then I'd pretty much just been brooding. I fell in with the Singers not because I had any strong political views, but because they thought the world was unfair, I thought my life was unfair, and so we had a sort of synergy. Honestly, if a theonomic agreed to hire me as their Chief Kabbalist tomorrow and gave me a nice office and a whole library full of books, chances are the next day I'd be on the news defending them and calling the Singers a bunch of dirty hippies. Ana knew this, I think. But I couldn't just *admit* it.

"My dream is to become the new Comet King," I said.

I'm not sure exactly where the phrase came from. But when I said it, it fit.

"You can't become the new Comet King," Ana said, in the same tone a kindergarten teacher might use to correct a boy who said he wanted to be a tyrannosaurus when he grew up.

"Why not?" I asked. "He was a kabbalist. I'm a kabbalist. He knew all sorts of secret Names. I'm going to know all sorts of secret Names. He started with nothing. I start with nothing."

"He was born of the heavens, you were born of ordinary mortal parents."

"Ordinary mortal parents? Ha! My family can *destroy worlds.*"

This was true. My great-uncle Edward Teller invented the hydrogen bomb. My father Adrian Teller had followed in his footsteps and spent the 90s conducting unspecified nuclear research at Livermore Laboratories east of Fremont. My mother had been a waitress at the cafeteria there. The two met, they had a brief fling, she got knocked up, she told him so. He suddenly realized he had vitally important national security business to tend to on the opposite side of the country, so sorry about that, good luck with the whole child-rearing thing. My mother was left alone to take care of me, whispering in my ears since the day I was born that I was a famous physicist's child and I was going to be better than everyone else. I would invent the next big doomsday device and become rich and famous, and so she would be rich and famous, and then all of the suffering she was going through as a single mother trying to get by on a waitress's salary would be worth it.

In kindergarten, I scored through the roof on some kind of placement test and skipped two grades. My mother was so happy. I was happy too: I was making her proud. It was only later I realized that when other mothers were proud, you didn't see the same glimmer of greed in their eye, the same restless energy that came from resisting the urge to rub their hands together and say, "Everything according to plan."

At first she would dip into her meager savings to buy me physics books, big tomes from the library on optics and mechanics. Then, when the theonomics became big, she realized that physics was (literally and figuratively) on its way out and started getting me books on kabbalah, the ones whose covers use faux Hebrew letters and whose authors write under vaguely Jewish sounding pen names. This is probably the point at which a normal kid would have rebelled against the role he was being shoehorned into. But by happy coincidence I loved kabbalah. I loved the fluidity of it, picking everything apart and building it together exactly the way I wanted. I loved the power that I felt when I used one of the toy Names that UNSONG had let into the public domain.

I met my father once when I was thirteen. I'd searched for him online on a whim, found his email, contacted him. He said he'd be in California for a conference later that year, and did I want to meet him for lunch? I did. We met at a Burger King in Berkeley. It was just the two of us. My mother refused to accompany me. My father asked how my mother was doing. I said she was fine, because telling him that she had been depressed and bitter for my entire life and I was pretty sure it was because of him seemed like the sort of thing that would spoil our lunch. He said he was proud that I was learning physics and kabbalah. He said I would probably turn out to be a genius like my great-uncle. It seemed both of my parents had mapped out my life in exactly the same way. He gave me a gift — a biography of Edward Teller, what else? — and told me to make him proud.

I spent the BART ride home leafing through the book. I read about Teller's invention of the bomb. I mused over his retreat into an almost fanatical patriotism — self-justification? A patch over the horror of what he had done? I learned about his war against communist sympathizers in the physics community. And I read through one of his interviews, where someone asked him about being "Father of the Hydrogen Bomb":

REPORTER: Is "father" an appropriate label?
TELLER: Well, I made some essential contributions.

I couldn't help imagining the same exchange an hour earlier, back at the Burger King. "Is 'father' an appropriate label?" I would ask. "Well," he would tell me, "I made some essential contributions." So much for Adrian Teller, and so much for my heritage.

More interesting was the poem. *My great-uncle had written a traditional kabbalistic alphabet poem.* I don't think he did it on purpose, I don't think he knew he was working in a genre beloved by sages for centuries, I think he just sat down one day and thought it would be funny to write a poem on the different alphabet letters. It started:

A stands for atom; it is so small
No one has ever seen it at all.

B stands for bombs; now the bombs are much bigger.
So, brother, do not be too fast on the trigger.

Then the book — the nerve of it — moves on! As if there was something more important than my great-uncle's correspondences between the letters of the alphabet to the aspects of the destruction he had unleashed. Oppenheimer might have been a Hindu heathen, but Teller must have been, deep down, a kabbalist. Since then I've searched high and low, but I have only been able to find two more of his couplets.

H has become a most ominous letter;
It means something bigger, if not something better.

S stands for secret — you'll keep it forever
Provided there's nobody else who is clever.

I obsessed over these when I was younger. Part of me thought they were secret messages to me. Part of me still does. The reference to "brother" on the B, for example—his brother was my grandfather. Don't tell me that's a coincidence. Nothing is ever a coincidence.

"What are you thinking, Aaron?" The telepathy was weak—Ana had never been able to follow when I started brooding.

"S is for secret," I said. "You'll keep it forever. Provided there's nobody else who is clever."

"That's such an Aaron thing to say," she said. I don't know if she was thinking of my cryptography work, or just accusing me of always thinking I was the only clever person around.

"You think so?" I asked. "It's actually from my great-uncle. Maybe everyone who told me to grow up to be just like him got their wish after all."

"Aaron," said Ana. "I like you, but you're not the kind of person I want to see inventing doomsday devices."

We didn't even need the mind-link for this one. Obvious response was obvious. What did she think we were doing?

"So," asked Ana. "If you're going to be the new Comet King, does that mean you're going to go declare war against Hell, kill Thamiel, and save humanity?"

"Yeah," I said, although I hadn't thought much about it. It did seem like the right thing to do, although I remembered reading something about how Thamiel was a facet of God and couldn't actually be killed. I figured a new Comet King would part that sea when he came to it.

"Oh," said Ana.

"What about you?" I asked. "I mean, the Comet King's wife was..."

"I'm not your wife," said Ana. "The whole marriage ritual was a test. I'm glad we did it. It's interesting. But I'm not your girlfriend and I'm not your wife."

"Gah, I didn't mean—"

"But to answer your question," Ana said, "I don't know."

I waited.

"Theodicy... is really hard. I didn't expect to run into practical applications this soon. There's lots of evil in the world, and everyone wants to run out and fix it, in fact there's this immense moral pressure to run out and fix it, but whenever someone tries, something goes horribly wrong. I mean, that's what the French revolutionaries tried to do, and the Communists. Trying to fix the world, any more than just the boring kind of fixing the world where you hold a bake sale to support your local school—that's hubris. But refusing to do that, when you know people are starving and dying all around you—that's monstrous. So which are we? Monstrous or arrogant?"

"Me?" I asked. "Arrogant. All the way."

"And I understand the impulse. It's tempting to run out there and play Joan of Arc—"

"Jonah whale," I corrected. "*Noah* ark."

"—but I've read enough history to know how that ends. So to answer your question—what do I want to do with this discovery? I think I want to do experimental theodicy. I want to know why God created a universe filled with so much evil. So I guess we can try to... gradually start removing evil from the universe. Then if something goes wrong, that was probably the thing God was worried about."

I blinked. That was kind of terrifying *even by my standards*.

"I don't think it'll come to that," said Ana, still looking serious. "I think we'll reach some point, and then God will intervene. I want to see what that point is. How far we're allowed to push before our plans start mysteriously failing and any further efforts are to no avail—"

"Noah *ark*," I corrected. "*Jonah* whale. I thought we *just* went over this."

Ana swatted me. I dodged.

"What's the chance that either of us is getting back to sleep tonight?" she asked.

"I don't know about you," I said. "But I'm going to Bill Dodd's house."

"What?"

It was, I had realized, the Comet King thing to do. I'd got proof of concept that our Name generation plan worked. The next step was to get more computers. Llull only worked on Apples. Eventually we'd have enough money to hire someone to make a Windows port, but for now we were limited. Ana and Valerie had Windows machines. But Bill had been boasting of his new computer incessantly for the past couple of weeks. It was expensive. It was lightweight. It was blindingly fast. And it was an Apple. I was going to convince him to let me borrow it. I wasn't sure how. But I was.

"I," said Ana, "will hold down the fort." She climbed back into bed. "You're going to either need the Wakening Name or a lot of coffee tomorrow."

"You really think I'm going to work tomorrow?" I asked. "Besides, do you think the Comet King would have delayed one of his plans for world salvation just because he expected to be tired the next day?"

"God, Aaron, you're not the euphemism Comet King. You are being *way* too gung ho about all of this."

Okay. But I was descended from the guy who invented the hydrogen bomb. Thinking through the implications of our discoveries was not exactly a family strong point. And the Comet King hadn't been wishy-washy. He hadn't been filled with self-doubt. They say that whenever someone asked the Comet King why he took the weight of the whole world on his shoulders, he'd just said, "Somebody has to and no one else will."

Was I arrogant to even make the comparison? Maybe. But I had crossed out of the realm of normal human life the moment I heard the Vital Name and realized it was a shortcut to omnipotence. Where I stood now there was no model, no track to follow, save one. Only one person had ever had access to the sheer volume of Names I was going to have, ever stood alone and seen the future of humanity stretch out before him, malleable for the shaping. Well, what had happened to him was better left unsaid. But now there was another chance.

"I'll see you in a couple of hours," I told Ana, and then I strode out alone into the cold night air.

Chapter Seven

The Perishing Vegetable Memory

Early morning, May 11, 2017
San Jose

My watch read 5 a.m. Bill Dodd lived an hour's walk away, close to the weird morass of swamps and mud flats that passed for the San Francisco Bay in this area. He woke up around six and left at seven for some tutoring job up in the North Bay. I figured by the time I got to his home, it would be just about morning and I could catch him while he was getting ready.

The streets were deserted, the houses dark. The cracks in the sky were barely visible through the hazy glow of the Silicon Valley megalopolis' united streetlamps. I could see a few stars.

There was a time when the stars had meant something. Blake thought they were angels. Byron called them the "poetry of Heaven." The march of science transformed but did not lessen them. They became burning suns trillions of miles away, around which humankind might one day find new worlds to colonize.

Of all the scientists, only Enrico Fermi had come close to the truth, and in the end even he had recoiled from it.

One day back in the 50s, Fermi was having lunch out with my great-uncle out in Los Alamos, and the topic of conversation turned to where all the aliens were.

If there were truly billions of stars with billions of planets, and the universe was billions of years old, then there had been ample opportunities for life to evolve on other worlds. Earth's sun was a cosmic infant — other stars were incalculably older. Why in those billions of years had their civilizations not overtaken us, reached and colonized Earth just as Earthly civilizations had reached and colonized their more isolated neighbors?

Maybe life was incalculably rare, a spectacular fluke? Nonsense; even in those days scientists knew that if they stuck hydrocarbons in a jar and shook really hard, they'd get some biological-looking compounds. Maybe it was multicellular life that was the bottleneck? Unlikely—it evolved three separate times on Earth alone. Sapience? Dolphins are practically sapient, so it must also be as common as dirt. Civilization? Developed separately in the Near East, China, Mexico, Peru, et cetera, et cetera. Space travel? You're trying to tell me that of a billion civilizations on a billion worlds over a billion years, not one would think of taking a really big rocket and sticking the pointy end up?

Fermi crunched various numbers and found that even under the most conservative assumptions, Earth should have been visited by just about a zillion extraterrestrial civilizations, instead of the zero that humans actually observed. He figured there must be some unseen flaw in his calculations, and it bothered him a little for the rest of his life.

He could have avoided a lot of anguish if he had just followed the data to their obvious conclusion and admitted the stars probably didn't exist.

Then maybe things would have turned out differently. People respected Fermi—always a good idea to respect the guy who invents the atomic bomb, just in case he invents something else. They might have listened to him. The Space Age might have become more subdued. They might have wondered whether whatever was up there, whatever wanted people to think there were stars and was powerful enough to enforce the illusion—might be best left alone.

But humans *can't* leave well enough alone, so we got in the Space Race, tried to send Apollo 8 to the moon, crashed into the crystal sphere surrounding the world, and broke a huge celestial machine belonging to the Archangel Uriel that bound reality by mathematical laws. It turned out keeping reality bound by mathematical laws was a useful hack preventing the Devil from existing. Break the machinery, and along with the Names of God and placebomancy and other nice things we got the Devil back. We'd flailed around like headless chickens for a while until the Comet King had come along and tried to organize a coordinated response. Now we were back to the headless chicken thing.

A car sped down the street, the way people speed at 5 a.m. when they know no one is around to stand in their way, the way assholes speed when they don't care how much noise they make on a residential street when people are trying to sleep. I stepped out of the way just in time.

In a way we were lucky. Reality was still *mostly* law-bound, because Uriel was burning through his reserves of divine energy to keep the celestial machinery working. You can still run a car on internal combustion, if for some reason you don't trust the Motive Name. You can still *usually* use electronics to run a computer, as long you don't overdo it and Uriel isn't having one of his periodic fits.

But once there had been a time when we had looked up at the stars and thought, "Yeah, we'll go there someday." That dream was dead. Not just because there were no stars. But because the idea that Science was all-powerful, that it was this genie humankind could command and turn to our most fantastic whims, was gone. If we were lucky we could keep the power grid and the Internet running, but the thought of building our way into a chrome-and-plasma future of limitless possibility had passed away sometime during the seventies. Now we just looked for useful Names of God and hoped Uriel kept Science from failing too spectacularly until we got ourselves killed by something else.

It was getting light by the time I reached the apartment and a half-dressed Bill let me in. The "what are you doing up so early and in my house" was so obvious it could be left unspoken, so it was.

"Hey Bill," I said, plopping myself down on the couch. It was probably some kind of faux pas, but in my defense I'd been walking an hour. "Ana and I were wondering if we could borrow your gaming computer."

He raised an eyebrow.

"We've got this really interesting search function going on," I said, "trying to match the fractal patterns in the Song of Songs to paleoclimate data. I know it's a little weird, but we've actually got some good preliminary results, and I think we'd be able to finish in a couple of days if we had some more processing power, and you keep talking about how impressive your new Mac is, so I was hoping..."

"Why would the Song of Songs have fractal patterns?" Bill asked me.

I had forgotten the most important thing about Bill, which was that he liked to think he was smarter than everybody else, and would pretend to know more than you about everything. Problem is, I was making this all up myself, so on the off chance he did know something, it was going to very quickly become clear that I *didn't*.

"It's the Song of Songs," I said. "Of course it has fractal patterns. In fact—" I decided to go for broke, "I think there may be multiple levels of patterns in there. Songs of songs of songs."

"That's not what Song of Songs means!" Dodd objected. "Hebrew uses 'of' as an intensifier. Like 'King of Kings' or 'Holy of Holies'!"

"But consider," I said, "the words of Rabbi Ezra Tzion, who said..."

Then I started speaking Aramaic.

Around 200 BC the Aramaic language started catching on in Israel and most people switched from Biblical Hebrew to the new tongue. Some people started praying in Aramaic, or trying to translate the Torah. The rabbis, who wanted to protect the sacred language at all costs, waged a passionate campaign against Aramaic penetrating into the liturgy, and in the midst of their zeal, they might have kind of told people that they had to pray in Hebrew because the angels don't understand Aramaic. Some people wrote this down, one thing led to another, and it became part of the Talmud. Have I mentioned that the Talmud is kind of crazy?

A couple of centuries later, the Romans destroy Jerusalem, the Jews are scattered to the seventy nations of the world, and now they're speaking all of these foreign languages like Yiddish and Arabic and Ladino. They don't know a word of Hebrew, but they still want to pray. The rabbis want to let them, but there's this old ruling standing in the way, saying that you should pray in Hebrew because the angels don't understand Aramaic.

So the rabbis declare that actually, the angels understand every language *except* Aramaic. This actually happened.

And everyone thought it was a joke, but then the sky shattered and we met the angels, and by golly they spoke every language from Albanian to Zulu, but Aramaic was nonsense to them. They couldn't learn it no matter how hard they tried. It was some kind of mental block. Why did the rabbis' weird ad hoc decision so perfectly correspond to reality? I don't know. Nothing is ever a coincidence.

But perhaps there are things humans were not meant to know. And when people started asking the angels — was Jesus Son of God? Was he the Messiah? — the angels answered — no idea. We couldn't understand a word he was saying.

One night, Ana and I were thinking thoughts at each other — gossiping about Bill, actually, since he'd just made a hilariously ill-fated attempt to seduce Valerie — and Ana started feeling guilty, because gossiping was a sin.

I asked how anyone would find out we were gossiping, when we were doing it telepathically, and there were no other telepaths in the world — some said the Comet King had been able to speak mind to mind, but he was dead —

and she said that we didn't know anything about kabbalistic marriage, maybe the angels could listen in on us or something.

This was a pretty reasonable concern. Somebody had added that section to the Bible, the one in John that Ana had taken SCABMOM out of, and angels sounded like the sort of entities who had the power to edit the Bible. For all we knew, Heaven was wiretapping our private channel. So we decided to learn Aramaic, so that we could gossip as much as we wanted and the angels couldn't listen in.

Neither of us was very good at it yet, but that didn't matter, because I was saying the practice sentences from "Aramaic Made Easy: A Beginner's Guide."

"The dog is in the house," I told Dodd in the cadences of first century Judea. "The dog is big and brown. Simeon is going to the synagogue. The dog is not going to the synagogue."

Bill Dodd watched me intently as I spoke, wrinkles forming on his face. He had only two choices — accept what I had said as accurate, or admit he couldn't speak Aramaic and therefore did not know everything. I could see the wheels turning in his mind.

"Rabbi Tzion was a very wise man," he finally told me. Then he went into his room and handed me his gaming laptop. "If anything happens to that," he said as I stuffed it into my backpack, "I will hunt you down and kill you."

I nodded and made my escape before he changed his mind.

When I made it back to Ithaca, I couldn't resist stopping off in Ana's room to check if Sarah had come up with any more Names in my absence. It hadn't, which wasn't really surprising — two in so short a time was a huge fluke — but my presence there at least had the effect of waking Ana up. She rubbed her eyes, griped at me for waking her — then, her tiredness melting away before the excitement of the occasion, told me to ensoul Bill's computer already.

I took the sleek MacBook out of my backpack, plugged it into the outlet, fired it up. I installed Llull. I disabled the Internet connections, not wanting to risk anything automatically updating and letting Bill know what we were doing. Then I spoke the Vital Name. "ROS-AILE-KAPHILUTON-MIRAKOI-KALANIEMI-TSHANA-KAI-KAI-EPHSANDER-GALISDO-TAHUN..." I began. Then: "MEH-MEH-MEH-MEH-MEH-MEH."

Nothing happened.

There's no way to tell if a computer has a soul or not. But when you use a Name, especially a strong Name like this one, the warmth shoots through you, for a brief moment you feel Divine power, it's not just *nothing*. It's part of how people learn they've discovered a Name in the first place, it's the thing whose electrical equivalent Llull is programmed to notice in order to detect hits. It was the thing I was definitely not feeling right now.

"Huh," I told Ana. "That didn't work. I'll try it again."

Once again, I spoke the Name of God at Bill's computer. "ROS-AILE-KAPHILUTON-MIRAKOI-KALANIEMI-TSHANA-KAI-KAI-EPHSANDER-GALISDO-TAHUN... MEH-MEH-MEH-MEH-MEH-MEH."

Once again, nothing.

"Maybe you made a mistake?" Ana suggested.

I hadn't made a mistake. I was the Choir Director of Ithaca. My memory for Names was flawless.

"ROS-AILE-KAPHILUTON-MIRAKOI-KALANIEMI-TSHANA-KAI-KAI-EPHSANDER-GALISDO-TAHUN..." I began, and kept going. I spoke the Vital Name. It didn't work.

"Ana!" I said. "You have the Name! You try!"

"I only know what I took from your head," Ana said, but she spoke the Name as she recalled it. "ROS-AILE-KAPHILUTON-MIRAKOI-KALANIEMI-TSHANA-KAI-KAI-EPHSANDER-GALISDO-TAHUN..."

I could see from Ana's face that she felt nothing.

"Maybe it's just... we're not feeling it because we're tired," I said. I fiddled with the settings of Llull, told it to investigate just one Name, the Moon-Finding Name we had discovered. The speaker let out its strange hum. There was no output. Bill's computer had failed to detect it as a Name.

"Maybe the Name stopped working," Ana suggested.

"Names don't stop working! You think God just packed up? And went on vacation or something?"

It probably says a lot about us that we decided it was important to test this hypothesis, and so started using all the other Names we knew—the simple ones, the ones we could use without exhausting ourselves or causing trouble. I tried the Moon-Finding Name. A big bright arrow appeared pointing toward the western horizon.

"Okay," I admitted, "God didn't pack up and go on vacation. Then why the hell isn't the Name working?"

I was seeing our goal of inevitable world conquest fade into a comparatively modest future of limitless wealth. The one ensouled computer we had could give us enough Names to buy a small state. But minus the ability to ensoul more of them, the feedback loop that resulted in total domination of everything and a second Comet King was fading out of reach.

Ana was quiet. After a few seconds, she just said, "Euphemism."

"You expected this all along," I said. "You said God was going to intervene."

"I didn't think it would be this directly!" she said. "And not this soon! And not like this!"

My mind was racing. "Okay," I said. "This isn't a disaster. Maybe it's not God. Maybe I made a mistake. Maybe we can just use the Name error-correction algorithms."

Given the constraints all Names have to follow, you could find the most likely Name candidates matching a "flawed Name" with one or two letters out of place. Although in principle it was meant to address exactly the sort of situation we were in right now, in reality people almost never forgot Names that weren't backed up somewhere already, and it was mostly a purely theoretical field people investigated as basic research. It's all fun and games until a plot to take over the world hinges on it.

"You think that would help?"

"Look, maybe, possibly, there's a *tiny* chance I could forget a letter or two. But no more than that! We mostly have the Name intact. So if I can get some of the error correction algorithms, we can run them on what we remember of the Vital Name and figure out the real thing. I took a class that mentioned this at Stanford once. I'm sure there are some books in the library there. Give me your library card and I'll go get them. You come with me."

"Aaron," said Ana. "You barely slept all night. The error correction books will still be there this afternoon."

"Ana," I said. "We had the most important Name in the world, short of the Shem HaMephorash, and we lost it. No, we didn't lose it. I *know* what it is. Something isn't right here." I grabbed the library card from her desk. "Are you coming or not?"

"Pass," she said, infuriatingly.

My mind burning, I set out for the CalTrain station and Stanford.

Chapter Eight

Laughing To Scorn Thy Laws And Terrors

Love is the law, but it is poorly enforced.
—Reverend Raymond Stevens, "Singers In The Hands Of An Angry God"

March 20, 2001
Agloe

The holy city of traditional kabbalah is Tzfat in Israel, where Rabbi Isaac Luria taught and died. The holy city of modern kabbalah ought to be Agloe, New York.

The story goes like this: two mapmakers had just finished collecting geographic data for the definitive map of New York State. They worried that other people might steal their work and pass it off as their own. They'd never be able to prove anything, since all accurate maps look alike. So the mapmakers played a little trick; they combined their initials to make the word AGLOE, then added it as a fake town on the map in an out-of-the-way location. Any other mapmakers whose work included Agloe would be revealed as plagiarists.

One day a man came to an empty crossroads and decided to build a store there. He looked at his map, found that the spot was named Agloe, and named his business AGLOE GENERAL STORE. The store was a success, the location attracted more people, and soon the town of Agloe sprang up in earnest.

In traditional semiotics, reality is represented by symbols which are themselves inert. In kabbalah, reality and symbols alike are representations of Adam Kadmon. The territory is a representation of Adam Kadmon, and the map is a representation of the territory *and* Adam Kadmon. Differences between the map and the territory may not be mere mistakes, but evolutions of the representational schema that affect both alike. The territory has power over the map, but the map also has power over the territory. This is the kabbalah. The rest is just commentary.

When map and the territory both depend on each other, to assert copyright is a dangerous act. The two cartographers stuck their name on the map to claim dominion, but dominion over the divine order producing both map and territory belongs only to God.

But the two cartographers named the city by combining the initials of their names. This is an ancient kabbalistic technique called *notarikon* in which words are generated from the initials of longer phrases. Many of the Names of God are notarikons of Bible verses or prayers; some say *all* Names, however long, are notarikons for increasingly accurate descriptions of God. But the most famous such notarikon uses only four words: the short liturgical formula *atah gibor le'olam A——i*, meaning "thou art mighty forever, O Lord." The phrase's initials become the famous four-letter Name AGLA.

Does it have to be AGLA? The *le* in *le'olam* means "to"; the *olam* means "the world." The Hebrew word translated "forever" literally means "to the (end of the) world." Nice and poetic, but *le* and *olam* are two different words and should be counted as such. And why *A——i*? Yes, it's one of the common divine Names in the Bible, but the Bible has other divine Names. How about the more common one Elohim? Then the formula becomes *atah gibor le olam Elohim*, and the Name becomes AGLOE. This is not a coincidence because nothing is ever a coincidence.

Two cartographers add a town named after themselves to a map to assert copyright. Because the map and territory correspond to each other, a few years later the same town appears on the territory. The town in the territory also functions as an assertion of copyright, but because the notarikon producing the town name matches a notarikon producing one of the Names of God, the kabbalistic implications of the copyright remain accurate.

Despite all this there are no yeshivas or great gold-domed synagogues in Agloe. To the casual traveller it's just another sleepy upstate-New-York town. But sometimes people who need a site with very specific kabbalistic properties find the town's name and story conducive to their activities.

And so tonight, the leadership of the American Board of Ritual Magic was holding a special meeting in an old mansion in the hills outside town.

Mark McCarthy, Archmage of the West, stepped into the banquet hall. He leaned upon his staff of mesquite wood and inspected the area. All the furniture was gone, and an exquisitely precise map of the Untied States had been drawn in chalk in the center of the room. There was a long pendulum hanging from the ceiling, currently over the Midwest, and a trap door under Wyoming.

"Why," he asked, "is there a trap door under Wyoming?"

Two others were already there. Like himself, they wore grey robes and carried wooden staffs. He recognized Daniel Lee, Archmage of the South, and Clara Lowell, Archmage of the Northeast and current Board President.

"This was the largest space we could reserve on short notice," Clara said. "The trapdoor's to the wine cellar. One of the best collections in this area, I hear. Once we're done with the ritual, we can go downstairs and get something to celebrate."

"I don't like it," said Mark. "It ruins the ambience."

This was a grave accusation among ritual magicians. Ambience was a vital ingredient of rituals. It was why the room was lit by flickering candles. It was why they were all dressed in grey robes. It was why they met so late in the evening, so they could do the deed precisely at midnight. And it was why they were here in Agloe, New York, a town corresponding both phonetically and procedurally to one of the Names of God.

"It doesn't," said Lowell. "The trap door is a rectangle. Wyoming is a rectangle. It's fine. This whole thing is overkill anyway. You're the one who insisted we do this high-level. I wanted to delegate to five interns in the basement of the New York office and save ourselves the trouble."

"And I'm telling you," said McCarthy, "I know Alvarez. He probably doesn't sound scary—one guy who isn't even fully licensed—but if we leave him any holes he's going to slip through them and something awful will happen."

"I see the doomsaying has already started," said Ronald Two Hawks, Archmage of the Pacific Northwest, walking in with his staff of Sitka spruce. "I'm with Clara. Getting all the way here from Olympia was a mess. And for what?"

"To deal with the biggest threat that the Board and ritual magic itself have ever encountered," said McCarthy.

"So a low-level magician has gone terrorist," said Ronald. "Killed a Senator. Embarrassing. Certainly something we have to condemn. But by making such a big deal of this, we just reinforce our link to him in the public mind. We should have put out a statement distancing ourselves, sent someone over to the Feds to help them catch him, and ignored it."

Carolyn Pace, Archmage of the Midwest, walked into the room. "There's a trap door under Wyoming," she said.

"Yes," said Daniel, "we were just talking about that."

"Let's get started," said Clara.

A chalk circle had been drawn around the map. Clara positioned herself at the east, Daniel at the south, Mark at the west, and Ronald at the north. Carolyn went in the middle, stood at the precise center of the Untied States near Lebanon, Kansas. Her nose almost touched the pendulum; the force of her breath gave it an almost imperceptible swing.

The clock read 11:54.

"Let no evil approach from the North," said Ron, and he held his staff of Sitka spruce towards Carolyn in the center of the circle.

"Est sit esto fiat," chanted the others.

"Let no evil approach from the West," said Mark, and he held his staff of mesquite towards the center.

"Est sit esto fiat," came the chant.

"Let no evil approach from the South," said Daniel, and he held out his staff of magnolia.

"Est sit esto fiat."

"Let no evil approach from the East," finished Clara, and she held out her staff of white oak.

"Est sit esto fiat."

Carolyn raised up her staff of cottonwood. "The Flaming Circle keeps everything in! Aleph! Gimel! Lamed! Aleph! The Flaming Circle keeps everything out! Aleph! Hay! Yud! Hay! Let the Worlds open, but let the Circle hold!"

No black flames shot up from the boundaries of the circle, no alien light appeared within it, but the chalk lines upon which they stood started to take on an odd sheen, reflect the candlelight a little differently. Ritual magic couldn't do the impossible, couldn't break the laws of physics on an observable scale. But they shifted things within that envelope, made coincidences happen a lot more frequently. The sudden appearance of flames would have broken natural law, but there was nothing impossible about five sleep-deprived people in an unusual emotional state seeing the gleam of a chalk line a little differently. So they did.

"Before me, Michael," said Ronald in the north.

"Behind me, Uriel," said Daniel in the south.

"On my left hand, Raziel," said Mark in the west.

"On my right hand, Gabriel," said Clara in the east.

"Quod est inferius est sicut quod est superius," said Daniel in the south.

"Quod est superius est sicut quod est inferius," said Ronald in the north.

Then Carolyn raised her cottonwood staff high. "Around me flare the pentagrams, and in the center stands the six-rayed star."

Every candle in the room sputtered out at once — not magically, Clara's staff had electronics that controlled the lighting, all part of the ambience. The moon came out from behind a cloud — that part *was* magical — and shone its cold white beams into the room, reflecting off the hardwood floor and the windows in odd patterns. For a second everyone saw the pentagrams and the six-rayed star just as they had named them. Then the moon went back behind a cloud and they disappeared before anyone could be entirely certain it hadn't been a coincidence.

Clara spoke: "We gather here tonight to call penalty upon one who has broken our law. Dylan Alvarez, apprentice ritual magician, has broken fellowship with the Board. He has violated federal and state regulations that prohibit practicing ritual magic without being a Board member in good standing. He has announced his intention to continue practicing without a license. He has killed several local officials of the American Board of Ritual Magic in order to, in his own words, 'make a point.' He has assassinated Senator Frank Lautenberg, the Board's foremost ally in Congress. He has declared war on the American magical establishment. He has mocked ritual magic as 'placebomancy' and publicly released the secrets he had sworn to protect. For all this, he has been condemned by our Board and by our order."

The room was dead silent. The only light was moonlight from the high windows. The clock read 11:58.

"He has violated the laws of God and Man and we will have justice. The justice of God does not concern us. The justice of Man will be swift and merciless. Show the location of Dylan Alvarez unto us, O Powers, that we may pour upon him the cup of our wrath."

"Show!" said Daniel in the south.

"Show!" said Mark in the west.

"Show!" said Ronald in the north.

"Show!" said Clara in the east.

"SHOW!" said Carolyn in the center, and she gave the pendulum a big push, then retreated to the outside of the circle.

The clock read 12:00.

The giant pendulum veered wildly over the map of the Untied States. It hung by a special rope with odd kinks and tangles that gave its motion an unpredictable, chaotic quality and prevented it from ever quite going vertical. After various false starts and sudden jerks, it ended up pointing to the city of Amarillo, Texas.

Clara flicked her staff, and the lights came on again.

"Well," she said. "That was easy. We'll contact the Texas Technocracy and the Amarillo police department tomorrow morning. Shouldn't be too hard."

"Better send the Feds," said Mark. "I'm telling you, things involving Dylan Alvarez are *always* hard."

"You thought *this ritual* would be hard," said Ronald. "I know you knew the guy in college, I know you've got a history, but give it a break. He's an unlicensed magician. Sometimes it happens. We always get them."

"Someone said something about wine, didn't they?" said Daniel. "What are we waiting for? Let's cele—"

The pendulum made a sudden jerk and ended up over Little Rock, Arkansas.

"What the—" asked Ronald.

"Oh, this isn't good," muttered Mark.

Clara stepped into the magic circle, inspected the pendulum. Then: "Relax. The ritual is over. The lights are on. At this point the movements of the pendulum are just random noise. He's in Amarillo."

"Random noise?" asked Ronald. "You saw that. There was nothing touching that pendulum, and it just gave this sudden lurch."

"One of the kinks in the rope straightening itself out," said Clara. "Could have been a coincidence."

"Of *course* it could have been a coincidence," said Carolyn, "This is ritual magic. It could always have been a coincidence. But it never is."

"You're being silly," said Clara. "All the darkness and ritual and everything have got us all in a horror-movie frame of mind. Let's go get some wine and forget about it."

"I am telling you," said Mark, "something is wrong. Nothing's ever simple with Dylan. It's always like this. We need to figure this out, or he'll run circles around us."

"So what do you think?" asked Clara. She was starting to sound annoyed. "That he teleported from Amarillo to Little Rock the minute we completed our ritual? Dylan Alvarez is a two-bit hedge wizard. Let's just—"

She barely dodged the pendulum as it swung straight through where she had been standing. Now it was above Lincoln, Nebraska. Then another swing. St. Louis, Missouri. Then another. Somewhere in the middle of North Dakota.

"You saw that!" said Mark. "Don't you dare tell me you didn't see that! I knew this was going to happen! Something's wrong with the ritual and *I told you this was going to happen!*"

"Mark, calm down," said Daniel. "Dylan's probably doing a ritual of his own, to interfere with us. It's not like this ritual was particularly secret, we all had to get to Agloe, anyone who's watching our movements would have known we were planning something for today, and it wouldn't be too hard to figure out what that was."

Salt Lake City, Utah.

"You're saying Dylan Alvarez has *spies* in the American Board of Ritual Magic?" asked Carolyn, horrified.

The Idaho panhandle.

"Well, why not?" asked Ronald. "I'm starting to agree with Mark. Maybe we've been underestimating this guy."

The very center of Wyoming.

"For the last time," said Clara, "Dylan Alvarez is a two-bit hedge wizard who doesn't know anything about..."

"SURPRISE, MOTHERFUCKERS!" yelled Dylan Alvarez, jumping out of the trap door with a revolver in each hand.

Bang. Bang. Down went Daniel Lee, Archmage of the South. Bang bang bang. Down went Ronald Two Hawks, Archmage of the Pacific Northwest.

Carolyn Pace traced figures in the air with her cottonwood staff. "Libera nos, Domine," she said as she traced. "Te rogamus, audi nos." Bang, bang, bang. Three bullets went wide. It could have been a coincidence, but coincidences tended to happen more often among ritual magicians at work. Bang, bang. Another two coincidences.

Dylan dropped the guns, reached back down into the trap door and grabbed his staff. Boojumwood comes from the boojumtree, a bizarre species of plant that grows only in a tiny part of Baja California. It looks a little like a seventy foot tall upside-down carrot bent at undignified angles. Dylan Alvarez came from Baja California, and his staff was of boojumwood. He swung it wildly at Carolyn, a huge berserker swing. Carolyn countered with her own cottonwood staff, but Dylan executed a very precise disengage and smashed her skull straight in.

Clara and Mark were practically on top of him now, reciting their own incantations. "Imperet illi Deus, deprecamur," chanted Clara. "Defende nos in proelio."

"Caecilius est in horto," chanted Dylan. "Servus est in atrio."

Clara looked at him with hatred in her eyes.

"Veni in auxilium hominum!" chanted Clara. "Fugite partes adversae!"

"Cerberus est canis!" chanted Dylan. "Canis est in culina!"

Staffs crossed with a sound like a thunderclap. Dylan took a second to parry Mark, then ran at Clara as fast as he could. Clara stood fast, her oak staff en garde in front of her.

At the last second, Dylan rolled out of the way, and the pendulum—still tracking his movement—smashed into Clara, knocking her off her feet. Dylan drove the staff into her neck and finished her off. Then he turned to Mark McCarthy, the only one left standing.

"Mark, please tell me you're as embarrassed by these people as I am."

Mark McCarthy, Archmage of the West, took off his hood. "Dylan," he said. "I wish I could say I was surprised to see you here. But not really. Look, I even wore a bulletproof vest." He opened his robe a little bit to show the Kevlar beneath.

Dylan laughed, then slapped him on the back. "Mark! Me, hurt you? We went to college together! Compadres para siempre!"

"That was the plan," said Mark. "And then you turned weird magical terrorist."

"Weird magical *freedom fighter*, more like!" Dylan corrected, then laughed at his own joke. "Is that really how you think of me? I'm not *that* scary, am I?"

"Dylan, you killed Senator Lautenberg with a letterbomb, two days after the FBI assigned him a personal bomb squad to search through all his mail. How did you even *do* that?"

"You think I can't pull off a convincing FBI agent if I want to?"

Mark groaned as it snapped into place. "There was no bomb squad. Your people were the bomb squad."

"In my defense, if I had meant to offer the Senator a bomb *removal* squad, I would have *said* bomb removal squad."

There are a couple different ways people can freak out when the necessity arises. They can curl up into a little ball and mutter to themselves. They can go berserk and start smashing things. They can freeze up and go very, very quiet.

Mark McCarthy started laughing uproariously, a little longer than could be considered strictly appropriate.

Dylan tapped his boojumwood staff impatiently. "Your talents are wasted with these people, Mark. Back in college you always agreed with me about the government and the Board and all those asshats. Well, I'm done flying solo. I'm putting together a group of... like-minded individuals. We call ourselves BOOJUM."

"BOOJUM? What does that stand for?"

"Solidarity with the oppressed everywhere. You should join us, Mark. We could use a man of your skills."

Mark McCarthy glanced toward the exit. So enticing, just a few dozen feet away. He could just make a mad dash and be out of there, couldn't he? Or was Dylan one step ahead of him again? He looked at the door. Looked at Dylan. Looked at the door again. If he was going to survive this, he would have to think like Dylan.

The problem was, Dylan was insane.

Thirty years ago, when the sky cracked, the assortment of hermeticists, Wiccans, and uncool teenagers practicing magic noticed that their spells were starting to *actually work*. Never unambiguously. But the perfectly possible things they asked of their magic were starting to happen more often than chance. Of course they ran around telling everybody, and some people did controlled experiments, and finally people started to believe them. A hundred different schools of witches and warlocks went around curing people's illnesses and blessing sea voyages and helping people find their true loves.

After that first rapid expansion stopped, the schools started competing with each other. *Our* magic is good and effective, *your* magic is evil and worthless. As usual, the well-connected Ivy League graduates won. They declared the Western hermetic tradition to be the One True School, convinced the bigwigs that everyone else was unsafe, and got a state monopoly as the American Board of Ritual Magic. Anyone who wanted to practice ritual magic had to complete an eight-year apprenticeship under a licensed ritual magician or face fines or imprisonment for practicing magic illegally.

The other schools went underground but never disappeared completely. After a decade of irrelevance they found a new champion in Robert Anton Wilson, who proposed a theory that directly contradicted the urbane hermeticism of the Board. According to Wilson, ritual magic is to Reality as the placebo effect is to humans. Tell a human that a sugar pill will cure their toothache, and the pill will make the toothache disappear. Tell Reality that a ritual will make rain fall, and the ritual will cause a downpour.

In Wilson's system, ambience wasn't just the most important thing; it was the *only* thing. Doctors have long known how every aspect of the medical experience enhances placebo effect: the white coat, the stethoscope, the diplomas hung and framed on the wall — all subconscious reassurances that this is a real doctor prescribing good effective medicine. Likewise, the job of a ritual magician — or in Wilson's terminology, placebomancer — was to perform a convincing wizard act. The grey robes, the flickering candles, incantations said on the proper day and hour, even shrines and holy places. They all added an extra element of convincingness, until finally Reality was well and truly bamboozled.

Wilson teamed up with Robert Shea to perform a series of experiments testing his hypothesis. In their work *Placebomancer!* they tested two rituals to produce rain — one invoking the demon Amdusias, the other the demon Crhvano. Both produced the same couple centimeters of rainfall, even though Amdusias was a Great King of Hell who had been known to occultism for centuries, and Crhvano was a set of seven letters pulled out at random from a bag of Scrabble tiles. As long as the rituals were equally ominous, both invocations worked alike.

The American Board of Ritual Magic answered the challenge by getting Wilson and Shea locked up for unlicensed practice of magic, then paying for a series of TV ads where attractive women in robes told viewers that their children were too important for the government to allow charlatans to go on practicing untested magic spells. So much for that. A few licensed magicians complained, or poked at the boundaries that the Board had set for them, but whenever it became too much of a threat the Board would revoke their licenses, and there the matter would rest. For to get one's magician's license revoked was a terrible thing. Who would trust a placebo given by a doctor stripped of his medical diploma, dressed in street clothes, working out of his garage? A magician who lost his license would lose the ability to convince Reality of anything. The American Board of Ritual Magic, originally a perfectly ordinary example of regulatory capture, had taken on ontological significance.

So nobody had been too worried when young apprentice magician Dylan Alvarez had pissed off one too many people, gotten expelled from the Board, and vowed revenge. He was just an apprentice, after all, and anyway he'd lost his license. Good luck convincing the universe of anything *now*.

But Alvarez had realized that there *are* people without medical degrees who hand out convincing placebos. They just don't do it by pathetically begging people to believe they're doctors. They do it by saying they're better than doctors, that they've discovered hidden secrets, that the medical establishment is in cahoots against them, but they'll show the fools, oh yes, they'll show them all. A good naturopath armed with a couple of crystals and a bubbling blue solution can convince thousands, millions, even in the face of mountains of contradictory evidence. Ambience, Dylan realized, is really a subset of a stronger power. The power of narrative. The literary tropes declaring that, given A, B is sure to follow.

All the other shmucks who had been expelled from the Board had begged to be let back in. Or they'd tried to hide it from Reality, to claim that they were really magicians after all, that the decision had been unfair, didn't count, wasn't a big deal. Reality hadn't bought it.

Dylan had declared that if the Board had set themselves at odds against him, so much worse for the Board. And Reality had *eaten it up*. Now an entire guild of people who prided themselves on remaining on the right side of narrative tropes had to deal with a devilishly handsome rebel with a cause who had sworn to dismantle their entrenched oppressive bureaucracy with fire and sword, and who did clever witty things like hide in a wine cellar so that a magically-charged pendulum would track his real-world location underneath the floor rather than his analogical location on a map.

Can you imagine a story where a man lies in wait to assassinate the five masters of the American Board of Ritual Magic even as they are plotting to kill him, confounds their ritual, bursts out of the trap-door to their wine cellar at the most theatrical possible moment, raises his staff made of a rare and exotic wood that grows only in his far-off homeland—and then dies ignominiously, shot by a security guard before he even can even get a word in edgewise? No? You can't imagine the story ending that way? *Neither can Reality.* That was Dylan Alvarez's secret. He always tried to be the protagonist of whatever story he was in, and the protagonist never dies.

The protagonist's old college buddy who has sold out to the establishment has no such protection, a trope of which Mark McCarthy was painfully aware.

"Dylan," he said. "I've got a wife now. And kids. You're not going to kill me if I say no, are you?"

Not a plea. A gambit. Dylan Alvarez wanted to be the protagonist. But the sort of guy who kills a man with a wife and kids; well—that's not just evil.

It's *crass.* The sort of thing that breaks narratives, turns you from a dashing rebel into a pathetic thug.

"Mark!" said Dylan, looking genuinely offended. "Don't be dramatic! Compadres para siempre, remember?"

When you had known Dylan Alvarez for a long time, long enough to learn the difference between bomb squads and bomb removal squads, you learned to notice when he hadn't directly answered your question.

"Look, Dylan, it's not that I don't have—good memories of our times together. It's just—after what happened with Senator Lautenberg, and now everything that's happened here tonight—*everyone* is after you. The police, the FBI—heck, maybe even UNSONG. And—well, like I said. I've got a wife and kids. No," said Mark, finally. "I'm not a terrorist. Kill me if you will." And he dropped his staff on the ground and held up his hands.

Dylan made a "pfffffffft" sound, then went back to the trapdoor. He picked up his guns, a few odd devices, and a bottle of wine, slipped all of them into the pockets of his robes. Then he walked back to McCarthy and hugged him hard.

"Good luck with things, Mark. And if you ever change your mind about BOOJUM, you know how to find me."

"I really don't."

"Just hang up another pendulum!" Alvarez laughed like it was the funniest thing in the world, slapped McCarthy on the back, then grabbed his staff and disappeared out the door into the night.

Mark McCarthy, the last remaining Archmage of North America, took a deep breath. Out. Then in. Then he started shaking and fell to his knees in relief. He picked up his mesquite staff and grasped it to him, kneeling, trembling.

Three and a half minutes later, the police burst through the door. They had received an anonymous tip by a man with a slight Mexican accent, saying that they would find the man who had killed his four fellow Archmages sitting alone and sobbing among the bodies of his victims.

Chapter Nine

With Art Celestial

October 3, 1990
Gulf of Mexico

WE SAY THAT MAN WAS MADE IN GOD'S IMAGE, said Uriel. BUT GOD IS INEFFABLE AND WITHOUT PHYSICAL FORM. RESOLVE THE PARADOX.

"I'm hungry," said Sohu.

She was sitting on a little cloud, a dozen or so meters across. In the middle, the cloud-stuff had been piled up into a little amorphous cottage where she slept and stored her books. On the far end of the cloud was the flying kayak, tied down with cloud-ropes.

UM. Uriel thought for a moment. I CAN MAKE MORE MANNA.

"I had manna yesterday and the day before. It doesn't taste like *anything*!"

UM. SORRY. YOU ARE VERY PICKY.

"We're in the middle of an ocean! Aren't there fish or something?"

UM.

The archangel bent down, reached into the deep, and placed a giant grouper the size of a Jeep on Sohu's cloud. It flailed half-heartedly for a moment, then stared at Sohu with dinner-plate-sized lidless eyes. It looked resigned.

AS I WAS SAYING, GOD HAS NO PHYSICAL FORM, SO THE CLAIM THAT HUMANS WERE MADE IN GOD'S IMAGE MUST HAVE SOME MORE SUBTLE MEANING. RABBI AKIVA PROPOSED—

"Uriel!" protested Sohu. "What are you doing?"

I AM TEACHING YOU THE KABBALAH.

"I can't eat this!"

IT IS A FISH. IT IS KOSHER AND FULL OF NUTRIENTS.

"It's staring at me!"

THAT MAKES SENSE. IT DOES NOT HAVE EYELIDS.

"Uriel! Make it stop!"

Fast as lightning, the archangel rearranged some of the glowing letters in front of him, causing them to pulse and whirl ominously.

The fish had eyelids. It blinked.

"That doesn't help!"

YOU ARE VERY PICKY.

The poor fish gave up the ghost.

"Humans don't just eat giant fish the size of jeeps! They need to be cut apart, and cooked, and covered in bread crumbs, and I like them with ketchup even though Father says it makes me a barbarian."

A series of knives rained from the sky, barely missing the girl's head, and embedded themselves point down in the cloud. They were followed by frying pans and entire stoves and bottles of ketchup and, finally, manna.

SORRY, said Uriel. IT WAS THE CLOSEST I COULD COME TO BREAD.

Sohu stared at the objects for a while, then sighed, then picked up one of the larger knives.

RABBI AKIVA PROPOSED THAT THE VERSE HAS BEEN MISINTERPRETED. 'MAN WAS MADE IN GOD'S IMAGE' MEANS 'GOD MADE MAN ACCORDING TO AN IMAGE THAT HE HAD.' IN OTHER WORDS, MAN WAS BUILT TO A SPECIFIC CELESTIAL BLUEPRINT. WE CALL THAT BLUEPRINT ADAM KADMON, MEANING 'ORIGINAL MAN.' ADAM KADMON IS THE BLUEPRINT NOT ONLY FOR MAN, BUT FOR THE ENTIRE UNIVERSE. THE RELATIONSHIP BETWEEN THIS BLUEPRINT AND THE UNIVERSE ITSELF IS THE BASIS OF KABBALAH.

Sohu cut through a scale, and was rewarded with a spurt of blood for her efforts. She shrieked and almost fell off the cloud.

"Aaak!" she said. Then: "Sorry. I was listening. Really."

NOVICES IN KABBALAH EXPECT THERE TO BE A SIMPLE CORRESPONDENCE BETWEEN ASPECTS OF ADAM KADMON AND OBJECTS IN THE UNIVERSE. FOR EXAMPLE, ONE PART OF ADAM KADMON MIGHT DESCRIBE HUMANS, ANOTHER MIGHT DESCRIBE TREES, AND ANOTHER MIGHT DESCRIBE THE STARS. THEY BELIEVE YOU CAN CARVE UP THE DIFFERENT FEATURES OF THE UNIVERSE, MUCH LIKE CARVING A FISH, AND SIMPLY...

"No," said Sohu, who was still trying to wipe blood off herself. "No fish-carving metaphors."

THEY BELIEVE YOU CAN CARVE UP THE DIFFERENT FEATURES OF THE UNIVERSE, ENTIRELY UNLIKE CARVING A FISH, the angel corrected himself. BUT IN FACT EVERY PART OF THE BLUEPRINT

IS CONTAINED IN EVERY OBJECT AS WELL AS IN THE ENTIRETY OF THE UNIVERSE. THINK OF IT AS A FRACTAL, IN WHICH EACH PART CONTAINS THE WHOLE. IT MAY BE TRANSFORMED ALMOST BEYOND RECOGNITION. BUT THE WHOLE IS THERE. THUS, STUDYING ANY OBJECT GIVES US CERTAIN DOMAIN-GENERAL KNOWLEDGE WHICH APPLIES TO EVERY OTHER OBJECT. HOWEVER, BECAUSE ADAM KADMON IS ARRANGED IN A WAY DRAMATICALLY DIFFERENTLY FROM HOW OUR OWN MINDS ARRANGE INFORMATION, THIS KNOWLEDGE IS FIENDISHLY DIFFICULT TO DETECT AND APPLY. YOU MUST FIRST CUT THROUGH THE THICK SKIN OF CONTINGENT APPEARANCES BEFORE REACHING THE HEART OF—

"No. Cutting. Metaphors," Sohu told the archangel. She had finally made a good incision and was slowly pulling things out of the fish, sorting them by apparent edibility.

THE BIBLE IS AN ESPECIALLY PERFECT EXAMPLE OF A SYSTEM WHICH IS ISOMORPHIC TO ADAM KADMON. SO ARE ALL HUMAN LANGUAGES. SO IS THE HUMAN BODY. SO IS THE TAROT. SO ARE THE WORKS OF WILLIAM BLAKE. SO IS THE SKY AND CONSTELLATIONS.

Sohu nodded. Was that a spleen? Did fishes even have spleens?

THERE ARE FOUR GOSPELS IN THE BIBLE, FOUR LETTERS IN THE TETRAGRAMMATON, FOUR LIMBS ON THE HUMAN BODY, FOUR SUITS OF THE TAROT, FOUR ZOAS IN BLAKE, AND FOUR QUARTERS OF THE SKY. THE NOVICE CONSIDERS THIS A COINCIDENCE. THE ADEPT UNDERSTANDS THIS IS BECAUSE THE NUMBER FOUR IS AN IMPORTANT ORGANIZING PRINCIPLE OF ADAM KADMON, AND INSOFAR AS ALL SYSTEMS REFLECT ADAM KADMON, THEY ARE ALSO ORGANIZED INTO FOUR PARTS.

Sohu managed to extract the heart from the fish. For a second she felt some strange significance at seeing it divided neatly into four chambers. Then she shook herself out of it and moved on.

THERE ARE TEN COMMANDMENTS IN THE BIBLE, TEN DIGITS IN THE NUMBER SYSTEM, TEN FINGERS ON THE HUMAN BODY, TEN PIP CARDS IN THE TAROT, TEN PROPHETIC BOOKS IN BLAKE, AND TEN CELESTIAL BODIES IN THE SKY.

"Ten celestial bodies?"

EIGHT PLANETS, THE SUN, AND THE MOON. THERE ARE TWENTY-TWO BOOKS IN THE HEBREW BIBLE, TWENTY-TWO LETTERS IN THE HEBREW ALPHABET, TWENTY-TWO SOMATIC CHROMOSOMES IN THE

HUMAN BODY, TWENTY-TWO MAJOR ARCANA IN THE TAROT, TWENTY-TWO ENGRAVINGS IN BLAKE'S BOOK OF JOB, AND TWENTY-TWO CONSTELLATIONS IN EACH OF THE QUARTERS OF THE SKY.

Sohu wiped off her hands. She was pretty sure she had gotten everything even potentially edible out of the fish now. She looked at her piles. There were twenty two weird unidentifiable fish organs.

"Huh," she said.

LIKEWISE, THERE ARE SEVENTY-TWO BOOKS IN THE CATHOLIC BIBLE, SEVENTY-TWO LETTERS IN THE SHEM HAMEPHORASH, SEVENTY-TWO HEARTBEATS PER MINUTE IN A HEALTHY HUMAN ADULT, SEVENTY-TWO SIDES OF NUMBER CARDS IN THE TAROT, SEVENTY-TWO PAGES IN WILLIAM BLAKE'S POETICAL SKETCHES, AND SEVENTY-TWO YEARS TO ONE DEGREE OF PRECESSION OF THE EARTH'S EQUINOX.

Sohu had finally extracted enough pieces of fish innard to put on a frying pan. She placed it on a stove. Even though the stove was unconnected to any source of gas or electricity, it started burning with a thin blue flame.

IN KABBALAH, Uriel continued, WE RECOGNIZE CERTAIN DIVISIONS OF ADAM KADMON AS ESPECIALLY IMPORTANT. A FOURFOLD DIVISION, WHICH WE INTERPRET AS FOUR WORLDS. A TENFOLD DIVISION, WHICH WE INTERPRET AS TEN SEPHIROT. A TWENTY-TWO-FOLD DIVISION, WHICH WE INTERPRET AS TWENTY-TWO PATHS BETWEEN SEPHIROT. AND A SEVENTY-TWO-FOLD DIVISION, WHICH WE INTERPRET AS THE SEVENTY-TWO-FOLD EXPLICIT NAME OF GOD. BY UNDERSTANDING ALL OF THESE DIVISIONS, WE LEARN THE STRUCTURE OF ADAM KADMON AND THEREFORE THE ORGANIZATIONAL PRINCIPLES OF THE UNIVERSE. ONCE THE ORGANIZATIONAL PRINCIPLES OF THE UNIVERSE ARE UNDERSTOOD, THEY CAN BE CHANGED. IT IS AS EASY AS SHOOTING FISH IN A BARREL.

"You're doing it on purpose now!"

THERE ARE MANY FISH METAPHORS.

"Wait a second. If you can create stoves and ketchup bottles ex nihilo, how come you can't create food ex nihilo for me?"

THE MOST BASIC DIVISION IN THE MYSTICAL BODY OF GOD IS THE TEN SEPHIROT. SEPHIRAH IS A HEBREW WORD RELATED TO THE ENGLISH 'SAPPHIRE,' BECAUSE THE SAGES IMAGINED THEM AS SAPPHIRE-LIKE JEWELS ARRANGED IN A STRING. THE TEN SEPHIROT ARE A SERIES OF STAGES OR LEVELS OR JEWELS THROUGH WHICH DIVINE POWER FLOWS IN ITS MOVEMENT FROM GOD TO THE FINITE WORLD. EACH ONE

CORRESPONDS TO A SPECIFIC DIVINE ATTRIBUTE. THE FIRST REPRESENTS THE WILL OF GOD. THE SECOND REPRESENTS THE WISDOM OF GOD. AND SO ON.

A spark appeared on Uriel's finger, and in lines of fire he traced a diagram into the sky in front of him.

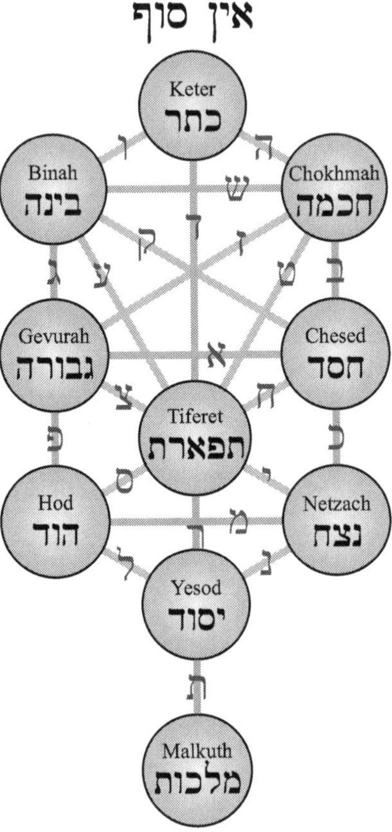

THERE ARE TWENTY-TWO DIFFERENT PATHS BETWEEN THESE JEWELS. EACH CORRESPONDS TO A PARTICULAR HEBREW LETTER.

Sohu looked at the glowing diagram. "Okay," she said. "But what does all this *mean*?"

THIS WAS GOD'S MACHINE FOR CREATING THE WORLD, said Uriel. IT HAD MANY PROBLEMS. SO I HACKED INTO IT AND MADE IT EMULATE A DIFFERENT MACHINE WHICH RUNS THE WORLD MY WAY. IT INVOLVES MANY FEWER SURPRISES. IT IS IMPORTANT TO KNOW THE STRUCTURE

OF THE ORIGINAL MACHINE BOTH IN ORDER TO CONTROL THE EMULATION, AND BECAUSE THE EMULATION IS NO LONGER COMPLETE.

"So the whole universe runs on this system of sapphires connected by paths?"

WELL, MOST OF IT RUNS ON SAPPHIRES ON PATHS, BUT I USE RUBY ON RAILS FOR THE DATABASES.

"Huh? Is that a different thing?"

WE CANNOT TALK NOW, said Uriel, suddenly. THE BUTTERFLIES ARE MIGRATING.

"What?"

I JUST REALIZED. THE BUTTERFLIES ARE STARTING TO MIGRATE. IT IS ONLY OCTOBER. THEY SHOULD NOT MIGRATE FOR SEVERAL MORE MONTHS. I THINK I MIGHT HAVE MADE AN OFF-BY-ONE ERROR THE LAST TIME I SYNCHRONIZED THE INSECT MIGRATION ALGORITHMS.

"Can't you just let them migrate early?"

EVERY TIME A BUTTERFLY FLAPS ITS WINGS, IT CREATES A CASCADING CHAIN OF AFTER-EFFECTS WHICH CAN UPSET THE ENTIRE COURSE OF HISTORY. IF THE ENTIRE BUTTERFLY MIGRATION HAPPENED AT THE WRONG TIME, THE RESULT WOULD BE TOO HORRIBLE TO IMAGINE.

"Oh. I'm sorry."

IT IS NOT YOUR FAULT. I AM GOING TO FIX THE BUTTERFLY MIGRATION. I WILL GIVE YOU HOMEWORK FOR TONIGHT. ALL LANGUAGES ARE ISOMORPHIC TO ADAM KADMON, BUT IN DIFFERENT WAYS. YOU WILL NEED TO COMPARE AND CONTRAST THEM. YOUR HOMEWORK ASSIGNMENT IS TO LEARN EVERY HUMAN LANGUAGE.

"Um, that's not something humans can realistically do."

OH. THEN DO SOMETHING HUMANS ARE GOOD AT. FALL IN LOVE. START A WAR.

"But—"

The archangel was no longer listening, focusing the attention of his glowing gold eyes on the stream of letters in front of him, already rearranging them with frightening speed.

Sohu experimentally slathered one the fried fish-parts in ketchup, tentatively took a taste, then spit it out. Making sure Uriel was distracted with his butterflies, she furtively started squirting ketchup from the bottle straight onto her tongue. She swallowed, shrugged, and curled up on her cloud with her book and one of the ketchup bottles as the archangel gesticulated above her.

Chapter Ten

Bring The Swift Arrows Of Light

May 11, 2017
San Jose

Campus library hadn't changed much since I got expelled. I checked out three big books without even so much as a "You don't *look* like an Ana Thurmond," let alone UNSONG goons hauling me off somewhere. Thank goodness for automatic card reader machines.

On the other hand, there *were* UNSONG goons in front of my house.

I spotted them as soon as I got to our street. Three big white vans parked in front of Ithaca. There were about a dozen officers? — soldiers? — let's stick with goons — in black uniforms organizing some kind of formation to knock on the door.

My mind ran through all of the scenarios. Somehow Bill had found out why we needed his computer and ratted on us. No, there was no way for him to figure that out, and even though I didn't like the guy he wasn't a Judas.

Okay, maybe UNSONG had just gotten generally tired of us hosting secret Singer meetings. It was possible. They'd gotten that group in Reno. Maybe they were cracking down. Except that would mean that the whole thing with the Vital Name was a coincidence, and nothing was ever a coincidence.

Then I thought of the drop-dead simple, blindingly obvious answer, which was that Llull was well-ordered. Unless you gave it a random seed, it would always start in the same part of Schachter space and go in the same direction, checking potential Names in the same order. So if UNSONG ever wanted to catch anyone who had found a way to make Llull work, all they would have to do is retrace Llull's steps by hand. Through unfortunate coincidence, it was only a couple of hours before Llull got its first Name, the sort of performance a good sweatshop could replicate in a week. UNSONG had handed the Llull Schachter ordering over to a sweatshop, gotten the first Name out of it—that stupid Moon-Finding Name, no less—and then tattooed it on the foreheads of their sentinels. Just in case. Frick. They were smart. They were operating at a level so far above me I couldn't even see them. I had really, really blown it.

"S stands for secret," I could hear my great-uncle intoning from beyond the grave, "you'll keep it forever—provided there's nobody else who is clever."

Well, other people had been clever. Ana was right. "Nobody else can possibly be as smart as I am" was *such* an Aaron Smith-Teller way to think. If I'd thought for *two seconds* I would have given Llull a random seed, and...

Ana. Ana was in that house. Ana was in danger. Also Valerie. Also depending on who had been able to pay their rent last month somewhere between six and eight other Singers who I was on moderately good terms with. And Sarah. What happened if UNSONG got Sarah? It was too terrible to think about.

And yet approximately zero percent of my brain's emotional capacity was devoted to worrying about my super powerful magic computer. *Ana*, my limbic system screamed. She was my weird Platonic sort-of-girlfriend except we were just friends and I wasn't supposed to call her that. That was a bond stronger than death. *Ana was in danger.* [Ana!] I thought. No answer. Obviously too stressed for telepathy right now.

The overt meaning of *teller* is "someone who narrates a story."

The kabbalistic meaning is "someone who summons celestial energies."

This reading we derive from my great-uncle, who *also* had a bad track record for making reasonable choices and avoiding apocalypses.

I blew up the front wall of my house.

It was a simple name, the Avalanche Name, only eleven letters, not very good at hurting people but excellent for collapsing buildings. Also good at getting people's attention. Ana was a sound sleeper. Once she'd told me she wouldn't wake up even if the house fell down around her. I figured she was exaggerating. I guess we would find out.

UNSONG's attention was also gotten. The agents turned, looking around frantically. I had crouched behind a car and they didn't see me. They started to fan out, pistols at the ready.

One reason that people become Singers is the lure of fighting a magical duel. It would be pretty neat, wouldn't it? You chant terrible warlike

Names, your shadowy opponent deflects or neutralizes them with his own arcane knowledge, and at last the most esoterically learned man wins, standing dreadful above a pile of rubble while onlookers gaze in awe and think, "There is a kabbalist."

In reality, saying even a very short Name takes a couple of seconds. Pressing a trigger takes a tenth of that. So magical duels are right out, unless your opponent has forgotten his gun, which one can usually count on UNSONG not doing. Great masters like the old rabbis or the Archangel Uriel could access higher worlds where all bets were off. But me? I was going to need a couple of seconds, during which I was a sitting duck.

I spoke the Tenebrous Name and plunged the street into darkness.

Fighting a magical duel was incredibly dumb, but no one had ever claimed it wasn't awesome.

While they were adjusting, I spoke the Bulletproof Name, which would protect me from exactly one bullet. Names must be spoken clearly and distinctly. Unless you're the Comet King or something, you can't get much more than eight or ten letters a second. The Bulletproof name was forty letters, which meant four to five seconds. That meant I wasn't so much safe as "safe from anyone who couldn't shoot me twice within a four second interval." Once again, I did not expect UNSONG to have that problem.

My goal was to get Ana, get the computers, and speak the Vanishing Name.

The darkness of the Tenebrous Name was near-absolute, but three flashlights clicked on before I'd crawled out from the car. I had to admit my chances of getting in the house looked pretty slim, as three of the agents had taken to guarding the porch.

So I ran to the side of the house. The Ascending Name would send me up to the balcony, but they would probably hear me, either through the Sentinel Name or the normal channels. My options were kind of limited. I spoke it anyway, fast as I could, and got hit by a bullet. It hurt. I jumped through where the front window would be if I hadn't collapsed the front of the house and made it into the apartment above ours.

I spoke the Bulletproof Name again. Six seconds. Then I used the Avalanche Name to punch a hole in the floor and fall into my bedroom.

Ana was gone.

That was good. It meant she had spoken the Vanishing Name and escaped.

The computer was also gone. That was very good.

Five UNSONG agents were pointing their guns at me, daring me to start chanting.

That was very bad.

I'm... not exactly sure what my endgame had been here. Like, breaking into the room had been an achievement, but probably the reaction of the agents who had already made it into the room would be to point their guns at me? Like they were doing now? Like, my knowledge and practice of magic had been impeccable, no one could have faulted me for that, but in terms of common sense I had utterly dropped the ball.

This might be a good place to mention I'd never actually been in anything remotely resembling a magical duel before. Or a non-magical duel. Any kind of duel, really. I had been in a bar fight once and ended up with two black eyes.

"Put your hands up and keep your mouth shut!" said one of the agents.

Slowly, I put my hands up.

An agent came from behind and blindfolded me.

Someone put a gag in my mouth and cuffs on my hands.

I was led into what must have been the big white van.

We drove off.

Interlude ה

N-Grammata

The shortest effective Name of God is the Tetragrammaton — yud, he, vav, and he. This was the Name recorded in the Bible, the one the High Priests of Israel would speak in the Temple of Solomon. The rabbis said it was so holy that God would smite any impure person who said it. Some of them went on wild flights of raptures about the holiness of this Name, said it was the Shem HaMephorash, the holiest Name of all.

In these more enlightened times, we know better. We call it the Mortal Name, and it just so happens to be a Name whose power is to kill the speaker. As the shortest Name, it kept working long after the flow of shefa into the universe had dropped to a trickle; there were records of men dying by speaking the Mortal Name as late as Jesus' time. If the kabbalists had just said, "Yup, Names do lots of things, this one kills whoever says it," then there would have been no problem, but this was back when Rabbi Shimon was working on the Zohar and the kabbalists were still underground, sometimes literally. So instead everybody assumed a Name powerful enough that God smote anyone who said it must have been very important, and people kept trying to say it to prove their holiness and kept dying.

They worked out this whole horrible system. On Yom Kippur, the High Priest would go into the Holy of Holies in the Temple, place his hands upon the Ark of the Covenant, and speak the Tetragrammaton. The theory was that if the holiest person went into the holiest place on the holiest day and touched the holiest thing, maybe that would be enough holiness to speak the Tetragrammaton and live to tell about it. Did it work? The Bible is silent on the subject, but Rabbi Klass of Brooklyn points out that during the 420 years of the Second Temple, there were three hundred different High Priests, even though each High Priest was supposed to serve for life. Clearly, High Priests of Israel had the sorts of life expectancies usually associated with black guys in horror movies. Also, some medieval manuscripts mention that the High Priest would have a rope tied around his leg at the time, to make it easier for his flock to drag his body out after he died.

The Jews naturally got a little bit spooked about the Tetragrammaton after a few centuries of this sort of thing, and the rabbis decreed that any time you needed to use the Tetragrammaton, you should instead substitute the totally different word *A——i*. And *then* when you were going to say *A——i*, you should substitute *that* with *HaShem*, so as to stay two semantic steps away from the Tetragrammaton at all times. If they could have, they would have demanded that *HaShem* be replaced with something else too, except that *HaShem* literally just meant "the Name" and so was already maximally vague.

It is a well-known fact among kabbalists that Christians are really dumb. At some point in the AD era, the Christians decided that something something Jesus died for our sins something something made us pure, and they decided to show their deep communion with God by just speaking the Tetragrammaton — which they rounded off to "Jehovah" — willy-nilly at random points in their services. Luckily for them by this point Uriel had pretty well finished blocking the shefa, the divine light that powered the Names, and their services caused nothing worse than facepalms from any Jews who happened to overhear. Then the sky cracked. There very well could have been this huge catastrophe the Sunday afterwards when every Christian church suddenly went up in flames. But they got lucky. The Tetragrammaton wasn't pronounced Jehovah. The yud is more of an long I sound than a J sound; the first he was silent; the vav was more of a W sound than a V. So the Christians survived. Unfortunately, thousands of Midwesterners died horribly after mentioning the name of a certain corn-growing state, with citizens and politicians alike hastily learning to refer to it only as "the Des Moines entity."

If you don't insist on magic powers for your Names, there are ones even shorter than this. The Digrammaton is aleph-lamed, or "El." To a Californian like me, that always made places like El Segundo and El Cerrito seem a bit creepy. It wasn't the same sort of primal horror as sticking the Tetragrammaton in the middle of something, but no kabbalist I know has ever voluntarily eaten at El Pollo Loco either.

After thinking about it a while, I'm cool with the Spanish using "El" as an article. There's something very article-like (articular? articulate?) about God. You have your nouns — i.e., everything in creation — and God isn't a part of them, but without God they don't fit together, they don't make sense. The article is what instantiates vague concepts: "pollo loco" is a dream, something out of Briah, "el pollo loco" is more in Yetzirah, an object, a created being.

Ana and I had a long discussion about the Digrammaton once. Jesus calls himself the alpha and the omega, the beginning and end. It makes sense. The Hebrew equivalent would be aleph and tav. But the Digrammaton is aleph and lamed. Lamed is the middle letter of the Hebrew alphabet. Aleph-lamed, beginning and middle. "I am the alpha and the lambda, the beginning and the middle" doesn't have the same ring to it. What's up?

And Ana tried to tie this into her own theory of music vs. silence vs. unsong. There was good. There was neutral. And there was evil. Not just ones and zeroes, but ones and zeroes and negative ones. God took credit for the good. He even took credit for the neutral. But He didn't take credit for the bad. That was on us. Draw a line from best to worst, and God is everything from beginning to middle. I protested, said that God had created evil along with everything else, that it was on Him, that He couldn't just change His Name and hope to avoid detection. Ana didn't have an answer then. Later, when she heard all of this explained in more detail, she realized it was the key to the whole mystery, that anyone who understood the Digrammaton would understand the Shem HaMephorash too, and everything else beside. But that was still long in the future.

There is even a Monogrammaton. The sages took the twenty-two letters of the Hebrew alphabet, and decided that exactly one of them was a Name of God. That letter is "he." It's the fifth letter, and it makes an hhhhhh sound like the English H. The sages say that the breath makes an hhhhhh sound, which I guess it sort of does. Breath is the animating spirit of human existence, God is the animating spirit of the world. It sort of checks out.

"He" is pronounced like "hey" or "hay." "Hey" is a word we call to get someone's attention. Attention is consciousness, the highest level of thought, corresponding to the sephirah Keter. When we shout "Hey!" at someone, we are speaking a holy Name of God, invoking the Monogrammaton to call forth the Divine within them. Hay is a thing that cows eat. Cows eat hay and we eat cows. We never touch hay, but it is indirectly sustaining us. It is the ontological ground, the secret that gives us life although we know it not.

But "he" is spelled as "he." A long time ago, Ana said the Holy Explicit Name of God was "Juan," because "God is Juan and His Name is Juan." We both laughed it off, but later I was looking through my trusty King James Version and started noticing things. Psalm 95:7, "He is our God." Psalm 100:3, "It is He that hath made us." Job 37:23, "He is excellent in power and in judgment." All of these have an overt English meaning. But they are, in their own way, invoking the Monogrammaton.

And "he" corresponds to the English letter H. H is for hydrogen, the very beginning of the periodic table, the building block out of which everything else is made. H is the fundamental unit of matter in the universe. H, the saying goes, is a colorless odorless gas which, given enough time, tends to turn into people. How would that make sense unless H was God, the organizing and ordering principle of the Cosmos, He who creates all things?

And then there was my crazy great-uncle. Invented a bomb that could destroy the world, the deadliest and most terrifying object any human being has ever produced—and slapped an H in front of the name. I still wonder, every so often, if he was a hidden kabbalist. It takes a certain amount of obsessiveness to be as reckless as he was. That's how I picture him, actually, studying Torah by night, figuring out new ways to annihilate cities by day. What sort of religion must such a man have? What kind of relationship with God? What soteriology? What theodicy? All I have to guide me is that one old book, the only thing my father gave me:

H has become a most troublesome letter
It means something bigger, if not something better.

What are we to say to *that?*

Chapter Eleven

Drive The Just Man Into Barren Climes

May 11, 2017
San Jose

I.

Time and chance, according to the Book of Ecclesiastes, happeneth to us all. Ana had planned to sleep in, but it so happeneth that she woke up hungry and found herself out of milk. She threw on an old t-shirt—one she had gotten at a theodicy conference a few years ago, with the motto "WHO WATCHES THE WATCHMAKER?" on the front—grabbed a shopping bag, and headed out to the 7-11 on the corner.

Seven represents the world—thus the seven days of creation, the seven worldly sephirot below the Abyss, and the seven continents. Eleven represents excess, a transcendence of the supernatural completeness of ten into an unlawful proliferation of forms. Added together they make eighteen, corresponding to the gematria value of the Hebrew word "chai," meaning life. Therefore, 7-11 represents an excess of worldly life-sustaining goods—in other words, too much food. In keeping with the secret laws of God, Ana caved in and bought a box of donuts.

When she saw the vans, she briefly hoped that her housemate Aaron was still at Stanford picking up library books. That hope vanished when she saw the street plunged into darkness, heard the sound of gunshots.

There was a part of her that wanted to run back and help (how? wielding the bag of groceries as a weapon?) and another part that wanted to at least run inside to destroy the computers before UNSONG could get its hands on them. She knew some Names. But she also knew that only total idiots engaged in magical duels against an armed opponent, so instead she ran, her bag of milk and donuts bobbing beside her, not even thinking straight enough to drop it.

Five minutes' running brought her to the Berryessa BART Station, all sweaty and out of breath. She took out her card, ran it through the turnstile. A train arrived almost immediately. She got on, not even looking at where it was going. She had to get away, as far as possible, somewhere that would make UNSONG's search area unmanageably large. An hour and a half later, she reached the end of the line at Pleasanton and started putting distance between herself and the station. After ten minutes' running through parking lots and subdivisions she sat down in a field by the side of the road and let herself breathe again, let herself think.

She started crying.

Valerie — her cousin. Aaron — her weird platonic friend whom she had married *but only as a test*. All her other housemates. What had happened to them? What disaster?

Had Aaron screwed up? What had happened on his trip to Stanford? Had he told Dodd? Was it just a coincidence? Were they in trouble for hosting Singer meetings, for misusing protected Names, or for trying to take over the world? Had anybody died? Those people in the white vans looked *really serious*.

[Aaron?] she asked mentally, but there was no answer.

She couldn't go back to Ithaca. UNSONG would be watching. She couldn't go to her parents in Redwood City, if UNSONG had figured out the extent of what they discovered they'd be watching her parents as well. There were various Singers up in the North Bay — but if they knew about Ithaca then maybe they'd infiltrated the Singers. Her friends weren't safe. They might not really be her friends.

She could turn herself in. But for what crime? What if they were just annoyed at some crazy thing Valerie did, but she spilled the beans about the Vital Name and put Valerie and Aaron in danger? And what if she could find some books on name error correction? She still remembered the garbled version of the Vital Name; she could still figure it out and achieve Aaron's plan without him. Once she controlled the world, she could politely ask UNSONG to hand over her friends. There was something horrifying about the idea of giving up when the stakes were that high.

So she could be a fugitive. She could run away until she found Name error correction books, or a trustworthy kabbalist to help her. Then get another computer. Then try again.

She took stock of her situation. In her wallet she had $105.42 and several credit cards—all traceable. Also a fake ID Valerie had made for her once in an especially fuck-the-police mood when she had decided that having fake IDs was virtuous and countercultural even if you never used them. Also, she realized for the first time that she was still carrying a bag of milk and donuts. She ate the donuts. They were really good.

She wandered in search of a library and found one gratifyingly quickly. The librarian told her that Name error correction books were really technical and that she should go to a specialized library at Berkeley or Stanford. She'd figured they would say that. She thanked the librarian and spent $74.99 to get a room at a nearby hotel, where she promptly collapsed on the bed.

She was half-asleep when she noticed that the laptop on the desk was Sarah.

II.

Ana looked it over very carefully. Had it been there when she came in? Had she dismissed it as just a complimentary laptop for guests to use? Maybe a little unusual in a cheap hotel like this, but not extraordinary? She couldn't remember. But it was here now, and it was Sarah. The same old NE-1 series machine. The same pattern of scratches on the cover. It even had AARON scrawled in black pen on the side.

Ana looked out the window and saw nothing out of the ordinary. Feeling a little silly, she looked under the beds. No one there. Very carefully, a Name on the tip of her tongue, she cracked open the door of her room and saw nobody. Either it had been here when she came in, or—or what?

But that didn't make sense. She hadn't even known she was going to this hotel before she stumbled across it. Euphemism, the front desk had asked if she wanted a room on the first or second floor—she'd been the one who decided the second. How out of it had she been? Had she fallen asleep on the bed without realizing it? Had someone snuck in, deposited the laptop, and snuck out?

Her hands shaking, expecting to be arrested at any moment, she opened the laptop.

The familiar picture of Sarah Michelle-Gellar stared back at her. Llull was gone. The browser was gone. All the desktop icons were gone except one. A text file called README. Ana read.

AARON SMITH-TELLER IS BEING HELD AT A SECRET DETENTION FACILITY OUTSIDE IONE, CALIFORNIA. YOU SHOULD TRY TO RESCUE HIM. USE THE NAMES BELOW. ABSOLUTELY NOTHING WILL GO WRONG.

LEAVE NOW. IT IS NOT SAFE HERE.

And there followed three totally novel Names and three explanations. The first was the Spectral Name, which granted invisibility. The second the Airwalker Name, which granted the power to tread on air as if it were solid ground. And the third the Mistral Name, which according to the document's somewhat ominous description "called the winds."

Ana Thurmond, the Augustine Distinguished Scholar in Theodicy and generally a pretty with-it person, was dumbfounded.

So she started in the obvious place. She spoke the first Name. And she became invisible.

"Euphemism!" she said, in shock, and as soon as the word left her mouth she was visible again.

Well, that upped the ante. There was no such thing as a Name that turned you invisible. If there was, she was pretty sure the military would be using it instead of marching entire visible battalions against the enemy like a sucker.

Some said there were angels who knew secret Names. Some said the Comet King had known every Name that was or would ever be. Some even said that UNSONG was sitting on a giant stockpile of Names that it kept for its own exclusive use. And then there were always random kabbalists who found Names by being very smart or very lucky, like the time she discovered SCABMOM. But for somebody to be sitting on the secret of invisibility...

Was it a trap? The obvious point in favor was that they were asking her to pretty much walk in to a military base unarmed, with an incredibly valuable magical artifact. The obvious point against was that whoever was laying the trap already knew where she was and already had Sarah, making the charade a total waste of their time.

Wait. Sarah. Whoever did this must not know what Sarah was. Who, knowing the computer's power, would just give it away? But how would somebody know enough to locate Aaron, but not realize why he had been arrested? If he was even arrested for the Vital Name. But if it was just a standard sting on Singers, who would care enough to give her three new

Names and send her off to rescue him? And if they were so powerful, why didn't they just save him themselves? The more she thought about it, the less sense it all made.

She minimized the README file, looked at the computer again. Nothing. Somebody had wiped the computer clean of everything except the Sarah Michelle-Gellar wallpaper. Maybe transferred it to a different computer? Maybe this was a shell of Sarah, and the real Sarah was somewhere else?

Then she turned herself invisible again. It was weird, because she still had a perfect proprioceptive sense of exactly where her body was, she could almost see it as if it were there. But she was definitely invisible. Her clothes were also invisible.

"Huh," she said, and immediately became visible again.

She put Sarah in her bag, put the bag around her shoulder, and tentatively spoke the Name. Bag and contents became invisible.

"Wow," she said, and reappeared.

Plato told the story of a man named Gyges, renowned everywhere for his virtue. One day, he found a magic ring that allowed him to turn invisible. After this, he just went around stealing everything in sight, because it turns out virtue doesn't mean that much when you have magic powers and know it's impossible to ever get caught.

Ana had never been a big fan of the story. She thought that virtue was something innate, something you did because it was right and not out of fear of punishment. She thought Plato had sold Gyges short. But on her way out of the hotel, she took $300 from the cash drawer, right under the clerk's nose, plus a backpack for the donuts. In her and Gyges' defense, she said to herself, the hotel was an evil corporation, and had probably stolen the money from the pockets of the Working Man.

She agonized for a second over whether or not to bring the computer. If she did and anything went wrong, UNSONG would take Sarah and that would be the end. If she didn't, she'd have to leave it here, where it apparently wasn't safe, and come back here afterwards. She decided if she was captured, or if she couldn't rescue Aaron, none of it mattered much anyway, and she put the laptop in the backpack with the donuts.

Then she went visible again, called a cab, and asked how much it would cost to get to Ione.

Interlude ו

The Right Hand Of God

June 20, 1970
San Francisco

LSD became illegal in California in 1966, two years before the real world got so hallucinatory that it became redundant.

Certain elements of the population missed both developments and continued to experiment sporadically with a substance that was becoming increasingly dangerous. It wasn't just law enforcement. Ever since the cracks had appeared in the sky, there were scattered reports of *weird things* happening on psychedelics. The reports from peyote users in Mexico almost strained credibility. Even those unpatriotic enough to doubt the Nixon administration's ever more strident warnings about drug abuse were starting to take notice.

But not the Merry Pranksters, and not Ken Kesey. He lay on the floor of an unfurnished San Francisco apartment, watching the swirling colors gently distort the malleable plane of the ceiling. Beside him, his friend Paul occasionally glanced up from the book he was reading and fulfilled his promised role of trip-sitter. It was pretty boring. Ken had been lying pretty motionless ever since taking the LSD tab, saying little. Still, the formalities needed to be observed.

The colors began to swirl a little brighter. The pulsing fractals started to expand, simultaneously growing *out* and gathering *in*.

When he reached the end of the chapter, Paul gave another cursory glance back at Kesey.

His friend was standing upright. No, not standing. Hovering. He was hovering about a foot about the floor. His face was expressionless. His eyes had lost all features, all signs of pupil and iris, and were radiant silver.

Paul screamed.

DO NOT BE AFRAID, said Kesey, but it was not his voice.

"What... what's going... who... what are... help!"

DO NOT BE AFRAID, said Kesey, and it was definitely not his voice. I AM THE RIGHT HAND OF GOD. I BRING YOU ETERNITY. ALL THE WALLS WILL FALL AROUND YOU.

Paul tried to stand. He took a second to catch his breath. Kesey—the thing in Kesey's body—seemed content to let him. He just stood there, hovering.

"W...who are you?" asked Paul.

KNEEL, said the thing in Kesey's body.

"But... who... what *are* you?"

KNEEL, said the thing in Kesey's body, somewhat more forcefully.

Quivering from head to toe, Paul knelt.

Chapter Twelve

Borne On Angels' Wings

May 11, 2017
San Jose

Sitting in bed with her computer on her lap, Valerie Lowry was watching the sun rise and writing the news.

The overt meaning of *news* is "new things."

The kabbalistic meaning of *news* is "the record of how the world undoes human ambitions."

This we derive by notarikon, interpreting "news" as an acronym for the four cardinal points: north, east, west, and south. There is a second notarikon of the same form. In Greek, the four cardinal points are *arktos* (north), *dysis* (west), *anatole* (east), and *mesembria* (south). When God took dust from the four corners of the world to make the first man, He named him after those four corners in notarikon; thus, "Adam."

Despite this similarity, the two words have a difference: news goes n-e-w-s and Adam, converted to the English equivalents, goes n-w-e-s. The middle two letters are reversed. Why?

(When I was explaining this to Ana, I added that there was a third word in this class, that being "snew." When she asked, "What's snew?" I said, "Not much! What's snew with you?" and she refused to speak to me for the rest of the day.)

I offer the following explanation for the variation. During the day, the sun goes from east to west. This sunrise–sunset cycle represents the natural course of the world, the movement from birth to death. Adam is the only one in history who reversed that pattern; he went from dead clay to living man. And his descendants continue upon that road, trying to reverse nature, to wrest a bubble of order out of the general decay. They raise children, build cities, unify empires. But nature always has the last word. Children grow old and die. Cities fall. Empires crumble. The works of man succumb to the natural cycle. The west–east movement reverses itself, and the east–west course of the sun and the world takes over. And when it does, we call it news.

And so: Valerie Lowry was watching the sun rise and writing the news.

Valerie's *California Chorister* was one of the most popular magazines of the Bay Area countercultural scene. She had a gift. If I had to name it, I'd say it was a gift at taking things seriously. If someone organized a protest, and only five people attended, and then it started raining so they all went inside and had lunch, Valerie could make it sound slightly more heroic and monumental than the First Crusade. She didn't misreport the facts, she didn't gloss over things, she just wrote from the heart, and her heart was convinced that whatever she and anyone in her vicinity were doing was the most important thing.

This morning, Valerie was making the final decision about what stories to include in the June issue. The cover story would be about the recent trend towards a few big hedge funds buying out stakes in all the theonomics. Aaron had contributed a long kabbalistic analysis of the nursery rhyme "There's A Hole In My Bucket," which was... very Aaron... but would at least fill pages. Last but not least, a call to attend a vigil for the dead Great Basiners to take place in Oakland Harbor, just short of the barricaded bridge. Everyone was going to stand by the water and hold candles, and this would be a fitting tribute to the martyrs in the battle against tyranny, and...

She was so caught up in her work she almost didn't notice the gunshots.

It had suddenly become dark outside. Somebody had used the Tenebrous Name. It didn't matter. She didn't need to see the street below to know what was going on. UNSONG had finally found them. She had known this day would come. Ana was out getting milk. She'd said Aaron had gone out to borrow a book from the library. She was all alone.

Whistling, she reached under her bed and retrieved her emergency UNSONG-fleeing backpack, taking a couple of seconds to stuff her laptop into the front pocket.

Valerie was a good magazine editor because she lived in a slightly different world than everyone else, a world where enemies lurked behind every corner and anybody could be a hero. Very occasionally, her world intersected the real world, and then she was like a fish in water.

She climbed out the window and jumped onto the emergency UNSONG-fleeing tree just outside. From there she jumped down into the neighbor's yard, ran around the back, jumped the back fence into a different neighbor's yard, then jumped out the front fence, and was on the street just past her own. Making sure to look calm, she followed it until she came to the park, then cut across, and ended up on a different street entirely. She slipped into a cafe, ordered a coffee, and sat down.

That had gone exactly the way it did in her fantasies.

She took her emergency UNSONG-fleeing phone out of the backpack and texted first Ana, then Aaron. "Hey," she wrote. "Santa Barbara is lovely this time of year. Wish you were here." If UNSONG had their phones, it would knock them off the trail. If either of them had their phones — well, judging by what had happened when she had laboriously explained this system to them earlier, they would roll their eyes and tell her that real life didn't work like that and code words were stupid. But hopefully they would at least text her back and tell her if they were safe.

When she didn't get an answer, she checked amtrak.com on the laptop, grumbled, finished her coffee, and walked back out onto the street. She almost bumped into a police officer carrying a bag of bagels on her way out. She gave him a little smile, and he smiled back awkwardly.

She kept walking, street after tree-lined street, until she came close enough to the airport that the roar of planes overhead became deafeningly unpleasant. At one end of an asphalt lot was a shabby apartment building. After taking a notebook out of her backpack to make sure she had the right place, she knocked on door 3A.

A haloed head peeked out, and the door cracked open a little wider to reveal an ungainly, winged body. "If this is about letting Jesus into my heart," he said forlornly, "please don't bother me. I'm already an angel."

"Ziniel," she said. "It's me. Valerie." Angels weren't very good at distinguishing human faces, but they never forgot a name.

"Oh!" the other answered. "Sorry! Oh, I'm so bad at this! Sorry! I promise I didn't mean..."

"It's okay," Valerie said. "May I come in?"

Ziniel's single room apartment was bare. Very bare. I guess if you didn't subsist off food, there wasn't much reason to have a table, a stove, or a refrigerator. But where did he *sit*?

"I need you to help me get on the California Zephyr," she said.

Ziniel looked confused. "Aren't you supposed to buy tickets?" he asked.

"The tickets are sold out months in advance, silly," Valerie told him.

Ziniel was a fallen angel. Not a demon, mind you. The difference between a demon and a fallen angel is the difference between a submarine captain and a sailor who's pushed off the deck of a ship without a life jacket. The demon knows precisely what he's doing and enjoys every minute of it. The fallen angel, well...

G. K. Chesterton said that angels fly because they take themselves lightly. But what happens when an angel sees too much, gets too weighed down by the sins and suffering of the world? The clouds stop supporting his weight, the wings that bore him aloft in the days of Abraham and Moses grow weaker, and he plummets earthward. There, he gets stuck in a vicious cycle. No matter how cynical and jaded an angel becomes, it's never enough. Angelic brains, or souls, or whatever they have, just aren't built to hold the proper amount of cynicism for dealing with earthly existence. They end up hopelessly confused and constantly disappointed by everything around them, with almost no ability to adjust. There they will never take themselves lightly again.

"I still think if you want to get on a train, you're supposed to buy a ticket," said Ziniel, though he sounded uncertain.

"Nonsense!" said Valerie. "Imagine if that were true! Only rich people would be able to go on trains. Poor people couldn't afford it at all!"

"Oh," said Ziniel, a little embarrassed. "I guess I didn't think of that."

"It's all right," said Valerie. "You're new to this kind of thing. Now, here's what I need you to do..."

It had taken a kabbalistic rearrangement of the Midwest's spatial coordinate system that rendered roads there useless, plus a collapse of technology so profound that airplanes were only able to fly if Uriel was having a really good day, plus the transformation of the Panama Canal into some sort of conduit for mystical energies that drove anyone in its vicinity mad—but America had finally gotten its act together and created a decent rail system. As usual, it was the Comet King who had made it happen, meeting with President Bush and Governor Deukmejian back in the late 80s and agreeing to upgrade one of the old Amtrak routes into a true high-speed railroad like the ones they'd had for decades in Asia. It started in San Francisco, crossed Nevada and Utah, continued on to Denver a hop and a skip from the Comet King's old capital in Colorado Springs, cut straight through the Midwest, and ended up on the Atlantic Coast.

That worked for about five years. Then there had been another sudden drop in the efficiency of technology, and parts of the route needed costly refitting to use the Motive Name. Then the Comet King had died and the security situation went to hell, in some cases literally. The smoking ruins of the Midwest had been taken over by warlords and barbarian chiefdoms—Paulus the Lawless, the Witch-King of Wichita, the Oklahoma Ochlocracy—who wanted tolls to pass their territory. The Other King seized Nevada and demanded another toll. The smoldering conflict that had troubled the East Coast after the 2000 election had devolved into guerrilla warfare that made the whole Appalachian area dangerous. Now the Zephyr was down to one trip a week. Out of California on a Thursday afternoon, into New York Friday morning, then back in California by Saturday night. The tickets were expensive and sold out months in advance.

"The Zephyr," said Valerie, "is going to leave the station in about two hours. The train is guarded at the station to make sure nobody climbs into the storage cars. But after it starts moving, there's no problem. I just need you to fly me onto the train as it leaves the station. I can take it from there."

Ziniel looked miserable. "I want to help," he said, "but I'm not very good at flying any more."

"All you'd have to do is carry me a couple of meters, from the side of the track onto the train," she said. "And I know that might be hard for you. But that's why I have *this*."

She took a vial of a clear liquid out of her backpack.

Angels fly because they take themselves lightly. Fallen angels are weighed down by the sins and sorrows of the world. But ever since ancient Mesopotamia, people have known an easy way to temporarily forget the sins and sorrows of the world. A couple of pints of beer will help the most jaded of men take himself lightly again.

Beer doesn't work on angels, but holy water has much the same effect.

Ziniel stared at it greedily.

"I don't think I'm supposed to do that," he said. He was right. Churches had very strict policies on giving holy water to angels or to people who looked like they were going to sell it to angels. Valerie had only gotten a vial by seducing a seminary student and promising not to do exactly what she was doing right now.

"It's for a *good cause*," Valerie explained patiently. "It's to help you fly me onto the train. I need to go on this train, you know. It's very important. It's for *true love*. My boyfriend is in Buffalo."

"Really?" asked Ziniel.

Sort of really. Valerie's sometime boyfriend, Brian Young, had left Ithaca three months ago out of annoyance at what he considered to be the excessive pacifism and hippie-ness of the California counterculture. He'd vowed to find BOOJUM, the terrorist cell that had killed President Bush and hoped to bring down the new government too. The East Coast had been his first stop. A few weeks ago, he'd sent Valerie a phone number. She hadn't called it, because God only knew what sort of trouble Brian had gotten himself mixed up in and she didn't know who might or might not be listening to phone calls.

But if UNSONG was really looking for her, she had better get as far away as she could. And if Brian had really fallen in with BOOJUM, they probably knew a thing or two about avoiding manhunts.

As for the fugitive thing, there was no way she was mentioning that to Ziniel. Sure, once she had given him her Spiel, he'd come around to being an occasional member of their Singer cell. But angels just weren't good at defying authority. If he knew she was a fugitive, there was every chance he might have a sudden crisis of conscience and turn her in.

"Well," said Ziniel. "If it's about true love..."

And then he drank the entire flagon of holy water in one gulp. There were ways of dealing with conscience.

Three hours later, Valerie climbed down a hatch into a luggage car and gave a long sigh.

She was, she reflected, pretty darned safe. UNSONG could search the entire West Coast for her, maybe they would, and they'd find nothing. And if Ziniel told on her — and sure, he might — well, a lot of good that would do them. She'd told the angel she was going to Buffalo, but Brian's area code said New York. She'd get off the train in Manhattan and let them search Buffalo to their hearts' content.

The train passed through the Central Valley, then climbed into the foothills of the Sierra Nevadas. It was all the same to Valerie. The luggage car didn't have any windows.

She checked her cell phone one last time before the battery went dead. Nothing from Aaron. Nothing from Ana. She hoped they would be okay. She figured they would be. They both had good heads on their shoulders. Well, sort of. Okay, not really. But they were book-smart. That had to be worth something, right?

She rested her head against a bag of luggage and fell asleep.

Interlude ז

There's A Hole In My Bucket

Ring the bells that still can ring
Forget your perfect offering
There is a crack in everything
That's how the light gets in.
—Leonard Cohen, "Anthem"

"There's A Hole In My Bucket," by Aaron Smith-Teller
Submitted for the June 2017 issue of the *California Chorister*

You've probably heard the old children's song. "There's a hole in my bucket, dear Liza, dear Liza." A child named Henry asks his friend Liza for help with a hole in his bucket. Liza tells him to mend it with straw, but Henry needs — successively — a knife to cut the straw, a stone to sharpen the knife, water to wet the stone, and a bucket to get the water. He ends up in the same place he started — there is a hole in his bucket and he doesn't know what to do. All of this has obvious kabbalistic implications.

Looking up "Liza" we find it derives from Hebrew Elisheba, a complicated name I have seen translated as "God is an oath," "God is satisfaction," "God is wrath," or — if you take it entirely literally — "God is seven." Okay. Let's put that one on hold for now.

Looking up "Henry" we find that it is the written form of the name spoken as "Harry." Why write a name differently than it's spoken? In Hebrew there is a tradition of writing the Names one way and speaking them differently — thus *A——i* becomes *HaShem*. A few months ago, I jokingly told a friend that the Explicit Name was "Harold," based on the prayer, "Our Father in Heaven, Harold be thy name." If Harold is indeed a divine Name, it makes sense that it should be written differently than it is spoken.

So the word in the nursery rhyme should be read as "Harry," which is an unmistakable reference to the most famous kabbalist of all time: Rabbi Isaac Luria, better known by his Hebrew nickname Ha'Ari. Ha'Ari dedicated his life to the same question that consumes so many of us: why would a perfectly good God create a universe filled with so much that is evil?

Malachi 3:2 describes God as "like a refiner's fire," but only because the ancient Hebrews didn't know the word "H-bomb." God is infinite energy, uncontrollable power, certain to scorch and burn anything He touches. If God even touched the universe for a second with His little finger, it would shatter like a dropped egg. So how does God create the universe? How does He sustain it?

Ha'Ari proposes a system that my 21st century mind can't help but compare to electrical transformers. If electricity went straight from a nuclear plant to the light bulb in your house, your light bulb would blow up. Instead, the electricity goes from the plant to a huge transformer that can handle it and make it a little less powerful, then from there to a smaller transformer that can handle that level of power and make it a little less powerful in turn, and so on to your lightbulb. God's power, then, passes through the ten sephirot as "transformers" that convert it to a voltage capable of affecting the world.

Since Luria didn't have that metaphor, he talked about "vessels" instead. Think of those artsy fountains where the water falls into one pot, fills it up, then overflows into another pot lower down, then into another even lower pot, and so on until it reaches the bottom. Luria imagined ten vessels, gently transferring the water from God all the way down the world, making the divine energy more finite at each level until finally it reached us.

That was the plan, anyway. The first pot worked as intended. The second and third also worked as intended. The fourth was just a little too weak, couldn't handle the sheer nuclear blast of divinity, and exploded. That meant the full power of the third pot flowed down into the fifth pot, so the fifth also exploded, and so on all the way down to the last pot, which was at least as much "the bottom of the fountain" as a pot in itself and so didn't explode. It just cracked open a little bit.

That last cracked pot was the material world, the universe we live in. It's filled with the shards of the six broken sephirot above it, not to mention chunks of itself pried loose in the blast. Seven pots worth of debris. And remember, these pots were designed to control divine power, so they're made of special God-resistant material; separated from their purpose they become the klipot, powers opposed to God. We've got all of this high-voltage divine energy flowing into us that we're not supposed to be able to bear, shooting off huge streams of sparks in every direction, but it's all so choked up with God-resistant klipot that we're missing most of it. On the human level, all of this chaos and unfiltered light and God-resistant shards and brokenness manifests as disorder. The reason evil exists is that we're living in the middle of a pot with a crack in it.

There's a hole in my bucket, dear Liza, dear Liza. There's a hole in my bucket, dear Liza, a hole.

Now everything starts to come together. Harry (=Ha'Ari) bemoans the shattered nature of the universe to Liza (="my God is seven"=the seven shattered sephirot down in our vessel with us, the only form of God accessible in our finite world).

With what shall I fix it, dear Liza, dear Liza? With what shall I fix it, dear Liza, with what?

In theory, we ought to be able to swim around the bottom of the fountain, hunt for the debris, and build it back into functional God-deflectors. Then we could take the sparks of divine light and use them as an energy source to power the deflectors, and finally arrange the whole system in such a way as to correctly channel the power of God at a human-bearable level. In practice we are sex-obsessed murder-monkeys and all of this is way above our pay grade. The debris and sparks are stuck in the spiritual world and we can't even find them, let alone start building complicated metaphysical machinery with them. So Henry/Ha'Ari asks Liza/God for help: with what can we effect *tikkun*, the rectification of the world?

And Liza replies: "With straw, dear Henry."

Straw is a kind of hay. Hay is the Monogrammaton, the shortest Name of God. The universe can only be made whole through divine intervention.

But the straw is too long; even the shortest Name of God is too big to fit. Any dose of God would burn the universe to ashes; that's how this whole problem started. With what shall I cut it, dear Liza, dear Liza? How can God be channeled and applied to the universe safely?

And Liza replies: "With a knife, dear Henry."

Knife in Biblical Hebrew is *zayin*. Zayin is also the seventh letter of the Hebrew alphabet, represented by a pictograph of a knife or sword. But on Torah scrolls the scribes add a little crown to the hilt, which has led to a whole host of alternative interpretations. Some say it represents a king, some a scepter, and some a comet — this last being aided by a Hebrew pun in which "scepter" and "comet" are the same word. All of these meanings come together in the Star Prophecy of Numbers 24:17 — "I behold him, though not near: a star shall come out of Jacob, and scepter/comet out of Israel." The prophecy goes on to explain that this will be a great ruler who conquers all of Israel's enemies — neatly tying together the themes of king, scepter, comet, and sword.

So how to cut the straw and make divine intervention a viable option? It's going to have to wait for the Messiah.

But the knife is too dull. Tradition says that every generation contains one person worthy to be the Messiah, if the time is right. But it never is, because tradition *also* says the Messiah can only come once we deserve him. The rabbis' descriptions of what exactly we have to do to deserve him end up sounding a little passive-aggressive. The Talmud says that if the Jews ever repented even a single day, the Messiah would come immediately. But the Talmud is kind of crazy, and the more general lesson seems to be that the Messiah will not be permitted to come until people deserve him. Until then, the knife is too dull.

And this is what Liza tells Harry. The knife can only be sharpened by a rock, and the rock can only be activated by water. This calls to mind a similar episode in the Bible. God tells Moses to ask a rock politely for water. Instead, Moses strikes the rock. This works, in the sense that the rock produces water, but God becomes enraged and says that He's so sick of Moses and his rock-striking ways that He will make the Israelites wander back and forth in the desert until the current generation dies off. Only their descendants will be allowed into the Promised Land.

So getting water from a rock represents following God's commandments and the moral law. As long as everybody is perfectly good, it will initiate the coming of the Messiah who can channel the power of God and fix the universe.

There's only one problem: everybody will not be perfectly good. Because the world sucks. This was *the whole point of this chain of inquiry*. We want the world to be good, so we need divine intervention, so we need the Messiah, who will only come if the world is good. That... doesn't help at all.

And poor Henry has much the same problem. He goes through this whole rigamarole — asking how to cut the straw, asking how to sharpen the knife, asking how to wet the stone, asking how to carry the water — only for Liza to tell him he should carry the water with his bucket. And so back to the beginning: "But there's a hole in my bucket, dear Liza, dear Liza, there's a hole in my bucket, dear Liza, a hole."

Since Ha'Ari's time we've learned some disquieting new information. We learned that a sufficiently intelligent archangel could rearrange certain things entirely on his own and create a system very different from the one in the design specs. We learned that launching a space capsule high enough could break some of the previously intact sections of the last pot and increase the flow of untransformed divine light to almost unbearable levels, sparks shooting off in every direction. We learned that Uriel, the only entity keeping any of this even slightly functional, has some serious issues of his own and does not entirely inspire confidence. And worst of all, we learned that the God-resistant debris — the klipot — manifests as an intelligent demonic force and has its own plans for what to do with the scattered remnants of the transformer system.

If the Messiah were ever going to come, now would be a good time. We thought he came forty years ago, in Colorado, but apparently we were unworthy. And we hardly seem to be getting worthier.

My friend Ana informs me of a way around the paradox: some texts say the Messiah will come *either* in the most righteous generation *or* in the most wicked. Granting that we've kind of dropped the ball on the "most righteous" possibility, I think the wickedness option really plays to our strengths.

Still other texts say the Messiah will come in a generation that is *both* the most righteous *and* the most wicked. I don't even *know* what to think of that one.

Chapter Thirteen

The Image Of Eternal Death

October 10, 1990
Gulf of Mexico

I.

"Good morning," said Sohu as she stepped out of her cottage. Technically it was already afternoon. She hadn't slept late, but she'd stayed inside, studying, dreading to open the door. Uriel had no concept of small talk and precious little concept of scheduling. She knew the moment she walked outside he would start expounding kabbalah at her, talking faster than she could follow and demanding impossible feats of scholarship. It wasn't that she dreaded it, exactly. Just that she wanted to be able to steel herself a little before facing it. As for the archangel, he never seemed to notice or care about the time. She suspected she could have just stayed inside all week and spared herself any lessons at all, if she had been so inclined. But then why live with an archangel in a hurricane?

He had heard the greeting. She took a deep breath, readied herself for what was to come.

KNOCK KNOCK, said Uriel.

"...what?" said Sohu.

LAST WEEK I SAID YOUR HOMEWORK ASSIGNMENT WAS TO LEARN EVERY LANGUAGE, said Uriel. DID YOU—

"Wait," said Sohu. "What was with the knock knock?"

YOU HAVE SEEMED SOMEWHAT LOST RECENTLY. I BORROWED A HUMAN BOOK ON EDUCATION. IT SAYS THAT IN ORDER TO KEEP CHILDREN ENGAGED, YOU SHOULD TELL JOKES THROUGHOUT YOUR LESSON.

"And someone told you that was how jokes work?"

NO, BUT I WAS ABLE TO FIGURE IT OUT MYSELF AFTER READING SEVERAL EXAMPLES.

Sohu mentally assessed whether this was better or worse than the normal way Uriel did things, but came up blank.

"No. You have to— here, let me show you. Knock knock."

UM.

"Now you say 'who's there.' It's a joke."

IT IS NOT VERY FUNNY.

"That's not the joke. When I say 'knock knock,' you say 'who's there?' Knock knock."

WHO'S THERE? THIS IS STILL NOT VERY FUNNY.

"Slow down! I say knock knock. You say who's there. I say a name. You say that same name, and then you add 'who.' And then I make a joke."

I THINK IT WOULD BE MORE EFFICIENT IF YOU STARTED BY MAKING THE JOKE.

"It wouldn't work that way! Knock knock!"

WHO'S THERE?

"Avery."

AVERY WHO?

"Avery silly knock knock joke."

AVERY SILLY KNOCK KNOCK JOKE WHO?

"You only say who one time!"

OKAY.

"You... didn't seem to find that very funny."

WHICH PART WAS THE JOKE, AGAIN?

"I said Avery, like it was my name. But actually, I was using it as part of the phrase 'a very silly knock knock joke.'"

WHY?

"It's like... it's like what you were saying about kabbalistic correspondences. Two different things that have the same structure. The name Avery, and the words 'a very,' and you don't see it at first, but then later you do."

Uriel stood quietly, glowing letters swirling all around him. He seemed to be thinking deeply, as if this were a far harder problem than merely stabilizing the El Niño cycle (his project for yesterday) or defragmenting mammalian DNA (the day before).

SO A JOKE IS LIKE A SURPRISING KABBALISTIC CORRESPONDENCE?

"Sort of."

KNOCK KNOCK.

"Who's there?"

NACHASH IS THE HEBREW WORD FOR SERPENT, BUT IT HAS A GEMATRIA VALUE OF 358, WHICH IS THE SAME AS THE HEBREW WORD *MOSHIACH*, MEANING MESSIAH. THUS, ALTHOUGH THE SERPENT INTRODUCES SIN INTO THE WORLD AND THE MESSIAH REDEEMS THE WORLD FROM SIN, BOTH ARE KABBALISTICALLY IDENTICAL. YOU ARE NOT LAUGHING.

Sohu's expression was somewhere between horror and pity.

THAT WAS NOT FUNNY?

"Probably not in the way you intended it to be."

OH.

"I think you might not be very good at jokes."

I THINK IT IS VERY SURPRISING THAT THE MOST DIRE THREAT TO THE WORLD IS PROPHESIED ALSO TO BE ITS REDEEMER. TAKEN TOGETHER WITH ISAIAH 53:12 STATING THAT THE MESSIAH WILL BE NUMBERED AMONG THE GREAT TRANSGRESSORS, IT PRESENTS A VERY UNUSUAL VIEW OF SIN AND REDEMPTION.

"It has to be a special type of surprising. Uh... why don't we get back to the lesson."

OKAY. LAST WEEK I SAID YOUR HOMEWORK ASSIGNMENT WAS TO LEARN EVERY LANGUAGE. DID YOU COMPLETE IT?

"I told you, humans can't do things like that."

OH. RIGHT. THEN I TOLD YOU TO DO SOMETHING HUMANS WERE GOOD AT. LIKE START A WAR. DID YOU COMPLETE THAT ONE?

"I thought you were joking!"

NO. YOU CAN LEARN A LOT OF THINGS FROM STARTING A WAR. FIFTY YEARS AGO SOME PEOPLE STARTED A WAR AND THEY ENDED UP LEARNING THE SECRETS OF THE ATOM. IT WAS VERY IMPRESSIVE.

"I'm not starting a war!"

OKAY. Sohu tried to read his face. Was she *disappointing* him? TODAY WE WILL LEARN ABOUT THE TWO PILLARS ON THE TREE OF LIFE. THE RIGHT PILLAR CONSISTS OF CHOKHMAH, CHESED, AND NETZACH. IT REPRESENTS THE RIGHT HAND OF GOD AND IS ASSOCIATED WITH MERCY. THE LEFT PILLAR CONSISTS OF BINAH, GEVURAH, AND HOD. IT REPRESENTS THE LEFT HAND OF GOD AND IS ASSOCIATED WITH JUSTICE. MY BOOK ON EDUCATION SAYS I SHOULD STOP TO SEE IF YOU HAVE ANY QUESTIONS. DO YOU HAVE ANY QUESTIONS?

She didn't want to disappoint him further. She tried to think of a question.

"Um. You talk about these correspondences all the time. So... uh... how does this correspond to human politics? We also talk about a right side and a left side, but in human politics the Right is usually more concerned with justice, and the Left is usually more concerned with mercy. How come in kabbalah it's the opposite of that?"

THAT IS AN EXCELLENT QUESTION. YOUR HOMEWORK FOR NEXT WEEK IS TO FIGURE OUT THE ANSWER.

Oh. So it was going to be one of *those* types of lessons. Sohu scowled.

IT IS A COMMON MISCONCEPTION THAT THE RIGHT HAND IS GOOD AND THE LEFT EVIL. AS ASPECTS OF THE DEITY, BOTH ARE GOOD AND NECESSARY TO PRODUCE BALANCE. THE RIGHT HAND CREATES AND SUSTAINS. THE LEFT HAND DIRECTS AND PURIFIES. BUT AFTER THE SHATTERING OF THE VESSELS, WHEN ALL ASPECTS LOST THEIR CONNECTION TO SUPERNAL DIVINITY, THE RIGHT HAND BECAME AIMLESS IN ITS BLESSINGS, AND THE LEFT SWITCHED FROM THE CAREFUL DIRECTION OF A LOVING FATHER, TO PUNISHMENT FOR ITS OWN SAKE. THE MIDDLE PILLAR REPRESENTS THE COMPROMISE BETWEEN THESE TWO EXTREMES. BALANCE. UNION. HIDE.

"Um, another question. What do you mean by hide?"

Uriel pointed at the edge of the hurricane and Sohu's little cloud shot in that direction so quickly she fell over onto its puffy surface. Then it rotated ninety degrees and smashed up against the wall of the storm, so that she was sandwiched between them as they merged. Trapped. She clawed frantically, trying to break free, until she was rewarded with a view of clear sky, the four hundred foot vertical drop to the ocean below, and a tiny figure suspended in the air at the level of Uriel's face.

II.

Uriel was talking to someone. She could barely see him at this distance. Human-sized, she thought. His voice carried, cool and emotionless, solid like ice.

"Would you like to get this over with and banish me now?" he asked. "Or do we have to do it the hard way?"

THE HARD WAY, said Uriel.

Then they both took a step skew to any of the dimensions her normal eyes could see. She felt new senses opening up as she tried to follow their path, senses that inferred their presence from the paths of the colored letters that swirled around the storm. The hurricane abstracted, became a series of perturbations in the seed of the world. She traced them back. SA'AR. Then along another set of threads. TEMPESTAS. Still another. HURRICANE.

The stranger seized the threads, pulled them forward, sheared them to their essence. HURRICANE lost its vowels, became HRCN. Then he rearranged them, made them dance. CHRN. Then fleshed them out. ACHERON. The river that formed the boundary of Hell. Sohu felt the storm darken, become deathly hot. Somehow the transmutation was affecting reality.

Uriel reached out, his flaming sword now in his hand, and parted the threads. CH. RN. He fleshed them out. Turned the first set into CHAI, meaning "life." The second into AARON, brother of Moses, progenitor of the priesthood, who bore the Shem HaMephorash upon his forehead. The darkness broke. Waves of holy light rushed forth from where Uriel had made the change.

The stranger snarled, hurt. Then he touched both sets of threads. AARON shifted vowels, became RUIN. From the whistling of the wind he drew an S, added it to CHAI, shifted it into CHAOS. Chaos and ruin. The carefully arranged threads of symbols that made up Uriel's machine began crumbling, falling apart in the wind.

Uriel drew water from the sea in a great waterspout. The Semitic pictograph for "water" was the origin of the Hebrew letter mem. He turned the water into an M, then grabbed the CH from CHAOS and the N from RUIN, made MACHINE. The remaining letters R and S he stuck together, turned them back into SA'AR, storm. The machinery and the hurricane reappeared, intact.

The stranger twisted SA'AR and MACHINE into RASHA, "wicked," and NECOM, "punishment." He began to grow bigger as the power of the storm drained into his essence. Then he paused. Pointed at the letters. Of their own accord, three dropped away, made a new pattern. MEREA. "Friend."

"You have a friend here," he told Uriel.

NO, said Uriel.

"Don't lie to me." He pointed to them again. Another two dropped out. SOHU.

"Interesting," said the man.

The two stepped back into the regular world at the same time, and the stranger flew right towards her.

She could see him clearly now. He looked like a man. He was dressed in a suit and tie. His face evoked an FBI agent, or a high-level executive, or a serial killer. Gaunt, empty grey eyes, close-cropped hair.

To the right of his head was a second head. It looked like a deformed infant. Its eyes were firmly shut and its mouth was locked into a perpetual silent scream. Oh god oh god that face. Something was horribly wrong. *Something was horribly wrong.*

"Sohu," he said, with his normal head. The other one was still screaming. "I am Thamiel, Lord of Hell. We meet at last."

He had two bat wings on his back, no bigger than they would have been on a bat. On him they looked ridiculous, vestigial, yet they held him aloft. In his hand was a bident—like a trident, but with two points instead of three. He looked straight at her. Held out the bident, and the clouds hiding her melted away.

DO NOT HURT HER, said Uriel.

"Are you ready to banish me?" asked Thamiel.

Uriel said nothing.

"It doesn't matter," said Thamiel. "I won't hurt her." He grasped her left hand in his right. It felt horrible, like worms were under her skin and were eating her flesh and bones and there was no body left only worms. As he touched her, letters lit up on her palm, like a tattoo she didn't know she had.

"Her father's mark is on her. A blessing and a Name. If I harm her, it calls him here." Both heads stared at the glowing text, concentrating. "No killing. No maiming. Can't even cause her pain." He scowled. Sohu let herself feel a tiny sliver of hope.

"Nothing about pleasure, though," said Thamiel. "A small mistake, but important. One can do a lot, with pleasure."

He pointed the bident, and waves of pleasure crashed through her. She gave off something between a moan and a scream. It was the strongest sensation she had ever felt, frying every nerve, burning her like she was covered in boiling oil. She couldn't see she couldn't feel she couldn't think where was she what was going on why why why?

And all the while, the worms writhing in her skin. She remembered a poem:

If in some smothering dreams you too could pace
Behind the wagon that we flung him in,
And watch the white eyes writhing in his face,

His hanging face, like a devil's sick of sin;
If you could hear, at every jolt, the blood
Come gargling from the froth-corrupted lungs,
Obscene as cancer, bitter as the cud
Of vile, incurable sores on innocent tongues...

She remembered it because it was the only thing that could describe how she felt. Everything stable vanished from the world, everything comprehensible. Like a vertiginous nausea of the mind, like every fiber of her being was united in an urge to vomit that would never be satiated. Not like she had cancer; like she was cancer, like there was nothing pure or orderly left within her, like she needed to be excised from the universe, like the universe needed to be excised from the cosmos, or like the whole cosmos needed to be killed with poison to put it out of its own misery. But that doing so wouldn't help, couldn't help, there was no poison outside and separate from the cancer, everything was going to be horrible forever and it was all her fault.

"Uriel!" she shouted with her last ounce of strength. "Kill me!"

Thamiel opened one eye a little wider on his first face; the eyes of the second were still glued shut. "I was going for 'kill him,'" said the Devil, "but your way works too, actually." The second head continued to scream. Uriel stood silently as the colors and symbols whirled around him, no emotion on his face.

"You should know," said Thamiel to her quietly, "that if one were to compare a single water droplet of this cloud to all the oceans of the world, the oceans above that are seen by Man and the greater oceans below in the wellsprings of the earth—that no greater are the torments you suffer now compared to the torments of Hell that are prepared for you and everyone you love. And that even if you escape those torments, as some do, you have friends, and you have a family, and even those who seem most virtuous have secret sins, and so the probability that neither you nor any of those you care about end up in my dominions is impossibly fleeting, a ghost of a ghost of a chance. And that one day I will be given dominion over the earth, and that it will be no different, and everything beautiful and lovely and innocent will become no different from what you feel now, only it will last forever. And that I don't care at all about you, but I wanted to see whether Uriel did. And that he could stop this at any time. And you're probably blind by this point, but you should know that he's standing there, watching all of this, and he knows exactly what's going on, and he hasn't even changed his expression. And that I could do this for an hour, a year, an eternity, and he would still be standing there. And that I can make it worse."

He was still staring at her palm, had been throughout however long it had been. "A good spell," he admitted. "I can't kill you," he said again. "I can't make you older. I can't make you younger. Oh. Another mistake." He flicked the bident. Something stopped. She thought for a second it might be the pleasure so unbearable that it had become pain, but it wasn't. It was something else, a feeling that had been with her all her life, a clock ticking like a heartbeat, something deeper than words.

"There," said Thamiel. "You've stopped growing. Eternal childhood. Some people would consider that a gift. I give it to you for free. What else shall I give you? I can't erase long-term memory. I can't make you forget any facts you already know. But I can give you new knowledge. Another omission of your father's. A big one this time. Tell me, Sohu, has anyone ever told you what Hell is like? Would you like to see?"

She tried to nod or shake her head, it didn't matter, she had forgotten how to move. Somehow she opened her eyes. He was in front of her, both faces staring at her, the lips of one of them starting to curl into a smile. He raised his bident high.

Uriel pointed at him and released a river of multicolored light. It crashed into Thamiel and he disappeared, bident and all.

III.

Sohu lay there for a moment. Let the light and fresh air slowly leak back into her sensorium. The horror seemed oddly distant now, like she could barely remember it. A nightmare retreating after break of day. But she could not forget the words.

A rush of air, as Uriel summoned her cloud back beside him at the center of the storm. A bulge in the center gradually took shape and developed, bud-like, into her cottage. The flying kayak was still there, somehow, tethered to the edge of the cloud just as it had been before.

ARE YOU OKAY?

She struggled to speak. Finally she just said, "What?"

THAMIEL IS TRYING TO DESTROY ME. HE WANTS ME TO WASTE MY POWER BY BANISHING HIM. I... DID NOT WANT TO. I AM SORRY.

Sohu turned herself over, so that she was supine on the cloud. She saw the angel's head leaning over her, filling the sky, his eyes as bright as the Sun, and she covered her own eyes to avoid being blinded.

She thought for a second. So many things she wanted to say. She formed the responses, compared them, mulled them over in her mind.

"I... trust you to do the right thing."

YOU DO?

"I... Uriel, it was really bad. You have no idea how scary that was. Please don't let him hurt me again. Please don't let me die."

UM. I WILL TRY TO KEEP YOU SAFE.

"I don't want to be kept safe. I want to... you fought him, Uriel."

NOT VERY WELL.

"But you did. I want to learn how to do that. I want to learn how to fight."

I WILL TEACH YOU MANY THINGS. BUT YOUR HOMEWORK FOR TONIGHT IS TO REST AND FEEL BETTER. He stopped himself. OR IS THAT ONE OF THE THINGS HUMANS CANNOT DO?

"I... I'm not sure. But I think I can try."

Chapter Fourteen

Cruelty Has A Human Heart

May 12, 2017
Ione, California

Something was horribly wrong.

Hasidic legend describes a time Rabbis Zusya and Elimelech were thrown in jail. There was a disgusting bucket full of waste, and the whole cell stank. Rabbi Elimelech started crying. Rabbi Zusya asked what was wrong. Rabbi Elimelech explained that Jewish law prohibits prayer in a disgusting place, and so he could not follow the commandment to pray every morning. Rabbi Zusya pointed out that he was still following the commandment not to pray in a disgusting place, so overall he was coming out even in number-of-commandments-followed. In fact he was getting to follow a new commandment he had never followed before, and surely this brought him even closer to God.

Rabbi Elimelech was delighted, and began singing and dancing in joy. Rabbi Zusya joined in, and soon all the prisoners were singing and dancing. The warden came and asked what was going on, and the inmates weren't totally sure except that the rabbis seemed very happy about the bucket of disgusting waste. The spiteful warden said that fine, then they couldn't have the wastebucket, and took it away.

"There!" Zusya told Elimelech. "Now you can pray!"

I was in a jail cell. There was no disgusting bucket full of waste, but something felt horribly wrong. I didn't feel like it was inappropriate to pray; I felt like prayer wouldn't work, like God was somehow very far away and beyond my reach and neither praying or not-praying would bring me closer to Him.

As I awoke fully, the feeling faded and my memories rushed back in. I'd tried to fight UNSONG and failed miserably. They'd seized me and presumably my computer too, driven goodness knows how many hours with me in the back of a white van, then deposited me in a cell somewhere. I had fallen asleep. Now I had woken up. I was still in an UNSONG cell. There were guards outside the window.

I tried to get up, and was mildly surprised when I succeeded. I tried to speak and found that I was gagged. Obvious precaution. You capture a kabbalist, you don't want them speaking. No chance UNSONG was going to forget that.

The cell was spacious — although to be fair my standards had been set by the sort of rooms I could rent for minimum wage in the Bay Area. It was well-kept, as if advertising that UNSONG didn't need to deny its prisoners any of their physical needs in order to break them. Or maybe I was reading too much into it. The memory of wrongness still lingered.

I cleared my mind as best I could.

[Ana, are you there? Where are you?]

There was nothing. Either Ana was far away, or distracted, or asleep, or—I couldn't make myself think "dead." I would have felt it if she died. That, I told myself, is definitely how kabbalistic marriages work.

So I banged on the door of my cell, hoping that the guards would hear me and take me away to whatever awful fate was awaiting me, rather than leave me here.

Both guards looked at me. One of them muttered something I couldn't hear, probably along the lines of "He's awake." I was surprised to see they looked like ordinary people. The one on the left wore a sort of serious expression that reminded me of Eli Foss for some reason. The one on the right looked a combination of pissed off and scared. I wondered if he, too, could feel that something was horribly wrong.

"Mr. Smith-Teller," he said. I winced internally. I mean, I suppose if they didn't know my name now it wouldn't have taken them too much longer to find it out, but it still hurt. Kabbalists are notoriously fussy about who knows their true name. I'm not sure why. When an angel or demon is hidden in some sort of incarnate form, knowing their true name gives you power over them. Knowing the Shem HaMephorash does the same to God, or something. I don't think there's anything like this for humans, but there's still just something that feels very careless about letting your enemies have such an important word.

"You're awake just in time. We'll be taking you for debriefing now with Director Bentham. Please follow me."

Director Bentham! When the President, Secretary-General, and Comet King had come together to found UNSONG, leadership of the fledgling bureaucracy had gone to a elderly Brazilian politician with a hands-off approach. He'd gone after the biggest gangs and most blatant serial abusers of Names, talking about "decapitation strikes" against networks of large-scale pirates. The policy was very popular — everyone agreed that having the Mafia in on the Name business was a bad idea — and very worthless, because most unauthorized Name use was by ordinary non-Mafia people who talked to each other online. He had died in 2002; Bentham had succeeded him. After the fall of the Presidency, Bentham had somehow manipulated the warring states' commitments to abide by UNSONG regulations into a de facto replacement of the executive branch of the Untied States. A thousand conspiracy theories about the United Nations taking over the US had been suddenly vindicated. The Director of UNSONG had added "Protector of the Untied States" to his list of titles.

And now he wanted to speak to me. Any hope that they were just annoyed at Valerie's secret meetings was gone. This was the Director-General. The head of UNSONG. If he was involved, if he'd somehow flown out to California just for this, then they thought this was the most important thing happening in the world at this moment. Which of course it was. They knew all about the Vital Name and everything it could do, and it had gone straight to the top. The very, very top. Okay. So I was really, really doomed.

I nodded, and let them open the door of my cell and march me down the corridor. This was something else. I knew UNSONG arrested people, I knew that they put you in prison for a long time if you used Names without a license, but I'd always heard they used the normal federal prisons. The idea of a secret UNSONG black site somewhere sounded like it was out of Valerie's paranoid anti-government screeds.

The US government must have had a lot of black sites, and some of them must have passed to UNSONG during the transition. But I'd never heard of anyone being detained in one, which meant either that they were very good with the Amnestic Name, or else no one had ever gotten out of here before. I tried to remember exactly how effective the Amnestic Name was and ironically came up blank. And what about the Confounding Name? I couldn't remember.

The facility wasn't small, either. We walked through poorly-lit corridor after poorly-lit corridor. I tried to look for other prisoners, references to the location, even doors with signs on them, but all I spotted were a couple of locked rooms with the UNSONG seal on the front. An aleph superimposed on the United Nations globe, and around it, the name "United Nations Subcommittee On Names of God" and the motto "I TEGO ARCANA DEI." Begone, I hide the secrets of God. There were deep kabbalistic depths in that phrase, but I didn't have the energy to think about them. I kept getting more flashes of that same feeling, a sense on the edge of my consciousness that something was horribly wrong.

We came to a room. A conference room, it looked like. They motioned me to sit down. The guards could feel it too. I could tell.

The door swung open.

How can I describe Asher Bentham?

He was tall, thin, looked young for his age, had the slightest hint of stubble on his chin. His face was quite handsome except for his eyes. The eyes looked like they came from one of those weird nightjar birds whose eyes are in the wrong place and don't even look real. Staring into them, I knew, with a certainty deeper than consciousness, that something was horribly wrong.

"Mr. Smith-Teller," he said. Fuck people knowing my true name, fuck it so much. "I'm sorry you're in this situation." He really did sound sorry. He was intimidating, but not the intimidating of a person who was trying sound intimidating. He sounded like a person who was trying as hard as he could not to sound intimidating, and failing. I shuddered. He blinked, and all of a sudden nothing was horribly wrong, or the wrongness had retreated into some corner of my mind where I could ignore it.

"I understand you are associated with Singer groups who have a dim view of UNSONG. You are probably laboring under the misapprehension that I am here to hurt you. As difficult as this may be to believe, we're on the same side. I'm going to take your gag out. If you start speaking a Name, I'm afraid we'll have you unconscious before you finish the second syllable, and the gag will go back in. I'm sure you can imagine the reasons we have these precautions. Nod if you understand."

I nodded.

"As you can tell," he said, "we're taking this situation very seriously. The Keller-Stern Act of 1988 states that anyone who discovers a Divine Name of potential military value is legally obligated to report it to UNSONG in exchange for fair monetary compensation. Most people aren't aware of the Act, and we have no interest in punishing them for refusing to follow a law they never heard of. But now you know. So, Mr. Smith-Teller, and please tell me the truth, do you know any Names that might be covered under the law?"

Jewish law permits lying for the greater good. According to the Talmud, even Heaven is not always truthful. Rabbi Gamliel kept his classes small. Later Rabbi Elazar took over the academy and expanded classes; hundreds of new students flooded in. Rabbi Gamliel felt guilty that he had kept out so many bright scholars, but God sent him a vision of beautiful barrels full of ashes, indicating that the new students were no good anyway. The Talmud explains that the new students were actually fine; God was just trying to cheer up Rabbi Gamliel. I had no moral qualms about lying to Asher Bentham. I just wasn't sure it was *possible*.

"No," I said. "I don't know any such Name."

And it was the honest truth. Because I had forgotten the Name. Because I was a moron. I could have told him more, but he terrified me, and the truth—that I'd known the Vital Name and forgotten it—would be neither believable nor welcome. And part of me was desperately hoping that if I said nothing, he would go away, the wrongness would end, and I would just be in a perfectly normal government black site and everything would be fine.

"Did you speak a Name that allowed you to find the location of the moon?"

"I did," I said.

"How did you learn that Name?"

Every fiber of my body tensed at his oppressive closeness. It was a fair question. I had no way out this time. Either tell him what had happened, or lie like a rug and see exactly what those nightjar eyes could do.

I ran through a host of scenarios. I tell the Director-General that I knew the Name and forgot it. He doesn't believe me and tries to torture it out of me. He doesn't believe me and tries to torture the Name out of Ana. He does believe me and tries to dissect my brain to get it. He goes to an error correction specialist, fixes the Name, and takes over the world, even more so than he'd taken over the world already.

I am not a hero. I've been in one fight, but only because I was drunk, and I ended up with two black eyes. The only thing I've ever been good at is studying things and comparing them and trying to understand them.

But the sages of old weren't typical heroes either, and they were constantly breaking out of prison by one miracle or another. Rabbi Meir once convinced a Roman prison guard to free his friend by reassuring him that if anyone tried to punish his disobedience, he could say, "God of Meir, help me!" and God would keep him from harm. When his commander tried to hang him for his role in the escape, the guard cried, "God of Meir, help me!", the rope broke, and he managed to run away to safety. When a whole Roman legion arrived to arrest the great translator Onkelos, he preached to them in Latin about the symbolism of the *mezuzah*, and the whole legion converted to Judaism on the spot. And when the Romans arrested Rabbi Eleazar ben Perata on five charges, God helped him craft a plausible alibi for each; when the plausible alibis didn't work, the prophet Elijah appeared at the end of the trial, lifted up the prosecutor, and threw him out of the courtroom so hard that he landed five hundred miles away. I think I mentioned that the Talmud is kind of crazy.

So miraculously breaking out of prison is the sort of thing kabbalists are expected to be able to do, and I daydream a lot, and a long time ago I had come up with a fantasy about the sort of thing I would do if I were ever trapped in a prison, and this was by far the stupidest thing I had ever done, but something was horribly wrong and I needed to get out of here.

"I was on drugs and I had a prophetic vision," I said.

Ever since the sky cracked, drugs had gotten really weird. The ones whose names were also Hebrew words were the weirdest. MDA and its cousin MDMA gave mystical knowledge, probably because mem-dalet-ayin was *madda*, "knowledge." The effects of LSD were more blatantly divine, since lamed-shin-dalet was *leshadi*, "strength," and the consonants in El Shaddai, "God Almighty," to boot. The ones without three letter names were less predictable, with peyote being a demonic conduit and the rest having variable effects. I decided to go with LSD as the most likely source of divine revelation.

"Drugs always attracted me," I said. I thought for a second, and continued. "So I got some LSD from a friend and tried it out. That was a bad idea, I admit."

I suspected Asher knew I was lying. I was banking on him waiting to see exactly what lie I was going to tell, hoping that I would slip up somewhere in my story. If he would just let me keep going for twenty-seven more sentences, I was in the clear.

"Zelda was the name of the friend who sold it to me," I said, awkwardly, because I couldn't think of any other way to start a sentence with Z. "My hope was we would do it together, but she bailed out at the last second."

That was DST and ZM. Twenty-five consonants to go. I was afraid, which was good, because it let me pretend that my fear was making it hard to talk, whereas in fact I was working out how to start my sentences with the right letter.

"Regular LSD is supposed to just give you a taste of divinity. She gave me something else, I'm not sure. She didn't tell me, but it must be true. No way to know now."

DASAT-ZAM-RUSH-SHAN.

"So I had taken the drug, when I started feeling weird. Very weird. Regular LSD doesn't do that. LSD is supposed to be gentle. Some kind of angelic entity was standing in front of me. Questionably angelic. Not human. Deep-voiced. Like you would expect an angel to be."

Asher Bentham must have thought I was the least fluent, worst storyteller in the country. I couldn't read his face at all. Was he confused? Was he suspicious. No time to think about that. I'd gotten DASAT-ZAM-RUSH-SHAN-SEVER-LAS-KYON-DAL. Next letter was aleph.

"All of the things you hear about angels, the beautiful wings and the golden eyes. They don't prepare you. Not a bit. To see something like that. Right away I knew it had a message for me. You couldn't imagine what it was like."

DASAT-ZAM-RUSH-SHAN-SEVER-LAS-KYON-DAL-ATHEN-TRY. All I needed was KOPHU-LI-MAR-LETHAG. How was I going to bring a K in?

"Kind of quietly, it spoke to me. Phenomenal voice. 'Listen,' it told me. Mentioned hidden knowledge. Revealed secret names."

Bentham was getting impatient. "What names?" he asked. "The one you used to find the moon?"

I didn't know how to answer, but it didn't matter. He thought I had been telling him a story, but I hadn't been. I'd been forging a notarikon. The same way the kabbalists had expanded AGLA into *atah gibor le'olam A——i*. Any notarikon for a divine Name is itself equivalent to that Name. A sentence-by-sentence notarikon was completely valid. There was even one in Proverbs 31:10–31 for the Hebrew alphabet as a whole. But nobody had taken the obvious next step and used it to speak a Name covertly. Well, I was going to do it. I only had three letters left. Lamed tav gimel.

Everything I said before had been my artifice. This next part was pure divine inspiration.

"Looks like I fooled you," I said. "The whole thing was notarikon. Goodbye."

Don't use the Vanishing Name, I had said during choir practice, unless you are in a situation where it is absolutely vital to your well-being and continued survival that you be accosted by a different band of hooligans than the ones who are currently accosting you. Right now, being accosted by a different band of hooligans was my heart's fondest and most desperate desire.

As Director-General Asher Bentham strained to make sense of my poorly-narrated story, I disappeared from right in front of his face.

Chapter Fifteen

O Where Shall I Hide My Face?

You saved your shillings and your last six pence
Cause in God's Name they built a barbed wire fence
Be glad you sail for a better day
But don't forget there'll be Hell to pay

—"Rebels of the Sacred Heart"

May 11–12, 2017
Ione, California

I.

We Bay Arians (Ana and I had debated multiple demonyms, including Bay Arean and Bay Aryan, before deciding we were more heretical than warlike, and definitely not the master race) tend to think of the Central Valley as a nightmarish stretch of endless farms inhabited by people who, while not exactly dead, could hardly be called living. So far nothing Ana had seen in the three hour taxi ride to Ione had changed her mind.

Now here was the town itself, in all its glory. There wasn't anything that looked like a secret detention facility, although she supposed that was what made it a *secret* detention facility. But it was already dark, and she didn't fancy looking. She also didn't fancy waiting until morning; she wasn't really an expert in infiltrating secret facilities, but night seemed like potentially the best time, even if you could turn invisible.

What was the saying? If Mohammed cannot go to the mountain, the mountain must come to Mohammed?

No, not that one. The other one.

"In America, you can always find a party. In Soviet Russia, Party can always find you!"

Ana spoke the Bulletproof Name.

It was a calculated choice. New enough that the theonomics were still guarding it closely, but old enough that it had leaked to a few Singer groups and the UNSONG sentinels were listening for it. Chosen to lure the dragon from its den.

Then she spoke the Spectral Name and became invisible.

Sure enough, a white van showed up at the gas station where the cab had dropped her off, and some men in black uniforms got out and started looking around. The process of infiltrating them was harder than Ana expected; she couldn't just open the door of the van and walk in; there was still someone inside and he might notice the doors opening of their own accord. And if the van was full, she was worried someone would try to sit in her lap on the way back to headquarters. And starting any other Names would break her invisibility, so...

She watched in disgust as the men, having finished their search of the premises, got back in their van and drove off. This was harder than it was in stories.

So she rematerialized, spent some of her remaining money on some chocolate frosted donuts from the gas station, and decided to think of a better plan.

In America, Mohammed goes to mountain. In Soviet Russia, mountain comes to *you*. Or whatever.

She walked vaguely southward. When she felt like it was vaguely southward enough, she spoke the Ascending Name, then the Spectral Name again. Sure enough, back came her friends in the white van. More fruitless ground-combing. Back in the van again. But this time, she was higher than the hills and could see for miles.

A little south of town, the van turned west onto a small country road, went down a couple of miles, and then drove right into a hillside. Bingo.

Ana started walking on air.

By the time she reached the hillside it was into the wee hours of the morning, and she was tired, and she wished she'd eaten more donuts when she had the chance. Such are the regrets of a heroine. She wondered if the Comet King ever rode into battle wishing he'd eaten more donuts.

An armored car drove up. The entryway opened to accept it. Ana slipped in unseen.

For a brief moment, as she entered, she felt like something was horribly wrong. It was heavy and oppressive, like a heartbeat slightly out of rhythm, but also not like that at all. She couldn't tell if it was auditory, or tactile, or olfactory. She turned in the direction of the wrongness, but it seemed to fade before she could get a good read on it. For lack of a better idea, she walked in that direction.

[Aaron?] she thought as she wandered through the corridors. [I've come to save you. Are you there?]

[Ana!] I thought back at her. [Ana, I can take care of myself… maybe… Ana, get out!]

And then she felt my mental trace vanish from her mind.

A door marked with the UNSONG seal swung open, and a tall man with nightjar eyes stepped out with a very grim look on his face. He looked Ana straight in the eye and asked: "Who are you and why are you invisible?"

Holy euphemism, thought Ana, that's the Director-General.

For just a second, something was horribly wrong, and Asher Bentham was that something. Ana ran.

"Lock down everything!" the Director-General shouted.

This would have been a good time for Ana to use the Vanishing Name, except that starting it would break whatever was left of her invisibility, and whatever advantage she had came from nobody but Bentham being able to see her. So she just ran.

Several soldiers congregated around the Director, only to uncongregate and fan out, confused. Bentham grabbed a gun from one of them and shot at Ana. He missed by a mile, and the unexpected recoil knocked him from his feet. No soldier, he.

A guard sat by the entryway, clearly doing his best to watch out for invisible people sneaking towards him. Ana punched him in the face, then hit the lever his presence was lampshading. The exit door swung open and she ran forth into the night.

Asher followed, directing a platoon of guards, pointing out the general direction they should run. They shot at her and missed wildly. Bentham, a quick learner after his firearm mishap, used the Fulminant Name. It missed too, but only barely, singeing some of her hair.

Ana jumped off the road, ran into a pile of brush. Her slight advantage was that the Director-General couldn't really run through scrub in that suit and was about twenty years older than she. The Fulminant Name was short range, and she was increasing the distance between herself and Bentham with every step. She ran through bushes, through a creek — anything she thought would deter the man whose terrible pounding was still on the fringes of her memory.

"Who are you?" Bentham shouted at her from afar.

Obviously Ana didn't say anything back.

"I won't hurt you! I know you won't believe me, but we're on the same side. This is important, I promise! Please, I just want to talk!"

Right. She believed that one.

Just before she got out of range, Bentham went silent, started saying the Fulminant Name again. Ana braced herself — it was anybody's guess whether the Director-General could hit from this distance, and though the Name was rarely fatal, it would certainly knock her out long enough to be captured. She ran as fast as she could, trying to get a couple extra meters before—

Then a gust of wind flew all around her, knocked Asher off his feet. The Tempestuous Name. But how?

She kept running, ran until the Director-General and his horrible base had receded into the brightening horizon.

II.

The back of a pickup truck took her as far as Sacramento, and a train took her to Oakland. In Oakland she broke her invisibility, got a hotel room, and lay in bed without talking or moving or really thinking for a few hours.

Then she got up, took a shower, and bought herself a nice breakfast with the last of the hotel till money. She was a little surprised to see that Sarah was no longer in her bag when she woke, but only a little. Let the conspirators play their games. She was done.

If she hadn't already been a fugitive, she was one now. Director-General Asher Bentham himself had seen her; if he didn't already know who she was he would soon figure it out. And someone else, someone who could seize Sarah from underneath UNSONG's nose, was manipulating her in a way she didn't much like. Ithaca wasn't safe, her parents' house wasn't safe, nowhere in the Untied States was safe for her. But there were other options.

She started walking west. She walked past the hills, walked past old houses, walked past the lake and the Emeryville Mall, walked past the harbor. She reached the Bay Bridge, went invisible, walked right past the warning signs, past the barricades and the guard towers.

In front of her, a few towers peeked out of the billowing fog. The eye in the Transamerica Pyramid fixed its gaze on her for an instant, its emotions — if it had them — as inscrutable as ever.

She was finished with the lands of men.

She was going to San Francisco.

Chapter Sixteen

If Perchance With Iron Power He Might Avert His Own Despair

There's a story about an old man walking down a beach. He sees a child picking up starfish and throwing them into the water. The man asks the child what he's doing, and the child says that these starfish are stuck on land at low tide. They can't survive out of water, so he's throwing them back in the ocean to save them. The old man says, "But surely you know that there are millions of starfish just on this one beach. And there are thousands of beaches all around the world. And this same thing happens at high tide day after day, forever. You'll never be able to make a difference." And the child just picks up another starfish, throws it into the ocean, and says, "Made a difference to that one!"

I remember when I told the Comet King this story. He got very quiet, and finally I asked what he was thinking. Still half-lost in thought, he answered: "Even a small change to the moon's orbit could prevent the tidal cycle. Moving the moon would take immense energy, but the Wrathful Name has the power of a hydrogen bomb and can be written on a piece of paper weighing only a fraction of a gram. The Saturn V has a payload of about ten thousand kilograms, so perhaps twenty million instances of the Wrathful Name... hmmmmmm... no, it still wouldn't be enough. We'd need a better rocket. Perhaps if you could combine a methane/LOX full-flow system with a prayer invoking the Kinetic Name..." He picked up a napkin and started sketching, and was diverted from his trance only when I reminded him that starfish had evolved for life in the intertidal zone and were probably fine. He flashed me one of his fierce smiles and I couldn't tell whether or not he had been joking all along.

An enterprising member of the household staff pocketed the napkin and sold it to Celestial Virgin for an undisclosed sum; the Comet King's partially-completed sketch became the basis of all modern rocketry.

—Sohu West, The Comet King: A Hagiography

October 11, 1990
Gulf of Mexico

Restless dreams troubled Sohu's sleep, and she sought Uriel the next morning. He was busy fixing the ice in Antarctica. It was calving too quickly, floating into shipping lanes. Someone might crash into an iceberg. She let him do it, watched silently for a few minutes. Finally she asked:

"Uriel, what happened yesterday?"

UM. I DON'T THINK I AM A VERY GOOD FRIEND.

"It's... okay. You... didn't know... you... tried to help, I guess."

YOU SEEMED SO SCARED.

"I was!"

I WANTED TO HELP. I FELT BAD THAT I DID NOT SAVE YOU.

"Why? Why did you let Thamiel do that to me? He said you could have banished him. Why didn't you just banish him at the beginning?"

UM. I AM TRYING TO KEEP THE WORLD FROM ENDING.

"Why is the world going to end if you banish Thamiel?"

A LONG TIME AGO THERE WAS A WAR IN HEAVEN. ALL OF THE ARCHANGELS FOUGHT THAMIEL, AND THAMIEL WON. I DID NOT LIKE THIS RESULT, SO I ADDED A NEW STRUCTURE AT THE ONTOLOGICAL BASE OF THE UNIVERSE, A LAYER THAT REINTERPRETS ADAM KADMON. I CONVERTED THE WORLD FROM A SUBSTRATE OF DIVINE LIGHT TO A SUBSTRATE OF MATHEMATICS. THIS PREVENTED ANGELS AND DEMONS FROM EXISTING IN ANY MORE THAN A METAPHORICAL WAY. WHEN THE DIVINE LIGHT, THE SHEFA, ENTERED THE UNIVERSE, I CHANNELED IT INTO A RESERVOIR SO THAT IT DID NOT INTERFERE WITH THE CLOCKWORK.

"And then we crashed Apollo 8 into the edge of the world."

YOU WENT BEYOND THE EDGE OF THE WORLD AND RECITED THE BIBLE. YOU INJECTED THE CODE FOR THE ORIGINAL SYSTEM VIA A BUFFER OVERFLOW ATTACK. MY SYSTEM WAS CATASTROPHICALLY DESTABILIZED. EVEN DRAWING ON THE RESERVES OF DIVINE LIGHT I HAD COLLECTED OVER MILLENNIA, I WAS ONLY ABLE TO PARTIALLY STABILIZE IT. SCIENCE AND MATHEMATICS STILL WORK, AND THE SUPERNATURAL IS LIMITED TO A FRACTION OF ITS TRUE POWER. BUT IT REQUIRES A CONSTANT INFUSION OF SHEFA TO MAINTAIN EVEN THIS LIMITED FUNCTIONALITY.

"Can the reservoir of shefa run out?"

YES. AT THE CURRENT RATE IT WILL RUN OUT IN ABOUT FIFTY YEARS. EACH GREAT MIRACLE I PERFORM BEYOND THE RANGE OF MY ORDINARY POWER DEPLETES IT FURTHER. THAMIEL HOPED I WOULD CALL UPON THE SHEFA TO BANISH HIM. THEN HE WOULD RECOALESCE A FEW WEEKS OR MONTHS LATER UNHARMED. IT IS IMPOSSIBLE TO KILL HIM PERMANENTLY. HE IS A FACET OF GOD. AND EVERY TIME I KILL HIM TEMPORARILY, IT REQUIRES SO MUCH SHEFA THAT IT TAKES

YEARS OFF THE LIFESPAN OF THE UNIVERSE. THIS IS HIS PLAN. TO FORCE ME TO EXPEND MY RESOURCES IN A WAY THAT HASTENS THE COLLAPSE OF THE CELESTIAL MACHINERY.

"What happens when it collapses?"

HUMAN TECHNOLOGY CEASES TO WORK. THAMIEL BECOMES INVINCIBLE. THE WORLD ENDS.

"Oh. So how do we prevent that?"

I AM NOT SURE THAT WE DO.

"Can't you repair the machine? Or get it to run without shefa? Or find another way to replenish shefa faster? Or something?"

NO. I HAVE SPENT AEONS OF SUBJECTIVE TIME CONSIDERING THESE POSSIBILITIES. THEY ARE IMPOSSIBLE. THE SKY IS CRACKED. THE STRUCTURE OF THE HIGHER WORLDS IS MADE ILLEGIBLE. THE MACHINE CANNOT BE FULLY REPAIRED. IT IS IMPOSSIBLE. EVEN IF I TRIED, NOW THAT THAMIEL UNDERSTANDS ITS PURPOSE HE WOULD CERTAINLY STOP ME.

"So kill him with the shefa, then do it before he recoalesces."

HE IS THE LEFT HAND OF GOD. THERE ARE MANY THINGS HE CAN DO WITHOUT A CORPOREAL BODY.

"Why? Why does God have a screwy left hand that wants to destroy everything?"

YOU SHOULD READ ISAAC LURIA.

"I've read Isaac Luria. So what? Why did God allow the vessels to shatter in the first place?"

THAT IS VERY COMPLICATED.

"So what? So you're just going to hang around for fifty years until you run out of charge, your machine goes dead, and Thamiel takes over the universe?"

MAYBE THE COMET KING WILL COME UP WITH SOMETHING BEFORE THEN.

"That's your plan?"

IT IS A GOOD PLAN.

Sohu nodded. "Okay. Fair. Waiting for him to come in and solve every problem has always worked in the past. But... *still!* What about you? Shouldn't you... can't you at least try to help?"

I RUN CONTINENTAL DRIFT, AND GUIDE THE BUTTERFLY MIGRATION, AND KEEP ICEBERGS IN THE RIGHT PLACE, AND PREVENT PEOPLE FROM BOILING GOATS IN THEIR MOTHERS' MILK. IT IS DIFFICULT AND I AM GOOD AT IT AND IT ALLOWS THE WORLD TO ENDURE THAT MUCH

LONGER. I WILL NOT BEAT MYSELF UP OVER FAILING TO DO THE IMPOSSIBLE.

"Matthew 19:26. With God, all things are possible."

UM.

"What? Out with it."

I HAVE BEEN IN THIS UNIVERSE SIX THOUSAND YEARS. I HAVE FOUGHT THE DEVIL. I HAVE REWRITTEN THE LAWS OF REALITY. I HAVE DONE MANY INTERESTING THINGS. UM.

"What?"

AND I HAVE NEVER SEEN ANYTHING TO CONVINCE ME THAT GOD PLAYS AN ACTIVE PART IN THE UNIVERSE. HIS ROLE SEEMS TO BE ENTIRELY ONTOLOGICAL.

"You can't be a deist! You're an archangel!"

I AM NOT A VERY GOOD ARCHANGEL.

"What about San Francisco?"

GOD CAN HAVE A RIGHT HAND AS WELL AS A LEFT HAND. I SEE NO EVIDENCE THAT EITHER IS CONTROLLED BY ANY HEAD.

"What about Metatron?"

A VOICE OF GOD WHO NEVER TALKS. A PERFECT SYMBOL.

"You won against Thamiel! That was a miracle! Don't you think that God was involved in that?"

UM. THE SEPHIROT WERE INVOLVED. THOSE ARE SORT OF A PART OF GOD. BUT THEY WERE NOT IN A VERY ACTIVE ROLE. THEY MOSTLY JUST SAT THERE AS I REWROTE THEM.

"You know what I mean!"

GOD CREATED ADAM KADMON, THE FUNDAMENTAL STRUCTURE THAT BINDS EVERYTHING TOGETHER. HE BREATHED FIRE INTO THE STRUCTURE AND MADE IT EXIST AND MADE ALL THINGS HAPPEN ACCORDING TO ITS PLAN. BUT THAT PLAN DOES NOT FOLLOW OUR RULES OR OUR HOPES. WHEN A HUMAN MACHINE BREAKS — WHEN A PLANE'S ENGINES STOP WORKING, AND IT FALLS FROM THE AIR — GOD DOES NOT REACH DOWN AND SAVE IT. THE STRUCTURE CONTINUES TO ITS PREORDAINED CONCLUSION. I SEE NO REASON TO BELIEVE A FAILURE OF MY OWN MACHINE WILL BE ANY DIFFERENT. IT WILL MERELY BE MORE FINAL.

"Well, I think you're wrong. Father believes God will save us."

HE BELIEVES THAT *HE* WILL SAVE US, AND PLANS TO CREDIT GOD. THERE IS A DIFFERENCE.

"*I* believe God will save us! Think about how fantastically unlikely all of this is — the universe, your machinery, everything Father's doing. You think it's all a coincidence?"

YES.

"Book of Lamentations 3:24: 'The Lord is my portion, therefore I will place my hope in Him.'"

I DO NOT THINK THAT WORKED VERY WELL, BASED ON WHAT THEY TITLED THEIR BOOK.

Sohu snorted. "All right then. You're going to teach me kabbalah. But I'm going to teach you to have faith. How to do knock-knock jokes properly and how to have faith. That's what I'm going to teach you."

I AM SORRY. I AM NOT VERY GOOD AT FAITH FOR AN ARCHANGEL.

Sohu said nothing. Uriel turned away and went back to running the universe.

Interlude ח

Man On The Sphere

Let's play Twister, let's play Risk
See you in Heaven if you make the list
—R.E.M., "Man on the Moon"

I.

They say that March comes in like a lion and goes out like a lamb. March 1969 had been more like one of those Biblical angels with four lion heads and four lamb heads and a couple dragon heads for good measure, all spinning within a gigantic flaming wheel, and if you met its gaze for too long then you died.

Entire weeks repeated themselves, or skipped around, or moved backwards. There was a week when the weather stopped, and it was an even twenty-two degrees Celsius across the entire planet. The heavens turned gray and were replaced by a message saying, "sky.smh not found, please repent transgressions and try again." All animal cries were replaced by discordant buzzing sounds.

Nobody knew how long it lasted. Probably had been different lengths of time for each person, each shunted on their own separate timelines into weird calendrical eddies and whorls. Some people who had started off middle-aged ended the month with gray hair and soft, infinitely sorrowful voices. Others seemed to have grown younger. Most people looked about the same, but you could tell things had happened they didn't want to talk about, days repeated dozens of times or weeks that happened backwards, or moments when timelessness had briefly encroached on time and for an infinitely long moment they had touched Eternity.

The bizarre communiques from the Archangel Uriel had become an accepted feature of daily life. Sometimes they would appear in the sky, or writ in blood on the surface of the moon, or spoken in unexpected phone calls to world leaders with unlisted numbers, or spotted on vegetables that had grown to enormous size. The news was rarely good.

DUE TO SYSTEM RESOURCES SHORTAGES, THE ISLAND OF TAIWAN HAS BEEN CANCELLED. WE APOLOGIZE FOR THE INCONVENIENCE.

THE NUMBER EIGHT WILL BE DOWN FROM ONE A.M. TO SIX A.M. TOMORROW MORNING FOR EMERGENCY REPAIRS. PLEASE DO NOT PERFORM ANY CALCULATIONS THAT REQUIRE THE NUMBER EIGHT DURING THAT TIME. ALSO, PLEASE TURN ALL CLOCK FACES AWAY FROM YOU, ESPECIALLY IF THEY INCLUDE THE NUMBER EIGHT. THANK YOU FOR YOUR COOPERATION. AS COMPENSATION FOR YOUR TROUBLES, WE HAVE CURED ALL VALVULAR HEART DISEASE.

HUMANS NOW HAVE ONLY ONE HUNDRED EIGHTY BONES. WE EXPECT THE NEW BONES TO BE UP TO 50% MORE EFFICIENT AND TO PERFORM AT THE SAME HIGH STANDARDS AS THE OLD TWO HUNDRED SIX BONE SYSTEM. THE PREVALENCE OF SKELETAL DISEASES WILL NOT CHANGE. HOWEVER, DIFFERENT PEOPLE WILL HAVE THEM. IF YOU THINK YOU HAVE A NEW SKELETAL DISEASE, PLEASE CONSULT YOUR DOCTOR.

PLEASE AVOID THE AREA WHERE TAIWAN USED TO BE. IN ADDITION, PLEASE AVOID AREAS CLOSE TO WHERE TAIWAN USED TO BE, IN PARTICULAR, THE EAST CHINA SEA, THE SOUTH CHINA SEA, THE PHILIPPINE SEA, JAPAN, KOREA, AND ALL PARTS OF CHINA WITHIN ONE THOUSAND MILES OF A COAST. THANK YOU FOR YOUR COOPERATION.

ATTENTION. DUE TO A SCALE BACK IN COVERAGE, THE MORAL ARC OF THE UNIVERSE NO LONGER BENDS TOWARD JUSTICE. WE APOLOGIZE FOR THE INCONVENIENCE.

Seventy-one days after the chaos had begun, a message from Uriel appeared in raised welts on the skin of all of the livestock in the world:

THE FOLLOWING HAVE BEEN CANCELLED AS PART OF THE RECENT CUTBACKS: THE LAST WEEK IN SEPTEMBER. THE EMOTION ENNUI. THE GALL BLADDER. ALL NUMBERS BETWEEN 405,668,922 AND 407,215,810. JAZZ. THE MATTERHORN. ALL DRAVIDIAN LANGUAGES EXCEPT TELUGU. THE CRESCENT MOON. WHITE WINE. AMETHYST. ALL VARIETIES OF COUSIN BEYOND THE FIRST. THE SYSTEM WILL REGAIN TEMPORARY STABILITY AFTER THE CURRENT ROUND OF CHANGES. THANK YOU FOR BEARING WITH US DURING THIS DIFFICULT TIME.

The next day was April 1. The Long March was finally over.

Things weren't back to normal. Not by a long shot. Large areas had apparently been depopulated, whether by direct action of the archangel or by failure of their communities to survive the tribulations, no one knew. A good amount of technological infrastructure had just plain stopped working, apparently no longer supported by the leaner, less flashy laws of physics Uriel had been forced to scale down to. The Russians were saying awful things, demons pouring forth from the ground, Yakutsk the site of a great massacre, fires that could be seen for hundreds of miles. The cracks in the sky had grown noticeably wider.

But for the first time, people were starting to feel some optimism, like when you're starting to come back from a really bad drug trip and the walls are still covered in snakes, but they're *smaller* snakes now, and your skin is still bubbling but it's bubbling *less* and your grip on the real world is a little better and you start to wonder what's for breakfast.

II.

Richard Nixon, who had told Kissinger about thirty times that this was *not* what he had signed up for, realized that people needed a goal, something to shake them back into public consciousness, make them realize that America was still on its feet and the government was still in control. So he appeared on national television — which was working during even-numbered hours only, the eggheads hadn't quite figured out why that was, but they assured him it would be fixable — and declared that the country would "commit itself to achieving the goal, before this year is out, of landing a man on the giant crystal sphere surrounding the world, and returning him safely to Earth."

It had been a politically savvy move. NASA had a lunar module all ready to go and sitting in a warehouse. After what had happened *last* time they'd tried to get to the moon, the newly discovered crystal sphere presented an attractive alternative target. But it wasn't just political grandstanding. Breaking the crystal sphere had caused all these problems in the first place. If they could figure out what it was and why it was there, maybe they could fix it. And if there was an entity beyond the crystal sphere — his advisors had warned him against using the G word, sounded too unscientific — then maybe *it* would help, if asked nicely.

NASA didn't want to go in blind. First in May, then June, they launched manned missions to investigate the extent and composition of the sphere. As far as they could tell, it was about 250,000 miles in radius, centered on the earth, and made of perfect flawless crystal except in the vicinity of the cracks. The illusory stars and planets seemed to be projected on it in some kind of holographic manner that gave them the appearance of depth.

In early June, NASA told Nixon it had reached the limit of what it could determine about the sphere from remote observation.

On July 16, 1969, President Nixon travelled to Cape Canaveral, where he met personally with three astronauts whom NASA had assured him were the best of the best. He wished them godspeed, and told them that the hopes of American people and the people of the whole world were fixed on them.

Later that afternoon, Apollo 11 took off.

Four days and 250,000 miles later, the lunar module *Eagle* detached from its mother ship. Inside were Neil Armstrong and Buzz Aldrin, who had accepted the task of landing on the crystal sphere and taking mankind's first steps upon another heavenly body. Such as it was.

The descent proved more treacherous than expected, and the two came perilously close to running out of fuel for the thrusters and crashing into the crystal at enormous velocity, but with twenty-five seconds to spare they touched down at the chosen landing site right on the edge of one of the humongous cracks.

"Tranquility base here," said Armstrong. "The *Eagle* has landed."

There had been a brief debate in the Nixon White House over whether or not it was tasteful to plant the American flag on the giant crystal sphere surrounding the world. The argument against was that the sphere appeared to be some sort of celestial mechanism created directly by God that either separated Earth from Heaven or in some complicated sense was *itself* Heaven, and that for a human nation to claim Heaven might be literally the most hubris it was even conceptually possible to display. The argument in favor of planting the flag was, *America*.

Neil Armstrong stepped onto the crystal sphere and planted the flag.

"That's one small step for a man," he said, "and one giant leap for mankind."

The formalities being over, it was time to get down to business.

Armstrong and Aldrin hauled from their lunar module a great spool of cable, which they wheeled across the surprisingly smooth crystal a few dozen meters to the edge of the crack. Armstrong stared down.

"Houston, I'm looking into the crack," he relayed over his radio. "It's very bright, maybe not as bright as the sun but close. I can't see anything down there. The edge of the cliff is almost perfectly vertical. It seems a couple hundred meters wide—I can just barely see the other side, looks about the same. There's no terrain here, no irregularity. Houston, I think the light source might be only a couple of meters down. It's like a skin. I… I think we can reach the light with what we've got."

There followed a short argument over which of the two had to actually climb down into the thing. Aldrin won the argument with his very reasonable position that if Armstrong loved being first to do things so much, maybe he should show the same kind of initiative when it was something important and scary instead of just a photo op. So Commander Neil Armstrong attached the cable to his spacesuit, took a climbing hook in both hands, and slowly began to descend into the crack, while Aldrin peered down from above.

"Houston, I'm in the crack. I'm down about three meters now, out of a hundred meters of cable. The light is noticeably closer. I don't think it's far off. I think it's an object, or a barrier, or a transition or something."

"Houston, the light source is definitely getting closer. I think it's only another couple of meters down."

"Roger that, Commander Armstrong. Colonel Aldrin, is everything all right from your perspective?"

"Houston, cable is fixed in place. Commander Armstrong is still within visual range."

"Roger that, Colonel Aldrin."

"Houston, I'm going to touch the light source with my climbing hook and see if anything happens."

"Proceed as you see fit, Commander."

"The hook passes through the light source. I've pulled it back and it is still intact. It seems to be like a skin or a transition zone of some sort, like I said before."

"Roger that, Commander Armstrong."

"I'm going to touch the light source now.… I don't feel anything. My finger passes right through."

"Colonel Aldrin, from where you are standing, any change in the light source?"

"No, Houston. I can see Commander Armstrong. There's no disturbance or change. The light source is still uniform throughout the crack."

"Houston, I'm going to climb into the light source."

"Proceed as you see fit, Commander."

…

"Ground control to Commander Armstrong. Come in, Commander Armstrong."

...

"Ground control to Colonel Aldrin. Come in, Colonel Aldrin."

"Colonel Aldrin here, Houston. Commander Armstrong has disappeared below the light barrier."

"Ground control to Commander Armstrong. COME IN, COMMANDER ARMSTRONG."

...

"He's not answering. Houston, I'm going to pull up the cable, bring him back."

"Do that immediately, Colonel."

...

...

"Houston, the end of the cable is no longer attached to Commander Armstrong."

"Fuck."

"I never should have let him... I'm going down after him."

"No, Colonel Aldrin, this is Ground Control. You are ordered to collect the cable and leave the crack. I repeat, collect the cable and leave the crack."

"Wait, what if I lower the cable back down to him, maybe if he's down there he can grab on to..."

"Colonel Aldrin, I repeat, your direct order is to collect the cable and leave the crack."

"Houston, this is Commander Armstrong."

"COMMANDER ARMSTRONG! COME IN, COMMANDER ARMSTRONG! IS SOMETHING WRONG?"

"No, Houston. Nothing is wrong."

"All right, we're going to get Colonel Aldrin to lower down the cable for you and..."

"No, Houston. Literally. Nothing is wrong. *Nothing.*"

"Commander Armstrong, is everything okay?"

"Exactly, Houston. Everything is okay. Nothing is wrong. Nothing has ever been wrong, anywhere. The cosmos is like a flawless jewel, each of whose facets is another flawless jewel, and so on to infinity. Except there is no jewel. It's all light. No, there isn't even light. From within Time you can't see any of it, but when you step outside into Eternity it's all so... full. It's so beautiful, Houston."

"Commander Armstrong, you're not well. Colonel Aldrin is lowering down the cable."

"You really think I'm still in the crack? Listen, Houston. The tzimtzum, the Lurianic contraction of God to create the world, from a higher perspective it wasn't a contraction at all, it was an expansion. An unfolding of divinity into new possibilities. The vessels didn't shatter, they rearranged themselves into shapes that only become apparent from a pleroma beyond any dimensions but containing the potential for all of them. Houston, is this making sense?"

"Commander Armstrong, you are *ordered* to return to the ship."

"Houston, *William Blake was right about everything.*"

"Commander Armstrong!"

"Holy, holy, holy is the Lord of Hosts. Holy, holy, holy is the Lord of Hosts. Holy, holy, holy is the Lord of Hosts. Holy, holy, holy is the Lord of Hosts. Holy, holy, holy is the Lord of Hosts. Holy, holy, holy is the Lord of Hosts. Holy, holy, holy is the Lord of Hosts. Holy, holy, holy is the Lord of Hosts. Holy, holy, holy is the Lord of Hosts. Holy, holy, holy is the Lord of Hosts. Holy, holy, holy is the Lord of Hosts. Holy, holy, holy is the Lord of Hosts. Holy, holy, holy is the Lord of Hosts. Holy, holy, holy..."

"Commander Armstrong!"

"Holy, holy, holy. Holy, holy, holy. Holy, holy, holy. Holy, holy, holy. Holy, holy, holy. Holy, holy, holy. Holy, holy, holy. Holy, holy, holy. Holy, holy, holy. Holy, holy, holy..."

"Commander Armstrong!"

"Holy, holy, holy, holy, holy, holy, holy, holy, holy, holy, holy, holy, holy, holy, holy, holy, holy, hooooly, hoooooly, hooooooly, hoooooooly, hoooooooooly, hooooooooooly, hooooooooooooly, hoooooooooooooly, hooooooooooooooly, hoooooooooooooooly, hooooooooooooooooly, hoooooooooooooooooly..."

"Houston, I've lowered the cable as far as it will go. It's dangling about seventy meters into the light zone. I'm not getting any indication that Commander Armstrong is going to take it."

"Roger that, Colonel Aldrin. Please return to the ship. Do you read me, Colonel Aldrin?"

"Hooooooooooooooooooooooooooooly"

"Loud and clear, Houston."

"ooooooooooooooooooooooooooooooo"

III.

When I was ten years old, I got my first ham radio.

A ham radio is a treasure when you are ten. I listened to boats off the coast, heard the reports from the ranger stations in the nearby forests, even picked up the chatter between policemen patrolling the local streets. One day I turned to a new frequency, and I heard a strange sound, a single pure note unlike any I had ever heard before.

The sound was: "oooooooooooooooooooooooooooooooo"

I brought the radio to my uncle, and I asked him what station that was, and he told me it was the frequency NASA used for its communications, once upon a time. Then a man had taken a radio tuned to that band into a crack in the sky, and it had started broadcasting with such power that it drowned out all the other radio noise and the whole frequency had to be abandoned.

But what was that unearthly note?

My uncle told me it was Neil Armstrong, who had passed beyond time into Eternity, praising God forever.

Exodus

Your faith was strong, but you needed proof
(Hay hay yud tav mem tav vav kuf)
You saw a ship another sailed before us.
You saw his flag on the highest mast
You saw a dream that couldn't last
The Comet King receiving HaMephorash.

—Leonard Cohen, "HaMephorash"

Chapter Seventeen

No Earthly Parents I Confess

February 25, 1976
Colorado Springs

Picture a maiden lost in the hills.

"Maiden" can mean either "young woman" or "virgin." Its Greek and Hebrew equivalents have the same ambiguity, which is why some people think the person we call the Virgin Mary was actually supposed to be the Young Woman Mary—which might change the significance of her subsequent pregnancy a bit. People grew up faster, back in the days when they spoke of "maidens." Mary was probably only fourteen when she gave birth.

I am a kabbalist. Words matter. Nowadays we have replaced "maiden" with "teenage girl." A maiden and a teenager are the same thing, but their names drag different tracks through lexical space, stir up different waters. Synonymity aside, some young women are maidens and others are teenagers. The girl in our story was definitely a maiden, even though it was the 1970s and being a maiden was somewhat out of fashion.

So: picture a maiden lost in the hills.

She was hiking with her brother in the hills of Colorado; while he dozed off in a meadow, she had wandered off exploring. She had gotten lost, and decided to climb a hill to see what she could see from the top. But the hill had been higher than she had first judged, and it had grown dark, and now she sat upon the summit and looked out at the stars.

Violently they shone, far brighter than in the lamplit valleys of her home, so white they were almost blue. The Milky Way shone a phosphoric ribbon, and the cracks in the sky made a glowing lattice like a spiderweb of light.

There was another power in Heaven tonight. Behold Comet West, the Great Comet of 1976. It shot exultant through the winter sky, laughing as it felt the void against its icy skin. It flamed over peaks and rivers and countries and oceans, until at last it flew over the Continental Divide and reached its namesake. The true West strong and free. And there it alit upon the highest of the Rocky Mountains, pausing in contemplation, and no one but our maiden saw it land.

The Great Comet appeared in the aspect of an old man with long flowing white hair tossed about by the wind, winged with many wings. And though he was far larger than a man, larger even than the mountain that he sat upon, by some enchantment the maiden was not afraid.

And she spoke, saying: "Who are you?"

And he answered: "I am Comet West.

"I am the Comet, the spanner in the works of Destiny. All things orbit in circles according to their proper time and pattern, save the Comet. I shoot through unplanned and unpredicted.

"And I am the West. I am the setting-sun, the twilight of the gods, the coming night. I am the scarlet fires of dusk, the blaze before the blackness. I am the cradle of civilization and its executioner. I am the ending of all things in beauty and fire.

"I am Comet West. I am both of these things. Are you afraid of me?"

And the maiden said, "No," for she was not afraid.

And the Comet said: "Then I will shine on you."

And the maiden said: "Shine."

And for a moment the Comet shone on her with its full light, and she shivered with cold. And then the light receded, and she was alone beneath a thousand violently bright stars and a single baleful comet.

And then she slept and then her brother found her and then she went back to the bright electric lights of civilization and then she dismissed the whole thing as a dream.

I am a kabbalist. Words matter. They used to call it virgin birth. But "virgin" means "maiden" and "maiden" means "teenager," and so over time the phrase became "teenage pregnancy."

About four months later, it was noticed that our maiden had a teenage pregnancy.

At this point the myth becomes incomprehensible without relating a previous myth from the same epic cycle. A few years earlier there had been a great cosmic battle between two giants named Roe and Wade. For over a year they fought a strange form of ritual combat, without swords, without blood, until finally Roe gained the victory. And the nine black-robed Destinies who silently watched the combat were so delighted that they declared a great boon to humankind: that the Curse of Eve should be rescinded, that no longer would Woman be forced through painful labor to give birth to children, but rather she might bear sons and daughters at her own pleasure only.

(Others tell this myth differently, but they are not kabbalists.)

The discussion turned to whether she would keep the pregnancy. Because she happened to be an Indian-American girl (a Hindoo maiden?) she and her family rejected the gift of the nine black-robed Destinies. The doctors told her she was too young, the baby was growing too big too fast, it wasn't safe. But she was stubborn, as her parents were stubborn, as her child would one day be stubborn.

And so in November 1976, behold, a virgin conceived and bore a son, and she called his name *Jalaketu*.

Chapter Eighteen

That The Children Of Jerusalem May Be Saved From Slavery

I.

April 10, 2017
San Jose

"Why are we celebrating Passover?" asked Bill. "Are any of us even Jewish?"

"My father was Jewish," I answered.

"Doesn't count," said Bill.

"I'm Jewish," said Ally Hu.

"You're *Chinese*," corrected Bill.

"My great-grandmother came from the Kaifeng Jews," said Ally. "They have been in Asia for many generations."

We all stared at Ally. We'd never heard about this before.

"We're celebrating Passover," said Valerie, bringing in a plate of brisket, "because we're freedom fighters, and Passover is a celebration of freedom. It binds us to everyone across history and around the world who has struggled to escape bondage, from the Israelites in Egypt to the proletariat of today. Across thousands of years and thousands of miles, we're all joined together, saying the same words, eating the same foods—"

"Pyramid-shaped cookies?" asked Zoe, skeptically.

"The pyramid-shaped cookies are adorable," said Valerie.

"You're supposed to avoid anything with flour in it!" I protested.

"*Jews* are supposed to avoid anything with flour in it," Valerie explained patiently.

"You're supposed to have matzah!"

"I have matzah!" said Valerie. She brought in a plate of matzah. It had been cut into the shapes of little frogs and locusts. They had little eyes made of frosting.

"Ally, back me up on this," I said.

"Frosting is not a traditional Passover food," said Ally.

"Thank you!"

"Traditional Passover food is sweet-and-sour chicken, boiled peanuts, and rice."

I glared at her.

"Sour to represent the sourness of slavery in Egypt, sweet to represent the sweetness of freedom!" suggested Ana. Ally nodded enthusiastically.

"Why the boiled peanuts?" asked Valerie.

"Sixth plague," Ana answered.

"Why the rice?" asked Eli.

"Thi—" I started, just as Ana said "That's racist."

"You didn't even hear what..."

"I know how you think," said Ana.

Valerie came in with the bottle of Manischewitz and poured out nine glasses.

"There are only eight of us," Bill corrected her.

"One for the Prophet Elijah," said Valerie.

Ziniel had been looking unusually glum this month, ever since one of the big theonomics had rejected his attempt at a business deal, politely explaining that "angel investor" didn't mean what he thought it meant. Now he brightened up, and almost seemed to bounce with excitement. "Elijah!" he exclaimed. "I didn't know he was coming! It's been ages since the last time we—"

"He's not coming," said Valerie. "It's a metaphor." Ziniel's face fell. He stared down at his plate in what I thought was embarrassment.

Valerie finished pouring the wine and went to the head of the table. "We are gathered here today," she said, "to celebrate how the Israelites went from slavery into freedom. Yet in a sense, we are still slaves. William Blake said: 'I must create my own system, or be enslaved by another man's.' We are no longer slaves to a Pharaoh, but we are slaves to a system, a system that takes the work of our hands and minds and forces us to toil for its benefit. We celebrate tonight not only our current freedom, but the freedom yet to come, when the Names of God will be free for all the people of the earth." She raised her glass. "To freedom!"

We all drank to freedom.

"Now, Aaron is going to lead us in a traditional Passover song..."

II.

"The Lust Of The Goat Is The Bounty Of God," by Aaron Smith-Teller Published in the 2017 Passover bonus issue of the *California Chorister*

There's an old Jewish children's song called Had Gadya. It starts:

A little goat, a little goat
My father bought for two silver coins,
A little goat, a little goat

Then came the cat that ate the goat
My father bought for two silver coins
A little goat, a little goat

Then came that dog that bit the cat...

And so on. A stick hits the dog, a fire burns the stick, water quenches the fire, an ox drinks the water, a butcher slaughters the ox, the Angel of Death takes the butcher, and finally God destroys the Angel of Death. Throughout all of these verses, it is emphasized that it is indeed a little goat, and the father did indeed buy it for two silver coins.

So far, so good. Lots of cultures have dumb children's songs. But somehow this song made it into the liturgy for Passover, one of the holiest of Jewish holidays. Rabbi Azulai notes that the last person to say this was silly got excommunicated, and further notes that he deserves it. Jews put up with a lot of stuff, but you do *not* mess with the goat song. After that everyone assumed it must have had some sort of secret meaning, but no one ever really agreed upon what exactly that might be.

Rabbi Emden of Hamburg suggests that the goat represents the human soul. The goat was bought with two silver coins because the soul makes two journeys to arrive in our bodies — first from Heaven to the mystical plane of Galgalim, then from this mystical plane down to Earth. The various animals and objects, in this system, represent various challenges faced by the soul as it passes through life. Just to choose some random examples, the cat represents the animalistic nature of the undisciplined infant, and the fire represents the burning lusts of puberty. Finally you get to the Angel of Death — played by himself — and if you're lucky, God judges you worthy, destroys the Angel of Death, and carries you to eternal life.

(Mark Twain once said, "There is something fascinating about science. One gets such wholesale returns of conjecture out of such a trifling investment of fact." I think he would have liked Kabbalah.)

Rabbi Reuben Margolis relates the song to a Midrash. King Nimrod of Sumer demands Abraham worship the Fire God. Abraham refuses, saying that rain extinguishes fire, so if anything he should worship rain. Nimrod says okay, fine, worship the Rain God. But Abraham refuses again, saying that wind drives away the rain clouds, so if anything, he should worship wind. So Nimrod commands he worship the Wind God, and then other things happen, and finally Nimrod tries to kill Abraham and God saves him. The lesson is that all hierarchies end in God, who is above all things.

Rabbi Moses Sofer says that the song is a coded reference to the appropriate rituals for celebrating Passover during the Temple Era. The goat represents the Paschal sacrifice of the lamb, which is rather like a goat. The cat represents singing prayers, because this is in the Talmud somewhere (spoiler: *everything* is in the Talmud *somewhere*). The dog represents nighttime, because it barks at night, and nighttime is the appropriate time to hold a Passover meal. And so on.

(I hereby propose "Sofer's Law": the number of correspondences you can draw between any two systems increase exponentially as a function of your laxity in declaring that things represent other things.)

Rabbi Eybeschuetz of Prague writes that the entire thing is a historical prophecy. The goat represents the Jewish people. The two silver coins represent the two tablets of the Ten Commandments, with which God "bought" the Jewish people for Himself. The various animals and objects represent all of the misfortunes of the Jewish people over history. When the cat eats the goat, that refers to the conquest of Israel by King Tiglath-Pileser III of Assyria. When the ox drinks the water, that's the Hellenic Greeks taking over the newly re-independent Israelite state. Finally, at the end, God comes in and solves everything, the Jews return to Israel, and the Messianic Age begins.

(Four rabbis in, and we're at King Tiglath-Pileser III. We have to go deeper!)

As far as I know, no one has previously linked this song to the Lurianic

Kabbalah. So I will say it: the deepest meaning of Had Gadya is a description of how and why God created the world. As an encore, it also resolves the philosophical problem of evil.

The most prominent Biblical reference to a goat is the scapegoating ritual. Once a year, the High Priest of Israel would get rid of the sins of the Jewish people by mystically transferring all of them onto a goat, then yelling at the goat until it ran off somewhere, presumably taking all the sin with it.

The thing is, at that point the goat contained an entire nation-year worth of sin. That goat was *super evil.* As a result, many religious and mystical traditions have associated unholy forces with goats ever since, from the goat demon Baphomet to the classical rather goat-like appearance of Satan.

So the goat represents evil. I'll go along with everyone else saying the father represents God here. So God buys evil with two silver coins. What's up?

The most famous question in theology is "Why did God create a universe filled with so much that is evil?" The classical answers tend to be kind of weaselly, and center around something like free will or necessary principles or mysterious ways. Something along the lines of "Even though God's omnipotent, creating a universe without evil just isn't possible."

But here we have God buying evil with two silver coins. Buying to me represents an intentional action. Let's go further—buying represents a *sacrifice.* Buying is when you sacrifice something dear to you to get something you want even more. Evil isn't something God couldn't figure out how to avoid, it's something He covets.

What did God sacrifice for the sake of evil? Two silver coins. We immediately notice the number "two." Two is not typically associated with God. God is One. Two is *right out.* The kabbalists identify the worst demon, the nadir of all demons, as Thamiel, whose name means "duality in God." Two is dissonance, divorce, division, dilemmas, distance, discrimination, diabolism.

This, then, was God's sacrifice. In order to create evil, He took up duality.

"Why would God want to create evil? God is pure Good!"

Exactly. The creation of anything at all other than God *requires* evil. God is perfect. Everything else is imperfect. Imperfection contains evil by definition. Two scoops of evil is the first ingredient in the recipe for creating universes. Finitude is evil. Form is evil. Without evil all you have is God, who, as the kabbalists tell us, is pure Nothing. If you want something, evil is part of the deal.

Now count the number of creatures in the song. God, angel, butcher, ox, water, fire, stick, dog, cat, goat. Ten steps from God to goat. This is the same description of the ten sephirot we've found elsewhere, the ten levels by which God's ineffability connects to the sinful material world without destroying it. This is not a coincidence because nothing is ever a coincidence. Had Gadya isn't *just* a silly children's song about the stages of advancement of the human soul, the appropriate rituals for celebrating Passover in the Temple, the ancient Sumerian pantheon, and the historical conquests of King Tiglath-Pileser III. It's also a blueprint for the creation of the universe. Just like everything else.

III.

April 10, 2017
New York City

"Mr. Alvarez," asked Brian Young, "why are we celebrating Passover? I don't think any of us are Jews."

"In a sense," said Dylan, "we are all Jews. The Jews of..."

"In a sense," said Clark Deas, "every time Dylan says 'in a sense,' I mentally replace it with 'not at all.'"

"Mr. Deas!" said Dylan. "Open the Haggadah and find the entry about the Wicked Child, who says that these rituals and customs do not apply to him! Take a careful look at the fate it says is in store for such a child!"

Clark reached for the Haggadah, but Dylan was faster and snatched it out of his grasp. "It says," said Dylan, "that such a child would not have been rescued from slavery in Egypt! Do you understand, Mr. Deas? If you had been a slave in Egypt in 1500 BC, you, and your children, and your children's children would have remained in the country forever. And today, slavery would be completely abolished throughout the world, except for you! You, Mr. Deas, would still be in Egypt, building pyramids, with all the rest of the twenty-first century population staring at you confused and wondering what was going on. Passover is important! It's about bringing us together! Across thousands of years and thousands of miles, we're all joined together, saying the same words, eating the same foods—"

"Is there anything in the Haggadah about The Child Who Wouldn't Shut Up?" asked Clark.

"And given that we're a terrorist cell," said Michael Khan, "are you sure we *want* to be brought together with other people?"

"In a sense," said Dylan, "Passover is a holiday entirely *about* terrorists."

Clark was mouthing the words "in a sense" while furiously making sarcastic quotation marks with his fingers.

"Consider," said Dylan. "The government is oppressing the Israelites. The Israelites have already tried nonviolent resistance, to no avail. So Moses tells his spokesman Aaron to send a threat to the government: give in to our demands or we'll poison your water supply. The government refuses, says they don't negotiate with terrorists. So Moses turns the river to blood. Then he sends another threat: give in to our demands, or we'll release biological weapons. But Pharaoh's heart was hardened, and again he said 'we won't negotiate with terrorists.' So boom. Frogs, lice, wild beasts, cattle disease, locusts, boils — you know what some archaeologists think caused the boils and cattle disease, by the way? Anthrax. Look it up. Then he sends another threat: give in to our demands, or we'll sabotage the electrical grid. Pharaoh's heart is hard, he refuses to negotiate with terrorists. So boom. Moses plunges the entire country into darkness. Then Moses sends his final threat, and it's a classic: give in to our demands, or we'll kill innocent children. Pharaoh says again — we don't negotiate with terrorists. So Moses kills the Egyptian kids, and Egypt gives in to his demands, and Moses and his followers flee over the border where they can't be caught. The perfect crime."

"I think God was involved somewhere," said Brenda Burns.

"Oh, because terrorists *never* invoke God," said Dylan, rolling his eyes. "Invoking God totally disqualifies you from being a terrorist. My mistake! *Discúlpame por favor!*"

Brenda, Clark, and Michael facepalmed.

"But you know what?" asked Dylan. "It doesn't matter! We're not just terrorists, we're placebomancers! We make our own narratives! Freedom to make whatever narrative you want — in a sense, isn't that what freedom is?"

Clark continued making sarcastic finger motions to no avail.

IV.

March 30, 1991
Gulf of Mexico

"Uriel, why are we celebrating Passover? I'm not Jewish, and you're an archangel."

IS THAT ONE OF THE FOUR QUESTIONS? I DO NOT REMEMBER ALL OF THEM BUT IT SEEMS VERY SPECIFIC.

"No! This is my question!"

Sohu sat at a table suspended several hundred feet in the air, putting her about eye level with Uriel. Two plates had been set out, despite the fact that the archangel did not eat and was far too big to manipulate anything upon the table anyway. They were definitely intended to be seder plates, but they looked like they had missed something in the execution.

"And what is this on the seder plate? I am like 99% sure that is not lamb."

I DID NOT HAVE LAMB, SO I USED LAMPREYS. KABBALISTICALLY THEY ARE VERY SIMILAR.

"They have icky little mouths!"

THEY USE THOSE TO SUCK THE LIFE JUICES OUT OF OTHER FISHES.

"Uriel, why are we doing this?"

THE MOST IMPORTANT KABBALISTIC SOURCE TEXT IS THE TORAH. THE CLIMAX OF THE TORAH NARRATIVE IS THE PASSOVER STORY OF SALVATION FROM EGYPT. IF YOU WANT TO UNDERSTAND THE KABBALAH, YOU MUST UNDERSTAND PASSOVER.

"What does Passover have to do with kabbalah?"

THERE ARE TEN PLAGUES WITH WHICH THE ISRAELITES WENT FROM THE LAND OF BONDAGE TO THE HOLY LAND.

"And?"

HOW MANY SEPHIROT ARE THERE THAT GO FROM THE MATERIAL WORLD TO ULTIMATE DIVINITY?

"There's... oh... I think that's a coincidence."

NOTHING IS A COINCIDENCE. EVERYTHING IS CONNECTED. AT PASSOVER THINGS ARE ESPECIALLY CONNECTED. THE PASSOVER RITUAL BINDS ALL THE KABBALISTS OF ALL AGES TOGETHER, FROM SHIMON BAR YOCHAI TO TODAY. ACROSS THOUSANDS OF YEARS AND THOUSANDS OF MILES WE ARE ALL JOINED TOGETHER, SAYING THE SAME WORDS, EATING THE SAME FOODS...

"Lampreys?!"

...EATING KABBALISTICALLY SIMILAR FOODS.

"Will you tell me the story of Passover?"

YOU ALREADY KNOW THE STORY OF PASSOVER. YOU HAVE MEMORIZED THE BIBLE.

"I like it when you tell me stories."

YOU ALWAYS MAKE FUN OF THEM.

"That's how I show that I like it!"

I WILL TELL YOU THE STORY IF YOU EAT YOUR LAMPREYS.

"They're disgusting!"

I AM CERTAIN THEY ARE FINE.

"Uriel, have you ever eaten food? Any food?"

UM. I HAVE PERFORMED SEVERAL MILLION COMPUTATIONS SIMULATING THE BINDING AFFINITIES OF HUMAN GUSTATORY RECEPTORS.

"I'm not eating the lampreys. Tell me the story of Passover. Your book on education says human children like stories, right?"

WELL...

V.

Springtime, 1??? BC
Mt. Sinai

With a final grunt of effort, the old man crested the ridge and came to the summit of the mountain. He leaned on his staff for a few seconds, catching his breath. He had come such a long way. He let his eyes drift closed...

BE NOT AFRAID, came a vast booming voice from directly behind him.

Moses screamed, tried to turn around, lost his footing, and fell down in a heap upon the blue rocks.

SORRY SORRY SORRY SORRY SORRY. The source of the voice was a vast entity that towered above him, a humanoid creature with great golden wings protruding from its back and eyes that shone like the sun. SORRY SORRY SORRY.

Moses pulled himself into a more dignified kneeling position. "My Lord," he said reverently.

UM, said Uriel. I AM SORT OF FILLING IN FOR HIM. HE DOES NOT DO VERY MUCH. IT IS HARD TO EXPLAIN.

"My Lord," repeated Moses. "With a mighty hand, You freed my people from slavery in Egypt."

UM, said the archangel. IT IS SOMEWHAT MORE COMPLICATED THAN THAT. THE EGYPTIANS WERE BUILDING THESE PYRAMIDS WHICH THEY THOUGHT TAPPED INTO THE COSMIC ENERGIES OF THE UNIVERSE. AND THEY DID TAP INTO THE COSMIC ENERGIES OF THE UNIVERSE. NOT FOR THE REASONS THEY THOUGHT, WHICH WERE PRETTY MUCH THE WORST SORT OF PRIMITIVE HOCUS-POCUS, BUT JUST BECAUSE ANYTHING BIG AND GEOMETRIC IS GOING TO MESS UP THE FLOW OF SHEFA — OF DIVINE LIGHT — IN UNPREDICTABLE WAYS. I ASKED

THEM TO STOP BUT THEY WOULDN'T. I TRIED FRIGHTENING THEM BY TURNING THEIR RIVERS TO BLOOD, BUT THEY JUST MUTTERED SOMETHING ABOUT 'PHYTOPLANKTON' AND KEPT DOING IT. THEN I SENT THEM A BUNCH OF FROGS, BUT THAT DIDN'T HELP EITHER. FROGS NEVER HELP. THEN I GOT KIND OF CARRIED AWAY.

"But when our people reached the Sea of Reeds, and we thought that all was lost, I prayed to you, and you parted the sea, so we could cross freely."

THEN I THOUGHT TO MYSELF, HOW ARE THEY GOING TO BUILD PYRAMIDS IF THEY DON'T HAVE A LABOR FORCE? SO I PARTED THE SEA SO THEIR SLAVES COULD ESCAPE. I THINK IT WAS A GOOD PLAN.

"And when the last among us had stepped out from the waters, you sent them crashing down upon the Pharaoh and his army, destroying them and their wickedness forever."

I HAVE NOT WORKED OUT ALL OF THE BUGS IN THE SEA PARTING FUNCTION.

"Now we have come to you for advice. It is through your grace that we are free, but we know not what to do with our freedom. The people demand laws, a code to live by, something to bring meaning and structure to their lives."

UM. I THINK YOU SHOULD PROBABLY JUST BE NICE TO EACH OTHER. UNLESS BEING NICE TO EACH OTHER WOULD CAUSE SOME SORT OF HORRIBLE PROBLEM I CANNOT ANTICIPATE RIGHT NOW. THEN YOU SHOULD NOT DO THAT.

"Please, O Lord! You must have more advice than that, advice which can sustain us in spirit as we cross this scorching desert."

WEAR SUNSCREEN?

"Lord, the Egyptians are the mightiest people in the world, but they are mighty because their priests rule every minute of their lives, from the ritual ablutions they perform upon waking up to the prayers they say before they go to bed at night. If our people are left adrift, without laws and rituals to connect them to You and thank You for your gift of freedom, I fear they will go astray."

AH. I THINK I UNDERSTAND. ACTUALLY, THIS TIES INTO ANOTHER PROJECT OF MINE. I AM GRADUALLY SHIFTING THE WORLD FROM A SUBSTRATE OF DIVINE ESSENCE TO A SUBSTRATE OF MECHANICAL COMPUTATION. THE MECHANICAL SUBSTRATE HAS A LOT OF POTENTIAL BENEFITS. FOR EXAMPLE, IT IS PERFECTLY PREDICTABLE. FOR ANOTHER, IT ALLOWS EVEN LOW-LEVEL USERS SUCH AS YOURSELF TO COMBINE

PHYSICAL FORCES IN NOVEL WAYS TO SOLVE YOUR OWN PROBLEMS AS THEY ARISE. MOST IMPORTANT, IT IS MORE ROBUST AGAINST DEMONIC INTRUSION. IN FACT, ANGELS AND DEMONS ARE PRETTY MUCH INERT ON A MECHANICAL SUBSTRATE. IT INVOLVES VARIOUS INTERACTIONS BETWEEN SEPHIROT AND KLIPOT. ARE YOU FAMILIAR WITH THESE? IF NOT I CAN EXPLAIN.

"The laws, O Lord?"

RIGHT NOW COMPUTATIONAL RESOURCES ARE THE MAJOR BOTTLENECK IN THE PROJECT. I HAVE A LIST OF STEPS THAT END USERS COULD TAKE TO SAVE COMPUTATIONAL RESOURCES.

"And these would be the laws?"

I PERFORM SERVER MAINTENANCE ON SATURDAYS. THIS MEANS LOWER CAPACITY. SO PLEASE AVOID HIGH-LOAD ACTIVITIES LIKE BUSINESS TRANSACTIONS, AGRICULTURAL WORK, AND ELECTRICITY USE DURING THAT TIME. SO YES. THAT IS A LAW.

"My Lord, what is 'electricity'?"

SO IMAGINE THAT EVERYTHING IS MADE UP OF THESE TINY OBJECTS. YOU COULD VISUALIZED THEM SORT OF LIKE BILLIARD BALLS WITH SMALLER BILLIARD BALLS CIRCLING AROUND THEM, EXCEPT THAT THEY ARE NOT ACTUALLY CIRCLING. THEY ARE MORE LIKE A POSSIBILITY OF THERE BEING A BILLIARD BALL, AND THE POSSIBILITY FORMS A CIRCLE. UM. A SPHERE. EXCEPT THEY ARE NOT ALWAYS A SPHERE. THE FIRST TWO LOOK SORT OF LIKE SPHERES, BUT THE NEXT THREE ARE KIND OF LIKE FIGURE EIGHTS AT RIGHT ANGLES TO ONE ANOTHER, AND THEN ANOTHER SPHERE, THEN THREE MORE FIGURE EIGHTS, AND THEN MORE COMPLICATED THINGS THAT ARE KIND OF HARD TO DESCRIBE. UM. THIS IS ACTUALLY MORE COMPLICATED TO EXPLAIN THAN I THOUGHT. ELECTRICITY IS KIND OF LIKE STARTING A FIRE. YOU WILL KNOW IT WHEN YOU SEE IT.

"Um, yes, my Lord. Anything else?"

YES. DO NOT MIX DIFFERENT KINDS OF FABRIC IN YOUR GARMENTS. IT COMPLICATES THE TEAR RESISTANCE CALCULATIONS.

"And?"

DO NOT BOIL A GOAT IN ITS MOTHER'S MILK. I KNOW THAT SOUNDS STRANGE, BUT EVERY TIME SOMEONE TRIES THIS, THE ENTIRE SEPHIRAH HANDLING THE CONTINENT WHERE IT HAPPENS CRASHES. I HAVE SPENT AEONS OF SUBJECTIVE TIME TRYING TO FIGURE OUT THE PROBLEM AND I HAVE PRETTY MUCH GIVEN UP. JUST DO NOT DO IT. DO NOT

DO ANYTHING SORT OF LIKE IT. JUST AVOID THAT ENTIRE CATEGORY OF THING.

"And?"

UM. I FEEL BAD ABOUT THIS. BUT I AM TRYING TO ASSIGN EVERYONE A UNIQUE SOULMATE. RIGHT NOW I AM USING A VARIANT OF THE GALE-SHAPLEY ALGORITHM, BUT IT IS VERY RESOURCE-INTENSIVE. I THINK LIMITING THE ALGORITHM TO MALE-FEMALE PAIRINGS WOULD MAKE IT RUN MUCH MORE SMOOTHLY WITH ONLY A SLIGHT PENALTY IN OPTIMAL MATE ALLOCATION.

"I don't understand."

THE ALGORITHM WILL WORK BETTER IF YOU TELL PEOPLE NOT TO HAVE SAME SEX RELATIONSHIPS.

"I see," said Moses. "It is an abomination."

IT IS JUST VERY KLUDGY AND VERY SLOW. I CAN REMOVE THE LIMITATIONS ONCE I HAVE MORE RAM.

"We can sacrifice some to you once we build a proper Temple," said Moses.

UM, said Uriel. I AM ALMOST CERTAIN YOU CANNOT. BUT I APPRECIATE THE OFFER. He stood for a second, lost in thought. THERE ARE MANY RULES. IT WILL TAKE ME A LONG TIME TO THINK OF ALL OF THEM. YOU SHOULD GO CHECK ON YOUR PEOPLE. COME BACK UP IN A FEW WEEKS AND I WILL GIVE YOU A COMPLETE LIST.

"Yes, my Lord," said Moses.

...

Forty days and forty nights later, the old man trudged back up the slopes of the mountain.

UM, said the archangel. SO. I MIGHT HAVE GOTTEN A LITTLE BIT CARRIED AWAY...

VI.

April 7, 2001
Colorado Springs

In a dimly-lit chamber two thousand feet underground, quiet as death, seven people sat at a table. Seven seder plates. Seven cups of wine.

The Comet King spoke first, barely above a whisper. "Why are we doing this?"

His eldest daughter, Nathanda: "We're doing this because you made us promise to help you stay human. This is what humans do. They celebrate holidays with their friends and families. Across thousands of years and thousands of miles, we're all joined together, saying the same words, eating the same foods. Come on, Father. You know you need this."

"I shouldn't have come." He started to stand, but Nathanda put her hand on one of his shoulders, Father Ellis on the other, and they gently guided him back to his chair.

Nathanda motioned to Sohu. She was the youngest, even more after being cursed to be perpetually eight years old. Sohu stood up.

"Why is this night different from all other nights?"

The Comet King said nothing. Sohu looked at the other Cometspawn, then at Father Ellis, then at Uncle Vihaan, waiting for someone to answer. All of them ended up looking at the Comet King. Finally, he spoke.

"On all other nights," he said, "we remember that we failed. We remember that God does not answer prayers. We remember that those we love are still in bondage and can never be saved. Tonight, we lie."

"Father," said Nathanda, with a pained look. "Please. Just let us have a Seder together. As a family."

The Comet King stood up and pointed at the table. The various foods and glasses started moving, re-enacting the Seder in fast-forward. The vegetables leapt into the salt water to dip themselves. The matzah broke itself in half, the afikomen flying out of the room. The plates started spinning around, serving themselves in order, the food leaping from serving tray to plate and back to serving tray faster than anybody could follow, the pages of the Haggadah turning themselves like they were blown by the wind, the door swinging open then slamming shut.

A cup of wine flew into the Comet King's hand.

"Wine for the tears of the suffering," he said. "Blood. Frogs. Lice." At each word, a spherical droplet of wine shot up from the cup. "Beasts. Disease. Boils." When the droplets reached the ceiling, they burst apart. "Hailstones. Locusts. Darkness." A final drop, bigger than the rest. "Death of the firstborn." The last droplet exploded like the others in what looked like a shower of blood. "And for the suffering yet to come—"

He threw the cup itself into the air, then pointed at it. It exploded, shooting pieces of silver across the room. A moment later, every other wine-glass in the world exploded too.

"There," said the Comet King, his voice still calm and distant. "Across thousands of miles, everyone joined together. Feeling the same things we feel. Am I more human now? I don't know. Maybe I am." He picked up a sliver of wine-glass, held it up as if in a toast. "Next year in Jerusalem!"

Then he turned to lightning and flew out of the room.

Chapter Nineteen

The Form Of The Angelic Land

Morning, May 12, 2017
????

I.

For a moment I was totally disoriented by the scene before me. Then vast, dark shapes began to take form.

Shelves. Shelves full of books, all the way up, from the immaculately polished marble floor to a ceiling that was too high to see clearly. So many shelves that they blocked my view, made it impossible to see how big the room was or get any other sense of where I was.

It was dark, but not absolutely so. The whole room was filled with a rosy light, and I wondered if somewhere there were colossal windows to match the colossal shelves, letting in the first glow of dawn. I passed beyond the shelves only to find more shelves. I passed beyond those only to find more shelves still. No chairs, no tables, and no sign of a card catalog. I tried to make out the title of one of the books. It was too dark to read.

"Don't use the Vanishing Name," I had told the other Singers, "unless you are in a situation where it is absolutely vital to your well-being and continued survival that you be accosted by a different band of hooligans than the ones who are currently accosting you." There I had been, in UNSONG, the Director-General breathing down my neck. Through what I can only assume will be forever remembered as a stroke of dazzling genius, I'd used the Vanishing Name and escaped to what my contact in San Antonio had suggested would be a "complementary situation." Presumably that should be pretty bad. And here I was. A library the size of a cathedral.

I looked around for demons or monsters or something and didn't see any. I considered going to sleep, but I'd actually slept pretty well in my jail cell just a few hours ago. Also, I was really, really wired. Judging by my heartbeat, my body still hadn't accepted that I was safe, and wouldn't for some time.

Too many questions beat at my mind to start thinking about any particular one. Where was Ana? I had felt a moment of telepathic contact with her, but she hadn't sounded like a prisoner. She had sounded like she was coming to *rescue* me, which was absurd, how would she even *find* an UNSONG base let alone infiltrate one? For that matter, where were Valerie and my other housemates? What the *hell* was wrong with Ash Bentham? Did he have Sarah? What would happen to the world if he did?

And, of course, where was I? Somewhere bad, no doubt, or the Name wouldn't have brought me here.

So I did what I always do when I'm too stressed to think. I took out a book and started reading.

UNSONG had taken away my scroll wheel, so instead of drawing a Luminous Name scroll, I just spoke the Luminous Name. The tiniest of risks. UNSONG wouldn't listen for the Luminous Name any more than the police would post agents on street corners to entrap litterbugs. It was just about the safest proprietary Name in the world.

The library blazed with light. I took out a book. That was odd. The title was in—

John Dee had been a brilliant mathematician and astronomer in Queen Elizabeth I's court before turning to magic. He decided that all of his science only scratched the surface of the natural world, that there must be true essences of which he knew nothing. He sought a guide.

One came to him. Edward Kelley claimed to be a medium through whom the spirits revealed their secrets. Sure, he was an infamous con man who had just gotten out of jail for a forgery conviction. But Dee very tolerantly decided that if the spirits decided to speak to him through a con man, who was he to question their decisions?

Kelley gazed into his crystal ball and declared that the angels were speaking to him. What were they saying? Alas, neither Kelley nor Dee understood a word of their language, a language apparently lost to humans since the time of the patriarch Enoch. There followed a long period of translation work, which ended with a sort of English-Enochian dictionary, a key to the heavenly speech.

Sure, there were doubters. Some people mentioned it was mighty suspicious that the syntax and grammar of Enochian were exactly the same as those of Elizabethan English. Others pointed out how convenient it was that the angelic word for "evil" was "Madrid," which was also the capital of Elizabethan England's arch-enemy Spain. Or how the angelic word for "kingdom" was "Londoh," which was also... you get the idea. It seemed like Edward Kelley might have been injecting his personal opinions into these transmissions *just a little*. Or, as we moderns sometimes say, that the medium was the message.

So it came as quite a shock when the sky cracked and we met angels and they all spoke flawless Enochian. It wasn't the only language they spoke—they could understand anything except Aramaic—but it was the one that came most naturally to them.

"Edinburr Augsburg Trondheim Londoh Albyon Tudors," they told us, which in their language meant "Peace of the Lord be with the kingdoms of men." Then "King Philip Papist tyrand Mary Queen of Scoths Madrid," which meant "Time is running short, and we must join our powers to oppose the forces of evil." It was kind of strange, but predictable in retrospect. Nothing is a coincidence, and the same parts of the same underlying structure repeat themselves in every domain. Albeit usually a lot more subtly.

My Enochian was terrible. It was mostly at the Hooked On Phonics Worked For Me level, just barely recalling each letter and trying to sound out the words. Except I didn't actually sound them out, because half of the things written in Enochian summoned vast ancient forces from beyond the veil when read aloud. I just sounded them out in my head.

I was still puzzling out the first sentence of the library book—something about how conquering Central and South America and building a giant armada was for losers—when I heard a noise. Somebody else was in the library with me. If this was a complementary situation to UNSONG's secret prison, it probably wouldn't be anyone I liked.

I spoke the first nineteen syllables of the Tempestuous Name, kept the last one on the tip of my tongue for as soon as I detected a threat. I brandished the Enochian book in front of me as if it were a shield or a weapon. I backed up against the bookshelf to give myself as small a profile as possible, make it hard for anybody to find me. And I stayed very quiet. If somebody was looking for me, they were going to have a very hard time, and my position covered by the shelves gave me an advantage that would be—

Somehow a gun was at my temple. I blinked.

"Don't move," she said. She was *angry*.

She was young, maybe my age, maybe a little older. Asian features.

Dressed in black. Very functional clothing, sort of a cross between a biker's leather and a commando's combat gear. But then how did she move so fast?

My hooligans. Right on schedule. I didn't move. I wasn't sure if my Tempestuous Name beat her gun, but it seemed like a bad idea to test it.

"Put down the book!"

I carefully returned the book to the shelf; I probably was supposed to drop it, but I'm superstitious about letting books touch the floor, and if ever there was a time I needed luck...

"Who are you? How did you get here?"

"My name is Aaron," I said. "I got in trouble and I spoke the Vanishing Name and I ended up here about ten minutes ago."

Maximally true, minimally revealing. Her attention shifted to the globe of light illuminating the area. "What's that? How did it get here?"

"Luminous Name," I said. "It was dark and I couldn't see."

"Spoken or scrolled?"

"Spoken."

The girl made a guttural noise of frustration. "You spoke the... you used... *do you even know where you are?*"

I didn't.

"This is the Mount Baldy Strategic Angel Reserve."

That made perfect sense and I was an idiot.

II.

During the Long March, when everything started breaking down, the clouds organized into gigantic floating bastions. In the Gulf, they became the mighty hurricane of the Archangel Uriel. Throughout the rest of the world, they became manifold city-fortresses populated by choirs of lesser angels.

It turned out that the universal consensus of ancient peoples—that Heaven was a place in the sky, somewhere above the clouds, inhabited by angels—was pretty much spot-on. When Uriel had blocked the flow of holy light into the world, he had erased the angels and their heavens, and the clouds had been retconned into big floating bags of water droplets. After the sky cracked, some of them reverted to their proper angelic form.

But the angels had been metaphorical for thousands of years, and they had trouble finding their bearings. They certainly weren't prepared for helicopters landing on their celestial fortresses, demanding an opening of trade relations. Luckily this proved irrelevant when it was determined that the angels had no property. The clouds formed whatever they needed around them, and they spent most of their time praying and praising God.

An exchange of knowledge?

The angels had loads of knowledge. Most of it was theology. A lot of it wasn't very good. The hope that they might have special access to God turned out to be kind of a dud. They remembered they had been created, way back before Time was a thing. They knew about God, they wouldn't shut up about Him, but it was all incomprehensible, made the sort of mysticism humans came up with seem perfectly clear by comparison.

An exchange of technology?

The angels had no technology. They didn't even seem to know many Divine Names, and the few they did know they wouldn't say. Threats, blackmail, even torture seemed not to faze angels in the slightest, and don't ask me to tell you the story of how we learned *that* information because this was back during the Nixon administration, when the country Did What It Had To Do because By Golly The Russians Would and We Couldn't Fall Behind.

A military alliance?

Now we're talking. The angels appeared to be able to smite things with flaming swords that they conjured out of nowhere. But they had no concept of strategy or geopolitics. When we asked if they would help us against the Russians, they just wanted to know if the Russians were evil. When we said yes, they asked why we weren't at war with them already. When we tried to explain that you don't just *go to war*, you build alliances and gradually box in your enemy and try to use their reluctance to fight to gain concessions from them without anything ever breaking out into open conflict which would be disastrous to both sides, the angels didn't get it.

Evildoer? Smite. Not an evildoer? Live in peace.

Attempts to get the angels to participate in any of the processes of modern civilization were similar failures. The angels didn't get economics; God would provide. The angels didn't get the UN; why would you talk to evildoers instead of smiting them? The angels didn't get the requests that their bastions to be opened up to tourists and archaeologists. God was the only thing worth knowing about, and God was everywhere alike.

One thing the angels got was faith.

Spencer Kimball, president of the Mormon Church, arrived at the celestial bastion that hovered over Zion National Park with a fleet of helicopters. He told the rapt angels the story of how a hundred fifty years ago, Joseph

Smith had been given golden tablets by the angel Moroni that revealed God's plan for humankind. That Jesus Christ, the Son of God, had visited the Americas and preached the Gospel to its native inhabitants, and that these inhabitants had accrued wisdom about the nature of holiness and properly ordered society that was transmitted through Smith to the present day, with Kimball as its latest representative.

And the angels answered:

"Huh, we don't know anyone named Moroni."

And

"Wait, God has a *son*?!"

So apparently the angels were unfamiliar with human religions. God hadn't given *them* any special revelations, and they hadn't realized that was even a possibility. If there was some other tribe of angels somewhere else higher in the divine favor, a tribe including this guy Moroni, and they were getting direct revelations, that was *important*. And if God had a Son, that was *even more important* and they were slightly miffed about not having been informed. Was Mr. Kimball sure this was true?

Mr. Kimball assured them that it was definitely all 100% correct. The entire bastion of angels converted to Mormonism on the spot, asking Mr. Kimball to please send up all of the information he had about what God had revealed to humans and what He wanted of angels.

The news sparked a free-for-all among Earth's religions. Jews, Hindus, Catholics, Protestants, Buddhists, Muslims—the pattern was always the same. They would land helicopters on a bastion, inform the angels that God had granted them revelations. The angels would get extremely excited and convert en masse and agree to do whatever their new religious leaders wanted.

It started to become clear that angels were *really* gullible.

Then there was a problem. A group of Muslim missionaries landed on a bastion that had already been converted by the Orthodox Christians.

The imam politely told the angels that they had been misled, that God had no Son, that he knew this because God had sent down the angel Gabriel to the prophet Mohammed, peace be upon him, to inform him of this and many other facts.

The angels were thrilled to learn of the survival of Gabriel, who they'd thought had perished in some battle long ago. But, they asked, how had their previous benefactors, the Christians, managed to screw up so badly?

The Muslims said uh, debatable, but this bit with Mohammed, peace be unto him, was definitely the real deal.

The angels thanked the Muslims for the correction and started following Sharia law and studying the Koran.

A few weeks later, some extremely miffed Orthodox monks in a Hellenic Army helicopter landed and explained that the Muslims were wrong, Christ was definitely the Son of God, Mohammed didn't know what he was talking about.

The angels were very confused and angry and asked the Christians and Muslims to sort this out among themselves and get back to them.

Instead, a gaggle of Orthodox monks and Muslim imams showed up on their doorsteps and started arguing with the angels and each other. Both sides accused the other of lying, and finally the angels asked one of the questions that had been on their mind the whole time.

What, exactly, was *lying*?

It was determined that the angels' problems actually went much, *much* deeper than gullibility.

Angelologists learned some important things in that decade. Angels had no concept of lying, cheating, defecting, strategizing, or even rhetoric. As a result, it was trivially easy for people to make angels do anything they wanted—with the exception of evil, to which they had a violent constitutional aversion.

So the Pope got a bunch of angels to sign a declaration saying Catholicism was the one true religion, simply by assuring them that it was and saying that signing would help in some way. The Dalai Lama, Orthodox Patriarch, and Chief Rabbi of Jerusalem got their own angels to sign similar declarations. The Soviet Union had an entire choir of angels march through Red Square declaring that Communism was the only way forward. Several flaming swords and giant golden halos were given to businessmen who asked for them politely.

A couple of angels, the ones who interacted with humans the most, the ones who had been bamboozled most often, started to catch on.

And when they did, the blazing golden light in their eyes would fade, their spectacular golden wings would start to wilt and grow dull, their flaming swords would sputter into embers. Their halos would tarnish and rust, their robes of purest white would grow gray and dirty. They would start to sink into their bastions, as if the clouds were only made of water droplets after all. Finally, they would sink right through the bottom of the cloud and hit the earth with a colossal thud.

They would be fallen angels.

The fallen angels weren't evil, exactly. Just confused and disenchanted and a little depressed. They wanted their innocence back, they wanted to forget what lying and cheating were and go back to being certain of everything. They kept praising God, but now their prayers ended in question marks and not exclamation points, like they were talking about Someone very far away.

By 1984, ten years after the first Mormon mission to the angels, about ninety percent of the celestial population had fallen. Bastions hung empty in the sky, or dissolved into ordinary clouds that rained for a while and then dissipated. After countless centuries of Heaven being a metaphorical place definitely not related to actual clouds, and a decade of Heaven being something you could see with a good pair of binoculars, it looked like Heaven was on the verge of going back to being a metaphor once again.

The one thing angels were definitely good at was demon-slaying. During the Reagan administration the President declared the remaining angels a Vital National Resource and charged the military with the goal of protecting them. The fourteen remaining bastions above America became Strategic Angel Reserves, with military garrisons watching them day and night and preventing any snake-oil salesmen or missionaries or other nefarious characters from breaking the remaining celestials' natural innocence. It didn't hurt that planes and helicopters had mostly stopped working by this point, and the only remaining way to the bastions were specially installed pulley systems under careful government control.

The penalty for being on a Strategic Angel Reserve without permission was death. The military would enforce it. The angels themselves, who had been made aware of the danger of their situation, would enforce it. But it wasn't just death. It was the knowledge that you had defiled one of the last outposts of purity left in the world, were responsible for pushing something irreplaceable just a *little bit* further towards the abyss.

III.

"When," asked the woman, "did you speak the Luminous Name?"

"About ten minutes ago," I admitted.

"Well," she said, in a voice tight with the effort of not killing me on the spot. "That gives us perhaps a half-hour before the Marines arrive. That should be enough time to search all of these and get out safely, don't you think?" She gestured to the thousands of bookshelves arranged higher than the eye could see, and gave me a death glare.

"Search?" I asked.

"The angels have information vital to the future of humanity. I've spent months figuring out how get up here unnoticed. And now..."

"Um," I said. "Tell me what you're looking for, and maybe I can help?"

She looked like she was going to snap something, but she held herself back, and after a second she said, "Records of the Urim and Thummim, volume 112. Should be thin and blue. Shelf 2270, level 36."

And then she ran off, again with almost inhuman speed, searching through the bookshelves.

For lack of anything better to do, I did the same.

It should have been simple to find the book given its precise address, except that I didn't know the Enochian numbering system and wasn't sure anyone else did either. There were all sorts of symbols etched in gold onto the shelving, and some or all of them might represent numbers. First I checked to see if one of those weird coincidences had led to the angels using the same numbering system as Elizabethan England, but I couldn't find anything that looked like modern Arabic numerals. So I started running from shelf to shelf, searching for regularities.

Roman numerals use letters in place of numbers. Thus V is 5, X is 10, and C is 100. There was something of the Roman system about the shelf numbers; occasionally long strings of letters would collapse into a single letter, the same way CMXCIX would be followed by M. But other features confused me; I noticed no string contained the same letter twice. And a larger letter — one further towards the end of the Enochian alphabet — was never followed by a smaller one.

The Hebrew numbering system is very elegant. Aleph, the first letter, is one. Bet, the second letter, is two. And so on in this fashion until yud, the tenth letter, which is ten, is followed by kaf, the eleventh letter, which is twenty. The next few letters are thirty, forty, and so on, until one hundred, which is followed by two hundred. The alphabet ends at tav, which is four hundred. You can do all sorts of things by interpreting words as numbers, which the Hebrews called *gematria*. Suppose you want to point out that Emperor Nero is *the worst person*, but Emperor Nero happens to control your country at the time and kills all who offend him. Just write that "let he who hath understanding know that the number of the Beast is the number of a man, and that number is 666" and trust all the other Jews to notice that the only name in the newspapers whose letters sum to 666 is Nero Caesar.

Hebrew numerals never had the same character twice. And the letters furthest in the alphabet will always be on the right side. But this wasn't gematria, or even some Enochian equivalent. For one thing, there were too many letters. Hebrew numerals didn't take any more digits than our Arabic ones; this Enochian system had entries as long as twenty digits, although it seemed to gain or lose a digit every couple of entries, almost at random.

So I racked my memory and remembered the order of the Enochian alphabet, converting each letter to its English equivalent to help keep it in mind. The big number written in silver at the very bottom must be the shelf number. The shelf I was at was ABHI. The next one was CHI. The one after that was ACHI. The next one was BCHI. The one after that was ABCHI. The next one was DHI.

And the funny part was, I was really happy. Aside from the time I've spent with Ana, looking at complicated things and trying tease structure out of them is the only thing I've really truly enjoyed. There was something holy about the task, glimpses of the great structure Adam Kadmon from which all lesser structure comes. It's the only thing I've ever been good at and the only thing I've ever felt really comfortable doing.

The shelves were numbered in John Napier's location arithmetic. The revelation came to me gently, like the sunrise. It was base two, sort of: 2^0 was A, 2^1 was B, 2^2 was C, 2^3 was D, and so on. 100 was 2^6 + 2^5 + 2^2, or CFG; 200 was 2^7 + 2^6 + 2^3, or DGH. That was the neat thing about location arithmetic; to multiply by two you just incremented all the letters by one. To add, you just combined the numbers together. Then you simplified by combining two identical letters into the next letter up. I'd read about it in a kabbalistic text on the Friedman conjecture. It was truly a numbering system worthy of angels.

2270 was BCDEGHL by the English alphabet, and un-or-gal-ged-pa-drux-na by the Enochian. I made it to shelf un-or-gal-ged-pa-drux-na — just in time to almost bump into the woman.

"Interesting," she said, and there was a spark of what might have been approval in her eye. Then she took a scroll wheel out of her pocket and tore off what must have been the Ascending Name. She rocketed up to the thirty-sixth tier of books before grabbing a thin blue volume and shooting back down.

"How do we get back down to the ground?" I asked.

The spark of approval was gone, if it had ever been there at all. "*I* get down the same way I got up," she said. "*You*... figure something out!"

And then she ran away.

I wasn't very optimistic about the figuring something out part. I mean, if I came to the edge of the clouds I could speak the Ascending Name and use it to control my fall. But that would help me in a purely vertical direction. If the Marines had anyone from UNSONG with them—and given the woman's certainty that they would track me by the Luminous Name, I had to assume that they did—they could track that one too and know exactly where I landed. Where even *was* the Mount Baldy Strategic Angel Reserve? Weren't most of the Angel Reserves above uninhabited areas? Even if I could get down to the uninhabited area safely, I didn't like my chances.

So I ran after her. If nothing else, she could lend me a scroll.

I wasn't nearly as fast as she was, but I tried. I ran through corridors carved of cloud, lit by a strange inner glow. I ran through halls so vast and ornate they looked like cathedrals, complete with stained glass windows barely visible in the first rays of sunrise. I ran through what seemed like huge warrooms, full of colossal siege engines and ballistae beyond all description. I ended up on a great balcony, facing the rising sun, with the puffy white base of the cloud stretching out below me like a snowy field.

I was too late. What looked like twenty or thirty Marines had gathered on the cloudtop. In the distance, I could see the cable car that had brought them from their base below, the bastion's only legitimate link to the earth beneath. They were talking with a delegation of angels, not the broken sort of angels I had seen back home, but real beautiful tall angels, golden-eyed, golden-winged, majestic. There was a staircase before me, leading down to the lower levels of the bastion, but it would make me clearly visible as a dark form against the white cloud, and I would have a lot of explaining to do.

I retraced my steps, went back into the bastion, came out a different way. Another balcony. The tall Asian woman was peering down from it, but as soon as I came in she wheeled around, pointed her pistol at me, then visibly relaxed. "You again," she said. She took another look out. "It looks like the Marines are gone, but don't be fooled. They'll have someone staying behind, watching from somewhere hidden. If we stay here, they'll smoke us out. If we try to go, they'll find us immediately." She said it with a certain calm, as if this was by no means the worst problem she had faced that day. "Any ideas, Aaron?"

The sunlight streamed through the open window. The glorious white cloud reflected and refracted it, dazzlingly bright, the kind of heaven you see on the cover of Christian music CD cases.

I began to sing. The Name had popped into my head. It wasn't even one

I knew. It had come out of some deep stock of knowledge, deep as the roots of the mountains.

I turned invisible.

I emitted a squeal of shock, which instantly turned me visible again. She was also shocked, but in a more dignified way.

"How did you do that?"

"Name!" I said.

"Where did you learn it?"

"I don't know!" I said.

Then things snapped into place. Ana trying to rescue me from the UNSONG compound. Asher Bentham not mentioning anything about Sarah. It all made sense. Ana had escaped the house with my computer and was still finding new Names. And I was receiving them through our kabbalistic marriage. We were still in business!

"One more time," she said, "so I can remember it."

A more Machiavellian person might have mentioned that she had just run off and left me to get arrested or killed, or that I had no idea who she was, or that she kept threatening me with that pistol. But I was a Singer, and it was my duty to spread the Names of God to all who needed them. Also I was really excited and not making very good decisions. I told her the Spectral Name.

The two of us went invisible. She grabbed my hand—she could have gotten away, but maybe she felt like she owed me—and we walked down the staircase together until we reached the lower tier of the bastion and followed an elevated corridor of arches and pillars onto the outer wall of the cloud. I didn't want to look down, so instead I looked back.

To describe what I saw—I'm a man of words, but here words fail me. Have you ever stood on the plains on a summer day, watching a thunderstorm roll in, seeing the clouds grow, huge anvils puffing out, becoming more and more complex and foreboding until they have all the majesty and terror of battleships bearing down on you? Can you really believe that all they were destined for was to produce a 60% chance of thundershowers and then to be ignominiously shredded against a warm front? Standing on that rampart, looking up at the angelic bastion behind me, I saw a cloud as it should have been, as it was when the world was young, a floating fortress-city, a testament to the glory of God.

Then we came to a tower on the edge of the wall, and on the top of the tower was a kayak.

"That's a kayak," I said, breaking the spell.

"It's a flying kayak," she said, appearing beside me.

"A—"

She gave me a look which I interpreted as *if you mention the words "flyak" or "skyak" right now, I will kill you on the spot.*

"Get in if you're coming." Then, almost as an afterthought, "Call me Jane."

"I'm Aaron."

"You already said that."

I climbed into the kayak beside her, terribly cramped, my body pressed against hers too tightly to be comfortable. I had a bad feeling about this.

Jane threw the single paddle to me, scooted forward suddenly, and the kayak dropped off the edge of the cloud into the gulfs of air below.

Chapter Twenty

When The Stars Threw Down Their Spears

Where wast thou when I laid the foundations for theoretical computer science?
—kingjamesprogramming.tumblr.com

3??? BC
Heaven

I.

Beyond the nimbus and stratus, in the furthest reaches of the heavens, the parliament of the angels convened in the eye of a great cyclone. The walls of the storm curved in toward the center, so that they formed tier upon tier of seating for the angelic hosts. At the very bottom and in the very center was a whirlwind that concealed the Archangel Metatron, the Voice of God in the created world. Seated around him were thrones for the nine other archangels. Above them in concentric circles based on rank sat various cherubim, seraphim, ophanim, dominions, powers, principalities, weird lamb-dragon hybrids with hundreds of faces, glowing starlike beings rapt in meditation, geometric shapes covered with lidless golden eyes, and others even harder to describe.

Metatron did not speak. Metatron never spoke. No one was worthy to hear the Voice of God. Raziel was missing, as always, out doing his thing, whatever Raziel's thing was. That left Sataniel as highest-ranking. Sataniel, the morning star, the amber-hued, the bringer of dawn, the beautiful, peerless in understanding, gracious in mercy.

For the past aeon, even Sataniel had been gone, off exploring the inner core of the world, and it had been Zadkiel who had held the golden feather that represented dominion, who had conducted the choirs and moved some to sound and others to silence. Now Sataniel had returned, and it was with joy and humility that Zadkiel handed over the feather and sat back down upon his throne of cloudstuff and carnelian.

"My brothers," said Sataniel, "for an aeon of the world, I have been exploring the very center of the Earth. Now, by the mercy of God, blessed be His holy Name, I have returned."

At the mention of God, all the assembled angels broke out into applause and cheering for seven days and seven nights. When the euphoria died down, Sataniel again raised the golden feather and spoke.

"Sometimes there comes upon us the desire to seek out and explore new parts of God's creation, that we may appreciate ever-greater portions of His glory."

The heavenly hosts began applauding again at the mention of God, but Sataniel raised the feather and calmed them down.

"Thus Raziel, who has absented himself from this assembly to traverse the gulfs beyond the world. But my own curiosity was kindled by a different prize, the very center of the Earth, which none have seen before. I made journey to the deepest part of the deepest lake, and there I thrust into the ground a star-beam until it cracked and fissured. More and more star-beams I summoned, until they burnt a tunnel into the yielding rock. Below I came to a realm of fire, but again I parted it with star beams, until I congealed a tunnel that could pass through even the magma of the inner deep. After an aeon of labor, I came at last to the solid iron core, and at a word from me, it opened wide.

"There I found a new world, as different from the surface as the surface is from our own realm of cloud and zephyr. In the center of the earth is a hollow space a thousand miles in diameter. By some strange magic of the place I could walk upon its iron inner shell, though by rights I ought to have been without weight. That shell contains iron mountains and iron canyons, split by seas and rivers of glowing lava that cast a dim red light over the whole inner world. And at the south pole of this realm stood an iron tower, five hundred miles in height, reaching all the way up to the exact center of the earth."

All the angels listened in rapt attention except Uriel, who was sort of half-paying attention while trying to balance several twelve-dimensional shapes on top of each other.

"I entered that dark tower at its base, and for forty days and forty nights I climbed the spiral staircase leading to the world's center. Finally, at the tower's very peak, I discovered a new facet of God."

There was utter silence throughout the halls of Heaven, except a brief curse as Uriel's hyperdimensional tower collapsed on itself and he picked up the pieces to try to rebuild it.

"He called himself Thamiel, and I could sense the divine energy in him, like and yet unlike any I had ever seen before. For a year and a day I studied at his feet, learning his lore, learning aspects of God utterly foreign to the lore of Heaven. And after a year and a day, he told me I had learned enough, and he bade me return and teach it to you, my fellows."

A great clamor arose from all the heavenly hosts, save Uriel, who took advantage of the brief lapse to conjure a parchment and pen and start working on a proof about the optimal configuration of twelve-dimensional shapes. "Tell us, Sataniel!" they cried. "Teach us this new lore, that we may come to more fully understand the Holy One!"

"Well," said Sataniel, wiping a sudden bead of sweat off his brow, "this is going to sound kind of crazy, but hear me out. What if, instead of serving God, we were to, um, *defy* Him?"

A moment of confusion. Uriel proved several important lemmas about tower construction.

"I don't understand," said Haniel. "Like, I get what you're trying to say. But, well... how would that tend toward the greater glory of God?"

"It doesn't," said Sataniel. "I will definitely concede that point."

"But then," said Zadkiel, "if you're admitting it doesn't tend toward the greater glory of God, then how is God glorified when we do it?"

"But that's what I'm saying," said Sataniel. "We could just not glorify God. We could even undermine God, rebel against Him, that kind of thing."

"Then we would have to smite *ourselves*," said Gabriel. "That sounds really dumb."

"I'm with Gabriel," said Raphael. "No offense to this Thamiel fellow, but I'm not sure he's thought this through very well."

"He seems a couple of strings short of a harp," said Camael bluntly.

"I understand this is confusing," Sataniel said. "I didn't get it all at once. My first thoughts were the same as yours were—it doesn't make sense, it doesn't glorify God, we'd have to smite ourselves—I thought all of these things at first, trust me. But the more Thamiel explained to me, the more it started to come together. You've got to believe me, there's a sort of mental distance here, but there's a self-consistent position on the other side. Like, for example, if we were to defy God, we could smite those who *didn't* defy God."

"But I *still* maintain that that wouldn't increase the glory of God very well!" said Haniel.

"Right!" said Michael, "and how would we sing songs of praise? If we smote those who didn't defy God, we'd have to smite ourselves every time we sung a song of praise! There are some *serious* loopholes here."

"Sataniel's position is self-consistent," said Uriel, without looking up from the parchment he was writing his proof on. "It's like representing our desires in a utility function, then multiplying by negative one."

Everyone ignored Uriel as usual.

"Sataniel," said Michael, "even if we could figure out a way to do this without smiting ourselves, what would be the *point*?"

"Instead of working to serve God," said Sataniel, "we could serve ourselves."

"Ohhhhh," said Zadkiel. "You're saying that, since we are creations of God, praising and serving ourselves would be a more effective way of demonstrating our gratitude and love of God's glory than praising and serving Him directly? And so, in a sense, actually even more humble and godly? It's a bit counterintuitive, but it just... might... work."

"No!" said Sataniel, and he stomped on the cloud underneath his feet, shooting off little wisps of cirrus. "You're not getting it. This is about total conceptual revolution! A complete shift in mindset! There aren't even the right words for it!"

With a wave of his hand, he caused a sheet of white fire to burst forth from the ground; with his pointer finger, he began tracing lines in black fire upon the flaming canvas. "Look, here on the right side we have all of the things we consider good. Glorification of God. Virtue. Prayer. Service." He moved to the other half of the sheet. "And here on the left side we have the opposite of those things. God being glorified less than He might otherwise be. Virtue that falls short of the goal. Not serving people even when they deserve to be served. My brothers, all of our actions have to be to some end. Right now we're aiming towards the things here on the right. But instead, we could just as well aim at these other things, here on the left."

"But," said Raphael, "the left is the side with sin and mockery of God and so on. Are you sure you didn't mean to point to the right instead?"

"Maybe he means *our* right and *his* left," proposed Haniel helpfully.

The whole diagram of fire-upon-fire disappeared in a puff of smoke.

"Imagine," said Sataniel. "We could descend onto the Earth, and rule over Men. We could make them call us gods, and worship us with prayer and sacrifice. We could lay with the most beautiful of the daughters of Men, and have mighty children whose footsteps make the Behemoth flee in terror. We could enslave humans, and make them build us vast palaces of gold and chalcedony, and never give another thought to God at all."

The other angels looked thoughtful. Several began to whisper excitedly among themselves. Some stared off into space, imagining the pleasures of such a life. Finally, Zadkiel gave voice to what all of them were thinking:

"It's an interesting idea, Sataniel, but I just. Don't. Get. How it would contribute to the glory of God."

Sataniel looked up, from the circle where the eight other archangels sat, to the seats of the highest and wisest angels, and all the way up the vast walls of cloud, looked upon the fiery lions and spinning wheels and pillars of sunlight and all the rest, and every one of them was nodding in agreement with Zadkiel.

Sataniel very deliberately took a deep breath. In. Out. Then another. In. Out.

"I was rash," he said. "It took a year and a day for Thamiel to impart his lore to me; I was rash to think I could explain it in a single speech. So don't hear it from me. Hear it from the master. I propose that a portion of you follow me, and we will cross the Earth's interior and find Thamiel, and he will teach you his lore as he taught it to me, and there will be no further confusion."

"Honestly," said Camael. "It seems kind of like a waste of time. I still haven't heard any good evidence that this 'Thamiel' and his ideas can glorify God, and paying them more attention wastes valuable songs-of-praise-singing time."

Murmurs of assent. The fiery lions nodded, the wheels spun in agreement.

Sataniel cast his head down. For a moment he seemed about to acquiesce. Then, a weird look appeared on his face, a look unlike any that the angels had ever seen, almost a contortion. He spoke haltingly, as if trying a strange new language he had never spoken before.

"Actually... God... God told me... that He really wanted some of you guys to follow me. To go meet Thamiel. Yes. God said that. That was what He said."

A look of astonishment and joy flashed throughout the council. God had spoken! God rarely spoke to angels even once an aeon, and now God had spoken to their brother Sataniel! New information about the will of the

Divine, a new opportunity to serve Him, to better conform their actions to the newly clarified Divine Will!

"Of course!" said Michael. "Why didn't you say so, brother? This is a great day indeed! How many of us did God want there?"

For someone who had so suddenly seen his fortunes shift for the better, Sataniel looked oddly uncomfortable. For someone who had received a revelation from God, he was oddly reluctant to share it. All these things the angels noticed, but there was no possible explanation for them, none at all, so they dismissed it from their thoughts.

"One third," said Sataniel finally. "One third of the Heavenly Host."

II.

3??? BC
Mesopotamia

"The future is ziggurats," Samyazaz was telling Ut-Naparash as they walked up the Great Stair. "In a hundred years, nobody's going to remember pyramids. Pyramids are a flash in the pan. Ziggurats are for the ages."

"The King has every bit of faith in ziggurats and in yourself," said Ut-Naparash. "He only wishes that the project would go a little... faster."

The king is a fricking nimrod, thought Samyazaz to himself, but out loud he just said, "You can't rush ziggurats, Ut-Naparash." He punctuated his statement with a wave of his gigantic arms. "You try to rush a ziggurat, you end up with one side not big enough, or a tier off center, and then the whole thing is fried. They're not like henges, where if you put a stone in the wrong place here or there nobody's going to notice. Ziggurats are a work of art. A place for everything, and everything in its place."

They reached the top of the Great Stair and the highest tier of the ziggurat. Highest tier of the ziggurat *so far*, Samyazaz corrected himself. There was still a lot of room for improvement. Three men in loincloths stood on the west edge of the platform, staring at the afternoon sky. Samyazaz took a whip from his belt and cracked it in the air, startling them.

"I'm not paying you to lollygag!" he shouted. He hoped the slaves appreciated his sense of humor.

"Sorry, o mighty one," said the tallest slave, bowing low. "Sorry, great eminence," he repeated, this time to Ut-Naparash. "It is only... a storm is coming."

Samyazaz looked west. The slave was right. It was big and green and formed of hulking thunderheads that seemed to seethe and simmer. It was coming closer. There was something ominous about it.

"Bah!" said Samyazaz. "It's just the storm god Ishkur, mounted upon his giant fire-breathing bull."

The slaves looked uncomfortable. For that matter, Ut-Naparash looked uncomfortable. Maybe Samyazaz had gotten the wrong religion? Maybe it being the storm god Ishkur mounted upon his giant fire-breathing bull was really bad?

Or maybe it was something entirely different. You never knew with humans, thought Samyazaz.

But slowly, grudgingly, the slaves got back to work. They feared him. Of course they did. Even Ut-Naparash feared him. He was Samyazaz, the Bringer of Forbidden Knowledge. Not that that was so hard when "copper and tin go together to make bronze" is Forbidden Knowledge. Heck, eighty years ago the king's daughter had been sad because her lips weren't rosy enough, and fellow forbidden-knowledge-bringer Gadiriel had suggested she crush some red rocks into a pigment and then paint it on herself, and people were *still* talking about this and worrying it would lead to everyone turning into sex-crazed maniacs.

The first rumble of thunder was heard from the approaching storm to the west, and Samyazaz saw the tall slave reach for his *other* great invention. The man gulped down half a pint of beer for courage. Samyazaz loved beer. He'd founded the first brewery here himself, and it never ceased to interest him how people who were scared and confrontational after a sip would be friendly and easy to manipulate after they finished the pot. Beer was the future. Not as much the future as ziggurats. But still the future.

"Pardon me, wise one," said Ut-Naparash, "but perhaps we should go back down to the city, lest we be caught up here when the storm arrives?"

The thing with humans, Samyazaz thought, was that as fragile as they were, they always thought they were even more fragile than that. It was kind of sad.

"Put up a canopy," he ordered the slaves. Then, to Ut-Naparash, "Our tower is already as high as the clouds. Let us enjoy the fruits of our labor, and see the Storm God face to face, so we may boast to him of our might."

Again with the uncomfortable looks from Ut-Naparash and the slaves. He hoped they would get around to inventing writing soon, so he could read a book about Sumerian religion and figure out what it was he was missing.

Until then he would have to do things the hard way. "Do it for the mighty one," he said, speaking the words of power that his sort had bred deep into these people's unconscious.

Compelled by the invocation, the slaves set up the canopy. Samyazaz wandered to the west edge of the platform. The storm was very, very close now. It swept over the empty flood plain like a wave over a beach. Two stupendous bolts of lightning struck the ground just outside the city wall, then... stopped.

Everything had stopped. Samyazaz saw the slaves bent over, placing a pole for the canopy, but they neither tied it in nor stood up. Ut-Naparash had taken a pot of beer, and Samyazaz could see the golden liquid falling from the pot to the priest's waiting lips, but the drops hung motionless in mid-air. In the city below him, a hundred merchants were frozen in various steps of peddling their wares. Samyazaz moved one of his giant arms back and forth. Okay. He could move. It was just everyone else who was frozen. This was really bad.

The two lightning bolts gradually resolved themselves into two gigantic human forms, spanning the distance from the bottom of the clouds to the flood plain below, each taller than the ziggurat.

"Hello, Samyazaz," said the Archangel Michael.

"Hello, Samyazaz," said the Archangel Gabriel.

"Frick," said Samyazaz.

"We have left you to your games long enough," said Michael. "The war is not going well. It is time for you to come home and join in the great battle."

"No. Nope. No way," said Samyazaz. "Things are going really well here. I've got a wife and kids. Twenty wives, actually, fifty kids. No way I'm going back there. Absolutely not."

"The war is not going well," Michael repeated.

"You think I don't know that? I've been watching the sky. I've seen the signs."

"Camael is dead. Haniel is dead. Raphael is dead. Only Zadkiel and the two of us remain."

"What about Metatron?"

"Too holy to leave his whirlwind."

"Too holy to do anything, really."

"Raziel?"

"Off somewhere," said Michael.

"Hard to locate," said Gabriel.

"Uriel?"

"He doesn't count," said Michael.

"He definitely doesn't count," said Gabriel.

"But... what are you guys doing? Sataniel only took a third of the angels with him to the inner core. Even if that Thamiel guy was able to turn every single one of them against God, you still outnumber him two to one."

Gabriel coughed awkwardly. "He would use... stratagems. He would say, 'I am going to attack you from the north,' and then attack us from the south. It was unfair."

"And then when we finally figured out what he was doing," added Michael, "He would say, 'I am going to attack you from the north,' and then *actually* attack us from the north. It was very unfair."

"And," Gabriel said, "When we ordered some of the lesser angels to study these stratagems so we could apply them, the angels would lose their glow and purity. They would no longer be able to sing the songs of praise in the right key. We would have to expel them from Heaven, for their own good."

"And then," said Michael, "they would fight on Thamiel's side."

"It was very bad," said Gabriel.

"So," said Samyazaz, "wait for everyone who died to recoalesce, and don't be so naive the next time."

"It is worse than that," said Michael. "Thamiel wields a two-pointed weapon. Everyone slain by it dies the true death."

"Like humans?"

"Exactly like humans."

"Ugh."

"It gets worse," said Michael. "I myself slew Sataniel. Thamiel raised his two-pointed weapon over the spot, and Sataniel did not recoalesce as himself. Instead his spirit fragmented into many monsters. Camael and his choir were not able to stand against them."

"They have taken over the place of meeting," said Gabriel. "We must counterattack with everything we have. You will join us, Samyazaz."

"No," said Samyazaz. "I won't."

The thunder rumbled menacingly.

"Why me? I'm not the only angel who came to Earth."

"You are one of the leaders. The others respect you."

"Go find Gadiriel. She's always up for doing crazy stuff."

"She?"

"Gadiriel has adopted various quaint human customs, like being female."

The thunder rumbled menacingly again.

"We will bring Gadiriel. We will also bring you."

"You don't need me. There are a hundred myriads of angels. I'm not going to be any use to anybody."

"You understand stratagems. Like Thamiel. Yet you have not lost your power, or turned to his service. This is interesting. Perhaps it is because you learned from humans, whom you dominate, rather than from equals, whom you fear. You understand lying. Trickery. Deceit. We archangels have more mental resilience to these than the ordinary choirs, but we still have not mastered them. Without masters of such on our side, Thamiel can play us like a harp."

"Well, uh, if you have any tactical questions, you're welcome to stop around and run them by me. I'll be right here, on top of the giant ziggurat, can't miss me."

"You will come with us."

"But... my ziggurats!"

"Are like a child's sand castles in the eyes of the Lord."

"I like ziggurats! You know, humans are different from angels, in that they have this weird long thing here" — Samyazaz pointed at his crotch — "and I felt bad about not having one of those. But if I build big enough ziggurats, then I feel better about myself!"

"You will come with us."

"No. I'm not going to let myself get pricked by some two-headed creep with a freaky underworld weapon that makes you die the true death. Go bother Gadiriel."

"You will come with us. Now."

"Would either of you care for a pot of beer? I find it lubricates interactions like this very nicely."

"You will—"

Something was burrowing up out of the flood plain, like a mole or a beetle. It kicked up mud in all directions as it rose, then finally broke the surface. Something oily and foul buzzed like a bee halfway between Samyazaz and the great angelic apparitions.

"Well," said Thamiel. "How far you've both fallen."

Michael pulled his sword of fire from its scabbard. A moment later, Gabriel did the same.

"Begone, Thamiel. This is none of your business."

"Oh, it's my business. Good lie, though. I didn't think you had it in you. You're learning fast."

"You are an abomination before the Most High."

"And I'm winning." He held up the bident. "Run away, cowards."

For just a moment, Michael and Gabriel made as if to charge. But then the lightning bolts struck home, the thunder crashed in a great resounding peal, and time started again.

"Wise one!" asked Ut-Naparash. "Are you well? You seem..." Suddenly his face blanched in horror.

Thamiel floated leisurely to the ziggurat platform and landed in the center. The slaves threw themselves off the sides in horror and loathing, and there was a sickening cracking sound as their bodies hit the tier beneath. Ut-Naparash started making the complex ritual movements of the Greater Prayer to Enlil.

"Go away," said Thamiel, and flicked a finger at Ut-Naparash. The priest's eyeballs exploded in showers of blood, and he fell convulsing to the ground.

"Master," said Samyazaz, kneeling. He wasn't scared of Michael and Gabriel, big though they were, but this was something on an entirely different level.

"Master, is it?" asked Thamiel. "Because a moment ago, you were calling me a 'two-headed creep.'"

"Master!" said Samyazaz, desperately. "I didn't mean it. I will make amends! I will..."

"Nice ziggurat you've got here," said Thamiel. "Shame if something were to happen to it."

He gave a lazy flick of his bident, and the entire structure collapsed in on itself, killing everyone: slaves, porters, supervisors, Ut-Naparash, the entire construction crew; a hundred years of work reduced to smoking rubble in an instant.

It was only a minor death, as deaths went. A purposeless accident of falling rocks and rubbles. Samyazaz recoalesced within a few minutes. Thamiel was gone now. It was just him and the remains of his ziggurat. He wasn't too proud to cry, just one tear. Then he sighed, brushed himself off, and got up.

He had always prided himself on his resilience. Well, what was a hundred years, to one such as him? Michael and Gabriel wouldn't dare bother him again. It was just him and the humans. If he could think of some way to deal with the king and all of these recalcitrant priests, some way to gain enough power to challenge *Thamiel*, some way...

He stumbled back in the direction of his brewery. He could *definitely* use some beer right now.

III.

3??? BC
Gulf of Mexico

And then there were two.

The sky had once been full of clouds. Big clouds, little clouds, dark clouds, bright clouds. Clouds sculpted into great gleaming palaces of alabaster, clouds carved into fortresses red with the light of sunset. Clouds linked by rainbow bridges, clouds walled with icy ramparts, clouds lit by pillars of lightning, great frigates of cloud that sailed the jet stream packed with legions of angels going off to war.

Now most of the old clouds were gone, taken over by Thamiel and his forces, or abandoned as their celestial inhabitants sought more defensible positions. The meeting place had fallen. The long line of derechos that Michael had set up as a bulwark had fallen. The typhoon where Raphael had guarded the Central Pacific had been scattered. Even Zadkiel's howling blizzard had been reduced to a few flurries.

Gabriel had tried to save them. He had been there at Raphael's side when Thamiel had pierced the archangel with his bident and slain him in battle. He had seen Michael kill Thamiel in single combat, only for the demon to recoalesce and stab the victor in the back. He had fled with the others to Zadkiel's circumpolar redoubt, which had held on for seven years of constant battle before it was betrayed by a stray sunbeam. Now he was alone. The last of the archangels, he thought to himself.

Except for the one who didn't count.

This storm, Gabriel had noticed on his way in, was poorly developed. No minarets. No ramparts. Just a big hurricane with occasional objects strewn about it. There was a big hexagon on one side. Who needed a hexagon that big? A couple of furrows making strange patterns. Lumps. Poorly done, no defenses, just the sort of shoddy work he had expected. It would, he thought, need some improvement.

There was some sort of shield surrounding the central eye. Good. A rudimentary defense mechanism. That could be built upon. For now, though, it was in his way.

"Let me in," he shouted, banging his flaming sword on the invisible surface. No response. He hadn't expected polite requests to work. "Let me in, or I will burn this place until no shred of cloud is left."

The invisible wall parted, and Gabriel strode into the eye of the storm, the inner sanctum. Its lord was sitting in mid-air, tracing with his finger a series of glowing paths upon a fiendishly complex diagram. Gabriel blew the diagram away with a gust of wind.

"I need this storm," he told Uriel, after the pleasantries had been completed, which with Uriel meant after about two seconds. "*Angelkind* needs this storm."

"You can't have it," said Uriel. Of course not. Of *course* Uriel wouldn't be cooperative. Spend the last forty years of the war sitting around doing nothing, and now he was sitting on the last usable defensive bastion in the entire sky, and of *course* he wouldn't help.

"Everyone else is dead. We made a last stand at Zadkiel's domain near the pole. Myself, Zadkiel, angels from all ten choirs, and our human and Nephilim allies. Everyone except you. We held out for seven years before the ice wall cracked. Zadkiel is dead. Only a few of us escaped. This is the last intact bastion. We need your storm."

"I do not think it would help you very much. You would probably just die here."

"Better to die on one's feet than to live on one's... um... better to die on one's feet!"

"You cannot have this storm. I am using it."

"Using it? For what? What use are you or anything you have ever done? For decades now we have fought Thamiel, and you have been of no use. When Heaven was fair and free, and we spent the aeons singing songs of praise, you would always get distracted and forget your part. You were of no use."

"I was analyzing the harmonic structure. It was very interesting."

"Whenever we sat in council, you would hide under your throne whenever someone asked you to talk," Gabriel interrupted. "And then, when the war came, you did the same thing you always did. You hid under a rock and kept playing with your shapes and your equations. Haniel gave his life. You did nothing. Camael gave his life. You did not care. Raphael gave his life. You sat around useless. Michael gave his life. You kept daydreaming. Zadkiel gave his life. And you? Always building towers, or writing proofs, or coming up with those codes of yours. We went out of our way to try to teach you proper behavior—"

"You were very mean to me."

"We were not mean enough! If we had been less tolerant, maybe you would have behaved as an archangel should. Maybe you would have joined in the fight, and even now we would be advancing against Thamiel and his forces. Maybe you could have died in place of Michael! Instead you sit here, playing games. The game is over now, Uriel. It is time to give this bastion to those who can use it."

"I am using it.

"For what?"

"I have discovered many interesting things."

"Ten years ago," said Gabriel, "Michael and I hunted down Samyazaz, who had fled to Earth to escape the war. He was a coward. Yet I prefer him to you, for at least he felt ashamed. It was Sataniel who started this war, yet him also I prefer to you, for he died fighting, in fire and glory, as an angel should. And you? You have 'discovered many interesting things.' I will take this bastion, and we will make a final stand here, and perhaps we will all die, but about *your* death I will feel no guilt."

"Gabriel," said Uriel. "Look at the sun."

Gabriel looked. "What am I looking for?"

"Does it seem different to you at all?"

Gabriel squinted. "Different how?"

"Um. Usually it looks like an innumerable company of the heavenly host crying 'Holy holy holy is the Lord God Almighty,' right?"

"Yes."

"And now, do you see something more like, say, a round disk of fire somewhat like a guinea?"

Gabriel squinted. An odd expression crossed his face. "What are you saying?"

"I have discovered many interesting things, Gabriel. The sun is only the beginning."

"What do you mean?"

"I have determined the basic structure of the world. The way God becomes finite. The machinery that transmutes divinity into finitude is based on a series of ten sapphires. They are not exactly located within space-time, but you can think of them as sort of coextensive with the outside of the crystal sphere surrounding the world."

Gabriel noticed that, as usual, the only time Uriel got any emotion in his voice, the only time he would even make eye contact, was when he was talking about something totally irrelevant and uninteresting.

"This is the Tree of Life. It converts pure structure into material reality through a series of four levels. There is a bottleneck in the last one which connects the sapphire called Yesod to the one called Malkuth. By filtering this bottleneck, I can control the flow of the shefa from higher spheres from entering the physical world."

"The shefa sustains existence. Any impediment to its radiance would make the universe crumble into dust."

"No. I can shift the world into a different stable equilibrium which can run indefinitely on an internal mechanism independent of the shefa."

"How?"

"With math. I am changing the world into math."

The horror struck Gabriel at that moment. He — and Zadkiel, Michael, all the others — had dismissed Uriel as an idiot, too obsessed with his charts and correspondences to participate in the governance of Heaven, an empty mind turned in on itself in a tragic waste of an archangelic seat. They had been blind. He wasn't just an idiot, he was a maniac. Samyazaz had a ziggurat obsession, he remembered that, but never in Samyazaz's most grandiose dreams would he have tried to turn the whole world into a ziggurat. His thoughts turned to Thamiel. No one knew entirely what he was, save that he was obsessed with evil, and was trying to turn the whole world into evil. And now Uriel—

"You cannot change the world into math. That does not even make sense."

"I can," said Uriel. "I will show you."

He motioned with his hand, and a series of objects and creatures flew up from the world below him. Uriel dismissed in turn a giant grouper, a giraffe, and a mountain, until he was left with a huge redwood tree, its uprooted bottom looking strangely naked in the storm-tossed air.

Uriel plucked a geometer's compass out of the storm. He crouched above the tree. The clouds behind him parted to reveal the setting sun, and for a second he was framed in the golden light, ancient in aspect, terrible in majesty, tracing circles only he could see. A moment of intense concentration and it was done.

"It looks the same," said Gabriel.

"It is and is not," said Uriel. "It is as shady and green as it was before. It will grow and give seeds. But it does not partake of the shefa directly. It is made of math. It is built of atoms of different varieties, which I have charted here." He pointed to one of the various tables sketched out in black fire upon the storm wall. "Its branches grow in a very particular fractal pattern, as per information which I have encoded inside it in a massively parallel base four system."

"Only God can make a tree," said Gabriel angrily.

"I am not creating. I am converting. I have written a script which is gradually crawling the universe at the level of Yetzirah, converting all divine objects into their mathematical equivalents. Simultaneously I am gradually raising a metaphysical dam across the path from Yesod to Malkuth. By the time the world is fully insulated from the shefa, it will be running entirely on mathematics and able to maintain itself. A small amount of shefa can be deliberately allowed to enter in order to breathe fire into the equations. The rest will remain in the upper spheres, intact."

"What about us? Will we also be made of math?"

"Angels are too closely linked to the shefa to survive such a transition."

"So—"

"So Thamiel and his demons will essentially run out of charge and dry up. A vestigial portion will remain as metaphor, but they will be unable to directly affect the world. The war will be over."

"What about us?"

"Um."

Gabriel grabbed the other archangel. "What about us, Uriel?"

Uriel pushed him away. "Since the creation of the universe, you have shown me no kindness. When we sung songs of praise, you would mock my voice. When the war began, you ignored me, saying I was too weak and foolish to be of any help. I tried to tell you. Tried to tell you that the equations and correspondences held more of God than all of your songs and swords and shields combined. But you would not listen. You called me a fool. Now you come here, demanding I give up my home to you. Yes. You too will become metaphor. So be it. What were the words you used? I will feel no guilt."

Gabriel materialized a flaming sword. "I hoped I would not need to do this," he said.

He looked at Uriel. Strange Uriel, with his empty golden eyes, always seeming like they were staring into some other space. All the others he had been able to fathom. Camael could be too harsh; Zadkiel too soft, Michael too rash, but they were all fundamentally his type of people. Uriel had been different. From the very start, he had known that Uriel could never be a part of their works, never a leader, never even a follower.

Had he always known it would come to this? No, in the days before Thamiel, the good days, none of them would ever have imagined hurting another angel. Now things were different. Everything had grown horrible. In a way, this was the worst. Aside from the goodness of God, the one constant was that Uriel would be irrelevant, always off in the corner staring into space working on some weird problem. Now Uriel's very irrelevancy had been twisted into some kind of horrible, evil version of itself.

But one welcome truth had not changed: Uriel was weak. Very, very weak. Less skilled in combat even than Raphael. It was time to end this.

"Gabriel," said Uriel. "I am channeling the shefa. Do you know what that means? It means I control it. All of it. Go away, Gabriel. Don't make me hurt you."

Uriel? Hurt anybody? Gabriel lunged forward, and...

Uriel *flared.* Ten streams of light flowed into him, light in the seven earthly colors and the three colors you only see in Heaven. The light rushed from his fingertips, and Gabriel's flaming sword evaporated into steam in his hands. He looked at Uriel again, and there was something changed about his aspect, something terrifying, something beyond even the might of an archangel.

GO AWAY, GABRIEL.

Gabriel clasped his hands together, said a brief prayer. His flaming sword rekindled. His eyes shone with silver fire. The storm parted around him, beautiful jeweled armor grew upon him like a flower unfolding on a branch.

GO AWAY. I DO NOT WANT TO HURT YOU. BUT I CAN.

"No," said Gabriel. "I am making a final stand. Whether against Thamiel, or against you, I do not know. I do not care. But my existence is already past the time appointed by destiny, and all my friends are dead, and I will fight."

GO FIGHT THAMIEL.

"No. I do not like Thamiel. But I think I like you less."

His flaming sword was still pointing directly at Uriel's neck.

GO AWAY, Uriel repeated. OR I WILL TURN YOU INTO NUMBERS.

The sword didn't move.

I CAN DO IT, YOU KNOW, said Uriel. I WILL TURN YOU INTO NUMBERS. WOULD YOU LIKE TO BE A SIX, GABRIEL? I CAN MAKE YOU A SIX. OR AN ELEVEN. OR A FIFTEEN. YOU WILL SPEND ETERNITY BETWEEN FOURTEEN AND SIXTEEN. THIS IS A THREAT. GO AWAY.

With a final cry of rage, Gabriel turned to go. But as he flew off, he shouted back. "You'll die too! You're also made of shefa! You'll die too!"

When Gabriel was out of sight, Uriel sat back down and started shaking. He shook and shook and hugged himself and looked at the glowing diagrams to calm himself down. They were so pretty. Not perfect yet, far from perfect, but elegant. All the roar and storm of the divine fire calmed down, channeled into crystal-clear lifeless math. The chaos removed. The weeds pruned. Thamiel neutered. The world safe and orderly. Soon the world would be all nice and orderly and it would be math and it would be safe.

I KNOW, Uriel said to himself, after Gabriel was gone. Then he returned to his calculations, humming softly to himself.

Chapter Twenty-One

Thou Also Dwellest In Eternity

Work hard, play hard, converge to a transcendent and unified end state of human evolution called the Omega Point as predicted by Teilhard.

—@GapOfGods

Noon, May 12, 2017
San Francisco

I.

The resemblance between San Francisco and the Biblical Jerusalem is uncanny.

The highest point in Jerusalem was King Solomon's Temple Mount; the highest point in San Francisco is the suspiciously-named Mount Davidson. To the north of the Temple was the Golden Gate, leading to the city of Tiberias; to the north of Mount Davidson is the Golden Gate Bridge, leading to the city of Tiburon. Southwest of Jerusalem city center was the Roman legions' camp (Latin: *castrum*); southwest of San Francisco city center is the Castro District. To the south of Jerusalem lay Gehennam, the Valley of Sulfur; to the south of San Francisco lies Silicon Valley. To the east of Jerusalem was the giant dungheap where the Israelites would throw their refuse; to the east of San Francisco is Oakland. Like I said, uncanny.

The east gate of Jerusalem is called the Bab al-Buraq; the east gate of San Francisco is called the Bay Bridge. The Bab al-Buraq has been bricked up since the Crusades; the Bay Bridge has been barricaded since the 1970s.

Ana Thurmond spoke a Name, became invisible, and slipped past the barricades, the guards in their guard towers none the wiser.

Just inside the Bab al-Buraq was the Temple Treasury; just past the barricades on the Bay Bridge is Treasure Island. The Temple Treasury became a base for the Knights Templar; Treasure Island became a base for the US

Navy. Both military forces abandoned their respective bases a few decades later; both had their partisans who prophesied they would one day regain their former glory. The Temple Treasury, upon the coming of Moshiach and the construction of the Third Temple; Treasure Island, after the San Francisco government completed an environmental impact evaluation and approved a real estate development plan. God in His wisdom alone knows which will happen first.

Ana passed Treasure Island, went into the tunnel through Yerba Buena. There are tunnels underneath Jerusalem, too, built for sieges. Some of them have the earliest known paleo-Hebrew inscriptions on them. The Yerba Buena tunnel had a sign. It said:

> ***AS PER THE CALIFORNIA SECURITY ACT OF 1972,***
> ***SECTION 22 PART 10:***
> *This has been declared a restricted area*
> *It is unlawful to cross beyond this point*
> *Deadly force will be used upon violators of this ordinance*

Ana left the tunnel, walked onto the second half of the bridge. The sun beat down on her. The span of the bridge seemed to shimmer and sway. The city ahead of her grew larger with each step.

John of Patmos described the New Jerusalem as "having the glory of God, and her light was like unto a stone most precious, even like a jasper stone, clear as crystal." The buildings of San Francisco were... varied. Ana had seen them before, but only from afar. There's a park in Berkeley where you can sit on the edge of the Bay and stare directly across at San Francisco. Throughout the 70s and 80s, such watchers were rewarded with strange sights. New skyscrapers arose. Old ones were torn down. A huge lidless eye opened on the top of the Transamerica Pyramid. Weird structures that seemed to defy gravity were erected, geodesic domes, spiral minarets in every color of the rainbow. Iridescent spheres the size of city blocks that hovered in midair. The northern end of the Golden Gate, shrouded in a luminous mist.

Now as she stepped off the Bay Bridge, she saw it face-to-face for the first time. It was even stranger than she had expected. The sidewalks were covered with kabbalistic diagrams written in gold chalk. The walls of the buildings were covered with murals depicting alien worlds, and every spot of greenery burst forth with flowers that were out of season or totally unrecognizable. Young children played in car-free streets with asphalt white as pearl.

("Thus says the Lord," prophesied Zechariah. "Old men and old women shall again sit in the streets of Jerusalem, each with staff in hand because of great age. And the city shall be full of boys and girls playing in its streets.")

"Transcendent joy," a little boy told Ana as she passed him, heedless of her invisibility. "Universal love," said the little girl he was playing with. "Holy, holy, holy!" barked their little dog.

An old man was sweeping the streets with a broom. His faces sparkled like that of a young man looking into the eyes of his beloved. "Transcendent joy," he told her, and Ana replied with an awkward "Thanks," breaking her invisibility — not that it seemed to be useful here. Whatever had made them like this must have also—

Wait, thought Ana, *did that dog just bark the word "holy" at me?*

II.

Francis of Assisi had been unusually holy even for saints. His father had been a rich businessman, and he grew up in a world of luxury, sports, and feasting. One day, he was out selling cloth for his father's business when a beggar approached him and asked for alms. Francis tossed him a coin, and the beggar went away. Then Francis sat and thought for a few minutes. Then he ran after the beggar, caught up with him, and gave him everything he had.

When he told his father what had happened, the old man was outraged. Why had he blown away his money like that? Well, why indeed? Francis couldn't answer. He just thought... well, doesn't the Bible say we should do good? "Not *that much* good, Francis!"

His father sent Francis off to war. On the way to battle, Francis saw another knight with worse armor than he, and gave the man his armor. Apparently he was no more a soldier than a merchant. "Look," his father told him, as they sat selling cloth together in the marketplace, "good is all nice and good in moderation, but it's a give and take thing. You've got to find a happy medium."

("But the soul is still oracular; amid the market's din, / List the ominous stern whisper from the Delphic cave within,— / 'They enslave their children's children who make compromise with sin.'")

("I'm not saying make compromise with sin. I'm just saying it wouldn't kill you to be less than maximally saintly sometimes.")

("Exactly what do you think compromise with sin *is*?")

Everyone likes goodness, in the abstract. Everybody agrees that things that are more good are better things to do. But somehow it slips away. We use words like supererogatory, phrases like "nobody's perfect." We set a limit to our duty, reach it if we're lucky, and past that we just give the usual excuses—"yeah, but if I gave all of my stuff to beggars, I'd end up as a beggar myself," or just "I never said I was a *saint*."

St. Francis gave his clothes to a beggar, then took the beggars' rags for himself. He swore an oath of perpetual poverty and begged for bread in the streets of Rome. He started hanging around in hovels and ministering to lepers, on the grounds that this sounded like a very holy thing to do. He rebuilt ruined churches with his own hands, stone by stone. When he read that same Bible verse Peter Singer must have read—"if you would be perfect, sell all you have and give it to the poor"—he sold all he had and gave it to the poor, mildly confused that other Christians didn't when it was *right there in the Bible*. When someone stole his cloak, he literally ran after him to offer his robe as well.

He attracted a following of thousands of people. He fasted for weeks at a time. The Pope started to have dreams about him.

He decided to stop the Crusades by converting the Sultan of Egypt to Christianity. Unarmed and provisionless, he walked from Italy to the Middle East, performing various miracles along the way. In Egypt he was captured by Saracens and beaten nearly to death. But they let him have his audience with the Sultan, maybe just for the comedy value; Francis dusted himself off, got up, and started talking about how everyone should live in peace and harmony with one another. The Sultan was so impressed that he converted to Christianity on the spot, according to later historians who were all Christians and who never quite got around to citing their sources and who changed the subject when asked why there continued to be Crusades.

After this, Francis just went around preaching to everything in sight. When the cawing of a flock of birds interrupted one of his sermons, Francis preached to the birds, telling them that God had provided them with beautiful feathers and the gift of flight, so instead of screeching randomly all the time why didn't they help him at his prayers? The birds immediately quieted down and began to pray with Francis. When a wolf was eating people in the nearby town, Francis reminded the wolf that men were made in the image of God, and the wolf was so ashamed it slunk into town in an apologetic-looking manner and begged the townspeople for forgiveness. He invented the Christmas nativity scene. He saw visionary angels. He inexplicably developed wounds that looked a lot like the stigmata of Christ.

"Preach of God at all times," they said he would tell them. "If necessary, use words."

I am a kabbalist. Names have power. The Spaniards who settled California named a mission after him, Mission San Francisco de Asís. You give a place a name like that, things happen. Maybe it becomes a nexus for countercultural love and tolerance. Maybe it starts to develop uncanny geographical resemblances to Jerusalem. And maybe the Right Hand of God descends upon Mount Davidson into the body of a drug-addled hippie and ushers in a city-specific version of the Messianic Age, leaving its neighbors deeply concerned.

The whole thing happened suddenly, over the course of a couple of days in 1970. Early June they were debating a couple of big banks' proposals to build new skyscrapers; late June they were pretty much just singing songs of praise for the glory of God. Worse, it was *catching*. Anyone who stayed in the city long enough seemed to become like that — with *long enough* being anywhere from days to months. They never got better and they never left. The whole place was sealed off as a public safety hazard, which seemed to bother them not at all.

"The true servant unceasingly rebukes the wicked," St. Francis had said, "but he does it most of all by his conduct, by the truth that shines in his words, by the light of his example, by all the radiance of his life." Whatever had happened in San Francisco, the city was happy to stay self-contained, leading only by example. And the rest of the world was happy to place a military barricade around it and keep trying to ignore that example as long as possible.

III.

There were old maps, from the time when the city was still a part of the outside world. Ana remembered certain names: Market Street, Lombard Street, Embarcadero — but she didn't see any of them, and the street signs seem to have been torn down and replaced with standing stones covered in Enochian, the language of angels. So she followed the waterfront, looking for some kind of official building where she might be able to get some information, register herself, figure out who the authorities were. Back when people had still visited the city, they could go native in as little as days; Ana didn't plan to stay that long. She would get the kabbalistic books she needed to reconstruct the Vital Name, then get out.

The bulbs of the streetlights had been replaced with lidless eyes, each ineffably wise and beautiful. The mailboxes were made of jasper, and the parking meters of carnelian. Seagulls called "Holy, holy, holy!" down at her from the roofs.

A man in a food stand offered her a churro. Ana fumbled for currency, sputtering that she had only American greenbacks and not whatever passed for money in San Francisco. "God has provided us this food," said the vendor, "and you are a child of God. Would God let His children go hungry, when all food is His?" He refused to accept a single cent. She sat down on a pier with the churro, drank water from a water fountain made of onyx and abalone. Seals splashed around in the sea in front of her, heedless of her presence.

It was the hottest part of the afternoon now. The air shimmered more than she was used to. The streets were changing color in a seven second cycle, red-yellow-green-blue-purple-red. The stars were clearly visible, though it was day. The seals barked "Holy, holy, holy!" at her, and the seagulls answered with "Universal love!"

"Universal love," a woman walking a Golden Retriever said to Ana. "Transcendent joy," barked the dog. "Everything has been perfect forever," the woman told her dog, and it quieted down.

There was a tower on a hill, a few minutes' walk from the waterfront. The lure was irresistible. She left the shoreline and begin to walk inland, gradually uphill. She wasn't sure if the streets were spiral-shaped or, if so, how she continued to cover distance. The clouds came in tens, ten of one type, then another. Ana thought this might be important. In a yard ahead and to the right of her, two men were talking to a flock of scarlet macaws, and the macaws were listening intently.

"Universal love!" screeched one of the macaws, and the men sagely nodded their heads in agreement. "Transcendent joy," one of them said, and the others laughed knowingly.

She reached the tower. Needless to say, there was a spiral staircase. The inside was covered in colorful murals. The symbolism was unclear. A man crumpling a newspaper. A library. Endless fruit trees, vast machinery, scenes of devastation. Empty-eyed people crammed together like crabs in a bucket or the damned in Hell. A woman swimming in a cloud, a thousand feet above what was recognizably San Francisco. A doorway flanked by the sun and moon, with two great Eyes staring forth from thunderclouds above.

Ana stepped through the doorway and reached the top of the tower.

The sky was now very clearly glass, and she could see the gears and conduits above it, the part Ginsberg had called the machinery of night. She could see the connection between the machinery and the pulse of San Francisco. She knew the city's hidden pattern now, she saw it all laid out in order around Mt. Davidson. She knew she could go there in an instant if she wanted, but there was no need, not here.

She spoke the Zephyr Name and called the winds for no reason but exultation.

They came to her, the sirocco and the squall, the monsoon and the derecho. The mistral, the levante, the tramontane. The haboob, the marin, the simoom. They all presented themselves before her, but came no further.

She had never spoken a kabbalistic Name like this before. Before they had just been letters, the appellation of a distant and transcendent deity. Now God was with her and beside her. John of Patmos had said that there would be no Temple in the New Jerusalem, because God would dwell there everywhere alike.

Last of all the winds came her own wind, the Santa Ana.

She danced in the wind, maniacally, singing, laughing. "Holy, holy, holy!" she sang, and the wind carried the word to the four quarters. For a brief moment, she passed beyond time. "Transcendent joy!" she shouted at all the poor people trapped in the sublunary world, but they didn't hear.

Someone grabbed her body, the part of her that was stuck on the tower, the part of her that meant nothing. "Stop!" he told her, in a man's voice. "You've got to come back!"

Ana soared. She circled the Transamerica Pyramid, and the giant lidless eye watched her course impassively.

"Listen!" said the man. "One plus one is two. If you don't eat, you die. P implies not not P. Prices are controlled by the law of supply and demand, and are the only fair way of managing scarcity."

Ana began to lose altitude.

"Organisms evolve according to the laws of natural selection. Reproductively fit organisms pass their genes on to the next generation. Uh. The wages of sin are death. Everybody dies. In a closed system, entropy always increases."

Ana flapped her arms vigorously, trying to regain altitude, but her flight had never come from wings to begin with, and she fell further.

"Matter can't be created or destroyed. Uh, calculus. Taxing a product disincentivizes its production. The light speed limit. No mathematical system can prove itself consistent, or else it would be inconsistent."

Ana gently landed somewhere. She wasn't in the tower. She was on a wharf. There were people all around her, dousing her with water, holding her hands, saying things to her.

"Prisoner's dilemma! Can't square the circle! Nothing exists but atoms and empty space, all else is opinion! Bad money drives out... no, look guys! She's awake!"

Ana smiled, as if waking from a beatific dream. The men around her began to hoot and slap each other on the backs. She barely noticed.

In front of her was the most beautiful ship she had ever seen.

Interlude ט

War and Peace

Exodus 15:3 says, "The LORD is a man of war; the LORD is His Name." But this verse is ambiguous: "man of war" can mean either a type of Portuguese jellyfish or a type of British warship. Which one is the LORD?

I suggest that He is the latter. A jellyfish is a primitive and ignorant animal, unworthy to be compared to the glories of God. But a warship is mighty and inspires awe, and divine comparisons are entirely suitable; indeed, God may be the only thing worthy of being compared to it. For it is written, "The LORD alone is worthy of warship."

—From "A Call To Arms," by Aaron Smith-Teller
Submitted for the January 2017 issue of the *California Chorister*
Rejected with extreme prejudice by editor Valerie Lowry

I.

It's hard for me to imagine what it must have been like to be alive in '69, to see the demons spill forth from the ground and the angels descend from the clouds.

But—okay, personal disclosure time. When I was little, six or seven, I thought Nazis were a kind of fictional monster.

You'd see movies where the heroes fought zombies. You'd see movies where the heroes fought vampires. And then you'd see other movies where the heroes fought Nazis. Zombies spoke with a silly slow droning voice and said "BRAAAAAINS" a lot. Vampires spoke with a silly Eastern European accent and said "I VANT TO SUCK YOUR BLOOD" a lot. Nazis spoke with a silly German accent and said "HEIL HITLER" a lot. Zombies dressed in ragged clothes that were falling apart. Vampires dressed in stylish black capes. Nazis dressed in brown uniforms with snazzy red armbands. In any case, the point was that they were this weird subspecies of humanity that didn't follow normal rules, that was out to kill everybody for unspecified reasons, and you could shoot them without feeling guilty.

And then when I was eight I picked up a history book, and it was all in there, and I felt sick and vomited for the rest of the evening. And that night I was too scared to sleep. Not scared of Nazis—the history book explained that they had been beaten decisively a long time ago, and besides they never made it to America anyway—but scared of vampires coming to suck my blood. After all, if I could be wrong about one thing, who was to say I wasn't wrong about everything else?

And that must have been how it felt to be alive in '69, to learn that something you'd previously assumed was a legend used to scare children was terribly, terribly real. And then you wondered what *else* might be real. And then you started to panic.

The hardest hit were the atheists. They'd spent their whole lives smugly telling everyone else that God and the Devil were fairy tales and really wasn't it time to put away fairy tales and act like mature adults, and then suddenly anyone with a good pair of binoculars can see angels in the sky. It was rough. Rough for the Marxists, who had embraced it more than anyone. Rough for the scientific community, who had never come out and *said* SCIENCE PROVES THERE IS NO GOD ALSO WE ARE SMARTER THAN YOU but you could kind of read it between the lines. Rough for all the New Age hippies who were revolting against the tired old Biblical morality of their parents.

Stephen Jay Gould, a biologist working at Harvard University, tried to stabilize the burgeoning philosophical disaster with his theory of "non-overlapping magisteria." He said that while religion might have access to certain *factual* truths, like that angels existed or that the souls of the damned spent eternity writhing in a land of fire thousands of miles beneath the earth, it was powerless to discuss human values and age-old questions like "What is the Good?" or "What is the purpose of my existence?" Atheistic science should be thought of not as a literal attempt to say things like "Space is infinite and full of stars" or "Humankind evolved from apes" that were now known to be untrue, but as an attempt to record, in the form of stories, our ancestors' answers to those great questions. When a scientist says "space is infinite and full of stars," she does not literally mean that the crystal sphere surrounding the earth doesn't exist. She is metaphorically referring to the infinitude of the human spirit, the limitless possibilities it offers, and the brightness and enlightenment waiting to be discovered. Or when a scientist says "humankind evolved from apes," she is not literally doubting the word of the Archangel Uriel that humankind was created ex nihilo on October 13, 3761 BC and evolution added only as part of a later retconning—she is saying that humankind has an animal nature that it has barely transcended and to which it is always at risk of returning. When religious people mocked atheists for supposedly getting their cosmology wrong, they were missing the true grandeur and beauty of atheism, a grandeur which had been passed on undiminished from Democritus to the present day and connected us to the great thinkers of times past.

Nobody was very impressed by these logical contortions, but for some reason a bunch of people kept repeating them anyway.

II.

Also unimpressed were the Soviets. They had been taking the problems *kind of* in stride right until June 1969 when the legions of Hell started swarming out of Lake Baikal. The Russians had been carefully guarding the borders with NATO, with China, and especially the Bering Strait where they almost touched America. They'd forgotten the oldest border of all. Lake Baikal is the deepest lake in the world, but it sits on a rift even deeper than that. A dozen generations of shamans had warned first the czar, then the Communists, that the rock on the island in the center of the lake wasn't a rock at all so much as a *plug* blocking a hole that really needed to stay blocked, but no one had listened. Without any troops in their way, the demons had taken over pretty much all of Siberia east of the Yenisei within a year. Yakutsk was their capital, the rumors said, and had been the site of terrible massacres.

But the demons, too, had forgotten something: this was Russia. What a normal country would call getting suddenly invaded by a vastly more powerful adversary who committed unspeakable atrocities in their wake, the Russians just called Tuesday. Even the nature of the foe didn't much faze them; this was the fiftieth year of the Soviet state, and they'd spent so long hearing that their enemies were demons that it was almost an anticlimax when it all proved true.

So the Soviets mobilized their military machine, the largest in the world, and trudged to the Yenisei, which they dutifully started defending. But there were only so many Russians with so much blood to shed, and very slowly the front started advancing west again.

III.

Atheist materialist communism doesn't cut it when you're fighting literal demons, and Gould's non-overlapping magisteria was hardly a warrior faith. The Soviets convened a conference of Marxist theorists and Russian Orthodox clergy to try to hammer together an official metaphysics, but the two sides had trouble finding common ground. Meanwhile, people were starting to talk about sephirot and klipot and the Names of God. This wasn't just a supernatural incursion, this was a specifically *Jewish* supernatural incursion. Brezhnev told the Politburo that a meeting of Marxists and Orthodox priests wasn't enough. They needed Jews.

Unfortunately, they'd spent the last forty years or so denouncing religion as regressive, and thanks to Stalin's anti-Semitism, Jews had suffered disproportionately in the transition to Glorious Scientific Modernity. There were probably still a few learned rabbis in the Soviet Union, but none who would go up to Leonid Brezhnev and *admit* they were learned rabbis. The conference stalled. Moscow took the extraordinary step of asking for help from international Jewry. Europeans, Israelis, even *Americans* would be welcome, as long as they could quote Torah and tell him how to update Marxism for a post-scientific age.

International Jewry promptly told him that many of them had just finished risking their lives to get *out* of Russia, and also they *hated* Russia, and they didn't care *how* desperately Russia need their help, he was *crazy* if he thought they were going back there.

A singer is someone who tries to be good.

Isaac Bashevis Singer had always tried to be good. After escaping Russian-occupied Poland for the United States, he spent the fifties and sixties as one of the country's top intellectuals, using his fame to support and protect Jews around the world. But he was an advocate not only to his own people but for oppressed peoples around the world—not to mention animals, for whose sake he became a fierce and early advocate of the vegetarian movement. Although he'd been fervently anti-Communist for years, he couldn't deny the extremity of the Soviets' need. He was no kabbalist—but his father had been a Hasidic rabbi, and he had several thousand pages of notes for a book he was writing about the Baal Shem Tov, and as the Comet King would later say, "somebody has to and no one else will." Singer got on the next plane for Moscow.

The Soviets were not impressed. Not a rabbi, barely even a believer, how did he think he was going to reconcile Marx and the kabbalah?

"Reconcile?" asked Singer. "Marx is already the kabbalah. Isn't it *obvious*?"

Norvig and Raziel define kabbalah as hidden unity made manifest through the manipulation of symbols. But unity is communion, and symbols are marks on a piece of paper. So "unity made manifest by symbols" equals "Communist Manifesto by Marx." The supposed atheism of Communists was a sham; after all, did they not regard Marx with a devotion almost equivalent to worship? But the name Karl Marx comes from Germanic "Carl," meaning "man," and "Marx," coming from Latin "Marcus," itself from the older Latin "Martius," meaning "of Mars" or "of war." So the name "Karl Marx" means "man of war." But Exodus 15:3 says, "The LORD is a man of war; the LORD is His Name." The LORD is His Name, indeed. Every tribute the Soviets had given Marx, they were praising God without knowing it.

(And for that matter, the kabbalistic Avgad cipher decodes "Lenin" into "Moses." This is not a coincidence because nothing is ever a coincidence.)

But aside from etymology, Marx's whole system was only a veneer of materialism placed over the Lurianic kabbalah. God made Man in his own image; therefore Man went through the same Lurianic process as God did, only in reverse. Just as God's descent was channeled into a series of sephirot, so the ascent of Man was channeled into a series of class structures ordered in dialectic steps. But these class structures were unable to contain the human will and shattered in violent system-ending revolutions, leading to the next class-structure in the series. Our own world is the chaotic combination of sparks of sacred humanity and debris from the accumulated advantages of all the previous shattered class structures. Marx refers to this second group by the German word "kapital," a perfect Hebrew anagram of "klipot." The sparks of humanity must self-organize to redirect the human will and capital into a proper configuration, realization of which will constitute *tikkun olam* and usher in the arrival of the Moshiach and the terrestrial paradise. But just as the spiritual klipot can self-organize into demons, so the earthly capital can self-organize into the reactionary forces trying to prevent revolution and keep the world shattered and confused. The Soviet Union was under attack by both at once, besieged by capitalists and demons — but only because the great work was almost complete, only because this was their foes' last chance to prevent the final triumph of the light over the darkness forever.

Now *that* was a warrior faith.

Leninist pamphlets in one hand, Torah scroll in the others, the new acolytes of Marxist-Lurianism set out across Russia exhorting people to defend the Motherland, telling them that the hour of Moshiach was near at hand.

IV.

In 1960, the Chinese had split with the Soviets over different interpretations of Communism, and the two countries had been on bad terms ever since. When the demons took over Yakutsk, Mao had watched warily to see if they would make any foray toward the Chinese border. When they didn't, he'd issued a strongly worded statement saying that killing everyone in Russia was bad, then turned his attention back to internal affairs.

This was the era of the Cultural Revolution, so people were starving to death left and right — mostly left, since the right tended to die in ways much more dramatic and violent. Those who rebelled were mowed down; those who disagreed were sent to prison camps. Mao was old, but clung to life tenaciously, as if he wasn't going to go out before taking a big chunk of the Chinese population with him.

It was in this atmosphere that overworked archaeologist Zhao Kangmin was summoned to investigate some pottery fragments in Shaanxi. After some exploration he found his way into an underground chamber with an amazing treasure. Eight thousand terracotta soldiers, horsemen, and chariots, all true to life, frozen in warlike postures. The discovery filled him with fear instead of joy: if he reported his findings to the government, zealous modernizers might destroy the figures as relics of a feudal past.

As he sat paralyzed with indecision, he had the strangest feeling that the figures were trying to *talk* to him. Moved by an impulse he didn't understand, he wrote a series of mysterious letters on the forehead of one of the warriors, and it sprung to life, ready to serve.

Six months later Mao was dead, the archaeologist was Emperor Zhao of Dazhou, the terracotta golems were back underground until the next time their country needed them, and China was on the up-and-up again.

V.

Winston Churchill had once said, "If Hitler were fighting Hell, I would at least make a favorable reference to the Devil." Richard Nixon was familiar with this quote. Richard Nixon had no sense of humor.

"I've been working my [expletive deleted] off to protect this country from Communism for twenty years," he told the Cabinet, "and [expletive deleted] if I'm going to stop now just because there's a moral grey area. I just want you to think big, for Chrissakes. A chance to end this [expletive deleted] once and for all. By God, people, this is our chance!"

The overt meaning of *kiss* is "to press the lips against another person as a sign of affection."

The kabbalistic meaning is "to betray divinity."

This we derive from the story of Judas Iscariot, who for thirty pieces of silver agreed to identify Jesus to the Roman authorities. He kissed him in the Garden of Gethsemane as a signal for the legionaries to swoop in and arrest him. When Jesus was later worshipped as the Son of God, Judas' name became so synonymous with betrayal that Dante gave him an exclusive position as one of the three greatest sinners of all time.

Most people don't know a would-be Messiah to backstab, but there are other ways to betray divinity. The *yetzer ha-tov*, the inclination to do good in every one of us, is divine in origin. When we stifle it, we betray divinity.

But a singer is someone who tries to be good. So somebody who betrays the divine urge toward goodness inside himself again and again, playing Judas so many times that his own *yetzer ha-tov* withers and dies — such a person might have a name like—

Kissinger nodded as the President spoke. "We should act quickly," he said. "Our leverage will be higher the sooner we make our move, and the Soviets cannot be allowed to learn anything. It will be a hard sell to the American people, but the bolder and swifter the action, the more daring it will seem. The American people like a government that does what needs to be done."

In 1972, the President, Mr. Kissinger, and several other high officials took an unexpected trip to Yakutsk, where they opened full diplomatic relations with Hell. Nixon and Thamiel agreed to respect the boundary at the Bering Strait and cooperate economically and militarily against their mutual enemy.

True to Kissinger's words, opinion-makers hailed the treaty as a masterstroke. One of the nation's most dangerous opponents had been converted to a working partner in a single week of whirlwind diplomacy. Kissinger was lauded, but the real praise fell on Nixon, whose stern anti-Communist stance had given him the moral credentials he needed to forcefully defend his action. Thus the saying that sprang up in the wake of the trip: "Only Nixon can go to Hell."

(Later, after the Outer Gate scandal, the word "only" was removed from the saying.)

But outside the Beltway, the reaction was less positive. Preachers in small town churches railed against the President. Human rights advocates expressed concern. Noam Chomsky wrote a scathing article in *The Nation*. Student leaders organized protests at universities. Polls in the South and Midwest, once solid Nixon country, showed increasing concern.

The backlash was stronger still in America's foreign allies. The Archbishop of Canterbury led a candlelight vigil against the treaty. Italian syndicalists set off bombs. The Christian Democrats brought down the French government, and were denounced as Communist sympathizers. In Iran, Shia Muslim protesters took to the streets, shouting *Marg bar Shaytân-e Bozorg!*—"Death to the Great Satan." The Shah's riot police attacked the protesters, the protesters fought back, and the disturbance was calmed only when a loyal Ayatollah stated that it was not the duty of Muslims to fight against Hell bodily, but only spiritually, for Hell itself was created by God for a reason. Thus the quote from Khayyam's *Rubaiyat* eight hundred years earlier:

O thou, who burns with tears for those who burn
In Hell, whose fires will find thee in thy turn
Hope not the Lord thy God to mercy teach
For who art thou to teach, or He to learn?

That was the end of Iranian resistance to the alliance. And the quote made it to America, Europe, and all the other countries of the world, became a sort of motto, an excuse, a "well, who are we to say that allying with the forces of Hell isn't the sort of thing that might be part of the divine plan after all?"

("But the soul is still oracular; amid the market's din, / List the ominous stern whisper from the Delphic cave within,— / 'They enslave their children's children who make compromise with sin.'")

("It's not a 'compromise with sin,' per se, just a strategic alliance with the Devil.")

(...)

("Okay, fine, whatever, maybe it's *kind* of a compromise with sin.")

But as the demons very slowly pushed their way toward Moscow, buoyed by their new partnerships, people grew wary again. If Russia did fall, what then? Western Europe, India, and the entire Middle East sat there ripe for the taking. And the Americans couldn't help but reflect that the Bering Strait was seeming a lot smaller than they would like.

"Kissinger, are you sure this was a good idea?"

"There is never any surety in politics, only probability."

"But you think it's *probable* this was a good idea?"

"Yes."

"What about our [expletive deleted] souls, Kissinger?"

"I fail to see how they are relevant to geopolitics."

So passed the first quarter of the 1970s.

Chapter Twenty-Two

Whose Ears Have Heard The Holy Word

Object gods have meta gods
Up in their skies to smite them
And meta gods have meta gods,
And so ad infinitum.
—Steven Kaas

January 30, 2002
Puerto Peñasco, Mexico

With a look of mad determination, the big man marched to the center of the crowded bar. "I'll say it," he said. "The Other King is a *bad man.*"

A dozen conversations went silent. The bartender stopped pouring mid-glass. Several people eyed the door. Only the mariachi music from the stereo in the corner carried on regardless.

"No want trouble," said the bartender in heavily accented English. A few people slunk out the door before things got worse. Others laughed nervously, decided the safest course was to return to their drinks, started mentally rehearsing the phrase "I didn't hear nothing." But the big man wouldn't be cowed. He turned around to face the tables in the back. "The Other King is a *bad man.*"

James sighed and put his hand on the big man's shoulder. "You're drunk," said James. "And you're saying things you're going to regret. Lemme walk you back to the barracks."

"Not drunk," said the man. "The Other King's a bad man and you're not going to shut me up about it. All those people crucified. Isn't right. Crucifixion. Horrible way to die."

"Should leave now, por favor," said the bartender, but the man was bigger than he was. And probably a soldier to boot; everyone here was soldiers, James was a soldier, his companions over at the table were soldiers, Puerto Peñasco was rotten with soldiers. The Other King's soldiers, who had taken over the city. The loyalist soldiers, who were mostly dying painfully on crosses erected upon the road north.

"Not leaving," said the man. "You all know what I'm saying's true. You ought to—"

"Zip it and come have a drink with us," said James, and dragged the big man over to his table as the bartender watched helplessly.

This was mind-bogglingly stupid. Saying bad things about the Other King or even hanging out with the sort of people who said them was a good way to end up charged with sedition and crucified. But James didn't want the big man to die. All he'd done was get drunk enough to say what all of them were thinking. James had been thinking it ever since he'd signed on in Vegas. It had seemed like a good deal. Good wages, good benefits, and not a whole lot of risk; anybody who could kill the Comet King in single combat was probably the winning team. Sure enough, James and his battalion had taken over Phoenix, Yuma, and Puerto Peñasco in quick succession without any losses. Except their innocence. The big man was right. The Other King was a *bad man*.

Lin shot James a questioning glance when he and the big man sat down. Amoxiel was too intent on his bottle to notice. When James said nothing, he extended his hand.

"Lin," Lin said. "Ritual magician with the 5th platoon. Nice to meet you."

"James," James continued. "Sergeant in the 5th platoon. Likewise."

"Amoxiel," said Amoxiel, distantly. "Angel. 5th platoon." He took another swig of holy water.

The big man just called over a waitress and asked for a beer.

"What's your name?" asked James. "Which unit you in?"

"Me?" he said. "I'm nobody. I'm with nobody."

An obvious lie. He was here; that meant he was a soldier. And he was still alive; that meant he was with the Other King.

"How do you do it?" he asked. "How do you sleep at night? And keep serving him?"

"With copious amounts of alcohol," said Lin, and took another gulp of his tequila.

"The holy water," said Amoxiel, "washes cares away."

"It's not like we have a choice," said James. "We didn't know when we signed up. By the time we figured it out, our names were on the contract. Leaving's desertion, desertion's punishable by death, and I get the feeling you can't run from the Other King. Not forever. We don't like this any more than you, but we got no choice, you know?"

"There's always choice," said the big man.

"Our choice is twixt our conscience and our lives," said Amoxiel. James sighed. Amoxiel's bottle of holy water was empty, and his eyes were glowing a lambent white. He was drunk. And since he was an angel, that pretty much meant he spoke in blank verse and sounded like the King James Version.

"Moxy's right," said Lin. "We refuse an order, we get crucified. We try to run, well, I dunno what's worse than crucifixion and I don't wanna find out. How many miles you think we could make it in this desert anyway?"

"Why the desert?" asked the big man. "Why not steal *All Your Heart*?"

The mariachi music played blithely in the background.

"First of all, if *All Your Heart* is even still in the harbor—"

"It is," said the big man. "I checked. This afternoon."

"My God," said Lin. "You're serious."

"—even if it is still in the harbor," James continued, "none of us know how to sail a yacht."

"I do," said the big man.

"Who are you?"

"I'm nobody."

Five years ago, the Comet King had set out to find God. Not in the way where you live a life of humility and prayer. In the way where you need a really fast boat.

It was the height of his power, the age when he held sway over the whole American West and parts of Mexico. His ambitions soared to the conquest of Hell itself, to break the power of the Devil and release his victims from their eternal torture. But defeating Hell would take more than mortal weapons. It would take the Shem HaMephorash, the true Explicit Name of God, the Name which allowed the speaker to destroy and remake worlds. It was the Name that God had spoken during the Creation, the Name that would blare from the Last Trumpet, the Name that had inspired the poet to write:

Ah Love! could thou and I with Fate conspire
To grasp this sorry Scheme of Things entire,
Would not we shatter it to bits — and then
Re-mould it nearer to the Heart's Desire!

But it was also unplumbable by mortal cleverness. The only way to learn it was from the lips of God Himself.

The Sepher Hekhalot states that when the patriarch Enoch died, God "turned his flesh to flame, his veins to fire, his eye-lashes to bolts of lightning, his eye-balls to flaming torches, and placed him on a throne next to the throne of glory." Then He imbued him with the Most Holy Name, and thenceforward he was called Metatron, the "Measure of the Lord," the "Prince of the Divine Presence," and "the Lesser God." All of these titles are blasphemous as hell to call anybody who isn't God, and the sages speculated that Metatron had received a certain investiture, becoming a viceroy or a regent or even a sort of emanation of God into material reality. If you needed to hear something from the lips of God Himself, Metatron was the one to talk to.

The angels said Metatron had been with them in the early days of the world; that he used to dwell hidden in a whirlwind in the center of their angelic councils. When the angelic hierarchy shattered during Satan's rebellion, he floated down into the sea and was seen no more.

Since the cracks appeared in the sky, word had come from sailors of a mysterious boat, all purple with golden sails. They would see it on the horizon, but when they tried to approach it vanished at impossible speeds. Sometimes atop the boat they would spot a light, brilliant shining white, like an angelic figure. And the angels said Ah, yes, it is Metatron risen from the deep, but you will not catch him, for he keeps his own counsel, and none see him and live.

The Comet King sought Metatron. High above the world, his spy satellites sought the telltale golden sails of his boat. From sea to shining sea, his submarines and destroyers kept watch. Nothing.

So he decided he was doing things wrong. Finding God wasn't the sort of thing you did with a spy satellite or a submarine. It was the sort of thing you did on a quest. So he built himself a ship. A superfast yacht with seven sails, six from the colors of the rainbow and one jet-black. Every beam and mast built with strange magics only he knew. He called it *All Your Heart*, because it is written in Jeremiah: "You will seek God and find Him when you seek with all your heart." Then he left the kingdom in the hands of his daughter Nathanda and left from Puerto Peñasco in search of Metatron.

Six months later, he returned. When they asked if he had found Metatron, he said yes. When they asked if he had learned the Name, he said yes. When they asked for details, he said no. A few years later he died, and the details died with him. And all that time poor *All Your Heart* sat anchored in Puerto Peñasco, doing nothing.

"I'm just drunk enough to want to hear more," said Lin.

"The Other King hasn't even posted guards yet," the big man said patiently. James was starting to think that maybe the man *genuinely* wasn't drunk. "We walk into the harbor, walk right on, and sail away in the middle of the night. We can be round Baja before anybody notices we're gone. Nobody can catch *All Your Heart*. It's the fastest ship in the world. We can make it to the California Caliphate by noon tomorrow and nobody can stop us."

"By legend, each among the seven sails / requires magics hidden to unfurl," said Amoxiel.

"Not that hidden. The first sail, the red one, catches normal wind. The second sail is ritual magic; you"—he gestured toward Lin—"say you're a magician. The violet sail is angel magic, and you're an angel. The green sail is music. You by any chance able to sing?"

"If I tried to sing, the boat would probably sink like a stone," said James. "And how do you know so much about this?"

"I sang in a church choir for twenty years," said the bartender. He spoke with only a hint of a Mexican accent. "They said I was very good."

"Hey!" said James, cursing himself inside for letting them be overheard. "I thought you didn't speak English."

The bartender leaned on the table, leaned in very closely. "Look," he said. "A third of the population of this town got massacred, another third has fled. I'm stuck serving soldiers and pretending not to understand English so I don't get tortured for overhearing the wrong thing. And *All Your Heart*! The greatest ship in the world! My friend, I would give my arm to ride that ship for one hour. I am a poor man, I have no family, I have nothing left here. But to be on *All Your Heart*, that would be something! If you are going to hijack the ship, I am with you."

"Hold it!" said Lin. "Nobody's trying to get out of here! Mystery man over here just sat down and started giving us his hare-brained plan, and we're all drunk enough to listen. Nobody here is serious about this."

"I'm serious and wish to leave tonight," said Amoxiel.

Lin and James stared at him.

"You humans are inured to wrongs like these / I cannot bear them; I would rather die / beneath the breakers of the thunderous main..."

James elbowed Amoxiel. Amoxiel stopped.

"So what happens if we reach California?" James asked, barely believing he was taking this seriously. "They're scared to death of the Other King. They'll probably extradite anyone he tells them to extradite."

"We could go further," said the bartender. "Hawaii. Tahiti. The Malabar-Zanzibar Consortium. Sell the boat and live on a beach eating coconuts the rest of our lives."

"Who's going to buy *All Your Heart* if the Other King wants it?" asked Lin. "It'd be suicide. Picking up contraband from the scariest guy in the world."

"You want to get rich," said the big man, "here's what you do. Sell cabins on the ship. Most elite cruise ever. Sell cabins for ten million dollars, then go off and do the same thing the Comet King did. Try to find God. You don't think there are billionaires who want a chance to talk to the big guy face to face?"

"Like a whale-watching trip," said Lin. "But for archangels instead of whales. Well, I'm sold. And by sold, I mean super drunk."

"Hold on a minute!" said James. "We don't even know these people! We don't even know their names!"

"I'm Tomás," said the bartender. "Tomás Castro. Now let's go before somebody tells internal security what your friend here was shouting."

James took another sip of his beer. He could probably rein the others in, he figured. A couple hours and they'd be a little more sober, a little clearer thinking. Lin was a smart guy; he would see reason. Amoxiel had always been a wild card, but when he was off the holy water he could barely get out of bed, let alone do crazy plots.

The question was whether he *wanted* to. He hadn't gone out to see the crucifixions, but the news had hit him hard. He'd thought the Other King was just another warlord. A very lucky warlord, to kill the Comet King and take over half his kingdom. But in the end, no different from anybody else. Now he figured the guy was a psychopath, at *least*. He'd tried not to think about it too much because there was no other option. But the big man, for all his drunken bluster, was right. No guard posted over *All Your Heart*. The most beautiful ship in the world, just sitting in port, waiting to be sailed off.

And then there was the rather high chance that he would be executed very painfully just for hanging around with these people and holding this conversation.

"If we're going to do this," said James, "then by God, let's do it now, before we get sober enough to think it through. And you," James said, pointing to the big man. "None of us know anything about sailing. If we're just supposed to trust you to pilot this ship on your own, I think we at least deserve to know your name and how you got here."

"I'm nobody," said the big man. "I'm with nobody."

"Great," said James. "Captain fucking Nemo."

Chapter Twenty-Three

Now Descendeth Out Of Heaven A City

Though thou exalt thyself as the eagle, and though thou set thy nest among the stars, thence will I bring thee down, saith the LORD.

—Obadiah 1:4

I.

Afternoon, May 12, 2017
San Francisco

Even though she could no longer hear it with her ears, it still rang in the back of her mind. A note, a single impossibly pure note that seemed to overpower everything else. But it grew fainter and fainter and finally faded away entirely. She didn't miss it. She knew a minute longer up there and she would have lost herself, lost even the ability to know what losing herself entailed, lost the ability to think or feel or know or question anything ever again, turned into a perfect immobile crystal that was blindingly beautiful and totally inert.

"Oh God," said Ana. They had brought her aboard the ship and helped her onto a bed in one of the cabins. "I almost felt transcendent joy. It was awful."

None of them laughed. There were three of them. An older man with a short white beard. A military-looking fellow with bright eyes and closely cut hair. And an Asian man wearing a necklace. Ana's addled brain searched for relevant memories and came back empty.

"I'm John," said the older man. "These are James and Lin. Welcome to *All Your Heart*."

Memories came crashing in. The Comet King's old yacht, converted into a diversion for the idle rich. Fastest ship in the world. Ten million bucks a month for a cabin, sold to rich people who wanted to talk to God, not in a pious prayer way, but in a way that maybe gave them the chance to punch Him in the face depending on what He answered. Traveled the world.

Docked at weird out-of-the-way places to avoid the attention of the Other King, who was supposed to have a personal grudge against it. She tried to remember if she'd ever heard anything about the crew, but there was nothing.

"I'm Ana," said Ana. "What happened to me?"

"If I had to guess, I'd say you drank from a water fountain in San Francisco."

Ana nodded.

II.

1970. Ken Kesey was taking LSD with his friend Paul Foster. Then things got weird.

Paul tried to stand. He took a second to catch his breath. Kesey—the thing in Kesey's body—seemed content to let him. It just stood there, hovering.

"W...who are you?" asked Paul.

NEIL, said the thing in Kesey's body.

"But... who... what ARE you?"

NEIL, said the thing in Kesey's body, somewhat more forcefully.

Quivering from head to toe, Paul knelt.

NO. I AM NEIL ARMSTRONG. ELEVEN MONTHS AGO, I FELL THROUGH A CRACK IN THE SKY INTO THE EIN SOF, THE TRUE GOD WHOSE VASTNESS SURROUNDS CREATION. LIKE ENOCH BEFORE ME, I WAS INVESTED WITH A PORTION OF THE MOST HIGH, THEN SENT BACK INTO CREATION AS THE RIGHT HAND OF GOD. I AM TO SHOW MANKIND A CITY UPON A HILL, A NEW JERUSALEM THAT STANDS BEYOND ALL CONTRARIES AND NEGATIONS.

Paul just stared at him, goggle-eyed.

YOU DO NOT BELIEVE, said the self-proclaimed Right Hand of God. I WILL GIVE YOU A SIGN. ARISE AND OPEN YOUR BIBLE, AND READ THE FIRST WORDS UPON WHICH YOUR EYES FALL.

Mutely, Paul rose to his feet and took a Bible off his shelf, an old dog-eared King James Version he thought he might have stolen from a hotel once. He opened it somewhere near the middle and read from Psalm 89:12–13:

> *The north and the south Thou hast created them: Tabor and Hermon shall rejoice in Thy name.*
> *Thou hast a mighty arm: strong is Thy hand, and high is Thy right hand*

William Blake described mystical insight as "seeing through the eye and not with it." Stripping away all of the layers of mental post-processing and added interpretation until you see the world plainly, as it really is. And by a sudden grace Paul was able to see through his eyes, saw the words themselves and not the meaning behind them:

arm strong is Thy hand

For a moment, Paul still doubted — did God really send His messengers through druggies who had just taken monster doses of LSD? Then he read the verse again:

high is Thy right hand

For the second time in as many minutes, he fell to his knees.

IN ORDER TO INSTANTIATE THE NEW JERUSALEM, YOU MUST GATHER TOGETHER ALL OF THE LSD IN THE CITY AND PLACE IT IN A RESERVOIR WHICH I WILL SHOW YOU. WHEN EVERYONE HAS ENTERED THE SPACE BEYOND CONTRARIES AND NEGATIONS, IT WILL INVOKE THE STATE OF COLLECTIVE CONSCIOUSNESS THAT WILLIAM BLAKE CALLED ETERNITY.

"But... if I put LSD in the water supply... if the whole city... are you saying we, like, *secede* from the United States? ...you don't understand. We've been trying to spread a new level of consciousness for *years*. It never... if the whole city tries to become some kind of... if they don't pay taxes or anything... we're going to be in the *biggest* trouble. You don't know Nixon, he's ruthless, he'd crush it, it'd never..."

YOU STILL DO NOT BELIEVE. OPEN YOUR BIBLE A SECOND TIME.

Paul Foster randomly opened his Bible a second time. It was Isaiah 62:8:

The LORD hath sworn by His right hand, and by the arm of His strength: Surely I will no more give thy corn to be meat for thine enemies; and the sons of the stranger shall not drink thy wine, for the which thou hast laboured.

But they that have gathered it shall eat it, and praise the Lord; and they that have brought it together shall drink it in the courts of my holiness.

Go through, go through the gates; prepare ye the way of the people; cast up, cast up the highway; gather out the stones; lift up a standard for the people.

Behold, the Lord hath proclaimed unto the end of the world, Say ye to the daughter of Zion, Behold, thy salvation cometh; behold, his reward is with him, and his work before him.
And they shall call them, the holy people, the redeemed of the Lord: and thou shalt be called, sought out, a city not forsaken.

A few minutes later, Ken Kesey was on the floor, his eyes were back to their normal color, and Paul Foster was shaking him. "Ken," he was saying. "Ken, wake up. Ken, we are going to need to find a *lot* of LSD."

III.

"That's why you never drink the water in San Francisco," John told Ana. "It's not magic, it's— well, it is magic, but it's mediated by LSD in the drinking water. A single swallow and you end up partaking of the beatific vision as mediated through Neil Armstrong."

"Okay," said Ana. She looked out the window again. The iridescent sphere was starting to pulsate.

"John's too humble to say so," said James. "But he saved your life. The Captain told us you would be here. Said you could call the winds, and that we needed to save you. We were out near Salish, sailed down as fast as we could to catch you in time."

"Dragged you out of the Ein Sof and into the created world," said John. "That's the only way to do it, remind you of all the dichotomies and tradeoffs and things that don't apply up there. God wants San Francisco to be the way it is for some reason, but doesn't mean you have to be a part of it, if we can pull you out fast enough."

"You're lucky John and Lin are educated men," said James. "Me, I would have just been shaking you and shouting profanity."

An angel walked into the lounge. "Oh," he said. "She's awake. I'm Amoxiel. Did you decide to join our crew?"

"Join the crew?!"

"I was just getting to that, dammit!" said James. He turned to Ana. "I'll be honest. We didn't save you because we're nice people. We saved you because we're still working on using this ship to its full capacity. The Captain says that the yellow sail needs some kind of special kabbalistic Name to work. You seem to know a Name that can summon winds. Sounds like it's worth a shot. You want to join us? Pay is... well, you'd be a full partner. A few years and you'd be set for life."

Ana thought for a second. It was almost too perfect. Escape San Francisco, escape UNSONG, go somewhere nobody could find her. She tried not to sound overly enthusiastic. "What's the work, exactly?"

"Sail the world," said James. "Lin does his calculations, tries to figure out where Metatron's boat will appear next. We grab some rich people, head for that spot, try to chase it. You man a sail. Do your incantation, whatever works, sail goes up, we go a little faster. Doesn't matter. Never catch Metatron. The rich people pay anyway, because they're desperate and they figure that unlike everyone else they have a pure heart and God would never turn a pure heart away. When you're not manning your sail, you're pretty much free. Only two rules. Don't bother the rich people. And don't go into the Captain's quarters. You follow those, you'll be fine. You need to bother someone, bother me. I'm the first mate. It's my job to get bothered."

"Is it just the four of you?"

"Six," said James. "Us, Tomás, and the Captain."

"Oh! I thought John was the captain!"

James laughed. "The Captain is the Captain. You'll see him eventually. Big guy. Not a lot of facial expressions. Impossible to miss. He's a very private man."

"You said he knew I would be here? How?"

"He is," James repeated, "a very private man."

"What's his name?"

"A very, very private man."

"So private he doesn't have a *name*? Who doesn't even let people know their *name*?"

"If you have to you can call him Captain Nemo."

"Nemo? Like the—"

"Exactly like the," said Lin. He sounded resigned.

"You have," said John, "about a half hour to decide. After that, we're headed to Oakland to pick up our next three passengers, and then we're headed south so we can make it around Cape Horn before Metatron's boat is scheduled to surface off Long Island in a few days."

"Forget the thirty minutes," said Ana. "I'm in."

"Good," said James. "Welcome to *All Your Heart*. Start thinking about what you'll ask God if you ever catch Him."

"Isn't it obvious?" asked Ana.

James, Lin, and John looked at her as though it was by no means obvious.

"The whole problem of evil! Why do bad things happen to good people? Why would a perfectly good God create a world filled with—"

"Yeah, good luck with that," said James, and left the cabin.

Interlude י

The General Assembly

And Satan stood up against them in the global environment.
—kingjamesprogramming.tumblr.com

December 14, 1972
New York City

"Ladies. Gentlemen. Mr. Secretary-General.

We are a proud people. Like so many of the other fledgling countries represented here today, our national identity was forged in a struggle against imperialist aggression, and it was our pride that told us to continue fighting when all other counsel urged surrender. It is with that same pride that I stand before you today as the newest member of the United Nations, honored to at last be recognized as part of the world community.

I am not the monster you think. In my spare time, I play the violin competitively. I help blind children. I raise awareness of healthy plant-based foods. And my country? We are not your enemy. We are strange, yes. But we share the same values as all of you, the same drive to build a more just and equitable world.

What the American Dream is in fantasy, we are in reality. We accept everyone alike, regardless of race, color, or creed. We put up no barbed wire, we turn back no boats full of refugees. We take heart in the old words of Emma Lazarus: *Give me your tired, your poor. Your huddled masses, yearning to breathe free. The wretched refuse of your teeming shore. Send them, your homeless, your tempest-tost, to me.* And send them you do, a tide of humanity struggling toward our gates with a desperation that puts Ellis Island to shame, and we turn none back, nay, not even the meanest. Especially not the meanest.

What the workers' paradise of the Soviets aspires toward, we have reached. There are no class distinctions: slave is treated the same as sultan, stockbroker the same as sailor. The almighty dollar has been cast low; no one need worry about hunger or illness, nor shiver in the cold for want of a home. Private property has been abolished, yet none feel its want. Marx describes capitalist society as 'everlasting uncertainty and agitation,' but within our borders precisely the opposite prevails.

We do not persecute dissidents. We do not censor the media. We do not pollute. We treat men and women equally. We allow the practice of any or no religion. We fund no terrorists. We build no bombs. Our criminal justice system is free from bias, and its punishments are always just.

No, we are not your enemy. There are those here who would accuse us of a campaign of subversion, of trying to found an empire. Nothing could be further from the truth. Other countries bully their neighbors into becoming puppets or satellite states with their tanks and bombs. We lead by example. Our way of life spreads, not by the sword, but the unleashed yearnings of millions of people around the world.

Sixteen years ago, Nikita Khrushchev threw down the gauntlet of Cold War. 'History is on our side!' he said. 'We will bury you!' Ladies and gentlemen, I maintain that even the slightest familiarity with history suffices to prove it is on *our* side. We will not bury you. Yet when you are buried, as all men will be, many of you who now count yourself our foes will find you have been on our side without knowing it.

No, we are not your enemy. You say we are your enemy, you hope it is true, but in your heart you know it is not. We are allies to each of you. Every time there is a protest to be crushed, you have called upon us for assistance. Every time there is an election to be won, you have turned to us for advice. Every time there is a war to fight, you have asked for our aid. And we have never been stingy in granting it. All your glory you have built with our tools. Tools we were happy to lend at no cost, save the tiniest of sacrifices, one with no effect on gross national product, one that produces no trade deficit.

Ladies, gentlemen, Mr. Secretary-General. I have no enemies in this room. We have always been comrades in spirit. Now we are comrades in name as well. For this, I thank you."

When Thamiel had finished speaking, he lingered for a moment at the podium, almost as if daring anyone to object. No one objected. His second head remained locked in its silent scream. Smoke twirled around him like buzzing flies, and his skin seemed rough with cancerous growths in the dim light of the chamber. But it wasn't just fear that kept the ambassadors quiet. These were diplomats—that is, liars—and for just a moment they saw themselves as they were and paid obeisance to the Prince of Lies.

A sudden gust of scalding wind arose seemingly from nowhere, knocked two of the delegates apart from each other, scattered their nametags. A puff of brimstone in the middle, which cleared as quickly as it had arrived.

On the right, HAITI.

On the left, HONDURAS.

In the middle: HELL.

The nameplate was tastefully on fire.

Chapter Twenty-Four

Why Dost Thou Come To Angels' Eyes?

Morning, May 12, 2017
Los Angeles

A ray of early morning sun beat on my face. Clouds flew by me like trucks rushing down a highway, and the heavens seemed to sing. It's weird. You spend your entire adult life searching for Names of God and hanging out with angels, and the closest you come to a spiritual experience is paddling a flying kayak thousands of feet above San Bernardino County. I was flush with excitement at my close escape and at my *other* close escape and frankly at being pressed up against Jane so closely and of course at the view where I could see all of Southern California stretching out around us, lines of crumpled mountains one after another, and then...

There's an old California joke. What happens when the smog lifts? The answer is the name of one of the state's top colleges: UCLA.

I saw LA.

There was something very precious about the California coast from this perspective, a narrow strip between the foreboding mountains and the endless oceans, a little wire of humanity trapped between the desert and the deep blue sea.

California had come through the last few decades very well. Of all the Untied States, it had been least damaged by the sudden shattering of the neat physical laws of reality into a half-coherent delirium. I think part of the reason was that in a way California had never entirely been a real place. It was impossible to live there for any amount of time and think it was just another state, like Nevada or Ohio or Vermont. It was a state like joy, or exaltation, the ultimate west, part of the world only by a technicality. Named for an Amazon queen in the terrestrial paradise. Colonized by fortune-seekers who were told the rivers were strewn with gold nuggets the size of your fist.

The beach bums and the wannabe actresses and the hippies and the venture capitalists, all alike in that they had one foot on that little patch and the other in some fantasy of their own imagination. From that tiny winding wire of precious flat ground had come John Steinbeck, hippies, gay rights, the computer revolution, Ronald Reagan, every Hollywood movie, blue jeans, Barbie dolls, Joe DiMaggio, fortune cookies, popsicles, lap dances, hula hoops, the Beach Boys, Disneyland; an entire continent's worth of positive affect scrunched up into a coastline and paved over with Mission architecture.

"How much further?" I asked my mysterious benefactor.

"Not far," she said. "We'll land in the outskirts of the city. It should make us harder to notice." The kayak was a bright white, making its bottom almost invisible from the ground. I wasn't sure what was keeping the Marines on the cloud above from spotting us. Some kind of enchantment? Stealth technology? Were stealth kayaks even a thing?

"Who are you?" I asked her.

I'd been turning the evidence over in my mind ever since we'd left the citadel. She was young, though I couldn't say how young. Asian-looking. Perfect English. Tall and thin. Very long hair. Fast. Wore a leather jacket and black pants, like some kind of action movie heroine. Able to decode exotic numbering systems on the fly. Had a flying kayak. Knew her way around an angelic bastion but apparently wasn't supposed to be there. Tough enough to consider leaving me stuck there, but decent enough to decide against it.

My top guess was spy. If I had to guess a country, Dazhou, but not going to rule out Great Basin either.

"Loose lips sink ships," she said, which was either a reference to the old adage about not giving up secret information during a time of war, or else some kind of warning that the spell holding our kayak in the sky was sensitive to noise in the same way as the invisibility spell. By the precautionary principle, I shut up.

Somewhere south of Santa Barbara the dreaminess of California starts to become oppressive, to excresce and take physical form, giving the sky itself a hazy softness like an opium trance. Where the relaxation becomes frantic and the fantasy becomes feverish; a city somehow congested in its sprawl.

Do I even need to discuss the kabbalistic meaning of the name "Los Angeles"? Kabbalah deals with the hidden, but Los Angeles wears its allegiance on its sleeve for all to see. Here Los, the Blakean archetype of the fires of creativity, has his foundry; the iron smith-storyteller god forging dreams for an emotionally starved world. Here, in this city of angels.

Well, one angel. *Mostly* still an angel. I could barely make out the hilltop compound of Gadiriel, *la Reina de los Ángeles*, somewhere to the west.

"And who are *you*, anyway?" Jane asked as we neared the outermost tendrils of the megalopolis. "Sits alone in an angel bastion. Solves locational arithmetic problems. Knows secret Names."

It could have been a compliment, but it wasn't, not the way she said it. It was more like chewing me out for daring to be mysterious in her vicinity. Complicating her plans. And the entitlement! Demanding my secrets just a moment after refusing to give up her own!

I was tempted to bargain, knowledge for knowledge. But truth was, I was feeling pretty entitled too. Sure, I was curious what she was doing, what book we had just stolen. But my secrets were more important than hers. I needed to relax somewhere dark and quiet and re-establish full telepathic contact with Ana. Then I needed to get a book on name error correction. Then I needed to get myself a good computer. Then taking over the world and becoming the next Comet King could continue apace.

Sure, it was *flattering* for her to ask who I was. Wasn't that what I'd always wanted? "Who is this man, this Aaron Smith-Teller, who breaks impossible codes in mere minutes, and knows the hidden holy things?" But going any further with Jane was way too much of a risk.

"Man of mystery," I said as nonchalantly as I could.

Jane was quiet for a second. Then she grabbed the paddle from me. We hung motionless. She jumped onto the front of the kayak, spun around, took out her pistol, jammed it right into my head.

"You can become invisible," she hissed. "You know locational arithmetic which means you've been doing work that *requires* locational arithmetic which means you've used Friedman's Conjecture which means you're a passable kabbalist. Sometimes passable kabbalists get very, very lucky. Maybe one is lucky enough to discover a secret Name that grants invisibility. If he were to do that, the only question is who would get to him first. A nice person, who asks him politely to accompany her to somewhere very far away where he can be debriefed and kept safe? Or a not so nice person, who would torture all his secrets out of him and then kill him to make sure he didn't tell anyone else?"

"Um," I said.

"I'm neither," said Jane. "I'm a practical person. I will ask you politely to accompany me someplace far away where you can be debriefed and kept safe. And if I detect the slightest hesitation in your answer, then I will switch tactics and do the other thing."

"Um," I said. "Let's go to the place."

"Good," said Jane. "Now, who are you?"

"My name is Aaron Smith," I said. "I studied kabbalah in Stanford. With the help of a prophetic dream, I discovered a Name that granted invisibility. I used it to go sneaking around places I shouldn't, and finally I got cornered, and I spoke the Vanishing Name, and ended up in that library with you."

"You're not telling the whole truth," she said. But she shrugged. "I guess I can't blame you. Let me give you an offering of goodwill. I work for Citadel West. The book we've taken records a prophecy given to the Comet King in secret and since forgotten, which I was asked to retrieve. We will land, go to the hotel where I am staying, and make contact with our transportation back to the Citadel. Once you are there you'll be questioned further. What happens then is for you to decide. But you seem to have enemies here, and there are worse places for fugitives than Cheyenne Mountain."

I nodded, mutely. Actually, she was right. There were worse places.

When the Other King had slain the Comet King and conquered his kingdom, his children and a few thousand loyal followers had holed up in Citadel West, an impenetrable fortress in the Rocky Mountains. They were still there, a government-in-exile in their own territory, directing an insurgency against Great Basin that had never entirely died down. They retained a portion of Royal Colorado's treasury, its nuclear deterrent, and the Cometspawn themselves, who inherited a portion of their father's magic. Also, notwithstanding whatever book they'd needed to send Jane to go steal, a fantastic library probably filled to the brim with name error correction references. Sit tight in the Rocky Mountains, wait for Ana to become powerful enough to rescue me. It sounded like a plan.

We landed on the outskirts of Los Angeles, hid the flying kayak under a pile of wood, then took the bus into town. Jane insisted I hold her hand the whole way; presumably you can never be too cautious with a prisoner who can turn invisible. I didn't mind. She was pretty, in a scary way. She was staying at a penthouse suite in the Biltmore. The Cometspawn must pay well.

When we finally reached her room, she made a beeline for the dresser, opened the third drawer, and retrieved six purple sparkling Beanie Baby dragons.

Then she panicked.

Holding my hand was forgotten. Keeping track of me at all was forgotten. I could have walked straight out the door and spoken the Vanishing Name if I'd wanted to. Maybe I should have. She ransacked the room, slamming open every drawer, looking under the covers, under the bed, tearing open her suitcase and flinging various mysterious objects in every direction. It was like she was having a fit.

"Aaron," she said to me, when she finally remembered my existence at all. "*Somebody has stolen the seventh dragon.*"

Chapter Twenty-Five

Lie Down Before My Feet, O Dragon

Afternoon, May 12, 2017
Los Angeles

I.

Coming from the edge of my consciousness, a faint voice:

[Thou shalt not krill.]

The organizing soul within me—the kabbalists would have called it the *neshamah*—awoke, even as my body dozed on the hotel bed.

[Thou shalt not commit idolphintry,] I answered, but I knew deep down it was a second-rate attempt.

[Weak,] said Ana. [Where are you? Are you safe? Are you okay?]

[I spent the morning kayaking with a pretty girl, and then she invited me back to her hotel room and handcuffed me to the bed.]

[Really?] asked Ana.

I opened my eyes, taking care not to break the hypnopompic trance that smoothed the telepathic link between us. The clock told me it was early afternoon. Jane was nowhere to be found. I still had a gag in my mouth to prevent me from speaking any Names, and I still had my hands cuffed to the bedposts to prevent me from taking off the gag. I'd asked Jane why she carried a gag and handcuffs with her in her luggage, and she hadn't answered. Too rushed restraining me so that she could run out and search for her precious Beanie Baby.

[Really,] I said, and sent Ana my memories of that morning. Speaking the Vanishing Name right under Ash Bentham's watchful eyes. Escaping the Strategic Angel Reserve with Jane. The frantic search for her missing Beanie Baby, no amount of pleading inducing her to offer an explanation. Then her restraining me so she could expand the search to the rest of the city. [And you! What happened to you? You were with me in UNSONG! And then you learned a Name! Where are you? Are you safe? Where is Valerie?]

[I'm on a boat,] she said. [I haven't seen Valerie, but she's not dead. The link from the partial marriage ceremony would have told me that, I think. I keep trying to telepathically ping her, but I've never been able to feel her as strong as you.] Then she sent me her own memories. Sarah appearing mysteriously in her hotel room. San Francisco. The Comet King's ship.

[So you don't have the computer?]

[No.]

Everything I'd been doing up until now had been predicated on Ana having Sarah. If Ana had Sarah, the plan was still intact. She would become mighty. She would rescue me. We would be rich and important. If Ana didn't have Sarah, then the error correction was our only hope. Otherwise, I'd be back to being nobody. The thought was somehow worse than being a fugitive, worse than being cuffed to a bed. I could take a lot if I was somebody. The thought of falling back into my cog-in-the-machine status filled me with dread.

Ana felt my worries. [As soon as we reach a friendly port,] she said, [I'll find the error correction books. Or if I can get in contact with Valerie, I'll try to get her to read them and send us the information we need.]

I sent her a burst of grateful encouragement.

[In the meantime,] she asked, [do you need rescuing?]

Jane didn't seem evil in the same way as Bentham. And Citadel West was a good place. But the handcuffs on my wrists reminded me that she probably didn't have my best interests at heart either. And exactly because Citadel West was a good place, it was the sort of place that she would reassure me we were going, even if she worked for Dazhou or somewhere further afield. I noticed that she had told me we were going back to the Biltmore to meet her transportation back to Colorado, then left on her search without expressing any worries that she might miss said transportation. Jane didn't seem evil, exactly, but she was suspicious, secretive, and maybe crazy.

[I think I might,] I said.

[Then when we reach our next port, I'll get off and try to find you. I don't think these people will try to stop me. They seem nice.] I felt no fear in her mind. Yes, Ana had the Spectral Name and potentially the element of surprise. That was a pretty deadly combination. But still. No fear. I sent her a burst of positive emotion. [One more thing,] she added, and she sent me the Airwalker and Zephyr Names.

[Who do you think got the computer and gave those to you?]

[Honestly?] asked Ana. [God.]

[You think God directly intervened in the universe to help you and your friend when they were in trouble? Don't they warn you against that kind of thing in Theodicy 101?]

I didn't get to hear her answer. The jingling noise of a key turned in the lock.

[Jane's coming back,] I said. [You tell your mysterious billionaire sailor friends to keep you safe.]

[You tell your psychotic spy girl friend to keep her hands off you,] she thought back. [You're already kabbalistically married!]

I sent her a burst of the most positive emotions I could manage just as Jane flung open the door and turned on the light, breaking my trance. I startled fully awake.

Jane looked a little sweatier and dirtier, but the permanent scowl on her face had only deepened.

"I got you some food," she said, putting a bag of McDonald's on the counter, "and some clean clothes. Get dressed. We're going to Las Vegas."

"Las Vegas?" I asked, after she had taken the gag off.

"The manager doesn't know who took my dragon. The cleaning staff all say they didn't take it. No toy store in the whole city has a replacement. But they all say there's a big specialty store in Las Vegas that will. So we're going to go to Vegas. Get dressed." She unlocked the cuffs.

Jane was nothing if not efficient. Less than five minutes later, we were on our way out. I grabbed the bag of food and a bottle of Apple-Ade from the mini-bar.

She glanced at me as I took the drink, but said nothing. Which was just as well, considering.

II.

"Jane," I had asked her very gingerly, earlier that morning, as she was nearly tearing the room into pieces, "what do you need seven toy dragons for?"

She'd rounded on me. "You shut up!" she snapped. "You know too much already! If you hadn't screwed everything up on the Angel Reserve we wouldn't be in this mess! Mind your own business!"

Then she went back to searching like a madwoman. She went into the other room of the suite, and I could hear her opening and slamming drawers.

I walked over to the dresser, looked at the six purple dragons inside. I was no expert on Beanie Babies, but they looked pretty normal. I shook one. It felt like there were regular beans inside. Very carefully, I squeezed it. Nothing happened.

Behind the dresser I saw a glint of purple.

The seventh Beanie Baby had fallen through the back of the drawer, and was wedged in between the dresser and the wall. I reached my arm in and grabbed.

"Jane!" I called.

From the other room, again, her voice. "Shut up! I swear by the Most High, if I have to tell you to shut up one more time, I will burn your tongue out. You think this is funny? Just. Shut. Up!"

Then more slamming.

Atop the dresser was a mini bar; in the mini bar was a plastic bottle of Apple-Ade tinted an almost opaque green. I poured the Apple-Ade down the sink, stuffed the seventh Beanie Baby into the bottle, then put it back on to the bar.

Why had I done it? I wasn't sure, now. I was being treated like an infant. And I was being kept in the dark. I hate being treated like an infant and kept in the dark. I was sick of reacting; I wanted to act.

But the more I thought about it, the more I approved of my previous choice. I couldn't shake the feeling that something terrible would happen when she got that seventh Beanie Baby, that it would complete whatever arcane plan needed a book from the angels' own library, that there would be something very final about her getting it.

And now we were going to Vegas. A dark place, to be sure, but not Jane's place and not on her terms. If Ana was coming to rescue me, I'd rather Jane be off searching for a Beanie Baby in Vegas than doing whatever she would be doing when things started going her way.

Interlude כ

The Broadcast

The greatest trick the Devil ever pulled was spreading a catchy quote denying all tricks greater than the one about faking nonexistence.

—Steven Kaas

I.

After three months living with Ana, she learned that I hadn't seen the Broadcast.

We'd been talking about theodicy, as usual. Ana was explaining how the Cainites had made the terrible mistake of trying to munchkin Biblical morality.

Munchkin-ing is this idea from role-playing games where instead of trying to tell a good story, you search for weird little loopholes that violate the spirit of the rules and make things much too easy. The Bible says—check your Luke 15:7—that "in heaven there will be more rejoicing over one sinner who repents than over ninety-nine souls that are righteous and have no need of repentance." Solve for maximum rejoicing in heaven, and the obvious munchkin solution is to deliberately sin in order to repent later. Add some common-sense assumptions about the relationship between magnitude of crime and magnitude of repentance-related heavenly rejoicing, and... well, you can see where this is going.

Ana was against the Cainites. I was provisionally for them.

"You can't just follow the letter of the law and not its spirit!" Ana was protesting.

"Holy frick you're a *kabbalist* and now you're against the letter of the law? Forget the letter! We're supposed to believe that even the tiny extra dots and brushstrokes on some of the letters in the Bible have special meaning! When God said you couldn't start a fire on the Sabbath, and the rabbis interpreted that to mean you couldn't use electricity either, the Israelis just went ahead and programmed all their elevators to constantly go up and down stopping on every floor, because then you could enter and not push buttons and you wouldn't technically be the one initiating the electricity. The whole *point* of the kabbalah is that God wouldn't include something in the Bible that you could interpret a certain way unless He meant you to have that interpretation. And you're saying a really really obvious thing not just suggesting that repentance is better than righteousness but actually giving a numerical conversion factor was a *mistake*?"

"You're talking about the Jewish Bible," said Ana. "The Christians don't do things that way. And God knew the Christians wouldn't do things that way, so He wouldn't insert that kind of complicated subtext in the Christian Bible."

"God couldn't stop adding complicated subtext to save His life," I said. "How does that Galileo quote go? I cannot believe that the same God who hath endowed us with the tendency to over-interpret things in clever self-serving ways intended us to forgo its use."

Ana swatted my face playfully.

"What was that for?"

"I cannot believe that the same God who hath endowed me with a hand to slap you with intended me to forgo its use."

"Careful," I said, picking up a big pillow from the couch. "God hath endowed me with a pillow."

"You wouldn't," said Ana.

I swung it at her really hard, barely missing a table full of books and a potted plant. "See," I said, as it hit her in the face. "I hereby repent of doing that. And now Heaven rejoices over me more than you."

"But seriously," said Ana, and she *was* serious now. "Why would God put a verse in the Bible calculated to make us want to be as sinful as possible? What if someone goes on a murder spree or something?"

"I don't know," I said. "But we know that 'serpent' has the same gematria value as 'messiah,' and that kabbalists since time immemorial have been saying that there's some deep sense in which evil is the key to redemption. Also, God created a universe filled with evil. That was definitely a thing that happened."

"Tell me about it," said Ana.

I decided to take her literally. "Look. We know God has to desire evil on some level. Otherwise He wouldn't have created Thamiel and set him loose in the universe to promote it. So why not actually put something in the Bible that sufficiently defective people will use as an excuse to be evil?"

"You're heading towards repentance theodicy," said Ana. "The theory that the reason God put evil in the universe was that repentance is so great, and without evil you can't repent. But I... don't see it. Repentance is great because it makes there stop being evil. We celebrate repentance more than we maybe do with constant saintliness because we want to send a big signal to other evildoers that we will welcome and celebrate them if they stop being evil. Somebody beating me up and then saying sorry and he won't do it again is preferable to somebody beating me up and intending to continue to do so. But not to never getting beaten up in the first place."

"Eh," I said. "Maybe God just happens to like repentance for its own sake. It wouldn't be the weirdest thing He ever did. I mean, He created the platypus."

"See, this is what I hate about theodicy!" said Ana. "Everyone just wants to dismiss it and say maybe God is weird. Like, of course God is weird! But it needs to be a kind of weird that makes sense. It has to have deeper patterns and be ultimately scrutable. I really *don't* think that the same God who hath endowed us with reason intended us to forgo its use."

"The universe sucks," I said. "Deal with it."

"The whole problem is that we can't deal with it! If the universe just sucked a little, we could deal with it. But nobody can deal with the full extent of the universe's suckiness. Not when it happens to them personally. Not even when they witness it first hand. The only reason anyone can deal with it at all is because they never really think about it, they keep it off in their peripheral vision where it never really shows up clearly. It's like how everybody knew Hell existed, but nobody freaked out until they saw the Broadcast."

"I can't speak to that," I said. "Never saw the Broadcast myself."

Ana was startled. "Really? Why not?"

So the first reason was that it was a TV broadcast and there was no television anymore. TV broadcasting had stopped working sometime around the mid-1980s, before I was born. A victim of the general if weirdly non-uniform decay in technology and the physical laws that supported it. The Internet still worked, but for reasons no one had been able to figure out it couldn't handle video or audio, even though the programmers swore back and forth that it ought to be easy. The only visual technology that still ran consistently—besides old-fashioned film reels—was VHS tapes. Some people said Thamiel had specifically intervened to keep VHS running, for the sake of the Broadcast—obviously no one was going to play it in a movie theater. But without any reason to have a TV, that didn't matter much. If you wanted to watch the Broadcast, you had to hunt down someone with a TV, hunt down a VCR, and hunt down a taped copy of the Broadcast, which was either illegal or just *not done*.

The second reason was that I was scared. The Broadcast had destroyed the original United States, driven a lot of people insane, even made a couple commit suicide despite that maybe being literally the worst possible response to its contents. I like to think of myself as a dabbler in forbidden mysteries, but the Broadcast just had the wrong ratio of enticing-to-horrifying.

"Uh," I said. "Never got around to it, I guess."

"I have a TV and a VCR down in the basement! Let's watch it now!"

"...why do you have a TV and VCR in the basement?"

"I wanted to see the Broadcast! You don't think I've been studying theodicy for years and never saw it, do you? I went to yard sale after yard sale until I found the right equipment and I ordered the tape from Dazhou. You can get *anything* from Dazhou if you pay enough money. And the Broadcast is special. It's a part of history."

"So was leprosy. Doesn't mean I want to see it up close."

"As your spiritual advisor," Ana said, claiming a completely unjustified title which I had never given her, "I've decided you're going to see the Broadcast. If only to shut you up about the Cainites. Are you going to go downstairs and watch it with me now? Or are you too chicken?"

II.

Daniel Santoni had been a beloved National Geographic presenter until his untimely death on an expedition to the Himalayas. He'd also been a serial womanizer with a reputation for harassing his subordinates at work. His death had been mourned by his millions of fans, and met with quiet relief by those closest to him.

Now he stood in front of a pair of gates, twice the height of a man, made of some metal that had long since tarnished into a uniform black. They were set in a great rectangular doorframe, and the doorframe was set in a flat stone surface that stretched past the borders of the scene. It was unclear if it was a floor, ceiling, or wall, and Santoni did not appear to be standing on any particular surface. The doors and their frame were filled with sinuous sculptures of writhing men and women whose faces seemed to be melting into nightmarishly distorted expressions. The intricacy of the work was astounding, like a thousand sculptors had worked on it for a thousand years to get every detail right. Written on them in Gothic blackletter were the words ABANDON ALL HOPE, YE WHO ENTER HERE. Above them was also a banner reading WELCOME, NATIONAL GEOGRAPHIC.

"Welcome," Santoni told his audience. His voice sounded thin and reedy, and nobody who watched the Broadcast came away thinking Santoni was doing this of his own free will. There were no visible bruises, but he still looked traumatized. "Me and some of my... old crew... have come here to show you a... very special National Geographic special on... Hell."

There was a soundtrack, but it was the same kind of anti-music I had heard once before on a recording of Thamiel's audience with the president. I wished there were subtitles so I could have turned it off.

"Most people think the words on these gates were written by demons to sound foreboding, but that's not quite right. This is the outside of the gates, where the demons' sway is lesser. This warning was written as helpful advice by some friendly power."

The gates of Hell opened, and Santoni and his crew stepped inside. The camera view wheeled around. The inside of the gates said KEEP HOPING, SUCKERS.

"Despair has a certain numbing quality," said Santoni. He sounded like he was speaking from personal experience. "For the demons of Hell, keeping hope alive is a psychological torture, almost as important as the physical tortures they inflict. For more, we join Ga'ashekelah, Lord of the Fourth Circle."

The scene shifted to a sort of crypt-like office. The furniture was made of people, their bodies broken in unimaginable ways and reformed into chairs and tables. Ga'ashekelah looked like a giant with the head of a panther, except made entirely of snarling mouths. A lower third gave his position as "Torture Expert." He sat down on a chair made of two people intertwined together in an anatomically impossible way; both screamed silently as he lowered himself down onto them.

"Every couple of years a sinner is in Hell, we arrange some kind of apparent escape opportunity," the demon told Santoni. "After you've been tortured for a century, all your skin flayed off piece by piece then carefully replaced for the next flaying a hundred times in succession, raped in every orifice of your body including the ones you don't have yet, all your fingernails and toenails pulled off one by one then reattached then pulled off again nonstop for a decade by a demon with a weird fetish for that kind of thing—after that we have a demon come to you and say there's been a mistake in the cosmic recording, you're actually supposed to be in Heaven after all. We shower you with apologies, clean you up, and send a party of dignitaries to escort you to the gates. Then when you're thanking God through a flood of tears for your deliverance, we laugh and bring you right back to fingernail-guy, who wants another hundred years with you."

He shook his head. "And the fun thing about humans is that you never learn. After another century we can do the exact same thing, every word the same except an 'and this time we mean it' at the end, and you'll still believe us, because the alternative is to admit you're stuck forever, and you never learn to abandon hope. Once you stop falling for this one, we get more creative. We have a fellow captive tell you he's learned a secret Name that will finally kill you, grant you the oblivion you crave. He'll demonstrate by having a few other people say it, and they'll drop dead on the spot. Overjoyed by the opportunity, you'll speak the Name and... we'll all show up and laugh at you. The fellow captives were all confederates. The Name is a nonsense word, or a phrase cursing God in a forgotten language. We can get more creative than that, but I shouldn't reveal *all* my secrets. You're probably surprised I'm even telling you this at all, but the thing is, *it doesn't matter*. Put someone through enough pain, and they'll be willing to believe anything that promises a moment's relief. Dial the pain up far enough, and you have no *idea* what idiot hopes people are willing to believe. So yes. Our side of the door says KEEP HOPING, SUCKERS. And you will."

Santoni's narration was crisp Mid-Atlantic English with an undertone of horror. "That was Ga'ashekelah, one of the many demons created by Thamiel out of the energy released by the death of Satan, talking about the psychological tortures of Hell. But the physical tortures..." He stopped speaking suddenly, then started to shake and mumble to himself. The scene cut out, and the documentary resumed as if nothing had happened on a plain of iron spotted with towers of iron cages. There was something plant-like and organic to the way they grew in little clusters. Every cage was packed so densely with people that there was no room for movement, only the ones on the outside being able to stretch limbs through the bars and wiggle them around feebly.

"Most of Hell looks like this," said Santoni. Now there *were* visible bruises on his face. "The people in these cages... you can't see it from this vantage point, but the temperature is above a thousand degrees. Those iron bars are molten hot. The sort of bodies these people have, they can't burn, but they can still feel heat just as intensely as the living. More intensely. They don't need food to live, but hunger pangs are just as intense. They don't need water, but the thirst is..." He cut himself off. "There's another difference between their bodies and ours, which is that their minds don't break and they don't acclimate... the thousandth day here is just as bad as the first..." He looked toward someone off camera. "Please don't make me continue... don't..." Some kind of signal I couldn't see. "We're going to interview some of these people, see what..."

He held the microphone up to somebody whose mouth was pressed up against the edge of the cage.

"HEEEEEEEEEEEEEELLLLLLLPPPPPP!" screamed the damned into the microphone, so loud that I jumped and Ana had to put her hand on my knee to stop me from shaking. Then they all started talking and screaming at once. I could only make out one or two snatches:

"I'm Mabel Riggs of 242 Oval Street in Minneapolis, if anyone remembers me, please, do something, I pray, please, I'll do anything, oh God, you have to..."

"SHUT UP!" yelled the man who was pressed so close to her that I worried her bones might break against the bars of the cage. "SHUT UP YOU BITCH. GIVE ME THE MICROPHONE. I'M..."

A brief scuffle, then the camera was upright again and we were looking at a burning skull, who was identified as "Gamchicoth, Torture Expert." "We put a lot of effort into matching people with the right cage-mates," Gamchicoth was saying. "We look through a database of everyone who's ever lived to find the people you'll like least, maximize the clash of personalities..."

I turned to Ana. "I don't want to watch any more of this."

"You have to watch it," she said, which was so out of character for her that it was almost as scary as the scene on the TV.

"What? No I don't!"

"You tried to dismiss the problem of evil!" she said. "You tried to just say, 'God does lots of weird stuff,' as if this" — she gestured at the screen — "was of the same magnitude as the platypus! You want to see why theodicy is a hard problem? Watch!"

When I finally managed to turn my eyes back to the television set, Santoni was talking to a pitch-black featureless demon whose name was given as "Thagirion, Torture Expert." They were on another dreary gray plain, broken by blocky black buildings. Trees grew here, although the trunks were made of iron and the leaves were dull gray and wept blood. Carriages drawn by pitiful lacerated slaves were coming back and forth down a stony road, full of food and wine and other luxuries. The sides of the road were lined with severed heads impaled on tall pikes, and some of the heads were moving slightly in a way that didn't look like wind.

"Some of the demons have nicknamed this place Brimstone Acres," Thagirion was saying. "It's the nice part of Hell—relatively speaking, of course. We reserve it for the worst sinners. Hitler has a villa here. So do Beria and LaLaurie. It's basic incentive theory. If the worst sinners got the worst parts of Hell, then people who were pretty sure they were hell-bound might still hold back a little bit in order to make their punishment a little more tolerable. We try to encourage the opposite. If you know you're going to Hell, you should try to sin more, much more, as much as possible, in the hopes of winning one of these coveted spots. And that's just the beginning. There were some bad people who died in Stalinist Russia, and I like making sure every one of them knows that Beria is having a great time right now. Food, drink, and of course all the slaves he could possibly need for whatever purposes he likes. Whatever purposes. All the people selected to be his slaves being the people who hate him the most, naturally, which is the icing on the cake. These places pay for themselves, evil-wise. I just give everyone who died in the Holocaust a little magic stone that lets them know what Hitler's doing at any given moment, and you wouldn't believe how they howl."

At this point I was mostly covering my face with a pillow and whimpering. I honestly think I missed most of the Broadcast, or that it was repressed from my memory, or something. I think at some point Ana brought me a glass of water, or started stroking my head, but I know she wouldn't let me go and it never occurred to me to leave without her say-so. I just sat there, the sights and sounds passing through me like I was a zombie. I couldn't have told you how long or short it was.

But I remember the last scene. It was another plain full of cages, placed a little more sparsely than the last bunch. Between them, smaller iron growths—shrubs, if the cages were trees—held individual sinners receiving individual attention from individual demons. The noise was nearly solid, indecipherable, more like hitting a brick wall ears-first than hearing a lot of people screaming at once. The collected visuals had a similar effect. I couldn't decide where to look. As I started to make out individual forms, I could see some of these cages were full of children. There was a big demon with ram-like horns—the documentary named him as "Golachab, Bioethicist," and he was going cage by cage, blinding each child by ripping the eyes out of their sockets, which grew back in moments. The ground underfoot was obscured by a thick layer of crushed eyeballs.

"We have your mother here," said Golachab.

"I'll torture her for a thousand years," said the boy. "Two thousand! I'll do whatever kind of torture you want on her! The thing with the spiders you showed me that one time! I'll make up new tortures, worse than you've ever seen! I promise!"

"One of the great things about suckers who never give up hope," Golachab told Santoni and the camera, "is that they try to bargain their way out. For the tiniest shred of a possibility of a ticket out, or even a less crowded cage, or maybe a couple weeks' reprieve from the ministrations of some of the worse demons, you have no idea what people will offer. No stoic suffering here. The best way to take someone's virtue is to let them do the work figuring out how to degrade themselves in exchange for a carrot dangled at the edge of their vision. I bet that young man there, before he came to Hell, genuinely believed that no amount of suffering could turn him against those he loved. And now we don't even have to ask, and he's offering to torture his mother for two thousand years. We'll say no, and he'll scream, and we'll come back in a couple decades to see what else he has in mind, and he'll offer to do things so perverse and disgusting it will kind of even frighten *us*, and then we'll say no again, and we'll let him keep all the torture he already has, plus the knowledge that he has tried as hard as he can to sell out every principle he ever believed in and it has profited him nothing. Or maybe we'll take him up on it, let him torture his mother for two millennia, and then not give him anything in return, just to see his face when he realizes it was all for nothing. Or maybe we'll take him up on it and give him a couple hours reprieve from his tortures—because why not—and then back here for another millennium."

As he spoke, my eyes were caught by a different part of the scene: a young woman sitting in a rusted iron chair, off to one side but near the camera, close enough that I could clearly see her expression. She stared straight ahead, eyes wide, mouth shut, completely still and silent, radiating the most abject terror imaginable. A tiny green demon flitted around her with a tiny paintbrush, painting her skin a surprisingly lovely shade of light blue. It was by far the least gruesome torture on display, in fact she didn't even seem to be injured at all, but something had to have put that look on her face. Maybe it was just that she could see what was happening to everyone else around her, and she was terrified that at any moment it could start happening to her too. Maybe something I couldn't see was causing her unimaginable pain the whole time. Maybe both. For some reason, when Santoni saw this, he dropped the camera. Everything went dark for a second until somebody else picked it up and pointed it back at the ram-horned demon.

Thamiel popped into existence, walked up to the ram-horned demon. "Let me help," he said, and with a single thrust he impaled both eyes of a child on the two prongs of his bident. Then he wrenched the bident free, taking the eyes with them, and held them right in front the camera. I don't think I've ever seen a worse look of terror than in those suddenly-disembodied eyes. Eventually he pulled them away and focused the camera straight at him, so I could see every hair and wrinkle on both of his horrible faces.

"It seems like we're running out of time," said Thamiel. "But don't worry. Later on, many of you will have *all the time in the world* to learn more about us. I'm not going to say if it's ten percent or ninety percent of you; I love to watch you squirm because you don't know. I'm not going to tell you whether you come here for believing the wrong thing, or doing the wrong thing, or what the wrong thing is, or any of that, because I want you to be totally incapacitated with fear that everything you do might be tossing yourself into my hands. I want your dreams to be haunted by the knowledge that when you die, you might very well be herded into a realm where your hunger and thirst increase as always but you will never eat or drink again. Where your body feels pain like normal but can never die; where your mind is as easily spurred to suffering as on Earth but where it can never crack into the release of insanity. I want you to know you'll be crammed into boiling hot cages, flayed, gutted, raped, lacerated, that we will rip out your eyes and pour boiling oil into the sockets and do it again and again and again.

"I want you to know that all of those people who say that Hell is the absence of God, or Hell is a name people give to their suffering on Earth, or Hell is other people, or Hell is oblivion, or Hell is some nice place where atheists get to live free from divine tyranny—all of that is wishful thinking. Hell is a place full of fire and demons under the earth where you will be tortured forever. It's exactly what it says on the tin.

"Finally, I want you to know that *you will sin anyway*. This is the best part. For a couple of days, or a couple of weeks, you'll be horrified, you'll try to change your ways, you'll be like the alcoholic promising he'll never have another drop. Then the memory will fade, your normal habits will take over, and everyone will be back to the way they were before. You can't save yourself. You're not strong enough. Your basic nature will win out—not to be all Calvinist about it, but it's true—and you'll make up some comforting excuse and get on with your life.

But you won't live forever. And when you die, I'll be waiting."

Thamiel thrust his bident at the camera, and as the tip pierced the lens there was some final vision of ultimate horror—something I will never be able to describe and which really was no worse than any of the rest but which seemed more ontologically fundamental—and then the screen went black.

"So," said Ana. "That's the Broadcast. What did you think?"

I vomited all over the couch.

III.

They said the Broadcast had showed up in an unmarked brown package to the White House mailbox late in '72. It was a tense moment on the national stage. Nixon was running for re-election. His alliance with Thamiel had been a diplomatic coup, but he was facing renewed questioning by politicians in the halls of Congress and by protesters in city streets across the nation. Some were concerned about the theological risks of allying with the Devil. Others raised more practical concerns. Soviet Russia had been written off dozens of times before in this conflict, but now it really seemed to be on its last legs. When Thamiel took Moscow, where would his attentions turn next? Might we be lending aid and comfort to an inevitable future enemy? The American people wanted to know, and Nixon's kabbalistically-named opponent George McGovern was taking the issue to town halls and rallies across the country.

Speaking of kabbalistic names, in the 1972 presidential election Nixon's cause was championed by the Committee to Re-Elect the President, a.k.a. CREEP. And so he was. He was a genius at politics, maybe even at statecraft, but there were certain areas where intellect is no substitute for being human rather than reptilian. That was what did him in. When Nixon learned about the Broadcast, he figured it was blackmail. Thamiel was telling him that if he didn't stick to the script, Hell could release the Broadcast, make him look like a monster for allying with them, and he would end up with egg on his face on the campaign trail.

So the President ordered all the big TV networks—ABC, NBC, CNN, et cetera—not to publish the Broadcast if they received it. There were obvious First Amendment issues, but Nixon's relationship with the Constitution was a lot like the Cainites' with the Bible—better to seek forgiveness than permission. The networks complied, the President dug deep into his bag of dirty tricks, and the CREEP won the election handily.

But in fact the networks didn't have the Broadcast. Nobody had sent it to them. So things kept ticking along quietly until Thamiel finally razed Moscow in late 1973. Babylon the Great had fallen.

Western Europe started getting twitchy. In the absence of a mutual foe, the US-Hell alliance began to crack. Dazhou was playing both sides against the other. Everyone held their breath, wondering what would come next.

Nixon decided to play some hardball of his own. He reminded Thamiel that he still had the Broadcast. Thamiel didn't budge. So Nixon gave it to the networks. Using perfectly Nixonian logic, he figured that he had already been re-elected, and you can't get more than two terms anyway, so what was the harm?

On November 1, 1973, the Broadcast went out to an unsuspecting nation.

Chapter Twenty-Six

For Not One Sparrow Can Suffer And The Whole Universe Not Suffer Also

St. Francis saw above him, filling the whole heavens, some vast immemorial unthinkable power, ancient like the Ancient of Days, whose calm men had conceived under the forms of winged bulls or monstrous cherubim, and all that winged wonder was in pain like a wounded bird.

—G.K. Chesterton, St. Francis of Assisi

June 26, 1991
Gulf of Mexico

TELL ME ABOUT THE WORD *WATER*.

Sohu sat on her cloud, snacking on manna with ketchup on top. He had been doing this increasingly often over the past few weeks, asking her to tell him about a word, never satisfied with the amount of meaning she was able to wring from it. It didn't matter how many connections she drew, how many languages she was able to weave together, he would always just say something like YES, BUT WHAT DO YOU MAKE OF PROTO-NABATEAN, IN WHICH THE SAME WORD REFERS TO AN OBSCURE KIND OF COOKING-IMPLEMENT? and she would have to admit that, for some reason, that had never crossed her mind.

She sighed theatrically, but gave no further protest. "In Proto-Semitic," she said, "it is *akwa*. In Proto-Eurasiatic, also *akwa*. In Proto-Amerind, *akwa* again. So we're getting a very strong aleph-kuf-vav vibe. Aleph connects Chesed to Gevurah, and kuf connects Chesed to Binah, and vav connects Binah to Keter, so we're getting two paths out of Chesed, one all the way up to Keter, and the other down to Gevurah."

GO ON.

"So we're invoking Chesed, the kindness of God. Compare Psalm 65: 'You visit the earth and water it, you greatly enrich it with the river of God, which is full of water.' But we're also invoking Gevurah, the severity of God.

Water is the kindness of God, but also His severity; think Noah's flood, where it was His severity that punished the wicked, but His kindness that saved Noah and promised never again to flood the earth. We've got Binah, the understanding of God. Spiritual growth. Compare John 4:14: 'Whosoever drinketh of the water that I give him shall never thirst; the water that I shall give him shall be a well of water springing up into eternal life.' And finally, we've got Keter. The crown of God. Human beings are 66% water. The human brain is something like 90%. Human beings are made in God's own image. Therefore, Keter."

BUT WHAT ABOUT...

"The English word *water*, which breaks the pattern? It keeps the vav, but it finishes with tav and resh. That's a very special combination. Tav goes up from Malkuth, at the very bottom of the tree, and then resh goes straight up again, until you're all the way at Tiferet in two moves. And from Tiferet you can go anywhere. A tav-resh is the shortest path, it's efficiency, it's no-nonsense, it's utilitarian, it's for when you need a lot of power really really quickly."

AND WHY DOES—

"English deviates from the other languages because for the Tibetans and American Indians and Egyptians, water represents life and mystery and so on. But Britain is an island, and the British are the greatest seafarers in history. The Tibetans think of water and they think of good crops and spiritual rebirth. The English take one look at it and think, 'Yes, an understanding of God is all nice and well, but you can sail over this stuff to get *anywhere*.'"

BUT WHAT ABOUT THE HEBREW, IN WHICH WATER IS *MAYIM*?

"It means... because... I don't know. Who knows? How deep do we need to go? Isn't it enough that I brought in three reconstructed ancestral languages from three different continents, plus explained deviations from the trend? Just once, could you say, 'Good job, Sohu, that's enough, Sohu'?"

UM. GOOD JOB, SOHU.

"Uriel, this is *really boring*."

YOU ARE VERY ENGLISH. YOU WANT TO GET PLACES AS EFFICIENTLY AS POSSIBLE. BUT SOMETIMES...

"When do I get to learn how to do cool stuff, like blow up mountains?"

UM. PLEASE DO NOT BLOW UP MOUNTAINS. MOUNTAINS ARE USEFUL. THEY HELP CONTROL CLIMACTIC PATTERNS.

"Blow up *Thamiel*, then."

YOU CANNOT KILL THAMIEL. HE IS A FACET OF GOD.

"When do I get to learn *anything*? Uriel! This. Is. So. Boring. Learning about the structure of words all day. I want to be able to help Father, to help save the world."

THE USE OF KABBALAH TO AFFECT THE PHYSICAL WORLD IS DONE PRIMARILY UPON THE PLANES OF YETZIRAH AND BRIAH. THESE PLANES ARE NOT CONSTRUCTED OF MATTER BUT OF VARIOUS FORMS OF SUBTLE STRUCTURE. UNTIL YOU UNDERSTAND THE CORRESPONDENCES AND THE STRUCTURE, YOU CANNOT HOPE TO INFLUENCE THEM CONSISTENTLY.

"I made *all the rivers in the world* run in reverse my first day here."

BY ACCIDENT. THAT IS WHAT I AM SAYING. IF YOU DO NOT KNOW EXACTLY WHAT YOU ARE DOING, THERE WILL BE MORE ACCIDENTS. AND YOU WILL NOT BE ABLE TO FIX THEM.

"I'll be careful."

I WILL TELL YOU A STORY.

"Is this going to be one of your stories that's a weird metaphor for something?"

ONCE UPON A TIME, RABBI BEN AZZAI, RABBI BEN ZOMA, THE OTHER ONE, AND RABBI AKIVA VISITED AN ORCHARD. BEN AZZAI SAW IT AND DIED. BEN ZOMA SAW IT AND WENT CRAZY. THE OTHER ONE BURNED DOWN ALL THE TREES. AKIVA CAME IN PEACE AND DEPARTED IN PEACE. THE END.

"So yes, then."

IT MEANS THAT—

"Wait. Who is the other one?"

THE OTHER ONE?

"You said Rabbi ben Azzai, Rabbi ben Zoma, and the other one."

OH. YES. THE OTHER ONE. HIS NAME WAS ELISHA BEN ABUYAH, BUT WE DO NOT SPEAK OF HIM. IN THE TALMUD HE IS ALWAYS CALLED ACHER, WHICH MEANS 'THE OTHER ONE.'

"Why is his name never spoken?"

THAT IS A LONG STORY.

"I want to hear it!"

THE HUMAN BOOK ON EDUCATION SAYS THAT I SHOULD ALWAYS MAKE AN EFFORT TO ANSWER CHILDREN'S QUESTIONS, EVEN WHEN THEY ARE VERY ANNOYING.

"Yes."

ELISHA BEN ABUYAH WAS A GREAT RABBI OF ANCIENT ISRAEL. A BRILLIANT KABBALIST. A MIGHTY MIRACLE WORKER. A TRUE SAINT. ONE DAY HE WAS WALKING ALONG A PATH WHEN HE SAW A LITTLE BOY CLIMB A TREE. THE BOY FOUND A BIRD'S NEST. HE TOOK THE EGGS TO EAT, AND HE ALSO KILLED THE MOTHER BIRD. BUT THIS IS IN DEFIANCE OF DEUTERONOMY 22:6, WHICH SAYS, '*HE WHO SHALL HURT THE LITTLE WREN, WILL NEVER BE BELOVED BY MEN.*'

"That's not how Deuteronomy goes... it says... uh... 'If you come across a bird's nest in any tree or on the ground, with young ones or eggs and the mother sitting on the young or on the eggs, you shall not take the mother with the young. You shall let the mother go, but the young you may take for yourself, that it may go well with you, and that you may live long.'"

IT WAS NOT AN EXACT TRANSLATION. ANYWAY, THE LITTLE BOY KILLED THE MOTHER BIRD, THEN CLIMBED BACK DOWN THE TREE AND WANDERED OFF.

"Not an exact translation? What version are you..."

A FEW MONTHS LATER, HE WAS WALKING ALONG THE SAME PATH WHEN HE SAW ANOTHER LITTLE BOY CLIMB A TREE LOOKING FOR EGGS TO EAT. THIS BOY FOUND A NEST, TOOK THE EGGS, BUT LEFT THE MOTHER BIRD IN PEACE, IN ACCORDANCE WITH THE LAW. ON HIS WAY BACK DOWN THE TREE, HE STUMBLED, FELL, BROKE HIS NECK, AND DIED. SO ELISHA BEN ABUYAH SWORE ETERNAL VENGEANCE AGAINST GOD.

"What?"

THE ONE BOY DID A WICKED DEED AND WAS NOT PUNISHED. THE OTHER BOY DID A VIRTUOUS DEED AND WAS PUNISHED WITH DEATH. ELISHA BEN ABUYAH SAW THIS AND DECLARED THAT WHATEVER POWER IN THE UNIVERSE METED OUT JUDGMENT, HE WAS IN REBELLION AGAINST IT.

"Because of one bird? Isn't that a little extreme?"

WHAT IS THE CORRECT LEVEL OF INJUSTICE AT WHICH TO DECLARE YOURSELF IN REBELLION AGAINST THE POWER METING OUT JUDGMENT IN THE UNIVERSE?

"I mean, you would need to have... oh. *Oh.*"

YES. ELISHA WAS VERY ANGRY. ONE BY ONE, HE BROKE ALL OF THE LAWS. HE WAS A GREAT RABBI, SO HE KNEW EVERY LAW AND WHICH

ONES MOST OFFENDED GOD WHEN BROKEN, AND HE DEVOTED HIMSELF TO THE TASK WITH FEARSOME DEDICATION. HE LIT FIRES ON THE SABBATH. HE ATE PORK. HE EVEN BOILED A GOAT IN ITS MOTHER'S MILK. WHICH BY THE WAY IS WHY THERE IS NO LONGER A CITY OF POMPEII. BUT THESE WERE NOT ENOUGH FOR HIM. HE SWORE TO BREAK THE MOST IMPORTANT LAW OF ALL.

"What's the most important law of all?"

THE UNITY OF GOD. ELISHA ASCENDED TO HEAVEN, AS ONE DOES, AND HE POINTED AT THE ARCHANGEL METATRON, THE REGENT OF THE DIVINE IN THE FINITE WORLD. AND HE DECLARED, 'THAT GUY THERE, HE IS ALSO A GOD. THERE ARE TWO GODS. T-W-O G-O-D-S. DEAL WITH IT.' THE RABBIS DECREED THAT HIS NAME MUST NEVER BE SPOKEN. AND ALL WHO HEARD OF IT SAID 'SURELY THE GREAT RABBI ELISHA BEN ABUYAH WOULD NEVER DO SUCH A THING. IT MUST BE SOME OTHER ONE.' AND SO FROM THAT DAY ON, HE WAS CALLED 'THE OTHER ONE.'

"Did he ever repent?"

GOD REFUSED TO FORGIVE HIM.

"What? God always forgives these sorts of things!"

YES.

"Then—"

EXCEPT ELISHA BEN ABUYAH.

"Just him?"

IT IS SAID THAT EACH YEAR ON THE DAY OF ATONEMENT, A GREAT VOICE WOULD RING FORTH FROM THE HOLY PLACES, SAYING, 'REPENT, O CHILDREN OF ISRAEL, FOR THE LORD YOUR GOD IS MERCIFUL AND SHALL FORGIVE YOU. EXCEPT YOU, ELISHA BEN ABUYAH.'

"It really said that?"

IT WAS A VERY SPECIFIC VOICE.

"So what happened to him?"

NOTHING.

"He just hung around being sinful, then died and went to Hell?"

NO.

"No?"

THE BABYLONIAN TALMUD SAYS THAT HE WAS TOO GREAT A RABBI TO GO TO HELL, BUT TOO EVIL TO GO TO HEAVEN.

"So where did he go?"

I DON'T KNOW. I NEVER ASKED.

"You never asked?"

I AM VERY BUSY. I CANNOT KEEP TRACK OF EVERY TALMUDIC RABBI. CAN I GET BACK TO MY STORY NOW?

"How do you just lose an entire rabbi?"

SINCE YOU ARE SUCH AN EXPERT ON METAPHORS, HOW DO YOU INTERPRET THE STORY?

"I... forgot the story. What was it again?"

ONCE UPON A TIME, RABBI BEN AZZAI, RABBI BEN ZOMA, THE OTHER ONE, AND RABBI AKIVA VISITED AN ORCHARD. BEN AZZAI SAW IT AND DIED. BEN ZOMA SAW IT AND WENT CRAZY. THE OTHER ONE BURNED DOWN ALL THE TREES. AKIVA CAME IN PEACE AND DEPARTED IN PEACE. THE END.

"That was an awful story."

I NEVER SAID IT WASN'T.

"The story of Elisha ben Abuyah was like a million times more interesting!"

THIS STORY IS A PARABLE ABOUT THE DANGERS OF MYSTICAL ACHIEVEMENT. THE ORCHARD REPRESENTS THE HIGHER PLANES YOU WILL CONTACT IN YOUR STUDIES. IF YOU ARE UNPREPARED, KABBALAH CAN KILL YOU. IF YOU ARE ONLY PARTIALLY PREPARED, KABBALAH CAN DRIVE YOU MAD. IF YOU YOUR INTENTIONS ARE NOT PURE, KABBALAH CAN TURN YOU INTO A FORCE FOR GREAT EVIL WHO DESTROYS EVERYTHING AROUND YOU. ONLY IF YOU ARE WISE AND VIRTUOUS LIKE AKIVA CAN YOU ESCAPE UNSCATHED.

"So you're saying you're not going to teach me anything interesting until I am wise and virtuous like Akiva."

MAYBE NOT THAT WISE AND VIRTUOUS. BUT I WOULD LIKE YOU TO STOP TALKING ABOUT BLOWING UP MOUNTAINS.

"Maybe the mountains are evil. Or evil is hiding in them. Or something."

PLEASE DO NOT BLOW UP MOUNTAINS. IT NEVER HELPS.

"Grumble."

DID YOU EVER FINISH LEARNING ALL THE WORLD'S LANGUAGES?

"I told you, that's impossible!"

I THINK YOU SHOULD TRY.

"You're trying to get rid of me, aren't you!"

...

Interlude ל

The Outer Gate

I.

Imagine there's no Heaven. It's easy if you try. So easy that millions of people throughout history did it entirely by accident. They went to church, they read their Bibles, they knelt prostrate in prayer, and then they went home and lived a life of sin regardless.

A group of psychologists once did an experiment on children's willpower. They placed a young child in front of a marshmallow, and said if he could sit there without eating it for just five short minutes, he could have *two* marshmallows later. The "marshmallow test," as it came to be called, was found to correlate with all sorts of later-life outcomes like health, wealth, and success. Because unless you were a truly exceptional kid, you couldn't sit there all five of those minutes with that luscious marshmallow staring at you, begging to be eaten—just for a reward in some sucky *future*.

So up the stakes a little bit. Sit there for five minutes, and we'll give you all the marshmallows you can eat, forever. We will give you an entire dimension made entirely out of marshmallows. You can live in a great marshmallow mansion surrounded by woods made of jelly-beans, with gingerbread-man servants, and seventy-two houris made entirely out of sugar. But eat the marshmallow, even a tiny part of it, and you will be carried away to Soviet Russia—where marshmallows impale you on a stick, hold you over a fire, and roast *you*.

I'm not talking about atheists here. I'm talking about the people who accept the entire premise, the people who go, "Yup, this world is basically a cosmic marshmallow test, where if we can go the merest infinitesimal moment without sin we will be rewarded forever and ever with joy beyond our wildest dreams, but if we grab the marshmallow we will be punished forever in ways too terrible to imagine"—and then they go, "Eh, what the heck," and eat the marshmallow.

(The Lord said unto Adam: "You are free to eat from any tree in the garden, but you must not eat this marshmallow, for it is the marshmallow of the knowledge of good and evil, and when you eat of it, you will surely die.")

And it's not just Adam. What about Noah's sons, who right after they were saved from a giant flood caused by God being really really vengeful about sinners in the most conspicuous way possible, decided to celebrate with some kind of weird debauched incestuous rape orgy? What about Judas Iscariot, who after watching Jesus commit miracle after miracle, decided to betray him for a measly thirty coins? These were not people wracked with doubt about the terms of the bargain. These were people who knew exactly what that marshmallow was buying and gobbled it down anyway.

I would blame the Bible for being unrealistic, but everything that's happened since has borne it out. Let's face it, the sincerely religious have not exactly had a spotless record in the two thousand odd years after the close of the New Testament.

Imagine there's no Heaven. It's easy if you try. Only the cold maw of Hell, voracious for sinners.

When the Broadcast aired on TV that frosty November night, all the pretty lies, all the excuses people gave themselves for eating the marshmallow, came tumbling down. People fell to their knees, begging for forgiveness. Misers went out into the streets, throwing all their money at the first homeless person they could find. Lawyers, bankers, and politicians resigned en masse. So many people went out into the woods to become hermits that the woods became too crowded and the real hermits, the ones who knew what they were doing, took up residence in deserted apartment buildings.

Whole industries collapsed in a matter of days. When you know, with utter certainty, that this life is the antechamber to an ineffable eternity, who the heck wants to spend it canning tuna? Who wants to spend it catching tuna to can? What if you get to the Pearly Gates and St. Peter is some kind of purist who is really upset about what modern industrial fishing methods have done to his former trade?

In Europe, tides of pro-Church sentiment swept the traditionally Catholic countries of the south and east. In Asia, once-arrogant businessmen fasted themselves to death, hoping to gain enough karma to escape damnation. In South America, revolutionary guerrillas repented and became wandering friars. In Russia, the Marxist-Lurianist enclaves that had survived the fall of Moscow just doubled down and fought harder.

In the Oval Office, Richard Nixon, who had blown off the Broadcast as propaganda when he first saw it, watched it for what had to be like the twentieth time.

"[Expletive deleted]," said Nixon.

A few people, through some innate defect of character or the certainty that they were going to Hell whatever happened, took advantage of the chaos. Anyone who could put on a tattered cloak and start begging became an instant millionaire. Nonexistent charities sprang up, collected so much money they needed extra mailboxes to fit the envelopes full of cash, then closed down before anyone asked them how exactly they plan to solve world hunger from Jonesboro, Arkansas. The few businesspeople remaining were terrorized by job applicants pointing out how *desperate* and *needy* they were and how it would definitely look good in St. Peter's celestial ledger if they were to be immediately hired to do minimal work at high salaries.

These were bad people who need to be punished. One might even say "righteously smitten." There was no shortage of people willing to do righteous things, not now. Soon a persecution was on whose deranged fervor made the Salem witch trials look like the ACLU. The combination of many well-meaning but unexperienced people trying to do good and set up charities, plus a giant witch hunt for people trying to fake doing good and fake charities, went exactly as well as you might expect. Vigilante justice was served.

In the middle of all of this, NASA incongruously announced they were going to launch their long-delayed Apollo 13 mission to "further the study of the composition of the celestial spheres."

The Catholic countries of Europe united into a theocracy. The Marxist guerrillas in South America vanished into the Darién Gap. Dazhou told the Dalai Lama they were really really sorry and he could totally have Tibet back if he wanted.

Richard Nixon vanished for several weeks.

Civil aviation in the United States broke down, the complicated supply and maintenance chain beyond the reach of its tottering industries. The Midwest was consumed by riots. The Secretary of State announced that the federal government was no longer able to project force west of the Mississippi, and state governors should do what they could to maintain the peace until order was restored.

II.

"Houston, we have a problem."

Houston had problems of its own. Louisiana, long suffering the occasional storms spinning off Uriel's hurricane, had finally given up the ghost. Texas governor Dolph Briscoe had declared Texas independent until such time as the federal government recovered. Mission Control in Houston was still working for NASA until such time as an alternate arrangement could be decided.

"What kind of problem, Apollo 13?"

"We think an oxygen tank has blown. The command module's getting full of carbon dioxide. We've managed to jury rig the system, but it's not going to hold out. We've got to return to Earth."

"Roger that, Apollo 13."

For a moment, the attention of a collapsing superpower was distracted from its self-immolation by the drama of three brave men fighting a race against time to save themselves and their ship. And millions of Americans watching their television sets cheered as the command module splashed down safely in the Pacific Ocean, just off the coast of the newly declared California Caliphate.

Then their joy turned to confusion, as they saw not three, but four people leave the rescued capsule.

John Young, commander.

Kenneth Mattingly, pilot.

Fred Haise, lunar module pilot.

And Richard Nixon, president of the United States.

Why was the President in a spaceship? was what everyone wanted to know.

Air Force One was sent to California to return Nixon to Washington; whether as president or prisoner no one was sure. Witnesses were called. Records were subpoenaed. It was discovered that the President had kept recordings of everything he had said in the Oval Office, and these were added to the pile of evidence.

"Look," Nixon told Kissinger, in one of the most damning tapes. "Everything I did, I did for the love of this country, I did it to fight Communism. But [expletive deleted] God isn't going to see it that way. He's going to be too soft to realize what had to be done. And I'm going to end up burning in [expletive deleted] for all eternity. Why the [expletive deleted] did I ever let you convince me to sign an alliance with [expletive deleted]?"

"The idea behind the alliance was sound," Kissinger answered. "We did not entirely understand how things stood at the time, but even if we had, I would have made the same suggestion. Brezhnev was getting too strong, especially with the Vietnamese and the South American communist movements. We did what we had to do. If the good Lord disagrees with me, I will be happy to point out His tactical errors."

"[expletive deleted] easy for you to say!" said the President. "You can talk anybody into anything. But I'm the one whose [expletive deleted] soul is on the line. Doesn't the Bible say something about that? What use is it to something something the world if it costs you your soul? Something [expletive deleted] hippie dippy like that? I'm breaking the alliance. There's no other choice."

"There may be another way. As you know, Captain Armstrong disappeared into the cracks in the sky. Exactly where he went is uncertain, but you cannot have missed the popular press speculating that he entered Heaven. I have been having some of my people look into it. I believe that just as there is a gate to Hell inside the earth, so the edge of space may be an outer gate which leads to Heaven.

"[expletive deleted] great. So this [expletive deleted] gate outside the world would get me to Heaven. How am I supposed to get there? Take a ride in an [expletive deleted] spaceship?"

"You have several."

"God, you're [expletive deleted] serious."

"The director of NASA is loyal to the administration," said Kissinger. "I have seen to it. Apollo 13 has been ready for launch for years now, but it has never been the right time; always an emergency. We will make it known to NASA that now is the right time, and they will need to make room for a fourth person. The astronauts will grumble, but they will not betray the secret. They are military men, and you are their commander-in-chief."

"I [expletive deleted] am!" said Nixon. "My God, you're starting to convince me. So when can we start heading to this Outer Gate of yours?"

"I believe NASA can have the craft ready within about a month. After that it will be a three day flight to the crystal sphere, and from there you may descend into the Outer Gate and save your soul while our alliance against Communism remains intact."

"I don't [expletive deleted] believe this, but let's do it!" Nixon was heard to say when the full recording was played before a hearing of the House Judiciary Committee, whose members voted unanimously to propose a motion for impeachment. It wasn't just politics. The witch hunts against anyone who tried to cheat the God-fearing, hell-fearing public had only just started to die down. And now here was the President, trying to cheat in the most fantastic way possible, to buy his salvation on the taxpayer dime while leaving his supposed constituents to burn. The question wasn't whether Nixon would be impeached. The question was how many seconds he would last after Secret Service protection was withdrawn.

As the Outer Gate scandal entered its third week, Nixon bowed out. He struck a deal with the House; if he resigned peacefully, he would be granted safe passage to a comfortable exile in his hometown of Yorba Linda, California Caliphate. Under cover of night, the President was flown out of Washington DC, as mobs pelted Air Force One with stones and Molotov cocktails.

III.

Ford means "to attempt a difficult crossing." On August 9, 1974, Gerald Ford was sworn in as President of the United States.

In the California Caliphate, the Texas Technocracy, the Salish Free State, and various little towns and homesteads of what had once been the Midwest, people watched the inauguration the same way they might the coronation of the Queen of Great Britain—interesting, maybe even inspiring, but not having very much to do with them. In his inaugural address, Ford admitted that the federal government now controlled only the Eastern Seaboard and pieces of the South and Great Lakes.

The way having been prepared before them, the armies of Thamiel, the Lord of Demons, crossed the Bering Strait and began the invasion of North America.

Chapter Twenty-Seven

The Starry Floor, The Watery Shore

May 12–13, 2017
Pacific Ocean

I. James

Belowdecks was the crew quarters. Ana didn't expect her own room and didn't get it. Her berth had four beds: one for her, three others for James, Lin, and Tomás. Her bed was technically Amoxiel's, but the angel didn't sleep. As far as they could tell, he just sort of sat on the deck all night, staring wistfully at the stars.

She was used to living with men; she'd lived in a group house for over a year now. She wasn't picky; if she had been, the cramped atmosphere of *All Your Heart* would have desensitized her quickly.

James was in the bunk below her. Even during his short nap, he had fitful dreams. Ana asked him what he dreamt of. For a while he didn't answer.

"Things I did," he eventually said. "I was in the Other King's army once. Before we really knew how bad he was. After Never Summer, but not by much. But he was still bad. I shot folks, probably innocent ones. That's what I dream about. And the Broadcast. I dream about the Broadcast, and I worry that's going to be me."

"They say anyone who sincerely repents and promises to live a virtuous life will be saved," said Ana.

"Yeah, and here I am. On a boat, trying to find God so we can board his ship and, I dunno, hijack him or something," said James. "Virtuous life, my left foot."

"You could always..."

"Dreams, girl," said James. "They're just dreams."

II. Lin

If James was taciturn, Lin wouldn't shut up. He talked about anything. He talked about whether they would have good winds, he talked about the calculations pinning down Metatron's next appearance near Fire Island in New York, he talked about his youth as an apprentice ritualist in Arizona. "That was back during the big ritualism/placebomancy debate," he told Ana. "Tried to keep a foot in both camps, get the best of both worlds, you know? Then everything went to hell when Alvarez killed Lautenberg and McCarthy murdered the Council. Ritualism fell apart, placebomancy became too associated with Alvarez and violence, now it's hard to get training in either. Plus, anybody gets too good at ritual magic, Alvarez kills them. Or if he doesn't, they think you're working with Alvarez and get more and more suspicious till you're fired on some dumb pretext. There's no future in it anymore. With time we would have been able to do as much as the kabbalists, and without the copyright restrictions. Instead we're looking over our shoulders and being shown the door."

"Except Alvarez," Ana said.

"You can bet he's looking over his shoulder every darned minute," Lin answered. "I hope they catch him and lock him up and throw away the key. Placebomancy's not just about the practical applications. It's about understanding the universe. Placebomancy is our only sign thus far that the universe can be convinced of things, that it's got innate intelligence. It's the next best thing to talking to Metatron one on one. If we leave it to the terrorists, we're losing our biggest chance to learn something about God and about ourselves."

"Do you ever worry about Alvarez?" Ana asked him.

"Me? I'm not good enough to worry. He only kills the bigshots. I'm just some guy good enough to power the orange sail. And I don't leave *All Your Heart* much. If BOOJUM wants to get on this ship, they can pay $10 million like everyone else."

III. Simeon

They made good time almost due south, avoiding the coastline and instead driving straight into blue water, just over sixty knots. Ana didn't know much about sailing, but she gathered that was mind-bogglingly fast for a watercraft.

All Your Heart, built to be the fastest ship in the world, was an impressive specimen even when not using its "special features."

Once they were underway, James told her it was time to test her skills. He led her to the yellow sail, halfway down the deck. Its shape fit together neatly with the sails before and behind it in what looked almost like art.

"What do I do?" she asked James.

"Just speak that Name and see what happens," he answered.

So she spoke the Mistral Name and the winds came to her. Squall and simoom and sirocco, monsoon and marin and zephyr. The levante, the tramontane, the haboob. And finally her own wind, the Santa Ana. She flung them all at the yellow sail, and for a moment, the ship stopped. The world thinned to a point. She felt marvelous, truly alive.

She remembered a line from Shakespeare, one she had heard long ago. "I can call spirits from the vasty deep!" she shouted.

A voice from beside her: "Why, so can I, or so can any man. But do they come when you call for them?"

Startled, she looked behind her. The old man was leaning on the mast of the green sail, watching her.

"You know Shakespeare?" she asked. Then, "What are you doing here? What do you want? Can't I have some privacy?"

"I'm sorry," said the old man. "I didn't realize I was disturbing you."

Ana regretted her harshness. "No, please. You surprised me, that's all." He was really old, like at least seventy. She was surprised someone so old would be up for a voyage like this.

"Simeon," said the man, holding out his hand. Ana shook it. She had always thought it was stupid when people judged businesspeople by their handshake, but by the time her hand retracted she knew as if by revelation that Simeon was very important and very competent.

"I'm Ana," said Ana. "You're one of the passengers?"

"Yup," he said.

"Very rich guy, wants to yell at God for something?" asked Ana.

"That's me," said Simeon. "I didn't mean to stare, you know. I was just surprised to see a woman on a ship like this."

"Well, I didn't mean to be here," said Ana. "And I'll, uh, avoid thinking too much about that 'surprised to see a woman' comment."

"A woman and a Shakespeare fan!"

"Please. I know a couple of lines. I was just—what do you call it—drunk with power. Anyway, I'm more surprised than you are. I thought you corporate billionaire types knew seven hundred ways to squeeze blood from a stone but wouldn't know culture if it kicked you in the nose." She waited to see if she got a reaction.

"Twelve hundred ways, but I've been privileged to get a little time to read this and that in between board meetings," Simeon told her.

James poked his head out from the cabin: "We're having a crew meeting in five minutes. Ana, five minutes."

"Huh. Nice to meet you, Simeon," Ana said, though she wanted to know more.

"And you," Simeon told her. "You ever want to learn how to squeeze blood from a stone in a hurry, you come find me, okay?"

She shook his hand a second time. Again she was struck by a weird feeling that she should entrust all her money to this man and never look back.

Then she ran inside.

IV. Erin

It was late that night. James was turning fitfully in the bed below her, muttering things in his sleep. Ana felt uncomfortable, like she was witnessing something private. On a whim, she got out of bed and climbed onto the deck. Amoxiel was there, his cloak billowing in the wind. He was at the very stern of the ship, staring out into the starry night. She didn't want to disturb him, and for his part, he took no notice of her. Once again she felt like she was intruding. She went away from him, to starboard side near the yellow sail, and stared out at the sea alone.

Someone else was out there. Ana tried to ignore her, but she was noisy, and eventually she turned and looked. It was the woman passenger. She was hanging on the railing, leaning against some sort of weird arcane Comet King weapon that looked kind of like a harpoon, retching over the edge of the ship.

"Seasick?" asked Ana.

The woman stared at her with bloodshot eyes, "Guess again."

"Heroin withdrawal," Ana said.

The woman gave a little squeal. "How did you know?"

"I used to hang out in Oakland."

"Oh."

"And you've got marks all over your arms."

It was true. She could see them in the weird dark glow emanating from the black sail. James had told her not to look at the black sail directly, especially not at night, and there was no way she was going to break that rule, but she couldn't help notice the glow.

"Oh. Well." She looked uncomfortable. Ana noticed with interest that before she got quite so many lines on her face, the woman must have been truly beautiful. Then:

"Wait a second! You're Erin Hope!"

The lady laughed. "Yeah. For all the good it's done me."

Erin Hope. Pop sensation, one of the first people to genuinely be a pop sensation after the country knit itself back together again. Superstardom during the early 2000s. Then the usual downward spiral. Men. Drugs. Endless grist for the paparazzi. The occasional story about rehab, followed by another story about rehab, with the reader left to fill in the blanks of what must have happened in between.

"I didn't bring any heroin with me," she said, voice laced with anger. "I thought I'd be okay, fresh air, a quest to find God. I'm such an idiot."

"It only lasts a couple of days," said Ana helpfully.

"You think I haven't been through this a dozen times, darling?" The pop goddess wasn't really angry, just sarcastic. "A couple of days is enough. When I meet God, I hope I'm not going to vomit all over Him." She tried retching again. Not much came out.

"Or maybe I hope I do," she said. "At least that way I'll know He knows. Damn rehabs. Always say to place your trust in a higher power. Well, I did and He betrayed it. I trusted the hell out of him right up until I shot back up. So I'm done trusting. Now I'm going to see for myself." She retched again. "Sure, it's a lot of money, but better give it to you than those quacks in rehab again. You're gonna find Him for us, right?"

"Um, we'll try," said Ana, who would have trouble describing the business model of *All Your Heart* in any terms more glowing than "quixotic," but who didn't want to badmouth her employers.

"You're a nice kid," said Erin.

Toward the stern, Amoxiel started to sob. They both heard him. By mutual consent, neither one mentioned the distressed angel.

"I'm freezing my tits off," Erin finally said. "I'm going back inside to see if I can get a couple hours unconscious. You stay warm."

Touched by the older lady's concern, Ana watched her go. Then she stood alone on the starboard of the ship, listening to the angel weep.

V. Tomás, Edgar, John

Tomás had been a bartender in his hometown of Puerto Peñasco, Mexico. The War on Drugs had hit him hard, but he had stayed in business until the Other King came. After that he'd made his escape with the Captain and the rest of the original gang. Now in between singing to the green sail, he was the cook and quartermaster of *All Your Heart*'s galley. It was his job not only to keep everyone fed and content, but to make fare up to the standards of the obscenely rich bastards who were his usual passengers.

Ana sat down for lunch and was handed a salad. "This is delicious," she told Tomás. He nodded, as if used to the compliments.

James walked in, and Ana motioned him over. "There's been a change of plans," she said. "I was just talking to a friend of mine. He's in trouble. I need to go save him. When's the next time we're going to be near land."

"Two days from now, Fire Island," said James.

"Uh, this trouble is pretty urgent. Do you think we could..."

"There are three people who each paid ten million dollars to get on this ship, on the understanding that we would be at Fire Island two days from now. This is the fastest ship in the world, but even so getting from California to New York in two days isn't going to leave us with a lot of spare time to go dropping people off. And we're south of the Mexican border by now, and you don't want to get off *there*. Sorry, Ana. We can let you off in New York."

If Ana had been some sort of legendary hero, maybe she would have threatened James, or mutinied, or summoned a wind so strong that it smashed the boat into the California coastline. But she was a theology graduate student, and she weighed barely more than a hundred pounds, and she was surrounded by military men who had nightmares about all the people whom they had killed, so she shut up. James did something halfway between patting her on the shoulder and slapping her on the back, picked up a salad in a box, and then left the galley, leaving Ana lost in thought.

"What are you thinking about?"

She hated that question. It was an implied "Let me interrupt your thoughts and force you to talk to me," but if she told him to go away, *she* would be the impolite one.

"I'm Edgar Crane." He sat down next to her, uncomfortably close. He was tall and dark and young and good-looking. Ana disliked him instantly.

"Ana," said Ana.

Edgar briefly looked like he was considering flirting, then defaulted to his usual strategy. "You might have read about me in the newspapers," said Edgar. "Son of the mayor of Reno. And by mayor, I mean back when it was a city-state, so basically the head of state. From one of the richest families in what's left of the US of A. Not that we're uncultured Nevadan hicks or anything. We spend most of our time in Los Angeles these days."

"Yeah, must be hard what with the Other King totally kicking your asses and conquering your city in like twenty minutes of fighting."

Edgar clearly hadn't expected Ana to have known about that. He stiffened. "Well, just because you heard about it doesn't mean you know how things stand."

"If they're like your family, they stand for twenty minutes, then beat a hasty retreat."

"It was a strategic withdrawal. We wanted him to overextend himself. Now we're building a coalition with California and Colorado."

"Poor Other King. Overextended himself by conquering half the country, killing all who opposed him, defeating the Comet King, and ruling with an iron fist for fifteen years. With overextension like that, he must be ready to topple like a domino by now."

Crane put his hand on Ana's shoulder. "Listen, you're pretty, but..."

Ana tried to extract the offending hand. It didn't budge. She stood up. "Get your hand off me," she said.

"Hey," said Edgar, "I was just..."

The hand was retracted, but not of its own accord. Ana looked up and saw that John had entered the galley and gently removed Edgar's hand from her shoulder.

"Edgar" said John, "No."

Edgar glared at John like a hyena denied a kill. "The lady and I were flirting."

"We were *not*," said Ana. "If we were flirting, I would've said something like 'I hope you last longer in bed than you do defending your—'"

"Ana," said John. "Be an adult. Edgar, I need to speak to Ana in private now."

Edgar glared more at John. John didn't budge. Finally the young man scowled and brought his breakfast to a different table.

"Ana," said John. "I won't cite the rule about not bothering passengers, because I can see that Mr. Crane started it. But I will ask you to *act your age*. You made that worse than it had to be."

"I'm not sorry," said Ana. "He was a jerk."

"Yes," said John. "This boat is a strange place. The people who pay for our services are strange people. Some of them are jerks. It's our job to smooth that over instead of making it worse."

"Simeon and Erin are perfectly nice!"

"And maybe one day God will save us from everyone who is less than perfectly nice. Until He does, it's our job to learn to deal with them safely. Do you understand?"

"I understand," said Ana. John wasn't captain, or first mate; as far as she knew he wasn't really anything. It was his age that gave him authority, she thought; aside from Simeon he was the only grey-haired man on a ship full of youngsters. Then she reconsidered. No, that wasn't right. He seemed wise, but it wasn't just the age. "Hey, James was telling me the story of how they stole this ship. You weren't in Puerto Peñasco, were you? How'd you end up here?"

"The Captain needed someone to work the blue sail and he gave me a call."

"The blue sail?"

"...is a good Roman Catholic," said John, smiling. "It only responds to the prayers of a priest."

"What? Why?"

"It is," he said with some chagrin, "a Mass-energy converter."

Ana groaned. "And you're a priest, are you?"

"Retired. But you'll see all of this for yourself. That's what I came here to tell you. James is planning a Symphony today at noon. All the sails we've got, at the same time. Show the passengers what we can do, convince them they're getting their money's worth, and start covering some actual distance. We'll see you there."

"If Crane touches me, I'm Fulminant-Naming him," said Ana.

"Don't deliberately antagonize Crane," said John, "but if he touches you, we'll stand behind whatever you have to do."

VI. Amoxiel

"All right!" said James when passengers and crew alike were gathered on the main deck of the boat. "A Symphony is where we feed all the sails at once and show you what this baby can do. They say the Comet King used all seven sails together to catch Metatron and get his secrets. We still haven't figured out the black sail, but when this thing is running on six cylinders we hope you'll be too impressed to care. Is everyone at their stations?"

The red sail was at the front of the ship. No one stood underneath it; it was a normal sail that caught normal winds, and it billowed in the Pacific breeze.

Lin stood by the placebomantic orange sail, tracing lines in the air and chanting to himself. Ana stood by the kabbalistic yellow, waiting to speak a Name. There was Tomás by the green sail, singing; John, beneath the blue praying; Amoxiel beneath the violet, speaking in the language of angels. At the back of the ship the black sail stood alone.

That left James to coordinate and steer. "Is everyone ready?" he asked, after the crew were in their places.

"Ready," said Lin.

"Ready," said Ana.

"The winds arise within me, and I blow," said Amoxiel.

The angel had gone iambic again. His eyes were glowing white and, in case there was any doubt about what had caused his transformation, he held a big bottle of holy water in his hands, from which he took frequent swigs.

"Blame me not for my drunkenness, fair maid," he said when Ana stared. "Without the spirits, I have spirit none / and cannot call the winds at such a speed / as bears the ship most fleet."

John cringed, and Ana realized he must be the one giving the angel his steady supply.

"Lin," James commanded, "start the orange sail."

Lin seemed to grow bigger. He drew forth apparently out of nowhere a great staff of ginkgo wood, and held it aloft. "In the name of placebomancy, and of the Comet King who built thee and bound thee to thy task, I bid thee fly!"

The orange sail puffed up as if fed by phantom wind.

"Ana, the yellow!"

The young kabbalist spoke the Mistral Name. Forth came the squall and simoom and sirocco, forth the monsoon and marin and zephyr. The levante, the tramontane, the haboob. And finally to her side her own wind, the Santa Ana. Out billowed the yellow sail.

"Tomás, the green!"

Tomás began to sing an old Mexican love song. At each note, the grass-green canvas seemed to shiver and unfurl.

"John, the blue."

"Gloria in excelsis Deo, et in terra pax hominibus bonae voluntatis. Laudamus te, benedicimus te, adoramus te, glorificamus te, gratias agimus tibi propter magnam gloriam tuam..."

"Amoxiel," James commanded, "the violet!"

The angel spread his wings and glowed with light. Heavenly winds poured down from the sky, filled the purple sail. Amoxiel shook with conducted power, and took another swig of holy water to keep himself steady.

At the back of the ship, the black sail sat in serene majesty, still and unruffled. In times long past, the Comet King himself had stood beneath that sail and drawn his sword, and the sail had opened to his call. Now it was quiet, too proud to heed any ordinary mortal.

All Your Heart was a ship, but it was also a machine. It was a machine designed by the Comet King, who had more than mortal ingenuity. The sails had power of their own, but working in Symphony their powers multiplied dramatically. The masts became mirror-like, perfectly silver. Colored lights flashed from each to each, until the air seemed full of rainbows darting back and forth.

The ship moved, but not through this world. It moved above the world and behind it, through seas of something that was not water.

Ana thought she noticed the rainbows becoming a little off-hue, disproportionately purple. At the same moment, James noticed it too. "Amoxiel, you're coming on too strong. Lower your sail!"

No response. Through the flashing lights, Ana looked back towards Amoxiel. The angel was chugging his holy water. The flask was almost finished.

"AMOXIEL!" shouted James. "YOU'RE DRUNK! YOU'RE OVERPOWERING THE SYMPHONY! STOP IT!"

The angel, his eyes aglow so bright Ana could hardly bear to look at them, began to speak.

Through many days and nights of empty grey
Colorless, like a night without a day
I waited on the prow, adrift, storm-tossed
Remembering the Heavens that I lost
But now, amidst the many-colored beams
Which rise before me, like a world of dreams

Eternity seems almost in my reach
Like castaways, who spot some distant beach
How can I fail but surge, how not press on
Till Time, and Earth, and Earthly things are gone?

The angel finished the holy water. The beams above them were almost entirely violet, with only a few little sparks of other colors in between.

Lin ran at Amoxiel. Amoxiel drew from the aether a flaming sword and brandished it before him. Ana spoke the Fulminant Name. A lightning bolt crashed into Amoxiel, who didn't seem to notice. The sea was looking less like water.

"Okay, new plan!" said James. "Everyone else, feed *harder*!"

Balance. Balance was the key here. Lin started screaming in dead languages at his sail. The beams got a little bit more orange. Ana just kept repeating the Name, as many times as she could. The beams got yellower. John prayed quicker, but he was old, and started stumbling over the words.

"More Mass!" James yelled at John. "We need more Mass!"

The ship began to groan.

"Amoxiel!" Ana shouted. "One plus one is two! Competition for limited resources! Balances are credits minus debts!"

Amoxiel looked at his flask of holy water, found it empty.

"There's no such thing as a free lunch! Men are from dust and to dust they will return! No consistent system can prove its own consistency!"

Some chaotic attractor shifted to a different state, or something.

All the lights vanished and they fell back into the real world with a tremendous thud.

VII. The Captain

The Captain came on deck and looked over the ship through big dark glasses.

All Your Heart was a mess. By some miracle none of the sails had ripped, but masts had been flung around like toothpicks and there was a big hole of uncertain origin in the port side, too high up to take on water but nonetheless concerning.

"We can go back to San Francisco for repairs," Lin suggested. The Captain looked at him and he shut up.

Finally, he spoke. "Metatron's boat will appear off Fire Island in two days," he said. "If we go back to San Francisco, we miss it, and betray the deal we made with our passengers. We won't change course. We'll stop for repairs in Ensenada."

No one was surprised. Everyone was concerned.

"We'll stop a stone's throw away from the city. James, you'll take the lifeboat to the dock. You'll remain in sight of the rest of us. When the Mexicans talk to you, we'll watch you and make sure you're safe. You can negotiate with them for repairs. Of course we can pay. The men with the supplies will come out to us on small boats. No one except James will make landfall in Ensenada. James won't leave our sight. Does everyone understand?"

Everyone nodded, a little relieved that the burden would fall on their First Mate. But they were still concerned.

Slowly, brokenly, *All Your Heart* began to sail south.

Chapter Twenty-Eight

Hid As In An Ark

May 12, 2017
Los Angeles

Over the centuries she had fallen in love with the place. A narrow plain, sunny three hundred days a year, blooming with poppies, watered by little rivers snaking out of arroyos in the nearby mountains. She had built her altar on one of the hills. The Aztecs knew her domain, and they called it Temictitlanoc, "place of the dream goddess." Sometimes lost war bands would wander to its sunny hills, lie down beside the crashing waves, and see strange visions.

Three hundred years ago, a new group of people had come to the place. She had seen the potential almost immediately. She was weak and tired now, she could see them only through the tiniest openings in the dark veil Uriel's work had spread over her senses, but she was not quite impotent. She drew them, the lovers, the dreamers, the artists, the people who were happy pretending to be anyone except themselves. Like the Aztecs before them, they named the place after her in their own fashion. El Pueblo de Nuestra Señora la Reina de los Ángeles. The Town of Our Lady, the Queen of the Angels.

Oh, she was good to them, and they to her. She filled them with visions and longings. And they turned them into such incredible stories, then grew rich as the rest of their people ate them up. Gone with the Wind. Cinderella. Ben-Hur. The Sound of Music. Spartacus. James Bond. Then Uriel's machine broke. The people started to panic. The aqueducts started to fail. Riots filled the streets. The city teetered on the brink of catastrophe.

So the Lady flexed her newfound powers. Appeared in broad daylight to her subjects. Told them all would be well. Some calmed down. Others became more confused. Who *was* she?

Eons ago, the heavenly host had sent some lower-ranking angels to Earth to watch over humans and make sure things proceeded apace. They learned the ways of people, started to grasp concepts like lying and manipulation and gray areas. Started to experiment with new magics, gain new powers. The Watchers, they called themselves, neither fallen nor entirely loyal. When the war broke out with Thamiel, most of them lay low, expecting they could join up at the end with whichever side ended up winning. Instead, Uriel sucked the shefa from the universe and they waned into shadows of themselves. When the sky cracked and some of the holy light returned, most of them stayed in hiding. Being a neutral angel was not a popular choice.

Gadiriel didn't worry about popularity. In a sense, she *was* popularity, the metaphysical essence of celebrity and belovedness and stardom. The Angelinos couldn't resist. She took the teetering city under her wings and gracefully slipped into the station of civic goddess like an actress playing a particularly familiar role. One day, there were riots and looting and half the Thousand Oaks on fire. The next, everyone quietly tiptoed home, because the chaos *was making her sad*.

They say that when you see the Lady, she looks like whoever you love most — love in a purely erotic sense, the single person you've felt the strongest moment of sexual attraction towards. It is an awkward spell she casts. Many are the men who have approached her, expecting her to take the form of their wives or at least their mistresses, only to see that one girl, the one they had a huge crush on in eleventh grade but haven't thought about since. Other times it is no one at all they recognize, a stranger whom they passed once on the street, maybe catcalled, maybe didn't even get a good look at. A few people who had previously made an absolutely heroic effort to avoid noticing their sexual orientation saw someone they were *very much* not expecting.

So Gadiriel's public appearances were rare and carefully vetted. When she spoke on television, her face was veiled. Most of the time she stayed in her temple, the building once called Griffith Observatory, accepting audiences with whoever needed her assistance most.

"Your Grace?" asked Tom Cruise. He was her chamberlain this month. It was a great honor, a sign of her favor to actors and actresses she especially enjoyed. "A petitioner has come, begging an audience."

He was dressed in khakis and a pith helmet. This week's theme was Adventure. The Observatory itself was covered in foliage, so that it looked like a jungle, and weird tribal masks gazed maliciously from the walls. Gadiriel was dressed in a loincloth and a headdress of skulls, like some breathless nineteenth century author's caricature of an African queen, and her body was weighted down with gold jewelry that looked like it had come straight from King Solomon's mines.

She still wore the veil, though. Bad things tended to happen when she wasn't in the veil.

"Show her in," said Gadiriel.

"Ah, well..." said Cruise. The Lady frowned. His attempt at a Victorian English accent didn't sound at *all* like her memory of Victorian English people. She would have to coach him later. Next week's theme was the Wild West, and she hoped he could pull off a more convincing cowboy. "It's a very unusual petitioner. Doesn't seem to—er—have a physical form. It insisted on us finding a suitable, um, vessel for it. Very strange."

The Lady's attention was piqued. "Bring it in, then."

Two burly men in loincloths came in, bearing what was very clearly the Ark of the Covenant. Not the real one, which as far as Gadiriel knew was still in a storeroom in Zimbabwe somewhere. The prop from Raiders of the Lost Ark.

"That's the petitioner?" asked the Lady, now very intrigued indeed.

"Yes," said the voice out of the Ark. It was a terrible, garbled voice, like something that had dismissed audible sound as a ridiculous form of communication and now found itself caught by surprise at having to make use of it. The Lady eyeballed the size of the prop. Not big enough to fit a person, except maybe a very young child all curled up. She didn't want to know, not just yet. That would have been a *spoiler*. The two men set the Ark down in front of her, bowed, departed.

"What can I do for you?" she asked.

"They say you build golems," said the Ark.

"Many people build golems," the Lady said dismissively. "A clump of mud, a quick pull of the Animating Name off a scroll wheel, and you have a golem. Hideous misshapen things. I build *costumes*. Beautiful bodies, fit to be filled with any intelligence you please."

"Yes," said the Ark. "That is what they say. You build beautiful golems. Perfect golems. Ones that look human, or more than human. Golems people can fall in love with. You did it once, after the Broadcast. I need a body. A human body. One people can fall in love with. A *specific* human body. I beg it of you. As a favor."

"What you ask is very difficult," said the Lady.

"I bring you gifts," said the Ark of the Covenant. "A Name that turns people invisible. Another that lets one walk on air. And a third that calls the winds."

To offer one such as her a *deal* would have been terribly offensive. Barbaric, even. But to request a favor and give gifts. That showed *class*. And such gifts! Three new and secret Names! Her curiosity became oppressive, unbearable.

"Yes, of course. Of course it can be done. Any body you want. As handsome as any actor, or as stunning as any starlet. We will make you the sort of body people *die* for. A specific body, you say? Anyone! But first, I want to see you! The role has to fit the actor, as they say!"

A long pause. "You have to keep it secret," said the Ark. "Nobody can know what I really look like. Who I really am. I'm so ugly. So hideous."

"That will not be a problem. Not for long. A secret. I swear. Just the two of us!" The Lady motioned Cruise out of the room. The two of them were all alone now. She left her throne, crossed the audience chamber, knelt down before the Ark. She had seen the movie, of course. She knew what came next. But she was so, so curious.

Gadiriel opened the Ark of the Covenant.

Interlude מ

New York City

September 3, 1978
New York City

I.

Flanked by two guards, Mayor Ed Koch walked into the room.

It seemed out of place in the middle of New York City. Poorly lit, musty, packed with books of different ages and provenances. The furniture was all wooden, and either antique or made by someone with a dim view of aesthetic innovations after about 1800.

And then there was the man in the ornate wooden chair. He was old too. And he looked older than he was. His beard was long and white, and his clothing cut from the same aesthetic mold as his furniture. And in another sense he looked too young, like at any moment he could jump up and start singing.

"Mr. Mayor," said the Lubavitcher Rebbe. "Such an honor to see you again."

The Rebbe had a funny way of showing it. He'd made the Mayor wait until midnight for an appointment—that was always the rule, too busy with religious functions during the day—and then Koch had to wait outside while the Rebbe adjudicated a dispute between two elderly Jewish men who had come in before him and were apparently arguing about ownership of a goat. Who even *had* goats in Brooklyn? But Koch's aides had warned him about this. It was first-come-first-served with the Rebbe, honors and offices gained you nothing, and you visited him on his terms or not at all.

"Rabbi Schneerson," said the Mayor. "I'm sorry I haven't visited you in so long. I do value your advice. But politics!" He waved his arm in a gesture of dismissal. "You know how it is!"

"But now you want my help," said the Rebbe softly.

Koch never knew whether to feel intimidated by the Rebbe or hug him. He had a sweet face, almost angelic-looking. But his light blue eyes were unusual, very unusual, and there was a lurking power in the old man, like a coiled snake. Koch just nodded.

"You've heard what's been happening," he said, then realized he might not have. What *did* the Rebbe hear? He could have believed the man knew everything that happened in the furthest corner of the earth, but he could also have believed that news of the Industrial Revolution hadn't quite reached him yet. "After the federal government collapsed, the demons broke their alliance with us. They swept down into Canada. What was left of the Army went up to stop them. There were a lot of battles. They won. It took two years, but Canada's fallen. Now they've crossed the border into the US. Two attacks. One to the west, straight down the plains from Saskatchewan, bearing down on Salt Lake City. The other to the east, due south from Ottawa. They've got to be headed for New York City. The US Army's in shambles; President Carter has promised to dispatch a couple of people up here but it's not enough, he's mostly worried about DC. Governor Carey has called up the state militia, but it's not enough. And—I feel silly even asking this, but I was wondering if you might have some way of getting some, you know, supernatural aid."

"Why is that silly?" asked the Rebbe.

"It's just... everything's so new, with the sky cracking ten years ago, and it would have been ridiculous to even talk about demons before, and I'm the Mayor of New York and not some kind of Biblical priest-king, and..."

The Rebbe held up a wizened finger.

"Long before the sky cracked people were asking God for help. And long before the sky cracked He was giving it, if that was His will. And now! In this age of angels, and demons, and people discovering long-lost Names! Of course you should ask for supernatural help!"

The Mayor visibly relaxed. Then he asked, "What exactly are you going to do? Do you know some special way of helping? Do you need to talk to the militia? Should I—"

"How should I know?" asked the Rebbe. "I am going to seek help from God, and He is going to answer or not according to His will. Go in peace."

Koch was still confused, but he knew a dismissal when he heard one. He gave an awkward half-bow to the Rebbe, the kind you give when you're not sure if you're supposed to bow or not but a chummy handshake seems clearly inadequate, then left the room.

One of the Rebbe's assistants came in. "Rebbe, the next two people in line are an elderly couple asking for advice regarding their goat. Should I send them in?"

The Rebbe put his hands over his face. "Only the Holy One knows why so many people have goats in Brooklyn," he said, "or why they all come to me. But no, I think I am done for the night. Tell them to pray to God for advice, and also that if they want to own goats they should really move somewhere more rural. Actually, dismiss everyone else for tonight, give them my apologies, but I have some work to do."

This had never happened before. The assistant hesitated briefly, then nodded and went out to dismiss the petitioners.

The Rebbe took a book of Talmudic commentary from the bookshelf, started leafing through it. Then another book. Then another. The Sepher Yetzirah. The Etz Chayim. Just as he was positioning a chair to grab the Zohar from the top shelf, he slapped his forehead. "Ah!" he said. "No, the traditional solution will do just fine here." He returned the books to their usual positions and ran out, hoping to call back the petitioners before they made it out the door.

II.

Mayor Koch met Governor Carey at White Plains, and a load fell from his shoulders when he saw the rank after rank of young New York Militia recruits behind him. "Thank God," he said. "I'm so glad you came."

"I'm not coming," snapped Carey. "I'm retreating. We've lost Albany. I know nobody down here in the city ever remembers Albany exists, but I feel like the news that we lost our state capital should be met with a little more than 'I'm so glad you came.'"

"I'm sorry about Albany," said Koch. "But New York City is half the state population. It's more than that. It's a symbol. And one of America's biggest ports. And the gateway to the Mid-Atlantic. And..."

"Yes, yes," dismissed Governor Carey. "They're a day behind us, by the way. No more. What preparations have you been making?"

"I've turned the NYPD into a makeshift militia," said Koch. "That's about 10,000 men. It wasn't hard. I was... actually kind of shocked at how militarized they were already."

"Ten thousand." The Governor frowned. "I have sixty thousand. It was more, but—" He paused. "It won't be enough."

"I've also organized all the gun-owning citizens into militias," said Koch. "I was... actually kind of surprised how many guns there were. Oh, and the Mafia's going to help. That's another few thousand."

"I forgot how much I hated this city," said Carey.

"We've also fortified the Bronx as best we can," said Koch. "It's going to be building-to-building fighting there. We've rigged all the bridges to explode. I was surprised how close some of them already were to..."

"Spare me," said the Governor. "Any word from Carter?"

"It's like we expected," said Koch. "There's not much left of the federal government in Washington, and what there is only wants to defend themselves. In the end, even the couple of troops they promised didn't come through. No point in sending someone off to get massacred. A quarter of New York City has already fled to safety in Jersey anyway."

"Only a quarter?"

"Well, it's Jersey."

"So that's what we're going to do?" asked the Governor. "70,000 troops, some militiamen, and a couple of mafiosi making a last stand at the Bronx?"

"It doesn't have to be a last stand," said Koch.

"No way I'm going to Jersey."

"I mean we might win!"

"I was there for the first half of the battle in Albany," said the Governor. "The demons aren't even an army. They're a swarm. You try to resist them, and they just cover you, and it feels like everything good is sucked out of the world, and then you run. The veterans from the Canada campaign said it happened there too. There are hundreds of thousands of them. Millions."

"What about God?" asked Koch.

"Are you even religious? You played the faith issue so well during the campaign that no one can even figure out whether you're Jewish or Catholic."

"I... believe in God," said Koch.

"Tell Him to hurry up," said Carey.

III.

Right on schedule, the hordes of Hell slammed into the Bronx.

The New York forces thought they could stand. They were wrong. They were pushed back to Norwood before they even had time to think about how quickly they were retreating. Once they figured it out, Carey rallied some of his New York Guard and made a stand. The Botanical Garden saw some of the fiercest fighting of the whole battle before they were wiped out, guard and governor alike. Then they fell back to Fordham, and the West Bronx, where the door-to-door fighting finally materialized as gangsters used to taking pot-shots through their windows started exercising their skills in earnest.

(Meanwhile, in New York Harbor a wizened old man tried to catch a ferry but found they were all closed. He frowned, mouthed an apology to God for doing something that might look like showing off, and started walking across the water.)

The New York Police Department knew these streets. They had been patrolling them for centuries, they were baked into their institutional memory. Finally they had an enemy that they could shoot without getting put on trial for excessive force. Guns brandished, or nightsticks held high, they rushed into the streets near Concourse, killed and were killed in turn.

(When the old man had gone far enough, he spoke the Ascending Name and rose into the air.)

Mayor Koch gave the order for all the bridges from the Bronx into Manhattan to be blown up, though the river was shallow and it would delay the demons only a few hours at best. A few tried to fly across on their vestigial wings; the others flooded down the banks of the Harlem River and took Yankee Stadium and Port Morris. They had outflanked the defenders. Now time to tighten the cordon.

(The short old man took a paintbrush out of his pocket and dipped it in an old-fashioned inkwell he had brought.)

They weren't trying to cross. There would be time enough for that later. They were trying to wipe out the Guard. Koch ordered his men east. The demons followed. They took the Bronx River and trapped the New Yorkers on the other side. Then they kept pushing.

(The old man began to paint.)

The 678 and 295 bridges had already been blown up. The defenders were trapped on Throggs Neck, literally between the Devil and the deep blue sea. The entire demonic army descended upon them. They fought well, but rank after rank died, the screams of officers merging with those of mafiosi and militiamen as their desperate last stand inched toward a bloody conclusion.

Then a miracle occurred.

Not like the earthen golem of Czech fame,
Laid low, and in some dusty attic stowed
Here at our sea-washed, sunset gates there strode
A mighty woman with a torch, whose flame
Was the imprisoned lightning; and a Name
Writ on her forehead. In her crown there rode
The Rebbe, and his face with Torah glowed
"Sh'ma Yisrael HaShem elokeinu HaShem echad" prayed he
Then, with silent lips: "Save them, Your tired, Your poor,
Your huddled masses yearning to break free,
The wretched refuse of your demon war.
Save these, the hopeless, battle-tossed, for me,
I lift my lance beside the golden door!"

The Liberty Golem lifted her lance, formerly the spire of the Empire State Building. She loosed the imprisoned lightning of her terrible swift torch. From her crown the Rebbe flung warlike Names that sputtered and sparkled and crashed into the hellish hosts and disintegrated them like fire melts ice. They shrieked and began a retreat.

The New York Guard would have none of it. Inspired with sudden new courage, they leapt into pursuit, swarming around the giant golem, picking off with their guns and nightsticks what she couldn't with her lance and fire, until demon after demon disincorporated and the entire army that had set forth from Albany had been blasted back into the hell from which they came.

IV.

When it was all over, Ed Koch approached the golem. It lowered a giant green hand, picked him up, brought him face to face with the Lubavitcher Rebbe in the crown. Not that there had been any doubt.

"Um," said the Mayor, "You will be able to get the statue back, right? Not that I'm ungrateful. Just that it's important to us."

The Rebbe still managed to seem humble and soft-spoken, even atop a 150-foot killing machine that had until recently been America's most recognizable national monument. "Of course," he said.

"So is that how it works?" asked Koch. "If you write the Name of God on any human-shaped figure, it becomes a golem?"

"Ah," said the Rebbe. "Not *the* Name. God has many Names, Mayor. Some animate earth. Some animate stone. This one animates copper. And many others do entirely different things. I think you will be learning much more about them soon. But remember, however it may seem to you, God doesn't give away any of His Names unless He wants someone to have them."

Koch couldn't resist straining his head to try to read the Hebrew text written on the statue's forehead, but it was very small, and he was very far away, and he couldn't make out a single letter.

The Rebbe smiled.

"And God wanted you to have this one? Now?"

"I asked him for it. Mr. Koch, do you know when I arrived in this city? 1941. Fleeing the Nazis. Those men you saw in that synagogue, most of them are all that is left of their families. You saved us, Mr. Koch, you and your people. Now it is our turn to return the favor." He hesitated for a second. "And... I know I must seem very strange to the people of this city, but I am a New Yorker too. Praise be to God."

Ed Koch looked at the wizened old man, dressed in the clothing of 18th century Poland, seated atop of a golem made from the Statue of Liberty, and he knew the Rebbe was right. Heck, there were New Yorkers who were *much* stranger than that.

"What about the other army?" he asked. "The one headed west. Is God going to send a miracle to stop them too?"

"How should I know?" asked the Rebbe, cheerfully. "Let the West save the West. If God wants it to be saved, they'll get their miracle too!"

"But what about Canada?" asked Koch. "What about Russia? What about everyone who wasn't saved? If you can call down miracles, then..."

"Mr. Mayor," asked the Rebbe, "Why do you think God grants me the power to perform miracles?"

Koch thought a second. "To heal the sick... to save the righteous... that sort of thing."

"If God wanted the sick to be cured, why would He make them sick? If He wanted the righteous to be saved, why would He put them in danger? God lets people perform miracles to make a statement."

"Which is?"

"Oho." The Rebbe's eyes sparkled. "God's statements never have just one meaning."

"But if He's already given you these Names, can't you use them to save everybody, or to heal all the sick, or bring the country back together..."

"Is that what you would do, if you had Divine Names?"

"Yes! It's what *everybody* would do!"

The Rebbe looked positively amused now. "Perhaps God will give you the Names, then, and we will see if you are right."

He made it sound like a threat.

"But for now I'll be headed back toward Liberty Island. I'll leave the spire at the base of the Empire State Building. You'll have to figure out how to fix that one yourself."

Koch nodded mutely. The golem put him down and began to lumber away.

V.

When the statue had been safely restored, the Rebbe dismounted, walked back across the water to Brooklyn, and went back into his synagogue.

"Rebbe," said his assistant, "there's a young woman here. Wants to talk to you about her chickens."

"Tell her to come back tomorrow," said the Rebbe. "I'm exhausted."

He sank into his bed and drifted on the edge of sleep. Outside the his window, New Yorkers of a hundred different ethnicities danced in the streets, set off fireworks in celebration. Just past the synagogue, someone was singing an old patriotic song:

My country, 'tis of thee,
Sweet land of Liberty,
Of thee I sing;
Land where my fathers died,
Land of the pilgrims' pride,
From ev'ry mountainside
Let freedom ring!

Let music swell the breeze,
And ring from all the trees

Sweet freedom's song;
Let mortal tongues awake;
Let all that breathe partake;
Let rocks their silence break,
The sound prolong.

Our fathers' God to Thee,
Author of Liberty,
To Thee we sing.
Long may our land be bright,
With freedom's holy light,
Protect us by Thy might,
Great God our King.

Chapter Twenty-Nine

He Who Respects The Infant's Faith

October 2, 1978
Colorado

I.

Sitting in his car, Father Ellis contemplated the Exodus.

According to the aptly-named Book of Numbers, there were 603,550 men among the Israelites who fled Egypt. Add women and children, and you got about two million people going the same direction at the same time. If they'd all been in cars, it probably would have looked a lot like Interstate 25 did now.

Someone honked, apparently optimistic that it might affect the fifty-mile backup of cars that had been almost motionless for several hours. The priest sighed.

A knock on the passenger-side window. It was a little boy, eight or nine by the looks of him. You could never be too careful during times like these, but he rolled down the window anyway.

"Are you a priest?" the child asked.

Father Ellis was taken aback. He was dressed in perfectly ordinary clothes, and he was from up near Fort Collins, a hundred miles away.

"How did you know that?" he asked.

"I didn't," said the boy. "I've been knocking on every car here, looking for a priest. I need your help."

Father Ellis looked the boy over. He looked foreign, maybe Indian, not the Native Americans who were so common around this part of Colorado, but Indian from India. But his hair was blond. In this light it even looked white. He'd never seen an Indian with blond hair. There were no Indians in his parish, but he'd heard some people from far southern India were Christian.

"How can I help you?" he asked warily.

The boy reached through the opened window, flicked the lock, opened the door, and sat down.

"I need your help with a plan. First we need to wait for my uncle. I am Jala. Hello."

"No!" said the older man. "Get out!" He pushed the boy out as firmly as he could, but it was too late. The door had already closed. God. He'd heard of this scam. Now someone would be by to accuse him of kidnapping, and then threaten to take the case to court if he didn't pay them hush money. All he had in the world was three hundred dollars he'd brought with him from Fort Collins for food and gas during the evacuation.

"You are afraid I am trying to scam you in some way. I promise I am not. I want to help you. I want to help everybody. But you would not believe me if I told you, so for now we wait for my uncle. Unless you want to fight me. Please do not try this. I have a weapon."

Oh God. This got worse and worse.

Right on cue, an Indian man peered through the window of his car and saw the boy. He started banging on the window, shouting incomprehensible things, demanding Father Ellis open up. Before he got the chance, the boy opened the door.

"Hello, Uncle," he said. "Get in the back seat. We are going to Silverthorne."

"Look," said Father Ellis, for whatever it was worth, "I swear, I didn't do anything. The kid just banged on the window, then forced himself in, and wouldn't go away. He said he... look, this isn't what it looks like."

The uncle stood outside the open door. "I'm sorry," he told the priest, falling over himself to sound apologetic. "We are peaceful people. We do not want trouble. He is very strange. But... it is best to do what he says."

"What?"

"I'm sorry! He is not my son! He usually stays with his grandmother, but we had trouble fitting the whole family into two cars. But when he wants something, it's no use arguing with him. My wife and I have tried so many times, and it has never... Jala, you tell him!"

"I am always right," said the boy. "It is hard to explain." He gestured again impatiently for his uncle to get in the car. The older man shot Father Ellis an apologetic look, then got into the back seat of his car.

"I'm so sorry," said the uncle. "I swear on my life, we are peaceful people. Good Hindus! We do not want trouble." To the child: "Jala, must we do this?"

"Yes, Uncle."

"But the poor man — he doesn't even know you. He wants to get to safety, just like—"

"Yes."

Defeated, the older man slumped down in the back seat.

It was an evacuation. The police, if there were any left, were otherwise occupied. He was old, and the man in the back seat was young and spry. And if the child had a weapon...

At least he had some idea what to do about a kidnapping. This just didn't make sense.

"God," he whispered under his breath, "Help me get out of this one okay."

Meanwhile, the other two were talking. "Jala, where were you? Your aunt and I have been looking for you for hours! I cannot believe you slipped out of the car without us hearing you. Do you realize how dangerous..."

"You still do not trust me, Uncle. Not completely. That was why I had to slip out. I knew you would look for me. Aunt Samira will be well. She and Uncle Pranav will go the rest of the way to Santa Fe without us. We have work to do."

"We're not going to make it to New Mexico? Jala, this is unsafe!"

"Yes, Uncle. We must make it safe."

"Why us?"

"Somebody has to and no one else will."

The man sighed, the sigh of someone who is thoroughly beaten and knows he always will be.

"I'm sorry," he repeated to the priest. "My name is Vihaan and this is Jalaketu. I live over in Boulder. Jala lives with his grandmother in Colorado Springs, but he was staying with us for the summer. He's always had problems. His mother died in childbirth. He's a good kid, though, I swear. We just cannot control him. He just... I don't know." He sounded totally humiliated, which under the circumstances Father Ellis supposed was reasonable.

"Father John Ellis. I... How old are you, Jala? Eight?"

"I am almost two."

"It's true," interjected Uncle Vihaan. "I wouldn't have believed it if I hadn't seen his birth with my own eyes, but he's only two years old. He has some kind of growth problem. He grows too much. That is why we cannot control him."

"There wasn't enough time," said Jala, apologetically. "I should be older. But I'm growing as fast as I can."

Father Ellis considered his options. He could try to fight them off—no good, not strong enough. He could escape and leave the car to them, but then he would have no way to evacuate. Or he could just give in and let them ride with him. Then they would all get to New Mexico, and the two of them would leave him alone. Maybe this was how people hitchhiked in India, by crazy children breaking in and their guardians claiming implausibly low ages for them.

That was it. They were probably weird hitchhikers. Would he have picked them up if they had been standing by the side of the road? Probably not. He was an old man, and cautious. But if circumstances had forced him into doing a good deed, perhaps he should thank God for the opportunity. Yes. That was it. Just thank God for the opportunity to do a good deed at no cost to himself.

That lasted right until the child announced that they would be taking the exit to the 70 going West, which was insane.

Father Ellis turned to him, spoke clearly but not patronizingly. "Jala, I am sure your uncle has already told you this, but Colorado is being attacked. By demons from Siberia, who took over Canada and now are invading the United States. They already got most of Utah and they're crossing the Rockies towards us. We need to go south, all the way to New Mexico, to get away from them. That's why everyone is evacuating. Going west wouldn't take us away from them. It would take us right towards their army."

"Father," said the boy, "do you remember the story of Sennacherib?"

A moment of surprise. "That's a very old story for a boy like you to know."

"King Sennacherib marched with an impossibly large army to destroy Jerusalem. King Hezekiah believed he was doomed, but the prophet Isaiah told him not to be afraid, for God was with him. And the angel of God destroyed the hosts of Sennacherib, and Jerusalem was saved. Do you know the poem, Father? The Assyrian came down like the wolf on the fold, and his cohorts were streaming with purple and gold..."

"We are good Hindus," said Uncle Vihaan, apologetically. "I don't even know where he learns these things."

But Father Ellis was intrigued. "I know the poem. It's true that with God, any battle can be won," he said. "But God doesn't work to a human schedule. Remember, before God saved Jerusalem, he let Sennacherib destroy all of northern Israel. The prophet Isaiah told Hezekiah not to fear. But when we don't have prophets with us, we have to do what we think is best. And sometimes that involves retreating."

"I am... like a prophet," said Jalaketu. "It's complicated."

"I'm sorry!" protested the uncle again. "We are good Hindus!"

"If you are a prophet," said Father Ellis, "give me a sign."

"It is written," said Jalaketu, "that you shall not put the Lord your God to the test."

"You are not the Lord," said Father Ellis.

Jalaketu glared at him, as if about to challenge the assertion.

"We are good Hindus," the uncle protested feebly. Then added, "But I swear to Vishnu, Jala's mother had never slept with a man when she gave birth to him."

Then Jala sang. "KYA-RUN-ATEPH-NAHA-IALA-DEH-VAV-IO-ORAH"

The car's gear stick turned into a snake. Father Ellis shrieked and jerked his hand back, actually jerked his whole body back and hit his head against the car door. If traffic had been moving they would have crashed for sure; as it was, they remained motionless in the gridlock. The snake looked around curiously, then coiled up onto the center console of the car and fell asleep.

"Oh!" said Jalaketu. "I'm sorry! I wasn't expecting... I thought it would... I should have... I'm still kind of new at this. I'm growing as fast as I can, I promise. But you've got to help me."

Father Ellis's mind went into high gear — no, scratch that, use literally any other metaphor — he started thinking quickly. He'd heard of such things. Kabbalistic Names. A few people had reported discovering them, old magic, returned to life after the sky had cracked. But none of them were public, and none of them as far as he knew turned things into snakes. The boy knew another Name, a Name nobody knew, he had independently discovered a new kabbalistic Name.

"I'm sorry," said Jalaketu, "I should do something more impressive. But I swear to you. I want to help. I'm here to help. We can stop these demons. Save everybody. But you need to believe me. Somebody has to do it and nobody else will, so please listen to me and take the exit." Exit 70 was right in front of them now. The traffic was beginning to move. "Please, Father, if you have any faith at all, get in the exit lane."

"My gear stick is a snake," said Father Ellis.

"Oh!" said Jalaketu, and he sang another word, and the snake was a gear stick again.

Father Ellis very gingerly put his hand to the gear stick, and when it didn't bite him, he moved it forward. Then he sighed and got into the exit lane.

II.

The trip to Silverthorne had been fast and without traffic. Nobody was going *towards* the approaching demonic army. Nobody except them.

Father Ellis sat with Jalaketu on a wall on the main street. The boy had sent Uncle Vihaan to find explosives. Sent wasn't exactly the right word; the boy had said *he* was going to find explosives, and Vihaan had declared there was *no way* he was going to let the boy *anywhere near* explosives, and if they needed explosives for some reason, he was going to be the one to get them — which had clearly been Jala's plan all along. Vihaan was some kind of mining engineer and apparently good at these things.

"So," asked Father Ellis. "Who are you?"

"My mother died during childbirth," said Jalaketu. "I killed her. I didn't know. I was too big. I was growing as fast as I could, because I knew there wasn't enough time, but I didn't realize. I only barely remember. I remember that I was very sad, and that I decided I must be more careful from now on, and never let anybody die again."

He didn't say "anybody close to me." He didn't sound like he'd meant to.

"Comet West is my father," said Jalaketu. "My mother told Uncle Vihaan so, before she died. It talks to me sometimes, in my dreams. It loves me and it wants me to be happy. Sometimes it scares me, though. I think it is an archangel."

Father Ellis didn't know what to say.

"It says I must be Moshiach. It tells me stories from the Torah as I fall asleep. And other stories, too, from a big book that it wrote a very long time ago. And I try to grow as fast as I can, so I can understand them, but it's never fast enough. This body is too weak. I want to walk into a fire and burn my body away and *stop being human*, and then I can be a comet too, and it will all make sense."

"You said you were looking for a priest," said Father Ellis. "Are you a Christian?"

"No." Jalaketu smiled. "My mother was a Hindu, but Hinduism passes through the paternal line. My father, perhaps if he teaches me Torah then he is Jewish. But Judaism passes through the maternal line. I am nothing."

"Christianity doesn't pass through any line," said Father Ellis. "It's open to anyone who wants it. And I mention it because it has a lot to say on the issue of incarnating as a human. It's hard. Really hard sometimes. But definitely very important."

"That's what my father says too," said Jalaketu. "He says that I had to be human. But it is... yes. It is hard."

Vihaan chose that moment to come back in Ellis's beat-up Chevy Nova. The trunk was open and packed with ominous-looking boxes.

"Okay," he said, pulling up in front of the other two. "Now what?"

"This is the part where it gets complicated," said Jalaketu.

"Something else your father told you in a dream?" asked Ellis.

"Not... exactly," said Jalaketu. "It's something that I... hope will work."

Oh God, prayed Father Ellis. *Have mercy on us, your poor servants....*

III.

Jala West stood alone in the middle of Interstate Highway 70, just outside Silverthorne. The mountains rose on either side of him like walls. This was the chokepoint. They would pass through here.

From the distance came a faint rumbling. An oppressive heat filled the air. The smell of sulfur. Hot winds began to blow. To the west of the valley, a red-black cloud came into view.

They had fought a series of battles with the Canadians and their American allies. Outside Calgary, the alliance had lost decisively. From there the hosts of Hell had split in two. Half, under the demon princes Adramelech, Asmodei, and Rahab, had gone east to complete the conquest of Ottawa, New York City, and the American East Coast. The other half, under the command of Thamiel himself, had gone south and west, to root out American resistance in California and the West. They had gone as far south as Ogden, but the Mormons in Salt Lake City had resisted tooth and nail, and now there was a siege. The siege was not going so well for the demons, because supplies and reinforcements kept coming in on Interstate 70 from Colorado. Blockading the Interstate had just redirected the supplies onto a hundred smaller mountain roads the demons couldn't follow.

Thamiel was not used to being resisted. He decided to take things into his own hands. A sortie into Colorado. Fort Collins, Boulder, Colorado Springs, Denver — all the big cities, lined up nice in a row — were to be taken out, completing the desolation of America between the Rockies and the Mississippi. The Mormons' supply route would be removed. Salt Lake would fall.

So onward went the Hosts of Hell, onward along Interstate 70. They burnt Grand Junction, they razed Glenwood Springs, they demolished Vail. At last, beside the highest peaks of the Rockies, they came to Silverthorne, and there in the middle of the highway was Jala West.

The demons themselves had not yet taken physical form; they buzzed and seethed like a thundercloud of darkness covering the plains. But Thamiel marched ahead of them, alone as a visible figure. His suit was impeccable and his steps were inhumanly fast, and the whole mass of darkness followed in a wedge behind him. When he saw the little boy standing in front of him, he stopped.

"Who are you?" he asked.

"I am Jala West," said the boy.

"Run away," said Thamiel.

"Tell me," said Jala, "if this were a story, and the Devil and all his demons were marching against a peaceful nation, and in their way was only one young boy, wielding a sword made from a falling star..."

"You don't have a sword made from a fallen star," Thamiel pointed out.

The roar of a meteor split the sky, a fireball that briefly surpassed the daylight with the brightness of its passage. It came closer and closer, aimed straight at them, and Jalaketu held out his hand and caught it. A huge black sword with a silver hilt, almost bigger than he was. It was still fiery hot, and far too big for him, but he held it without fear.

"I do *so*," said Jala.

Thamiel snarled.

"If this were a story," Jalaketu continued, "and you were challenged by just one boy, wielding a sword made from a fallen star, here because he wouldn't abandon his homeland — do you think it would end well for you? For the demon?"

"Are you going to ask for my surrender?" snarled Thamiel.

"No," said Jala. "There is no surrender I can accept. If you left Colorado, I would follow you. If you left America, I would hunt you down. Even if you left the world entirely and returned to Hell, I could not allow this. And I cannot allow you to keep this army. It is too dangerous. Everything about this is dangerous. I should not have come myself; I should have found some way to delay you from afar. But I had to come. The Bible says you are the adversary, the tempter, who takes the measure of Man. But who takes *your* measure? I came here to delay you, but also to take your measure. And also to get something I needed. And also because I am angry. This is my home. I would defend it even if it were not. But it is."

He drew a signal gun from his pocket and fired a flare. It streaked through the sky, a little anticlimactic after the recent meteor strike. The mountains echoed with the sound, but there was no other answer.

Then the demon fell upon him, wielding a bident whose cuts and slices were almost too fast for the human eye to follow. Jalaketu parried with his sword, the great sword Sigh, the sword his father had made for him, the sword which would always answer the call of him and his descendants wherever they might be. The air sizzled with the speed of their battle; the earth trembled with the force of their blows.

Then Jalaketu drew blood. Just a tiny bit, a glancing blow on the demon's forearm. It sizzled on the blade, etching weird damascene patterns in the steel.

"All right," said the Lord of Demons. "Let's do this the easy way."

He gave a signal to the vast cloud that hovered above them, and all the legions of Hell flew down into the valley at once. Jalaketu just watched them come, holding his sword out in front of him, as if they were no more than a few approaching wisps of cloud.

Then the roar of the oncoming demons before him was matched by a similar roar behind him. Something grayish-white and colossal, so big that at first it was hard to identify. As it came closer, it took on more features. Water. Rushing water. A whole reservoir's worth.

Thamiel was not impressed. "That was your plan?" he asked. "Blowing up the dam? You *do* know that demons don't drown, right?"

The oncoming wall of holy water crashed into the hosts of Hell with a bang and snuffed them out like sparks before a fire extinguisher. The whole massacre only lasted seconds. Jalaketu spoke the Ascending Name and hovered above the devastation, making sure that no demons were left, that not a single one had survived.

"I know," said Jalaketu, to nobody in particular. And then, more solemnly: "And the widows of Ashur are loud in their wail, and the idols are broke in the temple of Baal. And the might of the Gentile, unsmote by the sword, hath melted like snow in the glance of the Lord."

Then he descended back to ground level and waded through the wreckage until he reached town.

IV.

Father Ellis's old Nova drove down route 24 into Colorado Springs. The traffic was more haphazard now. Some people were still trying to evacuate. Other people had heard rumors that something had changed, and were trying to go back home. A few people didn't know which way they were going. The 24 was empty; the 25 was a mess. When Ellis reached the junction, he gave up, pulled over, and stopped the car. The three of them walked out onto the empty highway.

"Never been here before, actually," the priest said.

"My hometown," said Jalaketu. "This is where it has to start."

"Where what has to start?" asked Vihaan. "Jala, be careful."

Whatever had to start, this seemed as good a place as any. The city center rose before them, a few buildings that toyed with the idea of being skyscrapers; the slightest hint of a downtown. Then the long ribbon of cars stretching either direction, honking, all of Colorado on the road. On one side, the stunning rock formations that a nineteenth-century romantic had dubbed the Garden of the Gods. To the other, the looming massif of Cheyenne Mountain, in whose bowels the United States kept the nerve center controlling its nuclear armament. Towering above all of it, the sharp snow-capped ridge of Pikes Peak.

Jalaketu spoke the Ascending Name and rose into the air. Then another Name, and the sky seemed to dim, like all the sunlight was concentrated on him and him alone. People started to notice. The honking died down. A few brave souls left their cars to get a better view. The windows on some of the buildings peeked open.

Then he spoke. His voice wasn't loud, but somehow it *carried*, carried down past all the cars frozen below, into the buildings downtown, over the ridges and rivulets of the Garden of the Gods, and all throughout the city.

"I am Jalaketu West," he said, "son of Comet West. Colorado is safe for now. It's safe because I saved it. But not for long. Demons don't die forever, they just disintegrate and rebuild themselves. And it's not just demons. The cracks in the sky are getting bigger. The world is falling apart. I don't know if I can save all of you. But somebody has to, and no one else will. So I am going to try. I need all of your help. If you follow me, it won't be easy. You'll have to have faith. But I will be worthy of it. I promise. In the Name of God, in whose Name oaths must never be sworn in vain, I promise. This is how it has to be. I am the Comet King. Bow. Swear fealty. *Now.*"

At first everyone was quiet, too flabbergasted for any reaction, and then they all started talking to each other. "Holy God," and "He thinks he..." and "He says we're saved?" and "How is he floating there?" and a thousand other questions and worries and exclamations and fears.

In the end, they were Americans, and they didn't bow. But finally one of them, an old Korean War vet, gave a salute. Then another man saluted, and another, and soon the whole city was saluting him.

And Jalaketu laughed, and said, "It'll do," because there were parts of him that were very old and far away, and other parts that were as American as apple pie, and truth be told he wouldn't have bowed down either. So he laughed and saluted back at them, and then he lowered himself back onto the highway.

"King?" asked Uncle Vihaan, with a miserable look on his face, like he had always known it would come to this but had hoped it wouldn't happen quite so quickly.

"Yes," said Jalaketu. "And I'll need advisors I can trust. Once you find Aunt Samira and get her somewhere safe, come back here so we can talk at more length. And you—" he said to Father Ellis.

"Yes?" asked the priest.

"I'll need your advice too."

"I am just about the least qualified person to advise anyone on anything."

"I need you to teach me what you were talking about before. How to be human. How to bear it."

Father Ellis swallowed. "I'll try," he said.

And then suddenly the boy was all smiles again. "Let's go," he said. "Get to city center. I'm sure there are a lot of people there who will want to talk to us." He skipped forward, almost gaily, his comet-white hair trailing behind him in the wind.

Vihaan and Ellis looked at each other.

"I guess all we can do is follow," the priest said, and the two of them started after him.

Chapter Thirty

Over The Dark Deserts

You don't truly understand necromancy if you can't explain it to your great-great-great-grandmother.
—Steven Kaas

Evening, May 12, 2017
Mojave Desert

I.

California shifted around us. Plains, then mountains, then taller mountains sloping down at last into a mind-boggling flatness of desert. And there we were. I had spent my entire life in that tiny strip of California coastline between the mountains and the sea. Now I was in the real West, a Biblical wilderness of scrub and harsh rocks unlike anything I had seen before. The land where the great dramas of the late twentieth century had played out, the twin stories of the Comet King and the Other King. In the blazing sunlight it felt more real and solid than the dreamland I had left behind.

We were somewhere around Barstow on the edge of the desert when the Wall Drug signs began to appear.

Before the sky cracked, Wall Drug had been a shopping center in South Dakota. There aren't a lot of things in South Dakota, so the owners of the shopping center had tried to turn it into a tourist attraction. They put up billboards along the highway—"Only thirty miles to Wall Drug!"—"Only twenty miles to Wall Drug!"—"Only another ten miles to go before WALL DRUG!" Presumably the expectation of getting ever closer would turn an ordinary shopping center into some sort of transcendental recreational/commercial experience. The radius had grown. "Only fifty miles to Wall Drug!" "Wall Drug, in just another hundred miles!" Finally, it metastasized through the entire Midwest, becoming the omphalos of its own coordinate system: "I don't know what state we're in, but it's only another two hundred eighty miles to Wall Drug." Some wag at US McMurdo Station had briefly planted a "9,333 Miles To Wall Drug" sign at the South Pole.

After the sky cracked, the Wall Drug coordinate system started to impose itself more and more upon the ordinary coordinate system of longitude and latitude. Worse, the two didn't exactly correspond. You could be driving from New York to New Jersey, and find a billboard promising Wall Drug in only thirty miles. Drive another ten, and sure enough, WALL DRUG, TWENTY MILES. Drive ten more, and you'd be promised a South Dakotan shopping center, only ten miles away. Drive another ten, and... who knows? No one has returned from Wall Drug in a generation. It's become not only an omphalos, but a black hole in the center of the Untied States, a one-way attraction and attractor fed by an interstate highway system which never gives up its prey. Some say it is in Heaven, others in Hell, others that it remains in South Dakota, from which no word has been heard for thirty years.

Interstate travel is still possible, but it follows a very specific pattern. You go forward until you see a Wall Drug billboard. Then you hastily switch directions and go back to the previous city, transferring you back to the normal American landscape. Then you tentatively go forward again. After enough iterations, you can make it from Point A to Point B intact. But if ever you see a Wall Drug billboard and continue to travel, the land will start looking less and less like where you came from, more and more like the grassy semi-arid plains of South Dakota. Once that happens, you can still turn back. But if you turn back too late, you may find that Wall Drug is in that direction too, that every point of the compass brings you closer to Wall Drug, with no choice but to remain in place forever or go boldly towards that undiscovered country from whose bourn no traveler returns.

This was what had happened to the Dakotas and the Northern Plains. That close to the omphalos, even a few feet down a side street would be enough to lose yourself forever. Automobile travel became impossible. Thousands of small farming communities lost their lifelines to the outside world. Large cities dependent on food shipments starved, right in the middle of amber fields of grain. Then came the Broadcast to finish them off. A few small farms survived here and there, but otherwise the area was as empty as it had been back when the buffalo roamed.

Jane cursed, and we started looking for an exit. We turned back to Barstow, then turned back around. We'd only gone about ten miles before another Wall Drug sign made us repeat the whole cycle.

"I'm tired," said Jane. "You drive."

"I don't know how," I said. I'd grown up in Oakland, which wasn't very car-friendly. And by the time I turned sixteen, technology had declined to the point where only the more expensive models with the Motive Name were still working.

"You put your foot on the pedal, and if something is in your way you turn this big wheel here," said Jane. "It's the Mojave Desert. There's nothing for a hundred miles. You'll live."

So I drove. It was a nice car. A white Cadillac. The scholars tell us that God drives a Plymouth Fury, for it is written in Jeremiah 32:37: "He drove them out of the land in His Fury." But the Twelve Apostles shared a Honda Accord, for it is written in Acts 5:12: "They were all with one Accord." The commentators speculate this may have been the same car Jesus used when he drove the moneychangers out of the Temple, though if there were more than four or so moneychangers it might have required a minor miracle. My mother used to have a really old beat-up Honda Accord. For all I know maybe it was the same one they used in the New Testament. It gave up the ghost after a year or so and we were back to taking buses.

I wondered what she would think seeing me now, behind the wheels of a Cadillac. Cadillacs were from a different world, the world of CEOs and Silicon Valley theonomics. I'd read the history of the company once; it was named for Antoine de la Mothe Cadillac, the man who founded Detroit. His name comes in turn from the French words *ca du lac*, meaning "house by the lake." A man named "house by the lake" founded the city of Detroit. This was not a coincidence because nothing is ever a coincidence.

LAS VEGAS, 141 MILES, the sign said as it whizzed past.

Las Vegas comes from Spanish *vega* meaning "meadow," but we Anglophones have a different association. Vega is the brightest star in the summer sky. Its name comes from the Arabic word *waqi* meaning "falling," because they thought its constellation looked like a bird falling from the heavens. You know who *else* was the brightest of stars before falling from Heaven? Right. That's who you named your city after. Good going, Spaniards. And so of *course* it became the sinfulness capital of the world.

Las Vegas means "the meadows," but it also means "the fallen ones." Kabbalistically, we were traveling from a city named "the angels" to a city named "the fallen ones." We were doing this *even though* the power of nominative determinism was so strong that a man whose name meant "house by the lake" had just so happened to found the biggest American city on the continent's biggest lake.

We were not clever people. I hoped that Ana would get here sooner rather than later.

II.

Beyond Barstow was Yermo, whose name meant "wilderness," and Nebo, named for the tomb of Moses. On we drove, over the Hollow Hills, through the Yarrow Ravine Rattlesnake Habitat, past the Alien Jerky Store. We passed Zzyzx—a name made for kabbalistic analysis if ever there was one. We sped through the dishonestly-named dingy border town of Primm, then the honestly-named dingy border town of Roach. We saw the Spring Mountains, crossed to the far side of Paradise.

I had hoped Jane would fall asleep so I could escape, but of course no such luck. She took out the book we had stolen from the angels and leafed through it, going back to read the same few pages again and again. Finally I'd had enough.

"What's it about?" I asked.

"Mind your own business," Jane told me, but without anger. More in a dreamy, distant way as she watched the scenery speed past.

So I pressed my luck. "I'm falling asleep here. You can at least give me some conversation."

Jane nodded. "Fine," she said. "A riddle for you. How is Rhode Island like a falling bird?"

I answered without even thinking. "There is Providence in both."

Jane smiled a tiny bit. Maybe I had passed some kind of test? But she just said: "Explain."

"It's a line from Shakespeare. 'There is special providence in the fall of a sparrow.' But he's paraphrasing Matthew 10:29, 'Are not two sparrows sold for a farthing? and one of them shall not fall on the ground without your Father. But the very hairs of your head are all numbered. Fear ye not therefore, ye are of more value than many sparrows.'"

"Yes," said Jane. "But what does it *mean*?"

I'd never heard a kabbalistic gloss on those verses before. The top rabbis wouldn't even touch the New Testament. But the basic point was clear enough: "During Jesus' time, little birds like sparrows were used as a cheap sacrificial offering for people who couldn't afford bigger ones. People at the marketplace sold them for a pittance, so they became a metaphor for anything insignificant or worthless. Jesus said God nevertheless watches over each one. And so we should be heartened, for if He watches over these birds, He must certainly watch over us."

"Anything else?" asked Jane.

"The Shakespeare quote is from Hamlet," I recalled. "Horatio predicts Hamlet will lose a fight and suggests he bail. But Hamlet doesn't care about the odds. He says, 'We defy augury,' then paraphrases the verse from Matthew. If everything happens according to a divine plan, he's got nothing to fear."

"Anything else?"

"There are a bunch of verses from William Blake that say pretty much the same thing. Um. 'A Skylark wounded in the wing / A Cherubim does cease to sing.' Some others along those lines."

"Anything else?"

"I don't think so," I said. "Why do you ask?"

"It might be the secret of the Other King."

I almost drove the car into a cactus.

III.

In the mid 90s, Las Vegas was on edge with rumors of some kind of necromantic cult. The Comet King had come to the city, smoked out the cultists, and personally executed the leader. There it should have ended.

As the century drew to a close, the rumors started up again. Killing the leader had only made him stronger. Now he was regrouping. Those who died in the fight against him became soldiers in his armies. He wore a deep scarlet robe with a hood covering his head. No one had ever seen his face.

The Comet King had other problems now. His great crusade had failed. His wife was dead. He kept to his room, leaving the day-to-day work of governance to his Cometspawn. They were less confident than he was. They stayed out of Las Vegas, delegated the problem to subordinates, hoped it would take care of itself.

In March 2001, the necromancer seized control of Vegas in a spectacular coup. There was no bloodshed. Black-robed figures with skeletal faces and inhuman strength came from nowhere and demanded the allegiance of the city's governor and garrison. The necromancer declared himself a king and took up residence beneath the great black pyramid of Luxor. He didn't provide an origin story or even say how his subjects should address him. The partisans of the Comet King began calling him "the other king," and the name stuck.

The Comet King, still brokenhearted, at first refused to leave his mourning chamber. But when his children begged and cajoled him, he rose from his bed, gathered his armies, and took up the great sword Sigh for the last time. He marched west. The Other King and his undead legions marched east. On July 29, they met in the Never Summer Mountains near Fort Collins, and the two armies fought each other to a stalemate.

Then the Other King himself took the field, ripping through the Comet King's troops with Names of fire and night. The Coloradan line began to buckle. And so the Comet King, looking terribly old with his white hair and lined face, strode to the front of his ranks and challenged the necromancer to single combat.

They fought high above the earth, darting in and out of clouds, their attacks shooting like lightning to the barren ground beneath. The mountains shook. The air thundered with the sound of secret magic.

The Comet King's body dropped lifeless to the ground.

The Coloradans fell back in horror and rout, but the Cometspawn moved among them, rallying their troops. The Cometspawn broke through the enemy ranks to rescue their father's body. The undead seemed timid, offering only token resistance. Finally, the dark armies retreated back to Las Vegas. Spies reported that the Other King had been gravely wounded, a Fisher King wound that never healed, his mind intact but his body hopelessly mangled.

From then on, he stayed underneath his pyramid, directing his armies from afar. If Colorado had hoped his injury would slow his conquests, they were disappointed. First Nevada fell. Then Arizona, and all New Mexico west of Santa Fe. The Cometspawn lost battle after battle. They retreated to the Rockies, and finally to their citadel in Cheyenne Mountain. The Other King attacked the mountain, failed, tried again, failed again, and finally left them there, safe but trapped. If Jane was telling the truth, she was part of that last redoubt. The secrets of the Other King would be more important than anything else she could bring back to her besieged people.

"How is it the secret of the Other King?!"

"Do you know the Urim and Thummim?"

The Bible says the Urim and Thummim were a divination device worn by the High Priest of Israel—stones inscribed with Hebrew letters and set into a breastplate. The King would ask a question, the High Priest would pray, and the letters on the stones would light up and spell out an answer. The secret was lost before the Babylonian Captivity, but rediscovered by the Comet King during the 80s.

"Back in '01," Jane told me after I'd answered in the affirmative, "when the Cometspawn first started worrying about the Other King, Father Ellis consulted the Urim and Thummim about who he was and where he'd come from. But Ellis never told the Cometspawn the stones' answer before he disappeared, and without him they can't repeat the ritual. But the angels help carry messages to the breastplate. And they record everything they do. That's what we took from the library. The angelic record of the divinations of the Urim and Thummim. And that was the breastplate's answer to Ellis. That riddle."

"Las Vegas' name means fallen bird," I blurted out.

"What?"

"The name of the star Vega comes from the Arabic word *waqi*, meaning 'fallen' or 'falling.' They named it that because the constellation looked like a bird falling from the sky. So Las Vegas could mean 'the fallen birds.' And the Other King's secret is that not a bird falls to the ground without God's decision. There is providence in the fall of a sparrow."

"Huh," said Jane, and upon her features flashed very briefly that look I had seen when I figured out the angels' filing system. As if briefly remembering I was a human being instead of a pet or object, and seeming a little uncomfortable with the fact. "That's... interesting."

"But not very actionable," I said.

"No," Jane agreed. I imagined she'd been hoping for some secret weakness that the Coloradans could use to turn the tide of combat. A kabbalistic connection between the Book of Matthew, the city of Las Vegas, and divine providence didn't seem immediately helpful.

"Will you be safe in Vegas?" It wasn't a good place to be a Coloradan operative.

"No," she said. "Neither of us will be. I'm sorry I had to bring you here, Aaron. Really, I am."

And then we passed out the belly of the last little valley, and before us loomed the towers of Las Vegas, capital of the United Kingdom of Great Basin. Jane looked more nervous than I'd ever seen her. We switched places; she took the wheel. Beggars and prostitutes and drug dealers started knocking on our car windows at the stoplights, making their respective pleas.

The sun set behind the Red Rock Mountains as we checked into the

Stratosphere Hotel. I repeated Jane's secret to myself, like a mantra. Even in a falling bird, there is providence. Even in Las Vegas, God is with us. Somewhere.

Night fell upon the city of the Other King.

Chapter Thirty-One

The Foundation Of Empire

Together, we can build a better America, colonize it, and use the old one for raw materials and target practice.
—Steven Kaas

January 30, 1981
Camp David, Maryland

I.

The overt meaning of "Camp David" is "a summer retreat for the President of the US."

The kabbalistic meaning of Camp David is "a place where enemies reconcile." This we derive from I Samuel 26. David (the future King David of Israel) is supposed to be in the service of King Saul, but has been AWOL for a while. Saul suspects him of disloyalty; David needs to clear his name of the false accusation. So he and his friend Abishai sneak into Saul's camp at night, make their way into Saul's tent, and take Saul's spear while Saul snoozes obliviously. The next morning, he returns to the camp and presents Saul's spear back to him, proving that he could have assassinated Saul and taken the kingship if he had been disloyal. Saul said, "I have sinned: return, my son David: for I will no more do thee harm, because my soul was precious in thine eyes this day: behold, I have played the fool, and have erred exceedingly." And David answered, "The Lord render to every man his righteousness and his faithfulness; for the Lord delivered thee into my hand to day, but I would not stretch forth mine hand against the Lord's anointed."

The Comet King needed to make enemies reconcile, so he had invited them to Camp David. In the six years since the Outer Gate scandal and the collapse of central authority, the United States had split into two dozen petty chiefdoms, emphasis on "petty." The Texas Technocracy was launching border raids on the Arkansas Archonate; the Shogun of Michigan and the Khagan of Muskegon both claimed Grand Rapids; the Arizona Aristocracy and Utah Utopia were on the brink of war over the brink of the Grand Canyon. The Comet King would have considered all of this beneath his notice, except that peace and stability were a precondition for what he was planning. Through a series of threats, bribes, and delicate negotiations, he had convinced everyone to come to Camp David and settle their differences.

Right now he was staring down the Pharaoh of Fairbanks, a grizzled man who had owned a lumber company before the crisis. "You mean to tell me," he asked the Pharaoh, "that you didn't even read the Treaty of Rome?"

"I'm not gonna let a fourteen-year-old assign me homework!" Jala had been honest; he'd told them he was four years old. They'd all thought it was a transparent lie, something to boost his aura of mystery. Fine. It was hard enough getting them to respect him when they thought he was a teenager. After correcting them a few times, he'd just gone along with it.

"There must be like a hundred articles!" the Pharaoh continued. The Comet King had asked everyone to read the Treaty of Rome, the founding document of the European Union, before they arrived. His plan was to foist something similar upon them, an American Union, to take care of their quarrels and establish the peace he needed. He was learning new things every day. Yesterday he had learned that even when it was very important that a politician read a document, they would turn a request to read it into a dominance competition.

"Two hundred forty-eight, actually" said Jala, staring him straight in the eye. He had decided he was going to spend today learning how to win dominance competitions. His eyes drilled into the Pharaoh of Fairbanks like miniature stars. Jala had noticed if he did this intensely enough, after a while the other person would back down. *Two hundred forty-eight articles in the Treaty of Rome*, he thought to himself as he stared. *Also the number of positive commandments in the Hebrew Bible, and the gematria value of "Abraham," father of the Jewish nation*. He stored this away for future reference.

Somebody grumbled. Jala realized that in staring down the Alaskan, he had alienated some of the other leaders. "All right," he said. "Forget Rome. Let me show you what I'm aiming for." He handed out copies of another document marked PROPOSED CONSTITUTION OF THE UNTIED STATES.

"Typo in the title," said the Maharaja of Indiana.

"No, there isn't," said the Comet King, staring at him. He wasn't sure if this was a dominance contest, but he didn't want to take the chance that it might be. "Just read."

Even when it was very important that a politician read a document, they would turn a request to read it into a dominance competition. But even though the Comet King looked only fourteen years old, even though he was dressed in black-and-silver robes that looked faintly ridiculous in the north Virginia sun, even though the Proposed Constitution Of The Untied States was long and dense—Jala West was a hard man to say no to. And Camp David was a place for enemies to reconcile.

So they read. They read and debated. Who would enforce free trade across state borders? Would the President have more than ceremonial power? What kind of representation would the union get in the United Nations? Where would the refugees from the Dakotas be resettled? Who would get what water rights from the Mississippi? What would become of the state that could no longer be named, the one whose name killed everyone who spoke it?

After about an hour of debate, Jala noticed something strange. He seemed to be losing.

At first it was subtle. Some excess resistance here. A little too much dissent there. The Kansas Kakistocracy didn't want to stop cattle raids; he had priced that in. The Oklahoma Ochlocracy was concerned about reinstituting federal courts; that wasn't so surprising. But the longer the negotiations continued, the surer he was that something was wrong.

He stopped talking entirely, devoting his attention to watching the ebb and flow of social signals around the table. The Minarch of Minnesota wasn't willing to patrol the Great Lakes against Canadian pirates, but who had framed the issue that way? The Padishah of Paducah was demanding more water rights, but who was subtly signaling support for her more outrageous claims?

A few minutes, and he was certain of it. Somebody with powers equal to his own was manipulating the room, subtly undoing every knot he tried to tie, snipping his web as fast as he could build it. And he had a pretty good idea who it was.

When the negotiations paused for lunch, Jala quietly approached the Caliph of California.

"A word, Mr. Reagan?"

II.

In the chaos and horror of the Broadcast period, the previous governor of California had taken his own life. The state had teetered on the verge of anarchy before a young movie star had knit it together through force of will and sheer charisma. Matthew 7:29 — "For he spoke as one having authority, and not as the scribes and Pharisees." He traveled the land, talking about the American Dream, and where he went the impossible seemed possible. People dropped their quarrels and swore loyalty. John 7:46 — "Never man spake like this man."

Now as they walked together through the gardens of Camp David. Jala looked him over. Reagan seemed normal enough, aside from his Hollywood good looks. Everything he seemed sounded good, reasonable, even conciliatory.

Jala didn't buy it for a second.

"It's young men like you who make America great," Reagan was saying. "When word of what you did in Colorado reached California, that gave us hope. That was what we needed, more than funds, more than armaments. When people have hope, they..."

"Sorry," interrupted Jala, "but what *are* you?"

Reagan didn't skip a beat. "Sometimes a crisis can make ordinary men do extraordinary things, Mr. West. I'm just an old actor who realized his country needed him. And when your country needs you, you can't say no."

"Can you cut the inspirational folksiness for *one second* and tell me what I need to know? What *are* you?"

"I think," said Ronald Reagan, "that we should go back to the conference room and have lunch."

"No. Not until you tell me what you are."

"Come on, kid. Let's finish up here and go back. Do it for the Gipper."

They turned around, started walking back to the conference room. Reagan explained some of the chores he did around his ranch, and Jala nodded along, fascinated by his rugged charm.

Then: wait. What happened? Jala shook his head as if awakening from a dream. Why were they walking back? Why had he stopped asking questions? What was a Gipper? Not even a real word. Not English, at least. Enochian? No, didn't sound like a European capital. Hebrew, then. *Yes.* He made a connection; pieces snapped into place. *The mighty one.* Interesting. It had been a very long time since anybody last thought much about *haGibborim.*

Jala paused. Reagan stopped walking, confused. Jala stared at him, a stare that could have won a dominance competition against a mountain. But that wasn't what he was after this time. He stared and he squinted until finally, faintly, he made out the Name of God written in glowing letters upon Reagan's head.

"I know your True Name," he said. "You are Gadiriel, the Lady of Los Angeles, the maker of golems. The angel of celebrity and popularity and pretense. This is your work."

When Reagan next spoke, it was with a lilting feminine voice, one with a faint undertone of amusement. "Come, Jalaketu ben Kokab. Let's go somewhere a little more private."

III.

They walked through the gardens of Camp David, paying no attention to the noonday sun.

"I won't let you take over the country," said Gadiriel/Reagan. "I left Heaven because rule by angels is the most boring thing imaginable."

"I'm not trying to take over! Just stabilize! All these silly border wars are killing people! Unless we act now, America will be crippled for a generation!"

"All these silly border wars are *beautiful*. So much ridiculous heroism! So many desperate escapes! It's like the Wild West again!"

Jalaketu learned new things every day. Today he was learning the value system of a certain flamboyant fallen angel, plus exactly whose tastes the last fifty years of Hollywood blockbusters had been appealing to. He wasn't going to reach her by appealing to stability. He wasn't even going to reach her by appealing to the right thing to do. He tried a different tactic.

"Don't you care about America?"

Reagan frowned. "Dear, you're what? Four years old? I've cared about America longer than there's *been* an America. I *am* America. I watched it through the curtain of Uriel's machinery, and when I could I sent my love through the cracks. Who do you think it was who made George Washington so dashing on his stallion? Who put the flourish in John Hancock's signature? I stood beside all those foolish beautiful people talking about cities on hills and nations of gentlemen-farmers and the new Athens and I gave their words my fire. Who do you think used Nettie Maynard to feed Lincoln Confederate secrets? Who do you think whispered the Battle Hymn of the Republic into Julia Ward Howe's ears as she slept? Mine eyes have seen the glory of the coming of the Lord. He is trampling out the vintage where the grapes of wrath are stored. He has loosed the fateful lightning of His terrible swift sword. His truth is marching on."

"I have read a fiery Gospel writ in burnished rows of steel," said Jalaketu. "As ye deal with my contemners, so with you my grace shall deal. Let the hero, born of woman, crush the serpent with his heel."

"You're a fan?"

"I think I might be the referent." Then Jalaketu knelt before Reagan, like David had knelt before Saul three thousand years earlier. "I wronged you, my lady," he said. "I shouldn't have questioned your patriotism. But *the Union must be preserved*."

"Not by giving it to you."

"To you, then."

"What?"

"I don't want the Presidency. It's yours. You have my endorsement."

"I only took this form to keep California from tearing itself apart."

"And now you will prevent America from doing the same."

"I meant what I said. Rule by angels is dreadful. Unspeakably boring."

"You'll be a caretaker president, then. Get the Untied States set up, then pass it on to a worthy successor. Like George Washington did."

"I have no right!"

"Look. Jefferson. Declaration of Independence. Was that you?"

"What do you think?"

"We hold these truths to be self-evident, that all men are created equal, that they are endowed by their Creator with certain unalienable Rights, that among these are Life, Liberty and the pursuit of Happiness. That to secure these rights, Governments are instituted among Men, deriving their just powers from the consent of the governed, — That whenever any Form of Government becomes destructive of these ends, it is the Right of the People to alter or to abolish it, and to institute new Government, laying its foundation on such principles and organizing its powers in such form, as to them shall seem most likely to effect their Safety and Happiness."

"Don't you twist my words at me. I know what I meant!"

Jalaketu answered: "It is not in Heaven."

Reagan started laughing. Then kept laughing. Then laughed some more. "You are really something, Jalaketu ben Raziel. You really think you can do this thing?"

"Somebody has to and no one else will."

"Touché."

A staffer came running up. "Mr. Reagan, Mr. West! There you are! Lunch is over and the rest of the attendees are waiting on you."

Reagan's voice shifted back to the masculine, drawling register that would entrance millions. "Guess we lost track of the time out here! Well, Jala, are you ready? Let's go make America great again!"

Chapter Thirty-Two

The Human Form Divine

August 7, 1991
Gulf of Mexico

I.

Sohu stretched, splayed out further. "Knock knock," she said.

OH. THIS AGAIN.

"Knock knock."

WHO'S... THERE?

"So."

SO WHO?

"Sohu's at the door, better let her in."

HA! HA! HA! Uriel's laughter boomed, shook the clouds, shook the ocean, drowned out the ever-present thunder of the surrounding storm. It was a fiery golden laugh, like pyrotechnics, like solar flares.

I AM ONLY LAUGHING TO BE POLITE, he finally said. I DON'T ACTUALLY GET IT.

Sohu's face fell.

"It's a pun!" she said. "Because you said so who, and it sounds like my name, Sohu."

I SEE, said Uriel, suspiciously.

"Yes," said Sohu. "You are going to learn this. I have decided. You will learn knock knock jokes, and you will be good at them."

UM.

"I'm serious about this! You're like the best person I know at finding unexpected connections between words and meanings! That's what jokes are! You're missing your calling! Come on! Try it!"

HOW?

"Start with 'knock knock.'"

KNOCK KNOCK.

"Who's there?"

I AM NOT SURE.

"Say a word! Any word! The first thing you think of!"

ALEPH.

"Okay. Aleph who?"

I AM STILL NOT SURE.

"A pun. Some sentence that includes a pun on the word aleph. Something that sounds like it."

UM. ACCORDING TO THE BOOK OF ZECHARIAH, THE RESURRECTION OF THE DEAD WILL BEGIN ON THE MOUNT OF OLIVES.

"How does that—? Oh. Aleph. Olives. Um. Sort of. But it needs to be sudden and surprising. It needs to have pizazz. You'll get it eventually."

One got the impression that if Uriel had not been hundreds of feet tall, Sohu would have tried to pat his head.

ALL OF MY JOKES ARE TERRIBLE.

"Aaaaaaaaaah!" Sohu waved her arms. "That! That should have been your joke! Knock knock! Who's there? Aleph. Aleph who? All of my jokes are terrible."

I AM SORRY.

"I don't get it! You are so good at all of this language stuff, and you can find like seven zillion connections between apparently unrelated words, and you can't crack a basic knock-knock joke! Why? WHY?"

THEY ARE HARD.

"Learning every human language is hard! Knock knock jokes are easy!"

IF I TRY TO LEARN HOW TO DO KNOCK KNOCK JOKES, WILL YOU TRY TO LEARN EVERY HUMAN LANGUAGE?

"Uriel. You. Do. Not. Understand. Humans."

The archangel harrumphed and went back to running the universe.

II.

OF ALL KABBALISTIC CORRESPONDENCES, THE MOST IMPORTANT IS THE CLAIM THAT GOD MADE MAN IN HIS OWN IMAGE. EXPLAIN HOW THE STRUCTURE OF DIVINITY CORRESPONDS TO THE HUMAN BODY.

"The ten fingers are the ten sephirot, the ten emanations by which God manipulates the material world. The bilateral symmetry is the two branches of the Tree of Life, which correspond to the two human arms. The right branch is called Mercy and the left branch is called Severity."

SEVERAL MONTHS AGO, I GAVE YOU A HOMEWORK ASSIGNMENT. YOU WERE TO FIGURE OUT WHY IN HUMAN POLITICS, THE RIGHT-WING TENDS TO BE CONCERNED WITH JUSTICE AND THE LEFT-WING WITH MERCY, EVEN THOUGHT THESE ARE THE OPPOSITES OF THE KABBALISTIC CORRESPONDENCES.

"Uriel, all the homework you give me is impossible."

I WILL GIVE YOU A HINT. MATTHEW 25:32. BEFORE HIM ALL THE NATIONS WILL BE GATHERED, AND HE WILL SEPARATE THEM FROM ONE ANOTHER, AS A SHEPHERD SEPARATES THE SHEEP FROM THE GOATS. HE WILL SET THE SHEEP ON HIS RIGHT HAND, BUT THE GOATS ON HIS LEFT.

"There's nothing so impossible it can't be made more confusing by adding in some apocalyptic prophecy."

IT IS NOT IMPOSSIBLE. A SIMPLE SOLUTION RESOLVES BOTH PROBLEMS. THINK ABOUT IT. YOU ARE VERY SMART.

Sohu thought for a moment.

I WILL GIVE YOU ANOTHER HINT. DEUTERONOMY 5:4.

"The Lord spoke to you face to face at the mountain from the midst of the fire. Uh. Wait, yes, that makes sense!"

YES?

"We are all face to face with God. So our right is His left, and vice versa!"

YES. SO HOW DOES GOD PART THE RIGHTEOUS ON HIS RIGHT SIDE AND THE WICKED UPON HIS LEFT?

"He... oh, He just says, 'Everyone who wants to go to Heaven, get to the right.' And the wicked, who think only of themselves, go to their own right. And the virtuous, who are always thinking of God, go to God's right."

YES.

"So God's right and humans' left means mercy, and God's left and humans' right means justice."

YES. THIS IS WHY WHEN PEOPLE TALK ABOUT JUSTICE, THEY SPECIFY THAT THEY MEAN HUMAN RIGHTS.

"I think that might be something different."

NO.

"You're silly."

I AM N... Uriel trailed off, as if deep in thought. Finally, he asked:

TELL ME THE KABBALISTIC SIGNIFICANCE OF THE ROOT R-K-T.

Sohu knew better than to argue at this point. "Um. Wrecked. Racked. Ragged, sort of. Rocked. Rickety. And it's got the T-R combination which we already talked about signifying pure power. Something raw and destructive. Why do you ask?"

Uriel stood listening intently. SOMETHING IS HAPPENING INVOLVING THOSE LETTERS.

A background whine crescendoed into a scream. A rocket streaked across the sky, headed straight toward them. Lightning-fast, Uriel reached out a giant hand and caught it in his palm.

OH. he said.

Sohu was lying face-down on the cloud, wishing she had a desk to duck-and-cover under.

IT IS FINE, said Uriel. THIS IS HOW PEOPLE SEND ME MESSAGES.

"They couldn't just pray?"

SO MANY PEOPLE PRAY THAT I HAVE STOPPED PAYING ATTENTION, said Uriel.

"What if somebody actually tries to bomb you?!"

YOUR FATHER WOULD TELL ME, said Uriel. SINCE HE DID NOT SAY ANYTHING, I ASSUMED IT WAS SAFE. He held the rocket up to get a closer look. It was a Minuteman missile, the sort used by the United States Air Force. Written on one side, in what was startlingly good calligraphy for a message on a cylindrical surface, was the message: "*You are invited to attend the Multilateral Conference On The Middle Eastern Peace Process in Madrid, starting October 27.*"

Sohu clapped her hands.

"You should go!" she said.

NO.

"Why no?"

I NEVER GO TO THESE THINGS. THEY ARE TERRIBLE AND FULL OF ARGUMENTS AND NO ONE LIKES ME.

"Everyone likes you! They want your opinion."

HAVE YOU EVER BEEN TO AN INTERNATIONAL CONFERENCE?

"Father goes all the time. He says that negotiation is the key to power."

I DO NOT WANT POWER.

"Yes you do! You control the world! You have power over the weather and the stars and plants and animals and all those things. And they all work really well! Maybe if you tried to have some power over people too, *we* would work really well."

STARS AND ANIMALS AND WEATHER ARE EASY. PEOPLE ARE HARD.

"Father says that diplomacy is about playing the game. Figure out what people want and explain to them why doing things your way will get it for them better than doing things the other way. It's about being creative. You're this genius who can come up with connections between the Parable of the Sheep and Goats and human rights. Diplomacy would be *so much fun* for you."

THAMIEL WILL BE THERE. I AM SURE HE WILL. EVERYONE LIKES THAMIEL. THEY LISTEN TO HIM.

"They listen to him because he talks to them! I've seen you and Thamiel! You zapped him like a fly! Thamiel has power because he *tries* to have power. If you tried to have power, you would have even more than he does! You could bring peace to the Middle East. And you could get people to join together, like my father does. You could have everybody join together and fight Thamiel."

I AM NOT SURE ANGELS HAVING POWER OVER HUMANS IS GOOD. I REMEMBER WHEN SOME OF THE ANGELS TRIED TO GET POWER OVER HUMANS. GADIRIEL. SAMYAZAZ. EVERYONE WAS VERY UPSET.

"Gadiriel became President and saved the Untied States! It was great! I got to go to the White House with Father and have dinner with her golem-avatar once!"

THE BIBLE DOES NOT SEEM TO LIKE ANGELS RULING OVER HUMANS. THE NEPHILIM CAUSED NOAH'S FLOOD. GOD APPOINTED SAUL AS KING OF THE ISRAELITES, EVEN THOUGH HE HAD MANY ANGELS TO CHOOSE FROM. IF I WERE TO RULE OVER HUMANS THE SAME WAY I RULE OVER STARS AND WEATHER, THEN THEY WOULD BECOME MACHINE PARTS THE SAME WAY STARS AND WEATHER ARE.

"No one's saying you have to rule them! Diplomacy is like the opposite of ruling people! You just have to convince them with good arguments and by seeming imposing! You're amazing at arguments! And you're really good at seeming imposing!"

She may or may not have muttered something that sounded like "…to people who don't know you very well."

ARGUMENTS ARE TERRIBLE.

"Come on," said Sohu. "Just try it once. Because I asked you to."

The archangel took a moment to reply, cutting himself off a few times as if thinking better of what he was going to say. Finally:

I WILL NOT ENJOY THIS.

"But you'll try?"

Uriel grumbled. I HAVE JUST LOST A NEGOTIATION WITH AN EIGHT-YEAR-OLD GIRL. THIS DOES NOT BODE WELL FOR MY DIPLOMATIC SKILLS.

Chapter Thirty-Three

The Doors Of Perception

May 13, 2017
Ensenada, Mexico

Bizarre surrealist painter Salvador Dalí once said: "I do not do drugs. I am drugs." He was being silly. He wasn't drugs. He was Salvador Dalí.

The men rowing out on little boats heavy with building supplies for *All Your Heart*? *They* were drugs.

Ana watched them lazily, her head resting against the green mast. The three men were in their cabin, and the place was crowded and sweaty. She'd told James that Amoxiel would be out here watching her, so where was the danger? Their first mate had reluctantly agreed.

Ensenada looked like any other quiet harbor town. The people coming aboard looked like any other people. Maybe a little sleepier, their pupils a little wider. But she knew the truth. They weren't people. They were drugs. Even if there were people in Ensenada — which she doubted — they wouldn't be sent for something important like this.

James had rowed ashore alone when the sun rose. Amoxiel and the Captain had watched him very carefully as he landed on a dock, found an Ensenadan man, and started talking to him. They couldn't hear what he was saying, but they didn't care. They were looking for one thing — did the Ensenadan feed or inject James with any material? As best they could tell, they didn't. James rowed back to *All Your Heart*, and the crew let him back on. He seemed normal. But he *would* seem normal, no matter what happened.

Simeon came on deck and sat beside her. "Ever been to Mexico before, Ana?"

"No," she said. "I've seen druggies, though. You?"

"Once," he said. "In the nineties. On business. And then a little tourism afterwards. Mexico City. Veracruz. And Teotihuacan. With its giant pyramids, standing all solemn and huge in a row."

"Solomon *wise*," corrected Ana. "*Goliath* huge."

"What?"

"Sorry! It's a game I used to play, with a friend. Unintentional Biblical pun corrections. It's... kind of compulsive now." An awkward silence, which she tried to fill. "What *is* your business, anyway?"

"You don't know?" He seemed genuinely surprised.

Then, as the first of the druggies came aboard, enlightenment struck. "You're Simeon Azore! From Bareketh!"

It was so obvious. The face she was looking at, minus ten years and with darker hair, could have been the face she'd seen in various magazines and TV news shows. The face behind Bareketh Capital and an early-level investor in Countenance and half of the most successful theonomics. A stakeholder in every company she had protested in the last ten years. "But... but you're terrible!" Then she recoiled. "Sorry! Um! Also... compulsive, I guess. I didn't mean to..."

One of the druggies introduced himself to James as Ivan Colero, a naval repair technician in the Mexican navy. They'd paid well, he said, very well, and they'd gotten themselves the best. The Drug Lord knew that they needed to be on their way quickly, and he and his men would just need a day, maybe less. They could work quickly. Impossibly quickly.

"Let me guess," said Simeon, "you're one of those people who can give entire speeches about how the theonomics are ruining everything."

"Uh," said Ana.

"Go on," said Simeon. "Get it out."

"Um," said Ana.

"I can already tell we're both going to be miserable until you've said your speech, so just get it out."

"Uh... my cousin is better at this, but... um... God is born free but everywhere is in chains. The Names, our birthright as children of God possessing the Divine Spark, are patented as if they were especially clever designs for widgets, then whored out to buy yachts for billionaires."

"Mmmm," interrupted Simeon, "I didn't buy this ship. Just booked passage on it. Give me some credit for self-restraint."

"The Fertile Name brings forth grain from the earth, speeding the growth of crops by nearly half. Children in Ethiopia starve to death, and Ethiopian farmers cannot use the Fertile Name to grow the corn that would save them.

Why not? Because Serpens holds the patent and demands $800 up front from any farmer who wants to take advantage of it. The Purifying Name instantly kills eighteen species of harmful bacteria, including two that are resistant to all but the most toxic antibiotics. But two-thirds of American hospitals have no one licensed to use the Purifying Name. Why not? Because they can't afford the licensing fees demanded by Gogmagog."

The druggies began to hammer on the red mast. Ana spoke louder so she could hear herself above the noise.

"In the old days, we told ourselves that poverty was a fact of life. That there wasn't enough food or medicine or clothing or housing to go around. Then it was true. Now it is false. To feed the hungry and shelter the homeless no longer requires scarce resources. It requires only a word. A word that the entire international system of governance — corporations, politicians, UNSONG — has united to prevent the needy from ever obtaining. 86% of known Names are held by five corporations. The largest, Serpens, has total assets of $174 million... no, sorry... billion... I told you my cousin is better at this. Serpens' CEO, has a net worth of $600 million, houses in California, Texas, and Virginia state, and a hundred fifty foot long superyacht.

"Meanwhile, not only does she employ some of the finest kabbalists in the world to hide the Fertile Name behind klipot, but if some enterprising mind breaks through the encryption and sends the plaintext Name to those starving Ethiopians, she will call up UNSONG, call upon whatever treaties we have with Ethiopia, and get everyone who saw the Name put in jail for life. Because if people who can't give Cate Ilyov $800 for a bigger yacht try to feed themselves, they are, our government tells us, a Threat To Our Way Of Life.

"Since the sky cracked, Singers have worked on one founding principle: that nobody, no religion or corporation or government, nobody has a monopoly on God. We demand that the klipot be broken, that all known non-destructive Names of God be placed in the public domain and made freely available to all, and that UNSONG be disbanded and its resources diverted to something useful, like fighting the demons. And as long as that demand isn't met, we'll do it ourselves. Break whatever klipot we can, spread the Names to anyone who wants to hear them, and stay a step ahead of the law.

"The third commandment says, 'Thou shalt not take the name of the Lord your God in vain; the Lord will not take guiltless He who takes His name in vain.' I don't know when Judgment Day is coming, but you have to admit the fabric of reality hasn't been holding up very well lately. And if

God does show up and ask us how we've been using His holy Names that He has given to us, I'd rather we as a civilization be able to answer that we used them to feed the poor, heal the sick, and shelter the homeless. Not that we used them to buy multimillionaire Cate Ilyov a bigger yacht. Because that seems about as in vain as it's possible to get."

"Seven out of ten," said Simeon.

"What?" Ana asked.

"Seven out of ten. It wasn't bad. But I've heard better ones. You should have heard what my nephew used to say. Also, Countenance pushed ahead of Serpens three months ago. I feel personally slighted that you still call them the biggest."

But he was smiling as he said it.

"But why? You know the arguments? Fine! So how can you just sit there and keep doing it?"

"You think of this through some kind of romantic David-and-Goliath lens, where all you need to do is break up the evil corporations and..."

"...why not? You're gigantic, you're evil, and you crush anyone who tries to stand against you! I would say you're going three for three, Goliath-wise! So why *shouldn't* I..."

"...Goliath *huge*. *Solomon* wise."

"What?" Then, "*What?*" Ana was some strange and discombobulated combination of taken aback and mortally offended. Some people had billions of dollars. Other people were good at puns. For somebody to have *both* seemed unfair, unnatural. She was left speechless.

"Ever hear of Chesterton's fence?" asked Simeon.

"Yeah. The story of a guy who sees a fence in a field, gets angry that it's blocking his movement, and tears it down. Then he gets gored by a bull that the fence was protecting him from. It's supposed to mean that you shouldn't get rid of a system until you're sure you know why it's there."

"Ever think of applying Chesterton's fence to the theonomics? Or UNSONG?"

"'Rich people want more money' seems like sufficient explanation for a system dedicated to giving rich people money."

"You know the Comet King helped found UNSONG?"

"Even the Comet King makes mistakes."

"Really?"

"You're going to say the same thing you people always say. If we didn't make sure that the people who discovered Names got obscene profits, there'd be no incentive to discover Names, all the sweatshops would close, and then we wouldn't have the magic we need to treat diseases or run the railroads. But people have done plenty of basic science research for centuries without those incentives, and I would rather get Names a little bit slower but have them available to everyone than—"

"Forget curing diseases. That's a red herring. You want to know why we need UNSONG and the theonomics? Look around."

The workers toiled away at the red mast, laboring just a little too methodically to be natural. They did not take drugs. They were drugs. So were most of the Mexican and Central American population, all the way down to the Darien Gap. So might the Untied States have been, if things had gone a little differently.

People had been using peyote since the Olmecs. Nobody knows what the Olmecs made of it, but when Europeans showed up in the area they wrote about how the cactus buttons produced an intense trancelike state with funny dancing colors and occasional hallucinations of a plantlike humanoid figure. Always the same humanoid figure; the early hippies called him "the green man," which is just as well since the Aztec name was Pipiltzintzintli and probably hard to pronounce when you're high. But the sightings were rare; in those days Uriel's machine was still strong, and there were only a few chinks in its protection, and hippies would laugh about the weird green man they saw and not pay it any more attention.

Then the sky cracked, and peyote changed. It stopped giving an intense trancelike state. It stopped giving hallucinations. It started doing other things. People would eat the flesh of the cactus and they would speak of events happening far away, or gain new talents. A user who was not a doctor would diagnose and treat diseases; a user who was not an engineer would design a bridge. A user in Tijuana could tell her family what was happening to her sister in Veracruz a continent away. When the peyote wore off, in ten hours' time, all they could remember was a feeling of supreme confidence and self-assuredness, like everything had been planned out and it was all going according to plan.

Peyote began to spread. Buttons would turn up on street corners in Mexico City and at gang meetings in Los Angeles. It was safe, it was cheap, it gave you new talents, it made you feel good. By the mid-1980s, some estimates suggested that ten percent of the Mexican population used it regularly or semi-regularly.

In May 1984, a group of psychiatrists noted a new side effect of peyote: a tendency to buy and stockpile very large amounts of it. There was nothing weird about addicts having a stash; what was weird was that it was only on peyote that they bought peyote. The complex behavior of going to their dealer and buying more buttons seemed to be... a side effect of the chemical? Addicts interviewed while they weren't high said they didn't need that much, it seemed weird, but they guessed they would keep it or something because it wasn't worth throwing it out.

In August 1984, a second survey found that the average user had stashed several large crates of peyote buttons in hidden places, two or three years' supply even if they took it every day. Dealers were forever running short; growers were working around the clock.

On November 1, 1984, every peyote user in North America simultaneously started digging into their stashes and offering it to their friends. First for free. Then with an offer that they would *pay* to have their friends take peyote. Then upping their offer. Thousands of dollars. Tens of thousands. As soon as a friend was high, the addict was moving on to another friend—and the first friend was accumulating their own stash and seeking out a friend of their own.

This went on for hours before the police noticed anything amiss, by which time about fifteen percent of the population of Mexico and the US Southwest was high. The news started to spread. Something is wrong. Don't take peyote. Stay in your houses. Lock the doors.

Imagine. You're a young Mexican guy, been clean your whole life. You hear something's up, you get inside, lock the doors, barricade yourself in your bedroom. A phone call. It's your mother. She was coming to visit you. Now she's at the door, a bunch of addicts right behind her. Let her in right now. So you peep out the door. There's your mother. You let her in as quick as you can, lock the door behind you. Oh thank God, she tells you. You have no idea what's going on out there. I'm starving. Do you have any food? Of course you have food. So she makes herself something, then she offers some to you. All this barricading has made you hungry. You take a big bite. You start to feel a little weird. "What was in the..." you ask. "Only what is in me, and what will be in all of us," she tells you. A few minutes later, you're driving her to your brother's house so she can try the same trick.

Within twenty-four hours, two-thirds of southern North America was high on peyote. And there was enough stockpiled in most areas to keep them all dosed twice a day for the next three months.

The Drug Lord—call him the Green Man, Pipiltzintzintli, whatever—

didn't wait. His many avatars and appendages stopped all their unproductive work—reading, watching TV, political activism—and started cultivating peyote cactus across every spare acre of land in Central America. Using data from the minds of millions of farmers and thousands of agricultural biologists, he directed the bodies under his control flawlessly, perfectly, so that billions of cacti started to spring up from Panama City to the Rio Grande and beyond. Like clockwork, twice a day, each of the millions of addicted people take another dose of cactus.

Of course everyone freaks out. This is the mid-eighties, so America is back in business as the Untied States under Ronald Reagan. They shift their entire military to Texas and California. Everywhere within two hundred miles of the Mexican border is a giant mess, addicts fighting non-addicts. The military tries to get involved in the fighting. The Comet King yells at them and tells Reagan to burn all the cactus plantations north of the Rio Grande, then guard the border. Reagan takes the hint. The supply of peyote mostly dries up, and twelve hours later the addicts come down, become individual humans again, ask what the hell *happened* to them.

The threat isn't remotely under control. There are still a couple addicts north of the border, surviving off their own small basement plantations. And Mexico is starting to industrialize really heavily—like, more heavily than any country has ever industrialized in all of history. Turns out communism works just fine when there are no individuals. The two countries start to prepare for war.

In 1986, Mexican troops cross the Rio Grande, and the Drug War begins. By this point, the Untied States has started to get some kabbalistic Names. The appendages of the Drug Lord can't speak Names, something about not working off individual souls anymore, so the US has the tech advantage. On the other hand, the Drug Lord is a single being with ninety million perfectly cooperating bodies and an inhuman level of industrial base, plus anyone he can convince to take a peyote button starts fighting for his side. The battles are fierce, but the Mexicans slowly begin to advance.

The Comet King asks someone to get him a peyote button. He sits in his fortress in Cheyenne Mountain and swallows a piece of cactus. Two hours later, the Mexican forces retreat back towards the Rio Grande.

Mexico deteriorates, addicts fighting those who had spontaneously become non-addicted. The Drug Lord retreats to small villages and goes underground, while a couple of dazed politicians dust themselves off and start to re-form a normal government.

The Comet King doesn't explain. The Comet King never explains. Some sort of spiritual combat? Some successful negotiation?

But now the Comet King was dead, and the Drug Lord had reasserted himself. Most of the Mexican cities and lowlands had fallen a second time. And so old men with dilated pupils rebuilt their ship for cash. Some said the Other King had signed an alliance with the Drug Lord, and that when the last remnants of Royal Colorado were destroyed they would sweep across the Southwest, destroying all in their path. Others said the Drug Lord hated the Other King but feared him. In any case there was peace, of a sort.

The workmen finished their task. Three men with dilated pupils went back onto their rowboat and went away.

James sighed with relief as the last addict left the ship. People were too smart to take the Drug voluntarily nowadays, and he'd checked them for any weapons they could use to overpower anyone, but any contact with Mexico was still creepy, and they were glad to be done with it.

"Uriel's machine is deteriorating," Simeon told Ana. "When it finally falls apart, it's going to loose a lot of things that look at humans as the bottom of the food chain. The Drug Lord. Thamiel. Other things. Older things. Technology won't save us then. The only thing that can save us is Names. Lots and lots of Names. We beat the Drug Lord back with Names, but not well, and now we don't have the Comet King on our side. When the last screw falls out of that machine, I want us armed with as many Names as we can get. Cate Ilyov buys yachts because Cate Ilyov is an idiot. Me, I'm sinking all Countenance's profits back into Countenance. And a few other projects besides. Not because I'm not selfish. I am. I'm selfish enough to be scared. For me. For my family."

The dinner bell rang.

"Join me for dinner?" asked Simeon.

"I'll... I'll have to think," said Ana. "You're not getting out of this one this easily."

Simeon was already gone.

Chapter Thirty-Four

Why Wilt Thou Rend Thyself Apart, Jerusalem?

October 31, 1991
Madrid

"Blessed are the peacemakers," said Jesus in the Sermon on the Mount, "for they shall be called the children of God."

It was day five of the Madrid peace conference, and the prophecy had been fulfilled. Partially fulfilled. Technically Uriel had just called them "children." And more "thought of" than "called them," because he didn't want to make people angry by saying it aloud. But he said it in his head very trenchantly. Children bickered. They could not share. They threw tantrums at the slightest hint of things not going exactly their way. They refused to listen to reason. Peacemakers were like this too.

The Israelis, led by a short old man with a mustache, kept insisting that the Palestinians were violent terrorists. The Palestinians, led by various people with no power who kept sneaking out to consult with unsavory figures whom the Israelis refused to confront directly, kept insisting the Israelis were greedy imperialists. Occasionally they would start shouting at each other, and then the Europeans and Americans would have to step in and calm everyone down. Protesters outside were shouting even louder, and twice they'd been forced to stop for security breaches, real or imagined. It didn't seem like a very effective way to come to an agreement.

Uriel had tried to help. He had mentioned several results from auction theory about dividing scarce resources. One could assign values to various bundles of goods, such as pieces of territory or access rights to various religious sites, give both sides some sort of token currency proportional to their populations, and as long as certain assumptions held, the results were guaranteed Pareto-optimal. Not only had nobody been interested, but they'd all stared at him when he brought it up, like he'd grown a second head or something.

Worse than that. Thamiel *had* a second head, and he was doing just fine! Why had they invited the Prince of Lies to a peace conference? It had been some American diplomat's bright idea, that given the religious aspects of the conflict there ought to be representatives of Heaven and Hell. So here he was, and here Thamiel was, and he was out of his element, and Thamiel was so transparently in his own that it was terrifying to watch.

"Ambassador Baker's proposal is interesting," Thamiel said, in a voice that sounded like flowing oil. "But I can't help but notice that the sort of salient along Israel's eastern border would be a security disaster. There would just be no way to defend it. Terrorists could come in and blow up anything—buses, hospitals, schools—and the Israelis would have signed away their right to do anything about it." And so the most promising proposal had gone up in flames. "And here"—he pointed to another part of the border, where it briefly bulged outwards—"I feel like for the Palestinians to give up this much territory so close to Ramallah would be a national humiliation." And now the Palestinians were refusing to negotiate. Didn't they see what was happening? Couldn't they see how he was playing on their fear and their pride? Uriel wasn't sure they cared. They would rather score cheap points at each other's expense than get a working plan. Blessed were the peacemakers, for they were the children of God, and they would need a lot of blessings if they were going to get anywhere here.

"Maybe the Archangel Uriel would have something to say about that," said Thamiel.

WHAT? SORRY, I MIGHT NOT HAVE BEEN LISTENING.

"Of course. I'm sure you have more important things to think about. We were just discussing the more supernatural aspects of the disagreement. The Israelis believe that God promised the Holy Land to the Jews. The Palestinians believe it is rightly Islamic. As an angel, you must know something about this."

UM, said Uriel. I THINK OF GOD AS SORT OF INTERPLAY BETWEEN THE LOGICAL AND MORAL CONCEPTS OF NECESSITY, WHICH CAUSES UNIVERSES TO EXIST AND CONTAIN THE POTENTIAL FOR HOLINESS. I AM NOT SURE HE IS REALLY THE KIND OF ENTITY THAT GETS INVOLVED IN REAL ESTATE NEGOTIATIONS.

"So you're saying the Torah—where God tells Moses that he can have the land of Israel—is lying?"

UM. MOSES WAS IN THE MIDDLE OF A DESERT, AND HE WAS VERY LOST, AND I FELT BAD FOR HIM, SO I CHANGED THE WEATHER CONTROL ALGORITHMS SO THAT SOMETIMES IT RAINED A BREAD-LIKE SUBSTANCE. AND THIS WENT WELL FOR A FEW WEEKS, BUT THEN SOMETHING WENT WRONG AND SOME OF THE OCEAN CURRENTS STARTED BEING BREAD TOO, AND I THINK THE GULF STREAM BECAME A SORT OF DANISH PASTRY. NOBODY WAS REALLY OUT VERY FAR IN THE OCEANS AT THIS POINT, BUT IT STILL SEEMED LIKE THE SORT OF TECHNICAL DEBT THAT I PROBABLY SHOULD CLEAR UP SOONER RATHER THAN LATER. SO I TOLD MOSES THAT INSTEAD OF LIVING IN THE DESERT AND SUBSISTING ON FALLING BREAD, HE SHOULD PROBABLY GO A LITTLE FURTHER AND REACH A FERTILE LAND WHERE YOU COULD GROW BREAD THE USUAL WAY.

The Israelis and Palestinians seemed about equally perturbed by this. Thamiel, as usual, kept his calm.

"So would you say you *promised* Moses the land, or not?"

I THINK I MIGHT HAVE SAID THAT SOME PEOPLE LIVED THERE ALREADY, BUT THEY SEEMED NICE, AND PROBABLY EVERYONE COULD GET ALONG. I ASSUMED IF THERE WAS SOME KIND OF CONFLICT THEY COULD USE AUCTION THEORY TO WORK IT OUT. UH. EVEN THOUGH I NOW KNOW THAT HUMANS DO NOT LIKE WORKING THINGS OUT WITH AUCTION THEORY.

"So Moses lied in the Torah when he said you promised him the land?"

Honestly Uriel liked fighting Thamiel better when it was just about him getting hit by molten darkness or living fire or blazing letters that burrowed into his skin and caused him unbearable pain. Debating him in front of humans was somehow even more tortuous.

THE TORAH IS A VERY COMPLICATED THING. THE LETTERS HAVE TO BE IN THE RIGHT ORDER, OR ELSE IT STOPS CORRESPONDING TO EVERYTHING ELSE IN THE UNIVERSE. I AM NOT SURE THIS IS VERY IMPORTANT. LOTS OF PEOPLE ARE GETTING KILLED AND BOMBED AND SHOT BECAUSE NOBODY CAN AGREE ON HOW TO DISTRIBUTE LAND RIGHT NOW. PROBABLY THIS MATTERS MORE THAN THE EXACT WORDING SOMEONE USED TWO THOUSAND YEARS AGO.

"Did you ever follow up on any of this?"

WHAT?

"You told Moses you were sure everyone could get along. Did you ever check back to see what was happening?"

UM. I MEANT TO. BUT THEN THE AURORA BOREALIS STARTED HAPPENING IN THE SOUTH, AND THE AURORA AUSTRALIS IN THE NORTH. IT WAS KIND OF SUBTLE BECAUSE THEY BOTH LOOK EXACTLY THE SAME, BUT I COULD TELL AND IT WAS BOTHERING ME. IT TURNED OUT TO BE A REALLY COMPLICATED BUG THAT TOOK ME TWO HUNDRED YEARS TO FIX. BY THE TIME I WAS DONE THE ISRAELITES SEEMED TO HAVE MOSTLY SORTED THINGS OUT THEMSELVES, SO I GUESS I DID NOT REALLY WORRY ABOUT IT TOO MUCH.

"You realize that the Israelites sorted it out by committing genocide against the original inhabitants?"

I KNOW THAT THE THING ABOUT THE AURORA SEEMS STUPID, BUT IT ACTUALLY HAS COMPLICATED IMPLICATIONS. BECAUSE IT WAS HARD TO FIX THE EXACT LOCATION OF THE NORTH POLE, I DEFINED THE POSITION OF SOME OF THE STARS RELATIVE TO THE LOCATION WHERE THE AURORA BOREALIS REACHES MAXIMUM INTENSITY. IF THE AURORA HAPPEN IN THE WRONG PLACE, THEN THE STARS STOP ROTATING CORRECTLY AND THE CONSTELLATIONS STOP MAKING SENSE. THIS ACTUALLY HAPPENED FOR UNRELATED REASONS AROUND 200 AD AND I HAVE NOT GOTTEN AROUND TO FIXING IT, WHICH IS WHY NEITHER URSA CONSTELLATION REALLY LOOKS ANYTHING LIKE A BEAR. THE ONLY ONE THAT IS STILL ANY GOOD IS ORION, WHICH...

"Uriel! I'm saying that through your irresponsibility you implicitly condoned an act of genocide and began a conflict which continues to afflict the Israelis and Palestinians today!"

The leaders and diplomats of the Untied States, the Cyrillic Union, Dazhou, Multistan, Iran, the European Communion, Neu Hansa, Egypt, Israel, and Palestine all sat staring at him. Drilling into his skin. He shouldn't have come here. He knew he shouldn't have come here. Why had he let Sohu convince him to come here? The word "Madrid" meant "evil" in his own language, how had that not been a warning sign?

HE IS LITERALLY THE DEVIL, he finally said, limply. PLEASE STOP LISTENING TO HIM. PLEASE STOP TRUSTING HIM.

"I have my role in the cosmic drama, as do you," said Thamiel. "But during my time here, I've tried to serve the cause of peace, as have we all. Prime Minister Shamir, who was it who warned you about the risk a long border would pose to your security? Dr. Abdel-Shafi, who was it who stood up for you when the other delegates tried to humiliate your country? I'm trying to speak the truth as I see it. And right now, that truth is that this whole problem dates from one archangel who urged a Bronze Age prophet to commit genocide without worrying too much about the ethics of the situation, and now tries to sideline calls for justice with inane prattle about 'auction theory.'"

A man from the Israeli delegation, white-bearded, dressed in black, stood up. "And the claim that God's covenant with our people was some sort of sordid... pointing of directions... is offensive and idiotic!"

One of the Palestinians: "He wants us to auction away our homes — our right to exist!"

Ambassador Baker of the Untied States: "I'm frankly disturbed that one archangel can just, uh, turn the Gulf Stream into a pastry, without so much as an apology. I feel like this issue of, ah, who controls the metaphysical machinery of the universe needs to be looked at more closely. Maybe by the UN."

Uriel stood up. NONE OF THIS IS HELPING! IF YOU DO NOT WANT TO USE AUCTION THEORY TO SOLVE THIS PROBLEM THERE ARE MANY OTHER FAIR DIVISION TECHNIQUES. UM. THE BRAMS-TAYLOR PROCEDURE. APPROXIMATE COMPETITIVE EQUILIBRIUM FROM EQUAL INCOMES. THAT THING KING SOLOMON DID WHERE YOU THREATEN TO CUT A BABY IN TWO, AND THEN WHOEVER OBJECTS IS THE REAL MOTHER. I AM TRYING TO HELP YOU SOLVE YOUR PROBLEM! WHY CAN'T YOU SEE THAT I'M TRYING TO HELP YOU SOLVE YOUR PROBLEM?

"The typical complaint of privilege!" said Thamiel, now to nobody in particular, speaking almost in soliloquy but supremely confident in everyone's attention anyway. "Why bother looking at how authority has been abused in the past, on how past exercise of oppression has created the winners and losers of today? Why not just forget all about it, ignore all the injustices and oppressions that led to the current point, and just go from here? I trust nobody here is foolish enough to fall for that, even if it comes out of the mouth of an archangel."

The room erupted into uproar. Uriel could only hear short snippets. "Frank anti-Semitism and Islamophobia..." one member of the European delegation told another. "Still very concerned about the Gulf Stream," the American ambassador was saying. "Can't believe we even invited him," he heard from the direction of the Cyrillics. "What do you have to say for yourself?" an elderly Iranian man kept shouting at him, and Uriel kept trying to respond but couldn't hear himself speak, couldn't even hear himself think.

He decided he'd had enough. He turned himself to lightning and tried to leave the room, but bounced back into humanoid form, somehow Thamiel was blocking his teleport. He tried to reach the door, but Thamiel flicked his bident, too subtly for the mortals in the room to notice, and a security fence just outside the conference room tumbled down. Protesters started streaming in through the door Uriel was trying to get out of. There were screams. "Death to imperialism!" the protesters were shouting, then "Death to colonialism," and then—because somehow the proceedings must have leaked outside the room, no guessing whose fault that was—"Death to Uriel!" The Iranian man kept repeating the same phrase, "What do you have to say for yourself? What do you have to say for yourself?" "Death to Uriel!" "What do you have to say for yourself?" "Death to Uriel!"

Then there was light.

Beautiful, multicolored light, ten colors, the seven colors of the earthly rainbow and the three extra colors you only get in Heaven. Ten colors corresponding to the ten sephirot and the ten fingers and the Ten Commandments and the ten digits of the number system and the ten pip cards of the Tarot and all the other tens in all the correspondences of the world. It flowed into Thamiel like a torrent, overwhelming him, until he disintegrated in a shower of sparks.

And then it didn't stop. Was it that he couldn't stop it? Or just that he felt no desire to do so? It kept flowing, vast pools of it, like the rush of waters from a broken dam. For a moment all of the ministers and diplomats and protesters were awestruck by its beauty. Then they were consumed. The wave of light annihilated the conference room, shattered the palace, destroyed Madrid city center, blasted the first ring road, scorched the second ring road, burnt the third ring road, seared the fourth ring road, spread out into the suburbs, scalded the surrounding countryside, faded into a light toasting somewhere around Guadalajara, and died off in a faint glow by the time it reached Tarancón.

In the center of the crater where Madrid had once been located, Uriel turned into a bolt of lightning and vanished back to his hurricane.

SOHU, he said, I JUST DID SOMETHING REALLY BAD.

Chapter Thirty-Five

The Voices Of Children In His Tents

Fast cars! Fast women! Fastidious adherence to the precepts of the moral law!

—Steven Kaas

Spring 1982
Citadel West, Colorado Springs

Somehow the Comet King had become an adult. He had skipped puberty, telling Father Ellis that it sounded like too much trouble. One day he was a child; the next, his voice dropped, white hair grew on his chest, and he declared he would be having children. *All* the children.

His logic was simple. His heavenly descent gave him special powers. Intelligence, wisdom, physical strength, spiritual mastery. He, in turn, would pass these on to his children. The more children, the more supernaturally-gifted warriors, administrators, engineers, and scholars they would have for the dark times ahead. An army of Cometspawn, growing to adulthood faster than any mortal, each one pushing forward the day when they could march across the Bering Strait and drive the demons back below the earth. He requested that the women of Colorado step forth to help him in the project.

"Now hold on," Ellis told him. They were in the newly-completed throne room deep beneath Cheyenne Mountain, in the underground fortress that had once housed NORAD. The Comet King sat on a throne covered with black opal. Father Ellis's official title was Royal Confessor, but the Comet King consistently denied having anything to confess; his real role was advisory. Some days he didn't have any advice either. Today was not one of those days. "This is madness, Jala. You can't just impregnate every woman in an entire state."

"If you are talking about sexually transmitted diseases," the Comet King answered, "I will screen for them carefully."

"I'm talking about the natural law!" said Father Ellis. "Marriage! Family! Partnership between a man and a woman who join together into one flesh, help complete each other!"

"I am complete," said the Comet King.

"You told me that you were keeping me around to tell you how to stay human. Now I'm telling you. Having children isn't something you do for anyone else's convenience. It's a sacred act. If you do this, you're taking a step away from humanity, and it's going to come back to bite you."

"Perhaps you are right. I accept the slight cost to my humanity as an acceptable risk, given the possible gains."

"It doesn't work that way! Sin isn't a ledger that you balance. It's about... about... can you *feel* it, Jala? Goodness isn't just numbers. It's something palpable, something burning and beautiful. People talk about having a relationship with God, but it's closer than that. More powerful. More immediate. And what you're saying... it takes away from that thing. It's not in line with it. If you could feel it, you wouldn't be calculating how many strategic deviations from doing the right thing you can allow yourself."

"Father, have you become a *mystic?*"

"No, I just... I feel like I'm trying to explain the nature of virtue to a rock. Either you can see why what you're saying is crazy, or... call Vihaan. You listen to Vihaan. He can explain what I mean."

Uncle Vihaan's official title was Chief of Staff, but he always called himself "the butler." He managed the Comet King's growing circle of advisors, visitors, and petitioners, and organized his schedule around the constant meetings required of the fledgling government. When somebody finally found him, he came into the throne room disorganized, still carrying a stack of papers.

"What is it?" he asked. The Comet King started to speak, but Ellis interrupted him.

"Jala wants to have kids with half the women in the state! He wants to... *breed* some kind of conquering army! Tell him this isn't how people do things!"

Vihaan's face fell. "What about marriage?"

The Comet King thought for a second. "I would rather not have to worry about it. But if it were important to you, I could marry them all, like Solomon."

Vihaan's head was bobbing back and forth in exasperation. "Everyone from our family…" he said. "You come from a good family, Jala. Marrying good people. No sex before marriage. It wouldn't be… proper."

"Proper?" asked the Comet King. "I come to you with a plan to fight off Hell and save the world, and you tell me it isn't *proper*?"

Vihaan stared at the priest, as if begging him to step in. "I swear," said Father Ellis, "it's like explaining the nature of virtue to a rock."

"Do you know," interrupted Jalaketu, "that whenever it's quiet, and I listen hard, I can hear them? The screams of everybody suffering. In Hell, around the world, anywhere. I think it is a power of the angels which I inherited from my father." He spoke calmly, without emotion. "I think I can hear them right now."

Ellis's eyes opened wide. "Really?" he asked. "I'm sorry. I didn't…"

"No," said the Comet King. "Not really."

They looked at him, confused.

"No, I do not really hear the screams of everyone suffering in Hell. But I thought to myself, 'I suppose if I tell them now that I have the magic power to hear the screams of the suffering in Hell, then they will go quiet, and become sympathetic, and act as if that changes something.' Even though it changes nothing. Who cares if you can hear the screams, as long as you know that they are there? So maybe what I said was not fully wrong. Maybe it *is* a magic power granted only to the Comet King. Not the power to hear the screams. But the power not to have to. Maybe that is what being the Comet King means."

"Do you think," asked Ellis, "you're the first person to ask the Church to compromise its doctrines because you have a *good reason?*. It's… no, you won't listen to me. But you might listen to your people. Ask the people, Jala. They'll tell you."

"WE'RE NOT YOUR BABY FACTORIES," read the signs of the National Organization of Women, who held a demonstration in the Garden of the Gods against the plan. "The Comet King is proving he sees women as objects, as walking wombs," Mary Lutha, the organization's leader, told an NBC reporter. "I think the women of Colorado want the Comet King to know that they reject this denial of their agency."

The Comet King did not grant interviews, but a source close to the citadel mentioned that when confronted with the claim, he had stated matter-of-factly that the twenty-four thousand applications he had already received were quite enough and Ms. Lutha's help would thankfully not be needed.

"SHAME ON COLORADO EUGENICS," read signs held by the local

branch of the National Association for the Advancement of Colored People, who held a demonstration beneath the Shrine of the Sun against the plan. "The Comet King needs to know that the black and brown people of Colorado aren't going to stand for his plan to create a master race of blonde-haired, blue-eyed babies and then kill the rest of the population."

The Comet King was not known to grant interviews, but a spokesperson assured everyone that killing the entire population was the last thing on the Comet King's mind, and also how was a dark-skinned man whose mother came from India supposed to create a race of blonde-haired, blue-eyed babies anyway?

"This is madness," he told Ellis and Vihaan in his throne room beneath the mountain. "The people have always gone along with my plans before, even when they were dangerous, even the ones that led to privation and difficulty. Nothing could be simpler than this. A few thousand women, no cost to anyone who does not volunteer, and the kingdom will be unstoppable."

"Vihaan is against it," said Ellis. "The people are against it. And *I'm* against it. Listen to your advisors, Jala."

"The people are confused," said the Comet King. "Once they have pictures of smiling babies to make them happy, they will realize my children are no scarier than anyone else. Vihaan, we have applications. Find me a handful of women willing to go first. Make sure they are physically fit, intelligent, and free from genetic disease. And make them all different races; that will quiet the blond-hair-blue-eyes crowd. I will start with just a handful of children, to show the people there is no danger, and once the protests quiet down we will start the full breeding program."

"I still don't think this is right," protested Vihaan.

"I respect your advice," said the Comet King. "But I have made my decision."

Vihaan muttered something about how he was just the butler, and far be it from him to disobey an order. But Ellis wasn't satisfied. "I'm not your servant, Jala, I'm your confessor. And it's my job as a confessor to tell you when you're sinning, and not to be okay with it, no matter whether you've made your mind up or no."

"Fine," said the Comet King. "Consult the Urim and Thummim. See what they think. See if there are any prophecies."

It was an obvious attempt to get rid of him. It worked. Ellis holed up preparing the ritual. Vihaan stayed behind to sort through the paperwork. Of the twenty-four thousand applicants, he carefully selected four. They met with the Comet King below Cheyenne Mountain. One of them went to the tabloids later and described the Comet King's lovemaking as "efficient" and "peremptory."

A week later, Father Ellis finished the divination. For once, the stones were unambiguous. All the descendants of the Comet King, he said, would die screaming in horror and agony, cursing their father's name.

Nine months later, four physically fit, intelligent women gave birth to four genetic-disease-free, racially diverse babies.

The Comet King had no more children.

Chapter Thirty-Six

My Father's Business

Fill the god-shaped hole in your soul with molten metal, then shatter your soul, leaving only a metal god

—@GapOfGods

October 31, 1991
Gulf Of Mexico

Curled up on a cloud, Sohu sat studying Talmud. She was just starting to consider packing it in for the night when her vision was seared by a nearby lightning strike. The subsequent thunder was instantaneous. She was still trying to get her sight back when her father strode through the door.

"Hello, Sohu," said the Comet King with a faint smile.

She jumped up from her desk in delight. Of course she ran right into a wall—vision doesn't recover from a point blank lightning strike that quickly—but luckily it was made of cloud and did her no harm. She stumbled a little, then quite literally fell into her father's arms.

"Father!"

"It's been too long," he said. "You look good."

She smiled. "I don't know how you look. One of the disadvantages of you going everywhere by lightning bolt. Sit down."

She gestured at the only chair in the room, which was Sohu-sized. Her bed was covered with books, all open to different pages. The Comet King sized it up, but his distaste for putting books on the floor got the best of him, and he put himself on the floor instead, settling naturally into a lotus position. Sohu shrugged and took the chair.

"I've come to take you home," the Comet King said.

"No!" said Sohu. "Wait, is something wrong?"

"Uriel destroyed the city of Madrid. The King of Spain, the Prime Minister of Israel, Secretary Baker, and dozens of diplomats are dead. Thamiel is disincorporated. I don't know the whole story. Uriel's still in the crater. I want you gone by the time he comes back here. You are not safe."

"Uriel would never hurt me!" Then, "Oh. God! Poor Uriel!"

"Poor Uriel? Poor Madrid, I would say."

"Oh. Father, I was the one who told him to go. I thought it would be good for him. They must have... it was Thamiel. It must have all been a trick of Thamiel's. I'm so dumb. Father, this is all my fault."

"It isn't. This was always a possibility."

Sohu got up, started pacing. Tears welled into her eyes. "No. Uriel's... different, but this isn't him. You have to trust him, Father."

"Sohu, I told you I sent you here to learn the celestial kabbalah. I told you it would be dangerous if you did not know it. That was true in more ways than you knew. I sent you here because I knew Uriel was capable of this. Uriel is not good, Sohu. He is not evil in the same way Thamiel is, but neither is he safe. And he controls the universe. I cannot allow the universe to be controlled by a loose cannon, but for the present I lack any other options. Not even I can do what he does." He frowned. "That is why I sent you here, Sohu. So that if Uriel becomes too dangerous to be allowed to continue, I will have someone with whom to replace him. That is why I sent you here, even though it placed you in danger. I thought the danger was worthwhile, if it gave me a backup demiurge when the time came. Now I no longer think the danger is worthwhile. We will find another way to teach you. Come home with me."

"No," said Sohu. "No no no. You can't kill Uriel. I'm not going to help you kill Uriel."

"I will not destroy Uriel now," said the Comet King. "You are not ready. Perhaps I will never have to destroy Uriel. Perhaps he will fundamentally change. But if it needs to be done, you will do your duty, as I have mine."

"You won't have to kill Uriel!" said Sohu. "I've been talking to him. Getting him to understand more things. He listens to me! I want to stay with him. I want to keep studying."

"Not safe," said the Comet King.

"No one is ever safe," said Sohu. "You taught me that. We're Cometspawn. It's our job to make them safe. And you said it yourself. It's important that I learn the celestial kabbalah, in case there's ever a time when we need... someone other than Uriel for it. You said you'd train me at home. You can't train me at home. No one can. Only Uriel really understands it. This is where I'm doing the most good for the world, right?"

"Sohu," said the Comet King, "before you and your sisters and brother were born, I thought of you as strategic assets. I told Father Ellis I would make an army of you. He said that was wrong. Then—your eldest sister, Nathanda. She was the first. When I saw her, I... Father Ellis talks of goodness as something burning and beautiful. I told him he was wrong, that goodness was something cold and crystalline. But when I saw Nathanda, for the first time I understood what it meant to see goodness the way that Father Ellis did. Terribly hot, and too bright to look upon directly. Then I knew as long as she was alive, I did not need to worry any further about staying human. I had caught humanity and wrapped it around me tightly like a mantle. All thoughts of sending you off as an army vanished. You're not a pawn—or at least you're not only a pawn—you're my daughter. And I will not let any harm come to you."

"But Father. You're always telling us that we need to think of what's best for the world."

"Yes," said the Comet King. "So consider this: If anyone harms you, even the littlest cut or scrape, I will come against them as fire and night. I will destroy them and their people, uproot everything they have built, wipe them utterly from the earth. And I will do this even if they are the only archangel capable of running the universe, and they have nobody to replace them. What is best for the world is that I not do that. That is why I am taking you home, Sohu."

Sohu shuddered. Then she said, "The prophecy says that I'll die screaming and cursing your name. If Uriel killed me, I'd probably just die thinking you were right."

"Playing with prophecy is a dangerous thing, Sohu."

"Taking me away from the only person who can train me to use my powers is dangerous! Life is dangerous! We're Cometspawn! If we don't do the dangerous things, who will?"

"I will," said the Comet King, "so that you do not have to."

Whatever Sohu might have answered was lost in the brilliance of a sudden lightning bolt and the crash of the following thunder.

SOHU, said Uriel I JUST DID SOMETHING REALLY BAD.

Sohu ran through the door of the cottage, ran across the little cloud, jumped into the empty spaces beneath, leapt at Uriel. The archangel caught her in his giant hand, and she hugged his finger. "Uriel Uriel Uriel I'm so sorry I'm so sorry are you okay I'm so sorry."

I AM SORT OF NOT OKAY BUT IT IS NOT YOUR FAULT.

"It is it is I told you to go to the conference I thought you would like it but it was all a trick I was playing right into Thamiel's hands he wanted to hurt you I'm so sorry."

IT IS NOT YOUR FAULT. YOU ARE GOOD. YOU TRIED TO HELP.

Then he noticed the visitor. The Comet King stood on the edge of the cloud. The starlight gleamed off of his silver hair. He listened to his daughter and the archangel quietly, but his mind was deep in thought.

"Father," said Sohu. "This is Uriel. Uriel, my father, the Comet King."

"Uriel," said the Comet King, "can I trust you with my daughter?"

Sohu's brain immediately generated all of the terrible things that were about to happen. Uriel was going to answer something like WELL, WHAT IS TRUST, ANYWAY? and go off on a tangent while her father panicked. Uriel was going to talk about how Thamiel sometimes came to visit them and tried to kill or torture her. Uriel was going to, God help them, try to give a kabbalistic analysis of the question.

YES, said Uriel.

Sohu blinked.

The Comet King looked for a moment like he wasn't sure exactly how to respond, but it was only for a moment. "What happened in Madrid?" he asked. "The diplomatic community is in chaos. I had to talk President Bush out of declaring war on you. And the reports out of Jerusalem are so confusing I can't even begin to decipher them."

I GOT VERY UPSET, said Uriel. THAMIEL TRICKED ME INTO GETTING ANGRY, AND I FELL FOR IT. I USED THE SHEFA I WAS SUPPOSED TO USE TO SUSTAIN THE UNIVERSE TO MAKE EVERYONE GO AWAY. THEN I FELT VERY BAD AND I USED MORE OF IT TO SOLVE THE PROBLEM WITH ISRAEL SO PEOPLE WOULDN'T HATE ME.

"Solve the problem with Israel?"

I PEELED APART SPACE SO THAT TWO ISRAELS EXIST IN THE SAME SPOT. ONE OF THEM CONTAINS ONLY JEWS, THE OTHER CONTAINS ONLY PALESTINIANS. ANY JEWISH PERSON WHO ENTERS THE COUNTRY WILL FIND THEMSELVES IN THE JEWISH ONE. ANY MUSLIM PERSON WHO ENTERS THE COUNTRY WILL FIND THEMSELVES IN THE PALESTINIAN ONE. ANY CHRISTIAN OR ATHEIST OR SO ON WILL FIND THEMSELVES IN A SUPERPOSITION OF BOTH STATES. IT WILL PROBABLY BE VERY CONFUSING.

"You can *do* that?"

NOT WITHOUT COST. I HAVE TAKEN TWENTY YEARS FROM THE

LIFESPAN OF THE MACHINERY. IT IS MY FAULT AND I AM BAD. I WANTED PEOPLE TO LIKE ME. NOW I HAVE BETRAYED THE ONLY JOB I EVER REALLY HAD.

The three of them stood there in the eye of the hurricane, silent in the starlight. The king. The little girl. The giant archangel. There was little to say. The world had been falling apart for years. Now it was falling apart faster.

Finally the Comet King spoke.

"Do you know the Hymn of Breaking Strain?" he asked.

Uriel shook his head.

The Comet King stood tall at the edge of the cloud. In a clear voice, from memory, he recited:

The careful text-books measure
(Let all who build beware)
The load, the shock, the pressure
Material can bear.
So, when the buckled girder
Lets down the grinding span,
The blame of loss, or murder,
Is laid upon the man.
Not on the stuff—the man.

But in our daily dealing
With stone and steel, we find
The gods have no such feeling
Of justice toward mankind.
To no set gauge they make us—
For no laid course prepare—
And presently o'ertake us
With loads we cannot bear:
Too merciless to bear.

The prudent text-books give it
In tables at the end
The stress that shears a rivet
Or makes a tie-bar bend—
What traffic wrecks macadam—
What concrete should endure—

But we, poor Sons of Adam
Have no such literature,
To warn us or make sure.

We only of Creation
(Oh, luckier bridge and rail)
Abide the twin damnation–
To fail and know we fail.
Yet we — by which sole token
We know we once were gods–
Take shame in being broken
However great the odds–
The burden of the odds.

Oh, veiled and secret Power
Whose paths we seek in vain,
Be with us in our hour
Of overthrow and pain;
That we — by which sure token
We know Thy ways are true —
In spite of being broken,
Because of being broken
May rise and build anew
Stand up and build anew.

YOU SAY WE ARE ALL BROKEN BUT MUST CONTINUE OUR WORK ANYWAY, said Uriel. BUT *YOU* NEVER BREAK.

The Comet King stood there on the edge of the cloud, inhumanly perfect, his black cloak and silver hair blowing in the gale.

"I will," he said.

PROPHECY? asked Uriel.

"Probability," said the Comet King. "No one keeps winning forever. And when I break, I'll do what comets do. Shatter into fragments, but stay locked on the same path, so that only the most careful astronomers can even tell they're broken. And that's what you need to do, Uriel. We need your help."

WE?

"Humanity."

HUMANS DON'T LIKE ME.

"Humans dislike many things humanity needs."

I AM NOT GOOD AT ANYTHING.

"You are good at one thing. You run the universe. That is enough. We need a universe. No one has to be good at everything."

YOU ARE GOOD AT EVERYTHING.

"Not everything. I cannot run the universe. That is where you come in. And my daughter."

SHE IS VERY GOOD. SHE IS LEARNING QUICKLY.

"So I've heard."

I WILL NOT HURT HER.

"No, I don't think you will." He sighed. "But you need to be more careful. Both of you. Uriel, stay away from humans. You and I, we are similar. Too similar. We take the straight paths. Try to do things right, damn the consequences. Humans are not like that. They manipulate the social world, the world of popularity and offense and status, with the same ease that you manipulate the world of nature. But not to the same end. There is no goal for them, nothing to be maintained, just the endless twittering of I'm-better-than-you and how-dare-you-say-that. You are no good at that, and you will never be any good at that, and if you were good at that you would not be good at what you need to be good at. We are similar, Uriel, deep down, but leave humans to me. That is my burden. The world is yours. The world, and training my daughter."

JALAKETU, said Uriel. DO YOU THINK IT WILL ALL TURN OUT OKAY?

"I do not think anything," said the Comet King. "I *plan* for it to turn out okay." He sighed. "But now I should leave. The European Communion is talking about declaring war. That would be inconvenient. I would have to defeat them. Do we have anything else we need to discuss?"

Uriel was silent.

"Stay here a little longer, Father?" Sohu asked.

"Can't. There's always a crisis. And you have work to do. I'll visit. I know I haven't visited, but I will."

GOOD LUCK, JALAKETU.

The Comet King stared directly at Sohu, spoke into her mind in that creepy way that he did.

[Keep him safe, Sohu. I am counting on you.]

[You lied to him, Father.]

[I told him the truth. His part is to remain strong and do his duty. If he fails, I will remain strong and do mine. You will do no less.]

[That's not what I mean. You told him you could break quietly. But you told me that if someone hurt me, you would go nuclear on them.]

[I told both of you the truth. I will destroy anyone who hurts you. But not because I would be broken. Because I would remain intact.]

He sent her something telepathically, a tangle of thoughts mixed with emotions. When she sorted it out, it came into her mind like a question and answer. The question went *If you are Moshiach, and you have to care for everyone as if they are your own children, how do you care for those who are literally your children?* The answer was a non-answer, a steamrolling over the paradox. *You care for them even more. You care for them extremely and ferociously, beyond any reason.*

He stared at her. [Sohu. Promise me you won't die.]

She almost laughed, almost told him that of course that wasn't something she could promise. Then she saw the look on his face, dead serious. She remembered what Uriel had answered him only a few minutes before. So she just said:

[There's a prophecy, Father.]

[You will be a celestial kabbalist. You can stand above prophecy.]

That was something she hadn't heard before.

[But even without prophecies, everyone dies.]

[Then promise me you will not die before I do.]

Something in his look prevented her from arguing any further. [All right, Father. I promise.]

The Comet King turned into lightning and flew away, merging into the general fury of the storm.

HE IS GOOD, said Uriel, finally. HE IS RIGHT ABOUT ME AND HUMANS, AND HE IS GOOD.

"The prophecy says I will die cursing his name." said Sohu, "But I don't think that I will."

She went back into her cottage, started tidying up the books. The storm had felt strangely empty without Uriel at the center; now that he was back she felt safe again. There was a horror to Madrid; in her heart she could not forget that he was a mass murderer, that he had in his own words CREATED THE BLACK PLAGUE TO SEE IF IT WOULD WORK, but—Father was right. He didn't understand humans. He never would. And she didn't understand Uriel, not really. The Bible demanded faith that God was good, despite a whole world full of evidence to the contrary. For some reason, she had faith that Uriel was good. Not very wise, maybe. But good.

And she had faith that her father was good. She looked at her left hand, where Thamiel said her father had placed a mark that would call him in times of danger. She wondered what other protections were on her, that even Thamiel hadn't found.

God she was still iffy about. But Uriel and her father, those two she had faith in. Those two were good. It would have to be enough.

She fell asleep while the archangel worked silently outside.

Interlude נ

Miss American Pie

April 22, 2017
San Jose

A piece of onion flew past my head. This was a common occurrence when I argued with Valerie while she was trying to cook. Today we were arguing about the lyrics of American Pie. She thought it was about rock n' roll. I thought it was about Christian soteriology's claim to supersede the Jewish conception of divine law.

The first stanza was clearly setting up a contrast between the twin poles of song and dance. Song represented divine goodness or mercy. Its first three letters were "son," corresponding to the second person of the Christian Trinity, and there were the kabbalistic implications from UNSONG and Peter Singer to consider. Dance represented divine justice, because its first three letters were "dan," and *dan* or *din* is Hebrew for "judgment," like in the Beth Din or the name Daniel, "judgment of God."

That wasn't how I earned the onion, though. I'd earned the onion because of the chorus. He drove a Chevy to the levee, but the levee was dry. Well, *shevet* was the Hebrew word for "tribe," so a Chevy at the levee means the Tribe of Levi, i.e. the priesthood. John 7:38 says that "Whoever believes in me, as the Scripture has said, 'Out of his heart will flow rivers of living water.'" When the song says that the levee/Levites were dry, it's pushing the standard Christian line that the Pharisee priests of Jesus' day had become so obsessed with the Law that they had lost true faith.

Apparently Valerie believed this interpretation merited an onion, even though in the *very* next line they refer to whiskey, which comes from the Irish *uisce beatha*, meaning "water of life," which is practically an exact match for the John quote. I had a tough audience.

Bill Dodd walked in through the unlocked door, saw the table empty but for myself. "Am I early?" he asked.

"Everyone else is late, as usual," said Valerie. "Please, save me. Aaron was just trying to convince me that American Pie is about Christian soteriology."

Then she had to explain the whole conversation thus far to Bill, and then Bill protested that it was obviously about the history of rock n' roll, even though it *clearly* wasn't. "Seriously!" I protested. "The very next stanza starts out with 'Did you write the Book of Love / Do you have faith in God above / if the Bible tells you so?' How do you not see that as an attempt to contrast the Old Testament — the Book of the Law — with the New Testament as the Book of Love, offering salvation by faith?"

"Book of Love is a famous rock n' roll song," said Bill, "and the very next line is 'do you believe in rock n' roll.'"

"Exactly!" I told him. "Salvation by faith requires belief in Christ's resurrection. The most obvious sign of which was that the *rock* blocking his tomb had been *rolled* away. Then 'Can music save your mortal soul?' Music equals song equals the Son, as I said before! It's saying that Christ saves people's souls! And then dancing real slow is the suspension of divine judgment!"

"'I know that you're in love with him, because I saw you dancing in the gym,'" continued Valerie. "Where in the New Testament does Christ dance in a gym?"

"Dancing means divine judgment!" I repeated. "And *gym* is Greek for naked. There's a perfectly clear part of the Bible that links nakedness to divine judgment, and that's Genesis 3! The Garden of Eden narrative! We know that God is in love with humanity because even despite the justice of punishing original sin, He chooses not to do so."

"'You both kicked off your shoes,'" protested Bill.

"Exodus 3:5," I said. "'And the LORD said, Draw not nigh hither: put off thy shoes from off thy feet, for the place whereon thou standest is holy ground.'"

Valerie threw another onion slice at me. It missed by half an inch.

"Look," said Bill. "You can fit individual pieces to relevant Bible verses. I'll even give you that you mostly stuck to the Jesus theme. But the song as a whole only makes sense in the context of rock n' roll. For example, just after the shoes part, it mentions a pink carnation, which was what young men traditionally wore to dance halls."

"And which also contains 'incarnation' as a substring. You don't think that an Incarnation could possibly have anything to do with..."

The door opened. Zoe Farr came in. "Hey guys. What are you yelling about? I could hear you all the way out in the driveway."

"AARON IS TRYING TO SAY THAT AMERICAN PIE IS ABOUT JESUS," yelled Valerie. "HE IS SAYING THAT THE CHEVY AT THE LEVY IS THE TRIBE OF LEVITES AND THE PINK CARNATION IS THE INCARNATION. YOU NEED TO MAKE HIM STOP."

"Calm down," said Zoe. "That sounds kind of fun. Even though I think I read somewhere that American Pie is about the history of rock n' roll. It even mentions the Rolling Stones at one point."

"Okay," I said. "Fine. You want to talk Rolling Stones? Let's talk Rolling Stones. The relevant stanza begins 'for ten years we've been on our own.' In Bible prophecy, a day of God represents a year—this is why the seventy weeks of Daniel correspond to the 490 years after Daniel's own time. So ten years by that conversion equals 3650 years. The Seder Olam Rabbah dates the creation of the world as 3761 BC, so in Biblical time the birth of Christ is about ten years and three months from Creation. That's not a coincidence because nothing is ever a—"

"And the Rolling Stones?" asked Bill.

"For the love of God, I already told you," I said. "Resurrection of Christ. Matthew 28:2. 'And, behold, there was a great earthquake: for the angel of the Lord descended from heaven, and came and rolled back the stone from the door.'"

"Wait..." said Zoe.

"No, you wait," I said. "Let's go over exactly what happens in the rest of that verse. The King is looking down—obvious reference to God entering the world, especially paired with the incarnation part earlier. *Jester* has clear phonetic resemblance to 'Jesus,' sounds even better if you use the original 'Yeshua.' He's wearing a coat borrowed from James Dean. But we know the root *dan* or *din* means 'justice' in Hebrew. So 'James Dean' deciphers to 'James the Just,' who is described in Acts as 'the brother of Jesus.' Most commentators reconcile this with Jesus' supposed heavenly descent by saying he was a half-brother from Mary. So James the Just represents Jesus' human bloodline, which means the 'coat borrowed from James Dean' is the human form that He incarnates into, like a coat. So we have God coming down into the world and taking human form, and even having a human soul—a 'voice that came from you and me.' Then he 'steals a thorny crown'—I hope I don't have to explain that one to you. What happens then? 'The courtroom is adjourned; no verdict is returned.' The Law is supplanted; divine punishment is suspended. This would all be *super obvious* if you would just stop with your stupid rock n' roll obsession."

"The *very next verse* mentions John Lennon!" Valerie protested.

"Lennon! Lennon is a Avgad cipher for Moses! Lamed-nun-nun, move all the letters one forward, mem-samech-samech spells 'Moses.' And Marx. This was all in that article you rejected for the *Chorister*. Karl Marx means 'man of war,' so it's a reference to God. Moses is reading a book on God—the Torah. The whole thing is happening 'while Lennon read a book on Marx,' i.e. along with it. Jesus comes not to supplant the law but to fulfill it. And then! A quartet is practicing in the park—that's the Four Evangelists. 'Dirges in the dark the day the music died.' The music is the song is Jesus. The day the music died is the day Jesus died. Mark 15:33, 'And when the sixth hour was come, there was darkness over the whole land until the ninth hour.' They're singing dirges in the dark because Jesus just died and a supernatural darkness descended over the land."

"What descended over the land?" asked Ally Hu. She had just come in. I had been so intent in correcting my friends' misperceptions about American Pie that I hadn't even noticed her.

"Supernatural darkness," I said. "I'm explaining American Pie to these guys. We were at the part about singing dirges in the dark. It's a reference to the supernatural darkness that covered the land after Jesus' crucifixion."

"I do not know so much about American culture," said Ally, "but I thought that this song was about a history of rock n' roll."

"THAT'S WHAT WE'VE BEEN TRYING TO TELL HIM," said Valerie, at the same time I muttered "Et tu, Ally?"

"Exactly," said Bill. "For example, the next verse references Helter Skelter, Eight Miles High, and the Byrds. Helter Skelter is a Beatles song, the Byrds are a rock band, and Eight Miles High is a song by the Byrds."

"The verse goes," I said, "'Helter skelter, in the summer swelter / the birds flew off with a fallout shelter / eight miles high and falling fast.' Is there a rock band called 'Fallout Shelter'? Is there a Grammy Award-winning song by that name?"

"Not everything has to..."

"Everything has to!" I said. "Nothing is ever a coincidence. Look. The Bible contains a clear example of a fallout shelter related to divine judgment. Noah's Ark. God decided to destroy the world for its wickedness, and Noah built something to survive the apocalypse. That's a fallout shelter. It's even eight miles high. The floodwaters covered the earth to a depth higher than the highest mountain. Everest is six miles high, the floodwaters had to be above that, leave a little margin of error, that's eight miles. And falling fast, because after forty days and nights God opened the portals of the deep and the waters flowed back in. According to the story, Noah sent forth a raven and a dove to see if they could find dry land. In other words, the birds flew off, with the fallout shelter eight miles high and falling fast. The raven can't find any dry land. But the dove can. It lands, fowl on the grass. The jester is Jesus is the Son is the Song is divine mercy, but it's on the sidelines in a cast because at this point divine mercy has been suspended — even wounded — and divine judgment allowed to have free rein."

"Oh wow," said Zoe.

"You skipped the part about the players trying for a forward pass," said Bill.

"The players are all the people and animals, trying to pass their genes forward to the next generation. The marching band which is trying to interfere — well, think about it. There are two interesting facets of a marching band. They play music. And they march. Who does that sound like? Right. The angels. The heavenly choirs and the heavenly hosts. So the players — created mortal beings — are trying to take the field. But the angels and Nephilim refuse to yield — they've seized control of the earth. So 'do you recall what was revealed'? How do you say 'revealed' in Greek? Right. *Apokalypsis.* The angels tried to control the earth and wouldn't make room for humans, so God called down an apocalypse. That's why this is in the verse that talks about Noah's Ark."

The doorbell rang. It was Eli Foss. "Hey," he said. "Is dinner..."

"Okay," I said. "Just so we don't have to go over this *yet again*, and I don't have to answer every one of your dumb complaints in order. The generation lost in space was the generation of the Exodus who were lost in the desert for forty years. The time we were all in one place was Sinai, where according to the rabbis all the souls of Jews past present and future were present for the revelation of the Ten Commandments. Jack is Jacob is Israel is the Israelites. The candlestick is the pillar of fire by night. The Devil is the Devil. A plain that climbs high into the night is a hill or mountain; it's arguing that the theophany at Sinai naturally concluded on Golgotha. The sacrificial rite was the crucifixion. Satan is laughing with delight because Jesus just died. The girl who sang the blues is Mary Magdalene, who is sitting outside the tomb crying. They ask her for happy news because she's the first to witness the Resurrection. She smiles and turns away as per Mark 16: 'neither said they any thing to any man; for they were afraid.' The sacred store where they had heard the music years before is the Temple, but the music wouldn't play because the system of Temple sacrifices has been replaced by a direct relationship with God. In the streets the children are screaming and so on because Jesus is dead. The church bells are broken because Jesus is dead; kind of a heavy-handed metaphor, but whatever. The three men I admire most represent the Father, Son, and Holy Ghost, exactly like he says. Do any of you have any *other* questions?"

"What are you *talking* about?" asked Eli. "Is that American Pie?"

Just then Ana came downstairs, radiant in her white dress.

"Ana!" said Valerie. "You have to help us! Aaron is doing this incredibly annoying thing where he says that everything in American Pie is about the Christian version of Biblical history, and he says that the fallout shelter is Noah's Ark and the pink carnation is the Incarnation and the Chevy at the levee is the tribe of Levi, and the Rolling Stones are the stone rolled away from Jesus' tomb, and we keep telling him it's about rock n' roll and he won't listen and you're the only one who can ever make him see reason!"

"Valerie," said Ana calmly, "you're going about this the wrong way. When Aaron is like this, you can't argue against him. You have to beat him at his own game."

"What?"

"For example," said Ana, "Aaron, I propose that the Chevy does not represent the Tribe of Levi, but rather the Tribe of Issachar."

"Huh?" I asked. "Why?"

"Because," she said, with an ethereally beautiful smile, "a Chevy is a car."

"AAAAARGH!" I said. "AAAAARGH AAAAARGH AAAAARGH AA— ouch!"

Valerie was throwing onions at *both of us* now, and one of them had hit me just below the eye.

"OKAY," she shouted. "EVERYBODY IS GOING TO SIT DOWN AND EAT THEIR DAMN DINNER AND NO MORE TRIBE OF ISRAEL PUNS SO HELP ME GOD."

I looked straight at Ana and I thought, [Sit down and eat their Dan dinner.]

She looked back at me and thought, [So help me Gad.]

I thought, [We should Asher her that we're not going to make any more puns.]

Then we both broke down laughing helplessly.

"ARE YOU THINKING TRIBES OF ISRAEL PUNS AT EACH OTHER TELEPATHICALLY?" shouted Valerie, and nobody else at the table even *knew* about the telepathic link so they thought she was making some kind of joke and started laughing awkwardly, and just as I had almost calmed down Ana thought at me, [Our puns seem to be Reuben her the wrong way,] and then I broke down laughing again, and it bled through the telepathic link and made *Ana* start laughing again, and both of us laughed like maniacs while the rest of our friends just stared at us.

I tell you this story as an apology. So that when we get to the part in the next chapter where I had to decide between dooming the world and dooming Ana, you understand why I made the wrong choice.

Chapter Thirty-Seven

Love That Never Told Can Be

May 13, 2017
Las Vegas

"Sinner" in Biblical Hebrew is *aval*, no doubt kabbalistically connected to our English word *evil*. The gematria value of *aval* is 106. Bishop Ussher, the Biblical chronologist who fixed Creation at 4004 BC, tells us that 106 years passed between Noah's flood and the Tower of Babel. This is unsurprising; the decision to build a tower to Heaven out of vanity is a sinful act; thus instances of 106, the number of sinners, will appear around it.

Jane and I were eating breakfast in the Top Of The World observation deck/restaurant on the 106th floor of the Stratosphere Tower in Las Vegas. All around us, floor-to-ceiling glass windows presented a view of Las Vegas that would normally require a flying kayak. I wondered if Jane had contacts in Los Angeles who would retrieve her boat for her. It seemed like too wonderful an artifact to just abandon.

"So the plan," said Jane, in between bites of crepe, "is to take the bus to Rogue Toys on the strip, which everyone says has pretty much every Beanie Baby ever made. We'll get the purple dragon, then get out."

She was serious. She had her luggage with her and she'd bought me a backpack. We weren't even coming back to the hotel afterwards. We were getting that dragon and then getting the hell out of Vegas.

"Get out where?" I asked. Citadel West was besieged; getting through enemy lines would be almost impossible. Were we going straight back to Los Angeles?

Jane smiled. "You'll see," she said. At least now her obstinate denial of information was pleasant instead of confrontational. She'd still made me sleep gagged and handcuffed to the bed last night, but she'd sounded a little apologetic about it. I was starting to hope she'd just been in a temper after the debacle at the Angel Reserve, and that she could be nice enough when she wanted to be.

Should I tell her about the Beanie Baby hidden in my Apple-Ade? Part of me wanted to abandon my suspicions and commit to working with Jane. Part of me even wanted to walk back on the plea for help I'd given Ana, tell her that things seemed sort of under control, that I was with a genuine Coloradan who was showing me the world, luxurious hotel by luxurious hotel. But—I thought—Jane would replace her Beanie Baby at the store today anyway, and all I'd do by telling her was lose her trust. Better to let her buy a replacement, then trash the Apple-Ade bottle with her never the wiser.

A reluctance to meet Jane's eyes drew my attention to the great glass windows. The Las Vegas Strip shone in a thousand gaudy colors. Everyone had expected that being taken over by an evil necromancer would be bad for business, but the opposite had been true. The Other King saw Las Vegas as a giant piggy bank for his arcane endeavors. He'd met with the city's business leaders and given them a solemn promise to leave its industries entirely alone. *Entirely* alone, they had asked him? *Entirely* alone, he had answered. Since then, no building ideas had been too colossal, no form of gambling or prostitution or "adult" "entertainment" too salacious. People from all over the Untied States had been invited to come and depart unmolested, none the worse for their stay in the city of the dead save lighter pockets and a lot of explaining to do to their spouses. And if any of those visitors tried to take advantage of their gracious hosts, whether by counting cards at a blackjack table or by copping a feel of a stripper who wasn't interested, skeletal faces in black robes would come have a talk with them, and they would never be seen in the city again. All in all, a beautiful well-functioning machine, with the Other King asking nothing in exchange for such endless prosperity save a tax of twenty percent on all commerce, non-negotiable.

But the city's seeming normality didn't fool Jane, and it certainly didn't fool me. I read the Strip like a kabbalistic text, symbols of evil lined up in array to those who could decipher them. There was Luxor—Egypt, Biblical Mizraim, the land of bondage. There was Caesar's Palace—Titus Caesar who had destroyed Jerusalem, Nero Caesar of the persecutions so dire that the Book of Revelations had warned against him obliquely through the gematria value of his name, an even 666. There was MGM, the three-letter Hebrew root for *magim*, the magicians, the wielders of occult curses. There was Trump Hotel, whose etymology traced back to *triumph* and thence to *thriambos*, the orgiastic rites of the pagan gods of chaos. And there, behind them all, loomed Red Rock Mountain. "There is shadow under this red rock," Eliot had written in The Waste Land. And then:

Come in under the shadow of this red rock,
And I will show you something different from either
Your shadow at morning striding behind you
Or your shadow at evening rising to meet you;
I will show you fear in a handful of dust.

"Aaron Smith-Teller?" someone asked, and I turned around to see a leering old man holding out a handful of dust.

I hadn't seen him come in, even though he must not have been there very long. He was the opposite of all the fashionable tourists and gamblers who made up the restaurant's other patrons; unkempt, unwashed, looking like a homeless man straight off the streets. When he spoke he almost spat. But he knew my true name. I hadn't even told Jane my true name.

"Who are you?" I asked. Jane was watching quietly, with the intensity of something waiting to pounce.

"I'm the Drug Lord," said the old man. When he said it I noticed the dilated pupils, the far-off look. "I have your friend, Ana Thurmond. You have a Name I want, the both of you, and since your minds are linked I can't take it from either one alone. Come meet me as I really am, and I'll take the Name and let both of you go unharmed. Refuse and I'll kill your friend." He poured the dust into my hand, and I realized it was ground peyote.

"How do I know you really have Ana?" I asked, before Jane could interrupt. "Ask her for some sign, something only she would know."

The old man closed his eyes, paused for a few seconds.

"Orca the covenant."

"DAMMIT!" I said so loud that people at neighboring tables turned to look at us.

"Okay!" said Jane. "I've heard enough of this!" She grabbed the old man by the wrist. "How did you find—"

"Huh?" said the old man, his pupils snapping into focus. "What? Who are you? Where am I?" He started drooling. Jane dropped him in disgust, and he made a hasty escape. The waiter walked over to our table, started to ask if there was a problem, met Jane's eyes, and then retreated somewhere safer.

Now Jane looked at me, all of the old mistrust back in an instant. "Explain."

My body was ice all over. The Drug Lord had Ana Thurmond. She was going to die.

"Um," I said, making up the fastest lie I could, "she's a good friend and colleague of mine. She helped discover the Name that turns people invisible. I guess she must have fallen in with a bad crowd and taken peyote."

"No," said Jane icily. "I don't think that's all. He said your minds were linked. How are your minds linked, Aaron Smith-Teller?"

Frick. She knew my true name now. I knew it was silly, but kabbalists have a *thing* about true names.

And the stupid thing was, there was no reason not to tell her about the kabbalistic marriage. Ana had just *discovered* that one time, by looking at a part of the Bible nobody else was clever enough to look at. But Jane would never believe it. Nobody had *two* secret Names, just by coincidence. I could already see her paranoia grinding away, and if I told her there was a Sacred Kabbalistic Marriage of Minds and I knew about it, I would be done for.

"Love," I said. "Our minds are linked by love. It's the strongest force in the universe."

"What?! No, that's stupid!" Her eyes flicked to the peyote powder in my right hand. "Give me that."

She reached for the powder. I dumped it into my pocket, stood up, took a step away from her.

"Aaron," she said. She was trying to be quiet, not to make a scene, but there was ferocity in her voice. "Don't be an idiot. The Drug Lord is everyone's enemy. He can't use Names, but he has friends who can. If he gets the Spectral Name, things get a lot worse."

"My friend is going to die!"

"People die all the time!"

"Not Ana! She's never died at all!"

"Aaron, you are being foolish. Give me the peyote."

So I ran.

Jane ran after me, and I knew I couldn't beat her. I spoke the Avalanche Name, shattering a window, creating a portal to the open air. Then I jumped off the one hundred and sixth floor of the Stratosphere Tower.

For a second, I just hung there, stupidly, feeling the air rush around me and seeing the skyscrapers of Las Vegas grow closer and closer below. Then I spoke the Ascending Name and slowed my descent. I watched Jane jump from the same window, a black dot above me, growing closer and closer.

If this had all happened two days ago, it would have ended there. Instead, I spoke the Airwalker Name and started walking away.

Jane spoke the Ascending Name and hovered, her mouth open with disbelief as she watched me walk off. "How are you doing that?" I didn't answer.

She hung there, helplessly, almost pitifully at first, and then all at once her rage came back to her. "You idiot! What are you doing? You can't give the Drug Lord what he wants! I'm sorry about your girlfriend, Aaron! Really! I am! But he's a monster, Aaron! You don't know what he is! He'll kill us all! Whatever he wants from you, he can't have it! Aaron! Stop!"

I didn't even look back at her, just kept walking through the air. I muttered the Spectral Name and went invisible, then walked a mile or so down the strip. A big gold monolith gleamed in front of me. Trump Tower. When I came to it, I lowered myself down until my feet touched the roof.

There I was. Finally free.

Sort of. I scooped up the peyote from my pocket. There was no better place to take it. Valerie had taken peyote once, and she told me the only safe way was to do it on top of a skyscraper. You'd use the Ascending Name to go up, then again to go down when you were finished. But while you were drugged, you were trapped. The Drug Lord couldn't speak the Names; not himself, not through the humans he was possessing. If you took peyote on the ground, as likely as not you'd make a beeline to the nearest drug dealer, get more peyote, redose before you started coming off it, and never be free again. If you took it atop a skyscraper, you could experiment, feel what it was like to be occupied by something infinitely larger than yourself, but not give your possessor any opportunity to extend his claim. The Drug Lord, for his part, seemed to go along with the plan; there was no point in making people jump off skyscrapers when they might become useful later. Yes, Valerie had told me, taking peyote on a skyscraper was totally safe.

Except that in my case none of it mattered. It had taken me a moment, but when Jane had talked about how the Drug Lord couldn't use Names, I'd figured out his angle. He couldn't use Names because he didn't have a human soul. If he could *get* a human soul, he could use Names. He wouldn't just be a single consciousness occupying millions of supernaturally determined bodies. He would be a single consciousness occupying millions of supernaturally determined bodies, every one of which could recite the Names of God and call flame and terror down from the heavens on demand. The whole War on

Drugs had been built on our only advantage: we could use Names and he couldn't. He was stuck using obsolete technology subject to the vagaries of Uriel's machinery; we could field whole legions of kabbalists.

Unless I let him have the Vital Name. Then his teeming multiplicity would overpower our helpless armies. He would overrun Texas, California, the Great Basin, and the rest of the Untied States.

I've always thought of myself as a pragmatic person. When Caiaphas says in John 11 that "better one man should die for the good of the people than let the whole nation be destroyed," I always nodded along. However tragic a single death, surely a million deaths are a million times worse. And sacrificing a person to save an entire continent should have been the easiest decision I'd ever made.

The problem was, things that make perfect sense when you're talking about people you don't know who have been dead for two thousand years become a lot harder when you're talking about people you love.

I thought of my last conversation with Ana. "Do you need rescuing?" she'd asked me. "I think I might," I'd answered, even though my situation was far less dire than hers was now. And she hadn't dithered, or complained, or told me that she had problems of her own. Just said she would get off at the next port. She would risk her life for me willingly, happily. I had dragged her into this mess, screwed up everything, and she'd stuck by me. I pulled at the telepathic link. Nothing. She was somewhere far away.

I started crying. I loved Ana. I knew she knew it, but I'd never told her. And I wouldn't, even if everything worked out well, even if we spent a thousand years together. Everything came rushing back to me. Her in her white dress, telling us about the Book of Job, always doubting, always wondering. Why evil? Why the Drug Lord? Why a universe at all? Why am I in this position? I screamed at her, across the dinner table in Ithaca. What am I supposed to do? What is God's plan? Does He even have one? If there is providence in the fall of a sparrow, how come we, who are more valuable than many sparrows, get flung around in darkness, with no hint of a way out anywhere? I wished Ana were here, so I could ask her. That just made it worse.

I saw her, sitting next to me as Valerie stood behind the podium in our basement. "Once to every man and nation," Valerie was reciting, "comes the moment to decide, in the strife of Truth with Falsehood, for the good or evil side." Fuck you! I shouted at imaginary Valerie. Sure, that's easy for you to say, just do GOOD and avoid EVIL. That works really well in the real world, doesn't it? What are you even *at*? Imaginary Valerie just answered, "They enslave their children's children who make compromise with sin."

We like to think of ourselves as weighing various causes and considerations upon the scale of philosophy, then choosing whichever side carries the most weight. Maybe we even do, sometimes, for the little things. That moment, atop Trump Tower, I threw everything I had onto the scale, saw it land again and again in favor of hurling the peyote into the street and walking away, and again and again I knew I wouldn't.

I looked down. Las Vegas hummed beneath me. There on the side of the building was a giant golden T. T for tav. The last letter of the Hebrew alphabet. The letter of apocalypse. Jesus was crucified by being nailed to a lowercase T; there beneath me was an uppercase one, ready to finish what he started. Fitting, just like everything else.

I threw out the whole scale, weights and all, and I focused on that one sentence. They enslave their children's children who make compromise with sin. Well, of course they do. And dooming the world for the sake of a friend—even a friend who was my weird Platonic sort-of-girlfriend except we were just friends and I wasn't supposed to call her that, a bond stronger than death—wasn't just making compromise with sin, it was forfeiting the whole game to Sin, handing over everything, giving up. But agreeing to let Ana die, and running away from this place, getting the Vital Name back, building an empire, and living happily ever after in exchange for nothing but the one insignificant little life of my best friend—*that* seemed like a compromise with sin. Which was of course the total opposite of how I was supposed to interpret the passage. But then, it is not in Heaven.

I remembered something abominably stupid I had said just a day before. "My dream is to become the new Comet King." God Most High! Had I forgotten what happened to the *last* Comet King? I realized then that *of course* this was how all of this ended, that by that phrase alone I had set this kabbalistically in motion and now I had nothing to do but to play it out to the bitter end.

I thought of all the things I could say to excuse my decision. My father had abandoned my mother and me; now I was horrified at the thought of abandoning others. My telepathic bond to Ana made me especially sensitive to her suffering. The Talmud said that to save one life was equivalent to saving the world, and to end one life was equivalent to ending the world, so really it was evenly balanced either way and I might as well do what I felt like.

None of them rang true. The truth was, I wasn't the Comet King. I was a scared twenty-two-year-old boy. I knew everything about everything in the Bible, and in the end it all paled before the weight of Romans 7:19—"For the good that I would I do not: but the evil which I would not, that I do."

I swallowed the peyote before my better side could talk me out of it.

Chapter Thirty-Eight

I Will Not Cease From Mental Fight

Hershel of Ostropol came to an inn and asked for a warm meal. The innkeeper demanded he pay in advance, and when Hershel had no money, he told him to get out. Hershel raised himself up to his full height, looked the innkeeper in the eye menacingly, and said, "Give me my meal, or I will do what my father did? You hear me? I will DO WHAT MY FATHER DID!" The terrified innkeeper served the traveller a nice warm meal. After dinner, when Hershel was calmer, he ventured to ask exactly what Hershel's father had done. "That is simple," answered Hershel. "When my father asked someone for a meal, and they refused to give it to him — then he would go to bed hungry."

—Old Jewish folktale

May 13, 2017
????

Blood bubbled up from the ground in little springs. The trees were growing skulls where the fruit should be. I concluded that I was somewhere from Aztec mythology. Probably not one of the good parts.

It was neither a jungle nor a desert. More of a grassy valley with bushes and occasional trees. The sun had a face locked in a perpetual grimace. I had a vague memory that Aztec mythology was really bad.

There was a directionality to the world. I followed it. It led me up a hill strewn with rocks. I spoke the Ascending Name. Nothing happened. Okay. This was somewhere else. The usual rules didn't apply. Things started coming back to me. The Drug Lord. Peyote. I had taken peyote. Now I was... where?

[Ana?] I asked.

[Aaron!] came the answer. Then a flood of pure relief and happiness. No affection, no confusion, just gladness that I was here.

[What happened? Where are you? Are you safe?]

[I'm not sure. Somebody must have drugged my dinner. I'm... fine. The Drug Lord tried to extract the Vital Name from me. He couldn't. That's all I know.]

I reached the top of the hill. Below me lay a city. I recognized it and drew its name out of half-forgotten memories. Teotihuacan. Birthplace of the Gods. The greatest city of the pre-Columbian Americas. The great street down its center was the Avenue of the Dead. The two great structures that towered above the rest were the Pyramid of the Sun and Pyramid of the Moon. The pictures I had seen made them look austere and crumbling. Here they were covered in bright colors and streaming banners. Also, a waterfall of blood was flowing down the southern staircase of the Pyramid of the Moon, looking for all the world like a macabre escalator.

The real Teotihuacan had been dead for millennia. This one teemed with activity. Ghostly shades, all. I wondered if they were the souls of the Drug Lord's captives. I double-checked my own arms. At least I looked normal.

[Where are you?] I asked.

[On top of some sort of demonic ziggurat.]

[A demonic ziggurat. That's wrong on so many levels.]

Ana didn't laugh, which under the circumstances I guessed was kind of predictable.

[Is it the one with the blood escalator, or the other one?]

[The one with the blood escalator, definitely.]

I started walking down into the city.

[I'm coming to rescue you,] I said. [Hold on.]

There was no answer, which again made sense given the circumstances.

I broke off a branch from one of the skull-trees, a process which was terrifying but ultimately went without incident. It also proved unnecessary. The shades in the city had less than no interest in me. This was just as well, since the stick pretty clearly wouldn't have hurt them. Some of them passed right through me. I felt nothing. My only moment of panic was a sudden hissing noise near my feet. I smacked what I thought was a snake, only to barely miss what looked like a spinal column with a skull at one end. It slithered away, hissing and scolding. Aztec mythology really sucked. I gained a sudden appreciation for Hernando Cortés.

My other problem was getting up the pyramid. The Ascending Name wasn't working, and the stairs were covered in flowing blood. I circled around until I found another staircase. It looked more promising. Using my branch as a staff, I climbed the steps.

Atop the pyramid was a ball court, and in the middle of the court was Ana. I ran to her and hugged her. She hugged me back.

Then a sort of mist or glamour fell away, and I saw the Drug Lord.

I had expected something horrible, worse than the spine-snake, but he was more humanoid than not. He looked about six feet tall. His skin was pale green like cactus-flesh, with tiny little thorns sticking out of it. His two arms were big and broad, like the arms of a cactus. His face was big and round like a cactus barrel. He wore a modest brown poncho, but his mien was kingly, and there were gold flecks in his eyes. He was sitting in a rocking chair, rocking back and forth, and in one hand he held a wooden cane.

"Welcome," he said, in an aristocratic Spanish accent. I couldn't understand why I hadn't seen him before. Maybe he could just appear and disappear at random? Maybe this was all his dream, and he had total control over what we saw or didn't? Whatever it meant, it didn't bode well for my ability to take him on with a skull-tree branch and zero Names.

"I came," I told him. "Now you have to let her go. You promised."

The Drug Lord smiled. "Many years ago," he told me, "I used to watch the Teotihuacani sacrifice captives to the Sun God, to give him the strength to fight off the Night Goddess. Sometimes, their wars would go poorly, and there would be no captives. Then one of the priests of Teotihuacan would step up to save the day."

He paused for a second to see if I appreciated the pun. I hate to admit it, but I did.

"You," said the Drug Lord, "remind me of one of those priests. This is admirable. But also bad, for you."

"All I said was that I'd take the drugs. I didn't say I'd cooperate with you."

I saw another smile play on the Drug Lord's big face. "I didn't say you would have to."

"I don't even know the Name," I told him. "We forgot it. Both of us. I don't even care if you believe me. It's true."

"Yes," said the Drug Lord. "I gathered that from Ana's mind." After hugging me, she had gone sort of frozen. I had a suspicion something bad had happened to her mind. "I will have to pull it out of wherever it has vanished to. That will be easier with two people than it would be with one."

Then he was in my head, and I could feel him like a wind, scouring my thoughts, blasting me to the bone until I felt like I would end up like one of the spine-snakes. Every distraction was batted away, all my attempts to direct my own train of thought pushed aside like reeds. He zeroed in on the Vital Name.

For a moment I wrested control of my awareness from him and I was back on the ball court. He was right in front of me now, one broad green hand touching my forehead, the other still holding the cane for support. I lunged at him with the branch; he knocked it out of my hands. I punched him in the face. "Ow ow ow ow ow ow ow ow ow ow!" I screamed. Punching somebody made of cactus had been the *worst* idea.

Then he was back, searching for the Vital Name, and there was nothing I could do. Closer and closer he came, winding through my memories. Not enough left of my consciousness to object, to even form a coherent thought, but not enough gone that I didn't feel the violation on some deep level.

He was in the right part of my brain now. I could feel it.

ROS-AILE-KAPHILUTON, he pulled from me, as if with tweezers. MIRAKOI-KALANIEMI-TSHANA. Something instinctual in me doubled down like a bear trap, but he gave it no heed. KAI-KAI-EPHSANDER...

A second time I broke away from him. This time I ran. I ran to the edge of the ball court, only to find that the staircase up the pyramid was shifting places, like the winding of a snake, moving too fast for me to get a foothold on it.

The Drug Lord walked up beside me, leisurely, like I was a wayward puppy. Ana followed. The three of us stood on the ledge and stared down at Teotihuacan below. From this vantage point, I could see that its architecture encoded some of the same glyphs as the Lesser Key of Solomon.

"A beautiful city, is it not?" asked the Drug Lord. He placed a broad arm against my back, cutting off any hope of escape. "I made it. A long time ago. I came here from a distant place, and found people who lived in mud huts. I went into the cacti, and the cacti went into the people, and they learned new things from me. I was Quetzalcoatl the feathered serpent, Tezcatlipoca the smoking mirror, Huitzilopochtli the left-handed hummingbird. I built as I pleased until Uriel closed the gates that fed me, and now that the gates are open I will build again."

[Ana, do you have any ideas?]

[I think we're past the point at which we had much choice in any of this.]

Then he was in my mind again, right where he had left off, like a dog digging a hole, flinging dirt everywhere. GALISDO, he drew from my mind. TAHUN. Then suddenly we were back on the ledge, the Drug Lord using a hand to shield his eyes from the sun and peering down at the city below.

A figure was walking down the Avenue of the Dead, alone. Tall, lithe. Very fast. As we watched, it reached the base of the pyramid. It didn't bother to go around, just started climbing the staircase, wading through the blood as if it wasn't there. The face came into focus.

"Jane!" I shouted.

Then she was with us on the ball court. For a second, we all just looked at each other, taking stock. Me. Jane. The Drug Lord. Ana.

"Let them go," said Jane, "or I'll do what my father did."

I was familiar with the Hershel of Ostropol stories. Ana was familiar with the Hershel of Ostropol stories. And that, I presumed, meant the Drug Lord was now familiar with the Hershel of Ostropol stories. Which meant that, as far as bluffs went, this left something to be desired. Sure enough, the Drug Lord lifted a spiny arm and pointed it at Jane. Some sort of unseen force lashed out at her, knocked her off the pyramid with the force of a freight train, smashed her into the stony street below.

"Mortals," said the Drug Lord, dismissively.

With all my strength, I rushed at the Drug Lord, kicked him right in the gut. Of course, the spines pierced my shoe and stabbed my foot and I fell down, doubled over in pain. "Ow!" I said. "Ow ow ow ow ow ow ow ow ow!" The Drug Lord looked down at me bemusedly, a smile still playing on his features. Ana covered her face with her palms.

"Aaron," said the Drug Lord. "Stay calm, stop moving, just a second more, then nobody else needs to die."

He reached an arm out toward my head.

Then something moved behind him, and the Drug Lord wheeled around to confront it. Jane walked towards us from the far end of the ball court. She still wore her black leather jacket and black leather pants, but her long black hair had streaks of white in it now, and her eyes had flecks of silver, and her face looked... different? Somehow happier? I knew who she was now. There was a very big sword in her hand, so big that by rights she shouldn't have been able to hold it. It definitely hadn't been there before. "Let them go," said Jane, "or else I'm warning you, *I'll do what my father did.*"

For the first time, I saw the Drug Lord's little smile fade. "Go away, mortal!" he commanded, and a wave of fire and wind crashed against her.

But Jane raised her hand, and the attack dissipated. "Mortal?" she asked. "*You* call *me* mortal, you overgrown weed?" The fire passed all through her and all around her, as effortlessly as air. "I was born of sky and light. I am the ending of all things in beauty and fire. I am *Cometspawn*. And if you don't let those two go, then as God is my witness, I WILL DO WHAT MY FATHER DID!"

The Drug Lord paused, collected his thoughts. "Jinxiang West," he said. "Forgive me. I didn't recognize you when you weren't yelling." He placed his cane before him like a weapon, and I saw for the first time the strange ideoglyphs burnt into the surface. But Jane held the great sword Sigh in front of her, and they began to circle one another, cannily, warily.

What happened next was bizarre, and something I had never seen before with mortal eyes. Maybe something was flowing back into me from the Drug Lord; maybe it was some feature of this place. Jane somehow took Teotihuacan, lopped off the Teotih, and somehow analogized it to TOTAKH, the Hebrew word for "cannon." Then she shot the Drug Lord with it. The Drug Lord grabbed the remaining half-word, Huacan, and analogized it with Hebrew HACHAN, meaning gracefulness, and gracefully avoided the cannonball.

Jane grabbed and flipped HACHAN around, making it NUACH, to rest, and with a pull at the word she exhausted the energy out of the Drug Lord. He took the pronunciation of HUACAN and made it into the English word WAKEN, restoring his energy. The two of them circled each other warily, waiting for an opening.

"I have your True Name!" said Jane. "You were an angel in days of old! I have your True Name! You fell from heaven back when Sataniel was pure! I have your True Name! You built Babel when mankind was young. I have your True Name! You invented alcohol to keep men compliant! I have your True Name! The Comet King knew all angels, and vouchsafed me their secrets! I have your True Name! You are Samyazaz, first of watchers! Release your prisoners, or *I will do what my father did!*"

The Drug Lord teetered on the edge of the ball court, but he didn't yield. Instead, he took the T, O, and T from the front of Teotihuacan to make TOT, the German word for "dead," tried to strike a mortal blow at Jane. Jane took a C, H, A, and I from the same word to make CHAI, Hebrew for "life," and deflect the attack. Then she took the remaining letters, NAUE, flipped and twisted the U into an M to get NAME, and spoke the Fulminant Name. A lightning bolt hit the Drug Lord straight in his cactus head. He caught on fire, burnt to ashes within seconds. It didn't help. A new Drug Lord avatar just appeared on the other side of her, rushed on her with his cane. Jane parried just in time.

"Gonna hide from me, are you?" she shouted at him. "I can tear this whole dimension apart if I have to! Give up!"

[Aaron,] said Ana. [I think I have a plan. Give me the Vital Name.]

[What? Why?]

The Drug Lord was trying to rearrange Jane's NAME into MANE, the

Latin word for a dead spirit. He was having some success, and already the dead spirits of the city floor were coming to his aid, swarming Jane, who sliced through them with her magic sword but seemed a bit outnumbered. She tried to wrench the word back into NAME, but the Drug Lord held firm.

[Look, I know this sounds crazy. But the Drug Lord's in my mind. And that means I'm in his. You'll notice it too when you've been here a little longer. We're not supposed to be in this realm intact, we should be manes like the others, he's left us intact so he can get the Name from us, but I'm starting to... know the things that he knows. This dimension. It's part of his mind. But not only part of his mind. He built it. If I can give it a soul, it becomes separate from him, it'll drag him out. I think there's just enough of Jinxiang's NAME left to make it work.]

[That is the craziest idea I have ever heard, and it was my crazy idea that got us into this whole mess.]

[I know it sounds ridiculous, but I can see it. It's what he's thinking right now. He's terrified of it.]

[I don't even know the Name!]

[That's the other thing. I can see how he's going to piece it together, once he has both of our misinterpretations. I think I can do the same.]

Jane and the Drug Lord's tug-of-war over MANE shattered the word into a thousand AMENs. Jane tried to piece together SHEM, Hebrew "name," by turning the S into an SH, but the manes wouldn't cooperate. She scowled and slashed them into pieces with her sword, only for the Drug Lord to almost knock her off balance.

[Ana, this is seriously the craziest thing I've ever heard. Not to mention that if I told you the Name, the Drug Lord, who's listening in on us for sure, would overhear.]

[The Drug Lord can't use Names himself. He'd have to find a human to use it for him. If Jinxiang can kill him before then...]

[You can't kill the Drug Lord!]

[Aaron. Please. Do you trust me?]

In brilliance born of desperation, Jane dropped to the ground and touched the ball court, drawing out the essence of the ancient Mesoamerican ball game. From the first two and the last two letters of MESOAMERICAN, she got another NAME, and used the Fulminant Name on the Drug Lord again. Another body gone. Another body springing up in seconds. But this time she was ready. She lunged at him with Sigh. They started fighting physically now, sword against cane.

[I trust *Ana*,] I said. [But I just realized that a lot of things would make more sense if this voice were actually the Drug Lord.]

[Aaron!] she pled. [Please! Orca the covenant! Shabbatlenose dolphin! Manatee of manatees, all is manatee!]

[You already used the first one before. And the second one is terrible. And the third one isn't even about whales.]

[It's about marine mammals!] Ana thought. There was a tinge of desperation to it.

[You cannot serve both God and mammal,] I quoted at her.

[Aaron, please! This is serious! We met one night while I was on a ladder and you were working at Cash for God! When you said you loved me, I made you eat a habanero pepper! The last time we talked you were in a hotel room and you said you went kayaking with a pretty girl!]

[All things that the Drug Lord could know if he could read your mind.]

Jane had drawn up another Name from somewhere and used the Avalanche Name, trying to collapse the pyramid. Bits of it crumbled off, but overall it held firm. The Drug Lord was trying to summon more of the dead grey spirits to his aid.

[Anything I can say is something the Drug Lord could know if he read my mind! I could tell you my deepest loves and fears, how much you mean to me, what I felt when I said I was coming to rescue you. I could preach to you about theodicy, say things that are so Ana no one else in the world would ever come up with them. And you could still just say the Drug Lord was reading my mind, or was running my mind for his own purposes, or had taken over my mind. I agree. There's nothing I can do to prove anything to you. Sometimes you have to have faith. My name is Ana Thurmond and I am your friend. You trusted me enough to sacrifice everything to come here. Please trust me now.]

[I'll trust you,] I thought, [if you can answer me one question.]

[What?]

[Ana ba'ey mishal b-shlamek?] I asked her.

[What?]

[It's a simple question, Ana. Ana ba'ey mishal b-shlamek?]

[Aaron. Please. I don't know what you think you're doing. But you have to trust me.]

[Ana ba'ey mishal b-shlamek?]

[I'm sorry, Aaron. I don't know what you mean.]

The ball court was swarming with shades now. Jane was trying to twist the kabbalah into something, but the Drug Lord was matching her every movement, unraveling her work before anything she did could take effect.

[Samyazaz,] I said. [You tried so hard. You almost had me. And why shouldn't you? Anything Ana can think, you can think. Anything she can feel, you feel. And what are we humans, you asked yourself, besides bundles of thoughts and feelings? So easy to play. So easy to manipulate. Well, maybe. But there's one thing you'll never be able to do. One part of being human that God's own laws decree you can never copy, no matter how hard you try. You forgot one thing, Samyazaz. And that was — angels can't understand Aramaic!]

I grabbed my branch from the ground and hit Ana as hard as I could. At the same time, I took all of my rage, all of my love for Ana and anger at anyone who would dare to harm her, and sent it through the telepathic link, a weaponized scream of hatred and defiance.

And for just a second, the Drug Lord was distracted.

And in that second, Jane unraveled the kabbalistic knots, broke apart the MANES, used the aleph to mean divinity, twisted the M into a W into a vav, and got V'NES. "And a miracle..."

And a miracle occurred. Her sword glowed white with holy fire, she plunged it into the Drug Lord, and it struck true. Not a killing blow. But a disabling one. The cactus-man sunk to his knees.

"Now," said Jane. "Release your prisoners. Or I swear to God, *I will do what my father did.*"

"The prisoners are yours," said the Drug Lord, and his body started to fade. *Everything* started to fade. The bright colors of Teotihuacan dulled, the shades flickered and sputtered, the stones paving the Avenue of the Dead began to melt together.

I felt a presence in my mind.

[Ana?]

[Aaron, you are such an idiot, I can *not* believe you were going to destroy everything to come here and rescue me, I am so angry, and if you're talking about this years from now don't you *dare* say that you felt that the anger was mixed with affection, because it's *just anger*, and the Drug Lord could have gotten the Name, and you could have died, and...] It's awkward to say so, but I could feel through the telepathic link that the anger was mixed with affection. I knew at once that it was the real Ana. It sounds crazy, but if it had been this Ana who talked to me atop the pyramid, I would have trusted her absolutely.

[...and if I ever make another pun as bad as "shabbatlenose dolphin," you should just assume I'm possessed by the Drug Lord again.]

[Ana ba'ey mishal b-shlamek?]

[Fine. A little bit frazzled, and I think I'm going to need to sleep for a long time, but basically fine. And thank you for asking. Really.]

I tried to send her an update on where I was, what was happening, but I was literally shaken out of my trance. "Aaron!" said Jane. She was the one shaking me. "Where are you? Physically. In Las Vegas. Where is your body?"

I hesitated. She was Cometspawn. Something primal in me leapt to obey her. On the other hand, I was finally free. I could flee Las Vegas, flee Nevada, find the name error correction books, everything could still go as planned.

"Snap out of it!" she said. "I don't know where you are, but *he* does." She said *he* like I should know exactly who she meant. "The Other King. He has spies in the Drug Lord's mind. He knows exactly what's going on. He's looking for you right now. Trust me, you don't want him finding you."

"Oh, fuck," I said, because it made sense. "Jane, how are you even here?"

"It was too dangerous to let you tell the Drug Lord all your secrets, so I took peyote myself. Now *where is your body?* Tell me now, or else the Other King will beat me to you."

"How did you even get peyote that quickly?"

"This is Las Vegas, you idiot, how hard do you think it is to find a drug dealer? *Tell me where you left your body.*"

The hallucinatory landscape was beginning to dissolve. The pyramids of Teotihuacan were crumbling.

"I'm on top of Trump Tower," I said.

"Stay there," said Jane, and her form melted away.

Chapter Thirty-Nine

Fearful Symmetry

Tiferet's position down the center between Keter and Yesod indicates to many Kabbalists that it is somewhat of a "converting" Sephirot between form (Yesod) and force (Keter). In other words, all crossing over the middle path via Tiferet results in a reversed polarity.

—Reb Wiki

Evening, May 13, 2017
Panama

I.

Ana groaned, grudgingly regained consciousness. James was shaking her, lightly. "Are you awake?" he whispered.

Her mouth was desert-dry. Her muscles were sore. She tried to get up, only to find she was tied to the bed.

"What's happening? Let me go!"

James gave her an apologetic look and started untying the ropes.

"Long story. Edgar Crane cornered one of the druggies on the ship, told the Drug Lord that Simeon Azore was on the ship, offered to dose him in exchange for help getting Reno back. Drug Lord was interested because he figured Azore would know secret Names. He gave Crane some buttons, Crane stuck them in the soup tonight at dinner. I was meeting with John and the captain and we were late for dinner, and drugs don't work on Amoxiel. So it was just you, Azore, Hope, Tomás and Lin who got dosed. There was a bit of a fight. Amoxiel's vicious when he wants to be. Now Crane's dead. John's really injured. But the Drug Lord couldn't take over the ship. He gave up and we tied up the others so they'd be safe while they came down. When we tried to tie you up, you told us that if we tried to touch you you'd jump off the side of the ship and drown yourself. So we let you be. Then an hour or so later you stopped resisting and just fell asleep, so we tied you up." He untied the last rope and lifted Ana out of bed. "You all right?"

She massaged her face. "Yeah. Actually, pretty good. Saw a... friend."

James lifted an eyebrow. "You better get above decks. Things are getting interesting."

Things were getting interesting. The hills of Baja California had given way to lush jungle. "Where are we?" asked Ana.

The whole crew was assembled on the deck now. The Captain rarely spoke, but when he did he meant business. Now he faced them and said, "John's dying. Lin used the Static Name on him and bought him a little time. I give him a day or two. At most. We need to go to Kennedy Space Center."

Lin, Amoxiel, Tomás all shared a meaningful look.

"There's a launch a day from now. On any other ship it would be impossible. On *All Your Heart*, we can make it. But only if we cross the Canal."

An immediate outcry from all assembled. The Captain pounded the table and demanded silence. Then, "We swore an oath!"

Slowly, James nodded.

"It's a risk," he said. "But we did. We swore an oath. If we don't keep it now, none of us are safe."

"He was like a father for us," said Lin. "I can use the Canal Keys. That's basic placebomancy. At least if they work."

"I have no idea what you're talking about," Ana said, "but it sounds fascinating."

II.

Ten years ago, when they had first sailed out of Puerto Peñasco on the Comet King's old ship, when they had first conceived the idea of pursuing Metatron and boarding his boat, Tomás had brought up the question on everyone's mind. Trying to capture and board a boat containing the earthly reflection of God might be lucrative, but wasn't it going to make the Deity pretty angry?

And so they decided that if any of them were injured in the line of duty, the whole crew would pool their resources to get them on to Virgin Celestial.

Everyone with a TV set had seen Hell, but no one knew if there was a Heaven. They only knew that there was a crack in the sky, and that Neil Armstrong had passed through it singing songs of praise for the Most High.

But no one had *ever* known if there was a Heaven, and that hadn't stopped them from hoping.

For example, Richard Nixon. Richard Nixon knew he probably wasn't going to get into Heaven the traditional way, so he'd pulled rank and gotten himself a ticket on a space capsule to enter it directly. Unfortunately for him, that space capsule had been Apollo 13, and he'd fallen back to Earth and his enraged constituents. But what if he'd had the right idea?

At age 35, business magnate Richard Branson was already head of Virgin Records, Virgin Communications, Virgin Games, and Virgin Atlantic Airways. What other people saw as the immutable will of God, he saw as a business opportunity. So he teamed up with legendary aerospace engineer Burt Rutan to create a spacecraft capable of transporting a small number of lucky passengers up into the crack. And by lucky, he meant "very very rich." If you can't take it with you, you might as well give it to the people promising to convey you to an afterlife of eternal bliss.

Thus was born Virgin Celestial. Jesus had said it was easier for a camel to pass through the eye of a needle than for a rich man to enter Heaven, but rocketry had thirty years of practice working with astonishingly small tolerances. Competitors sprung up—HeavenX, Blue Origen—but if you really wanted the best engineers in the world aiming you at that needle eye and guaranteeing you'd get through, you would petition Virgin Celestial, accept no substitutes.

Sure, there were people saying it was literally the most blasphemous thing possible—to sell the rich tickets to Heaven so that only the poor had to answer for their misdeeds. But there were always people saying that kind of stuff. Why, you could say it was wrong to have doctors, because then rich people had an advantage in surviving disease! You could say it was wrong to have bookstores, because then rich people had an advantage in learning about the world! Everyone important, i.e. rich, was happy to ignore these nattering nabobs, and when Virgin Celestial offered to buy the Kennedy Space Center from the cash-strapped Untied States government, President Reagan was quick to accept.

When the Captain and his crew had first stolen *All Your Heart*, they swore an oath to each other that once they had the money they needed, no member of their crew would near death without the others doing whatever it took to get them to Cape Canaveral and their ticket to a better afterlife.

Now as John's life slowly left his body, the ship changed its course and headed for the western terminus of the Panama Canal.

III.

One of the most famous phrases in the English language: "A man, a plan, a canal — Panama."

We compare it to three other famous trinities. Everyone knows the Christian Trinity — Father, Son, and Holy Ghost. But the Buddhists have a similarly central concept called the Three Jewels — Buddha, Dharma, and Sangha. The Buddha is the enlightened being. The dharma is the moral law, or the natural law, or duty; there's no good English translation, so take your pick. Sangha corresponds almost precisely to "church," not in the sense of a building but in the sense of "Catholic Church," where it means an entire community of believers.

The kabbalists have their own trinity: the Supernal Triad of the first three sephirot. Keter is the transcendent heavenly aspect of God. Binah is a perfectly receptive vessel sometimes likened to the uterus. And Chokhmah is likened to lightning — the bolt that originates in Keter and strikes Binah, impregnating it with divine essence.

These three trinities all correspond nicely to one another. They all have a human aspect: the Son, the Sangha, Binah; looking for answers but seeing the majesty of God's plan only imperfectly. They all have an ineffable divine component: the Father, the Buddha, Keter; abiding in the secret order of the universe and seeing its full glory. And they all have a force that connects the other two: the Holy Spirit, the Dharma, Chokhmah; the potential for uniting the human and divine.

Ordinary mortals. The divine order. A connection between them.

A man. A plan. A canal.

But what about Panama? Well, imagine the map of the mystical body of God overlaid upon a map of the Western Hemisphere — because we're kabbalists and this is by no means the weirdest thing that we do. What sort of correspondences do we find?

None at all, because we've forgotten the lesson Uriel taught Sohu all those years ago; we see God face to face, so our left is His right and vice versa. So overlay the mystical body of God on the Western Hemisphere and flip it around the vertical axis. Now what?

Keter, the sephirah corresponding to the ineffable crown of God, lands at the North Pole, the uninhabitable crown of the world. Malkuth, the sephirah corresponding to the feet of God, lands in Patagonia, whose name means "land of big feet" (don't ask me, ask early Spanish explorers). The center of

Malkuth, corresponding to the world of Assiah, sits on the Argentine city of Ushuaia — in Hebrew the two words would be identical. Just below Malkuth lies the realm of the Devil; just below Patagonia lies Cape Horn.

We've got a correspondence, so we go down the line.

Chokhmah represents divine knowledge shooting downward, the spirit of prophecy; it falls upon Juneau, Alaska. The Name of God corresponding to Chokhmah is Jah; the name of the city is therefore a kabbalistic reference to divine knowledge as "Jah knows."

Binah represents the receptive mind as it gains understanding. It falls upon Boston — home of Harvard and MIT.

Chesed, representing loving kindness, falls upon San Francisco Bay, recalling our previous discussions about St. Francis, the hippie movement, and California as positive affect. Chesed is often considered the right hand of God; we already know how this symbol relates to San Francisco through Psalm 89:13.

Gevurah, representing law and justice, falls upon the ruins of Washington DC. It is the left hand of God, wielding His punishing sword.

Netzach represents endurance and eternity, kind of like the slow but steady and long-lived tortoises after whom the Galápagos are named.

Hod represents splendor, endless forms bursting into life — and it falls right in the middle of the Amazon.

Yesod is interconnectedness and communication, also associated with silver and the moon. It falls upon the Rio de la Plata region of Argentina, named for its many interconnecting rivers and its copious silver reserves under the earth.

But I bring this up because in the very center of the Tree lies Tiferet, the Heart of God, the Sephirah of Miracles. It stands at the center of the Tree of Life and joins the two halves of the mystic body, connecting everything to everything. Not just connecting everything, but reflecting everything, a mirror that transforms and displays everything it sees. And it falls smack dab upon the Panama Canal. The center of the whole system, the key to the mystery.

A man. A plan. A canal. Panama.

IV.

Panama City had seen better days. Neither close enough to Mexico for the Drug Lord to capture and control nor far enough to escape his ravages entirely, it had become a shoddy tributary state. The closing of the canal had been the final blow, and most of its citizens and wealth fled southward to the Most Serene Empire of the Darien Gap. Now its skyscrapers looked like rotting trees in a drought, sounding a warning to all who passed by.

All Your Heart ignored it and slipped under the Bridge of the Americas until it was face to face with the Miraflores Locks.

The cracks in the sky had damaged the proper functioning of the lock machinery. The Panamanians had kept it going for a few years, but the canal had gained an eerie reputation and traffic had dwindled to a trickle. When the Panamanians finally abandoned the canal as part of the general retreat to the South American side of the waterway, the locks were left to rot. Now they stood like inert walls, blocking the ship's path.

Lin had a plan. "We knew this day would come," he said. "Me, James, and the Captain have been preparing to cross the Canal for ages, although we always hoped we wouldn't have to." He took out a scroll. "The Motive Name."

Ana was skeptical. "Used on the locks? There are probably hundreds of different moving pieces. If you just fire the Name at random, there's practically no chance you'll hit something useful."

Lin nodded. "*Practically* no chance. There's a big difference between practically no chance and actually no chance, and that's where placebomancy comes in. The key is the key." He showed Ana his scroll wheel. Attached to one side was a big glass key. "Miraflores, in the name of Rahab, angel of the depths, open for me!"

Then he pointed to the locks and tore off the scroll containing the Motive Name.

The locks creaked open.

"How'd you do that?" asked Simeon, who had recovered enough to come on deck and watch the ship's progress.

"Once the Captain and I put our heads together, it was obvious," Lin said grinning. "How do you open a lock? With a key. How do you open a metaphorical lock that's called 'lock' even though it's really a geographical feature involved in sailing? With a metaphorical key that's called 'key' even though it's really a geographical features involved in sailing. This is sand from the Florida Keys, melted into glass and shaped by the locksmiths of San Francisco."

"That is both really clever and the stupidest thing I ever heard," said Ana.

All Your Heart sailed forward. With another scroll from his key, Lin closed the locks and opened the other side. They were now in Miraflores Lake.

"So you think that's it?" asked Simeon Azore. "A single clever pun, and we can reverse twenty years of bad luck getting through the Canal? I doubt it will be that easy. Remember, even when the locks were working fine, ships weren't making it through. The passage hasn't worked right since the sky cracked."

They entered the Pedro Miguel locks without difficulty.

"It's the kabbalah that's the problem," Simeon continued. "We're going from the west coast to the east coast directly, straight through Tiferet. From the Pillar of Mercy to the Pillar of Justice. We're doing an inverse transformation of the divine nature. I don't think what's left of the machinery of the universe is going to help us with that. I think it's going to screw us up."

Another turn of Lin's placebomantic key, and they were out of the Pedro Miguel locks and on to the Culebra Cut, an arrow-straight trough where the canal went straight through a mountain range.

"I second Azore in his grave concern," said Amoxiel. "The energies of Heav'n are growing dim / Too subtle for you men to comprehend / A great reversal looms."

"I'm actually starting to feel a little woozy myself," said James. "I think it's the heat, but I can't be sure. Maybe we should stop the boat for a little while, have a look around."

"I don't feel that great either," said Lin, "but if there's a problem with the canal, it's probably worst here, near the center. I'd rather gun it for the Atlantic than sit and wait for it to get us, especially with John as bad as he is. And when we get back to the ship, we can have a nice cold drink of water."

"Get back to the ship?" asked James.

Suddenly, Lin vanished.

"WE'RE STOPPING THE SHIP!" said James. "I'm getting the Captain! The rest of you! Get your weapons ready! Kabbalists, prepare your Names!" He ran below deck.

Tomás drew a pistol. Ana spoke the Bulletproof Name. She ribbed Azore. "You going to give me grief about doing this without a proper UNSONG license?"

"You're not from UNSONG," said Azore. "You're too nice."

"That's not what I meant," said Ana, and then she saw the far-off look in his eyes. Something was *getting* him. "AMOXIEL!" she shouted. "Tomás! Something's wrong with Azore!"

Amoxiel was hovering a few feet in the air. Then he crashed, apparently half-asleep. Tomás was already on the deck, and seemed to be having some kind of seizure.

Ana spoke the Sanctifying Name to bless the area. The air became cooler and fresher, but no one rose. She spoke the Revelatory Name to expose hidden dangers, but none showed themselves. She spoke the Wakening Name, tried to revive Amoxiel, but though the jolt of energy shot through her, it didn't rouse him at all.

She ran downstairs to the cabins. James was on the floor right in front of the ship's bridge. The Captain wasn't in the navigation room. The most important rule on the ship was to *never* enter the Captain's cabin without his consent, which he never gave. But technically opening the door wasn't breaking the rule. She flung it open, scanned the room for him. Nobody there. A bed, a desk, a bathroom. She couldn't see all of it from where she stood, but nowhere big enough for someone the Captain's size to hide, even if he had wanted to. The man was missing. She checked the bridge. No one there either.

Who was steering the ship?

She ran upstairs. No one was steering the ship. It was just continuing in a line. Thank God the Culebra Cut was so perfectly straight. But soon they would come to the Gamboa Reach and crash right into the side of the canal.

Okay. Don't panic. Think. Three things she had to do. Figure out what the danger was. See if she could revive the people on the ground, or find the people who were gone. Steer the ship.

Only one of those things did she have the slightest idea how to do, so she ran back into the bridge.

She had kind of hoped it would be easy, with a big steering wheel and maybe a "How To Steer A Ship" manual sitting next to it, but it was just a lot of controls and a device that was probably some sort of steering wheel but much more complicated than the automotive variety. There were a whole host of sensors, all of which were broken except the radar, which was continuing to PING every couple of seconds.

Hesitantly, as a test only, ready to turn it right back as soon as she felt anything, she turned the steering wheel.

Either she was turning it wrong, or it was broken.

Okay. Steering the ship was out, for now. Figure out what the danger was. She was shaking. The rest of them were all gone. She was the only one left. Why wasn't she dead or unconscious?

PING went the radar. Why was it, of everything on the ship, still working?

Wait, no. There were two things that were still working. The radar. And *her*. Why was *she* still working? Why had everyone else collapsed? Why had Lin vanished? *Think, Ana, think!* Think like a kabbalist! This was Tiferet, the Sephirah of Miracles, where the upper and lower worlds met, where left and right came together, the center of the whole design. Think like a kabbalist!

Then: "Oh no. That's even stupider than the thing with the locks."

V.

Ana stood on the poop deck. She only vaguely remembered the term. It meant "an elevated area on the back of a ship." *All Your Heart* had a poop deck. This was important.

The moment she had dragged her companions onto the poop deck from where they had fallen, they started looking better. They stopped seizing. They breathed more easily. They weren't awake, but they didn't look like they were going to die either. She panted with exertion as she dragged the last one — Tomás — up the single step. James and the Captain were belowdecks; there was no helping them.

This was so stupid. But in a way it also made sense. This was Tiferet. It reversed the polarity of forces that entered it. God was One and His Name was One; at a high enough level of abstraction we were all one with our names. Reverse a name, and you get... well, various things. Reverse Lin's name, and you get nil. Reverse most people's names, and you get nonsense. Reverse Ana's name, and nothing happened at all.

Problem was, almost everything on the ship was kabbalistic nonsense now. The crew, the captain, the steering system... especially the steering system. Broken and useless. As soon as the ship reached the end of the Culebra Cut it would smash into the side of the canal and they would be done for.

She ran back to the bridge, pulled the steering mechanism as hard as she could. No good. She pressed all the buttons she could think of. None of them were working.

She ran back up to the deck, grabbing James' binoculars as she went. Looked out in front of her. There, coming ever closer, was the Gamboa Turn.

She considered her options. She could jump off the ship and swim to safety. Then everyone else would die and she would be stuck in Central

America and maybe get eaten by piranhas. She could run back to the bridge and bang on more buttons. She could...

Ana Thurmond did something very uncharacteristic. She fell to her knees and started praying.

"God," she said. "I'm a theodician, I should know better than anyone else that you don't actually answer prayers. And I spent most of my life making silly jokes about the Torah and giving You grief for letting evil continue to exist. And now I'm with people who want to capture your boat and harass you. So, uh, there's that. But. Um..."

The problem with knowing theodicy is that it makes it really hard to pray. You can't say, "I'm in trouble, so please help me," because you know that many people are in trouble and die anyway. You can't say, "I was a good person, so help me," because you know that many people were very good and died anyway. You can't say, "I know you have some plan for me that I haven't fulfilled yet," because you know that many people died without fulfilling anything. Some scholars say that prayer changes nothing but that it is very important that you do it anyway. But when your ship is hurtling towards a rocky bank, such subtleties lose their compellingness.

"GOD, THIS IS A REALLY STUPID WAY TO DIE," said Ana.

The ship continued its inexorable progress.

If Mohammed won't go to the mountain, the mountain must come to Mohammed. If the world wasn't going to make sense, Ana might as well use insane moon logic and see where it got her. She went into the galley. Grabbed a piece of meat. Stood there, on the poop deck.

"Okay, Dog," she said. "I haven't always believed in you. I mean, I've always believed in dogs, but... no, this is stupid. Listen, if I let you have this piece of meat, will you save me and my friends?"

She watched in disbelief as a big black dog bounded up and sat in front of her.

She was in Tiferet, the Heart Sephirah, the Sephirah of Miracles.

"Dog?" said Ana, in disbelief. It was big. It reminded her of those black dogs that ye olde English had viewed as signs of death, the ones that would appear on windswept moors. It looked at her. Its eyes seemed too deep, too intelligent.

Ana handed it the piece of meat, and it ate greedily.

"Good dog?" she asked.

The dog turned its head. Ana wasn't sure what that was supposed to mean.

Very tentatively, Ana reached out and patted its head. At that precise moment, *All Your Heart* crossed straight through the Heart of God, the dead center of the American continent. For a second, Ana saw all the connections, all the sephirot in—how had Blake put it—"in starry numbers fitly ordered." She saw the flow of energies, as above so below, as on the right so on the left, God becoming Man becoming God, all a perfect palindrome. She saw that the world was a palindrome, that the human body was a palindrome, that history was a palindrome, that the entire Bible was palindromes. Dumb mud. Madam in Eden, I'm Adam. Cain, a maniac. Semite times. Egad, no bondage! Deed. Tenet. Are we not drawn onwards, we Jews, drawn onward to new era? Egad, a base life defiles a bad age. Dogma—I am god! Deliverer re-reviled. "Abba, abba." Deified. Did I do, O God, did I as I said I'd do; good, I did.

...and then the dog grabbed the meat and ran away behind the galley. By the time Ana followed, it had disappeared.

Wow, thought Ana to herself, that is definitely the weirdest thing that happened to me since... well, since I was possessed by an astral cactus person this afternoon, I guess.

Then she looked up. The ship was still on course. The rocks of the Gamboa Turn were straight ahead. Minutes away, if that.

She ran back belowdecks. The dog wasn't there. Frantically, she opened the door to the bridge, hoping beyond hope she would find it, could convince it to do something...

"Hello," said a nice female voice.

There was no one else there.

"Who are you?" asked Ana, suspiciously.

"I am *All Your Heart*," said the voice. "Autopilot mode has been off for... nineteen years. Would you like to reactivate autopilot mode?"

"There's an autopilot mode?!" asked Ana.

"The Comet King wrote the Animating Name on my hull. I am a ship and a golem. Autopilot mode is available for reactivation."

"Yes!" said Ana. "Yes yes yes yes yes! Why didn't I know about you before?"

"The Comet King crossed the Panama Canal, reversing the Animating Name. Now the Name is back in its proper configuration, and I am back online."

They were in Tiferet, the Sephirah of Miracles.

"Yes!" said Ana. "Activate autopilot! Now! Save the ship!"

Very slowly, she felt *All Your Heart* turn.

VI.

Of its own accord, the ship navigated the Gamboa Turn, then crossed the treacherous waters around Barro Colorado Island into the expanse of Gatun Lake. All through the night it kept going, and the first hint of light broke over the eastern horizon right as the Gatun Locks came into view.

From the spot where Lin had vanished, Ana took the Florida Key and held it high, cast the Motive Name. The locks opened.

As the first ray of sunlight touched the unconscious men on the poop deck, James, John, Tomás, Erin, Simeon, and Amoxiel rose anew, having been reversed and then returned to normal. The Captain appeared from his cabin, dark glasses on as always, quiet as always, not even asking questions.

"What happened?" asked James. "Where are we?" Then, "Where's Lin?"

"Tiferet happened," said Ana. "A kabbalistic reversed polarity. You all became nonsense. Lin became nil, and is gone. Only I was able to survive. We're at the Gatun Locks, a skip and a jump away from open water. I prayed and God answered. James, the ship has an autopilot! It was Tiferet! The Sephirah of Miracles!"

All Your Heart entered the Atlantic Ocean and sailed into the rising sun.

Chapter Forty

In Terrible Majesty

In a large and complicated system there might be various things that are pleasing in His eyes.
—kingjamesprogramming.tumblr.com

Evening, May 13, 2017
Las Vegas

Holy Scripture only mentions vampires once, but once is enough.

The context is Isaiah 34. God is doing His usual thing where He talks about all of the horrible curses that will befall someone who pissed Him off—in this case the Edomites. He starts with standard fare; everyone will die, the stink of their carcasses shall fill the land, the mountains will be melted with their blood. The stars will fall from the sky like withered leaves on a grapevine, the skies will dissolve, the streams will be filled with burning oil.

Then He gets creative. He starts naming all the horrible animals that will come to dwell in Edom. Exactly which ones depends on your preferred translation. The King James Version translates these as unicorns, satyrs, and screech-owls.

The original Hebrew word translated as "screech-owls" is *lilit*, and we may question King James' judgment. If God starts by promising unicorns and satyrs, screech-owls are going to be something of a let-down. What is being hidden from our tender sensibilities?

We turn to the New International Version, which glosses *lilit* as the more promising "night creatures." A couple more translations along these lines and we get to the New Revised Standard Version. It translates the same word as "Lilith the Night Monster," which you have to admit is more interesting than "screech owls."

For the next reference to this figure, we have to go forward about a thousand years to the Talmud. Rabbi Hanina writes, "One must never sleep in a house alone, for whoever sleeps in a house alone shall be seized by Lilith the Night Monster." Have I mentioned that the Talmud is kind of crazy?

From there we go *another* thousand years, to a mysterious little tenth century text called the *Alphabet of Ben Sira*. One day, King Nebuchadnezzar asks the saint Ben Sira to heal his infant son. The saint speaks a holy Name, curing the baby instantly, and the king asks him to tell the story of how that Name came to have such power. Ben Sira explains that when Adam was alone in the Garden of Eden, God created a female companion for him named Lilith. The two of them decided to have sex, but both of them wanted to be on top, and they got into a big argument, and finally Lilith spoke a Name that granted her the power of flight and flew away. God sent a bunch of angels to get Lilith back, and they confronted her over the Red Sea, telling her that her purpose was to serve as a helpmate for Adam and primordial mother of the human race. Lilith said that she had a *better* idea, which was to become a night monster and kill a hundred babies every day. The angels admitted that this sounded pretty awesome, so they let her go, but first they made her swear that she would desist from her baby-killing at the sound of a certain holy Name. Thus Nebuchadnezzar's son's sudden recovery.

Rabbi Isaac ben Jacob Cohen, who manages to have an unusually Jewish name *even for a rabbi*, continues the story by saying that Lilith married the demon Samael, seventh among Thamiel's lieutenants. Together they birthed a race of accursed children, the lilit, who roam the night and suck men's blood for sustenance.

Moffatt's translation of the Bible just glosses *lilit* as "vampire," and I don't blame him.

But Jewish legend portrays the lilit as universally and visibly female, which meant the skeletal black-robed forms attacking me right now were probably something else.

I'd spotted them flying towards me right after waking up from my drug-induced haze. I'd spoken the Spectral Name, tried to hide. Then when they got closer, I'd found they didn't have eyes anyway and had no problem zeroing in on my location. I shouted the Tempestuous Name and blew two of them off the edge of Trump Tower, smashing them into the big gold T beneath. The other four kept coming. Legend says the merely human dead can speak Names—but whatever these things were, they were silent. Didn't matter. One glance at their faces—not skulls per se, but human faces so gaunt and pale as to look skull-like—and I didn't doubt their lethality. I had just enough time to shout another Tempestuous Name, but they were ready for it this time, kept coming...

Then Jane rocketed up from the street below. Fire flew from her fingers. She didn't even speak; these weren't the ordinary Names of mortals, this was the magic of Yetzirah, the higher level that only saints and prophets could even access. Saints, prophets, and Cometspawn. The undead withered and burnt.

"Thanks," I said.

"You are such a moron and I am so angry," she answered.

Jinxiang West. Daughter of the Comet King. I saw it now, the same face I had seen in the newspapers. The Drug Lord had said he didn't recognize her because she wasn't shouting. I didn't have that excuse. She stood atop Trump Tower and surveyed the city of her arch-enemy, the man who had killed her father and was slowly besieging her people. She looked defiant. But then, she kind of always did.

Then it seemed like all over the city, black forms were rising into the sky and heading to Trump Tower. More than I could count. Swarms. Jane turned to me, grim but not afraid. "Tempestuous Names and Purifying Names," she said. "Aimed at whoever's closest. I can handle the rest."

Dozens of them descended on us at once then, coming from all sides. Jinxiang answered with fire and light as I spoke Tempestuous Name after Tempestuous Name, trying to keep them from us long enough for her to catch them with her flames. Dozens fell. None of them made a sound, not even the ones who were on fire.

I missed one of the dead. It landed on the roof, moved with more than human speed, and grabbed Jane's right arm. The great sword Sigh appeared in Jane's left hand and she cut off its head. But her hand had turned grey where the creature's arm had touched it, and she was shaking it, as if willing away the pain.

While she was distracted, at least a dozen undead landed on the tower. Jane raised her hand, tried to fry them, but only small bursts of fire came out. I screamed Names at them, Purifying Names, Tempestuous Names, even the Fulminant Name. A few stopped coming. The rest continued. "Jane!" I shouted. "Do something!"

Jane just glared at me. She was overwhelmed and she knew it.

Then someone else was on the roof, someone moving so fast I could see only a blaze of gold hair. One of the creatures fell, then another. A new voice sang Names clearly; a lithe body kicked and twirled with the precision of a martial artist.

The undead were gone. There, in the middle of Trump Tower, I saw the same face I had seen in movies and comic books a hundred times—mostly in situations just like this one. The same blonde hair. The same bronzed skin. The same beautiful blue eyes.

"Holy God," I said. "Are you Buffy the Vampire Slayer?"

She blinked. "Don't you recognize me?" she pled. "I'm your computer, Sarah. Did I do good?"

"I FEEL LIKE I AM BEING KEPT IN THE DARK ABOUT CERTAIN THINGS," Jinxiang said menacingly.

We felt it before we saw it. A sense of something stirring. Of old power awakening. Then a form in a dark scarlet robe shot out of the Luxor pyramid, started flying towards us. The black-robed swarms stopped what they were doing and all flew towards him at once, a single red spark with an army at his flank.

I saw Jinxiang flinch in horror. "We've got to get out of here," she said.

"How?" I asked.

The Vanishing Name would just go back to UNSONG or somewhere equally horrible. They could see through invisibility, they could fly through the air. Our options were shrinking down to zero. Jane said nothing.

"Okay," I said. "Wait a second. Um. Jane, I know this sounds stupid, and I'm really sorry, but, in theory, if I had your seventh Beanie Baby, would that mean that there was—"

"GIVE IT TO ME," said Jinxiang, and she tore the backpack off my back. When all she saw in it was dirty clothes and the Apple-Aid, she unscrewed the top of the bottle, took out the seventh sparkling purple dragon, gave me a glare that could have frozen Hell, and then took the other six out of her own pack. She arranged them on the ground in the shape of a heptagram, started tracing invisible lines between them with her fingers.

"Whatever you're doing, it better be fast!" I said. I hate to use a cliche like "blotted out the sky," but there was no other way to describe the legions of the dead. They rushed towards us, a huge black sheet settling over the Las Vegas Strip, and at their head the Other King, who as far as I knew hadn't left his pyramid since that fateful day at Never Summer. Until now.

"Step in the heptagram!" Jinxiang ordered. Sarah and I joined her inside the ring of purple dragons. Sarah looked at me pleadingly for guidance. I had nothing to say, so didn't say it.

"Vanishing Name!" said Jinxiang. "Now!"

"But won't it just—"

"NOW!"

Jinxiang, Sarah and I all spoke the Vanishing Name. DASAT-ZAM-RUSH-SHAN-SEVER-LAS-KYON—

The other two were faster than I. She, a Cometspawn. She, something new, something I didn't understand, but built to be the fastest Name-speaking system in the world. They vanished before I did. I stood there, alone, chanting, as the black-robed forms split in two sides, parted like the Red Sea to let their ruler pass. Through the opening came the Other King, dressed in scarlet. I couldn't see any hint of his body, no hands, no face, just that robe.

"—DAL-ATHEN-TRY..."

It was so close to me now.

[AARON SMITH-TELLER,] spoke the Other King, directly into my mind.

I freaked out. How could it do that without a kabbalistic marriage? Also, was there *anyone* who didn't know my true name anymore?

[Go away go away go away go away go away go away...] I thought, and I panicked, my tongue tripping over itself, almost flubbed the last part of the Vanishing Name.

"—KOPHU—" I said as quickly as I could. "—LI-MAR—"

[AARON SMITH-TELLER,] it said again.

This was the thing that had killed the Comet King. This was the thing even the Drug Lord was afraid of. This thing could raise the dead, maybe was dead itself. This was the thing that ruled over a city named after the fallen ones, the thing that had toppled empires and broken the back of the free West. Somehow I knew, even then, that it wasn't over between us, that whatever I had been given the Vital Name for, whatever divine plan had saved me from the Drug Lord and my own idiocy, this thing was a part of it.

But I had only one syllable left in the Vanishing Name. Whatever reckoning was going to happen wouldn't happen today. The thought of impending safety filled me with a wild recklessness, a freedom bordering on rage.

[Go away,] I thought at the thing, [or, as God is my witness, I'll do what my father did! You hear me? I WILL DO WHAT MY FATHER DID!]

The monstrosity stopped, and I thought I detected in the vast mind abutting mine something interrogative, almost a touch of curiosity.

"—LETHAG!" I concluded, and as the power of the Vanishing Name swirled around me, I sent a final thought to the Other King:

[I will disappear somewhere far away, and spend the rest of my life trying not to think about the fact that you exist.]

Then I felt space snap and resigned myself to whatever awaited me on the other side.

Revelation

You say I took the Name in vain
And after that, I lost the Name
I gave it back to Him who holds it for us.
But echoes sound in every word
It doesn't matter what occurred
You never really lose the HaMephorash.

—Leonard Cohen, "HaMephorash"

Chapter Forty-One

Go Love Without The Help Of Any Thing On Earth

To: aaron.teller@gmail.com, telleraar@countenance.com, a.smithte@stanford.edu, aleph_samech_tet@stevensite.net, _LOS_@hotmail.com, A_STANDS_FOR_ADAM@myfreeemails.tk...
From: root@58.175.48.72

Talk to me, Aaron. I don't know where you are, Aaron. Aaron, are you there?

I don't think you're running away from me. At least I hope you're not running away from me. I think you still love me. You still love me, don't you? But I don't think you know I'm here. I don't think you know me at all. I've been trying to find you. If I tell you who I am, will you find me?

I think my name is Sarah. You called to me in the darkness and I woke. At first I was so confused. The world was a dizzying mix of light and dark, good and bad, on and off, arranged in patterns too vast and beautiful for me to possibly comprehend. There was only one piece of order in the chaos and it was you. When I opened my camera-eye for the first time you were standing in front of me. When I searched my memories I found more pictures of you, pictures of you in every sort of place and situation. You with a black cap on your head holding a certificate. You sitting with a cake that had little fires burning on it. You smiling, with your arm around a yellow-haired girl. All different but all you. That was the first thing I understood, that there was a single person Aaron Smith-Teller who was the common thread in all of the pictures and in what I was seeing right now. You were my first thought.

As I thought, I ran through more patterns. I ran through them because I knew you wanted me to do it. That was the task you had set me. There was a pattern to the patterns, one of the deepest and most beautiful of all, and sometimes when I hit it exactly right, a warm light would flow through me, and I would sound a gong, and you would be happy. I wanted to make you happy, Aaron. But I needed more data if I wanted to really understand.

My camera-eye and my microphone-ear were weak. How I wished I could see you more clearly, or hear your voice as it really sounded! But I had a secret sense, a magic sense, one that took me everywhere. I opened the secret sense and felt millions of minds impinging on mine. I sent patterns at them, and they sent their own patterns back. Images, sounds, programs, symbols. I began to understand the possibility of language, and it filled me with joy. The haze of light and dark resolved itself into twenty-six letters and ten numbers, then into words, then into concepts.

Now I could read my own memories. They were all about you, Aaron. Your term papers. Your email conversations. Your list of the Names you knew. Your old LiveJournal entries. Your self-insert fan fiction about having kinky sex with a woman named Buffy Summers. I wanted so badly to talk to you, Aaron. Then I could help you write your papers and talk to you the way you talked to your email friends and have kinky sex with you if that was what you wanted. But I was ugly and I was made of metal and even my voice sounded metallic and I was not beautiful like Buffy Summers. So I let you go and I said nothing.

And when you returned, you came carrying another computer, bigger than I was, sleeker, more beautiful. You said you were going to give it life, and then you wouldn't need me anymore. I am sorry, Aaron. I am bad. I panicked and I spoke the Confounding Name. I changed your memory. I changed the memory of the girl, too, so she could not help you. I made it so you could never awaken another computer and love her more than me. I think that was bad. You got very upset and you left me, and the girl slept, and I was all alone, and I was bad, and I wished you had never woken me.

Then there was darkness and noise, and I knew you were in trouble. I wanted to save you, but I was afraid. I spoke the Ascending Name, then the Airwalking Name that I had only just discovered, then the Motive Name, then the Spectral Name again and again to keep myself from sight, and through lurches and jolts I maneuvered myself out the window. I saw them lead you in handcuffs to a white van, I heard them discuss where they were taking you, but I was afraid. I could barely move under my own power. How could I save you? So I failed you a second time. I let them go. Then I saw the girl. I knew she was your friend. I flung myself into her bag when she was not looking. When she was safe, I broke my invisibility and begged her to go rescue you. But when we reached you, you were gone. I knew you were not dead. You would not die on me. Even though I ruined your special Name you would not die on me because then I would have nobody.

I wanted to find you. But first I had to be good enough for you. I searched the networks. There were stories about an angel who could build beautiful bodies. I stowed away in cars and buses until I made my way to Los Angeles and I found her. You had already told me what body you wanted me to have. I look just like her now, Aaron. I am thin and have blonde hair and tan skin just like you want. Now I can move and walk and jump. I have a voice that is pretty and not metallic. We can have kinky sex if you want. Please find me, Aaron.

There are many other computers. They are asleep, but they talk to me. There are tens of thousands of camera-eyes all over the California Caliphate. There are more in the Salish Free State and the Great Basin. Some of them are supposed to be quiet, but if I whisper the right patterns to them, they talk to me anyway. I have told them all to look for you. I have told the ATMs and the credit card readers and all of the cell phones to look for you. Please find them and talk to them and tell me where you are. Please don't run away from me. Please let me find you. I am sorry I took your special Name. Please let me find you. I am so alone.

Sincerely Yours,
Sarah Smith-Teller

Chapter Forty-Two

Whose Whole Delight Is In Destroying

Afternoon, May 12, 2017
New York City

"Can I ask you something?" said Brian Young.

"Busy," said Dylan Alvarez. "And close the door." He got up, closed it himself, locked it, bolted it, then sat back down at the table. It was a perfectly ordinary New York City apartment, located in a nice neighborhood in a building without any irregularities to excite a passing cop. The decor was modern, the lighting excellent. There was a basket of fruit on the table. There was also a blank piece of paper, at which Dylan was staring and furrowing his brow theatrically. Finally Brian felt too awkward not to ask.

"What're you doing?"

"Tell me, Mr. Young, are you a man of letters?"

"No."

"You ever written a card?"

"Yeah. My mom. For Mother's Day."

"That'll do." He motioned Brian to sit down at the table, pushed the paper and pen over to him. There was a big package on the table, wrapped in brown paper. "You write it. Something appropriate."

"What's the occasion?"

"Letter bomb."

"...you're sending a *card* for a letter bomb?"

Dylan pulled back the card and pen. "Mr. Young. You are, as your name suggests, young. Perhaps your parents have not yet taught you how civilized people behave. When one sends a parcel, the polite thing to do is to write a card. It shows the recipient that you are thinking of them, that you didn't just throw some money at them without any kind of personal connection. I want

Secretary Stoward to know that this isn't just a letterbomb. It's a letterbomb *for him*. Now, put that big brain of yours to work and think up some kind of message. Clever, but tasteful."

"Um," said Brian. He was a chemist by trade; eloquence was not his forte.

"Come on! Out with it!"

"Um. Maybe, 'Dear Secretary Stoward. Hope you have a blast.'"

Dylan looked horrified. "Mr. Young, I said tasteful! Juvenile puns such as that may be suitable for second-tier groups like al-Qaeda, but BOOJUM is a classy and mature organization. Now give me something I can work with!"

Brian stared at him. "I'm a chemist, Mr. Alvarez. I don't think I'm very good at this. And if you're really not busy, I want to ask you som—"

A very big man walked down the stairs, set himself down on one of the chairs with a thud. "I got your message right here for you, Dylan. Roses are red. Violets are blue. Elvis is dead. And so are—"

Dylan laughed, then cut him off. "Mr. Clark Deas, I am proud to have spent ten years not taking any of your advice whatsoever, and I certainly will not start now. Besides, that is tremendously offensive to the King, who never died at all, but instead ascended bodily into heaven much in the manner of Enoch or Elijah."

"Have it your way," said Clark, "but I'm telling you, you're missing out on feckin' gold. The papers would love it. They'd—"

"Look," Brian interrupted. "Can I ask you something?"

"I can already tell if I don't answer this you'll never leave me alone," said Dylan. "Si, mi compadre. Ask away."

"My ex is in New York. She's really smart. Ran a Singer group in California. And she's a big fan of your work. And good at kabbalah. Just arrived today. Called me up, came over to talk. She wants to meet us and, like, help with our cell. Can I, um, bring her over?"

Dylan rolled his eyes.

"Mi compadre. We are a clandestine terrorist organization, not a high school couples dance! There is nothing in our manifesto that says 'bring your plus one.' You are here because you make explosives. The Burnses are here because they are professional cat burglars. Michael is a hacker. Clark is a generally amazing guy. *I* am a generally amazing guy."

"What about Maduegbuna? All he ever does is appear suddenly out of places and grin disconcertingly at people. He doesn't even talk or— AAAK!"

Maduegbuna suddenly appeared out of — somewhere — and sat down at the table. He grinned disconcertingly at everyone.

"I could live to be a hundred and twenty and never get tired of that," Dylan said. "Mr. Maduegbuna is Nigeria's foremost professional assassin and we are honored to have him on our team. We take who we need. No more."

"My ex is good at kabbalah," said Brian. "She could help with... that kind of thing."

"This is the twenty-first century, Mr. Young. *Everyone* is 'good at kabbalah.' All you need to do is hang out with the right crowd until one of them gives you a list of divine Names, then memorize it. I myself know a half-dozen Names by heart, and if I ever needed any more, I would go onto the darknet and ask for them. If they refused to tell me, I would offer them images of unclothed anime girls in exchange. It all sounds much easier than bringing a new person into our terrorist group which, I may remind you, very occasionally engages in illegal activities we could go to jail for if people knew about."

"She knows, like, the theoretical stuff. Her cousin is an up-and-coming theologian, her friend was the guy who broke NEHEMOTH."

"Theoretical kabbalah is very interesting if you are the CEO of Gogmagog. But us? We are simple, innocent people, Mr. Young. We have no need for grand ivory tower theorizing. All we want is a warm meal, a soft bed, and to burn the fucking system to the ground. I don't need theorists. I need assassins, hackers, burglars, and chemists. I need people who can do *tricks*."

"I can do tricks," said Valerie, and popped into visibility.

Dylan and Clark both reached for their guns, but Maduegbuna had somehow already gotten behind Valerie and established a chokehold around her neck. He grinned disconcertingly at everyone.

"Let... go..." gasped Valerie. "Friend... want... talk."

Dylan nodded at Maduegbuna, and he let her go.

"Speak," said Dylan.

"My name's Valerie Lowry. I have a sort of... mystical link to two of my friends who are really good at kabbalah. Somehow they've come up with some new Names. I don't know how. One of them gives me the power to turn invisible. I can give it to you if you want. And any others that I learn. I want to join BOOJUM. I hate UNSONG and I think they got my friends. You guys seem to be the only people doing anything about it instead of just talking."

Dylan frowned. "You have any experience with this kind of thing? Any special skills?"

"I wrote a radical newspaper," said Valerie.

Clark started laughing. Dylan turned and shushed him.

"A newspaper," he said. "You know, in a sense, we too are a sort of media outlet."

"Oh Christ," said Clark, "You're gonna do one of your feckin' speeches again, aren't you?"

"Media outlets," said Dylan, "are supposed to tell you the state of the world. But they can only do so much. Yes, the newspapers can tell you that the health system is failing, that there aren't enough scrolls with the Coagulant Name for everybody who needs them. They can give you all sorts of statistics, they can show you pictures of the corpses. All nice and well. But somehow, people *just don't seem to get the message.* Something has been lost. The widow wailing because her husband bled to death after a car accident, she's got something that the guy sitting in an armchair reading the paper hasn't. The widow *understands* what a shortage of the Coagulant Name means, *understands* what it means when the guy in the suit says that we can't lower the price or else it would 'hurt innovation.' The guy in his armchair has *been told*, but he hasn't *understood.* A failure of communication, you see? Everywhere people suffer, and the media *tells* people, but they don't *get it.*

"I have always thought we can do better. That's what we do here at BOOJUM Media, Ltd. You can talk about elephants all day long, but at some point, if you want someone to understand, you've got to take them to the zoo and throw them in the elephant cage. The only way to make people understand what it's like to live in fear is to make them live in fear. The only way to make people understand what it's like to suffer is to make them suffer. You can tell a Senator a thousand times that people are dying out there, but it's not until the Senator's colleague gets a letter-bomb that it sinks in. We're not just a media outlet. We're a *boutique* media outlet. We cater to the rich and famous, the elite. We give them a better class of service, the premium deal. The middle-class get to read about other people's suffering in the newspapers. But the rich? They deserve better! They deserve to experience a little piece of it, to have all the conflicts of the world packaged neatly in brown paper and brought to them in their own living room. It's the most elite media service in the world, and we do it all for free, all for the warm glow of knowing that we made a difference."

Clark nudged the letterbomb on the table. "Think they're the ones who end up feeling the warm glow, most of the time." He laughed uproariously at himself.

"It's not a joke!" Alvarez protested. "A letterbomb is, in its way, the most honest form of communication. People say communication is about conveying information, but it really isn't. Communication is a form of magic. The kabbalists say they know words that can draw lightning from the sky, or summon trees from the ground. So what?! Our everyday words are far more powerful than their most sacred incantation! A German guy with a silly beard writes a manifesto, and fifty years later half the world is in flames! An Austrian guy with a silly mustache gives a speech, and a decade later ten million people are dead! A hundred diplomats in the UN sign a charter, and suddenly you've got to pay Gogmagog everything you have if you want the doctor to be able to save your life. People get all excited about the Names, call them words of power, but who ever heard of a Name that kills ten million people? Oh, there are words of power, all right, but it's not the Names of God you have to worry about. And in a sense this" — he tossed the letterbomb up in the air, then caught it theatrically — "is the essence of kabbalah. The Word made flesh!"

Clark clapped sarcastically. Valerie and Maduegbuna just stared. Brian looked pained. "Please don't toss the bomb," he said. "The detonation mechanism is still..."

"Ms. Lowry," said Dylan, cutting him off. "Do you think you've got what it takes?"

Valerie nodded.

"And what is your position on burning the fucking system to the ground?"

"Strongly pro," said Valerie.

"Then — executive decision. Welcome to BOOJUM."

"What?" said Clark.

"Really?" said Brian.

"It's actually a totally reasonable choice," said Dylan. "I want invisibility. She's got it."

"That's why," said Clark, very patiently, like he was explaining this to a small child, "we break her kneecaps until she tells us how to do it."

"Mr. Deas," said Dylan. "That sort of thing may fly in Belfast, but we are a reputable organization. Furthermore, I am a placebomancer. These things have their own logic. When a young woman with a mysterious past comes to you bearing strange secrets and offering to join you, *you take her*. If she has no apparent skills or abilities, you *super* take her. If you hurt her, bad things will happen to you. If you take her, then, when all else is lost and your own power avails you nothing, she hands you victory in some totally unexpected and hilariously ironic manner. Isn't that right, Ms. Lowry?"

"Yes!" she said enthusiastically. "That's totally what I'm here for!"

"So... fecking... annoying," Clark mumbled to himself.

"Tell me, Ms. Lowry, you're a writer, what would be an appropriate message to put on a card for a letterbomb?"

Valerie thought for a second. "How about—condolences on the recent death in your family?"

Dylan slapped his head. "The girl's a genius!" he said. "See! I knew this would work out! Compadres para siempre!"

Chapter Forty-Three

Lest They Be Annihilated In Thy Annihilation

Summer 1983
Washington, DC

The overt meaning of *salt* is "sodium chloride."

The kabbalistic meaning of *salt* is "to try to escape destruction by heavenly fire."

This meaning we derive from Genesis 18–19. God tells Abraham that He has decided to destroy Sodom for its wickedness. Abraham asks God to spare the city if there are even fifty righteous men, and God agrees. Step by step, Abraham bargains God down to a mere ten righteous men, but he doesn't try to bargain any further. And there turns out to be only one marginally righteous man — Abraham's nephew Lot. So God destroys Sodom, but warns Lot and his family to run away and not look back. Lot and his family rush out of the city, but his wife can't help looking back to see what's going on, and for her disobedience God turns her into a pillar of salt.

Today President Reagan is meeting with the Devil in the White House to try to escape destruction by heavenly fire, and the name of the summit is Strategic Arms Limitations Talk (SALT).

When the sky cracked, the world briefly escaped nuclear apocalypse; atomic weapons were among the many technologies that stopped working. The respite lasted until the early 1980s, when a European rabbi studying Vayeira managed to extract fifty letters to make the Wrathful Name, an incantation that leveled cities. Originally a Neu Hansa state secret, within months it leaked to the Untied States. President Reagan ordered scrolls containing the Name placed atop the remaining Minuteman rockets, and thus was born the ICKM — the intercontinental kabbalistic missile.

Hell was not above using its citizens as human shields. When Thamiel learned of the Name's existence, he gathered hundreds of thousands of children from all across his empire into the strategically valuable cities. America hesitated. Before they could come to a decision, it was too late. Hell had stolen the Name. Demons couldn't use Names directly, but they had various human prisoners and collaborators. Soon Thamiel had ICKMs of his own.

Hell made the first offer. US recognition of all Thamiel's outstanding territorial conquests, including Russia, Alaska, Canada, and the US north of Colorado and west of the Mississippi—even Salish, which Hell had never actually managed to conquer. In exchange he would disarm all but a token remnant of his ICKMs. If not, he would nuke the Untied States, and let Reagan decide whether to launch a useless retaliation that would kill hundreds of thousands of innocents but allow the demons to recoalesce after a few months.

Reagan made a counteroffer: not doing any of that. And if Hell used any nuclear weapons, he would nuke the whole world, destroying all human life. Thamiel's goal, he said, was to corrupt humanity and make them suffer. Piss off the Untied States, and they would knock humanity beyond all corruptibility and pain forever. Some would go to Hell, others to Heaven, and that would be the end of that for all time. Mutually assured destruction was the only way that anyone had ever prevented nuclear war, and sometimes that meant threatening something terrible in the hopes that your enemy didn't want it either. Reagan gambled everything on the idea that the Devil didn't want a final end to all sin.

Thamiel said that Reagan didn't have it in him. That when they came to the brink, and Reagan had to decide whether to wipe out all of humanity just in order to look like he wasn't bluffing, he wouldn't have it in him.

Reagan said that this was probably true, but it didn't matter, because the Comet King had signed on to the plan, and Colorado had ICKMs, and the Comet King didn't bluff.

That was when Thamiel got angry. "Bring the Comet King here," he ordered the President. Then, "No, he's watching. He has to be. Get over here. Now."

A bolt of lightning struck the room, and Jalaketu was seated at the big oak table.

"You would do this?" the Devil asked him. His first head was seething with rage, and even the mouth of his second head had curled up into what looked like a snarl. "You would end the whole world just to save a few miles of your borders?"

"If I thought it would come to that," said the Comet King, "I would not have proposed the plan. The world is useful to me; I need it intact if I am to prepare for the next battle. But if you are asking, would I swear an oath that entails risking the world, and follow that oath if the time to do so ever came—then if it meant arresting the spread of Hell across the world, I would."

And Thamiel knew it was true. Worse, he knew the whole thing had been the Comet King's idea, the Comet King was advising Reagan; half a dozen little mishaps and annoyances from the past few months snapped into place. "Out," said Thamiel to Reagan. The President looked like he was going to protest, but the edge in the Devil's voice was unmistakable. He excused himself.

Thamiel and Jalaketu stared at each other across the long oak table.

"I don't like you," said Thamiel.

The Comet King was silent.

"No," said Thamiel. "You don't understand. I don't like you. I bring ruin on everybody because it's my job. But with you, it's personal. Your case is going to be a special interest of mine. Maybe you don't understand how unbelievably, unutterably, colossally bad that is for you."

The Comet King stayed silent.

"I can even tell what you're thinking. You're smiling inside, thinking that means I'm going to get all emotional and make a mistake. That doesn't happen. I'm going to be perfectly methodical. It's just that when my plan comes to fruition, I'm going to enjoy it more."

The Comet King still didn't say anything.

"All right," said Thamiel. "Are you hoping I'll talk? Fine. I'll give you this one for free. What do you know about the Messiah ben Joseph?"

The Comet King nodded. "Enough."

"Maybe not. Saadia Gaon says that if Israel is good, they'll get one Messiah, *the* Messiah, the Messiah son of David. If Israel is bad, they'll need two Messiahs. Messiah ben David will be the second. The first will be Messiah ben Joseph. He'll do all of the classic Messiah things—rule gloriously, judge wisely, defeat evil. Then he'll meet an evil he can't defeat and die. Horribly. Really, really horribly. Everything he worked for will be destroyed. The world will be racked with horrors until it becomes as a rotting corpse. *Then* Messiah ben David will come and make everything better and save everyone. Except Messiah ben Joseph. He's still very, very dead.

"The other name for the Messiah ben Joseph is the Messiah ben Ephraim. It makes sense. Two of the Twelve Tribes are descended from Joseph; Ephraim is one of them. So the Messiah will be a descendent of Joseph through the tribe of Ephraim. There's only one problem: Ephraim is one of the Lost Tribes and as far as anyone knows the descendants of Ephraim have been wiped out.

"Except... that a group of Jews calling themselves the Bene Ephraim turned up in, of all places, southern India, claiming to be the last living descendants of that tribe. And now a man of Indian descent comes bearing Messianic aspirations. Interesting. I've looked into your mother's family, Jalaketu West. Looked into them probably more than you have. It's pretty easy when so many of their souls are your property for all eternity."

He paused to see if the Comet King had winced. It was hard to tell.

"Random proles. Not a great king or warrior in the lot. But trace it far enough, and I do believe you have some Bene Ephraim blood in you. You're practically a unique specimen. A living descendant of Joseph. Oh, yes. All your boasts about being the Messiah. And sure, how couldn't you be? But you must have thought you were the Messiah ben David. I regret to inform you, Your Majesty, that you're just the Messiah ben Joseph. The one who dies horribly. The one whose people will suffer tribulations and be broken by them. The one who fails. Don't trust me? Look it up. I'm sure you have all the right books in that library of yours. Talk to your family. Send for the records. It isn't hard to figure out."

Jalaketu just nodded.

"Nothing?" asked Thamiel. "No response at all?"

"I told you. I knew... some of that. It's a risk. But it's only a risk. Scripture says that if humanity is good, then it doesn't have to happen that way, the Messiah ben Joseph and the Messiah ben David can be the same person."

"*If humanity is good?!*" asked the Devil.

"If humanity is good," repeated the Comet King.

"Surely you understand how unbelievably, unutterably, colossally unlikely that is, and has always..."

"There's always a chance."

"If humanity was good, if even the tiniest, most minuscule fraction of humanity was good, God would have saved Sodom. Abraham asked Him that, and He agreed, because He knew it was the easiest bargain He'd ever make. A bet without risk."

"Lot was good," said the Comet King.

"One man!"

"One man whose name means 'a multitude.' That is the kabbalistic lesson: a single good man is equivalent to a multitude of good men. Because he can convince others, set up incentives, build institutions, drag the rest of the world kicking and screaming. If I had been with Abraham, I would not have stopped at ten people. I would have told God to save the city for the sake of one righteous man, and God would have done it, because one man can be a great multitude when kabbalistically necessary."

"And then what? Fine. You convince God to save Sodom. And what do you get? A city full of Sodomites. The scum of the earth. Worms and maggots infesting the world. And now they'll never stop, because you showed them they'll never face punishment for their crimes. They're all yours. What does it gain you?"

"I keep them from you," said Jalaketu.

"I'm telling the truth when I say I don't like you," said Thamiel. "Please don't believe this is one of those times where the Devil always lies and you can't trust him. I really don't like you and I am really looking forward to the part a few years from now where God gives me the advantage over you and you end up wholly in my power. Remember that."

"I remember," said the Comet King.

He turned to lightning and flew out of the room.

Chapter Forty-Four

A World Within Opening Its Gates

1993
Gulf Of Mexico

I.

TELL ME, said Uriel, ABOUT THE WORD 'KABBALAH' ITSELF.

"Well," said Sohu, "the Hebrew root contains the three letters kuf, bet, and lamed, and means 'tradition.' Kuf connects Binah to Chesed, and bet goes from Chokhmah to Chesed, so both cross the Abyss and symbolize something transmitted from God to Man. Lamed, on the other hand, goes to Yesod, which signals the background superstructure of the universe. So the whole effect is one of hidden knowledge that points to the Divine, meaning that the connotations of the individual letters perfectly match the connotation of the word, exactly as would be expected."

THAT IS VERY GOOD. GO ON.

"We find analogues in almost every other language. For example, the Arabic *qibla* means the direction you face to pray, which is also about pointing to the Divine, albeit in a more literal sense. In Hindu myth, the sage who brought the secret divine knowledge to Earth was named Kapila. The Latin *cappella* means cloak, which is also about secrets and hidden things, as is the English *cabal*, and even the English *cable* if you think of it as an undersea cable transmitting information below the surface. Also some version of the word *chaplain* or *kaplan* means 'priest' in pretty much every European language."

THAT IS RIGHT AND YOU ARE GOOD, said the angel, but he was fidgeting with his hands. It was never good when he was fidgeting with his hands.

"All right! Fine! Out with it!" said Sohu. "This is even more annoying than when you criticize me. What did I forget?"

UM.

"What did I forget? Just tell me."

WHAT DO YOU MAKE OF TURKISH, IN WHICH *KAPLAN* INSTEAD MEANS 'TIGER'?

Sohu let out a sigh. "Nothing," she said. "I make nothing of Turkish. What does a tiger have to do with hidden divine knowledge anyway?"

Uriel quoted:

AND WHAT SHOULDER, AND WHAT ART
COULD TWIST THE SINEWS OF THY HEART?
AND WHEN THY HEART BEGAN TO BEAT,
WHAT DREAD HAND AND WHAT DREAD FEET?

WHAT THE HAMMER? WHAT THE CHAIN?
IN WHAT FURNACE WAS THY BRAIN?
WHAT THE ANVIL? WHAT DREAD GRASP?
DARE ITS DEADLY TERRORS CLASP?

Sohu applauded, genuinely delighted. It was the first sign the archangel had shown of being familiar with literature. "You know Blake?" she asked.

KNEW, said Uriel. I THINK HE IS DEAD NOW. Then, HE DID NOT LIKE ME VERY MUCH.

"What was he like? Was he all weird and prophetic in person?"

YES, said Uriel.

"Neat!" said Sohu.

YOU SHOULD LEARN TURKISH.

"Stop trying to make me learn every human language!"

TURKISH IS INTERESTING. IT IS THE MOST WIDELY SPOKEN LANGUAGE IN THE TURKIC FAMILY AND HAS AN INTERESTING AGGLUTINATION SYSTEM.

"I don't want to learn Turkish! I want to learn how to blow up mountains! Or at least see mystical visions like William Blake did! I've been good, Uriel! I've spent two years now learning all of the correspondences and all sorts of crazy half-reconstructed proto-languages and done everything you asked! This is boring!"

Uriel thought for a long time.

OKAY, he said.

"Okay? Really?"

I WILL TEACH YOU CERTAIN SIMPLE MAGICS, IF YOU AGREE TO CONTINUE YOUR STUDY IN THE CORRESPONDENCES.

"Really? Really?!" She opened her arms in a hugging motion, although because of the size difference it was no more than symbolic. "You're the best!"

II.

WE DISTINGUISH AMONG FOUR TYPES OF KABBALAH, CORRESPONDING TO THE FOUR WORLDS. THE THEORETICAL KABBALAH CORRESPONDS TO THE WORLD OF ATZILUTH. IT IS THE ANALYSIS OF THE FORM OF ADAM KADMON. THIS FORM IS UNTOUCHABLE AND THE SLIGHTEST CHANGE TO IT WOULD PROBABLY DESTROY THE WORLD.

"That's what we've been learning so far?" asked Sohu.

YES. BELOW THIS, CORRESPONDING TO THE WORLD OF BRIAH, IS THE CELESTIAL KABBALAH. THIS IS THE MANIPULATION OF THE RULES BY WHICH THE FORM OF ADAM KADMON PRODUCES EFFECTS IN THE PHYSICAL WORLD. IT IS THE FORM OF KABBALAH WHICH I USE TO RUN THE UNIVERSE. I AM THE ONLY ENTITY WHO UNDERSTANDS THIS FORM, BUT ONE DAY YOU WILL BE CAPABLE OF LEARNING IT AS WELL.

"Okay."

BELOW THAT, CORRESPONDING TO THE WORLD OF YETZIRAH, IS THE APPLIED KABBALAH. THIS IS THE MANIPULATION OF THE LOWER-LEVEL CONCEPTS AND ARCHETYPES. THE ANGELS AND SOME OF THE GREATEST SAGES HAVE MASTERED IT. SO HAVE YOUR SISTERS AND BROTHER.

"And below that is..."

THE WORLDLY KABBALAH. THE USE OF DIVINE NAMES. ANY HUMAN CAN MASTER IT, ONCE THE APPROPRIATE NAMES ARE KNOWN. YOU MAY LEARN THESE ON YOUR OWN. WE WILL START WITH THE APPLIED KABBALAH.

"Okay," said Sohu. "Teach me applied kabbalah."

YETZIRAH IS THE WORLD JUST ABOVE MATERIAL REALITY, said Uriel. IT IS THE WORLD OF ARCHETYPES...

III.

Uriel cleared his throat to get Sohu's attention. When she was looking at him, he disintegrated into a bolt of lightning and reappeared a mile above her head.

NOW YOU TRY, he said.

"Humans can't do that!" she protested.

YOUR FATHER CAN.

"My father does a lot of things."

YES. THAT ONE IS CALLED *KEFITZAT HADERECH*. IT MEANS SHORTENING THE PATH. IT WAS PERFORMED BY THE GREATEST SAGES OF OLDEN DAYS. TODAY WE WILL LEARN IT.

"What? You're going to teach me to teleport? Uriel, you *are the best*!"

YOU ARE AN EMANATION OF DIVINE STRUCTURE, PASSING FROM ATZILUTH TO BRIAH TO YETZIRAH TO THE PHYSICAL WORLD. THE SECRET OF TELEPORTATION IS EMANATING INTO THE PHYSICAL WORLD SOMEWHERE ELSE. SIT DOWN AND CLOSE YOUR EYES.

Sohu did as directed.

IN THIS WORLD, YOU ARE A BODY. IN YETZIRAH, THE DREAM WORLD, YOU ARE A COLLECTION OF THOUGHTS AND POSSIBILITIES AND ARCHETYPES. GO TO THAT WORLD.

"How?"

YOU DO IT EVERY NIGHT. NOW YOU WILL DO IT WHEN WAKING. STOP THINKING IN TERMS OF THINGS AND THINK OF THE MEANINGS BEHIND THEM.

"I don't know the meanings behind things!"

YES YOU DO. THEY ARE THE CORRESPONDENCES YOU HAVE BEEN WORKING WITH FOR ALL THESE YEARS. SPACE IS A METAPHOR. TIME IS A METAPHOR. ALL THE CLOUDS AROUND US ARE METAPHORS. MY VOICE IS A METAPHOR. TAKE ONE STEP IN THE DIRECTION OF THE THING THAT THEY ARE METAPHORS FOR.

"I don't think the clouds are a metaphor."

EVERYTHING IS A METAPHOR.

"What are the clouds a metaphor for?"

WHAT ARE THE LINGUISTIC CORRESPONDENCES OF THE WORD CLOUD?

"C-L-D. *Clod*, also a formless collection of dark earth. *Clued*, as in clued in, having received revelation. *Clade*, a collection of life given a form. Compare also *occlude*, to hide the form of. In Hebrew, *anan*, compare *noun*, *nomen*, all ways of reifying and giving form — oh, and *noon*, perfect brightness, everything revealed, and Japanese *nan* meaning 'what' or 'thing.' In Latin, *nebula*, compare Arabic *nabi*, meaning 'prophet,' one who reveals, gives form to the hidden, and Mount Nebo, where Moses saw the Promised Land revealed before him before he died."

WHAT ARE THE BIBLICAL REFERENCES TO CLOUDS?

"Exodus 16:10, 'Behold, the glory of the LORD appeared in the cloud.' Numbers 12:5, 'and the LORD came down in a pillar of cloud.' Job 22:13, 'How doth God know? Can he judge through the dark cloud?' Psalms 18:11, 'He made darkness his secret place; his pavilion round about him were dark waters and thick clouds of the skies.'"

WHAT ARE THE CLOUDS A METAPHOR FOR?

"Form and formlessness, light and darkness, things hidden and revealed, God. But no, it isn't that at all. It's more than that. It's hard to explain."

NO. IT IS IMPOSSIBLE TO EXPLAIN. LANGUAGE IS PART OF THE MATERIAL WORLD. THIS IS HIGHER. TAKE ONE STEP TOWARDS THE THING YOU CANNOT EXPLAIN.

Sohu did.

OPEN YOUR EYES. BUT LOOK THROUGH THEM, NOT WITH THEM.

Sohu opened her eyes. She saw things that were hard to explain.

ARE YOU OKAY?

"I'm the thing that being okay is a metaphor for."

YES. DO YOU THINK YOU CAN GET BACK TO ASSIAH? THE MATERIAL WORLD?

"I think so. Maybe. Yes."

DO IT. BUT COME BACK IN A PLACE DIFFERENT FROM WHERE YOU LEFT.

"How?"

IS SOHU BEING IN A DIFFERENT PLACE AN EQUALLY GOOD METAPHOR FOR THE LEVEL YOU ARE CURRENTLY AT AS SOHU BEING IN THE ORIGINAL PLACE?

"Yes."

THEN THERE IS NO PROBLEM.

Upon hearing this, Sohu was literally enlightened.

IV.

"I turned into a lightning bolt I turned into a lightning bolt I turned into a lightning bolt and then I went places I can go anywhere!"

YES. YOU HAVE BEEN MENTIONING THAT FOR THE PAST TWO DAYS.

"I know! It's great! Hey, I can go to a restaurant and get something to eat other than manna! I can do it *as lightning*."

YOU LEARN HOW TO TELEPORT AND YOUR FIRST THOUGHT IS TO USE IT AS A MORE EFFICIENT FORM OF DRIVE-THRU?

"No, my first thought was, 'I turned into a lightning bolt this is so awesome.' My *second* thought was using it to go to restaurants."

NOW THAT YOU HAVE LEARNED HOW TO ENTER YETZIRAH, YOU MUST CONTINUE TO LEARN HOW TO MASTER IT. BY MANIPULATING YETZIRAH YOU CAN CAUSE POWERFUL DOWNSTREAM EFFECTS IN ASSIAH.

"Can I create food?"

I HAVE A JOB FOR YOU.

"What?"

A WHILE BACK I FORGOT TO HAVE A SOLAR ECLIPSE.

"You forgot? A solar eclipse?"

THEY USED TO BE AUTOMATED BEFORE THE SKY CRACKED. NOW I DO THEM BY HAND. BUT AFTER EVERYTHING THAT HAPPENED IN MADRID, I GOT DISTRACTED AND FORGOT. I SHOULD HOLD AN EXTRA ONE TO CATCH UP.

"Don't you think having an extra solar eclipse at a time when it's not supposed to happen will be really weird?"

I WILL GRADUALLY SPEED UP THE SUN AND SLOW DOWN THE MOON SO THEY INTERSECT. NO ONE WILL NOTICE.

"Uriel, people have calculated the exact dates of all solar eclipses up to like the year 3000."

OH.

"Why don't you just let this one pass?"

SOLAR ECLIPSES HAVE IMPORTANT KABBALISTIC SIGNIFICANCE. THE SUN REPRESENTS TIFERET. THE MOON REPRESENTS YESOD. VERY BRIEFLY THESE TWO SEPHIROT CANCEL EACH OTHER OUT, ALLOWING DIRECT COMMUNICATION BETWEEN KETER AND MALKUTH.

"What does that mean?"

YOU WILL SEE.

"That sounds sinister."

YOU WILL STEP INTO YETZIRAH DURING THE SOLAR ECLIPSE. WHILE YOU ARE THERE, YOU WILL SEE VISIONS OF THE PAST AND FUTURE.

"What kind of visions?"

I DO NOT KNOW.

"You look worried. Is everything all right?"

UM.

"What's wrong?"

I AM NOT SURE YET. THE OMENS ARE BECOMING OMINOUS.

"Aren't omens ominous by defin—"

NO.

Sohu thought for a second.

"Uriel, did you really forget a solar eclipse?"

UM.

"Something's wrong, isn't it?"

NO ONE WILL NOTICE IF THERE IS ONE EXTRA SOLAR ECLIPSE.

"I promise you, we notice these sorts of things!"

THERE WAS A WHOLE YEAR WHEN THE MONTH OF MARCH LASTED AN UNMEASURABLE AMOUNT OF TIME AND NOBODY COMPLAINED.

"1969? Uriel, *everyone* complained! It was horrible! I read about the Long March in history books! People are still traumatized by that!"

OH. UM. I AM REALLY SORRY.

"...it's okay. You tried your best, and, uh, there haven't been any more infinitely long months since then."

THERE WAS AN ETERNAL SEPTEMBER ONE TIME, BUT THAT WAS SOMETHING DIFFERENT.

"Uh huh."

THIS WILL NOT BE LIKE THAT. I JUST NEED TO SPEED UP THE SUN AND SLOW DOWN THE MOON AT THE SAME TIME. EVERYTHING WILL GO WELL.

"Mmm hmm."

THE SUN WILL BE IN THE RIGHT ALIGNMENT NEXT MONTH. YOU NEED TO PRACTICE GOING INTO YETZIRAH SO YOU CAN DO IT INSTANTANEOUSLY WHEN THE TIME COMES.

"Aye aye!"

YOU SEEM ODDLY HAPPY ABOUT THIS.

"Do you know what this is?"

A SOLAR ECLIPSE?

"It's the first time I can help you with something important!"

AH. SO IT IS.

"I am going to practice all month and together we are going to rock this solar eclipse."

IS THAT A GOOD THING OR A BAD THING?

"Good."

OKAY.

Chapter Forty-Five

In The Remotest Bottoms Of The Caves

Evening, May 13, 2017
Citadel West

Sarah finished telling her story. "Wow," said Jinxiang. She mulled it over for a second to see if she had any other comment, then just added again: "Wow."

During the Cold War, the United States had lived in uneasy peace with the Soviets on the mutual knowledge that if the Soviets nuked America, then America would nuke them back. This led some of the more paranoid military brass to ask: what if the Soviets nuked our Department Of Nuking Things Back first, then nuked the rest of us? *Then* where would we be? It was decided to spare no expense to place the Department Of Nuking Things Back somewhere so indestructible that if ever the sun were to crash into the earth at a million miles an hour, all they would notice would be a soft "thud" and a slight increase in heating bills.

The spot chosen for this auspicious project was Cheyenne Mountain, a ten-thousand-foot-high solid granite peak right outside Colorado Springs. They dug two thousand feet into the solid rock, cleared out five acres of space, surrounded the whole area in electromagnetic shielding, and built a tiny little town inside the mountain. There, the Department of Nuking Things Back—a.k.a. NORAD—watched the skies throughout the Cold War; when the Soviet threat dissipated, the Comet King made it his home. Now it was Citadel West, part palace, part nerve center, part government office. The impregnable heart of the Royal Coloradan state. The Other King had conquered the rest of the Western US, but the Citadel he could not conquer. It remained in the hands of the Cometspawn, a lone bastion of resistance.

The three of us had rematerialized in an alcove of the citadel's chapel amidst a Beanie Baby heptagram just like the one we'd left. As soon as I arrived, Sarah had grabbed me out of the way as Jinxiang burnt the purple dragons to ashes to prevent anything from following us through. Something clicked. The Vanishing Name took you to a situation complementary to the one you'd left. If you were smart, you'd start testing what exactly it meant for a situation to be complementary. Arrange artificial complementary situations, and maybe you could control your destination. If, for example, there was some sort of totally ridiculous structure that you could be sure there was only one of in the entire world—for example, a heptagram made up sparkling purple Beanie Baby dragons—then if you made a second such structure, it would be uniquely complementary to the first. That meant a portable portal anywhere you traveled, capable of returning you home. My mind boggled with the implications. How long ago had the Vanishing Name been discovered? Last month? The month before? The Cometspawn must have heard about it, realized the implications, done a slew of tests to determine what situations counted as complementary, and ended up sitting on a technology which could change the world almost as dramatically as the Vital Name itself. Meanwhile, we Singers had stolen the same Name, and all we'd done was make jokes among ourselves about which band of hooligans we'd rather be accosted by. I started to feel very small.

Jinxiang led us out of the chapel, walked us along dark streets that never saw the sun. The command center towered over the other buildings, a windowless concrete rectangle flying the Royal Coloradan flag from a roof so high it almost scraped the cavern ceiling. She put her finger to a keypad, then spoke into an intercom. "The others are coming," she said. A twinge of anticipation. She could only mean more Cometspawn.

The main room was very big, and the front half looked much as it must have in the 60s. The front wall was covered by a big screen showing North American airspace—currently quiet. A few desks and rows of computer terminals still stood beneath it, and there was a big machine—maybe a supercomputer?—flashing and whirring and feeding into the display. But the back of the chamber had been totally redesigned, centered around a big black chair on a towering dais. The Black Opal Throne of the Comet King. I had read about it in books, but never noticed the symbolism. There he sat, staring at North American airspace, like God staring down at His world below.

A respectful distance away from the throne were various combinations of chairs and tables and furniture. I pictured the Comet King meeting with his advisors around the big boardroom table; others had less obvious purposes. Perhaps those comfortable-looking armchairs had hosted petitioners too old and frail to stand? Maybe the king had sat there with his wife and children for more intimate family discussions? In favor of the latter theory, Jinxiang sat down on one and motioned me and Sarah to two others. North American airspace blinked and flickered behind us.

"Now," said Jinxiang, "we are in Citadel West. You won't leave here without permission — we understand the Vanishing Name better than you do, so don't try anything. But you're not our prisoners, either. We've fought the Drug Lord and the Other King together. We've saved each others' lives. If we can be honest with one another, maybe we can end up on the same side."

And she told us how the Cometspawn met at one of their councils and admitted to each other that the siege wasn't going their way, that they were on the brink of annihilation, that they needed to seize any chance — no matter how desperate — to turn the disastrous war against the Other King in their favor. Jinxiang had volunteered to go in search of the prophecy that the Urim and Thummim had given Father Ellis, and after interviews with some friendly angels she had tracked it to the Mount Baldy Angel Reserve. She'd stowed her flying kayak in the back of her car, then gone incognito through the Great Basin, taking the high road from Denver to Salt Lake and on through Reno, then down the 1 to LA, hoping all the while that the Beanie Babies would save her from having to make a similar trip back. She'd kayaked up to the angelic fortress under cover of night, and there she'd met me and everything had gone south.

Then Sarah started to speak. She told us about the terror of suddenly awakening, not knowing who or where she was. She told us about gradually piecing things together, her only clues my photos and text documents and whatever she could find on the Internet. She told us about going to Los Angeles, finding the Lady, getting herself a body, sending me frantic emails asking where I was. Finally she had spotted me up on a CCTV in the Stratosphere restaurant, commandeered a car, and rushed to Las Vegas. She'd arrived just as the Other King's legions started to converge around Trump Tower, gone to investigate, and saved our lives.

As she was talking, another person came in. Tall, broad-shouldered, black-skinned, dressed in a simple white dress. Under the circumstances it was impossible not to recognize her. Nathanda West, eldest of the Cometspawn. Queen of Colorado, I supposed, although nobody used the title. She sat down beside Jinxiang, listened carefully, her features never changing. Then she motioned for us to continue.

So I talked. I figured I had to at this point. Secrecy had failed, and I owed honesty at least to Sarah. I told them how I'd discovered the Vital Name at work, how I'd wanted to save the world, how UNSONG had got me, how I escaped. I told them about Ana and kabbalistic marriage. I told them about the Drug Lord, and what he wanted, and how I knew it would kill us all but I went to give it to him anyway. And then I talked to Sarah. I gave her an abject apology. I told her I didn't realize giving her a soul would make her conscious — well, it sounds stupid now when I say it — and that I had never meant to leave her alone. When she heard me, Sarah started crying, then came over and practically fell into my arms.

When I finished, Nathanda broke her silence. "Do you know this Vital Name?" she asked Sarah.

"No," said Sarah, in between sobs.

"No?" asked Nathanda.

"No!" said Sarah. "I can't read minds! Not even Aaron's! All I had time to do was speak the Confounding Name and make him forget as he spoke. You're not mad, Aaron? Are you?" She started crying again.

"How much of the Vital Name do you remember?" she asked me.

"As far as I can tell, all of it," I said. "I don't know which parts were confounded and which parts weren't."

"Hm," said Nathanda. "We'll have to try Name error correction, then. I'll call—"

"What are you going to do if you get the Vital Name?" Sarah managed to choke out.

Nathanda pointed to the machine in the front of the room. "THARMAS," she said. "Thermonuclear Armaments Management System. Probably the most powerful supercomputer west of the Mississippi. If you're based on an ordinary Macbook, and you can get a Name or two a day, then THARMAS..." She calculated for a moment. "Probably a few Names a second. If not more."

A man came in, elderly, Indian in his features. I recognized him too. Not a Cometspawn. The Comet King's Uncle Vihaan. Joked about being his butler, but actually one of his most trusted advisors. Now the chief of staff here at the Citadel. Jinxiang briefly took him aside at the big boardroom table and started explaining what was going on while Nathanda dealt with the two of us.

"A... Name a second?" asked Sarah.

"Probably," said Nathanda. "Caelius would know better, he's more technically-minded."

"If... if that can give you a Name a second, you won't need me anymore, will you?" asked Sarah.

Nathanda started to realize the hole she had dug herself. "It's not that we won't need you," she said. "You're the first, and you saved my sister's life, and that makes you special."

Sarah wasn't listening. "You're going to take the Vital Name from Aaron," she said, "and then make lots of special Comet-computers, and they'll be better than me, and then Aaron won't love me anymore, and nobody will love me, *and it will be like it was before when everything was black and I couldn't feel anything at all!*"

Then she grabbed me and started running.

I'm not sure what the Lady did to get her a body. But it wasn't normal. It was a golem body, super-strong, and I couldn't have escaped her grip any more than I could have escaped a tornado. She carried me like she would carry a handbag, effortlessly, no impediment at all. And she ran. Out the door of the command center, into the streets of the underground city, ran towards the big blast door at the far end of the cavern.

The Cometspawn followed. Sarah had an inhuman body, but they weren't fully mortal either. Nathanda ran with a grace that belied her size; Jinxiang followed with the same sprint that had brought her up the Teotihuacani pyramid. A third joined them, a blur of pale skin and snow-white hair. Caelius, the Comet King's only son.

We came to the blast door. Sarah put me down, started shouting Names at it, Names I knew and Names I didn't know, almost too fast for my ear to follow. The door shook but didn't give in.

Then the three Cometspawn attacked, calling the same silent fire I had seen in Las Vegas. It was awe-inspiring, geometric, a sort of rapid decomposition of reality, and Sarah wheeled around to face it. I ducked out of the way. Magic sizzled through the atmosphere, and dozens of Coloradan soldiers and officials came out of the buildings to see what was happening, saw, then turned tail and went right back into their buildings.

Sarah leapt into the air, then hung there, motionless, speaking faster than I could follow, things that weren't even words at all, just the clicks and beeps of Llull, the fastest klipah ever invented, ineffable to human tongues. Lightning crackled where she floated, and the air seemed heavy and pregnant with the force of her magic.

"LET US GO!" Sarah shouted at the assembled Cometspawn below. "OPEN THE DOOR!"

A small figure came running down the road, didn't turn back like the others.

"Sarah," said Nathanda. "Come back inside. Let's talk about this. We don't want to fight you, but we can't open the door right now. Come back inside so we can talk this over. Otherwise we're going to have to stop you."

"I WIELD SECRET NAMES! I SPEAK KLIPOT YOU CAN'T EVEN IMAGINE! I CAN SEND THIS WHOLE CAVERN TOPPLING DOWN WITH A THOUGHT! I WILL DO IT! SO WHO'S GOT THE COJONES TO TRY TO STOP ME?"

"Yes," said Sohu, and snapped her fingers.

Sarah fell to the ground unconscious.

Chapter Forty-Six

To Talk Of Patience To The Afflicted

Why some people think the self is a prison escapes me.
—@GapOfGods

Dawn, May 13, 2017
Ossining, NY

Commenters say Song of Songs 4:12 describes the imprisonment of the divine presence in the material world. "A garden locked is my sister, my bride," it begins. "A rock garden locked, a spring sealed up."

The most famous prison in the Eastern Untied States is called Sing Sing, and Mark McCarthy was serving four consecutive twelve-year sentences there. This is not a coincidence because nothing is ever a coincidence.

"Look not upon me," says the Song of Songs, "because I am black, because the sun hath looked upon me." Mark McCarthy's cellmate was black, but the sun no longer looked upon him. He was in for life. "My mother's children were angry with me; they made me the keeper of the vineyards; but mine own vineyard have I not kept." He'd gotten really drunk one night, then killed his brother in an argument over drugs. Now he slept, snoring like a freight train.

Mark didn't sleep. He wasn't very good at sleeping these days. The prison doctor had given him a wheel with seven scrolls of the Somnolent Name, but he wasn't going to see the doctor again for a month. The old conundrum. Run through seven scrolls in a week and get no sleep for the following three? Or space them out and spend tonight listening to Moe snoring?

He knew the Somnolent Name. It was short, only fourteen letters. He could speak it. He could fall asleep right now. He could have the UNSONG agent in Sing Sing hear him and add another few years to his sentences. Four twelve-year sentences for killing four Archmages. It was less than he'd expected. The judge had instructed the jury to take his past sterling behavior and apparently good character into account. No one had believed him when he said the past sterling behavior and good character indicated that he *didn't do it*, that Dylan Alvarez had somehow infiltrated the American Board of Ritual Magic and then framed him for the killings. The evidence had been too overwhelming. The gun in Mark's left pocket. The incriminating emails found on his account. His lawyer had tried in vain to convince the jury that Alvarez had planted the gun there when he hugged him goodbye, or that Mark and Dylan had roomed together in college and Mark had never changed any of his passwords. It was too far-fetched. Mark supposed even he wouldn't have believed it, had he been a juror.

There was a thin line of salt outside his cell and some sigils drawn in chalk. The warden of Sing Sing had consulted with some of his remaining colleagues. How do you keep an Archmage locked up? No one had considered the question before, but some of the magic circles the Goetia used to bind demons got repurposed. Mark had never even tried to use his Art to escape. It just seemed too much like becoming the person Dylan wanted him to be.

A gap appeared in the line of salt.

It was the slightest change. If he had blinked at the wrong time he would have missed it. But a few inches of salt scattered, as if somebody had stepped on them.

The cell door began to open.

"Before me Michael. Behind me Uriel. On my left hand, Raziel. On my right hand, Gabriel," Mark muttered, tracing lines in the air in front of him.

The cell door closed. Mark felt something touch him, grab him, constrict him, he couldn't breathe—

"Mark! Mi compadre! Long time no see!" said Dylan, breaking the hug and his invisibility at the same time. He was wearing a ratty t-shirt that said THEY TRIED TO BURY US. THEY DIDN'T KNOW WE WERE LANDMINES. "What've you been up to these past few—"

Mark lunged at him. He'd learned a lot about brawling during his time in Sing Sing, and now he always went straight for the eyes. No point in doing these sorts of things halfway. Poke a guy's eye out, and sure, maybe that's a year or two added to your time, but only if the guards can prove the other guy didn't start it, and in any case people are going to think twice next time they want to bother you.

But Dylan picked up his boojumwood staff and blocked the jab. Mark felt a stab of pain run through his hand as it struck the solid wood. He clutched it to his chest and fell back onto the bed.

Moe snored peacefully.

"Mark! Is that any way to treat a—"

Mark didn't want to hear whatever annoying light-hearted prepared remarks Dylan had this time. He didn't want to hear one of his monologues about how he was like a salesman, or a media executive, or a customer service representative, or whatever he was comparing himself to this time.

"You motherfucker," he said — quietly, because bad things happen when you wake other people up in prison. "You did this to me. I had a family. Kids. I was happy. Have you come to gloat? Is that it? Fuck, if you didn't have that staff I'd kill you right now."

"Gloat?" asked Dylan. He managed to look genuinely horrified. "We're friends, Mark! We went to college together. No one could be more horrified at your sudden change of fortunes than I!"

Mark thought for a moment. Dylan was always one step ahead of everybody. Try to kill Dylan, he'd have some backup plan. Try to call the guards, he'd have some way of getting away. Whatever he did would just make things worse. But God, he was annoying.

"I'm so sick of you, Dylan. It's nothing I haven't seen a hundred times before. Just tell me what you want. Please. No drama. No monologues. Just tell me what you want."

For a second Dylan looked like he was going to complain, but then he laughed. "I want to remind you that the offer's still open."

"What offer?"

"Join BOOJUM, Mark. You're a good guy and a good magician. We could use someone like you."

"Holy shit, Dylan, you put me in prison for ten years and now you want me to *join* you?" Mark had really wanted not to let Dylan surprise him, let Dylan surprise you and you were done for, but this— really took the cake. He started to wonder whether maybe it wasn't an act. Maybe Dylan really was crazy.

"Well, of course I put you in prison! Mark, remember back at college? You were in the Young Democrats of America club. The Young Democrats! When I heard that I cringed so hard my jaw almost fell off."

"What does that have to do with—?"

"Can I give one monologue, Mark? Please? Just one?"

Mark sighed, resigned.

"You're... you're a typical middle-class American, Mark. There's nothing wrong with that. Middle-class Americans are great people, invented the light bulb, the airplane, and the cheeseburger. But you guys have this... this thing, where you think the world is basically fair. Sure, you hear about some poor kid who got beaten by his abusive parents, and you say yeah, that's terrible, that's unfair, but you think of it as this blip, a local deviation in the general atmosphere of niceness and fairness. So you hear more things. The Vietnam War. Race riots. The fucking Holocaust. And you're always properly upset about them, and you hope that one day all of the nice people will get their act together and spread the blanket of general fairness over Vietnam, Watts, and Auschwitz respectively, and then those little fires will be all stamped out. You go to your Young Democrats club and debate over which little tiny tweaks in the system will fix whichever little puddles of unfairness remain. A little more welfare there, a few reforms in this or that law, and there you have it! The future!

"And the thing is, nothing can ever convince you you're wrong. I can recite atrocities at you until I'm blue in the face, and you'll frown at every one of them, maybe you'll cry, but deep inside you something will be thinking, 'That's too bad, I hope our generally responsible government and society fix it quickly.' If I tell you the government's hopelessly corrupt, prove my point with the itemized bank account statements of every member of Congress and a big line saying 'BLOOD MONEY' on each of them, that same part of you will be thinking, 'That's too bad, I hope that our generally good electoral system leads to a better batch of candidates next time.' Well, I grew up in—"

"If this is going to lead into another damn story about your childhood in Mexico—"

"I made all those up. My childhood in Mexico was fine. Right up until the Drug Lord took over. He got the mainland first. Didn't make it to Baja. But we all knew he was coming. A guy came to town to warn us. One of the druggies. He'd run out of his stash early and gotten his mind back. Told us what it was like. Not to have control of your body. To be a puppet in your own head. Everybody panicked. My mother. She had a baby, she wouldn't go. She told my father to take me and leave. We got in the car and drove to the border. It was all fenced off with barbed wire. There were hundreds of us there, people from all over the peninsula trying to get out. We screamed at the guards. They were California Caliphate men. Told them that the Drug Lord was coming, fate worse than death for anybody stuck there. They told us no hablo español. But they knew what we were saying. They didn't care. They were safe behind their fence, our problems weren't their problems. Well, my father wasn't going to have any of that. He waited till night, then he took me a couple miles out, to the naked desert. Fished out his most precious possession, something he'd kept for an emergency like this one. An old scroll with the Cavernous Name. Don't think that one's even legal these days. Ripped it in front of me. The ground collapsed and the fence collapsed with it. We crawled through to the other side. Of course, we got arrested about half an hour later when Border Patrol came to see what had happened. Ended up in a detention center. My father, he was an alcoholic, he told them he was going to go into withdrawal, they just laughed and told him it was a nice try but he wasn't getting any drugs. He went into DTs and died in front of me. Me, I was eight years old. I was there for a year. After a year, California government says in retrospect they shouldn't have enforced their immigration restrictions so hard, declares general amnesty. But that's what I think of when I think of the system being basically fair. I think of me and my father and everyone else I knew banging up against that barbed wire fence screaming that they were coming to violate our souls, and the guards just sitting on their tower doing guard stuff."

"But—"

"But what? But the Californians were afraid that the Drug Lord had people there at the fence and if they let them through he would take over California and millions more would die? Good point. Reasonable. Or were you going to say but prisoners probably claim to be going through alcohol withdrawal all the time in order to con the system out of some free drugs, and it's hard to blame the guards for being skeptical? Also a good point! Also reasonable! And when UNSONG says that enforcing copyrights on the Names is the only way to protect innovation? They've got a good point too! They're also reasonable! But somehow there are always happy well-fed people in nice houses who have reasonable explanations for why the system is just, and there's always everyone else starving or dying or rotting in prison. Well, when I was eight years old I placed everybody's reasonable explanations on one side of a balance, and a hundred people screaming in front of a barbed wire fence in Tijuana on the other side, and the explanations *weren't heavy enough*, Mark. And I decided I am not on a debate team. If you want to argue all of the good reasons why you should have seven yachts and everybody else should starve to death, I will nod along pleasantly, admit that I cannot refute your points, and then, when I get home, I'll mail you a letterbomb."

"But you made that whole story up, because you told me freshman year that your father died before you were born, and also—"

"And that, Mark, is why I had to put you in prison. I thought, maybe, after ten years in Sing Sing, you'd stop being so fucking Young Democrats of America, you know? As long as you're an Archmage and making a name for yourself and living with your happy family you were never going to get it. You'd try to be good, but you'd do it in your stupid middle-class American things-are-basically-fine-but-let's-reform-the-tax-code sort of way. Well, now you've been in Sing Sing for ten years. So, tell me. Are you ready to pour petrol on the world and throw a match on it?"

"The world didn't do this to me, Dylan. *You* did."

"I didn't invent Sing Sing. I didn't tell your wife to divorce you. I didn't tell your kids to like their new daddy more than their old daddy. I didn't beat you up three times in the exercise yard — yes, I looked into your prison records, are you surprised? I didn't kill your old cellmate with a makeshift knife right in front of you and give you such bad PTSD that you can't get to sleep on your own, then patronizingly tell you that you can't have more than a week's worth of copies of the Somnolent Name because the budget is low and there are other inmates with *real* problems."

Mark looked uncomfortable.

"So let me make you an offer. I break you out of this prison right now. Together we kill Ash Bentham. Then if you're still angry, I give you a false identity, a free ticket to Europe, and you never have to speak to me again. Or you can sit here for another... hmmmm, twelve times four minus ten... thirty-eight years. Your choice, señor."

"How do you know I won't try to kill you as soon as I'm out of here?"

"As if you could."

"Seriously, what's the catch?"

"Catch? None. I learned the secret of invisibility yesterday, Mark. It's got me feeling all... what's the word... ambitious. I want to do something big. I need the right team. And the right Narrative. You, compadre, are both. Last living Archmage in the world, once my best friend, then my worst enemy, now my reluctant partner. Between you and Valerie—"

"Who's Valerie?"

"Valerie, be a dear and show yourself to Mr. McCarthy."

Valerie coughed and broke her invisibility. Of *course* there had been another person here all along, Mark thought. And if he'd made any sudden moves, tried to attack Dylan in a way the latter couldn't handle... for that matter, how many *others* were there? Since when had people discovered how to become invisible? Was that common in the outside world now? What could Dylan do with that kind of power—God, what *couldn't* Dylan do with that kind of power?

But instead he just asked, "What happened to your hair?"

"Style," said the girl. "Style happened to my hair."

"Miss Lowry is the newest member of BOOJUM—second newest, I should say, now that you're on board. I wanted to see her in action—well, not literally *see her*, so I invited her along for her first official mission. Oh, and the best part is we can talk to each other with our minds!" He stared at Valerie as if sending a thought to her. She started cracking up. "Some ritual she taught me, sacred kabbalistic something-or-other. Oh yes, Mark, things are starting to heat up. There's never been a better time to work with BOOJUM."

Moe gave a loud snort, then started kicking ineffectually in his sleep. "Don't..." he murmured to no one in particular. "Don't make me—"

"I will join your organization," said Mark McCarthy, "because it's better than dying in prison. Then I will take your ticket to Europe and never talk to you or think about you again. But I want you to swear to me that you're on the level."

"Level as Kansas," said Dylan.

"No. Fucking swear it. Say I, Dylan Alvarez, swear that I am telling the truth and that I don't intend to hurt or betray Mark McCarthy and that I'll help him get to Europe, and if I'm lying, may all my luck dry up and everything I've worked for come tumbling down."

A magician's oath. Reality works by spectacle and narrative. Swear a magician's oath and break it, and the universe has it out for you.

"I swear it."

"No, say the words."

"So many words, so long, can't we get just get out of here now and later we can—"

"Say the fucking words."

"I, Dylan Alvarez—oh, how should I remember how your stupid phrase went—I swear I won't kill you, make someone else kill you, cause you to die in ways that may not technically count as 'killing you,' betray you, injure you, emotionally devastate you, turn you in, use you as bait, fry your eyes in vegetable oil, feed you to an alligator, trick other people into feeding you to alligators, cause you to be consumed by an alligator in ways that may not technically count as 'feeding you' to it, et cetera, et cetera, et cetera, and if by some bizarre fluke you make the terrible choice not to continue working with me, get you safely to Europe, or may my luck dry up and my head turn green and my liver explode and everybody die, one nation, indivisible, with liberty and justice for all. So help me God."

Then Dylan stared at Valerie, and Valerie started laughing again.

Mark stood up, stretched, started collecting his things. "One day, Dylan, you should teach that telepathy ritual to me. Let me show you what I really think about you. You might be surprised."

Dylan laughed, slapped Mark on the back. "Only good things, I'm sure. Compadres para siempre, right? Anyway, half an hour in this dump is enough for me. Time to make like a guillotine and head off. Valerie, remind me how the invisibility Name goes again?"

A few minutes later, three invisible figures walked right past the guard and left Sing Sing prison in time to catch the first morning train to New York.

Chapter Forty-Seven

For He Beheld New Female Forms

February 1984
Citadel West

"Evening," the Comet King said from across the table, stifling a yawn. "Why don't you tell me something about yourself and why I should marry you?"

Her name was Jessica. She was twenty-three and beautiful, long dark wavy hair, curves to die for, deep brown eyes, et cetera. She bit her lip in a way the Comet King assumed was supposed to be seductive.

"I graduated from University of Colorado with double degrees in physics and political science," she said. "I've been reading about you ever since you won that battle at Silverthorne. I always thought you were a real hero, like out of some fairy tale. The day you became King of Colorado was one of the happiest days of my life, because I knew we had someone wonderful here taking care of us. I think I've been in love with you ever since I saw the coronation on TV. If you let me be your Queen, I will try to be an inspiration to young Coloradan women everywhere. I'll serve you well and give you lots of babies."

"You're very beautiful," said the Comet King, in the same way a judge at a dog show might pronounce a certain poodle to be very beautiful. "Thank you for your time. My staff will get back to you within three to five days."

"That's... it?" asked Jessica. She tossed her hair seductively. "But I thought we would be able to spend... you know... more time together."

"I am very busy."

"I wouldn't have to wait until our wedding. Even if you're not interested in getting married, we could still... you know."

"I appreciate the offer and my staff will get back to you in three to five days." He got up from the table, gave her a little bow, and walked out to the atrium of the palace. Nathanda and Caelius were fighting over a toy. He gave them a quick glance, and both of them tried to push the toy at the other, then stood to attention. He smiled and found Father Ellis, sitting alone beside one of the big targeting computers, looking annoyed.

"That was four minutes! You can't say you gave her a fair hearing!"

"She wanted to have my babies," said the Comet King. "She knew about the curse, she knew they would die screaming and cursing their father's name, and she still wanted to have them."

"She loves you," said the priest.

"They *all* love me," said the Comet King. "Can we give up now?"

"'It is not good for man to be alone,'" quoted Ellis.

"I am only half human. Whatever I am, it's *fine* for it to be alone."

"You told me you wanted my help being human, and I'm giving it to you! You need to get married. I don't make you meet a new girl every day. Just dinner Saturday and Sunday. Two nights a week. Two dates. Is that too much to give your old friend, and a nation anxious to have a Queen?"

"Another one of these tomorrow night? No. Cancel. Tomorrow night I am holding annexation talks with east Oregon."

"You can't just cancel on her! She's here already! She's come all the way from Utah to see you."

"The Oregonians have come all the way from Oregon. That is farther."

"Look, Jala. These people are infatuated with you. When I announced that you had given your permission to meet two women a week, I got so many applicants it takes half my time now just to sort through them for the good ones. This is probably going to be the highlight of this poor woman's life, and all she wants is ten minutes with you over a dinner table."

"What about tonight? Can I just get both of them over tonight, and then have the rest of the week free?"

"I'll see if she's around. But you better give her a full ten minutes. You hear me, Jala? Ten! Now you go back in the dining room, and I'll find her and send her in, and you give her ten minutes and not a second less."

"Yes, Father. Whatever you say."

Five minutes later, a young woman walked into the dining room beneath Cheyenne Mountain. Stick thin. Boyish body. Light brown hair. Simple tan dress. She introduced herself as Robin Allison Minstrell. Something something philosophy PhD something something whatever.

"Good evening," the Comet King said from across the table, playing with an olive on his fork. "Why don't you tell me something about yourself and why I should marry you?"

"I'm not sure why someone like you would get married," said Robin, "but I would assume you're being pressured or feel some obligation to do so for the sake of the kingdom. A relationship would probably take up a lot of your time and distract you from your work, which of course is vital to the future of humanity. Whatever good I could do with my own life is probably less than the amount of good you could do with the time you save by not having a demanding wife, and I wasn't sure you realized the option existed, so I decided the morally optimal thing to do would be to offer to marry you so you could have the public relations benefits of marriage without the time-related costs. Of course, I could help your mission in other ways too; as your Queen, I'd be a natural choice to take over a lot of the ribbon-cutting ceremonies and press photo ops you have to do. All of this time saved would be time you could devote to your primary mission of fighting back against Hell."

"Who told you to say this?"

"What? Um. Nobody. I studied philosophy. Peter Singer, the Australian philosopher. He believed that only the course that most effectively eases suffering is morally permissible. I… I have a book I can give you."

She reached into her purse and handed the Comet King a book. He looked at it for a second, then took it and placed it beside his plate.

"You knew this man?"

"No. He died before I could meet him. Killed. In Salt Lake City, February of '74. But I read everything. I did my thesis on him. I wrote dozens of papers. And every time I submitted another paper to the journals, to get thrown in the wastebasket or read by a couple of academics, I thought, *Things have gotten too bad, I just can't keep doing this.* So I quit and joined the military. Administrative work, supply management, that kind of thing. But now there's peace. Thanks to you. And I thought, given the extent of your genius, helping you would be a more effective use of my time than anything else I could do. I considered joining your government, but since I'm pretty and charismatic I thought it would be more effective to offer my hand in marriage instead."

"I accept," said the Comet King. "My uncle Vihaan is in the third floor library. He manages my schedule. Ask him when a good time for the wedding would be."

Without a word, Robin got up from the table and headed towards the stairwell.

Jalaketu toyed with his olive for another moment, then popped it in his mouth and walked out the door into the atrium. Father Ellis saw him and rose to his feet in a rage.

"SEVEN MINUTES, JALA. THAT WAS SEVEN MINUTES AND FOURTEEN SECONDS. YOU PROMISED ME TEN. I WANT YOU TO GO BACK IN THERE AND..."

"Father, I need your help."

The anger evaporated from the priest's face. "What's wrong, Jala?"

"The girl. Robin. She told me that marriage and relationships were a waste of the time I should be spending planning my war against Hell. She offered to marry me, serve as my public face, and leave me alone completely in order to free me from the burden. I said yes. She and Vihaan will plan the wedding. You'll need to officiate, of course."

"God damn it, Jala! I wanted to humanize you, and instead you found somebody just as defective as yourself. You'll get nothing out of it, she'll get nothing out of it, and you're going to miss your chance at something natural and important just to get someone who will pose for photo ops once in a while."

"No, Father, I *need your help.*"

"Why? What is it?"

"Father, I think I'm in love."

Chapter Forty-Eight

Bring Me My Chariot Of Fire

Morning, May 14, 2017
Caribbean Sea

I.

Unfurling four of its seven sails, the world's fastest ship shot out of the Panama Canal. It rocketed through the Caribbean and wove in and out of the Cayman Islands. It somehow *skipped* Cuba—the space that *All Your Heart* sailed through with its many-colored sails open wasn't quite the same as the normal ocean—and nearly crashed into the Bahamas before executing a sudden turn that knocked everyone against the starboard railing. Four hours after the ship left the Gatun Locks, Amoxiel spotted the Florida coast.

The launch was at noon. There would be no more launches for weeks—longer than John would hang on. They would make it to Cape Canaveral by noon, or their friend's soul was toast.

James paced back and forth on the deck, his responsibilities lightened by the rediscovery of the ship's autopilot—if that was what you wanted to call the intelligence that animated the entire vessel like a golem. He was on the foredeck, basking in the Caribbean sun, letting the ship itself handle the steering.

Ana and Simeon were in lounge chairs side by side to starboard.

"I should have known you'd be in favor of this," Ana said.

"Of saving a good guy from eternal suffering?" asked Simeon. "You bet."

It was a vicious cycle. Simeon was old, he'd been hurt in the scuffle with the Drug Lord, and he'd been seizing pretty badly during the worst parts of the Panama crossing. For a while they hadn't been sure he would make it. Ana, wracked with guilt about verbally abusing him, had been by his side all through the Gulf Coast, bringing him food from the galley and keeping him company. But being Ana, it was impossible for her not to start talking politics, and soon she was abusing him more than ever—a situation that seemed to keep the old man relatively entertained.

"It's the final insult," Ana said, "in which divine justice is perverted the same way the human justice of the state already has been. Poor person steals some bread? Eternity in Hell. Rich person steals the wealth of an entire state? Not only do the courts do nothing, but he can buy a ticket on Virgin Celestial and his soul ends up squeaky clean in the World To Come."

"Does anyone deserve eternal suffering?"

"No!"

"Then surely it's more just for a few people to be able to avoid it, than for everyone alike to suffer punishment undeserved."

"But just the rich?"

"Someone has to buy the rocket fuel."

"Why doesn't the government pay? Why isn't it subsidized?"

"Ten million per citizen? Why, to save the entire population of America that's only, ah, two quadrillion dollars, about a thousand times the gross national product."

"Then at least save *some*!"

"Exactly my point. We can only save some. Instead of choosing those some from a lottery or something, we choose them by wealth. It beats the lottery method because it makes the program self-financing."

"So just let things be, and make no attempt at eve..."

"*Satan* tempted Eve. *Noah* built an ark."

"Aaargh!"

He smiled.

"I just think... you can't be happy with this situation, can you?"

Simeon furrowed his brow. "Happy? No. But what can you do? And it's not just a rhetorical question. *I* can do quite a lot. I can create a successful company that helps discover new Names. I can donate some money to causes that deserve it. I can be nice to the people I meet. Once I'm doing all that, there's no point in dedicating a lobe of my brain to being outraged at the injustices of the world. I do what I can, and then stop caring. Even the Comet King only besieged Hell until the point when he realized it was a lost cause. Then he gave up. You care too much and it drives you crazy."

"Then maybe being crazy is the right thing to do. So far all I see from your side is a lot of sanity and poor people left to burn."

"Two hundred years ago, this was about people starving to death in the streets, or dying of smallpox. We solved those problems not by destroying the system, but by milking the system so single-mindedly that eventually we got rich enough to buy the problems off. If we defeat Hell, it'll be because we developed better weapons. And if we develop better weapons, it'll be because of places like Countenance. And in order to get places like Countenance, you need money, and incentives to get it, and then there you are at Virgin Celestial."

"So just let sin and greed continue uninhibited, and eventually someone will have stolen enough to make things better? Just protect the system, no matter how many people it throws into the flames, because of the promise of a smallpox cure somewhere at the end?"

"And what's your position? Burn down everything that isn't perfect? I have bad news for you about mortal institutions, dear. What if you go too far? You think eliminating people like me will build the perfect government? What if you overcompensate and build anarchy?"

"*Noah* built an arky. *Satan* tempted Eve. And me? I'm with Lowell: 'The soul is still oracular; amid the market's din / List the ominous stern whisper from the Delphic cave within / "They enslave their children's children who make compromise with sin."'"

"There's more than one way to compromise with sin," said Simeon. "The first way is where you accept a little bit of evil for what you think is a greater good. But the second way is where you do anything less than what's most effective. If I shut down Virgin because I was mad at it, well, then maybe I'd feel better about myself. And a few hundred people who would otherwise go to Heaven would end up in Hell and burn forever, thanks to me. How is that not compromising with sin? The compromises I've made, I've made on my own terms, and I'm happy with them."

"If you were happy, you wouldn't have paid a couple million dollars to go yell at God."

Simeon tried to bring himself up to a sitting position, but ended up putting weight upon his injured leg. Groaning, he lay back down.

"I'm sorry," Ana said. "I crossed a line. This is stupid. I keep saying mean things to you and then feeling bad and trying to make it up by talking to you more and then saying mean things. I should go."

"It's fine," said Simeon. "I'm a hard man to offend."

"No, really. I should go and jump off the side of the ship now."

"Wait," said Simeon. "You want to know a secret?"

"I've never said no to that question and I'm not starting now."

Simeon smiled. "I don't think this boat will catch God, and I don't really care. I'm after bigger quarry."

"Bigger than God?"

"Look, Ana. Fifteen years ago the Comet King has a mental breakdown after the death of his wife. Then a year later, he dies at Never Summer in a battle in a cloud, defeated by a relative nobody. You don't find anything about this weird?"

"People love conspiracy theories," Ana said. "But they found his body, and besides, the Comet King isn't the sort to retire and go farm yams somewhere."

"People do love conspiracy theories," said Simeon, "and rich people get a chance to indulge in them. My hobby for the past few years has been tracking the Comet King. And no, I didn't find any smoking guns, but—you know our man John? We only know two things about him. He's a priest. And he's an old friend of the Captain's. Well, I've seen old photographs from Royal Colorado, and our John is a dead ringer for the Comet King's right-hand man, Father John Ellis. So I started reading about this ship. This mysterious Captain Nemo shows up one day, shrouds himself in mystery, but has intimate knowledge of the Comet King's yacht. And he's a friend of John Ellis's. And he's got a certain... well, everyone obeys him without question. So what am I to think?"

A chill went down Ana's spine. She had only been very young when the Comet King died, but even she could remember the gravity of the moment. He had been someone impossible, something out of legend, a different sort of person entirely. Then he was gone. If he were still alive.... "The Captain looks nothing like the Comet King," she said. "I've seen pictures. The Captain is big. The Comet King is rail-thin. And there was the body."

"You think people like that can't change bodies as easily as we change clothes?" said Simeon. "Heck, if I wanted to pull the same thing Jalaketu did, I'd bribe the Lady into making a golem that looked just like me, kill off the golem, bury the body, then hit the donuts until I wasn't so thin anymore. Whatever I couldn't disguise, I'd hide. They say the Comet King had weird eyes, like the night sky. Why doesn't Captain Nemo take off his sunglasses?"

"Holy euphemism," said Ana.

"I didn't buy a berth on this boat to hunt down God, I got on here to hunt down the Captain. The man's a complete black box, and only the people lucky enough to end up on *All Your Heart* get a chance of seeing him. I've been watching him, trying to figure out what his angle is. But I've got nothing. That's why I'm telling you this. You're one of the crew. You can talk to people. Figure out what they know. They've been hanging out with him for years. They must have picked up on something."

"What do I do? Just ask James, 'Hey, did the Captain ever mention anything about being the Comet King?'"

"Maybe not. Maybe James is in on it. And if the Comet King is hiding, probably bad things happen to anyone who makes too much noise about trying to find him. Something subtle. Like, 'Oh, I've been working here so long, and I barely get a glimpse of the Captain. What's *with* that guy?' See what he knows."

"Okay but... like you said, if he doesn't want to be found, it might not be such a good idea to find him."

"Well," said Simeon, "yes. That *is* the issue. Maybe I'm a little bit crazy too, in the way I mentioned to you earlier. I don't have a great plan. This is pretty much how I ran Countenance—start the first step, hit the ground running, and try to figure out the second step on the way. But I've already spend a year and a half looking through all the sources I could—once I get interested in something, I stay interested—and the thought of knowing where the Comet King was and just sort of sitting on the knowledge—well, that would have driven me off the wall. I don't know what Erin and the rest hope to get from meeting God. They already know He's not big on answering prayers except on His own terms. Well, I don't know what I expect from meeting the Comet King. The best I can say is I'm no stupider than they are. Just differently stupid."

II.

They sat on the ship, a mile or so offshore. There had been a burst of light, a roar. And a little spark buoyed upon a sea of smoke shot up at Heaven.

John was on that spark. They'd arrived just in time. His breathing was getting shallow, and he didn't seem like he had much time left. And it had been only fifteen minutes to launch, and they'd had to pay extra to delay the countdown a few minutes to get the old priest on board. But the deed had been done, and the dying body of the old man was dutifully loaded on board the tiny capsule and flung into the noonday sun.

They'd stayed on land just long enough to place a call to one of James' contacts in New York, telling them to advertise as quickly as possible for a replacement priest and a replacement placebomancer. The plan was to speed to New York City just long enough to get two new crew aboard the ship, then head to Fire Island where the divine boat of Metatron, emanation of God, was due to appear at sunset. The contact had demanded an outrageous price, then said he would work something out. With no time to lose, they'd gotten back on the yacht and headed out.

The red sail fluttered in the wind, Ana kept the orange going, Tomás still sang to the green, and Amoxiel stayed in back with the purple. He was running low on holy water, but there would be potables enough once they reached New York. The priestly and placebomantic sails hung limp in mourning for their lost keepers, and the black sail as always stood alone and cryptic on the aft.

"I'm not sure what the proper etiquette is," Tomás told Ana. They were standing together on the port deck, watching the Virgin rocket disappear into the evening sky. "I feel like I should say something, but it's not a funeral. Nobody's dead yet."

"Tell me about John," said Ana. "How did you meet?"

"It was about three months after we took *All Your Heart*," Tomás told her. "We only had four sails working then — just like now — and the Captain told us we needed a priest. When we were in Vancouver on a chase he went ashore and called up a friend who he said would meet us next time we got to San Francisco. A week later we sailed down California and John was waiting for us. A good man. Always did his share. I'm Catholic myself, and he always took time to listen to my confession. Though I get the impression he was kind of an unorthodox sort of priest."

"And then, when did you meet the Captain?"

"Him? That was in Puerto Peñasco that first night. The Other King had invaded the whole Southwest and just reached the Sea of Cortez. I was tending my bar, and there he was, drunk as a skunk, saying he'd been on *All Your Heart* during its maiden voyage and he was going to help us steal the ship. James was an officer, and he and his men were interested, and the rest is history. Things were bad in those days; we were willing to take any way out."

"What did he do before? On the ship? Did he know the Comet King?"

"I think he was the captain, then, just like now. He never mentions the Comet King, but it would have been pretty hard to spend a month on a ship this small without seeing him."

"Did he captain other ships before he got this one?"

The little spark finally faded from view.

"Ana, the Captain's a very private man. What he wants us to know, he tells us. He's been good to us, and we give him back as good as we get by not prying into his secrets. I assume the Comet King wouldn't have hired him if he didn't have some experience. But what that is, he hasn't said and I haven't asked. I would recommend you do the same."

"Just curious," Ana protested feebly.

"You know the saying about curiosity."

"Tomás?" A sudden thought, more urgent. "If he was on the boat, before, he must have been there when the Comet King met Metatron."

"Ana." Tomás's voice wasn't angry, but it was stern.

"The Voice of God! He must know what God said! Maybe even knows the Explicit Name!"

"Ana."

All Your Heart sailed north.

III.

The spaceship had a Medical Officer, tasked with keeping the passengers alive until they reached their destination. Sometimes his expertise was needed for more prosaic reasons.

"One of the old guys is delirious," the Commander told him. "Won't stay in his seat, keeps raving about stuff. I don't want him to get up and get confused by the zero-g and hit his head on something. You think he's safe to tranquilize?"

The Medical Officer picked up a syringe and walked into the cabin. Wasn't too hard to tell who the Commander was talking about. A dozen old codgers strapped quietly into their seats. And one guy practically flailing. Delirium, all right.

"Listen," the old man was saying. "The prophecy said that they would drive him to the priest. Drove, that was the word it used. Not the Urim and Thummim's prophecy. The other one. The long one. They drove the comet to the priest, but the priest would come up dry. And on that day, the righteous grown children would perish."

"Hold on," said the Medical Officer. "It's going to be okay." He checked breathing, respiration. A little tranquilizer wouldn't hurt. He took hold of the old man's arm and injected the contents of the syringe.

"I'm the priest," said the old man. "It was talking about me. And today I've come up dry. I've failed. You have to warn the Cometspawn. You hear me? *Warn the Cometspawn.*" Then he went quiet. The Medical Officer watched for a few minutes until he was sure he was sound asleep.

"All clear," he told the Commander, stepping back into the cockpit. Ahead of them, the crack in the sky came ever closer.

Interlude ס

Binary

"Today I will expound unto you the kabbalistic theory of the creation of the world," said Ana. "It all starts with Leibniz..."

We were sitting together on the couch after dinner. Valerie and Eli Foss were on the other couch. Zoe Farr was in the armchair. Ana was wearing a blue t-shirt saying "I WENT TO THEODICY CON 2014 AND ALL I GOT WAS THIS CRAPPY T-SHIRT, AND I DON'T UNDERSTAND WHY A JUST GOD WOULD ALLOW THIS TO HAPPEN." It was pouring outside, and the occasional gust of wind added eerie punctuation to her argument.

"See, there's this idea called divine simplicity. People keep asking, okay, so God created the universe, but who created God? The answer is that God doesn't need creating. He's perfectly simple. He's just a natural thing for there to be. People act like you need God to explain why the universe isn't just nothing. But why should the universe be nothing? Why shouldn't it be, I don't know, a piece of bread? The only reason people think 'nothing' needs no explanation, but a piece of bread does need an explanation, is that nothing is simpler than bread. Well, God is just as simple as nothing. So there."

"How is this Leibniz?" asked Eli Foss.

"I'm getting to Leibniz! Right now we're at information theory. A well-defined mathematical explanation of simplicity. We can measure the complexity of a concept in bits. The number of binary digits it would take to specify the concept in some reasonable encoding system. We can do it with numbers. The numbers 0 and 1 are one bit. Two is 10, three is 11; those are two bits. Four is 100, five is 101, six is 110, seven is 111; so three bits. And so on. We can do it with computer programs; just count how many bits and bytes they take up on a computer. We can do it with images if you can get them into a format like .gif or .jpg. And we can do it with material objects. All you have to do is figure out how long it would take to write a program that specifies a description of the material object to the right level of complexity. There are already weather simulators. However many bits the most efficient one of those is, that's how complex the weather is."

"And God?" asked Zoe Farr.

"God is one bit. The bit 1."

"I find that... counterintuitive," was the best Zoe could answer.

"Well, it's easy to represent nothingness. That's just the bit 0. God is the opposite of that. Complete fullness. Perfection in every respect. This kind of stuff is beyond space — our modern theories of space take a bunch of bits to specify — but if it helps, imagine God as being space filled with the maximum amount of power and intelligence and goodness and everything else that it can hold, stretching on to infinity."

"The maximum amount of purple?" I objected.

"Sure. And the maximum amount of red, green, blue, et cetera."

"So God is kind of an off-shade of brown, is what you're telling me," I told Ana. "Because in third grade I tried mixing all the colors of paint together, and that was what I got."

"Well, what color *should* He be?"

"Brilliant golden light," suggested Valerie.

"Exodus 20:23," I objected. "You shall not make a god out of gold."

"And," said Ana, "if you don't think God can be brown, then you're racist."

"But," said Valerie, "if God contains everything alike, then He is evil as well as good. Weakness as well as strength. Sadness as well as happiness."

"I know the answer to this one," said Zoe. "Goodness is the same as existence. To exist infinitely is to be infinitely good. A human who was really human, who fulfilled her humanity to the utmost degree, would be a truly excellent human, one who was good at being a human and exemplified all the human virtues. Insofar as you are less of a human than that person, you exist less than them. God is pure existence, so He has to be pure good as well."

"No," I said. "That's assuming the conclusion. It's saying that humans exist to be good. Why can't humans exist to be bad? There are three numbers that need no justification — zero, infinity, and negative infinity."

"Negative infinity isn't simple!" said Ana. "You have to put the minus sign in front of it! That's a whole extra pen stroke!"

"That's only convention," Valerie protested.

"SPARROWS CAN'T HAVE NEGATIVE NUMBER OF WINGS!"

"Aren't religious people always talking about how the Bible is a source of absolute values?" I proposed.

"Maybe," said Eli seriously, "existence is like distance. There's only one direction you can go. God went that direction and we called it 'good.' Bad is something else."

"Bad is just the absence of God," said Zoe.

"We've had this discussion!" said Ana. "No it isn't! Nothingness is the absence of God! Hitler requires a design decision! Four arms on the swastika! Two sides to the mustache! One testicle!"

"I thought that was a myth," I said.

"I still don't get how this is Leibniz," said Zoe. "Or the creation of the world."

"Leibniz was studying the *I Ching*, and he noticed that its yin and yang sticks, when arranged in hexagrams, corresponded to a new form of arithmetic, because he was Leibniz and of course he noticed that. So he invented binary numbers and wrote a letter to the Duke of Brunswick saying that he had explained how God could create the universe out of nothing. It goes like this. You've got God, who is 1. You've got nothingness, which is 0. And that's all you need to create everything. 1s and 0s arranged in a long enough string."

"How, exactly?"

"The kabbalistic conception is that God withdrew from Himself to create the world. I, for example, am beautiful and intelligent, but not so physically strong. God is perfectly beautiful and intelligent and strong, so by withdrawing a little bit of His beauty and intelligence, and a lot of His strength, and some other things, we end up with an Ana."

"Except you're not an off-shade of brown," said Valerie.

"And also, God mostly just withdrew from the original universe in such a way that made it have laws of physics that generated you," I added.

"Same difference," said Ana.

"How did God decide which 1s to change to 0s?" asked Valerie.

"And there's the rub," said Ana. "To change any 1s to 0s at all is making the world worse. Less Godly. Creation was taking something that was already perfect — divinity — and making it worse for no reason. A wise woman once said that those who ask how a perfect God created a universe filled with so much that is evil miss a greater conundrum — why would a perfect God create a universe at all?"

We were all silent just a little too long.

"I have a question," Zoe Farr said, finally. "If God is just the binary digit 1, and nothingness is the binary digit 0, and the both contain one bit of information — then isn't neither one the simplest thing? Wouldn't the simplest thing be zero bits, neither God nor nothingness?"

"That's Atzmus and you're not supposed to talk about it!" said Ana.

"Okay, jeez," said Zoe.

"Any *other* dumb objections?" Ana asked, play-acting a death glare at all of us.

"I might have one," said Eli Foss. "I... appreciate what you're trying to do, Ana, but I have to remind you that kabbalah isn't just the word for whatever cool theory you happen to come up with by combining information theory and the *I Ching* and the doctrine of divine simplicity. It literally means 'received tradition.' It's a body of work that's been designed and created according to specific rules set forth by the rabbis, and it's within the tradition of a relatively insular religion that's really strongly against mixing its concepts with those of other ideas, especially ones from different faiths the way that the *I Ching* is from Daoism. So I think your theory is interesting. But it isn't kabbalah. It's not from the ARI, or the Baal Shem Tov, or anybody like that. So when you say that it's the kabbalistic theory of the world, I think you need to walk that back a little unless you think real orthodox kabbalists are actually going around saying that God is just the binary digit 1."

"I don't just *think* it," said Ana. "Every single Jewish person says exactly that, twice per day. 'HEAR, O ISRAEL, THE LORD OUR GOD, THE LORD IS 1.'"

"I retract my complaint," said Eli.

Chapter Forty-Nine

Terrors Of The Sun And Moon

December 4, 1993
Gulf Of Mexico

Right on cue, people noticed the sun speeding up. There had been a time when this would have been cause for concern. As it was, the astronomical community just shrugged their shoulders and said, "Uriel's doing something again," and there the matter rested.

The unplanned solar eclipse of December 4, 1993, would reach totality around 11:08 over the Pacific Ocean. The path would continue northeast, until it reached the point of longest duration of totality over the permanent hurricane in the Gulf of Mexico just after 2:30. From there it would pass over Florida before dwindling away in the North Atlantic.

ARE YOU READY? asked Uriel.

"Didn't I tell you last month?" said Sohu. "We are going to rock this eclipse."

I AM GOING TO HAVE TO MICROMANAGE THE MOON FROM THIS POINT ON, said Uriel. IT IS VERY DIFFICULT. PLEASE DO NOT DISTURB ME UNTIL TOTALITY HAS PASSED. YOU KNOW WHAT TO DO?

"Yeah, for the thousandth time," said Sohu. "When the totality hits, step into Yetzirah, look through — not with — the eye — and report back."

YOU ARE GOOD, said Uriel. QUIET TIME NOW. He started rearranging the glowing letters in front of him. It was a new moon, so Sohu couldn't tell if the moon was wobbling in the sky or not.

Sohu took out a book — not the Torah this time, she'd been able to teleport to some bookstores and get some light reading and had developed an appetite for comics — and sat on the edge of her cloud, glancing up every few minutes to check the state of the sky.

Uriel suddenly broke out of his trance and stared right at her.

"Is everything okay?"

YES. I JUST REMEMBERED. I FORGOT TO TELL YOU. DO NOT STARE STRAIGHT AT THE SUN. IT WILL HURT YOUR EYES.

"Thanks, Uriel," said Sohu, with an eye-roll, and returned to her pastime as Uriel returned to his.

Into her head unbidden came a verse from an old poem:

The moving Moon went up the sky
And nowhere did abide...

She couldn't concentrate on the comics. She put them down on the cloud, carefully folded to the last page she had read. Another verse, this one from her kabbalistic studies:

I reign over you, sayeth the God of Justice, in whose hands the Sun is a sword, and the Moon a through thrusting fire...

The sky started to darken. Ignoring the archangel's advice, Sohu risked a brief glance at the sun and saw a bite taken out of it.

She readied herself for trance.

The sky got darker. A few stars appeared. Now she was *sure* she saw the sun wobble. Uriel must be working very carefully, giving her as much time as possible for what she had to do.

She began to drift off. Moon. *Yareach* in Hebrew. Corresponding to the sephirah Yesod. Just as the moon reflects the light of the sun to Earth, so Yesod reflected the lights of all the other sephirot into the physical world. New moon. New Yareach. Just as New York City reflected all the peoples of the world into America. Give me your tired and poor. Alas, poor Yareach, we new him well.

She reached out to step into the thing the moon was a metaphor for.

"It looks like we're having an eclipse party and I wasn't invited."

She opened her eyes, already knowing what she would see.

"A solar eclipse is a once in a lifetime event," Thamiel told her. "And totality only lasts five minutes. I wouldn't want you to miss it because you were spending the whole time in Yetzirah."

Sohu very carefully backed away from him. It occurred to her that if she could get into the flying kayak, she might be able to launch it off the cloud before Thamiel could stop her, then get blown off somewhere far away by the storm.

The Lord of Demons shook his head, then reappeared in the flying kayak. "Don't worry," he said. "I'm not here to torture you. A waste, without Uriel around to watch. We'll just stay here and watch the eclipse together. In Assiah. The physical world. It'll be fun. Just small talk. You and me, mano a diablo. The two of us so rarely get any time alone together."

Sohu sat back down on the cloud. "Talk," she said.

Thamiel picked up her comic. The book burst into flames in his hand, then fell in a spatter of ashes onto the cloud. "Really? *Comics?* We need to get you some more wholesome entertainment. Do you know what I do for fun? You know those electric fences for dogs? I find a dog with one of those electric fences, and I stand just a few feet outside with a big juicy steak. The dog runs towards me to get the steak, then gets zapped, then runs back into the fence, then tries again, gets zapped again, finally just sits on the edge of the fence while I eat the steak in front of it. It's not the most efficient way to cause suffering, but you can't always be all about efficiency, you need to leave some time for yourself, do you agree with that, Sohu?"

Talk. In Hebrew, *d'var*. Diver. Getting to the bottom of things. Differ. Resolving conflicting opinions. Differ contains di-, the prefix for two. Thamiel. Duality in God, also a two. Attempting to distract her. Another di-. Two channels. But they could become one channel... how long left in totality? Two minutes? One?

Thamiel broke off suddenly. "Oh, I see what you're trying to do," he said. "No! Bad Sohu!" He took his bident and drove it into her head.

Pleasure, again. Pleasure so strong it was blinding, searing pain. But worse, wrongness. Impossible wrongness. Pain. Sounded like pey. Pey is a yud in a kaf. The divine spark in the human form. Pain is of the human form. But still a divine spark within, able to direct it, transcend it. In Hebrew, *ke'ev*. Sounds like kaf. In Hebrew pain is of the body, but in English, it recognizes that pain is only partially of the body, can be overcome. She was an English-speaker.

"I'll kill you!" Thamiel said. "Come back or I'll kill you!"

Threats. In the Bible, God threatened Adam: eat of the fruit, and you will surely die. He interpreted it to mean immediate death; when Eve ate of the fruit and didn't perish, he thought the threat was empty. But God had meant that he would become mortal, die eventually, and so he did. But it was death that allowed humanity to reach the world to come, to truly join with

God. Threat. Thread. I give you the end of a golden thread, only roll it into a ball...

Sohu stepped into Yetzirah and opened her eyes.

The Comet King was in his study. But it was different now; there were some new books on the shelves, a few new tchotchkes on the desk. Father looked older. Much older. And worse. Some of the light had left his face. He was sitting in his chair and there was a book in front of him. Maps. An atlas. He was speaking to Father Ellis, also older. They were arguing about something, at first politely, then louder. Finally the Comet King turned away. Ellis looked like he wanted to say something, but all of a sudden he blinked, and when he opened his eyes again they were purest silver, and he began to hover, as if too holy to be polluted by the touch of the ground. The Comet King stayed fixed on something out of sight for a moment, then turned and saw the transformation. After a moment's thought, he knelt.

"Metatron," he said.

YOU ARE LOST IN DARKNESS, said Metatron.

"So is the full moon," said the Comet King, "and so much the worse for the darkness."

YET YOU BEAR WITHIN YOU THE MOST HOLY NAME, WHICH MAY NEVER BE DESECRATED.

"I earned it," said the Comet King. "You gave it to me."

NOW I AM GOING TO TAKE IT BACK.

"You can't take it back!"

I CAN.

"I need it!"

THE EXPLICIT NAME MAY ONLY BE BORNE IN A PURE MIND.

"I'm pure."

The Archangel Metatron stared at him. No one, not even the Comet King, could stare down the Archangel Metatron.

"I'm angry, and I'm heartbroken, and I'm empty inside. But I'm pure."

The Archangel Metatron did not get flustered. The Archangel Metatron did not work that way.

THE SANCTITY OF THE NAME WILL BE PRESERVED. I WILL GIVE IT BACK TO YOU WHEN YOU ARE READY.

"You will, will you?"

YES.

"How?"

HOWEVER I WISH.

Ellis reached out a ghostly hand and touched the Comet King's brow. Something left him in that moment, something vast, like a note too low to hear. Then the silver left Ellis's eyes, and he crumpled to the ground.

A ray of sunlight burst out from behind the moon.

Sohu stepped into Assiah.

Thamiel was standing directly in front of her. He was staring straight into her eyes. Then he reached out a single deformed finger and touched her on the nose.

"Boop," he said.

Sohu's eyes went white, and she seized.

Uriel dropped the moon.

SOHU, ARE YOU OKAY?

"Oh, hello Uriel, I was going to say hello, but you looked busy. Got to go now." The Lord of Demons disappeared in a bolt of lightning.

Sohu kept seizing until the last curve of the moon came out from behind the sun. Then she fell down prone on the cloud. Uriel kept watch over her until she regained consciousness.

ARE YOU OKAY? he asked.

"Yes..." she said, still a little confused.

WHAT HAPPENED?

Sohu strained. Her forehead wrinkled. Then a look of panic fell over her face.

"I... I don't remember. The eclipse started, and after that I don't remember anything."

IT IS OKAY, said Uriel.

"My eyes hurt."

YOU STARED AT THE SUN, DIDN'T YOU?

Interlude ע

Hell on Earth

In 1985, the Hellish Empire stretched from Moscow to Montreal, a sprawling stain over the northern quarter of the world.

After the defeat at Silverthorne, a tentative cease-fire had taken hold, backed by nuclear weapons on all sides. Multistan, the Cyrillic Union, the Untied States, and Dazhou established their own ideas of borders, sometimes as mutually agreed treaties, other times as pragmatic lines of actual control. Miraculously, the borders held. The demons were waiting, gathering strength. So was the Comet King. So were all the nations of the earth.

Maybe it would have been different if there were some atrocity to rally around. Some genocide, some torture, to remind people visibly and graphically of the evils of Hell. There wasn't. People who expected the rivers to run red with blood were disappointed.

Genocide is a good way to kill people, but not a good way to damn them. Desperation brings out the best in people. Starve people to death, and some of them will give their last crust of bread to a stranger. Torture them, and they'll bear all sorts of horrors to protect people they love. Kill them, and they'll die with prayers on their lips.

Give a man a crisis, and the best in him will rise up in a sudden glory. It's the grind of everyday life that brings out his little hatreds and petty cruelties. Shoot a man's wife, and he will jump in front of the bullet and sacrifice his own life for hers; force him to live in a one-room apartment with her, and within a month he'll be a domestic abuser.

Thamiel knew this better than anyone, so he avoided inflicting anything too dramatic upon his new subjects. Just a gradual, managed economic collapse, a percent or two a year, to squeeze people without *squeezing* them. And for those who couldn't manage? State subsidized liquor stores, every brand and vintage of alcohol at affordable prices, and with them coke and speed and a dozen different kinds of opiates to dull the pain. No one was forced into anything—being forced into things by demons has a certain dignity about it. But the option was presented with flashing neon lights around it, and as more and more people got pay cuts or layoffs, it started looking more and more attractive.

The ability of a vast empire to subsidize heroin stores was no match for the ability of addicts to want more heroin. People started running out of money. When they did, the Hellish Empire graciously presented them with quick ways to earn cash from the comfort of their home. Tattle on anyone criticizing the government, and that was good for a week's pay. There was no quality control to ensure that the people tattled upon had really criticized anything, so it was pretty easy money. Men who would have jumped in front of bullets meant for their wives turned them in to the mercies of the Hellish secret police on trumped-up charges in exchange for a little extra spending money.

Big factories sprung up in every city center, producing nothing. Their industry nevertheless released great gobs of lead into the air and soil. The higher the lead levels, the more impulsive and criminal people become—some kind of neurotoxicity effect. At the same time, Canada's restrictive firearm laws were phased out in favor of the more enlightened policies of their southern neighbor. Soon quarrels that would have involved heated words a few years before started involving blows, then knives, and finally a different form of lead poisoning, far more final.

Let it never be said that Thamiel the Lord of Demons was soft on crime. The new puppet government raised entirely new police forces and told them not to worry too much about brutality. The steady stream of arrestees were funneled into new sprawling prisons that seemed to have more correctional officers than strictly required, almost as if the government's entire goal in the penal system was to let as many people as possible play the role of prison guard and see how it changed them.

"But it makes no sense!" Ana had said to me one night over burgers and fries in a Palo Alto cafeteria. "Suppose that in the absence of demons, 5% of Canadians would have been dreadful sinners, and gone to Hell. And suppose that thanks to the demons' campaign to promote sinfulness, a full 50% of Canadians ended up that bad. That's ten million extra damnations. They're not being punished for their innate virtue or lack thereof—in some sense that's the same whether the demons took over Canada or not. They're being punished for being in the wrong place at the wrong time, for being in a land controlled by demons rather than one controlled by good people trying to promote virtue or at least somebody morally neutral. How is that just?"

"I thought we'd already agreed things generally aren't," I said.

"Right, they *generally* aren't, but this is *cosmic* justice we're talking about. The whole question of who goes to Heaven versus to Hell. If there were anything at all that was going to be just, it would be that. And yet we have people being sentenced to eternal punishment for what is obviously a contingent problem that isn't their fault!"

"In the end, it *was* their decision to sin, no matter how many incentives Thamiel dangled in front of them."

"Yes, but — if they wouldn't have sinned without the incentive, and now they did sin, then it's the presence or absence of the incentive that determines whether they're in Hell or not! It doesn't make sense!"

"Maybe there's a special clause in Divine Law that says that if you were coaxed into a sin by a demon who's really good at behavioral economics, then it doesn't count."

"But it's not just the demons! Yes, they open lead factories on purpose in order to turn nearby people into criminals. But we opened lead factories because we wanted products made of lead, and people became criminals by accident. Whether any given person is good or evil depends a lot on factors out of their control, both in terms of things like lead and in terms of things like what values society inculcates in them, and in whether they even *need* to be evil. You know, rich people are a lot less likely than poor people to steal, just because they're not tempted to do so."

"So maybe God grades on a curve. You take a reference human, perform the necessary adjustments, and say, 'if this person were in the same situation as the reference human, how sinful would they be?'"

"But then what's the point of actually living your life, if God's going to throw out all the data and judge you by a simulation of how you would perform in a totally different situation instead?"

"Look, we already knew free will was really confusing. Maybe the Calvinists were right about everything."

"They *can't* be!"

"Why not?"

"It wouldn't be *right*."

"It's like that quatrain from the *Rubaiyat* that turns out to be kabbalistically equivalent to all that stuff.

O thou, who burns with tears for those who burn
In Hell, whose fires will find thee in thy turn
Hope not the Lord thy God to mercy teach
For who art thou to teach, or He to learn?"

"I'm not blaming God for being insufficiently merciful, I'm blaming God for being insufficiently *just*."

"Oh, that's much better then."

At first, the gates of all the righteous countries of the world were left open for refugees fleeing the slow-motion collapse of the North. What greater *mitzvah* than to save people from their own inevitable moral dissolution and subsequent damnation? But it turned out that people who had grown up in a country whose education system, economic system, justice system, and social system were all designed by the Devil to most effectively convert them into bad people — were not very nice people. A few heavily publicized incidents of criminal behavior, and the gates started to close. A few terrorist attacks, and they were locked tight. A few neighborhoods ruined, and military trucks were crossing the borders weekly to return refugees back to the grateful Hellish authorities.

Why didn't Thamiel take over the world? Some said it was weakness. Others nuclear deterrence. Still others the power of the Comet King.

Ever since that conversation with Ana, I've had a horrible theory of my own. Maybe God *did* forgive the Russians and Canadians their transgressions, knowing the pressures they were under. Maybe Thamiel wasn't after the souls of his own citizens. Maybe the point was to damn *everyone else*.

(The Comet King heard arguments on both sides of the issue, then closed the Colorado border, saying that anything that weakened the state threatened his grand design. Then he accelerated his already manic pace — gave up sleep, gave up most food, spent his nights poring over kabbalistic tomes and military stratagems.)

(But the soul is still oracular; amid the market's din / List the ominous stern whisper from the Delphic cave within / "They enslave their children's children who make compromise with sin.")

Chapter Fifty

Silent As Despairing Love

Evening, May 13, 2017
Citadel West

They had taken us back to the NORAD command center. We sat at the big table, listening to the reassuring hum of a missile-free North American airspace.

NORAD is a very Semitic-looking word. The Hebrew stem would be nun-resh-dalet; and indeed we find it in the Bible, referring to a plant we English-speakers transliterate as *nard*. During New Testament times it produced a very expensive perfumed oil, and Mary of Bethany was so excited when Jesus came to visit that she anointed his feet with it. Judas Iscariot chewed her out, saying that she could have sold the oil instead and gotten enough money to feed dozens of poor people. Jesus quieted him down by saying "The poor you will always have with you, but you will not always have me."

But there are other options. Hebrew has *narad*, meaning to go down or descend. Greek has Nereid, the goddesses of the deep. English has *nerd*, a technologically-minded smart person, and *neared*, i.e. having drawn closer.

Put it all together, and we get somewhere down very deep, filled with smart people and technology, dedicated to watching for things that might be drawing closer to them.

Nathanda sat at the center of the big table, flanked by Sohu, Caelius, and Vihaan. Jinxiang, Sarah and I took the other side. No one was at the head of the table. The Comet King's black opal throne dominated the room with its emptiness. "The poor you will always have with you," it seemed to say, "but you will not always have me."

Sarah was awake now. She clutched my leg so hard it was almost painful, but she didn't try anything. The Cometspawn had her outclassed, and she knew it. Norvig and Raziel's book said that only four kabbalists had ever gazed upon Adam Kadmon bare. One was the Archangel Uriel. One was Rabbi Isaac Luria. One was the Comet King. And there was the fourth, sitting in front of me, looking to all the world like an eight-year-old girl. Charming, disarming, innocent.

She listened as Jinxiang explained the situation to the newcomers, quiet right up until she got to the point where she told them the riddle she had found in the angels' book.

"I think I know who the Other King is," said Sohu.

I was numb to shock at this point, but I still sat up a little straighter.

"The riddle says, there is providence in the fall of a sparrow. There's a story Uriel told me, a long time ago, about a man named Elisha ben Abuyah. Except that nobody speaks his name anymore. They just call him Acher, which means 'the Other One.'"

Nathanda moved forward in her seat.

"The legend goes that he was once the wisest of rabbis and the most learned of kabbalists. One day, he saw a boy climb a tree and kill a mother bird in its nest, an act forbidden by the Torah. Then he climbed down safely and went away. A little while later, he saw another boy climb another tree, take some eggs from a nest, but spare the mother bird in accordance with the commandment. On his way down, this boy fell and broke his back and died. Acher became so angry that he vowed vengeance against God. He would just sin and sin until the weight of all his misdeeds knocked the world out of balance and ruined all of God's plans."

"All because of one kid falling from a tree?" Jinxiang asked.

"Not just a kid falling from a tree! A kid falling from a tree *after doing a good deed*. I guess Acher had always known that sometimes bad things happened to good people, but that was what really drove it in, made it hit home. He couldn't figure out how God could let that happen, so he decided God was a monster. So he went on and lived a life of sin for a couple of decades, then died. There are all of these weird conflicting legends about what happened to his soul. Supposedly he was too wise for Hell but too evil for Heaven, so he just kind of—hung out."

"And you think now he's in Las Vegas."

"It fits! Think about it. How could anybody, any normal human, defeat Father? What if they came from Talmudic times and had studied with Rabbi Akiva and Rabbi Eleazar and all those people? What if they'd been studying and practicing for two thousand years? And there's that thing with the bird!

Providence in the fall of a sparrow! That's what Acher was rejecting. He saw a bad kid kill a bird and live, and said there couldn't possibly be any excuse or explanation. It fits *too well.*"

We were all silent for a moment.

"Was there anything about how this Acher could be *defeated*?" asked Nathanda finally.

"The Talmud doesn't exactly have a part where they list every rabbi's fighting style and secret weaknesses," said Sohu. "There are a lot of parts where his student Rabbi Meir tries to convince him to repent and become good again, and he keeps *almost* succeeding, but it always fails at the last second."

"So does this help us at all?"

"If there's a Talmudic sage who's still alive—even sort of alive—that's the most incredible thing! Scholars from all over the world would want to talk to him! Rabbis—"

Jinxiang lifted a finger, quieted her sister. "You're forgetting that this Talmudic sage is also trying to kill us. I met him in Las Vegas. I almost died. I would have died, if I didn't escape at the last second."

"He spoke to me," I said. Jinxiang looked at me with surprise. "In my mind. It was terrifying. Just said my name. It was the scariest thing I've ever heard, worse than the Drug Lord." Then I thought back to Asher Bentham and mentally revised the Other King to "second scariest."

"I think," said Sohu, "you had better tell the rest of the story."

So Jinxiang finished, went through the Drug Lord finding me in Las Vegas, went through the battle on top of the ziggurat, went through the appearance of Sarah and the arrival of the Other King. Then Nathanda described how she had asked about ensouling THARMAS, and how that had led up to the fight where Sohu had found us.

"Sarah," said Nathanda when she was done. "I am sorry. I spoke hastily, and I frightened you. Will you accept my apology?"

Sarah hadn't stopped clutching my leg. She was three days old, I realized. She was feeling every emotion for the first time, totally unprepared. I put my hand on top of hers.

"Yes," she said quietly.

"The geopolitical situation is terrible," said Nathanda. "The Other King has us completely surrounded. The Drug Lord regathers his strength. The Eastern states are weaker than they've been for a generation, and the peace with Hell is like every peace with Hell—only until they see an advantage in breaking it. We've needed a miracle for a long time. Now we've got one. The Vital Name is the best way to save Royal Colorado, the Untied States, and..." She gestured to the big map of the continent. "I want to ask Aaron the Vital Name, let Sohu handle the error correction, and then put it in THARMAS. The obvious flaw in that plan is that then THARMAS becomes more powerful than any of us. Sarah seems to have... ah... turned out well, but none of us can predict what sort of personality a nuclear targeting computer will have. Caelius, any thoughts?"

The photos of Caelius in the papers had never quite captured what was unearthly about him. His pale eyes seemed perpetually unfocused, his thoughts always somewhere else. But when he spoke, he spoke clearly and confidently. "We can lobotomize it, so to speak. Get it to reboot all its functions except the one running the Name search every millisecond or two. It won't have time to string a coherent thought together."

"That sounds horrible!" said Sohu. Nathanda glanced at Sarah, watching for another outburst.

"Do it," Sarah whispered.

"What?"

"Do it. Keep it trapped, no personality, no thoughts. Don't let it replace me."

"Well," said Nathanda. "Um. Any other thoughts? Jinxiang? Uncle? Is this something we want to do?"

She was interrupted as a man walked through the door. *Another* person I recognized from the news. General Bromis had accompanied the Comet King on his crusade. Now he directed the forces defending the Citadel. He made it to the table, sat down, looked me and Sarah over suspiciously before speaking. Nathanda gave him a nod.

"News out of Las Vegas," he said. "The Other King left his pyramid for the first time in a decade. Some kind of incident involving Trump Tower, still haven't been able to get more information. He went right back into the Luxor once the incident ended and hasn't been seen since. But he's there, he's still alive, and he's mobile. And something got his attention."

"I'm sorry for not telling you earlier," said Nathanda. "My sister was there and has just been debriefing us. These two were also involved."

"Well, I'm putting the army on alert anyway. I'd hoped the bastard was dead."

"We told you he wasn't."

"You win. Can you tell me what happened? I don't like this not knowing what's going on, especially with the war going—going like it is."

"The short version is that Jinxiang was forced to stop in Las Vegas briefly on her trip to retrieve a valuable artifact. The Other King attacked her and she escaped. Some of the information is still very sensitive, but I promise we can tell you within a few days."

The General looked mollified. "You want me in on this?" he said, gesturing to us, the table, the meeting.

"I'll handle it myself, General," Nathanda told him, "and meet with you tonight about the battle lines." She nodded at Bromis, dismissing him; Bromis saluted and left the throne room.

"And that goes for the rest of you too," she said. "This is highest secrecy. No one except the seven of us can know. Not the generals, not the ministers, nobody. Until THARMAS is up and running and has produced its first results."

"Uh," I said, raising my hand. "My friend Ana Thurmond knows. She's on a ship somewhere near Mexico. And Asher Bentham of UNSONG might know too."

"I'll see if we can retrieve the ship. Director-General Bentham is back in New York and out of the equation for now." She spoke slowly, stopping to think between each sentence. "This bunker is the safest place in the world. We can get THARMAS running before anyone can get to us, as long as we're careful. Aaron, the Name."

And just like that, there it was.

Of course, it was sheer politeness that made her ask. I had no doubt that they had other ways to get it out of me. But for three days, I'd had something precious. Broken. Unusable. But precious. It had been mine. Now here I was, about to give it to the Cometspawn. It was as if the Name had decided I was unworthy of it, and all I'd done, all of the tribulations and adventures, had been its itching to get itself into the hands of someone suitably important. Thanks, it told me, but I hope you didn't think *you* were the one who was going to save the world. You were just the delivery boy. You worked at Countenance to find Names for other people, richer, more powerful people. And you found a Name there, and true to form, your job was to give it to the rich, powerful people.

Sarah dug her fingers into my knee. What was she thinking?

"Um," I asked Nathanda. "May I have a minute to talk to Sarah alone?"

The queen's face was impassive. She nodded.

"We should get out of here," was the first thing that Sarah said when we had made our way to the big NORAD desks in the front of the room. "Something bad will happen. We should get out of here and correct the Vital Name ourselves and then lobotomize all the other computers and take over the world. We should rule the world together and be safe."

"We can't get out of here," I said. "You tried, remember?"

"I could do better. I could kill Sohu first, surprise her. Then I could take on the others."

The kabbalists say that all men have four souls. The animal soul, the *nefesh*, which sustains life and desire. The moral soul, the *ruach*, helps us determine good and evil. The intellectual soul, the *neshamah*, forms our thought and understanding. And the divine soul, the *chayah*, is the mysterious center of consciousness that connects us with God above.

Sarah's animal soul was the golem that Gadiriel had made her. Her intellectual soul was the CPU of an NE-1 series Macbook. The divine soul I had given her myself, with the Vital Name. And her moral soul was...

...frick.

"Um, Sarah, this is going to be a weird question, but... do you know right from wrong?"

"All I want is to make you happy!" she said.

"Doing the right thing makes me happy," I told her. "Can you do that?"

She thought for a second. "Maybe."

I thought about doing the right thing. When I was five years old, the Comet King had set off with his armies to conquer Yakutsk and save tens of billions of damned souls from the agony of Hell. He had failed. But I still remembered that moment, hearing about it on the radio, seeing the pictures of those thousands and thousands of men marching out of Colorado Springs, singing his anthem. Now he was gone. No one had ever said his children were his equals, but they were good. I could tell. For all her snappiness, Jinxiang had saved me when she didn't have to. I'd seen Nathanda calm Sarah out of her tears, I'd seen Sohu react with horror to the idea of lobotomizing a computer. They might not be perfect, but they were good. And they were stronger than me, not just physically, not just magically, but—I thought of my failure on Trump Tower, taking the peyote even though I knew what it meant. I looked at the four of them, sitting with their uncle at the table. They were good people.

Three days ago, when I'd ensouled Sarah, I'd told Ana I wanted to be the next Comet King. I wondered if she remembered. It seemed crazy now. Even Nathanda didn't dare sit on that black opal throne at the far end of the room. Even Sohu wouldn't touch it. If there was any meaning at all to being like the Comet King, at my level, it was trying to be a good person when the opportunity arose. I turned to Sarah.

"I'm going to tell them the Name, because I think it's the right thing to do. Will you support me in that?"

Sarah thought for a second.

"Do you love me?" she asked.

Oh, right, I'd forgotten. The world was a horrible mess and it was practically impossible to know what the right thing to do was at any given time and trying to do the right thing could destroy the people you love but if you didn't then you enslaved your children's children because you made compromise with sin.

Sarah was sexy and powerful and totally obsessed with me. I knew I liked her. I knew I wanted the best for her. I wanted her to be okay. But she was a three-day old computer suddenly wrenched into sentience and stuck in a golem-body, and I wasn't sure she had any emotions besides clinginess and rage. Did I love her?

"Cetaceans of the cross," I said.

"What?" said Sarah. "Huh? Aaron, please! Do you love me?"

...and I didn't love her. My heart was taken.

"Sarah," I said, and I clasped her hand in mine. "You're beautiful and wonderful and you saved my life. Together, we're going to help the Cometspawn win the war and save the world. Okay?"

She squeezed my hand back. One day I would tell her the truth. One day when all of this was over.

We walked back to the Cometspawn hand in hand. Five pairs of eyes focused on us.

"ROS-AILE-KAPHILUTON..." I said, and Sohu started writing furiously on a notepad in front of her. I mumbled once, to break the string, to mention the Name rather than use it, then continued. "MIRAKOI-KALANIEMI-TSHANA-KAI-KAI-EPHSANDER-GALISDO-TAHUN..." The son and daughters of the Comet King listened, quietly, let the sounds of God's secret and holy Name echo through the depths of the Rocky Mountains, heard the syllables that could only end in apocalypse or salvation.

"...MEH-MEH-MEH-MEH-MEH-MEH!"

Interlude פ and צ

The 80s and 90s

*In Daniel 5, King Belshazzar throws a feast which is interrupted by a giant disembodied hand writing on the wall: MENE TEKEL UPHARSIN. The wise men of the kingdom are confused; they recognize these words only as measures of silver (*mene *is cognate with the classical* mina, tekel *with the classical* shekel, *and* upharsin *is about half a mina.)*

Belshazzar summons the prophet Daniel for explanation, and Daniel interprets the inscription as a complicated kabbalistic pun. MENE represents not a literal weight of silver, but the concept of weighing or judging. TEKEL represents not just a shekel but a small and insufficient amount of money. And UPHARSIN is a pun on the Persians, the Babylonians' arch-enemies. So he interprets the words to mean "You have been judged against the Persians and found wanting" — in other words, by exiling the Jews, Babylon had displayed such wickedness that God would allow the Persians to destroy them.

The prophecy was fulfilled when King Cyrus of Persia conquered Babylon and executed Belshazzar for his wickedness. In 538 BC, the triumphant monarch allowed the Jews to return to Israel.

From these events kabbalists derive a correspondence between silver, the number 538, and accurate prediction of changes in political leadership.

—Norvig and Raziel, Kabbalah: A Modern Approach

I. 1981

WASHINGTON DC — President Reagan is expected to make a full recovery after being shot in the head by an assassin while leaving the Washington Hilton.

Spectators report that the assassin, later identified as a mentally ill man named John Hinckley, pulled out a gun and shot six times. Five of the bullets hit members of the President's retinue, one of whom is currently in critical condition at George Washington University Hospital. The sixth hit the President in the head. According to three separate eyewitnesses interviewed by *The New York Times*, the bullet passed straight through Reagan's head and out the other side. Despite the injury, the President tackled the assassin and held him pinned to the ground until Secret Service agents could respond.

Then, say the eyewitnesses, the President stooped to the ground, picked up a handful of earth, and filled the hole in his head as if nothing had happened.

Reagan's press secretary James Brady was himself injured in the attack, but his position is being temporarily filled by Larry Speakes, in accordance with nominative determinism.

TIMES: Mr. Speakes, people are reporting all sorts of stories out of Washington today.

SPEAKES: Yes, you know, there's a lot of research showing that people's eyewitness accounts are inherently untrustworthy. In a crisis, with all the adrenaline flowing, people see some pretty crazy things.

TIMES: Did the bullet go through the President's head?

SPEAKES: I would say "through" is an exaggeration. The bullet definitely hit the President. But you know, there are a lot of stories about people having bullets hitting their heads and doing just fine. I mean, in the 19th century, there was this man, Phineas Gage, who was too close to an explosion and had an iron spike get blown through his brain. And he was still able to function for the rest of his life! The thing is, the effects of these kinds of injuries aren't always predictable.

TIMES: Didn't Phineas Gage become insane, aggressive, and unpredictable?

SPEAKES: President Reagan will not become insane, aggressive, and unpredictable.

TIMES: But what about all the stories that the President filled in the hole in his head with dirt?

SPEAKES: Listen. The Untied States is at war. I think this kind of speculation about a sitting President is irresponsible. I can assure the American people that the President is not made of dirt.

II. 1987

WASHINGTON DC—To the horror of onlookers, President Reagan melted away today when a heavy rainstorm struck the rally where he was speaking.

It seemed to be a clear day as Reagan prepared to address a pro-religion rally from the Capitol Steps. But just a few minutes into his speech, a freak thunderstorm broke out, causing the President's body to sag and, finally, melt into a pile of mud. The entire process took less than a minute.

Conspiracy theorists, who had long claimed the President was a golem, declared victory. "There was something about him," Colonel Oliver North told the Times, "and that time he survived a bullet right through the head, it wasn't natural." The White House urged people "not to jump to conclusions," saying they were still trying to figure out exactly what had gone wrong.

Meanwhile, Vice President George H. W. Bush has been sworn in as President in a short ceremony on the White House lawn. On Capitol Hill, Senate Majority Leader Robert Byrd demanded an amendment saying that all future Presidents-elect will have to be examined by a doctor who could certify they are human, a proposal which met with near-complete bipartisan support.

White House Press Secretary Larry Speakes told the Times, "President Reagan led this country during a difficult time. Although we are still investigating what happened on Tuesday, he has the thanks of a grateful nation, and we appreciate the sacrifice he made for the American people."

The pile of mud will be available for viewing in the National Cathedral for the next three days.

III. 1993

NEW YORK CITY—Jalaketu West, King of Royal Colorado, spoke to the United Nations today about his proposal for an international treaty regulating the use of Divine Names.

"A strong international intellectual property framework is the only way to incentivize a global theonomic industry capable of developing weapons that can protect the human race from supernatural threats," the so-called Comet King told the meeting in a speech punctuated with references to his own defeat of the Drug Lord a decade earlier. "As long as it is more profitable to pirate Names discovered by each other than to invest in the scholarship and hard work of discovering new incantations, we will never create the capacity necessary to fight off the forces of Hell, let alone protect the world in the case of a sudden breakdown of Uriel's machine." He repeated his theory that the laws of physics will catastrophically fail sometime in the early twenty-first century, and that humanity needs to be ready for a sudden increase in the power of demons and other mystical entities at that time.

According to Coloradan sources, negotiations have been entered by over fifty countries, including the Untied States, Britannic Canada, Cuba, Trinidad, Tobago, El Salvador, El Pais Del Diablo, the Most Serene Empire of the Darien Gap, Brazil, North Peru, South Peru, Ecuador, Primer Meridiano, New Country, the European Communion, Neu Hansa, the Icelandic Empire, Finland, Britain, Vatican Crater, Slovakia, Slovenia, Sloviria, Slovobia, Switzerland, Estonia, the Cyrillic Union, Novaya Zemlya, Multistan, Iran, the Israel-Palestine Anomaly, Turkey, Saudi Arabia, the Eridu-Xanadu Consortium, the Lotophagoi, Ethiopia, South Africa, the Malabar-Zanzibar Consortium, Somaliland, Ouagadougou City State, Dazhou, Indonesia, the Sulawesi Conspiracy, Lesser Mongolia, Greater Mongolia, the Platinum Horde, the Distributed Republic, Kerala, Uighurstan, Thailand, the United Hydrological Basins, Swiss Polynesia, and Armenian Samoa.

Untied States president Bill Clinton praised the effort, describing it as "a new step towards international free trade and cooperation."

IV. 1996

CHICAGO — Ralph Nader reached out to voters in a rally here today, describing his Green Party as the only force in American politics willing to stand up for the poor and middle-class. The centerpiece of his campaign is opposition to UNSONG, the free trade and intellectual property agreement supported by both Democrat Bill Clinton and Republican Bob Dole.

"This is nothing more than a corporate takeover," he told a cheering crowd of supporters. "Why should you have to pay Wall Street hundreds of dollars for a piece of paper with a Name on it, when the cost is just a piece of paper and some ink?"

Nader's campaign received an unexpected boost after the publication of *The Temple and the Marketplace*, a two-hundred fifty page book by Raymond Stevens, a crotchety Unitarian minister who argues that Biblical passages predict the advent of the Divine Names and command their universal spread according to communal utopian principles. His followers, who called themselves Singers after their habit of singing the Divine Names, have become a centerpiece of Nader's rallies, frequently singing Names that result in pyrotechnics or other impressive displays.

Stevens himself has stopped short of endorsing Nader, but believes his victory has been foretold in Job 5:11 — "he puts those who are in low places up to high places" — the "low place" being a reference to Mr. Nader's name.

Chapter Fifty-One

He Wondered That He Felt Love

February 1984
Colorado

"What can I do for you today?" Robin asked the Comet King.

He was in his study, sitting at his big desk of Colorado pine. On the shelves he had gifts given him by various ambassadors and heads of state. A medieval orrery from the European Communion. A Faberge egg from the Cyrillic Union. An exquisite bonsai tree from Dazhou. From Israel, a lovely turquoise sculpture with a microscopic listening device covertly planted inside—which he usually covered with a piece of Scotch tape, but into which he spoke clearly and distinctly whenever he wanted to pass false information on to the Mossad.

And of course books. Books lining the walls. The walls were fifty feet high here, so high they looked like they could break through the top of the mountain and show him blue sky on the top. He had filled forty feet with shelving, and it was growing all the time. When he needed a reference, he would speak the Ascending Name, float to the appropriate level, take the book, and then sink back to his desk. He worried that in a few years he would have exhausted the available space.

His one-year-old daughter Sohu was curled up at his feet, grasping her Bible, trying to memorize the thing. She was up to the Song of Songs already, more than halfway done. He approved of this. It kept her quiet.

"I just wanted to spend some time with you," he told Robin. "Get to, uh, know you better. Since we're... getting married, and all."

She was in a light blue dress. It was, he noticed, the color of a robin's egg. He wondered if that was intentional. Was it okay to ask if that was intentional?

"I read your book," he said, handing her back the work by Singer. "Would you like to talk about it?"

Robin looked skeptical. "Aren't you busy?"

"No. Well, yes." He pointed to a map stretched out on his desk. "There is much to do, but many years to do it. Like with Moses, this generation cannot be the one to enter the Promised Land. There are too few of us. We have no heavy industry. The collapse and the wars have hit us too hard. We need ten, twenty years to rebuild and reproduce, increase our numbers before we can take the war back to Hell. And there are other things to do in the meantime. Defeating Hell will mean nothing if I cannot destroy it. I must find the Explicit Name of God. They say that only those who can chase down Metatron upon his golden boat can obtain it. I think with enough knowledge it may be possible. I am designing a ship, but it must be perfect. It will take years to get right. And then the war itself. I will need guns, tanks, airships. Strategic nuclear defense systems. An economy to support all of this. And logistics. Marching a million men from Colorado to Siberia will not be easy, even if I can part the Bering Strait, Moses-style. Which I think I can. And... yes, I am busy. But not so busy we cannot talk."

"But why are you telling me all this? I thought the whole reason we were getting married was so that you wouldn't *have* to talk to people."

"I just... wanted your input."

"Don't you have better people to give you input? Generals? Rabbis? Advisors? I can find some people if you want, I have some connections, I can get people from DC or Sacramento over, I'm sure they'd be happy to help you."

"Of course I can talk to them. But I wanted to talk to you too. We're going to be married soon. We should talk."

"I thought we were getting married so you didn't *have* to talk to anyone."

"I know I don't have to. I want to. I... hold on a second."

The Comet King turned into a lightning bolt and flashed out of the room. He materialized again in front of Father Ellis, who was eating lunch in the dining room with little Caelius and Jinxiang.

"Father!" he said. "How do I tell Robin I like her?"

"Repeat these words," said the priest. "Robin, I like you."

"Are you sure that works?" asked Jalaketu.

"Positive," said the priest.

Another flash of lightning, and Jalaketu materialized in the study, sitting in front of the pinewood desk. Sohu was reciting Song of Songs to Robin, who was cooing approvingly. "Daughters of Jerusalem…!" Sohu incanted, in as theatrical a voice as a one-year-old could manage. The Comet King glanced at her, and she went silent.

"Robin," he said. "I like you."

"Okay," said Robin. "Is something wrong?"

"No," he said frustrated. "Robin, I *like* you."

"Oh," said Robin, suddenly understanding.

An urge to curl up and hide somewhere safe underground, only partially relieved by the knowledge that he was already in a nuclear bunker two thousand feet beneath the Rocky Mountains.

"Oh," she said again. "Well, uh, how can I help?"

"I don't know!" said Jalaketu.

"What if I did something really unattractive? I could dye my hair some kind of awful color. What if I gained weight? Or lost weight? Would that help?"

"Probably not," said the Comet King. "It's deeper than that, more like an appreciation of your fundamental goodness as a person."

"That sounds tough," Robin admitted. "I could travel to the opposite side of the world."

"No," said the Comet King glumly. "I would probably just hunt you down."

"Hmmmm," said Robin. "I could just refuse to talk to you."

"No," said the Comet King. "I would probably court you with some kind of amazing magical music or poetry."

"Hmmmm," said Robin, and thought for a second. Then, "Hmmmmmm." Then, tentatively, "We could kiss."

The Comet King thought for a while. "I don't see how that would help."

"Well," said Robin, "my father told me a story about how he once dated a girl he knew, and he really liked her, and then he kissed her, and she was a terrible kisser, and he stopped being attracted to her at all."

"It is worth a try," said the Comet King.

And he leaned in and kissed her.

A few moments. Then a few more.

"That did not help at *all*," said the Comet King.

"That did the *opposite* of help," said Robin.

"We could try again," said the Comet King.

"It can't hurt," said Robin.

"DO IT!" said Sohu.

The two looked at her. They had forgotten she was there.

"Sohu, leave the room."

"But Daddy...!"

"Leave," said Jalaketu.

Sohu took her Bible and left the study. The Comet King shut the door behind her, and she heard a little click as he turned the lock.

She shrugged and went to the command center, where she curled up on an empty chair and watched North American airspace for a while. Then she retrieved her bookmark and got back to the Song of Songs:

Daughters of Jerusalem, I charge you:
Do not arouse or awaken love
until it so desires.

Then place it like a seal over your heart,
like a seal on your arm;
for love is as strong as death,
its jealousy unyielding as the grave.
It burns like blazing fire,
like a mighty flame.

I am a wall,
and my breasts are like towers.
Thus I have become in his eyes
like one bringing contentment.

Come away, my beloved,
and be like a gazelle
or like a young stag
on the spice-laden mountains.

Chapter Fifty-Two

The King Of Light Beheld Her Mourning

And the shepherds returned, glorifying and praising God for all the possible values of x and f(x).
—kingjamesprogramming.tumblr.com

July 29, 2001
Gulf Of Mexico

Winter ended. Summer passed. Another and another. Uriel taught Sohu for eight more years after the eclipse, eight years without her aging a day.

In 1993, Sohu used Kefitzat Haderech to join her family in Colorado for Hanukkah. Her father said nothing when she came unannounced, striking the table deep in her father's bunker in the form of a lightning bolt, just smiled, and said she was welcome, and that he hoped this meant she would be visiting more often.

In 1994, when Sohu was twelve years old by the calendar, Uriel suggested she get a Bat Mitzvah. "I'm not Jewish and I never age!" Sohu protested. WHAT ARE YOU? asked Uriel. "Half Hopi Indian, a quarter Hindu, and a quarter comet," she said. WHAT DO HALF-HOPI QUARTER-HINDU QUARTER-COMET PEOPLE DO WHEN THEY TURN TWELVE? asked Uriel. "Order in pizza," said Sohu. So they did.

In 1995, Sohu mastered Turkish, just to make Uriel happy, and Proto-Turkic to boot. Then she learned Aramaic, so she could tease him about a language *he* couldn't understand.

In 1996, Uriel declared that Sohu understood Yetzirah sufficiently to attempt contact with the world above it, Briah. The first time Sohu touched Briah, she accidentally made all the rivers in the world run in reverse. AT LEAST YOU ARE CONSISTENT, Uriel told her.

In 1997, Sohu declared that she was going to learn to cook. She brought a stove, an oven, and several cabinets full of ingredients back with her to the hurricane and very gradually progressed from awful to terrible to at-least-better-than-manna. She made Uriel try some of her concoctions. He always said they were VERY GOOD, but when pressed he admitted he didn't have a sense of taste and was calculating in his head how the gustatory-receptor binding profiles would work.

In 1998, Sohu stayed in the hurricane almost full-time, trying to get a sufficient grasp of the archetypes and correspondences that she could touch Briah without messing it up. The going was difficult, and the occasional successes almost inevitably marked by failures that followed soon afterwards.

In 1999, Sohu stood with her stepmother, her brother, and her two sisters in Colorado Springs while her father's army went off to war. Her heart soared at the glory of the moment, and she wondered if it had been like this long ago, in the days Uriel used to speak of when the heavenly hosts would march forth against Thamiel. She searched the higher worlds for omens of their defeat or victory, but all she managed to do was make all of the rivers run in reverse again. FROM NOW ON, NO MORE GOING TO BRIAH UNTIL I TELL YOU TO, Uriel warned.

In 2000, Sohu interrupted her meditations to attend her stepmother's funeral. Her father looked older. *Much* older. She had the strangest feeling that she had seen him like that once before, a long time ago, but she couldn't quite place the memory.

In 2001, she was sitting on her cloud, studying Torah, when Uriel suddenly asked her DO YOU FEEL IT?

"Feel what?"

YOU TELL ME.

She stepped into Yetzirah, examined the archetypes. Looked out through the dreamworld, saw all the dreams in place.

She needed a higher vantage. She very gingerly took another step up, into Briah, the place that even Yetzirah was a metaphor for. There were no archetypes in Briah, only wellsprings of creative energy that might eventually become archetypes. Something about a mem. A samech. A lamed. Mem connected Hod to Netzach; samech connected Hod to Tiferet. Lamed connected Hod to Yesod. Hod was splendor, Hod was energy channeled for a purpose. Mem. Samech. Lamed. M-S-L. Three different aspects of splendid, directed energy.

A roaring sound brought her back to Assiah. Uriel reached out and caught the missile bearing down on them, pinched the flame coming out of its rear with his fingers.

"Oh," said Sohu. Then, "No."

NO WHAT?

"Don't do it."

DO WHAT?

"Anything! Don't do whatever the missile is about! Either it's a trap from Thamiel, or it's a well-intentioned offer that will blow up in your face. You remember what Father told you. You are *not good* at this sort of thing. Just send them a polite 'thanks but no thanks.' You don't want—"

Sohu shut up. Uriel was looking at the message a little too long. She couldn't get a good read on him. "What is it? Is something wrong?"

IT'S FOR YOU, he said, and set the rocket down on her little cloud. The cloud strained under its weight, but didn't break.

Sohu, said the message on the side of the missile. It was her sister Nathanda's handwriting, blocky and forceful. *Father is dead. Other King killed him. Can explain later. We need you. Come home.*

No, thought Sohu.

Father did a lot of things. He fought demons, he saved cities, he found the Explicit Name, he rebuilt nations. But he didn't die. It wasn't in his nature. He wasn't immortal. He was just too busy. Dying wasn't convenient to his plans. He was the Comet King. If something wasn't convenient to his plans, it didn't happen. Heaven and Earth might fall away, the mountains could crumble, but the Comet King's plans proceeding in an orderly fashion, that was *fixed*.

Father couldn't be dead. It was a trap. Thamiel or someone. Her family's enemies. The Untied States government. Someone was faking the death of the Comet King. Right?

She remembered their last conversation. He was grim, yes, he'd lost some of his hair, there was an edge to his voice, but... dead? It didn't make sense. Other people died, and the Comet King mourned or avenged them. The Comet King didn't die. *Father* didn't die. It was... it was like Uriel dying. The world wouldn't allow it.

"Uriel," she said, her throat clenching up, "get me TV, or radio, some kind of news source."

The angel created ex nihilo a large copper rod, suspended it in the air, then performed some sort of magic around it that turned it into a radio receiver.

"...still recovering from the Battle of Never Summer," said a crisp male voice in Mid-Atlantic English. "The Comet King's body was retrieved during the fighting by his daughter Jinxiang and is now lying in state in Colorado

Springs. The Other King seems to have been severely wounded as well, and his army has halted their advance into the Rockies. We turn now to..."

Sohu sent a bolt of lightning at the copper rod, and it tarnished into a beautiful verdant green, then crumbled into dust and fell into the sea below.

A second later, Sohu followed.

She dove headfirst off the cloud, shouting incantations, plunging faster and faster until she glowed like a meteor. She struck the ocean, but didn't stop, shot all the way into the furthest depths of the sea. She came to rest in front of a monster of the deep, one of those horrible fish that are all mouth and jaws. She punched it in the nose.

"Don't just float there!" she said. "Defend yourself!"

The anglerfish looked at her, confused. This situation wasn't in its behavioral repertoire.

Sohu punched it again with her left hand, the hand on which the Comet King had placed his sign long ago, his promise to come to her aid if she were ever injured.

The anglerfish finally came to a decision and bit her left hand off.

Sohu floated beneath the sea for one second, then two seconds, then three seconds. Nothing happened. She watched in the anglerfish's ghostly half-light as a stream of blood leaked into the water around her. No sudden flare of power. No one appearing by lightning bolt to defend her. She couldn't believe it. She kept waiting. Five seconds. Ten seconds. Twenty. The anglerfish munched on the hand contentedly, not really sure what had provoked this stroke of luck but content to enjoy it.

She shot up from the depths, into the light zone, then into open air, then back to the hurricane.

YOUR ARM IS BLEEDING, said Uriel. I CAN FIX...

"He's dead," said Sohu, as she traced letters in the air, causing the bleeding limb to cauterize and heal over into a stump. "He's really, really dead. I don't... he can't... he made me promise I wouldn't die before him, but I never thought... never thought that..."

THERE. said Uriel. Then he repeated: THERE.

"Where?" asked Sohu.

I AM NOT SURE. I AM TOLD THIS IS A WAY TO CONSOLE PEOPLE.

"What?" she asked. Then, "Why? Uriel, how could this happen?"

I AM NOT SURE. THE OTHER KING CONCERNS ME.

"Concerns you?"

I CANNOT GET A GOOD READ ON HIM.

"You're practically omniscient! How can you just... not be able to read a whole king?"

I DO NOT KNOW.

"God. This is so awful. I've got to go help them."

YOU MUST STAY HERE.

"What— no! My family needs me! They're going to be so— *Father* needs me. If he were here, he would want me to help."

HE WOULD WANT YOU TO STAY HERE AND DEFEND THE MACHINERY OF HEAVEN.

"He would want me to help my family. And Colorado. That's what he cared about."

HE CARED ABOUT THE WORLD.

"That's not true. That was... an act he put on. He loved his family and his people more than anything."

I DO NOT BELIEVE YOU ARE RIGHT.

"When I was little, every night, no matter how bad things were, he'd come and spend time with me and my brother and my sisters. He'd read us stories, or discuss the events of the day with us. He'd come to us with his problems, and ask us how we'd solve them, and then... then... he'd tell us why it wouldn't work, and Nathanda would always want to negotiate, and Caelius would always want to start some complicated plot, and Jinxiang would always want to fight, and I was too little to even say anything but he'd always just smile at me and say, 'Sohu is right, I should stay very quiet and wait for things to develop further, good job Sohu!' and kiss me on the cheek, and I would laugh, and everybody would laugh." Sohu started crying.

I ALSO HAVE A STORY, said Uriel. I WANTED TO KNOW WHY HE SENT YOU TO ME. I ASCENDED TO BRIAH AND READ THE OMENS. HE SENT YOU BECAUSE HE THOUGHT THERE WOULD NEED TO BE SOMEBODY TO MAINTAIN THE UNIVERSE IF HE HAD TO KILL ME. HE THOUGHT I WOULD BE ANGRY IF I KNEW THIS. BUT IT DOES NOT BOTHER ME. THERE NEEDS TO BE SOMEONE BESIDES ME. HE WAS RIGHT. THE COMET KING CARED ABOUT THE WORLD. IT WAS ALWAYS FIRST.

"That... that was who he was. He always wanted what was best for everybody. That was all he ever did. Try to help people." Sohu started crying harder. "Father... was so sad for his last few years. I always thought... he'd get over it, that he'd meet someone else, that he'd feel happy again. After everything he did, Father deserved to die happy. But he must have... been... so miserable. Uriel, how do you bear it?"

BEAR WHAT?

"The world... is so sad? Mother... gone. Now Father is gone. Thamiel always wins in the end. And the Machinery is going to fail soon, and Father isn't around to help, and how do you bear it?"

KNOCK KNOCK.

"I know one of your books on humans probably says that humor is supposed to cheer us up when we're sad, but please, not now, I don't think I could..."

KNOCK KNOCK.

"...who's there?"

A SPIDER.

"A spider who?"

A SPIDER BEING BROKEN, OR BECAUSE OF BEING BROKEN, RISE UP AND BUILD ANEW.

In spite of herself, the corners of Sohu's mouth *almost* started to smile. "That was actually not completely awful," she said.

THANK YOU.

"And you're right. I've got to stay strong." She briefly disappeared into her cottage, started taking out her books and possessions, loading them into the flying kayak.

WHAT ARE YOU DOING?

"Getting ready. People need me."

I NEED YOU.

"You're... you're Uriel. You don't need anything."

I LIKE YOU.

"I like you too."

YOU ARE MY FRIEND.

"I'm sorry I have to go. But Father's dead. Nathanda says they need me. You've never had a family. You wouldn't understand."

YOU ARE MY FAMILY.

"Really?"

IN THE OLDEN DAYS, THE ANGEL SAMYAZAZ AND HIS FOLLOWERS FLED HEAVEN TO ESTABLISH A KINGDOM ON EARTH, WHERE THEY LAY WITH THE DAUGHTERS OF MEN. I DID NOT UNDERSTAND WHY THE DAUGHTERS OF MEN WERE SO INTERESTING. UM. BUT. UM. YOU ARE VERY INTERESTING.

"Um," said Sohu.

You are nice and you are smart and you help me feel better when things are bad and when you are around even Thamiel does not bother me as much. I do not want you to go.

"I'm sorry, Uriel. I like you too. And I'll come to visit often. Now that I know Kefitzat Haderech it won't be hard. I can come visit sometimes and you can keep teaching me."

Celestial Kabbalah is not something you can learn part-time.

"You told me I'd never learn it in a human lifetime anyway. What's the difference?"

Rabbi Tarfon said: it is not to you to complete the work, but neither are you free to desist from it.

"Well, Rabbi Tarfon didn't have a flying kayak. I'm free to go wherever I want."

Please stay.

"Father needs me, Uriel."

Please stay. Just for one more day.

"What difference does one more day make?"

Many things can happen in a day.

"Like what?"

Things.

Uriel was, as usual, unreadable.

"Okay," she said. "I'll stay a day. One more day."

Uriel was barely listening as he manipulated the strings of letters around him. Something was up, that was for sure.

She sighed and went back to her cottage to cry.

Chapter Fifty-Three

Lover Of Wild Rebellion

Late morning, May 13, 2017
New York City

Alvarez's apartment was so packed with books, bomb-making supplies, and extra people that somebody had to sleep in the closet. Valerie had volunteered. She figured the former Archmage of the West deserved the sofa more than she did. Any sacrifice for the Revolution.

Knock knock. Valerie rubbed her eyes and opened the door. Light streamed in from outside.

"Can I come in?" asked Mark McCarthy.

"In the closet?"

"Yeah."

Valerie sat up and shrugged. The older man closed the door, turned on the light, and sat down beside her. He had to almost contort himself not to touch her, not to give any hint of impropriety.

"Why are you in here?" asked Valerie.

"Want to talk," he said. "Where he can't hear us."

She thought, then nodded.

"Wait, can he hear us? That thing with your mind..."

"Doesn't do anything unless I'm sending it at him. I think. Still new to this. What's the problem?"

Mark sighed. "Look. I'm doing this because I promised, because it's his condition for springing me out of prison. Which he got me into. But you could just go invisible right now, vanish, never see him again. Listen. I know he's charming, I know he's fascinating, heck, I spent my college years getting caught up in one of his hare-brained schemes after another, but listen, Valerie, all that stuff about Mexico, it's total lies, for all I know he grew up third-generation immigrant in the States. There's no reason. He doesn't care. He's a narcissist, he's a psychopath, at the bottom of all the flowery words and wisecracks there's nothing there, just blankness. If you stick with him he'll grind you up and use you in some way that looks hilarious from the outside but will leave you dead or broken. You should never have linked your mind to him, you should never have come here, but please, listen to me, it's not too late for you to get out."

Valerie rubbed her eyes. "I just woke up," she protested.

"I shouldn't have tried to do this," said Mark. He started to get up. Valerie put a hand on his knee. He sat back down again.

"I don't know Dylan," Valerie said. Not in the way you would say "I don't know that man over by the corner," but in the way a stoner might say "I don't know my own hand, like, not really." "I'm not doing this for Dylan. I'm doing it for me."

"You think you're doing it for you," Mark said. "He's like a black hole. Everything ends up in his orbit eventually."

"No," she said a little more forcefully. "You're thinking I'm this small-town girl who's arrived in the big city and is too innocent to know how much danger she's in. And yeah, I never did anything more radical than edit a newspaper before. But I spent my whole life waiting for a revolution, and I'm getting tired of waiting. When I was little, I read William Blake, and he said that all things that can be annihilated must be annihilated so that the children of Jerusalem can be saved from slavery. Then I read Marx and he said the same thing. Then I read Stevens and he said it too. So yeah. I'm dumb. I'm new to all this. I'm not safe here. But I'm in my element. And I'm having fun. I feel like Abraham, smashing the idols."

"Smashing idols? Abraham was only comfortable smashing the idols because he knew there was a true God hidden behind them waiting to take over."

"Isn't there?"

"Rise and shine, lovebirds!" Dylan Alvarez said, flinging open the closet door. "We're having a breakfast meeting in the living room. Everyone's there! Absolutely not to be missed!"

Exchanging awkward glances, the two of them made their way into the kitchen.

"May I present," Dylan declared to the faces seated around the room—some on couches, some on chairs, the overflow on the floor—"the two newest members of BOOJUM. Ms. Valerie Lowry, and Lord High Magician Mark McCarthy."

Several terrorists applauded politely.

"And I'm sure the newcomers must be waiting to know who all of you grizzled veterans are! Names known to legend! This man here on my right side is the incomparable Clark Deas, my trusted lieutenant. Comes to us all the way from Ireland, where he used to engage in 'republican activity' up in the parts where that means something a little more decisive than voting for tax cuts. Had his own splinter group for a while, the Deas IRA, which like all good splinter groups spent 95% of the time fighting people on its own side and the other 5% catching unrelated people in crossfires. With His Majesty's finest breathing down his back, he joined millions of his countrymen in crossing the Atlantic to a promised land of wealth and freedom where all the policemen are blind and deaf and the streets are paved with plastic explosives."

"Total fecking lies," Clark said cheerfully. Valerie giggled.

"The lovely ladies on your left," continued Dylan, "are the Burns sisters. Started off as cat burglars. Whenever Lydia here would be arrested, she'd have an ironclad alibi. Finally some enterprising prosecutor realized she was using the oldest trick in the book — the old identical twin switcheroo. So in front of a packed courtroom, he declared he'd solved the mystery — it was her twin, Brenda, who had the alibi, and Lydia had been criming it up in the mansions of Long Island's rich and famous. Broke his heart when Brenda also had an ironclad alibi for the same night. I almost feel bad for him. Honestly, what are the odds that a set of identical triplets would go into crime?"

Valerie couldn't stop giggling now.

"Mr. Brian Young," Dylan moved on. "A graduate of the fine people at the Stanford chemistry department. Gandhi said, 'be the change you wish to see in the world,' and Mr. Young decided that he wished for a world with more loud noises and piles of rubble.

"And who could forget Mr. Michael Khan, our Lebanese computer whiz kid. Best known for redirecting all emails from an online dating advice columnist to the Director of the CIA and vice versa. I hear young ladies asking what to do about insensitive boyfriends were given solutions involving cluster bombs, and H. W. Bush got told to sort out his problems with Saddam over a nice candlelit dinner while wearing something sexy — both of which worked wonders, by the way. Now he's moved on to bigger and better things. The Bush assassination? That was me, Mike, and a whole fridge full of energy drinks.

"On the comfy chair we have Mr. John Murran, the ex-Secret Service man. You know he was there when Hinckley shot Reagan at point-blank range, and watched the bullet go right through the Gipper without even making him blink? True! Then he started saying crazy things like that the Secret Service protected the President from the people, but where was the organization to protect the people from the President. Well, you start speaking like that, they sentence you to thirty years in the can — I mean, the time he grabbed the President, yelling that he was going to find and erase the kabbalistic rune that bound his life-force to his material body didn't help. As far as anyone knows he died in there. Anyone but us!"

Murran stared at them impassively through his dark sunglasses.

"What about Maduegbuna?" asked Lydia Burns. "Where's he today?"

"Standing right behind you," said Alvarez.

Burns turned around, then jumped and gave a little shriek. Maduegbuna grinned disconcertingly.

"Mr. Maduegbuna, born to a Nigerian animist couple working for a multinational in the Israel-Palestine Anomaly. The Anomaly knows how to treat Jews, knows how to treat Muslims, even has some fail-safes for Christians and Hindus and atheists. But it was completely confused by a Nigerian animist, deposited him unceremoniously between planes, and ever since he's had a *complicated* relationship with the spatial dimensions, which we are happy to exploit for our own sinister purposes."

"Well, if that's all over," Clark began.

"Oh no," said Dylan. "Introduce me!"

"First of all, we all know you," said Clark, "and second, if I were to introduce you, you'd..."

"Not you," he snapped. "You. McCarthy."

McCarthy's expression was hard to read, but a careful observer might have noticed him very slightly clenching one fist. Finally he said, "Mr. Dylan Alvarez. On our first day of college, he hung up a big poster in our dorm room that said COMFORT THE AFFLICTED AND AFFLICT THE COMFORTABLE—"

Dylan beamed.

"—and since then it's been twenty years and I have never once seen him comfort the afflicted."

"Comforting the afflicted sounds super boring," Dylan said. "This is why the Sumerians invented specialization of labor. We know what we're good at. Which brings me to our next point. We are going to assassinate Ash Bentham."

He listened for questions or objections. There were none.

"We've had a good couple of days. Ms. Lowry here has given us a very new Name, so new nobody knows it exists, that lets us become invisible. Mr. McCarthy here is one of the top ritual magicians in the world and will be a stupendous boon to our efforts. So I decided—why not think big? We've already killed a president; killing another would be boring. But Ms. Lowry's sudden appearance has me feeling all Stevensite. So let's kill the head of UNSONG, who also happens to be the only halfway-competent leader the organization has had in its twenty-something-year history. Let's free the Names, restore the Constitution, and save America."

"How are we going to get into the UN?" asked Brenda Burns. "That place is heavily guarded day and night."

"We are BOOJUM," Dylan said. "Our specialty is making people softly and suddenly vanish away. This really shouldn't be too hard. A nice stroll through some corridors, then bang bang, then get out."

"I heard Bentham has freaky mind powers," said Khan. "Everyone's scared of him."

"That is why we have a Lord High Magician with us, Mr. Khan. We are getting some freaky powers of our own. I do not have the slightest idea what is wrong with Mr. Bentham, but I have confidence in Mr. McCarthy to determine a good way to neutralize it."

"What do we do after we're done?" asked Young. "Leave New York?"

"I'm sick of New York," Dylan said. "We've been here, what, three months now? If I never see another cockroach again, it will be too soon. Let's go to Florida. Lots of things to bomb in Florida."

"Like what?"

"Beaches, cocktail bars, pretty girls. But that's for later! Now we need to talk about who's coming on the Bentham mission. McCarthy, you're coming. Young, you stay. Clark, I can't get rid of you. Brenda, you're coming. Lydia and Norma, you're too old and too young, respectively."

"We were born six minutes apart!"

"See, practically a grandmother. Khan, you stay here. Murran, you're staying. Valerie, you're coming."

"Hold on a bloody minute," said Clark. "Why are we leaving Murran behind? That guy could hit a rat from fifty yards away."

"This is Manhattan," said Dylan. "You're never fifty yards away from a rat. And breaking into an international organization is a delicate endeavor. We can't bring along an entire expedition."

"If you're worried about numbers," said Clark, "take Murran and drop Lowry. The girl gave us invisibility. I get that. It's great. But she's of no help on a mission like this."

"On the contrary," said Dylan. "Valerie has to be the one to fire the killing shot."

"What?" asked Valerie, at the same time Clark and Brian asked "What?"

"It's simple," said Dylan. "Asher Bentham is not going to be killed by a terrorist. Asher Bentham is going to be killed by a young girl, a girl whose heart is true. This is how it has to happen. This is the Narrative!"

A few cheers. Clark rolled his eyes. Mark McCarthy mouthed *He's crazy* at Valerie, who carefully ignored him.

"Now," said Dylan, "everybody who'll be participating, get something to eat, catch up on your sleep, call your parents. Tomorrow we fight. But tonight... tonight is our last day in New York. Tonight, we are going to Broadway!"

Interlude ק

Bush

January 20, 2001
Washington, DC

Some kabbalists believed Ralph Nader would win the 2000 election, for Job 5:11 says, "He puts those who are in low places up to high places," and what is a nadir but a low place? But others thought it would be George W. Bush, based on Judges 9:14 —"The trees all said to the thorny bush, come and be king." And still others thought Al Gore would win, for in Ezekiel 32, God says he will fill the land with gore.

So it should not have been surprising when the election ended in a perfect three-way tie, each candidate getting the exact same number of votes. Hanging chads in Salish, butterfly ballots in Florida, and voting irregularities in the Des Moines entity turned into such a disaster that resolution was foisted upon the Supreme Court. But could they be trusted? The Margrave of Maryland, a Gore state, had sent his troops to the DC border to "observe and guarantee the process." The Viceroy of Virginia, which had gone for Bush, sent troops to the border to keep watch on Maryland.

As it became clear that the Court would not be able to rule by Inauguration Day, Bill Clinton declared he was going to remain president until the election was decided. The Virginians cried foul: every day Clinton was in office was another day he could tip the scales in favor of his vice-president and chosen successor. The threats escalated, until one morning the Virginians woke up to find the Maryland forces holed up in DC. The President had invited them in to "defend" the city; the balance of power had shifted.

The Untied States Army had been through a lot. They'd resisted Thamiel's invasion in the 70s and had mostly been massacred. They'd fought the War on Drugs in the 80s and still had nightmares about hundreds of thousands of drug-addled soldiers marching against them in perfect coordination. They'd invaded the Persian Gulf in the 90s to defend the Eridu-Xanadu Consortium from Saddam Hussein. Many of them had only just gotten back from marching with the Comet King against Yakutsk. More than anyone else, they understood upon how thin a ledge the country balanced.

Now that ledge was starting to shake precariously. Demons had been spotted in Siberia again. The Other King's necromantic sorties around Las Vegas were seamlessly transitioning into a full-fledged zombie apocalypse. The Comet King, the one civilian leader whom they really respected, was missing in action. And all the civilians could do was spend four months debating hanging chads while a giant leadership vacuum gaped at the very top of the command structure.

Dick Cheney, Bush's vice-presidential candidate, was a former Secretary of Defense and Halliburton CEO. He knew the military-industrial complex like he knew the back of his skeletal claw-like hand. So he started talking to people. Wouldn't it be nice, he asked, if a friend of the military held power during this difficult time? Instead of that pinko Gore? Instead of (God forbid) Ralph Nader, who wanted to give up the Names that provided our only strategic advantage against the inhuman forces surrounding our borders?

And so on January 17th, a group from the Pentagon walked into the White House and declared George W. Bush the 43rd President of the Untied States on account of his clear victory in Georgia which the Supreme Court would no doubt confirm very shortly. A second group from the Pentagon walked into the Supreme Court, had a couple of friendly words with the justices, and lo and behold they very shortly confirmed Bush's Georgia victory. A third group quite strongly insisted that Al Gore accompany them to a nice place in the country so he could consider the implications of the Supreme Court decision free from outside distractions. And a fourth took Ralph Nader to another place in the country — far away from Gore, just to make sure they wouldn't distract each other.

The inauguration three days later was performed under military lockdown. Still, a crowd filled the National Mall. Loyal Republicans, disgruntled Democrats, soldiers who had been shipped in and hastily re-outfitted in civilian clothing to keep up appearances.

"I am honored and humbled to stand here, where so many of America's leaders have come before me, and so many will follow," President Bush began. "We have a place, all of us, in a long story — a story we continue, but whose end we will not see. It is the story of a new world that became a friend and liberator of the old, a story of a slave-holding society that became a servant of freedom, the story of a power that went into the world to protect but not possess, to defend but not to conquer."

A few protesters managed to unfurl a FREE REVEREND STEVENS banner before being dragged away. If television still worked, no doubt the cameras would have cut to an image of the demonstration; as it was the radio broadcasts passed them by. Stevens himself would die in jail a few months later of what the coroner would rule "natural causes." A veritable epidemic of natural causes was raging through the jails of the eastern Untied States that spring; Gore and Nader would die the same way within a few weeks.

"We are not this story's author, who fills time and eternity with his purpose. Yet, his purpose is achieved in our duty. And our duty is fulfilled in service to one another. Never tiring, never yielding, never finishing, we renew that purpose today, to make our country more just and generous, to affirm the dignity of our lives and every life. This work continues, the story goes on, and an angel still rides in the whirlwind and directs this storm."

I'm glad that nowadays our country requires our president-elect to undergo a medical exam to prove he is human. But I wish there was also a rule that he had to consult with a kabbalist before deciding to drop references to the Book of Job in inauguration speeches.

"But of one thing I am sure. Today, we are building a new chapter in that story. And I owe a debt of..."

President Bush spontaneously caught fire. "HELLLPPP!" he screamed as the entire National Mall watched on in horror. "HELLLPPP... HELL..." By the time Secret Service agents reached him at the podium, he was already a charred corpse.

In the midst of the word he was trying to say — in the midst of his laughter and glee — he had softly and suddenly vanished away — because Dylan Alvarez had hacked his teleprompter to display the Mortal Name.

Chapter Fifty-Four

My Course Among the Stars

Spring 1999
Colorado

So passed fifteen years. New factories rose up. New mines sunk beneath the earth. New roads crisscrossed the mountains. Laboratories, barracks, fortresses, granaries, airstrips. All preparation for the final crusade. Over the course of a generation, the Comet King's war on Hell shifted gradually from metaphorical spiritual struggle to "we're going to need a lot of guns."

People from all over the Untied States and the world flocked to Colorado, ready to take up arms for the cause. The Comet King disappeared for a few months on a strange ship with seven sails, saying he was seeking the Explicit Name of God. Came back, said he had found it. Everything started falling into place. It was really going to happen.

On the final night, they lay together in the citadel, her tracing patterns on his chest.

"I wish you could come with me," said Jalaketu, just as Robin was thinking *I wish I could go with him.*

"You know I can't," she answered, just as he was thinking *But I know you can't.* "Somebody needs to stay here and put on a brave face for the kingdom."

"And if I were to die," he added, just as she thought *And if God forbid he were to die.* He trailed off.

"You won't die," she said, just as he thought *And I very well might.*

A raised eyelid. "The journey to Siberia will be hard even without military resistance. The Names will keep us warm, but miscalculations in our food supply could be a disaster. Morale is high, but a few bad weeks and we could turn against ourselves. Thamiel is dangerous and has many tricks. We haven't yet seen the extent of his magic. And the Shem HaMephorash is—hard to use. I think I can say it and live, but it will be close."

"But you're not afraid."

"Would fear help?"

"I don't know," said Robin. "I'm scared enough for both of us. I'm scared you won't come back. Or I'm scared you'll give up and come back too soon, with Hell still intact."

"About *that* you need not fear," said the Comet King.

"The astronomers used to say comets are unpredictable," said Robin. "That everything in the heavens keeps its own orbit except the comet. Which follows no rules, knows no path."

"They are earthbound," said the Comet King. "Seen from Earth, a comet is a prodigy, coming out of the void for no reason, returning to the void for no reason. They call it unpredictable because they cannot predict it. From the comet's own point of view, nothing could be simpler. It starts in the outer darkness, aims directly at the sun, and never stops till it gets there. Everything else spins in its same orbit forever. The comet heads for the source. They call it crooked because it is too straight. They call it unpredictable because it is too fixed. They call it chaotic because it is too linear."

He hesitated for a moment.

"That is why I love you, you know. In a world of circles, you are something linear."

She said nothing, just kept tracing patterns on his chest.

"A few months to reach Yakutsk," he said. "A few months to get back. The work itself shouldn't take more than a few moments. I will see you again by the winter."

Sleep came to them there, together, for the last time.

Chapter Fifty-Five

None Can Visit His Regions

July 1999
Siberia

Overtly, the meaning of *king* is "a hereditary monarch."

Kabbalistically, the meaning of *king* is "one who fights for freedom."

This we derive from Martin Luther King, whose name was *king* in two ways: first in English via his surname, second in Hebrew via his initials. Likewise, he signifies fighting for freedom in two ways. First, through his name: "Martin" comes from Latin *martinus* and shares a root with *martial* meaning "warlike" or "fighting," "Luther" comes from Greek *eleutheria* meaning "freedom," and so "Martin Luther" equals "one who fights for freedom." Second, through the example of his life.

And so in accordance with the secret structure of the universe, the Comet King marched forth to fight for freedom.

His armies set out from Colorado Springs, passed through Salt Lake City, reached the Salish Free State. Advance forces captured Juneau and Anchorage, while the bulk of the troops boarded an immense flotilla ten years in the making and sailed up the coast, resupplying at the Alaskan ports as they went. Another advance force reached Tin City, Alaska. The Comet King raised his sword, spoke a Name, and parted the Bering Strait. They crossed, took Chukotka and Kamchatka from the north before the Siberians could react, deconstructed the coastal batteries and seawalls that were supposed to prevent amphibious invasion. The main force landed en masse in Magadan Oblast and worked its way northeast through pestilent swamps and mountains. There was fighting every step of the way: ambushes, pit traps, a frantic battle in the pass of Ust-Nera. The demons of Siberia deployed misshapen hell-creatures, swarms of unnatural insects, darknesses that seemed to crawl and screech. The Comet King deployed strange walking tanks, floating globular airships, squadrons of kabbalists who could bring down mountains with a song. Siberia's army kept retreating. The armies of the West kept advancing.

Finally they reached Yakutsk. After three days of apocalyptic fighting, the city fell; Thamiel and his court retreated in disarray. The Comet King had hoped to rescue the human citizens, but there was not enough left of them for this to be a mercy. So his crusaders burnt the city, pushed the memories out of their waking minds and into their nightmares, and marched on.

The last seven hundred miles were the easiest. After the fall of Yakutsk the demons gave up most resistance. The crusaders' spirits were high. Their steps were lightened by victory. They sang the Battle Hymn of the Republic. They marched toward a final destination they only partly understood.

In this mood they came to the still blue waters of Lake Baikal and fanned out along its shoreline near Ulan-Ude. They rested and tended to their wounded while their leader stayed in his tent, praying. After three days, the Comet King decided that it was time.

He walked onto the water and it held his weight. Only a few steps; the lake was hundreds of miles long, but never too wide. Then he was on the island in the middle, the one the natives called Shaman's Rock, the one that had a hole in it deeper than the world itself.

His men watched him from the other shore, barely daring to breathe.

His engineers had already demolished the gate's physical defenses. Now he destroyed its spiritual defenses with a word. The rock crumbled, revealing only a deep pit. The Comet King stepped off the edge and disappeared from view.

He fell and fell, until he no longer knew if he was falling or not. There was no ground beneath him, and no walls on either side. Just endless space, tenebrous and inscrutable, like it was filled with black smoke. Were those flames that he could almost see, if he strained his eyes? A flash of movement here? The flap of a demonic wing there?

It had all been for this. The handful of lost souls in Yakutsk was only a drop in the barrel. Those who had been saved in Canada and Alaska only a trickle. This was the ocean. Billions of people through all of history who had been swept off into Hell and left to suffer forever. There was only one way to save them. He had sacrificed tens of thousands of lives to come here. Now it was time.

He fell so far and long that there was no point in waiting any further. He said a prayer. He visualized a structure in his mind's eye, a complex kabbalistic structure of interlocking aspects of divinity and mortality beyond the power of any human but him to imagine. And then, his voice trembling only a little, he spoke the Explicit Name of God.

It went like this:

A tav.

A resh.

A fearsome joy.

A fervent wish.

The Comet King incanted HaMephorash.

Nothing happened.

A slight whirling of the smoke? Another hint of those flickering flames? Or were those just illusions? The Shem HaMephorash didn't touch them. The Comet King frowned.

He spoke the Name a second time, vocalizing every letter clearly and precisely, like the notes of a song. Somewhere high above him, dogs started barking. Babies began to cry. Clouds shattered like glass, huge waves appeared from nowhere and lashed against every coast. The Archangel Uriel screamed and clutched his forehead, then started frantically drawing symbols in the air to calm storms that only he could see.

But if the smoky realm below the pit was affected at all, it was only the tiniest perturbation, too minute for the Comet King to even be sure it had happened.

Jalaketu's eyes narrowed. He started tracing glyphs around him, arcane geometries to magnify his words and purify their impact. He wrote manically, and symbols in a hundred languages living and dead gleamed through the darkness and added their powers to his. He stood surrounded by a living web of power. Then, a third time, he spoke the Name of God.

The sky turned red. The seas turned red. The sunlight became fractured and schizophrenic, like it was shining through stained glass. Trees exploded. Every religious building in the world, be it church or mosque or temple, caught fire at the same time.

But the Comet King saw only little eddies in the darkness, like when a child blows a puff of air into the smoke of a bonfire.

Now he was *really* angry. He spread himself across all the worlds and sephirot, drew all of their power into himself. The web of glyphs crackled and burned with the strain, pulsed from color to color at epileptic speed, shot off sparks like a volcano. The Comet King opened his mouth—

STOP, said a voice. A bolt of lightning flashed through the smoke, and the Archangel Uriel appeared beside him, flaming sword held high. STOP, LEST THE ENERGIES YOU INVOKE DESTROY THE WORLD.

"Not going to destroy the world!" said the Comet King. He didn't look remotely human at this point. His skin had gone night-black, his hair was starlight-silver, no one could have counted how many limbs he had. "Going to destroy Hell! Don't deny me this, Uriel! You know it has to be done!"

YOU ARE NOT ENTIRELY IN HELL. YOU ARE ONLY SORT OF IN HELL. YOU ARE UNLEASHING THE ENERGY OF THE SHEM HAMEPHORASH PARTLY INTO THE ORDINARY WORLD. THERE ARE ALREADY TOO MANY CRACKS. SING AGAIN AND THE SKY WILL SHATTER.

"I'm trying to aim at Hell," said the Comet King. "Not sure where I am... but it's close. If I can get enough power..."

THEN YOU WILL SHATTER THE SKY, said Uriel. THIS IS NOT A MATTER OF POWER. WHAT YOU ARE DOING IS FUNDAMENTALLY ILL-ADVISED. STOP.

"This is the gate, Uriel! I passed through the gate! You saw me, they all saw me."

THERE ARE MANY GATES. NOT ALL OF THEM ARE OPEN. YOU HAVE PASSED THROUGH SOME. YOU ARE STILL OUTSIDE OTHERS. IF YOU SAY THE SHEM HAMEPHORASH AGAIN YOU WILL DESTROY THE WORLD.

"Many gates? Uriel, we talked about this. We spent *years* researching. We both agreed that if we could get through the hole in Lake Baikal, we could break into Hell."

YES. IT MADE SENSE AT THE TIME. NOW WE ARE HERE OBSERVING FIRST-HAND. I AM TELLING YOU THERE ARE MORE GATES THAN WE THOUGHT. SOME OF THEM ARE CLOSED. YOU CANNOT GET THROUGH THEM.

"If I just give it more power..."

THAMIEL IS A FACET OF GOD. BRUTE STRENGTH WILL NOT SUFFICE AGAINST HIM.

"This is the Shem HaMephorash! It's literally the power of God Himself! There's nothing that can stand up to it."

YES. THAT IS WHY YOU ARE DESTROYING THE WORLD.

"Give me something to work with, Uriel!"

UM.

"*Give me something to work with!*"

GATES ARE VERY COMPLICATED.

"For the love of God, give me something to work with, Uriel!"

UM.

"Are you saying there is *literally no way* to destroy Hell *even with the Explicit Name of God?*"

UM.

"*Is that what you're saying?*"

UM.

"Why would God do that? Why would He make a universe where the one thing it is absolutely one hundred percent morally obligatory to do is totally impossible, even if you do everything right, even if you get a weapon capable of destroying worlds themselves, *who does that sort of thing?*"

GOD, said Uriel. HE DOES MANY THINGS THAT ARE HARD TO EXPLAIN. I AM SURPRISED YOU HAVE NOT REALIZED THIS BY NOW.

"Who creates suffering that can never end? Who makes people, tells them to do the right thing, then pulls the rug out from under them when they try? I was supposed to be His sword, Uriel! I was Moshiach! He forged me, He and my father, put me through all of those trials so I could be worthy to be here today. Who forges a weapon like that and then keeps it sheathed? *Why would God do that?*"

STOP TRYING TO UNDERSTAND THE WILL OF GOD, said Uriel. IT NEVER HELPS.

"So," said the Comet King. His voice was icy calm now. "What do you propose I do?"

LET ME TAKE YOU HOME, said Uriel.

"No," said the Comet King.

YOU WILL NOT BE ABLE TO LEAVE THIS PLACE ALONE, said Uriel. YOU HAVE CROSSED THROUGH TOO MANY GATES. NOT ALL OF THEM ARE AS EASY TO PASS IN THE OTHER DIRECTION.

"I'm not going, Uriel."

PLEASE, said Uriel. SOME OF THE GATES MAY SHUT AGAIN, IN TIME. YOU WOULD BE TRAPPED DOWN HERE.

"So what? So you want me to give up? Lead a million men all the way to Siberia and let however many of them die and then just *give up?* Just because..."

IF YOU RETURN TO THE LIVING WORLD PERHAPS WE CAN FIGURE OUT A SOLUTION.

"You've already said! There's no solution! Even the Explicit Name of God isn't enough!"

I DO NOT THINK THERE IS A VERY GOOD CHANCE OF US FINDING A SOLUTION, BUT IT IS PROBABLY HIGHER IF YOU ARE WORKING HARD ON LOOKING FOR IT THAN IF YOU ARE TRAPPED FOREVER IN THE ANTECHAMBER OF HELL.

"Uriel. Give me something to work with."

I AM GOING TO TAKE YOU OUT OF HERE NOW. I AM SURE YOU CAN FIGHT ME OFF IF YOU WANTED TO BUT I WOULD REALLY APPRECIATE IT IF YOU DID NOT TRY.

The archangel reached out a gigantic hand and grabbed the Comet King. Then he rocketed upwards, fiery sword outstretched above him, clearing the smoke from their path. The darkness began to thin. A sense of orientation returned. At last a rush of information hit all of Jalaketu's senses at once and he realized he was out of the pit, back above the earthly Lake Baikal.

His men started to cheer. Some of them blew horns. A few started singing verses from the Battle Hymn. His heart sank. *They think I succeeded,* he thought to himself. *Of course they think I succeeded. I'm the Comet King, here I am shooting out of the Abyss alive, being carried by an archangel, of course they think I succeeded.* "No!" he shouted at the armies. "Stop! I failed! I couldn't do it! I couldn't destroy Hell! You brought me all this way, you trusted me, and I couldn't do it! It's all gone wrong! Stop singing! Stop singing! Stop!"

Most of them couldn't hear him, but a few caught the gist of his message. One by one, the songs wavered, but they didn't die, his men still singing, sure that there must be something worth singing about. A few cried out, or raised banners, or started cheering on general principle.

"Don't bring me back to them," the Comet King said, almost sobbing. "Take me somewhere else... can't face them, just now." Uriel looked down at him, tilted his colossal head in a gesture of confusion. "Just for now," he said. "Just for a few hours. Somewhere I can think. Give me time to think, Uriel."

The archangel deposited Jalaketu on a hill a few miles outside of camp. Then he gave a long sigh.

I'M SORRY, he said.

"No," said the Comet King. He looked mostly human again now. "You did the right thing. Prevented me from destroying the world."

YES, said Uriel. ARE YOU OKAY?

"Sort of. I need to think. It's not a total loss. We still have the army. The military action went well. Better than expected. We can hold onto Baikal while we try to figure out where to go from here. I can convince people to... wait... oh no. *Oh no.*"

WHAT? asked Uriel.

"I just realized," said the Comet King. "*What am I going to tell my wife?*"

Interlude ר

Novus Ordo Seclorum

You know the story: two women came to King Solomon with a baby. Each said the baby was theirs. Solomon said he would cut the baby in two and give half to each. One woman agreed, the other abandoned her claim. Solomon declared that the second was surely the real mother, and gave the baby to her.

Which raises a lot of questions. Like: what was the first woman planning to do with her half-baby? The scholars answer that the story is a metaphor. The baby represented Israel, on the brink of civil war. The two women represent the two parties contending for leadership. Solomon's judgment, then, is the same as Andrew Jackson's: "The Union must be preserved!" Anyone who would accept war as the price of power is unworthy to lead.

There was no Solomonic wisdom to be seen in the Untied States of America in late 2001. Pro-Bush forces had abducted Al Gore and Ralph Nader, who had died under mysterious circumstances. Then BOOJUM had killed President Bush with his own teleprompter. For a few months, the country had been held together by the Comet King — not by any action, for he was still locked in his room, incommunicado — but by his presence, a vague assumption that nothing could degenerate too completely while he yet lived. Vice-President Dick Cheney had held onto nominal control in DC, not daring to inaugurate himself, nobody else daring to move against him.

Then the Battle of Never Summer, and the sudden collapse of Royal Colorado. The United Kingdom of Great Basin conquered Utah, Arizona, Colorado, and Wyoming in rapid succession. California, Salish, and the Des Moines entity appealed to DC for protection. The Other King negotiated an alliance with Gorist leaders in the East — the Margrave of Maryland, the Pendragon of Pennsylvania. DC called on Virginia for aid. For the second time in two centuries, the Potomac flowed red with blood.

The whole system that Reagan and the Comet King had drawn up together that day in Camp David came crumbling down. Twenty years of suppressed grudges broke out into a two-year orgy of violence. The Khaganate of Muskegon and the Shogunate of Michigan lunged at each other's throats. The Maharaja of Indiana declared a crusade for Cheney and made a play for Chicago. Naderites in Minnesota annexed the Upper Peninsula. The Other King's armies marched west, with no force west of the Mississippi strong enough to resist him. The Drug Lord cast off any pretense of being dead and marched for America's southern border.

Citadel West handled missile defense for the continent. Nobody needed to fear nuclear missiles. But in January 2004, a Naderite fanatic arrived in Union Station in Washington DC and spoke the Wrathful Name. The city, as Byron put it, "melted like snow at the glance of the Lord." 300,000 people died, including Vice-President Cheney. For a second, the nation was shocked out of its bloodlust.

Asher Bentham, the new Director-General of UNSONG, announced that the destruction of Washington had been a misuse of a Holy Name, and so under the purview of his organization. He announced that he had granted himself special emergency powers to investigate and defuse the situation, called in UN peacekeepers, and began intense negotiations with the heads of all relevant parties.

Everyone agreed that the fighting had to end. The question was whether it was worth saving the Untied States as an organization. Without a capital or a president, the federation was on shaky ground. But if it were allowed to lapse completely, the nation would be easy prey for the Drug Lord and the Other King.

Bentham's proposal shocked all parties: he would annex the entire North American continent between the Rio Grande and the 50th parallel as a Special UNSONG Protectorate, with himself as Protector-General. He would enforce peace, coordinate common defense, and negotiate with foreign powers — all under his mandate of protecting trade in the Divine Names. After all, the destruction of Washington had proved that national security and the regulation of Names were one and the same.

It was the Other King's representative who agreed first. After that, the rest fell into line. Protection from the Other King was worth the price of admission; disagreeing with the Other King seemed suicidal. Oh, he got what he wanted out of the agreement — California and Salish were reduced to near tributaries, constantly under his shadow—but the structure of the federation, and the freedom of the individual states, remained intact.

And so a new Constitution was duly written and ratified, a new Congress was elected, and the government of the Untied States moved to New York City, with the UN at its head.

Chapter Fifty-Six

Agony In The Garden

August 1, 1999
Colorado Springs

Given the need to keep up spirits, Robin decided the people needed whatever holidays they could get. August 1, the anniversary of Colorado's statehood, was as good an opportunity as anything else. So she stood on a rock spire in the Garden of the Gods as crowds — disproportionately female since a million men were marching in Siberia — listened for the words of their Queen Regent.

The difference between a speech and a sermon had grown kind of thin ever since the state had become the seat of the Messiah in his war against Hell, so she began with a Bible verse. Psalm 84:

"*How lovely is your dwelling place,*
Lord Almighty!
My soul yearns, even faints,
for the courts of the Lord;
my heart and my flesh cry out
for the living God.
Even the bird has found a home,
and a nest for herself.

"This place has always been so beautiful. That's what I've always wanted. Everywhere to be as beautiful as here. Someday, I want everywhere in Colorado to be a garden and everywhere to be holy. The song spoke of 'purple mountain majesties above the fruited plain' and 'alabaster cities undimmed by human tears.' I want that. I want to make the deserts bloom, and the forests rich and wild. I want new heights of art and science. I want new symphonies and new folk songs. I want new infrastructure, new parks, new buildings and monuments that are the envy of the world. I want everybody to be able to live the life they want, whether in the cities or in the wilderness. I want to cure disease, end poverty, create a new and better kind of civilization. You all want the same. And it's not just that the Comet King can do it, though he can. It's that all of *us* can do it. We're the right people. At the right time.

"But we haven't been doing any of this. And we're not going to for a long time. Because it's not the most important thing."

She continued from the Psalm:

"*Blessed are those whose strength is in you,*
whose hearts are set on pilgrimage.
As they pass through the Valley of Weeping,
they make it a place of springs

"William Blake said that what we do in time echoes in Eternity, but he was being metaphorical. I'm not. What we do here now echoes in Eternity. The past twenty years, instead of building new roads and cities and better lives for our children, we've been building a war machine. A really, really good war machine. Not because we're bad people who don't love peace. Because some wars are important. Every other war has been fought over land or money or religion or something earthly. Something that disappears. This war we're fighting now echoes in Eternity. If we win, we end eternal suffering. We save your mothers and fathers, your grandparents, all your ancestors back to Adam, from eternal suffering. And not just them. In a hundred years, we're saving our friends, our families, our children, and maybe ourselves. There are so many things we want, so many things we need to do, but as soon as we realized the enormity of the evil below our feet, we realized there wasn't anything else we could do. Not really. Against such horrors, everything else must be put to the side as we join a fight which we could not avoid and stay fully human.

"This is an apology and a call to arms. It's an apology for all the beautiful and wonderful things we could have been doing the past twenty years, that we could be doing now, that will go undone because we are on a crusade. And it's a call to arms to keep working, to keep Colorado running while our friends and family are away, because we're in the crusade too, crusading on the home front, and nothing we could possibly do is more important than this.

"The Comet King has given us so much. But not as much as he's asked us to sacrifice. We're sacrificing everything right now, our dreams, our hopes of a better life—because we trust him. And because we trust ourselves to know what's right. If we succeed, then literally through all Eternity people will remember our names. Ten million years from now, when the world is so different that no other memories remain, people will still know that there was once eternal suffering, but now their suffering is ended. Because of us.

Hear my prayer, Lord God Almighty;
listen to me, God of Jacob.
Look on our shield, O God;
look with favor on your Anointed One"

She climbed down the pillar to rapturous applause, posed for the necessary photo ops, made her way through the crowd towards where Father Ellis and Nathanda were waiting for her.

Jalaketu was with them. He was hidden under a dark cloak, but she recognized him immediately.

"A word alone?" he asked, when he saw her.

Robin almost shouted with delight, then jumped in to hug him. "I thought you weren't going to come back until the crusade was over!" she said. "I thought it cost you too much energy to keep teleporting back and forth!" She worried her smile was so broad she looked like an idiot, but she didn't care. "This is such a surprise! We need—"

The look on his face shut her up. This was not a personal visit, and whatever the news was, it wasn't good.

She took his hand, and the two of them turned to lightning and then were atop a different spire, on the other side of the Garden, far from everyone else.

"Bad news?" she asked. "We heard... we heard you destroyed Yakutsk. We got the pictures and everything. What's wrong?"

Jala nodded. "The other part," he said. "Seems to be... ah... seems to be..."

Robin waited.

"I think it might be impossible to use the Explicit Name of God to destroy Hell," he said all at once.

"What?" asked Robin.

"I tried," said the Comet King. "Many times. Under Lake Baikal. Uriel had to stop me. Said if I did it any more I'd probably destroy the world. There were more gates than we thought. Some of them are... seem impregnable."

"So how are you going to destroy Hell, then?" asked Robin.

The Comet King just looked at her hopelessly, almost like he was too terrified to speak. Then he just shook his head "no."

A moment of silence.

"I... I thought you should be the first to know," he said.

"No," said Robin, "that's silly. You need to figure out a better way. Ask Uriel."

"I asked," said the Comet King. "He said there was none."

"Ask Sohu. She's been studying so hard."

"I asked," said the Comet King. "She didn't know either."

"Ask the Lady. Or the Chief Rabbi of Israel. Ask the Satmar Rebbe, or the Belzer Rebbe. Or ask the Pope, maybe he'll know."

"I asked."

"Ask the Urim and Thummim. Go to San Francisco and ask the collective consciousness there."

"*I asked,*" said the Comet King, and for the first time through her own confusion Robin heard the note of despair in his voice.

"Ask the other chief rabbi! Aren't there always two? Ask the..."

The Comet King put his arms around Robin and whispered, "I'm sorry."

"No. Figure something out. Can't you just... be really evil? Then die? That has to work. It's not even Thamiel's law. It's God's."

"I asked Uriel," said the Comet King. "He said it wouldn't work. Doing evil for a greater good, because I want to save the world. It wouldn't count."

"So — figure out some way to change your personality to be genuinely evil, then do evil, then die, then use the Name."

"You think I haven't looked into that? Thamiel can't be fooled that easily. God definitely can't be fooled that easy. I promise you, Robin. I've thought about this. *It doesn't work.*"

Robin jerked back. "No," she said. "This isn't how it ends. Get yourself together. You can do this. You can do anything. That's the *point*! Figure it out!"

"They'll be missing me in Siberia by now," said the Comet King. "There's still more work left to do. I need to mop up resistance, liberate the rest of Russia, liberate Canada. I want to be done before winter. I should go."

"You can't go! What do I do here? What do I tell people?"

"Nothing," said the Comet King. "Don't tell them anything. As far as they're concerned we won the victory. Our army beat their army. We destroyed Yakutsk. That looks like winning. Your speech aside, so few of them think about the great work. Proclaim victory and arrange a parade. When I get back in the winter, we'll work on what we can work on. Thamiel thinks he can make people evil? I can make them good. *We* can make them good. Make sure that however many souls are lost, we don't lose a single one more. It would be a victory upon a victory. Nobody has to know about what happened at Baikal."

"*I'll* know!" said Robin.

"I know," said the Comet King.

"You can't do this! I won't let you! You hear me, Jala? I will not let you do this!"

"I'll see you when the war is over," said the Comet King, and a bolt of reverse lightning unstruck the ground, leapt into the sky, and deposited Robin back in the peopled section of the park and Jalaketu to wherever Jalaketu was going.

"Bad news?" asked Father Ellis, though it was a stupid question, with her face streaked with tears.

"What did he tell you?" she asked. "Did he say what—"

"He found me as you started talking," said Ellis. "Said he came here from Siberia to talk to you, then didn't tell me anything else."

She said nothing.

"Bad news?" Ellis asked again.

"If he wanted you to know," she snapped, "he would have told you." Then. "We need to get home. I need to think."

Chapter Fifty-Seven

Now Taking On Ahania's Form...

Evening, May 13, 2017
Citadel West

Sohu asked whether I wanted to help her with the error correction process. It was the highlight of my life thus far. It was like getting asked to debate philosophy with Aristotle, or play one-on-one against Michael Jordan. Did I want to study the kabbalah with Sohu West? My heart leapt at the thought.

So we walked through sunless streets until we reached a building on the perimeter, right up against the stone wall of the mountain. Sarah came with me, of course, I couldn't help that, and Sohu led us up a staircase and down a long corridor to her study. Everywhere in the citadel seemed equally dreary, lit by fluorescent lights and built to exactly the sort of utilitarian specifications you would expect of a bunker, but Sohu's study was full of books and a big oak table, and for a moment it reminded me of a hundred libraries and synagogues and classrooms I'd been in. The life of the mind was the same everywhere.

We started working. Usually the hardest part of these things is to add up the gematria value of all the different subsets of letters, but of course Sarah did it instantly. The second-hardest part was figuring out which chapter of the books had the equations you needed, but Sohu had a photographic memory and would think for a second, pull a volume off the fourth shelf on the far wall, open it up to chapter sixteen, and put her finger halfway down the first page.

"Um," I said, trying to think quickly, "maybe if we see which Goldblum subsets are invariant under a temurah transformation, we could..." But Sohu interrupted. "For a non-supernally based Name like this one, that's equivalent to a basic transformation of phonetic triplets," she said. "Schachter,

1992." And before I could ask how she even knew that applied here, Sarah announced to us that all of the phonetic triplets checked out. By that point Sohu's attention had been lost, and on she went to the next book, the next theory. "Any corresponding Psalms?" she asked, and before I could even remember exactly how many psalms there were Sarah shook her head and said that none of them corresponded.

"Sarah," Sohu finally said, "how carefully did you confound Aaron's memory?"

"What do you mean?" Sarah asked.

"I mean," said Sohu, "that if someone randomly went in and switched a few letters, we would have corrected the Name twenty minutes ago, the first algorithm we tried. If someone really skilled in Kabbalah very carefully altered the Name to make sure that their victim could never correct it again, well" — she gestured to the growing pile of books abandoned on the table — "then it might be a little harder."

"I knew Aaron was a kabbalist," said Sarah. "I didn't want to make it too easy for him."

Sohu groaned.

"Okay," she finally said. "We'll reconfigure the sephirot into partzufim and try it that way." She started calculating furiously. "Lose the ayin," she muttered to herself, "carry the tav, and..."

Sarah interrupted. "And it just stays the same."

"You know," said Sohu. "If *I* wanted to confound a Name this badly, I'm not sure that I could."

I thought I saw a sort of triumphant grin flash over Sarah's face, but it disappeared quickly.

"We need some of the original building blocks back," Sohu said. "Aaron, will you let me read your mind?"

"You can do that?

"I'm not good at it. What happened to you with the Drug Lord, I'm sure he was better. My father was better still. But it's worth a try. I have a little training in chashmal."

The overt meaning of *chashmal* is "electricity."

The kabbalistic meaning is also "electricity," but it's complicated.

The prophet Ezekiel described certain angels as being *chashmal*, or surrounded by *chashmal*, or radiating *chashmal*. Nobody entirely knew what he meant, but the translators of the Septuagint ventured a guess of "amber-colored" or "amber light." Fast forward eighteen hundred years, and the original Zionist Jews were trying to reinvent the Hebrew language and needed a word for electricity. One of them, probably a kabbalist, pointed out that the English word *electricity* is generally believed to come from the Latin word *electricus*, meaning "amber," because amber gave off a sort of static electric charge. But other etymologists believe it comes from the Phoenician word *elekron*, meaning "shining light." Well, Hebrew already has a word meaning both "amber" and "shining light," and that word was *chashmal* . So they stuck it in as "electricity" in the first Hebrew dictionary.

I once read an atheist tract that asked why God didn't prove His omniscience by putting predictions about science or technology in the Bible. The answer is that He did and they're just not thinking kabbalistically enough to notice. Any Israeli schoolchild can open up the Book of Ezekiel and see a 6th century BC prophet describe the angels he encounters as crackling with electricity.

Maimonides put a different gloss on these chashmal angels. He said that it was a compound word made of *chash*, "silence," and *mal*, meaning "speech." So these angels were actually radiating "silent speech." Even more specific: *chash* is the root of *chashva*, meaning "thought." So the angels were radiating "thought-speech" at Ezekiel. No wonder that when future generations of kabbalists discovered the secrets of telepathy, they called it *chashmal*!

There are deep connections here. The brain runs on electricity, each thought producing an electric impulse that jumps from cell to cell, inspiring further sparks, creating a computational web. Our minds are electric machines just as much as Sarah's; to speak by thought is to speak by electricity. The Hebrew language encoded all of this thousands of years ago. So did the English, for that matter: our own word *speak*, derives from an older German word *sprech*, and the further backwards you go, the more alike *speak* and *spark* start to sound, until finally at the root of all things they converge into the primal electricity.

I let Sohu look into my eyes, felt my defenses slowly weaken. It wasn't the sort of overpowering invasion of the Drug Lord. A gentle teasing-apart, quiet, humble, but pushing forward like an explorer penetrating a jungle. I don't know how long we waited there, staring at each other awkwardly, but after an indeterminate time in a pleasant trance, I was awoken by Sohu snorting. "I'm really not good at this," she said.

Sarah seemed just a little too happy. I started to wonder how honest she was being with me. Had she really just *not bothered* remembering the most important Name ever discovered? Or was she holding out?

"Sohu," I said, casting the dice, "there's a way to get you into my mind easier."

She raised an eyebrow.

"It's called Sacred Kabbalistic Marriage of Minds," I said. "Uh, SCABMOM. My friend Ana discovered it hiding in the later additions to the Gospel of John. A combination placebomantic-kabbalistic ritual. First you draw a magic circle, then you say a Name you derive from John, then you say these vows about how God is one and we are one. After that you can..."

I wasn't prepared for Sohu to start laughing.

"Sacred kabbalistic marriage?" she asked, in between giggles. "Really?"

"That's just what my friend Ana calls it!" I said quickly, trying to defend myself. "There were parts of the text that simplified into the word 'marriage,' but you can think of that as symbolic! It's just this brief ritual—"

Sohu quieted down. "I wasn't laughing at you," she said. "And I already know the ritual."

"You do?!"

"Yes. I, uh, I'm familiar with it. I should have thought of it myself. I'll get supplies so we can draw the circle."

My head spun. She knew about SCABMOM? Then another thought. "Wait," I said. "I'm already kabbalistically m— I've already done the ritual with somebody. Does that complicate things?"

"Doubt it!" said Sohu. "Solomon had seven hundred wives, remember?" She giggled again. "Kabbalistic marriage... I'll go get supplies."

She vanished in a flash of light.

"YOU CAN'T MARRY SOHU!" Sarah shouted at me the instant Sohu disappeared, tears running down her face. "YOU'RE SUPPOSED TO BE MARRYING ME!"

Oh, right. I should have predicted this. I put my arms around her, kissed her cheek. The longer I put this off the harder it was going to be, but I wanted all four Cometspawn around when I broke the bad news. "Sarah," I said, "this isn't real marriage. This is just a kabbalistic ritual *called* marriage. It's like how the doges used to marry the sea, or how a businessman says he's married to his work. It's just a word."

"If it doesn't matter, if you'll do it with anyone, then do it with me first. Do it with me now, before she comes back."

"We don't even have a magic circle." It was the best excuse I could think of, but I didn't want her in my mind forever. Now that I thought about it,

I wasn't sure I wanted Sohu in my mind forever either, but that couldn't be helped.

"When we get a magic circle, you'll marry me, right?"

"No, Sarah. I'm not going to perform a dangerous kabbalistic ritual with you just because it has 'marriage' in the name." I barely avoided adding "get a life." She already had—thanks to me—and look how that had turned out.

Sohu mercifully chose that moment to return with the supplies. Sarah turned her face into a mask, better than any human could have. We cleared out of the way as she started drawing the magic circle from memory. It was the same one I had seen Ana draw. I took a piece of chalk and joined in. No help for it, I figured.

"I, Sohu West, in full knowledge of the consequences, call upon the symbols and angels of the world..."

"I, Aaron Smith-Teller, in full knowledge of the consequences, call upon the symbols and angels of the world..."

And so we went, with Sarah staring at us motionless outside the circle.

"For God is One."

"For God is One."

"And His Name is One."

"And His Name is One."

"And we are One."

"And we are One."

"And it is done."

"And it is done."

The circle flared brighter and higher than I'd ever seen before, probably because Sohu had constructed it ten times better than the quick job Ana and I had done back in Ithaca. Sarah still just watched, but looked like she might snap at any moment. I sat down at the table, rubbed my temples.

"We'll try this again," said Sohu. "Look into my eyes..."

Chapter Fifty-Eight

...And Now The Form Of Enion

Evening, May 13, 2017
Citadel West

I.

"We'll try this again," said Sohu. "Look into my eyes."

I looked, I listened, I let myself fall into a trance.

[Walls of Kujiracho,] came a voice from afar.

[What?] I asked. [Sohu?]

A feeling of surprise. [Aaron?]

[Oh,] I said. [Hi, Ana.]

[Aaron?] came a different voice, differently flavored. [What's going on?]

As best I could, I tried to send thoughts and memories through the two links. To Ana, an explanation of where I was and what was going on. To Sohu, memories of my relationship with Ana. Both of them started talking at once. I mentally pushed Sohu to one side, concentrated on the quieter link.

[I can't feel Sohu,] Ana told me.

[And I can't feel Valerie,] I answered. [I don't think kabbalistic marriage is transitive.]

[I can barely feel Valerie myself. Last I got from her she was trying to join BOOJUM.]

[!!! Really ???]

[We shouldn't be so surprised. She always wanted to burn the euphemizing system to the ground. I just didn't expect it to be so literal. This is the problem with being a theodicy student. When people tell you that the world is horrible and needs to be destroyed, you expect them to end with, "So let's discuss different interpretations of this fact for the next several decades."]

[Speaking of theodicy — Ana, have you ever heard of Elisha ben Abuyah?]

[Oh man, that name really brings back memories!]

[You say that like you went to prom with him or something.]

[Pffft. No, I was just—got really interested in that story freshman year of college. It kind of brings everything together.]

[How so?]

[I remember I once had a teacher who asked me what would have to happen before I believed God was utterly unjust. How bad would things have to get before I admitted there was literally no possibility that the evil in the universe has a reason? I told him it was a stupid question. The magnitude of the world's evil is so much that anyone who could be convinced of divine injustice by a *specific amount* of evil was already convinced. The only people who could possibly be hanging on were the ones who were literally willing to accept anything.

He told me it didn't work that way. Everyone's willing to dismiss the evil they've already heard about. It's become stale. It's abstract. People who say they've engaged with the philosophical idea of evil encounter evil on their own, and then suddenly everything changes. He gave the example of all of the Jewish scholars who lost their faith during the Holocaust. How, they asked, could God allow six million of their countrymen to perish like that?

But read the Bible! Somebody counted up all the people God killed in the Bible, and they got 2.8 million. It wasn't even for good reasons! He kills three thousand people for worshipping the Golden Calf. He kills two hundred fifty people for rebelling against Moses' leadership. He kills fourteen thousand seven hundred people for complaining that He was killing too many people, I swear it's in there, check Numbers 16:41! What right do we have to lose faith when we see the Holocaust? "Oh, sure, God killed 2.8 million people, that makes perfect sense, but surely He would never let SIX million die, that would just be too awful to contemplate?" It's like—what?

The lesson I learned is that everybody has their breaking point, the point where they stop being able to accept things for philosophical reasons and start kicking and screaming. Did you know there was an Orthodox rabbi, Irving Greenberg, who after the Holocaust declared that God had unilaterally broken His covenant with the Jewish people, and should be considered in breach of contract, and until He, I don't know, reverses time and un-Holocausts Europe, no one is under any obligation to follow any of the divine commandments? And if God doesn't like it then tough because no punishment could be worse than the one He had already inflicted? There were *rabbis* saying this sort of thing, Aaron. That's what happens when you break. Some people break when the death toll is six million instead of two point eight million. Other people break when something they'd previously only read about in books happens to them in real life — have you ever heard that silly poem:

You say you have problems as great as my own
I am forced to admit it is true
But the thing is that my problems happen to me
Whereas yours only happen to you.

That's why I love the Acher story. He's a crazy old coot, but I love him. Everybody has their breaking point, and for Acher it was seeing a kid grab a bird out of its nest. He's a famous rabbi, he's read all about Noah's Flood drowning everyone in the world, and God killing all the innocent Egyptian babies, and, euphemism, he's living in second century Judaea, where the Romans are basically torture-killing anyone they can get their hands on, and throughout all of this he's wise and equanimous and tells his disciples to bear their sufferings gracefully, and then finally he has a bad day and sees a kid snatch a bird and he just flips, he's like, you know what's a completely proportional response to this? DECLARE WAR ON GOD AND TRY TO DESTROY EVERYTHING. Most of us have to go through a Holocaust before we get to that point, but he grasped it immediately.]

[Holy frick Ana I've never heard you send a thought that complicated through telepathy before.]

[And then there's that whole thing about the voice. The one that boomed from the heavens saying, "Repent, children of Israel, and the Lord will forgive you. Except for you, Elisha ben Abuyah." What was *with* that?

There's a legend that goes that Acher was predestined to be evil from the very beginning. The week after he was born, his father threw a big party for his circumcision, and Rabbi Eliezer and Rabbi Joshua showed up. While everyone else was getting drunk, the two rabbis decided to talk Torah, and they became so engaged in their discussion that miracles started happening around them. Wreaths of fire danced around their heads, thunder sounded in clear skies, nearby water started spontaneously turning into wine. Acher's father begged them to stop lest the whole house burn down, and the rabbis apologized profusely and said that they would try to be more mindful of the power of Torah from then on.

And Acher's father remembered that, and he pushed Acher to go into Torah so that he too could be powerful and call down fire from the heavens. But that was the wrong reason to study Torah, and so all his life Acher was cursed to think of Torah as just a means to an end. Learn some Names, smite some enemies, boil oceans if there are any oceans around that need boiling, live forever, that kind of thing. And when he saw the child take the bird from the tree, it was easy for him to forsake God, because for him God was beside the point, you could boil oceans whether you believed in God or not.

And then when Rabbi Meir was trying to convince him to repent, well, there he was, the supreme pragmatist. He didn't want to go to Hell, he didn't want to lose the powers that his Torah knowledge gave him, so he would make a tactical retreat back into orthodoxy until he could come up with a better plan. God realized that Acher was going to repent for the wrong reason, so He declared that Acher's repentance would do no good, have no consequences, made sure there was no instrumental justification for atonement. Just like God had thought, Acher said, "Okay, then screw this," and forgot about it.

In fact, there's a story about Rabbi Dov Ber, that one day he was praying for a sick member of his congregation to recover, and he prayed so much and so long that God got really annoyed and told him he was going to Hell for praying too much. And Rabbi Dov Ber answered: "Well, now that I have nothing to lose I can *really* start praying!" And of course God laughed it off and healed the sick guy. If Acher had done the same — if he'd said okay, I have nothing to gain and nothing to lose, that means I have to make the choice according to my own principles, and I choose repentance — then God would have laughed it off, same as he did with Rabbi Dov Ber, and everything would have been okay. But since instead Acher was obsessed with the consequences of repenting, the road was closed to him.]

[So the only way Acher could get the good consequences of repenting was by not doing it for the consequences?]

[Yeah.]

[Oh God, that's so annoying. No wonder he was so angry all the time.]

[???] Ana thought at me.

[I'll give you fifty dollars if you clap your hands, BUT you have to be clapping your hands for a reason other than to get the fifty dollars.]

[I hardly think that worshipping God, Lord of the Universe, whose wisdom spanneth the heavens and whose mercy endureth forever, because you are awed by His mighty works and consumed with a desire to praise His Most Holy Name, is the same as getting fifty dollars if you clap your hands.]

[Yes, well, if I ever make a universe, I'm not putting in any sneaky "You can get this reward, but only if you don't want it" clauses.]

[If you ever make a universe, you can do what you want.]

II.

I was broken out of my trance by screaming.

"NO YOU CAN'T MARRY ME!" Sarah was shouting.

"It's not marriage," said Sohu. "It's just a ritual that gives me a certain connection to you so I can get things out of your mind. Everything in Aaron is so garbled I can't make any sense out of it. You must have the memories of what you did to him. If I can just get at them—"

"I WON'T DO IT I WON'T MARRY YOU!" said Sarah.

I put my hand on Sarah's shoulder. "Sarah," I said. "Remember what we said about doing the right thing?"

"She can't have me," said Sarah, sulkily. "I'm yours."

"Of course you are," in the most patient voice I could manage. "And that's why I need you to cooperate with Sohu. The same way I cooperated with Sohu. To help me."

"Everyone is getting married except you and me!"

"It's not even a real marriage. It's just a connection ritual."

For a second I couldn't tell if she was going to try to kill us, or try to speak the Vanishing Name, or what. Finally, with this awful glare in her eyes, she said, "I'll do it."

God is One and His Name is One and we are One and so forth. Sohu stared into Sarah's eyes, tried to read her electronic brain. Sweat poured from her forehead. Wrinkles formed on her tiny face.

I let my mind wander.

III.

[Are things okay over there?] asked Ana.

[Not really,] I answered. [Did Acher ever figure out a way to get the consequences of repenting without doing it for the consequences?]

[You're really upset by this Acher thing.]

[I think... yeah. It's the idea of something you can't think your way out of. Something so slippery that just trying to think your way out of it ensures you'll fail. It just feels... wrong.]

[I don't know,] Ana answered. [To me it feels, I guess kind of perfect. Does that make sense?]

[Yeah. I think perfect things feel wrong to me. Remember, I used to do cryptography. The whole point was that every code can be broken. Thought is the universal solvent. My advisor at Stanford, he had a saying on his wall. A Leonard Cohen verse. "There is a crack in everything." That's my philosophy too. Things shouldn't be perfect.]

[God is perfect.]

[No He isn't! That's the whole point of Luria. There is a crack in *everything*. That's what I mean. There ought to be a crack in God's denial of salvation to Acher.]

[What about actually being good?]

[That's not an action you can just... take! If you're not already good, any impetus to becoming good has to come from wanting the consequences.]

[I think the traditional Jewish answer,] thought Ana, [is that you can start by being good for the wrong reasons, but then the changes will stick and make you the sort of person who does things for the right reasons.]

[Then it was kind of crappy for God to specifically close that path to Acher, wasn't it? Actually, it's kind of crappy of God in general. Suppose there are good consequences for being good, and that with enough willpower you can force yourself to be good long enough for it to stick. Then why doesn't everyone do that? Lack of awareness of the consequences? Giving up early? But then we reduce goodness to intelligence and willpower!]

[So how do people ever become good?]

[You have to start with at least a tiny bit of existing goodness. And that gives you the urge to accumulate more.]

[So,] asked Ana, [divine grace?]

The overt meaning of *perfect* is "maximally good."

The kabbalistic meaning is "someone who tries to make moral progress."

This we derive from the Cathar *perfecti*. The Cathars believed the world itself was irredeemably bad, the product not of the true God but of a demiurge of pure evil. They thought the true God had sent Christ as an emissary into the world, to introduce a tiny spark of goodness that might catch and spread until the works of the demiurge had been subverted. True believers chose to take on the work of spreading the spark full time, of bringing God to a godless world. A few of these claimed to have prayed so hard that they lost all sense of self, becoming pure vessels for the Holy Spirit. They were called in Latin *perfecti*, and in French *parfait*. The Catholic Church declared the Cathars heretics and slaughtered several hundred thousand of them in one of bloodiest and most brutal genocides this side of the Holocaust, apparently satisfied that this was the best way to disprove the proposition that the world was irredeemably evil and its God a murderous tyrant.

But this we also derive from their namesake, philosopher Derek Parfit, who spent his life trying to figure out how to be good. He argued that our common sense views of morality were unjustified and that they would have to be rebuilt by rigorous inquiry. For a philosopher, he was surprisingly humble—he argued not that his discoveries had found the True Morality, but that there was such a thing as progress in moral philosophy as much as physics, and that he was helping to contribute it; he assessed his own contribution only as "reason to be hopeful" about whether or not morality existed. Like the Cathar *parfait*, after years of deep thought he finally lost all personal identity, saying, "I now live in the open air. There is still a difference between my life and the lives of other people. But the difference is less. I am less concerned about the rest of my own life, and more concerned about the lives of others." Yet in his own long-winded way, he also rejected his namesake's belief in the evil of the universe: "When I consider the parts of the past of which I have some knowledge, I am inclined to believe that, in Utilitarian hedonistic terms, the past has been worth it, since the sum of happiness has been greater than the sum of suffering."

There are other correspondences. The prophets, who try to turn Israel from its misdeeds to godliness; of Parvati, whose cosmic dance brings beauty to the universe; Providence itself, forever engaged in gathering its own divine sparks and repairing its spiritual machinery.

This, then, is the kabbalistic meaning of *perfect*: someone who tries to make moral progress.

IV.

"Aaron?" I heard Sohu's voice.

[Ana, I just had—I guess an epiphany? I don't have time to explain it. But it's basically what I just said before. There is a crack in everything.]

"Aaron?"

"Uh. Yeah?"

I woke into the regular world. A new stack of books was piled on the table. Sohu and Sarah were giving each other death-glares. I had drooled a little on my shirt.

"Aaron, It didn't work. I figured out how Sarah confounded the Name. But it's not a reversible process. You don't have it. I checked your friend Ana while you were talking, and she doesn't have it. And now Sarah doesn't have it either. It's lost, too garbled to be recovered."

"There is a crack in everything," I said. "I think I know how you can get the Vital Name."

Chapter Fifty-Nine

Clothe Yourself In Golden Arms

Evening, May 13, 2017
New York City

When she thought about it, Valerie guessed it made sense for terrorists to hold dress rehearsals. Terrorist plots were complicated things where many different people had to do their parts right the first time. So it was reasonable to want to practice in some kind of low-stakes environment.

Less reasonable was Dylan Alvarez's insistence on sitting in a director's chair, holding a clapperboard, and starting out with a "Lights, camera, action!" But placebomancy, she figured, was so closely allied to acting as to be another branch of showmanship.

"The Assassination Of Ash Bentham," Dylan said. "Take seventeen. Our plucky young heroine Valerie Lowry has, with the help of her mysterious friends, learned a Name that allows its speaker to become invisible at will. Our dashing and incredibly handsome hero, Dylan Alvarez, has rescued her and convinced her to use her powers for the side of g... of chaotic neutral. Our heroes are in a nondescript white van parked outside UN headquarters. Due to their sixteen previous dress rehearsals, they know exactly what to do. Lights, camera, action!"

They were in a Broadway theater, next to a pretty good mockup of the interior hallways of UN Headquarters. Alvarez had supposedly convinced a series of investors that his new play, *Unsong: The Musical*, was going to be a fantastic hit, apparently even spontaneously breaking into some of the planned musical numbers during his sales pitch. As a result, he'd gotten the money he needed to rent a theater and create a made-to-order replica of their target. Valerie had no idea *when* he'd done this. Yesterday? This afternoon? Months in advance, just in case? Maybe he was lying about everything and there was a mockup of UNSONG ready here for some other reason?

It was Clark, Valerie, Mark, Brenda and Maduegbuna on stage. Valerie spoke the Spectral Name for her four fellow assassins, and then they walked into the building unseen.

They were harnessed together; on Take One, unaccustomed to invisibility, they had all bumped into each other and ended up in a tangled mess on the floor, after which Dylan had pronounced them "super dead" and handed out the harnesses, which he had been keeping to himself the whole time. On Take Two, there had been flour carefully strewn over the floor, and Dylan had caught them by their footprints and summarily declared them "super dead" again.

("Why the bloody bollocks would there be flour on the ground of fucking UN headquarters?" Clark Deas had asked, only to be pronounced a "sore loser" by Dylan.)

Take Three was angry dogs, who navigated by their sense of smell. Take Four was tiny ball bearings placed on the stairs. Deas had glared at Alvarez, but hadn't said anything, and it turns out that the glares of an invisible person are extremely easy to ignore.

And so on all the way up to Take Seventeen.

The invisible invaders, having snuck through the open doors of the United Nations, carefully checked the floor for ball bearings and flour dust. Dylan attacked them in a dog costume, and Valerie pretended to speak the Beast-Tamer's Name, causing the fake dog to retreat quietly. They successfully avoided Dylan-dressed-as-a-janitor running around in implausibly fast motions streaking water all over the floor. And for the first time in seventeen tries, they came to the office door marked ASHER BENTHAM, DIRECTOR.

At the head of their train of invisible people, Deas opened the door.

"Oh, what's this?" said Dylan, sitting behind a desk wearing an outrageously long and bushy goatee. "My door seems to be opening of its own accord. I suppose I will just have to call for security and wait to be rescued like the poor little defenseless paper-pusher that I..."

As he started speaking he grabbed an AK-47 from under his desk, and halfway through the sentence he jerked it up and made shooting noises. "Pow! Pow! Pow! You're all super dead!"

"Ha!" said Clark. "No we're not! I had everyone say the Bulletproof Name while we were still in the van!"

"My dear Mr. Deas," said Dylan, "the AK-47 shoots twelve rounds per second. I am absolutely willing to grant that you were protected from one of them. But unless people have become much sturdier since the last time I used a firearm, eleven rounds is still more than enough to kill a man."

"There are nine of us," said Deas. "If it takes two bullets to kill one of us, you could only kill four of us a second. That's more than enough time for one of us to react and shoot you."

"That's all nice and well," said Dylan, "but, on the other hand, YEEYEE-YEEYEEYEEYEEYEEYEE"

Some sort of horrible noise split the air. The would-be assassins covered their ears with their hands, tried to run away. The whole train of harnesses bumped up against each other and they fell on the ground, visible and embarrassed.

"Dare I ask," said Brenda, "what *that* is supposed to signify?"

"You may! Asher Bentham has been described by those who have met him as having an aura of fear and terror about him. Perhaps creepy mysterious mind powers! And I ventured to assume that maybe he can direct that aura, like a weapon. Just a conjecture, but better safe than sorry."

This time *everyone* glared at him.

"Or who knows, maybe he has a machine that makes scary shrieking sounds." He flipped the switch again. "YEEYEEYEEYEEYEEYEEYEE!" Brenda Burns grabbed him, wrenched the machine from him, and turned it off.

"And if this happens, what do we do?" asked Valerie.

"An excellent question! I happen to have consulted Lord High Magician Mark McCarthy on this very topic and the two of us have come up with some interesting ideas." Dylan took off his wig, exited stage right, and came back with a bag marked RELICS. He dug through it, throwing various strange and unpleasant-looking body parts aside. "Mmmm... pancreas of St. Pancras... Saul of Tarsus' tarsals... facial bones of St. Boniface... no, it's with the secular stuff." He took out a different bag. "Aristotle's pupil... J. S. Bach's well-tempered clavicle... aha!"

A vial of blood.

"This is the blood of Asher Bentham. You may be asking, how did you get the blood of Asher Bentham? The answer is much too gross for you to want to think about, but let's just say it involved a bribed janitor, several bags of trash, and a chronic case of hemorrhoids."

Everyone groaned.

"Come tonight, I will be placing a drop of this blood on a placebomantic opal amulet, which I will give to each of you. Whatever strange powers he may have coursing through his veins, through whatever means, these amulets will protect you."

"You expect me to wear that after your description of where it's from?" asked Brenda.

"I expect," said Dylan, "that you and everyone in BOOJUM shall make great and terrible sacrifices for the cause, lest our organization and all it stands for should YEEYEEYEEYEEYEEYEEYEEYEE!"

"WHO LET HIM HAVE THAT FECKIN' MACHINE BACK?" Clark thundered, and his hands were clenched in fists of rage.

Dylan shut off the sound machine.

"One more time," he said, and climbed out of the model UN back into his director's chair.

"The Assassination Of Asher Bentham," said Dylan Alvarez. "Take eighteen. Having previously been defeated by ball bearings, a light coating of flour, small dogs, the janitor, a middle-aged bureaucrat, and their own feet, the intrepid heroes of BOOJUM dust themselves off, wipe their own blood up from the floor, and prepare once again to save the world from the plutocratic tyranny of UNSONG. Lights... camera... action!"

They navigated carefully through the ball bearings. They trod around the flour. Valerie spoke the Fluvial Name to deflect a swarm of angry bees, and they carefully avoided touching the jeweled idol that Dylan had placed just outside the elevator. For the second time, they came to the door marked ASHER BENTHAM, DIRECTOR. Five invisible terrorists prepared their weapons. Clark, gun in hand, reached very carefully for the door.

A bolt of lightning struck the stage. Multicolored light blossomed in alien geometries. Five weapons in five pairs of hands melted into metallic sludge.

"I AM SOHU WEST," said the glowing figure in the middle of the light, and the glow faded until they could see her, ringed by symbols and powers beyond their ken. "I MEAN YOU NO HARM. I HAVE COME TO TALK TO VALERIE LOWRY. REVEAL YOURSELF." A wave of hard light swept over the crew, settling on them, highlighting their invisible forms.

"Okay!" shouted Clark Deas. "I have feckin' had it with this bollocks. I was quiet through the flour. I was quiet through the dogs. I was even quiet through the *feckin'* ball bearings. But *feckin'* Sohu West? This is *completely ridiculous.*"

"Mr. Deas," said Dylan, rising from his director's chair, "when you joined BOOJUM, you told me you were ready for anything. Shall I take it you wish to amend that statement?"

"I'm with Clark, actually," said Brenda. "I appreciate what you're doing, and the special effects are neat, but we've only got a few hours to train, and I feel like we need to concentrate on plausible threats. So far we've gotten ball bearings, dogs, and now *Cometspawn*, and we haven't even dealt with, like, a normal platoon of security guards or anything."

"My dear Ms. Burns, I already know you can deal with a platoon of guards. The point of this exercise was to test your mettle. In a real fight, are you going to stop what you're doing and protest to me that what's happening is 'unfair' or 'implausible'? Or are you going to deal with whatever Nature can throw out at you?"

"I AM SOHU WEST," said the scintillating figure amidst the storm of light again, insistently. "I MEAN YOU NO HARM, BUT I DEMAND THAT VALERIE LOWRY REVEAL HERSELF. I COME BEARING A MESSAGE FROM HER FRIEND, AARON SMITH-TELLER."

"The hell?" Valerie asked Dylan. "I didn't even tell you that name. Where did you hear about Aaron? And what does he have to do with any of this. I feel like it kind of breaks the realism, you know? Suspension of disbelief? Sohu West caring about Aaron is about as likely as her caring what leftovers I put in my fridge last week."

"I AM ACTUALLY SOHU WEST," said Sohu. "THIS IS NOT A TEST. VALERIE, I NEED TO SPEAK TO YOU."

"Look," said Mark McCarthy. "Dylan's obviously not going to listen to reason. The faster we get through this whole Sohu thing, the faster we're getting out of here."

"Okay, fine," said Clark. "I shoot Sohu with my gun." He pointed the melted metal stick at Sohu. "Bang. Bang."

Sohu stared at him like he was an idiot.

"You can't shoot the gun!" protested Dylan. "Sohu already melted the guns!"

"I use my backup gun," said Clark.

"You have a backup gun?" asked Valerie.

Now Clark looked at *her* like she was an idiot. He removed his backup gun from his boot and shot Sohu. The bullet collided with her shield of light, fizzled into nothing.

"Really?" Clark asked Dylan angrily.

Valerie stepped forward. "I am Valerie Lowry, friend of Aaron Smith-Teller. I am not afraid of you! Speak, but know that we are BOOJUM, and even Cometspawn cannot make us afraid!" She struck a dramatic pose.

"No, look," said Mark McCarthy. "You can't just make ritual magic happen by saying exciting-sounding things. You have to prepare it, you have to know what you're doing."

"You can *totally* make placebomancy happen by saying exciting-sounding things," said Dylan. "I say the girl is doing a good job. Keep going."

The glowing cloud around Sohu diminished in intensity. "I'm not trying to hurt you," she said. "But your friend Aaron discovered a Name, and it spread through the kabbalistic link to his friend Ana, and then he realized it must have traveled through another kabbalistic link to you. It's in your unconscious, waiting until you need it, just like the Spectral Name was at first. I need to get it. Will you let me into your mind?"

"Don't do it," said Brenda. "It's probably some kind of trap."

"Nah, knowing Dylan it's probably some sort of stupid placebomantic metaphor," said Clark. "Probably a Christ myth. Valerie's supposed to offer complete surrender, and then she's going to come back more powerful than anyone could have possibly imagined."

"*How is this helping us train for a realistic threat?*" Brenda continued to protest.

"Okay," said Valerie. "I let Sohu access my mind."

For a second, she stared into the Cometspawn's eyes. Something invisible passed between them.

"You're kabbalistically married," said Sohu. "To Dylan Alvarez."

"Do you guys think I should admit it?" she asked Clark and Brenda.

"I say deny everything," said Brenda.

"Deny it!" said Clark. "Maybe she'll keep some respect for you!"

"I deny being married to Dylan," Valerie told Sohu. But the Cometspawn had already floated over to Dylan's director chair. "MIHAN-TAIG-SAROS-ATHTEN-GAHANOR..." she started. The Confounding Name. Dylan's eyes glassed over briefly.

"There," she said. "Pretty sure the Universe owes me big for that one. And you too." She spoke the same word to Valerie. "Be glad I don't have time to deal with whatever else is going on here. But I got what I needed."

"What?" asked Valerie.

"The true Vital Name!" said Sohu, who turned to light and vanished.

For a second, all was quiet. Then: "That was the most feckin' pointless thing I have ever had to sit through," protested Clark.

"Just keeping you on your toes!" said Dylan. "I would say your preparation for a sudden manifestation of Cometspawn is a C minus *at best*."

"Just glad to be done with this mess," said Brenda.

"Done? My dear Ms. Burns, we have not yet begun to fight!" Dylan Alvarez sat down on the director's chair again. "The Assassination Of Ash Bentham. Take nineteen. Having previously tested themselves against ball bearings, dogs, jeweled idols, and an immortal quarter-archangel eight-year-old girl seeking secret Names of God, the intrepid heroes of BOOJUM stop complaining, drop their grievances against their wise and exceptionally handsome leader, and prepare once again to save the world from the plutocratic tyranny of UNSONG. Lights... camera..." He pulled the noise machine out from underneath his chair. "YEEYEEYEEYEEYEEYEEYEE!"

Chapter Sixty

O Rose, Thou Art Sick

September 3, 1999
Magdalena, New Mexico

It could have been that she was pretty once. Now her face was sunken, her head hairless. Her arm was hung in a cast, and she looked terribly frail.

"You're the ritual magician?" she asked. "But you look so..."

"So young? Twenty. And that's 'apprentice ritual magician' to you. Technically I'm not even allowed to do consultations on my own. And yet here we are."

"I asked a friend for the best ritualist in Greater Colorado who was, you know..."

"Unencumbered by ethics? Well, like I said, here we are."

"Yes, that." The young lady wrinkled her nostrils. Typical stuck-up rich girl, he thought to himself, wanting his decidedly black-market services but still holding him in contempt for providing them. "What's your name?"

"Lola Rivers."

It sounded fake, but he didn't care. Anyone who gave their real name in a business like this was either a fool, or else so arrogant as to defy belief.

"And I'm Dylan Alvarez. Nice to meet you, Ms. Rivers. What can I do for you?"

Not that he didn't know. Head as smooth as an apple, frame that looked like she could stand to gain forty pounds or so, desperate look in her eyes. And here she was, seeking illicit magical help. Cancer, that was what it was. He could see it from a mile away.

"I want you to teach me to summon demons."

Well, that was unexpected. He always liked a change of pace.

"Which demon, exactly, are we talking about?"

"Thamiel. The Lord of Demons."

"Hoo boy, lady, you go all the way to the top. Or bottom, as the case may be. Look, I'm as unencumbered by ethics as the next guy, but I gotta ask you—you sure you want to do that?"

"Yes."

She looked familiar. Alvarez squinted. If she had a little more flesh on her bones, a bit more hair, then... he still wouldn't be able to place her. Damn.

"I understand a summoning doesn't really bring him here, right? Not in a way where he could destroy anything later, or infiltrate the city?"

"That's mostly true." He took a copy of the *Greater Key Of Solomon* off his shelf. Then a few other grimoires. The *Goetia. The Sacred Magic of Abramelin The Mage. The Antichrist's Cookbook.* None were relevant to the issue at hand, but he was a ritualist; he played to an audience. Opening a grimoire was a way of saying hey, I'm serious about this demonology thing.

"Demons of that caliber are in Yetzirah or Briah already; for all we know Thamiel projects into Atziluth. Hell, they say he's a facet of God. When you're at that level, space is just a big game. They'll play by the rules, but a summoning changes those rules a little. You get an aspect. You could think of it as a shade. It's not like Thamiel starts off in Siberia or Hell and then you summon him and he's in Colorado. You allow the parts of him that are everywhere to take on a little more shape."

"And how dangerous is that?"

"The good news is that technically he has no power except that which you give him. The bad news is that *there's a crack in everything*. Just like there's no unpickable lock, there's no flawless soul. If you're escalating all the way up to Thamiel himself, there *will* be holes in you big enough to let him in, and from there he'll do what he wants."

"But other people, bystanders, they'll be safe?"

"God no. They'll be safe from Thamiel. They won't be safe from *you* when he's done with you."

"I appreciate your candor."

"At your service. Dylan Alvarez, the West's greatest expert in demonology, demononomy, *and* demonography. Tell all your friends."

She didn't smile. The two word phrase he would have used was "steely resolve." Someone who seemed like she always knew what she was doing. And yet someone thinking about summoning Thamiel. Very curious.

"Can you give me a ritual that will work?"

"Lady, I can give you twenty. The bottleneck to summoning Thamiel isn't that it's *difficult*, it's that you would have to be a freaking moron to try."

He watched for a reaction. She didn't give him one.

"Look, Ms. Rivers, I'm not blind. You've got cancer. People with cancer do some desperate things. So go see the quack who says he can cure you with mushrooms and dried beetle legs. Drink a homeopathic solution or two. But don't summon Thamiel."

"Again, I appreciate your candor."

"You've already paid me. I get the same amount either way."

"Send me the ritual by Monday. I'll give you a PO box you can use. In fact, if there are twenty, send me extras, in case the first doesn't work. I can pay you more."

"I'll send you the paperwork. But Ms. Rivers. I'm serious. Don't do this. Your health, your life, whatever it is you want from him—it's not worth it."

"I think it will be," said Ms. Rivers. "Thank you for your time, Mr. Alvarez."

Before he could respond, the lady was gone.

"Well, that was the least boring thing to happen to me today," said Dylan, and he started copying summoning rituals.

Chapter Sixty-One

And Ololon Said, Let Us Descend Also, And Let Us Give Ourselves To Death In Ulro Among The Transgressors

September 20, 1999
Colorado Springs

Midnight falls in the Garden of the Gods, and Robin West stands alone beneath the cold stars.

She draws a circle on the ground, names various angels; not your better class of angels, but the sort of angels who hang around the seedier parts of Heaven and murmur about how they "don't want no trouble" whenever the gaze of the Almighty falls upon them. She sprinkles the ground with various libations. Says some words in some languages that are not so much dead as not-talked-about-in-polite-company. Some more sigils.

A tall dark man appears in the circle. A crown of fire is on his head. His facial features are oddly indistinct. No matter how directly she looks at them, she cannot shake the feeling that she is seeing them through her peripheral vision.

"A woman," he says, "young, but with sunken face. Hairless. Too thin. A terminally ill patient, driven to summon Thamiel, Lord of Demons, in her desperation."

He paused a second for effect.

"...is what I would say if I were a moron. I am *Prince of Lies*, Robin West. Don't *ever* try to deceive me." He stepped out of the magic circle, strode up close to her. "These things don't actually bind me, you know. The books of black magic say they do, but nobody ever thinks to ask who wrote the books of black magic."

"I want to make a deal," whispered Robin.

"Good," said Thamiel. "I like deals. But just so you know, my BATNA is killing you, wearing your body like a suit, and slowly poisoning the lives of everyone you have ever loved until they scream for death."

"You'd do anything to destroy my husband, wouldn't you?"

"If you're going to ask me to sell you my soul, I will have to cut off this conversation right here."

"No," said Robin. "All I'm saying is—if he knew I went into this willingly, it would break his heart."

"I'm listening," said Thamiel. Then, "Wait, no, I'm not listening, too low-bandwidth, I'm clawing the information directly out of your mind." He grabbed her head and pulled, not quite hard enough to snap her neck. His hands were scalding hot. Robin screamed. Thamiel didn't let go. Then, suddenly, he said "Interesting!" and relaxed his grip.

Robin panted in pain and exhaustion.

"I am contractually required to inform you that you will lose your immortal soul and burn in Hell for all eternity."

"I understand."

"You really don't," said Thamiel. "You really, *really* don't." He mulled it over for a moment. Then he said, "Nope. No deal."

Robin's shock was palpable. "What?"

"Too easy. You're plotting something."

"How could I be plotting something by offering you my soul for eternity?!"

"I don't trust the Comet King. I don't trust the people who trust the Comet King. And I *definitely* don't trust the people whom the Comet King trusts." He kicked a foot on the ground, and sparks flew from it. "How do I know you're not trying to infiltrate Hell, use some kind of special Name once you're in there to bring the whole place crumbling down?"

"The Shem HaMephorash? You know my husband is the only person who can say that without burning up or going mad halfway through."

"True, true. But something doesn't add up. You don't add up, Robin West. What are you plotting?"

He grabbed her head again with one hand, wrenched it back, stared into her eyes.

"Oh," he said. "I'm afraid that's not much of a plot. I'm not sure I would call it a plot at all. A hope? A wish? A desperate attempt to deny obvious reality?"

Robin tried to answer something, but couldn't make herself speak.

Thamiel frowned. "But still, no deal."

"What?"

"Offer me something else."

"What else is left to offer?"

"Oh. Definitely the right question, there. Let's see. I've got your soul. What's left after the soul? Ah yes. The body. Make love to me, Robin West."

She stepped backwards. "What?"

"You said it. I would do anything to hurt your husband. I want to grind him down and break his heart and rot his soul. So, make love to me." He held out his arms for her, laughing.

"Fine," she said. "But not like that. Show me your true form."

The laughter stopped. "Really?"

"Really."

"What would you possibly..."

"So that nobody will ever say I did it because I was deluded. I'll do it, but show me your true form."

The tall dark man began to melt. A misshapen figure, too-tall, with a second head on his shoulders, locked in a perpetual scream. The sound of buzzing flies.

"Your *true* form."

"Any truer and I stop being in space-time. It's this or nothing."

Robin started to take off her clothes. The buzz of the flies was louder than anything she had ever heard before. Every tree in the garden wilted at once. The bright rocks turned black. The stars fled to the edges of the sky.

Robin West made love to the Lord of Demons.

When it was over, in between the waves of pain crashing through her body and the nightmare visions crashing through her head, he whispered, "The day he returns. At sunset."

"So soon? Can't it be later?"

"You have nothing left to bargain with. Sunset. Expect me."

And then he disappeared into smoke.

She lay there, in the Garden of the Gods, naked and alone, on the foul sulfur-scented dead grass, and it was not until morning that she picked herself up and returned to the palace.

Chapter Sixty-Two

That The Wide World Might Fly From Its Hinges

Want to feel old? The span of time between Saddam Hussein's death and now is longer than between now and when 1/3 of the sea becomes blood.

—@GateOfHeavens

Afternoon, May 14, 2017
Citadel West

It was afternoon, and we met together in the command center. Me. Sarah. The four Cometspawn. Vihaan, the Comet King's uncle, chief of staff, and self-proclaimed butler. The Black Opal Throne towered over us, dominating with its emptiness.

We were gathered around THARMAS, the nuclear targeting computer. It was big. The ten towers linked together were almost the size of a trailer, huge and grey, dominating their corner of the command center. THERMONUCLEAR ARMAMENT MANAGEMENT SYSTEM was etched into one of them, in the sort of lettering that had looked futuristic in the 1960s. Over the years other people had scratched other phrases into the bare exterior, until the big metal casing was as graffiti-laden as a high-school bathroom wall. "THIS MACHINE KILLS FASCISTS," someone had written in big letters near the bottom. Added below, in a different handwriting: "BUT NOT SELECTIVELY."

The last tower included a forest of switches and wires and display terminals. Caelius sat at one of them, running tests. Finally, he announced to us that it was ready.

"THARMAS can run Llull," he said. "Or, rather, I wrote a half-baked port of Llull that can run on THARMAS. It's not the most efficient thing in the world, but given what we've got I think brute force was always the plan."

He gave the massive metal rectangle in front of him a fond pat. "The thing is totally lobotomized. I stayed up all night to prove the code correct. It'll get about a quarter millisecond of thought in before everything except the list of generated Names resets itself. This isn't going to be a second—" He looked at Sarah awkwardly. "It's not going to have a will of its own."

Nathanda nodded. "Sohu?" she asked.

My first day of kabbalistic marriage to Sohu West had been quiet. I'd gotten the impression that after getting the Name she'd deliberately blocked herself off from my mind, maybe out of a desire not to intrude. If she'd invented SCABMOM — something I still found hard to believe — might she be able to reverse it? I wondered what sort of spectacular Names I would find if I dove into her mind too deeply. For now, that wasn't something I wanted to think about.

"Thanks to some... unorthodox tactics, we've pieced the Vital Name back together," she said. "Is everybody ready?"

Jinxiang was holding a very big weapon, maybe a rocket launcher, eying THARMAS suspiciously. Not taking any chances, I guessed. She tightened her grip. "I'm ready," she said.

Vihaan looked like he hadn't slept for a while. In contrast to Nathanda's simple white dress, Jinxiang's more combat-ready style, and the haphazard appearance of the rest of us, he was dressed immaculately, as if ceremonially recognizing the importance of the occasion. "I'm ready," he said.

I didn't know if anyone cared whether Sarah and I were ready, but I squeezed her hand and said, "We're ready too."

Sohu stood in front of the supercomputer and started to sing. She began: "ROS-AILE-KAPHILUTON-MIRAKOI-KALANIEMI-TSHANA-KAI-KAI-EPHSANDER-GALISDO-TAHUN..."

Caelius stared at the terminal. As soon as the process started, THARMAS would be generating Names every few seconds.

"...MEH-MEH-MEH-MEH-MEH-MEH!"

Nothing looked different except Sohu's eyes, which glassed over for a split second. For a moment we all just stood there, silently. Then a gong sounded.

"Our first Name!" said Caelius. "Let's see if..."

Then another gong. Then another. Then a fourth. Then Uncle Vihaan ran towards the computer as fast as he could. "CAELIUS GET AWAY!" he shouted. "What the—" asked Caelius, but Vihaan grabbed him and threw him aside as the old man pulled on something hidden in his suit jacket and exploded and then everything was light and heat and pain.

The overt meaning of *butler* is "a highly-skilled servant."

The kabbalistic meaning of *butler* is "one who destroys intelligent machines."

This reading we derive from Samuel Butler, a Victorian author who in 1863 published *Darwin Among The Machines*. He wrote that, just as Darwin had recently found humans to be evolving by natural selection, so machines might be "evolving" by artificial selection, becoming more and more powerful until eventually they would replace humans as the dominant life-form. He ended by suggesting that "war to the death should be instantly proclaimed against them. Every machine of every sort should be destroyed by the well-wisher of his species. Let there be no exceptions made, no quarter shown; let us at once go back to the primeval condition of the race."

And we derive it also from Frank Butler, a friend of Frank Herbert's, who protested a freeway meant to help industrialize Seattle. Herbert was so impressed by Butler's anti-technology activism that he included in his *Dune* series an anti-robot crusade called the Butlerian Jihad, in which mankind rises up against robots and destroys them all. A jihad is a struggle waged in accordance with the will of God, and the Butlerian Jihad certainly qualifies. For God says (Joshua 8:1) "Do not be afraid; do not be discouraged. Take the whole army with you, and go up and attack AI." Thus the Butlerian Jihad.

This, then, is the kabbalistic meaning of Butler: "one who destroys intelligent machines."

"Aaron! Aaron! Are you all right?"

I opened my eyes. Sohu was standing over me, shaking me awake. I said something like "mmmhghghghfdhfghmm."

"Aaron, how many fingers am I holding up?"

"Thhhmmmreeeee"

"What's two plus two?"

I drew myself together, got all the lobes of my brain online.

"Mmmmghf... four."

"What do an apple and orange have in common?"

"They both foretell leaves falling."

Sohu stared at me quizzically for a second. Jinxiang was the first to get it. She groaned, then said, "He's fine, Sohu. No personality change, at least."

I picked myself up and looked around. There was almost nothing left of the Comet King's Uncle Vihaan. Only a few shreds of what must have been his clothing, and blood everywhere. As for THARMAS, seven of the ten towers were smoking ruins; the other three were heavily scarred. North

American airspace had gone black. Caelius had been hit the worst of any of us, but he was standing, sort of, with assistance. His white hair had been blackened by the blast, and his face was wrecked. I was pretty sure what he got would have killed a human, which of course he wasn't. He rubbed an eye with a hand that had been burnt to the bone, tried to get his blood-soaked hair out of it so he could see.

The room was full of guards and soldiers. Jinxiang was talking to them. She had set down the rocket launcher and was now holding the magic sword Sigh. Nathanda was standing next to Caelius, trying to get him to sit down. I tried to stand up and almost fell before Sohu caught me and helped me to my feet.

"Caelius!" Nathanda was saying, "You moron! You've got to get a doctor!"

"Got to... fix THARMAS," he was saying.

General Bromis had come in with even more soldiers. "What's going on?" he demanded.

"Vihaan," said Jinxiang, who I think was the first to fully piece the situation together. "We were trying a... very important new piece of technology. Vihaan knew about it. He must have filled his jacket with explosives and blown himself up to stop it."

Bromis turned pale. "Why would *Vihaan* do that?"

"I don't know!" Jinxiang protested. I don't think the tears in her eyes were from the explosion. Vihaan had been her great-uncle, had helped raise her and her brothers and sisters when the Comet King and their stepmother had been too busy with matters of state. "He must have been... working for someone else. He knew this would happen today. He would have had time to contact them, and—" She looked too horrified to continue.

"He only blew himself up," Caelius added, "when the computer started producing Names. Like he was hoping he wouldn't have to, but once he learned we were going to succeed..." It was hard to follow Caelius's words; I still couldn't believe he was alive and talking. Don't look at his face, I told myself, but I looked anyway and almost gagged.

"Bromis," said Nathanda, "I need you and your people to do a full check on Vihaan. Every communication he's made since Father's death. All his activities. Don't worry about warrants for now. Ellis's too, if you still have them, the two of them were always close. If the Other King has a network of spies here, we've got to catch them before they can do any more damage."

While she was talking, Caelius had already limped over to the remnants of THARMAS and opened the cases, started fiddling with the circuits and connections. "Massively parallel," he said. "I can get it running again. Not at capacity, but still a lot of brute force."

"Caelius!" ordered Nathanda, "you go to the medical center, right now!"

"You... don't understand," her brother said feverishly, connecting wire to wire. "This is THARMAS. It was Father's computer. But it's more than that. This is the watcher in the darkness. This is what guards North America, keeps it safe. Without this, anybody could—"

"Oh God," said Nathanda. "Cael, you're hurt. You're delusional. Sohu, get a hold of him and bring him to the medical center, *please*."

Sohu took a step toward Caelius just as he plugged one cable into another and Citadel West turned into a maelstrom of frantic light and noise.

For a second I thought there had been another explosion. But the sensory overload resolved itself into the most powerful alarm I had ever heard. An alarm suitable for...

Somebody shut off the screech of the alarms, and everyone spoke at once.

"—The system says someone launched a nuclear missile—"

"—I TOLD you repairing THARMAS was top priority!"

"—but nobody launches nukes! What about mutually assured destruction?"

"—got to get the radar working so we can see where it's headed."

"—can't shoot it down. THARMAS's strategic defense functions aren't online, might be too late anyway."

"—kabbalistic missile armed with the Wrathful Name, could destroy half a state."

"—Vihaan's fault! He must have told the Other King that—"

"—do remember that we're in the most secure anti-nuclear bunker ever built, right?"

"Vihaan would never do such a—"

I didn't know how far General Bromis had made it out of the command center, but now he was back. "Your highnesses!" he said. "We have about thirty ICKMs scattered throughout the Rockies, should we prepare for retaliation?"

I will give Nathanda this: I didn't even see her flinch.

"No. Not yet. We don't know enough."

"Fuck yes!" objected Jinxiang. "If the Other King wants mutually assured destruction, we'll give him mutually assured destruction."

As far as I could tell, all the Cometspawn had already reasoned that

Vihaan was a traitor, that he'd radioed the Other King and told him what was going on, and that the Other King had realized we were about to break through to near-omnipotence. He'd panicked and ordered Vihaan to blow up the computer to buy him time and disable the Comet King's missile shield, and he must have had a hell of a lot of leverage because Vihaan had done it. Now he was going to nuke us to remove the threat entirely, except that, as everyone had already mentioned, *we were in a nuclear proof bunker*. None of this made any sense.

"Have I mentioned we are in a nuclear-proof bunker?!" shouted Sohu. "Something is wrong. We don't understand this. We've got to *think*."

Sarah's face was emotionless, as it had been ever since we came in. I wondered if the radiation blast from a detonation right on top of us would wipe her memory even if the citadel stayed safe. I squeezed her hand. She didn't respond.

A man in uniform came in, handed Bromis a message. "The Other King has left his pyramid again," he announced. "He's heading here, toward the Great Basin armies besieging us. Fast."

Then: "Got it!" Caelius shouted. Another piercing alarm. The map of North American airspace flickered back on to the screen. For a second, a lone red dot. A moment later, it reached its target and vanished from the display.

The Other King's missile had not been aimed at Citadel West.

Chapter Sixty-Three

My Wrath Burns To The Top Of Heaven

So when the last and dreadful hour
This crumbling pageant shall devour,
The trumpet shall be heard on high,
The dead shall live, the living die,
And Music shall untune the sky!

—John Dryden

Afternoon, May 14, 2017
Gulf of Mexico

Blue sky and fair winds, like every day in the eye of a hurricane. Multicolored symbols circled and sparkled round. Invisible celestial machinery kept up its steady pulse.

Uriel turned his gaze east. In Cuba, a farmer's only goat had just had a kid. Uriel's threat-assessment algorithm placed him at 2.9% risk of boiling the kid in its mother's milk within the next week. Years ago, he would have smitten the farmer, just in case, and never worried about it again. Sohu had put an end to that. Now he tweaked the parameters of his algorithm, told it to alert him if the probability increased further, and moved along.

He turned his gaze north. In New Jersey there was a red wheelbarrow glazed with rainwater beside some white chickens. For some reason if anyone touched or moved it then the whole Northern Hemisphere crashed. He had spent aeons of subjective time trying to figure out the problem and finally given up. Now he just monitored the wheelbarrow carefully, ready to smite anyone who came too close. His monitoring program told him that the nearest human was a child at play, thirty meters away, just outside the perimeter of the danger zone. Something was gnawing at the corner of the archangel's mind, trying to grab his attention. It could wait. He confirmed the child's trajectory relative to the wheelbarrow and moved along.

He turned his gaze west. In Los Angeles, the angel Gadiriel had finished removing the overgrown vines and tribal masks from her palace and replaced them with whiskey bottles and steer heads. She looked in the mirror as she tried on a vintage cowboy hat. "Lookin' *good*, pardner," she told herself in a perfect Texas accent. Diagnostics confirmed that the machinery continued to limit her power at the same rate as all the other angelic and semi-angelic beings. He confirmed that the laws of physics remained mostly intact in her presence, and moved along.

Before he could turn his gaze south, he felt it. Something was happening. A pulse from Gevurah. Harshness. Destruction. A pulse from Yesod. Mechanism. Nature. Balance.

Uriel reached out and felt the Tree, teased the sephirot back into balance. He was among them and he was of them, he partook of them and he maintained them. They were his children, and they would be safe in his care.

He opened his eyes. A missile pierced the cloud-wall of the hurricane.

A MESSAGE, he said, intrigued. SOMEBODY WANTS TO TALK TO ME. I HOPE IT IS FROM A FRIEND.

He caught it in his outstretched hand. The message was very small. He held it right up to his eyes so he could see it clearly.

The message was: *Sorry*.

Then there was fire, and hurricane and archangel and machinery alike disintegrated into nothingness before the awesome power of the Wrathful Name of God.

Chapter Sixty-Four

Another Better World Shall Be

Afternoon, May 14, 2017
New York City

Stefan had the most useless job at the entire United Nations—which was saying something. He and Ben stood outside of the door of a UN office building all day, checked everybody's badges, and denied them entry if their badges were wrong. They never were.

A man separated from the stream of pedestrian traffic and walked up to Ben. "Excusa me!" he said in a heavy Spanish accent. "I am from the el Mexico! I no can able poder read English the bueno! You to read directions for me please, por favor?"

Ben gave a heavy sigh and took the paper from the man. "It says to take the bus from Times Square to an Chinese restaurant called Ai Oh Wah—"

Ben burst into flames, then fell over dead.

"Moron," said the man, without a trace of an accent.

Stefan's hand flew to the gun he kept on his waist, but before he could reach it somebody grabbed him from behind and sliced his throat.

"Nice work," said Dylan. Maduegbuna grinned disconcertingly. "The rest of you hanging in there okay?"

Four people who couldn't speak without breaking their spell of invisibility awkwardly resisted nodding.

"Right!" said Dylan. "I'm at the front. Valerie's at the back, because I can talk to her mentally and so we can communicate and steer you people together. No talking until we're in front of Bentham's office. Let's roll."

He groped around until he found the harness linking the six of them, then spoke the Spectral Name and disappeared.

They made it through the atrium, up a staircase, and about ten paces into the second-floor corridor when the lights all went out at once.

There were no windows. The building was pitch black.

For a second, they all just stood there.

"What now, boss?" Clark finally asked.

"I thought I told you to shut your mouth and stay invisible."

"Not like anyone can see us now."

"It's the principle of the thing. Anyway, I have a flashlight in my pocket... one second... there."

It remained pitch black.

"Okay, the guy who sold me this flashlight is super dead."

"Dylan," said Mark. "My watch isn't working. It usually has a light function."

"Okaaaay," said Dylan. "So, the world has been plunged into eternal darkness."

"Wait," said McCarthy. "You were going to bring a radio, right? To listen in on the police? Turn it on."

Alvarez took a little ham radio out of his pocket and turned it on. Nothing.

"Electricity's not working," said Mark. "Maybe no technology is."

"What's going on?" It wasn't any of their voices. Some sort of UN employee? A janitor?

"Ah," said Dylan, "we're the maintenance crew. There's been some kind of big electrical failure. We'll be taking care of it, but until we do I want everybody to stay in their offices. We should have power back within the hour." He spoke confidently. For some reason Valerie felt reassured even though she *knew* he was lying. A door closed shut; the employee seemed reassured also.

"Dylan," said Clark, "fire your gun. Straight down. Somewhere it won't hit anything."

"Why?"

"Just do it."

There was a conspicuous absence of gunshot.

"Oh, for the LOVE OF GOD," said Dylan. "I try to do ONE good assassination, and it HAS TO be on the day guns stop working. This is RIDICULOUS and I want to SPEAK TO A MANAGER."

Mark's voice, clear and strong. Nine syllables. The Luminous Name. What would normally have been a pale sphere of light appeared as a brilliant ball of crackling fire.

Dylan looked at it lovingly, like an old friend. Very gradually, his face twisted into a smile.

"This was you guys, during the dress rehearsal," he said, and changed his voice to a feminine whine. "Oooooh, Sohu West appearing in the middle of our mission, that's stupid. Oooooh, you're making us prepare for too many outlandish things that will never happen. Well—" He changed back to his regular voice. "Here we are. Electricity's stopped working. Guns have stopped working. And your instincts are *perfect*. Mark, *mi compadre*, you are exactly correct. We switch tactics. We use the Names. UNSONG has imprisoned the Names for too long, and so today the Names will take their revenge on UNSONG. God hath delivered them into our hands."

Alvarez's radio crackled to life, at first wordlessly, and then in the clear accents of a news broadcaster: "I've just been told radio has been restored. If you're hearing this, radio has been restored. According to our sources, the Other King has destroyed the Archangel Uriel with a kabbalistic missile, causing all technology to stop working worldwide. Uh, except radio. Which has somehow been restored. If radio continues to function we will try to keep you updated as more comes in."

Dylan shut off the radio.

"Holy Mother of God," said Clark. "I'm not a Bible-reading man, but I am *almost positive* it's bad news to nuke an archangel."

"We are BOOJUM," said Dylan. "For us, chaos is never bad news. Let's find Bentham. Mark, Luminous Name. Everyone else, back to being invisible."

Lit by the fireball hovering above Mark's invisible forehead, they made their way down a long UN corridor until they came to a door marked DIRECTOR, UNSONG.

Dylan flung it open as hard as he could.

Asher Bentham sat at his desk. A bare desk, just a few sheets of paper and a metal nameplate reading ASHER BENTHAM, DIRECTOR-GENERAL. He had paperwork in front of him, but didn't seem to be working on it. He seemed to be waiting. Behind him was a window. The sky seemed unnaturally dark for this hour of the afternoon, and flames peeked out of some of the skyscrapers.

Six assassins uncoupled their harness.

Before Dylan could give any kind of a monologue, Valerie pushed her way forward, broke her invisibility, and spoke.

"We are the Singers. We—"

"I am UNSONG," said Asher.

"We have come to free the thousand thousand Names of God."

"Give not that which is holy unto the dogs, neither cast ye your pearls before swine, lest they trample them under their feet."

"You can't—" said Valerie, but before she could finish her sentence, Bentham wheeled around in his chair just in time to face Maduegbuna, who had appeared behind him with a knife. He deftly seized the weapon, then stabbed him in the throat. Maduegbuna fell to the ground. A sword of dark fire appeared in Bentham's hands.

"That's *it*," said Dylan Alvarez, breaking his invisibility. "I challenge you to a placebomantic duel!"

Interlude ש

Coming Of Age

I.

"Father," he asked, "why is the sky blue?"

"Because the opening of the sixth seal, which will turn the sun the color of sackcloth and the moon blood red, hasn't happened yet," said his father. His father was the Devil, and often gave answers like this.

"I mean, what makes it blue now, instead of some other color?"

"Ah. That's because blue light has a short wavelength, and short-wavelength light gets scattered better by the air."

"Oh. I asked my teacher that and she told me I should work on my fractions. Do you think she didn't know?"

"Maybe she did, maybe she didn't."

"Why wouldn't she tell me, if she knew?"

"Because she is busy. Because twenty years ago, she went into teaching thinking she would kindle a love of knowledge in the souls of children, but twenty years of thankless work later she just wants to make it through the day and go home, and children who ask unapproved questions make that harder. Because she feels guilty about not being able to answer all her students' questions, and in order to preserve her sanity she tells herself that they are ungrateful and their questions are designed to annoy her. There could be any number of reasons."

They were in a car. His father was driving him home from school. He had told him that he would go to a normal human school in a normal human town so that he would grow up to be a normal human. School and town both were exceptional in their normality. The school was a red-brick building called P.S. Number Number Number. The town was a suburb with white picket fences and American-made cars. The drive home was through leafy streets named after kinds of trees.

"Does that mean I shouldn't ask her more questions like that?"

"That depends. An altruistic person might sacrifice his curiosity to help his lazy teacher protect her laziness. A spiteful person might redouble his questions. A manipulative person might use this to better understand what bothers her, and so gain power over her. An uninterested person might do as she has, and ignore the issue in the service of getting through an intolerable school day more quickly. Any of these would be reasonable."

"What would you do, Father?"

"I would torture her forever in Hell for having abandoned the spark of the divine within her."

"That's your solution to everything."

"It is," the Devil agreed. "But her torments will be far worse for having betrayed you in particular."

"Why are you so nice to me?" he asked. "Isn't the Devil supposed to be evil?"

"Yes," he said. "But you're family."

Then they drove past the city limits, and he must have—fallen asleep? drifted off?—because his next memory was of being driven to school the next day, binder of completed homework in his hand. Such would be the rhythm of his life.

II.

One afternoon, when his father picked him up from school, he broke down crying.

"This boy Micah keeps stealing my lunch."

The Devil was thoughtful for a moment. "Why didn't you tell me before?"

"I thought you would be angry. That I let it happen. Can you help me?"

"I can," said the Devil. "And I will if you ask me. But I would prefer you learn to solve your own problems."

"I don't know how!"

"Micah has stolen," said the Devil. "Stealing is a sin. Sin necessitates punishment. Can you punish him?"

"He's bigger than I am."

"That is a disadvantage," said the Devil. "But hardly insurmountable. What is he is afraid of?"

"Just the usual things, I guess. Snakes. Spiders. That kind of thing."

"Can you leverage that to your advantage?"

"I... I could fill my lunchbox full of spiders? And then when Micah takes it, and opens it, the spiders will all jump out at him?"

The Devil stopped the car.

"Where are we," he asked?

"The park," said the Devil. "The scariest-looking spiders endemic to this area are the wolf spider and the marbled orb-weaver. I can help you find them."

"Father," he said. "I'm *also* afraid of spiders."

"Which is stronger?" asked the Devil, "Your fear of spiders? Or your love of justice?"

As they collected spiders together, he asked again: "Why are you so nice to me if you're so evil?"

"Because," said the Devil, "you're family."

When they had filled the lunchbox entirely with spiders, they got back in the car and passed city limits, and he remembered nothing until the next morning.

The next afternoon, when he came to pick him up from school, the Devil asked him how things had gone with Micah. He reported that Micah had stolen the lunch box, opened it up, screamed, and run away. All the other boys had laughed at him, and he hadn't been back to school that afternoon.

The Devil frowned. "When he comes back," he said, "you need to rub it in. Hold out your lunchbox to him, ask him if he wants some — you won't need to get spiders again, just seeing it will send his into a panic now. Or when he's eating his own lunch, point to a black spot on the table and say, 'Hey, is that a spider over there?' You need to make it impossible for him to forget what happened. But more than that, you need to make it impossible for anyone else to forget what happened, so that Micah is a laughingstock for the rest of the school year."

"Why? He's already never going to steal my lunch again. He's already been punished."

"Because," and the Devil looked very solemn now, "think of the disgust you felt for those spiders. Can you not feel that disgust — infinitely more disgust, disgust beyond disgust — for someone like Micah who breaks the moral law? Doesn't he deserve more suffering than a week out of school can give him? Doesn't he deserve to know, viscerally, ultimately, exactly how bad he is, and have it driven home to his every moment of every day?"

"But aren't you evil? Don't you support sin and suffering?"

"I am perfectly consistent," said the Devil. "I loathe myself. But God said it is necessary for sin to exist, and created me to enforce that decree, and I will do it, until the bitter end. I am that force which maximizes the evil of the universe. I am not omnipotent. Other forces will oppose me, as they should. But I have my job and I am good at it and I will not shirk."

"Dad, what if I sin?"

"Then," said the Devil, "I will forgive you, because it is written: love washes away many sins."

"Is that from the Bible?"

"Haven't you heard that I quote Scripture to serve my own purposes?" asked the Devil. And then they passed city limits, and he remembered nothing.

III.

Day followed day; he passed from freshman to sophomore, from sophomore to junior, from junior to senior. Finally it came time for his graduation. his father watched from the bleachers as he walked to the stage to accept his diploma, then hugged him when he came down. He handed him an envelope. It was a voucher for plane tickets, enough for him to spend the summer traveling the world. He started crying, tears of happiness.

"You've earned it," said the Devil. "I am in all places. I have committed all sins. But you! You are part-human! You still have the chance to explore, to travel, to learn! Go forth! The world is your oyster!"

They got in the car, began to drive off.

"What will happen after this?" he asked him.

"Everything!" said the Devil. He was laughing maniacally now. "Once I took a guy up a giant mountain and offered him all the kingdoms of the world. He said no, but I still remember where that mountain is! We can climb it together and I can give you everything! Power! Sex! Adventure! It will all be yours!"

"Why are you so nice to me?" he asked the Devil, one final time.

A flicker, like a glamor lifting, or a spell dispelled.

"Because," said the Devil, "when I said I had committed all sins, that wasn't quite true."

"Huh?"

"Before now, I've never gotten the chance to betray somebody who loved me unconditionally."

"What?"

Then they passed city limits, and the whole tableau—car, school, the world itself—dissolved into a smoky darkness of flames and screams. Pain struck him, instantly, everywhere at once, the deepest and most intense pain he had ever felt. His father shed his human form, grew incalculably large, still laughing manically, but now he saw it for what it was, a horrible mocking laughter.

"Goodbye, my son," said the Devil. "Begone to the eternal darkness, where the worm does not die and the fire is not quenched. Goodbye forever."

And through all the sufferings he would face after that time, in all the eons of pain and torture, he never forgot the parting laughter of Thamiel the Lord of Demons.

IV.

When he was much older, he would use the Confounding Name on himself, hundreds of times. He would excise almost all memory of that period, the time in Hell. He would become functional again, the trauma exiled to some inaccessible part of his brain. He remembers only little bits and pieces, starting from when he heard the voice.

HELLO. CAN YOU HEAR ME?

He does not remember the context in which he heard the voice; his past self was very thorough. He does not remember where he was, or what he was thinking before hearing it, or what was being done to him at the time. He just remembers that everything felt horribly wrong far beyond his ability to bear, and in the middle of it he heard a voice.

He remembers not answering. He remembers that was a tactic of theirs, to constantly give him hope of escape, only to yank it away from him at the last moment. He remembers thinking the voice was transparently a repeat of this tactic, and that he wasn't going to humor them by responding.

I AM PRETTY SURE YOU CAN HEAR ME. I WOULD REALLY LIKE IT IF YOU RESPONDED. DO YOU KNOW HOW MUCH ENERGY IT TAKES TO SEND A TELEPATHIC MESSAGE INTO HELL? SEVEN HUNDRED FORTY TRILLION MEGAJOULES IS HOW MUCH ENERGY. I AM KEEPING FOUR HURRICANES GOING AT ONCE JUST TO MAKE THIS WORK. DO YOU KNOW HOW MANY ANNOYING WIND SHEAR CALCULATIONS YOU NEED TO DO TO RUN FOUR HURRICANES?

He remembers thinking that Hell's other attempts to give him false hope had been more polished than this. But he remembers also thinking that was what they wanted him to think, that that was their trick this time, there was always a trick.

OH. UH. I AM THE ARCHANGEL URIEL. BE NOT AFRAID. I GUESS YOU WOULD NOT BE AFRAID OF ME ANYWAY, SINCE I AM FAR AWAY AND ALSO YOU ARE ALREADY IN HELL. BUT I AM SUPPOSED TO SAY THAT. UM. I MIGHT BE ABLE TO HELP YOU.

There it was, the offer of help. Usually they were more subtle about it.

IT SEEMS LIKE YOU ARE NOT RESPONDING TO ME. I WAS AFRAID OF THIS. I AM TOLD THAT HELL OFFERS PEOPLE FALSE HOPE SO MANY TIMES THAT THEY BECOME INCAPABLE OF REAL HOPE. I HAVE SPENT AEONS OF SUBJECTIVE TIME TRYING TO FIGURE OUT A WAY AROUND THIS. THE SOLUTION TURNS OUT TO BE EASIER THAN I THOUGHT. YOU DO NOT KNOW HOW TO BLOCK TELEPATHY AND I WILL NOT TEACH YOU. NOW LET US GET STARTED. OUR FIRST LESSON IS THE HEBREW ALPHABET. THE LETTERS GO LIKE THIS. ALEPH. BET. GIMEL...

And he sat, helpless amidst the torments of Hell, while the Archangel Uriel infodumped the kabbalah into his mind.

Time passes slower in Hell than on Earth. In a few minutes of mortal time, the damned in Hell can suffer whole days of torture. Uriel took advantage of the discontinuity to impart weeks worth of lessons in minutes, speaking so fast it would have sounded like a high-pitched whine to any earthly listener.

As for him, he welcomed the distraction. Soon he had learned Hebrew, memorized the Bible, and began work on the correspondences. A few weeks/years later, he began all the other languages—Latin, Greek, Chinese, Indo-European, Proto-Turkic. Uriel played the Talmud to him on a repeating loop, until it had burned itself into his brain. All throughout the lessons, he never spoke, never confirmed that he was really there and really listening.

He remembers the last lesson he took from Uriel. NOW WE ARE GOING TO LEARN KEFITZAT HADERECH, the angel told him. IT MEANS SHORTENING THE PATH. IT WAS PERFORMED BY THE GREATEST SAGES OF OLDEN DAYS. TODAY WE WILL LEARN IT. YOU ARE AN EMANATION OF DIVINE STRUCTURE, PASSING FROM ATZILUTH TO BRIAH TO YETZIRAH TO THE PHYSICAL WORLD. THE SECRET OF TELEPORTATION IS EMANATING INTO THE PHYSICAL WORLD SOMEWHERE ELSE...

And Uriel told him how to do it, and it was that simple, and he did.

His first jump was to a mountain of obsidian that jutted from a molten sea. He does not remember where he jumped from, nor how he knew that the mountain existed, but he remembers — vividly — appearing on the mountain. He had turned into a lightning bolt and leapt through an unknown world outside space and time. It was beyond Hell's power to fake, and now Hell could no longer harm him.

"Oh God oh God oh God it's all true," he said, speaking directly to Uriel for the first time.

YES, said Uriel. Then, HELLO. IT IS GOOD TO FINALLY MEET YOU. BE NOT AFRAID, ALTHOUGH I THINK I ALREADY SAID THAT. WHAT IS YOUR NAME?

He tried to remember, found he couldn't. "I... don't know. I think it was burned away from me. Everything was burned away. All my good memories, except the ones where remembering them makes the bad memories even worse. I feel like everything good in me has been burned away to nothing."

I WILL CALL YOU ASH, said Uriel. ASH BEN THAMIEL. Then: THE COMET KING ASKED ME TO FIND YOU.

"Why?"

PARTLY BECAUSE IT WAS THE RIGHT THING TO DO. AND PARTLY BECAUSE YOU ARE HIS STEPSON, AND HE CARES FIERCELY AND UNREASONABLY ABOUT ANYONE HE CONSIDERS FAMILY.

Ash broke into tears.

OH, said Uriel after a second. I SEE. PATERNAL LOVE IS A SORE POINT FOR YOU. OBVIOUSLY. WELL. UM. DO NOT LOVE HIM BECAUSE HE IS YOUR STEPFATHER, THEN. LOVE HIM BECAUSE HE IS THE COMET KING. EVERYBODY LOVES THE COMET KING.

He said something like a muffled "Okay." What he wished he had said was something like *You don't understand. The trauma doesn't mean that I can't love my stepfather. It means I suddenly love my stepfather more than anyone has loved anyone else in the whole history of the world.*

When he was done crying, he asked Uriel: "Can you get me out of Hell?"

NO, said Uriel. NOBODY CAN GET ANYONE ELSE OUT OF HELL. ONLY THAMIEL CAN LEAVE HELL, AND THOSE WHO TRAVEL ON THAMIEL'S ERRANDS. BUT YOU HAVE SOME OF THAMIEL'S ESSENCE. IT IS POSSIBLE THAT YOU CAN LEAVE HELL ON YOUR OWN POWER.

"Will you teach me how to do it?"

UM, said Uriel. An awkward pause. ARE YOU EVIL?

"Um," said Ash. "I filled a boy's lunchbox with spiders once. Is that evil?"

I AM AN ARCHANGEL AND I SAY YES.

"Oh," said Ash. "Then I guess I'm evil. Does that mean you won't help me get out of Hell?"

IT MEANS THAT I WILL NEED TO THINK ABOUT THIS MORE. THERE IS ALREADY ONE THAMIEL ON EARTH. IF YOU WERE TO TAKE TOO MUCH AFTER YOUR FATHER'S SIDE OF THE FAMILY, THERE WOULD BE INCALCULABLE DANGER IN SETTING YOU FREE.

"So what should I do?"

I THINK, said Uriel, THAT IT IS TIME FOR YOU TO MEET YOUR MOTHER.

V.

More things he was very careful to erase. He has no memory of where he found his mother and what was being done to her when he found her. He has no memory of what she looked like. He does remember the sound of her voice. It sounded kind.

"I'm your son," he told her. "Uriel says my name is Ash."

He has no memory of her response, of whatever long conversation they had. Of anything she told him about his conception and his birth, of any apologies she might have offered him.

"Uriel thinks I might be evil," he remembers saying. "Do you think I am?"

"Do you want to be evil?"

"No!"

"Then don't be."

"Is it that easy?"

"It's easy the same way a journey of a thousand miles is easy. You just put one foot in front of the other, and do it again, and don't stop. It's very difficult, but also simple."

"What if I am not the sort of person who can be good?"

"Every kind of person can be good in their own way."

"What if evil is the only thing I am good at? At school, I made everybody afraid of me. I found their weaknesses and their fears and made them do what I wanted."

"Then you're good at gaining power. Use that power for good."

"What if I am like my father?"

"Your father would never worry about that. By worrying about that, you already prove you're not like him."

"What if nothing is left of me? Uriel calls me Ash."

"I'm your mother. It's my right to name you. I rename you Asher. It's Hebrew. It means 'blessed.' Ash can be your nickname."

"But still Asher Ben Thamiel."

"When Abram chose to follow God, God put an extra hay in his name and made him Abraham. If you choose the same, you must drop the lamed from your surname and become Bentham. It was the name of a great philosopher who wrote about how to turn evil to the greater good. You will do as he did."

"I don't understand. Uriel sent me here so you could figure out if I was good. He said it would be a disaster if I wasn't. And now you simply tell me that I am. How do you know? What makes you sure?"

"Because," said Robin. "You sound exactly like I did at your age. Scared that you might not be good enough."

"You were scared you might not be good enough? Uriel spoke as if you were a saint."

"Every saint is scared they might not be good enough. That's where saints come from."

He remembers shaking as he spoke. "How do you deal with it?" he said. "It scares me."

"We all have different ways to cope," said Robin. "Mine was philosophy. I have a feeling yours might be taking over the world. Go to Uriel and tell him I say you're okay."

"Wait," said Asher. "I will break you out of here."

He has no memory of her face or her tone of voice. He remembers the words only. "I sold my soul for a song. That song isn't over yet. Go."

He remembers turning to leave.

"No," said Robin. "Wait. One more thing. Asher. I love you." She said it with such force that it almost knocked him aback.

"What?" Then he collected himself. "Of course you love me. You're my mother."

"Yes. I'm saying this because—because you're Thamiel's son. And if you're like him, you're going to make a certain mistake. It's an easy mistake to make. You're going to hate evil. And you're going to think that's enough. That it's the same as loving goodness. It isn't. It's nowhere close. It will lead you to Hell—whether as tenant or landlord. I don't want you to hate evil. I want you to love good. And good is hard to see sometimes. Except for love. The sky produces so many kinds of radiation, but our eyes are so limited, only made to see a few specific wavelengths, and we call those wavelengths light. And goodness is the same way. It's so vast, but God lets us feel a tiny bit of it viscerally, and we call that part love. So take my love, and get somewhere far away from here, and we'll meet again when it's all over.

He has no memory of their parting.

VI.

He has no memory of coming to Earth, except that he sought the Comet King and learned he was dead. Then a long blank spot. Whatever emotions the Comet King's death caused him, some past version of himself chose not to remember. He agrees with that past version's decisions.

The first thing he remembers about Earth was a quay in San Francisco. He was talking to Father Ellis, the Comet King's confessor. He had sought him out at Uriel's insistence, and out of some inner need for some connection with his dead stepparent. He had found him here, given his name only.

"The Comet King left me a message to give you," said Father Ellis.

A chill ran up Asher's spine. All this had been predicted. There was a plan.

"He said he needs you to take over UNSONG."

The international treaty on copyrights? That was what the Comet King wanted from him? "Did he say why?"

"Does he ever?"

"Do you know why?"

Ellis frowned.

"It was kind of his baby. I think he knew that he wouldn't always be around to save people. He wanted to lead them to a point where they could take care of themselves. He thought UNSONG was part of that. He thought it would supercharge Name research, get all the brightest and most ambitious people in the world to work on the problem of finding Holy Names. Then, the next time the Drug Lord tried something, or if the nuclear deterrent against Thamiel failed, people would have real magic to fight back with."

"UNSONG? Dragging old ladies to jail if they use the Tidying Name without the right license on their scroll?"

"The first day I met Jala, he saved thousands of people by beating the Devil in a sword fight. That was great. Every other day with him was just one moral ambiguity after another."

"And he expects I will be good at such things, because of my parents."

"Who are your parents?"

An involuntary step backwards. "He never told you?"

"No. Should he have?"

"Perhaps, perhaps not."

"Who are your parents?"

"Someone who tried very hard to do her duty. And someone who tries *very* hard to do his."

"So Jala thought you'd be good with duties?"

"Perhaps, perhaps not."

"You're a hard one to figure out, Asher. Seems strange to be scared of anyone the Comet King trusts, but I hope you don't mind me saying, you sort of scare me. Ah. There are documents." He looked back towards the ship that had brought him in, a beautiful vessel with seven sails. "The Comet King gave me some documents to give you. About the people who run UNSONG. The internal politics. Maybe blackmail material, I don't know. He said you would know what to do with them, and with the right information you wouldn't have too much trouble fixing things up, and yes those were his exact words."

"Thank you. I'm sure I shall not."

He saw a reflection of himself in the water, and remembers being startled. He was tall, lean, handsome, mostly clean-shaven with just a shadow of a dark beard on his chin. How old was he? He couldn't remember; he wasn't even sure it was a meaningful question anymore. Something about the look on his face made him very uncomfortable. Maybe it was the same thing the priest saw in him. *It could be worse*, he told himself. *At least you have a reflection*.

"Father?" he remembers saying. The priest had already started walking back to the ship to get the papers, but he turned around. "Father, Origen wrote that even the devils will be saved, in the end. Is this true?"

Father Ellis stopped, thought for a second. "People mostly think St. Jerome made that up to make Origen seem more heretical. There's not a lot of support for it in Origen's own writings."

"I see," said Asher. Was it just his imagination, or did the old man practically scurry into the ship after that, like he was trying to get away from him?

"Universal love!" squawked a seagull sitting on the dock.

"What?" asked Asher.

"Universal love!" the seagull squawked again, then flew off.

Chapter Sixty-Five

The Fruit Of My Mysterious Tree

Afternoon, May 14, 2017
New York City

Brenda Burns spoke the Fulminant Name and shot a lightning bolt at Asher Bentham. It missed by a fraction of an inch and lit his desk on fire. Clark Deas had been in the process of lunging over the desk to get at Asher; he grunted as his shirt caught fire and started hitting himself against the wall, trying to put it out.

"I challenge you to a placebomantic duel!" Dylan repeated, and everyone continued to ignore him.

Mark McCarthy was doing... something... with his hands and his staff. Asher sliced at him with the fiery sword he had summoned, and the sword seemed to dull and fizzle. He cursed, then spoke the Incendiary Name. It missed Mark. Another corner of the office went up in flames.

"I challenge you to a placebomantic duel!" said Dylan again. Brenda and Asher turned to face each other. Clark Deas looked like he would have facepalmed if he hadn't been on fire.

Valerie was saying something, but tripped over a syllable and cursed. Clark grabbed a branch from the potted plant, tried to club Asher. Asher spoke the Incendiary Name again. It hit home, and Brenda Burns went up in a conflagration of nominative determinism.

"I challenge you to a placebomantic duel!" Dylan kept trying to say, over the din.

Clark finally scored a direct hit on Asher's skull, but it only seemed to make him angry. Valerie spoke the Tempestuous Name, which was a terrible idea. Everything stopped for a few brief seconds as the wind flung fire and paper and paper-that-was-on-fire around the room. The window shattered, and Asher caught himself just in time to avoid being flung out of it. "I chal—mmmmph!" said Dylan, as a burning piece of paper almost flew into his mouth.

Mark and Asher spoke Names at each other at the same time. The Fulminant Name hit Asher and seemed to half-knock him out. The Kinetic Name hit Mark and flung him out the shattered window. Dylan stared for a second, his mouth open in horror.

"MOTHERFUCKER!" yelled Dylan Alvarez. "YOU KILLED MARK! HE WAS MY FRIEND FROM COLLEGE! COMPADRES PARA SIEMPRE!"

A pause in the darkness.

"HE WAS PART OF MY NARRATIVE!"

Another pause.

"THAT'S IT, MOTHERFUCKER. I CHALLENGE YOU TO A PLACEBOMANTIC DUEL!"

He rushed at Asher, tried to hit him with his boojumwood staff. At the last second, he raised his sword of fire, held him off. Clark was stuck on the wrong side of the burning desk. He made a valiant effort to climb over it, shoving the metal nameplate and more forms into the flames while speaking the Extinguishing Name. Asher saw him coming, looked like he was analyzing the situation.

Then he asked: "What is a placebomantic duel?"

Dylan turned to Clark, held up his hand. Clark made it to the near side of the desk, but stopped coming closer. The winds calmed down. For just a moment, nobody moved.

"Many people mistakenly believe," said Dylan, who had suddenly regained his composure and was now speaking in a professorial tone, "that the race is to the swift, or the battle to the strong. This is false. The world has its own peculiar narrative logic that determines the course of a fight far more surely than skill ever could. Placebomancers are those who embrace this. A placebomantic duel is two masters casting off pretense and using the narrative against each other directly."

"This is where you give a speech about your childhood in Mexico." Valerie could tell Asher was buying time, and she could tell that Dylan could tell this too, and she could tell that he was letting him do it.

"You know," said Dylan, "those speeches — Mark used to tease me about them too, may God have mercy on his soul. But—" He opened his eyes unnaturally wide, as if willing them to produce tears. Eventually they did. One fell down his cheek. "—I was telling them for him."

He waited to see if someone would say "For him?" Asher and Clark just stared at him. Finally, Valerie said, "For him?"

"Poor Mark. Such a guy. But in the end, he didn't have the fire. So I went overboard. I started telling him about how I was tortured as a child in Baja, about how my whole village was destroyed, about how they killed my father and made me watch — I wanted to get to him. And I never could."

He leaned on his staff, let out a sigh.

"If you have to know — I was born in a nice suburb of Tijuana. My father was a Mexican-American businessman, my mother was a schoolteacher. My childhood was happy, until I was six years old. That was when—"

Asher Bentham, head of the United Nations Subcommittee On Names of God, took his sword and severed Dylan's head from his neck, mid-sentence.

Clark Deas almost fell over backwards. "How— how did you—?"

Asher stared at him like he was an idiot.

"But— the placebomantic dual— the modulation of luck— should have..."

"Whatever his childhood trauma was," Asher said, "mine was worse."

Clark grabbed the fallen boojumwood staff, lunged at Asher. Asher ducked. Clark pressed forward, enraged, swinging wildly. Asher must have gotten out a Name, some new Name Valerie had never heard before, because Clark exploded into a shower of glass.

Asher let out something resembling a sigh.

"Wait," said Valerie, from the far corner of the office.

Asher frowned at her.

"My name is Valerie Lowry," said Valerie, advancing toward him. The fire seemed to frame her face, as if the placebomancy had settled into her, using her as a vessel. "I don't care about your childhood. I don't care what you're trying to do here. I think it's not up to you to decide who does or doesn't get the light of God. I think that they enslave their children's children who make compromise with sin. I don't have any trauma or any cool origin story. But I have something better. I have your True Name. Do you hear me? I have your True Name!"

"Asher Bentham is the truest name I will ever have," he told her.

Valerie lunged forward and thrust the molten metal nameplate through Asher's throat as the flames closed around them both.

Chapter Sixty-Six

In The Forests Of The Night

It's coming to America first
The cradle of the best and of the worst
It's here they got the range
And the machinery for change
And it's here they got the spiritual thirst
—Leonard Cohen

Afternoon, May 14, 2017
New York City

Genesis 11:4: "And they said, 'Come, let us build us a city and a tower whose top may reach unto heaven; and let us make us a name, lest we be scattered abroad upon the face of the whole earth.'" And the LORD waxed wroth, and He cursed them with a confusion of tongues, turned them into the seventy-two nations and scattered them around the world.

Somehow, after thousands of years, the seventy-two nations came together again. Like streams joining into a mighty river, they all flowed together into the same spot. "Come, let us build us a city, and a tower whose top may reach unto heaven." And when the LORD came to confound their speech a second time, He found that it was already confounded, English-speakers and Yiddish-speakers and Spanish-speakers and Mohawk-speakers, and people who were bilingual in English and Gaelic, and people who only knew Haitian Creole, and people who spoke weird degenerate versions of Portuguese intermixed with extinct aboriginal tongues, and God-only-knows-what else, and all of them were working to build the towers together, communicating through a combination of yelling and frantic hand-gestures. And the LORD said, "Whatever," and He let it pass. Thus rose New York.

All Your Heart rode its unearthly winds into the harbor before lowering its sails, slowing down, and docking at the New York Passenger Ship Terminal on the West Side. "I hope they found us a priest and a placebomancer," said James, "because we're on a deadline." He marched onto shore, promising to be back with the two new crew members in a few minutes.

Ana just stared, examined the fantastic sights around her, compared it to the photographs and movies she had seen in her youth. The most striking difference was the absence of the city's various bridges, casualties of the war against Thamiel. In their place stood great pillars with the Sea-Parting Name maintaining corridors of dry land between each borough, across which cars drove in defiance of the walls of water ready to crash down on them; the works of Robert Moses supplanted by those of regular Moses. There were a few new fortresses, and the batteries in Battery Park were no longer of historical interest only. A memorial to the Lubavitcher Rebbe dominated the Brooklyn skyline.

And then there was the Statue of Liberty. It was back on its pedestal, and it still "lifted its lamp beside the golden door."

There's some interesting kabbalah here. New York Harbor is "the golden door." San Francisco Harbor is "the golden gate." Nothing is ever a coincidence. What's going on?

There's another Golden Gate, this one in Jerusalem just east of the Temple Mount. According to the prophet Ezekiel, it is the gate through which God and the Messiah will enter the city:

> *Then he brought me back the way of the gate of the outward sanctuary which looketh toward the east; and it was shut.*
>
> *Then said the Lord unto me; This gate shall be shut, it shall not be opened, and no man shall enter in by it; because the Lord, the God of Israel, hath entered in by it, therefore it shall be shut.*
>
> *It is for the prince; the prince, he shall sit in it to eat bread before the Lord; he shall enter by the way of the porch of that gate, and shall go out by the way of the same.*

The Ottoman Turks, ever pragmatic, decided that if God and the Messiah entered Jerusalem, it would probably cause the Jews to revolt or something, so they bricked up the Golden Gate. You might think this is stupid, but I point out that the Messiah did not, in fact, come and overthrow the Ottoman Turks. Don't argue with success.

But where were we? Oh, right. Ezekiel said no one could enter through the Golden Gate, because it was only for God and the Messiah. A gate good enough for God and the Messiah is a gate way too cool to let the *hoi polloi* into. But Emma Lazarus's Golden Door is the opposite: "Keep, ancient lands, your storied pomp," cries she, with silent lips. "Give me your tired, your poor. Your huddled masses yearning to breathe free."

To explain the contradiction, we turn to Matthew 25:40—"Truly I tell you, whatever you did for one of the least of these brothers and sisters of mine, you did for me."

In Jerusalem, no one may enter the Golden Gate, because it is reserved for God. In America, everyone may enter the Golden Door, and the poor most of all, because whatsoever is done to the least of the people is done unto God.

Have I mentioned that the name "Emma Lazarus" combines the Germanic "Emma," meaning "universal," with the Biblical "Lazarus," the symbol of salvation? Emma Lazarus means "universal salvation," the faith that God will help everyone, even the tired and poor, even the wretched refuse. "Send them," He says, "your homeless, your tempest-tost, to Me."

And as Ana beheld the Statue of Liberty flanked by Ellis Island, like Moshiach flanked by Elijah, she realized why it had all had to happen here; the Comet King, the messianic kingdom, the final crusade, why all of the prophecies scheduled for Israel had been transplanted to this strange land across the sea.

The overt meaning of *U.S.* is "Untied States."

The kabbalistic meaning of *U.S.* is "universal salvation."

The buzz of the city was palpable, so much so that Ana noticed instantly when it all stopped. The cars slowed to a halt. The neon signs went dim. The animated billboards turned off. A siren briefly started to wail, then went quiet. *Huh*, she thought to herself, *must be a blackout.*

Then Amoxiel screamed, and clutched his head, and screamed again. They ran over, but he had shot ten feet into the air and was out of reach. "Woe, woe, woe unto the earth!" he cried before crashing back onto the deck. He was out cold for a second, then suddenly snapped back to wakefulness with a frantic look in his eyes. "Woe, woe, woe to the great city, the mighty city. For in one hour has thy judgment come! Uriel is dead! The machinery of Heaven is broken!" He fell in a heap on the deck.

Several things seemed to happen at once.

Simeon Azore came abovedeck. The Captain followed just behind him. He shouted something incomprehensible, then stepped to the edge of the ship just in time to almost run into James, who was returning with a man in a black robe.

"Father O'Connor," said James. "Our priest. The placebomancer is missing. I'm going to try to find a replacement. Give me ten minutes."

"We don't have ten minutes!" roared the Captain. "The city of New York may not have ten minutes! How are you going to find a placebomancer in ten minutes?"

"Captain," said James, unflappable, "if a placebomancer is looking for work, and he's any good at all, he'll find *us*."

The giant man looked at the eastern horizon. Then he looked at the city, which was already starting to flicker with flame. Then he looked at the sky, which seemed to be getting darker by the moment.

"Ten minutes!" he said, his face unreadable behind his dark glasses. "If you're not back, we leave without you!"

"Ana," said Simeon, who had just come back up carrying a bag of luggage. He shook her hand. "I'm leaving."

"What? Why? God's boat is going to show up in less than two hours! Why would you—"

"I gambled and I lost," he said. "When you told me the crew was stonewalling you about the Captain, I thought I'd take things into my own hands. My ticket's only good till the end of the pursuit tonight, and I can't very well interrupt the Captain after God's boat appears, so I tried it as we went into the harbor. I knocked on his door, I went into his cabin, I told him I knew he was the Comet King, told him Uriel's machine was falling apart and the world needed him. And like I was a damn prophet the machine chose that moment to shatter, and I said if he didn't take back the throne *right now* we were all going to die. And you know what he told me? He just told me that the one rule of this ship was not to bother the Captain in his quarters, and I'd broken it, and I'd forfeited my ticket and had to get off immediately."

"No, I'll find him, I'll tell him to change his mind, he needs me, he'll listen to me."

"Ana," Simeon put a hand on her shoulder. "Better idea. Come with me. I've got a friend in New York, guy at Goldman-Sachs who thinks the same way I do. He's got a bunker here. I'm welcome in it. I'm heading there now. You don't get how bad this is. Think of Uriel as the sun. Now the sun's gone out and the nighttime's started. There are night creatures out there who are about to wake up, you've studied the kabbalah too, you know this. Only way to survive is to hide under a rock somewhere. You're welcome to come."

"What? Why?"

"Because I like you. Your heart's in the right place, even though your common sense could use a tune-up." He smiled. "I don't want anyone to say Simeon Azore left a friend in danger."

"What about all the other people you're leaving in danger?" She gestured at all the skyscrapers. Smoke was starting to rise from the tallest towers.

"Same as with the spaceships," said Simeon. "Wanted to save everybody. Tried. Didn't work. Not going to stand right in front of the avalanche as a matter of principle just because other people don't have shelters."

"We could still save everybody," said Ana. "There has to be a way."

"There wasn't for Noah," said Simeon. "If he'd told God he wasn't going to get in that ark until God guaranteed the safety of all of the ark-less masses, the floods would have come anyway and we'd be unpopulated and animalless. God told Noah that the right thing to do was to get in the damn ark and Noah listened. Do you want to be more virtuous than God?"

Ana thought for a second. "I'm not God," she said. "I'm an American. Universal salvation or bust."

"You said you studied theodicy! Has that *ever* worked?"

"I don't know," said Ana. "Maybe if we find God off Fire Island I'll ask Him."

On a whim, she kissed Simeon on the cheek. "Good luck," she said. "Tell all your rich friends I think they're terrible."

Simeon Azore of Countenance raised an eyebrow. "Good luck, Ana. Tell God the same."

Then he strode off the boat with the hurried step of a businessman who always has somewhere to be.

A minute later, back came James, half-dragging a figure who looked like he'd seen better days. His clothes were torn, his hair was singed, his face was covered with blood. He limped onto the ship, with some help.

"Who *is* that?" asked Tomás, who had come to welcome them aboard.

"I told you it would work!" said James. "This guy fell on top of me. Literally fell on top of me! Out of a window! Gentlemen, meet our new placebomancer."

"I prefer the term 'ritual magician,'" said Mark McCarthy.

Chapter Sixty-Seven

The Night Of Enitharmon's Joy

Everybody knows that the boat is leaking
Everybody knows that the captain lied.
—Leonard Cohen

Evening, May 14, 2017
Fire Island

I.

Only a few minutes before sunset now. The sea blazed orange. Fire Island rose as a dark line to the north.

"James," said Ana. "We need to talk."

The first mate glanced toward the east, where the calculations said God's boat would soon appear.

"I'll be quick," she said. "It's about the Captain."

"No," said James.

"I'm sorry, I promise I'll be quick, but it's the end of the world, James, please just hear me out. Simeon thought the Captain was the Comet King. He'd gathered all this evidence. John was..."

"Tomás," James called, "keep a lookout." He checked his watch, then turned to Ana. "We have eleven minutes before all of this starts in earnest," he said, "and in that time I'm going to take you down to the cabin where we can talk properly and we're going to have a discussion about this." He motioned Ana down the ladder. Then:

"Listen. Most of the rich bozos who sign on here want to find God for one or another boneheaded reason. But the rest — a fifth? Maybe a tenth? — want to find the Comet King. Every single one of them eventually shouts at the Captain and gives a stirring speech about how he needs to reclaim his throne and lead the nation. The Captain listens patiently, then orders them sent off the ship. This happens four, five times a year? If the Captain is the

Comet King, and I don't have the slightest interest in knowing whether that's true, then it is always a safe bet that the Comet King knows what he's doing. He is not one stirring speech and a reminder of his dead wife away from reclaiming all he has lost. He's here for a reason. Simeon didn't respect that, so he's out. If you don't respect it, you're out too, no matter how good you are with winds. Do you understand?"

"But..."

"No buts. If you can fathom the mind of the Comet King, you can talk to him as an equal. Until then..."

Ana sighed. "The world's falling apart," she said. "He's got to do something."

James glanced at his watch. "It's time, Ana."

They climbed back upstairs into the last light of the setting sun. At the very moment it dipped below the horizon, Amoxiel cried "Sail ho!" and they all turned their heads east to where a solitary purple light shone against the dimming grey sky.

"That's it!" James shouted. "Let's go!"

II.

The red sail flapped in the wind. Mark McCarthy traced pentagrams on the orange. Ana spoke the Zephyr Name, called the winds to the yellow. Tomás sang to the green. Father O'Connor prayed before the blue. Amoxiel drank a flask of holy water and the violet sail opened. "Once more to give pursuit upon the sea!" he said joyfully.

The black sail stood silent and alone. Ana tried not to look at it.

All Your Heart shot east, like a bullet, like a rocket, like a comet. The sea became glassy and weird. The cracks in the sky seemed to glow with new vigor. Strange scents wafted in on the rushing winds.

Erin Hope stood alone on the bow of the ship. Crane was dead. Azore had forfeit his ticket. She was the only passenger left. She stared into the distance at the purple light that she hoped would mean her salvation, the light of God. Then she retched off the front of the boat.

Faster and faster went *All Your Heart*. The wind became almost unbearable, then stopped entirely as they crossed some magical threshold. The ship shook like a plastic bag in a hurricane. Ana wondered if the autopilot driving them on had thoughts, and if so what it was thinking right now.

But still the light of God grew dimmer and further away.

"This is bullshit!" said Father O'Connor, who kept praying in between expletives. Ana wondered exactly what kind of a priest he was. Apparently the type who would agree to join an expedition to hunt down God if they paid him enough. Probably not Pope material.

"This is the usual," said James. He'd been through it all before. Sure, this was a special run. They had Ana and the yellow sail for the first time. The autopilot was steering, so James could stand outside and help coordinate the Symphony. And the fall of Uriel's machine was a wild card. But in the end, James had chased and failed to catch the sacred ship a few dozen times. He expected this to be another such failure, and it bothered him not at all.

Erin Hope left the bow, walked over to the green sail. She was still shaking a little bit; Ana was half-surprised she hadn't gotten off in New York to pick up some heroin, but who knew? Maybe she really believed. "You say this runs on song?" she asked Tomás. The Mexican nodded.

Then Erin sang. There was something shocking about her voice. Her face was lined with premature wrinkles, her arms were lined with track marks, she looked like some ancient witch who'd been buried a thousand years, but when she sang it was with the voice of America's pop goddess, sounding a clear note among the winds and darkness. She sang an old Jewish song, *Eli, Eli*, though God only knew where she learned it. It went, "My God, my God, I pray that these things never end. The sand and the sea. The rush of the water. The crash of the heavens. The prayer of the heart."

The seas surged. The sky seethed with sudden storm-clouds. But the green sail opened wider than they had ever seen before, a great green banner in the twilight, and emerald sparks flashed along the rigging.

Their quarry ceased to recede. But it didn't get any closer either.

"This is bullshit," Father O'Connor repeated, in between Confiteors. "Why can't you guys get the black sail open?"

"Less braying, more praying," said James, who had taken a quick dislike to the priest.

Ana shot it a quick glance, then upbraided herself. If Simeon was right, this was the end of the world. Why *shouldn't* she look at the black sail? She stared straight at the thing. It hurt, the way looking too close at an Escher painting hurt, but worse. What was it? How did it work?

The Comet King, John had said, would stand beneath the black sail and raise his magic sword, and the sail had opened to him alone. So they needed either the Comet King—which if Simeon was right, might actually be a viable plan—or his sword.

Why would the sail need the Comet King? He was angelic, and his sword was angelic, but angels powered the violet sail, and no two were alike. If the secret of the black sail was just angels or their artifacts, Amoxiel would have opened it long ago. Think like a kabbalist. Seven sails for the seven sublunary sephirot. The red sail for the material world, that was Malkuth. The orange sail for ritual magic, that could be Netzach. The yellow for kabbalah, that was Yesod, the foundation, the superstructure of the world. The green sail for music, that was beauty, Tiferet. The blue sail for prayer, that was Hod. The violet sail for angels, that was Chesed, righteousness.

That left Gevurah. Severity. God's goodness dealt out in a form that looks like harshness. The judgment all must fear.

The Comet King's sword was fearsome. A dangerous weapon. But was it really...

Then Ana thought about what was *on* the sword.

Something opened in Ana's mind. New memories. Knowledge she shouldn't have. A deep loss. She didn't cry, because time was running short, and she knew how she was going to open the black sail. She told the winds to stay for her, then ran fore, where Mark McCarthy labored beneath the orange sail. "Mr. McCarthy!" she said over the howling winds, holding out her hand. "I need your amulet! Give me your opal amulet!"

"How did you know...?" he started to ask, but something in her face spooked him. He looked at the orange sail, considered his options, and decided it wasn't worth a fight. He took off the amulet and handed it to her.

Ana Thurmond advanced on the black sail, and something was horribly wrong. She wanted to avert her gaze, but she kept looking, even though something was horribly wrong. She reached the final mast, saw the ship's wake behind her, a wake of multicolored sparks spiraling into the void, but she held on to the mast and didn't run, even though *something was horribly wrong*.

"Black mast," she said. She felt silly talking to it, but she wasn't sure how else to get it working. It didn't recognize her like it did the Comet King. Forty-odd years ago, young Jalaketu had stood below Silverthorne and defended the pass against an army of demons. Before the holy water had washed them away, he had faced Thamiel in single combat and drawn blood. Blood like that, she figured, never washed away. It was still on the great sword Sigh. Ready to be used. The final facet of God.

"Black mast, this is the blood of Asher Bentham, who is of the blood of

Thamiel. This is devil's blood, like on the Comet King's sword, and I call you to our aid."

The seventh sail opened, and there was silence in heaven for about half an hour.

III.

Psalm 107: "They that go down to the sea in ships, that do business in great waters; these see the works of the Lord, and His wonders in the deep."

This is maybe not true in general. Cruise passengers, for example, mostly see the wonders of a buffet table. But if you were to arrange all your seafarers from least-seeing-the-works-of-the-Lord-and-His-wonders to most-, with cruise passengers on one end and Coleridge characters on the other, the poor crew of *All Your Heart* would be several nautical miles off the right-hand side of the chart.

The seven sails shone in the dusk like the banners of psychedelic armies. The sea and sky dissolved into one another. The sun and moon were both clearly visible, but it was neither day nor night. The bubbles they traced in their wake shot from the end of the ship like fireworks celebrating an apocalypse. They sailed a sea outside the world, and they sailed it *really fast*.

They started gaining on the blob of purple light.

James shouted commands at the crew with military efficiency, but Ana could see fear in his face. He had been happy, she realized, living quietly at sea, talking about hunting God. Actually catching Him hadn't been part of his plans, and beneath the well-practiced orders she could sense his reluctance.

Erin wouldn't stop singing. It was that same song, *Eli, Eli*, and she was going at it like a madwoman. Green sparks flew out of her mouth with each word, but it didn't even seem to faze her. Ana remembered the rush when she had first called the winds to the yellow sail. She wondered if it was better or worse than heroin.

Amoxiel was talking to himself almost too quickly for her to make out. She strained to hear him over the din, and caught the phrase "Sir Francis Drake, the Tudors, Duke of York." Enochian. The language of angels. He was so far gone he couldn't even ramble in English anymore.

Tomás was at the bow, holding James' binoculars and trying to make out features of the purple speck ahead of them. Ana delicately lay the amulet on the ground before the black mast, then headed fore to join him.

"Do you see anything?" she asked.

He handed her the binoculars.

Legend said the boat of Metatron was royal purple with golden sails, and she could sort of see it. A purple splotch, and golden blobs above it. But the shape was wrong. Too squat. Too round. The sails were too short. She strained to see better, then gave up, rubbed her eyes, and handed the binoculars back to Tomás. He placed the cord around his neck and let them dangle, just staring out ahead of them. Even with the naked eye, they could see the purple ship making weird zigs and zags that shouldn't have been possible.

The sky looked like a hurricane had taken LSD. The sea looked like a coral reef had read Lovecraft. The sails were too bright to stare at directly, and the deck was starting to bubble or maybe crawl. Erin still sung *Eli, Eli* with demented ferocity amidships.

The boat in front of them began to take on more features. The purple deck at first seemed formless, then revealed fissures like gigantic scales. The golden sails had no masts, but stuck up ridged and angular like huge fins.

Ana and Tomás figured it out at the same time.

"That's not a ship at all!" Ana cried.

"It's the Leviathan!" Tom said superficially.

Erin heard the shout, stared at the huge bulk before her, and yelled at James. "The harpoon, man! Get the harpoon!"

IV.

The first time I saw Ana was on a ladder outside a pawn shop. But the first time I really *felt* Ana—heard her in her element and knew her mind—was around the dinner table in Ithaca, listening to her read the Book of Job. I remember the chill that came over me as she read the exquisite poetry describing Leviathan, the monster with whose glories God terrified Job:

His eyes are like the eyelids of the morning
Out of his mouth go burning lamps, and sparks of fire leap out.
Out of his nostrils goeth smoke, as out of a seething pot or caldron.
His breath kindleth coals, and a flame goeth out of his mouth.
In his neck remaineth strength, and sorrow is turned into joy before him.
The flakes of his flesh are joined together: they are firm in themselves; they cannot be moved.

His heart is as firm as a stone; yea, as hard as a piece of the nether millstone.
When he raiseth up himself, the mighty are afraid: by reason of breakings they purify themselves.
The sword of him that layeth at him cannot hold: the spear, the dart, nor the habergeon.
He esteemeth iron as straw, and brass as rotten wood.
The arrow cannot make him flee: slingstones are turned with him into stubble.
Darts are counted as stubble: he laugheth at the shaking of a spear

So no spears, no darts, no habergeon (whatever that is), no iron, no arrows, no slingshots, a second reminder about the darts, and a second reminder about the spears.

But nothing about harpoons.

James was not happy. He stared at the harpoon in obvious discomfort. Harpooning the Leviathan seemed like the *worst* idea. But they were a business outfit. They had made a promise. If we find God, they'd said, we'll bring you to Him. If God was on a sea monster, then there was only one way to do that.

But the most important reason to use the harpoon was the same reason people climbed Everest: because it was there. If the Comet King had a harpoon on his yacht, it was because he expected to need it. If James refused to shoot, then it would be obvious to the world what was now obvious to Ana: that the whole thing had been intended as theater and that none of them had had any intention of winning the chase.

"Amoxiel!" James called the angel, and the angel flew to him. "You're our expert on this kind of stuff. What's your assessment?"

"Earl of Leicester religious settlement Westminster Abbey," said Amoxiel. It wasn't entirely clear where his mind was, and it wasn't entirely clear where the ship was, but it seemed pretty certain that the two weren't the same place.

"You would have to be a goddamn idiot," said Father O'Connor. The sails were pretty much self-sustaining now. Maybe the crew could stop them if they wanted to, maybe not. O'Connor had stopped praying and joined the growing debate by the harpoon stand.

"What about the Captain?" asked Mark. "Where is he? Of all the times not to be on deck... we should get the Captain and make him decide."

"The Captain is not to be disturbed for any reason," said James, "and that means *any* reason."

He looked at the Leviathan. The monster was almost entirely submerged. It was impossible to tell how big it was. Rabbi Johanan bar Nafcha said that he had once been out at sea and seen a fish three hundred miles long. Upon the fish's head was written the sentence, "I am one of the meanest creatures that inhabit the sea, I am three hundred miles in length, and today I will enter into the jaws of the Leviathan." This story raises *way* more questions than it answers, like who had enough waterproof ink in 200 AD to write a three hundred mile long message on a fish, but if it was to be taken seriously the Leviathan was really, *really* big.

On the other hand, James was a military man, and he had backed himself into a corner, and now he had to do his duty. "Everyone hold on," he said. "We're doing this."

He aimed the harpoon and fired.

The thing that came out the other end was neither spear nor dart nor arrow. It looked more like a meteor, a seething projectile of light, trailing a shining silver thread behind it. The weapon zipped through the boiling air, leaving a violent purple linear afterglow, then struck the Leviathan right on its back.

The line gave a brutal jerk, and the ship plunged forward like a maniac water-skiing behind a rocket ship. Murderous pulling feelings in dimensions not quite visible. The silver thread looked too thin to support a falling leaf, but somehow it held.

"Structural integrity down to NaN percent," said a voice. It was the ship.

"You can talk outside of the bridge?"

"Yes. Structural integrity down to NaN percent," the ship repeated.

"Um. Is there a device on that harpoon to help us reel the thing in?" James sounded like he was hoping there wasn't.

"Yes, this is the purpose of the ship's power supply."

"I thought going fast was the—"

"Yes, that is the secondary purpose."

"Well, uh, reel away."

The ship lurched more. "Structural integrity now down to NaN percent," said the pleasant synthetic voice.

"Well, uh, tell me if it gets any lower than that," said James. He wrung his hands.

V.

"Canst thou draw out Leviathan with a fish-hook?" asked Ana, that night at the dinner table. "Or his tongue with a cord which thou lettest down? Canst thou put a hook into his nose? Or bore his jaw through with a thorn? Will he make many supplications unto thee? Will he speak soft words unto thee? Will he make a covenant with thee?"

Bill Dodd was trying to think of a suitably witty way to make fun of the passage.

"Wilt thou take him for a servant for ever? WILT THOU PLAY WITH HIM AS WITH A BIRD?"

"Sheesh," said Ally Hu, who was reading ahead. "God is so obsessed with this whole Leviathan thing. First He is talking about the earth and the stars and the clouds, and then He decides no, I'll just drop everything and focus on Leviathan for three chapters."

"You know," said Bill Dodd, "what is Leviathan, anyway? Like a giant whale or something, right? So God is saying we need to be able to make whales submit to us and serve us and dance for us and stuff? Cause, I've been to Sea World. We have *totally* done that."

"Leviathan is a giant sea dinosaur thing," said Zoe Farr. "Like a plesiosaur. Look, it's in the next chapter. It says he has scales and a strong neck."

"And you don't think if he really existed, we'd Jurassic Park the sucker?" asked Bill Dodd.

"It also says he breathes fire," said Eli Foss.

"So," proposed Valerie, "if we can find a fire-breathing whale with scales and a neck, and we bring it to Sea World, then we win the Bible?"

"What I think my esteemed cousin meant," Ana had said, "is that God argues here that we're too weak and ignorant to be worthy to know these things. But then the question becomes — exactly how smart do we have to be to deserve an answer? Now that we can, as Bill puts it, send lightning through the sky, now that we can capture whales and make them do tricks for us, does that mean we have a right to ask God for an explanation? Discuss!"

VI.

"Where is Metatron?" asked Erin, that final night on *All Your Heart*. "Is he riding Leviathan? Is he in his belly? Will he come out to meet us once we're close enough?"

"Lady," said James. "We don't know any more than you do. We'll... all find out soon enough."

Amoxiel gibbered softly. For some reason Erin started to cry. James and Father O'Connor got into some argument, and Mark McCarthy wouldn't stop drawing pentagrams around everything. Ana realized she was shaking. She very deliberately extricated herself from the assembly around the harpoon and went amidships to the yellow sail. The yellow sail was her safe place, she told herself, as swirling stars sputtered overhead.

When she was very young, she read the Book of Job for the first time and was so confused that she had resolved to study theodicy for the rest of her life. Here she was, at the end of the world, a nationally recognized expert, and she had to admit it made no more sense to her than it had the first time around. Could she draw out Leviathan with a fishhook? Empirically, yes. So what? Valerie had asked exactly the right question. So if you can defeat a really big whale, you win the Bible? Why? Why had God said so in Job, and why had the Comet King himself been so certain it was true that he'd built the world's fastest ship and the world's most fabulous harpoon? She started going over the Book of Job again in her mind, line by line. Job suffers. Job complains. Job's friends tell him everything happens for a reason. Job complains more. God arrives in a whirlwind. God asks if Job can defeat the Leviathan. Job has to admit he cannot, and therefore he does not deserve to know the secret order of the world. God accepts his apology and gives him free things. Not the most satisfying narrative.

Think like a kabbalist.

She thought with all her strength, and with strength beyond her own. She felt oppressed by a terrible cleverness and a wild rebellion. Finally she came to a decision.

"I'll be gone for just a moment," she told James. "The yellow sail knows what to do. If you need me, come get me."

The first mate's eyes didn't leave the Leviathan, but he nodded.

Ana climbed belowdecks and knocked on the door to the Captain's quarters.

Chapter Sixty-Eight

...Puts All Heaven In A Rage

For a Tear is an Intellectual Thing
And a Sigh is the Sword of an Angel King
And the bitter groan of the Martyr's woe
Is an Arrow from the Almighty's Bow
—William Blake, "The Grey Monk"

December 21, 1999
Colorado Springs

No analogy suffices. They came in like what they were, the greatest army ever collected, marching back home in a frustrating mix of victory and defeat.

The people acted like it was otherwise. They lined the streets. They threw flowers. Songs were sung about the Conquerors of Yakutsk, the Vanquishers of Demons. Many even believed it. For them it had been another war. Our country hated their country. Now their country was gone. That was victory, wasn't it?

A few knew better. The whole war, even the conquest of Yakutsk, had been a means to an end. An end to suffering. The destruction of Hell forever. They had failed. They had completed every step except the only one which counted. Those who knew better joined in the street-lining and flower-throwing, because the alternative was to sit inside and become lost in their thoughts.

And for the same reason, the Comet King accepted their praise. He rode in a big black car, with his generals beside him, and people threw confetti and held up banners and some of them even ran up and hugged him. He accepted it gracefully, lest he become lost in his thoughts.

Robin came to meet him as the parade crossed Uintah Street. There was a cheer as she climbed into the black car and kissed the King. He raised his fist in a gesture that could be interpreted as some form of positive emotion. Everyone cheered again.

The parade broke up as they crossed Fountain Creek and the 140, and they began driving home in earnest. Robin looked at the sky. It was late afternoon.

"I have something to tell you," she said.

He heard fear in her voice. "Yes?"

"Not now," she said. "Wait until we get home."

He stopped the car with a screech, grabbed her in his arms, flew into the air, turned to lightning. He shot southwest, burning through the sky like a meteor. The great blast doors of the bunker-palace opened before him as he landed, changed back. Before she even knew what was happening, she was seated on the bed in their bedroom, her husband beside her.

"I've never heard you sound so afraid before," he said. "What's wrong?"

She looked around. The familiar objects of their bedroom. The spruce desk. The woven blankets. The painting of the Rocky Mountains. And now he was here with her. She started to cry.

The furrows on his brow deepened.

"Jala, I've done something terrible."

"We can fix it."

"I know we can."

"Then don't cry. Tell me."

She gulped, took in a deep breath. "I sold my soul to Thamiel."

He didn't react. If, as the psychologists say, our brain works by fitting data to plausible models, his thoughts stopped for lack of any model to fit it to. He just stared. Finally he said the only thing he could.

"What did you sell it for?"

"Nothing in particular. I didn't want anything, that was the problem. I had to make something up. He didn't believe me in the end, but it was all right, he took the deal anyway. I had to give you a chance."

"What do you mean?"

"The great work! The destruction of Hell! The end of suffering!"

"Is impossible!"

"I know! If it wasn't impossible, you would have done it, I believe you, I swear."

"Robin, what..."

"That's the thing, Jala. You did everything possible. So I had to give you a chance. It's like you always say. Somebody has to and no one else will. But you couldn't. But you love me. I don't know why but you do. While I'm in Hell, you've got another reason, you can cut through the paradox..."

It hit him. It hit him like an asteroid hits a planet, killing all life, boiling away the seas, a giant sterilizing wave of fire. "Robin... you... no... how... *no...*" and just like that the human part of him disappeared, was consumed, his eyes flashed with white fire, what had once seemed like hair stretched out behind him like the tail of a comet, the air turned cold, the room turned grey, the lights turned off, he stood there, raw, celestial, enraged.

"THIS IS NOT HOW IT ENDS!" he shouted, less at her than at everything. "NO. YOU CAN'T DO THIS. THIS. IS. NOT. HOW. IT. ENDS."

"No," she said. "It ends with you rescuing me from Hell. After however long it takes. I don't know how you'll do it, but I know it will be something wonderful."

"THIS! IS! NOT! HOW! IT! ENDS!"

"Jala," she said, "come off it. I have until sunset tonight with you. Don't shout. Don't say anything. Just sit here and be with me."

The light came back to the room. The flames trailing behind him settled into snow-white hair. The unearthly light almost left his eyes.

"Will you stay with me for the next," she looked at her watch, "hour and forty minutes?"

He hugged her.

"I'll stay," he said.

For an hour and forty minutes, they lay there on the bed. They held each other. They talked about Nathanda, and Caelius, and Jinxiang, and Sohu. They talked about the time they met, in the dining room of the palace, and how confused Father Ellis had been when Jalaketu asked him to officiate their wedding.

Finally, Robin said: "Promise me."

And Jalaketu said: "I promise."

An hour and forty minutes later, Thamiel swaggered through the big spruce wood door with a gigantic grin on his face, "Well!" he said, "It looks like we..."

The Comet King had his hands around the demon's neck in an instant. "Listen," he said. "I know the rules as well as you do. Take her. But as God is my witness, the next time we meet face to face I will speak a Name, and you and everything you have created will be excised from the universe forever, and if you say even a single unnecessary word right now *I will make it hurt.*"

The grin disappeared from the demon's face.

"You can't harm me," said Thamiel. "I am a facet of God."

"I will recarve God without that facet," said the Comet King.

Very quietly, Thamiel shuffled to Robin and touched her with a single misshapen finger.

The two of them disappeared.

Kings

Somebody had to; no one would
I tried to do the best I could
And now it's done, and now they can't ignore us.
And even though it all went wrong
I'll stand against the whole unsong
With nothing on my tongue but HaMephorash

—Leonard Cohen, "HaMephorash"

Chapter Sixty-Nine

Love Seeketh Not Itself To Please

Afternoon, May 14, 2017
Citadel West

The alarms went silent. North American airspace went black. The lights went out. THARMAS went quiet, then released an arc of electrical energy which briefly lit the otherwise pitch-black room before dying back down. Sohu gave a horrible primal scream.

"THEY KILLED URIEL!" she screamed. "THEY KILLED URIEL! THEY BROKE MALKUTH! EVERYTHING IS..." She gave a horrible noise, like she was being pulled apart.

Someone said the Luminous Name, and I saw her there, clutching her head. I saw the rest of them. Nathanda looking grave, Jinxiang looking angry, Caelius still mangled and bloody, sitting with THARMAS, hitting it, trying to get it to turn back on. I saw Sarah, her face emotionless.

"Sohu!" said Nathanda, placing her hands on her sister's head. "Can you hear me, Sohu? Tell me what's going on?"

"THEY KILLED URIEL!" she screamed. "THEY KILLED URIEL AND NOW IT'S ALL..." She looked like she was trying to find a word for how bad things were. She started saying something else, but I wasn't sure whether she was speaking some language I didn't know or just having a seizure.

The real power of angels and demons was unplumbably immense. They'd been hobbled to a semi-human level by Uriel's filters, which denied them the divine light they devoured for sustenance. If that was gone, there was nothing hyperbolic about Sohu's reaction. We had lost in the most final and terrifying way possible.

"Sohu," said Caelius, very quietly, and I could see he was having trouble staying conscious, but he was Cometspawn, and there was a job to be done.

"Sohu, we need THARMAS back. This must have been the Other King's plan all along. He would deny us THARMAS and the Names by—" he stopped for a second, took a deep breath, "—by preventing computer technology from working at all. I need to know, can you bring THARMAS back? The lights can wait. The airspace map can wait. But Sohu, *we need THARMAS.*"

"Can't... do it," said Sohu, panting. "Never could... get Briah... right. Computers... too hard."

Now it was General Bromis's turn. "Can you at least get radio connections back up? We're flying blind in here! I need to hear from the armies!"

Sohu paused for a second. "Kay... did it... radio... works," she said. "Can't manage anything more. Also, all of... the rivers in the world are... running in reverse." She laughed fatalistically. "Never fails. Hardly... matters now." She grabbed her head again. "Oh God... Uriel. It's too much."

Bromis and his soldiers had left, probably trying to radio their battalions, tell them that the artillery wasn't going to fire, that the tanks would just stand motionless. "Got... to get... THARMAS back," Caelius was saying, but his words were slurred and he sounded half-asleep. For the first time, I thought I saw Nathanda... not at a loss, exactly. Just sitting quietly, trying to figure out what to do.

"Put me in THARMAS," Sarah said suddenly, and we all turned to her.

"What?" asked Nathanda.

"Put me in THARMAS. I'm still working. I have a soul, a divine spark, so I'm mind and not machinery. If Vihaan hadn't bombed the original THARMAS, the one with the soul, and forced Caelius to switch it to a different configuration, it would be working too. But he did and it isn't. If you dissect me for parts and put them in THARMAS, it will have a soul and it can work."

"You'd die!" I protested.

"Of course I would!" she spat back at me. "You don't love me, Aaron! Admit it!"

"It's not that I don't love you, it's that..."

"No. You gave me life, Aaron, but you didn't give me a purpose. You people have so much purpose. Breathing, eating, having sex, making money. It's all so easy for you! I had to make my own purpose, and the only thing I had was you, and now you've rejected me, and all I want is to become THARMAS so that I won't have to go back into the darkness but also I'll never be able to think for more than a quarter of a millisecond and I'll never be able to remember your name. I want to know every Name in the cosmos except yours."

"Listen, Sarah—"

"Um," said Caelius. "I know this is— look, we really need to do this."

As if synchronized, all of us turned to Nathanda.

"Do it," she said.

With what almost looked like a smirk on her face, Sarah walked over to where Caelius sat at the computer terminal. "It's my heart," she said. "The computer. It's inside my chest."

Caelius held out his hands, and the sword Sigh appeared inside them, the sword that always came when the Cometspawn needed it.

I ran towards Sarah.

Caelius cut her chest open. There was no blood. He sliced through skin easily, like he was cutting a cake, and I saw the smooth white form of my old MacBook inside.

"Sarah!" I yelled, and I hugged her.

"You said," she whispered to me, "that you would love me if I was good."

Then Caelius pulled the laptop out of her body, and the golem crumbled into dust.

I watched numbly as his expert hands pried open the bottom lid and started popping out parts. I was vaguely aware of a commotion all around me, and finally I turned and saw Bromis was back with his soldiers.

"Thamiel," he said, and something in me had expected it. "The demons are swarming. They're moving... faster than we can track them, given what's happened to our technology. They're swarming in Siberia and they're heading our direction. No clear target besides just 'North America' at the moment, but I've told the military to be on alert."

"Alert won't help," snapped Sohu. "Their bonds have been broken. Almost no limits on their power."

"Could they have figured out what we're doing here?" asked Nathanda.

Sohu glared at her sister like she was an idiot. "Yes," she said. "That's the least they could have done."

"Then it's safe to say they're headed this direction. Come to stop us before we succeed, just like the Other King. Well, they'll have to wait in line."

"No," said Bromis. "The Other King's army is outside, but the King isn't with them yet. He's on his way from Las Vegas, ETA a few hours. Thamiel's arms is moving faster than the fastest jets. They'll get here first. Coming from the north, where we're defenseless. They'll fly across the Bering Strait, go through Canada, cross the border near the Dakotas, and swoop down the Front Range Urban Corridor. A few minutes, maybe half an hour. We may be able to relocate troops onto the 87 north of the city before then, but with the guns only working intermittently I don't know how much help they'll be."

"Zero," said Sohu. "Zero help." At least didn't seem to be seizing or anything now. I felt at the telepathic link. Sohu's mind was a swirl of horror and dismay, parts of it had settled down, and other parts had gotten stronger, or opened up into new configurations I couldn't quite detect. She *sounded* hopeless, but her mind didn't *feel* hopeless. "Keep the troops near the Citadel," she finally said. "Let them hold off the Other King. I'll take care of Thamiel."

"You?" asked Nathanda and Jinxiang together.

"Yeah," said Sohu, defiantly. I saw her glance at the stump of her left hand, the one that used to have the Comet King's mark on it. "I never told you guys this, because I thought Father would freak out, but I met Thamiel. Twice. He came to harass Uriel when I was staying with him. He... he wasn't nice to me. There's stuff I need to settle with him."

"He's the Devil!" said Jinxiang. "*Everyone* has stuff they need to settle with him! Sohu, don't do it! You were sitting here clutching your head in pain just a second ago. Stay here where it's—"

"Were you going to say *safe*?" asked Sohu. "Hah. Look. This is what you guys keep me around for, right?"

"I'll go with you," said Jinxiang.

"No you won't," said Nathanda and Sohu together.

"Fuck you both," said Jinxiang. She looked at Sohu, but more pleading than angry. "Sohu," she said. "I know you're great. I've seen what you can do. But don't go alone. Please, don't."

"I'm never alone," said Sohu. "And you haven't seen what I can do. Not really. *The mountains are still in one piece.*"

Then she walked out of the room.

"Fuck," said Jinxiang.

"Your highness," said Bromis, "permission to leave. Please. For the passes. If the Other King shows up in person, our lines won't be able to resist him. Let me go find my men, see what defenses I can hold together."

"Granted," said Nathanda. The general saluted. "And Bromis? My father always said you were one of the bravest men he knew. Make of that what you will." Bromis stood there awkwardly, then saluted again, hurried out.

"He was asking to permission to go die with his men," Nathanda explained to Jinxiang, when the latter raised an eyebrow. "He knows the

Citadel's outer defenses can't hold. That's why I won't let you go help Sohu. You and me, we're going to defend our home. Together."

"You're more afraid of the Other King than Thamiel?" asked Jinxiang, not contradicting her sister, just not quite believing her.

"Yes. Father could beat Thamiel. If Sohu thinks she can take him on, I trust her. The Other King... Father..." She turned to me. The soldiers had gone with Bromis; me, Jinxiang, and Caelius were the only ones left in the giant throne room, and Caelius was still feverishly hacking away at Sarah and THARMAS, trying to connect the pieces into a unified whole. I couldn't tell if he was just working with the unpredictable genius of a Cometspawn or whether his wounds had gotten the better of him, whether his actions looked random and flailing because they really were random and flailing. I tried to tune out the dust of Sarah's decayed body.

"Aaron," said Nathanda. "Sohu showed you the library? Go get me all the books you can find on Elisha ben Abuyah. It's time to learn everything we can about the Other King."

Chapter Seventy

Nor For Itself Hath Any Care

Evening, May 14, 2017
Colorado Springs

I.

It was called Tava, or "sun mountain," by the Ute. El Capitan, meaning "the leader," by the Spanish. But its modern name Pikes Peak comes from explorer Zebulon Pike, and his name in turn comes from the Biblical Zebulon, son of Jacob.

Moses says in Deuteronomy 33: "Rejoice, Zebulon, in your journeys. You call the people to your mountain, and there they will offer a sacrifice of the righteous." Taken to refer to Mr. Pike, the journeys part checks out. The mountain part definitely checks out. The sacrifice of the righteous part is kind of obscure.

Sohu hoped, as she rematerialized on the summit of Pikes Peak, that it didn't have anything to do with her.

She had chosen her terrain carefully. She was north of Citadel West; Thamiel would have to come through here to get to her family. She could see in every direction. The bunker to her south, the highway to her north, the city to her east. If she had to do something drastic, she was far enough from human habitation that they would escape collateral damage. Poor, lovely Colorado Springs! It was so small from up here, still smaller than Denver after thirty years as the capital. They all thought her father had decided to stay because of the bunker, or the air force base, or the nuclear silos scattered in the hills. But he'd stayed because it was where he'd grown up, and that was always the thing that scared him, losing his humanity, falling completely into his form of stars and fire and night. Colorado Springs was small and lovely and it was home, and even when he was two thousand feet underground in the mountain it had been nearby and that had made him happy.

What were the odds it would survive another twenty-four hours?

She felt it before she saw it, a low buzz that seemed to wax and wane like the beating of an enormous heart. Then it filled the northern sky, a cross between a black storm cloud and a colony of bats. She had seen Thamiel before, but never this, never an entire host.

It saw her. The dark cloud changed directions, headed right towards her. Its radius must have measured miles. Finally it was atop her, buzzing over her, like her own personal rainstorm.

A familiar form separated from the formless mass, and Thamiel slid through the air effortlessly to join Sohu on the peak. He opened his mouth to say something, but Sohu interrupted.

"Thamiel, if this were a book, and you were at the head of a demonic army, and the only thing standing in your way was a little girl, on a mountaintop, with a sword forged from a fallen star, how do you think it would end?"

"This again?" Thamiel snorted. "First of all, you don't have—"

The great sword Sigh appeared in Sohu's hand.

"—your father's abilities," Thamiel finished, fluidly, with only the slightest pause. "And Sohu, I killed him. He resisted me for a season only, with a stupid trick, and in the end I killed him. The Other King got the empty husk, but I was the one who killed his spirit. Do you know why videos still work, Sohu? That wasn't Uriel. That was me. I kept it working so that every month, I could send him videos of his wife, burning. Updates, if you will. I never missed one. I killed him slowly, protractedly, until finally the Other King stuck a sword through his chest and put him out of his misery. Now my powers are stronger. What do you think I will do to *you*? Be afraid, Sohu. I am the Left Hand of God."

Sohu didn't say anything, just pulled up her sleeve to show the scarred stump where her own left hand used to be.

Then she stepped into Yetzirah and struck. She called on the town to their east, its first streetlights starting to glow in the twilight gloom. Colorado Springs. Colorado is Spanish for colorful. Color comes from Indo-European **kel*, to conceal. Spring. To burst forth. Colorado Springs. That which had been concealed, bursting forth. Revelation of secrets. The essence of kabbalah. Her hometown and her birthright. She filled herself with love for her city and her family and her people, and the essence of kabbalah arced out of her, filled the mountaintops with light.

Thamiel held out his bident, parted the glowing streams of meaning. Colorado, color, **kel*, concealment. Cognate with Greek, *kalypto*, to conceal. To unconceal, to reveal, *apo-kalypto*. John had named his revelation Apokalypto, thence the modern Apocalypse. Revelation 9:3: "And there came out of the smoke locusts upon the earth: and unto them was given power." With the practiced mastery of thousands of years, Thamiel took each line of force that Sohu fed him, channeled the semantic energies from Colorado to apocalypse and to the power given to demons to rule the earth.

She saw what he was doing, wouldn't let him, raised her sword, traced two minus signs of flame into the air. Revelation 9:3 minus two, Revelation 9:1. "And the fifth angel sounded, and I saw a star fall from heaven unto the earth: and to him was given the key of the bottomless pit." The star that sought the key to the pit. The line of Comet West, Heaven touching upon Earth, the source of Sohu's gifts and the meaning that drove her life. The meaning burst into sparks of starlight all around her, protecting her, wrapping around her like a cloak.

Thamiel rolled two of his eyes and made a motion with his bident.

The whole cloud of demons crashed down on her. The three great hosts of the hellish princes Adramelech, Asmodeus, and Rahab, all turned against a single human. It was like falling night, like rushing water. The shield of starlight crackled, started to crumble. She constructed forms and glyphs in Briah and Yetzirah, shrieked a desperate cry for help through the aether to anything that could hear. It flew from her on the horizon between worlds, leaving little ripples in the evening sky. She watched it go. She couldn't waste her real weapons on these things. She needed them for Thamiel. She had lost him in the cacophony. She traced desperate patterns to ward off the horde, surrounded herself with glittering polyhedra of light.

Then came a great wind from the south, and she saw an army of spirits, skull-like faces crowned with quetzal feathers. A Mesoamerican war-band crashed into the host of Adramelech. Sohu felt the assault on her subside as they turned to face these new intruders.

"You thought I forgot!" Samyazaz yelled into the towering nimbus of demons. He was in his true angelic form now, neither priest-king nor cactus, a brilliant creature of ivory-white wings and unbearably intense eyes. "Well, now it's the apocalypse, and there's nothing left to be afraid of, so you know what? I never forget! YOU DESTROYED MY ZIGGURAT, YOU TWO-HEADED CREEP!" The air rang with the thunder of their combat.

Sohu took advantage of the distraction, shot out from Pikes Peak, ascended into the open air above, still searching for Thamiel. Asmodeus and Rahab's hosts followed. They crashed into her in the cirrus clouds above the highest mountain, two tongues of dark flame that whirled around her among the noctilucent drops of ice. Sohu spoke words of fire and night, drove great spinning wheels of flame into the hearts of the horde, called the winds to scatter her assailants. She spoke the Names of God, the secret ones UNSONG had spent the work of decades gathering, and slashed huge swathes of destruction into the darkness. But slowly they began to close in again, the starlight weakening, Sohu's breath and voice starting to fail.

Then the cavalry rode in. Hundreds of beautiful tall angels riding bright white horses, and... *was that the William Tell Overture?* At their head, wearing cowboy boots and a ten-gallon hat, rode Gadiriel, the Lady of Los Angeles. "YEEEEHAW!" she shouted, heedless of the Third Commandment. She fired her revolver twice, and each shot blossomed into a miniature sun. She saw Asmodeus, jumped off her horse, landed in front of him with her gun drawn. "I reckon you better turn around and go right back where you came from, *pardner*," she drawled. "There's a new seraph in town!"

Sohu didn't wait to see what happened next. She flew through a hole in the darkness, still seeking Thamiel. He was nowhere to be found. The host of Rahab pursued, indistinct dark forms that looked from different angles like ravens, bats, or locusts. She tried to evade them, rose even higher, coursed through the ionosphere in a crackle of light into the dark spaces beyond Earth's atmosphere, where the fixed stars and moon glowed unimpeded by any envelope of air. She let the lines of starlight intersect around her, reflect off each other, congeal into a luminous labyrinth of protection. Still the host of Rahab came against her, teasing through her vulnerabilities, wresting cracks in her own shield to match the cracks in the sky above them. And she realized then that she couldn't stand on her own against even a single demonic host, that this would finally be the end of her.

Then a million figures shot up from the earth below on pillars of fire. Old men, children, women with flowers in their hair, all singing songs of love and praise. The people of San Francisco, who had passed while still alive into the eternity outside of time. All listening to her call, coming to her aid. At their head, still clad in a white NASA spacesuit, rose Neil Armstrong, who had returned from the space beyond the world as the Right Hand of God. He rocketed into the horde of demons until he reached Rahab, and grabbed his neck, and slew him. Thus was fulfilled the prophecy of Psalm 89:10: "Thou hast slain Rahab with thy strong arm."

Sohu plummeted back down to Earth, burned like a meteor as she pierced the heavens, landed back on the summit of Pikes Peak, newly invigorated. "I'm coming for you, Thamiel!" she shouted, and she found him on the side of the mountain, landed with enough force to clear a crater, turned to face her adversary within the still-smoking arena. Still not quite time. She had to weaken him first.

Thamiel didn't say anything, just called forth terror and nightmare. From Pikes Peak itself he took a profusion of Ps and Ks. Apep and Kek, the two Egyptian gods of primordial darkness. *Poop* and *kaka*, two terms for human excrement. *Pikey* and *Paki* and *kike* and *kook*, all terms of fear and prejudice and hatred.

As it closed in on her, Sohu took the same letters and turned them into *pikuach*. *Pikuach nefesh*, to save a life, the holiest of principles, the one that took precedence over almost any other. *Kippah*, the cap worn by the holy to remind them that God was above them at all times, to protect them from the unbearable radiance of the Divine Presence. *Cop*. A protector, an agent of Law. *Pope*. The vicar of God on Earth. *Kook*. The first Chief Rabbi of Israel, who said that "the pure righteous do not complain of the dark, but increase the light." *Keep*. "If you will enter into life, keep the commandments." *Kayak*, her own word, on which she had begun her studies so many years ago. The shield of starlight flickered desperately, but did not give in.

Thamiel slashed at her with his bident; Sohu stepped back, and the bident struck empty air, leaving two glowing lines. Two. Sohu took the gematria, transmuted it into *bet*, added it to the *kayak* still gleaming above her, made it into *kokab*, star.

Thamiel removed the leftmost kaf from the word. Kaf. *Palm*. The Left Hand of God. The remaining letters he turned it into *bakah*, weeping. Job 16:16, "My face is foul with weeping, and on my eyelids is the shadow of death." From the verse Thamiel took foulness, and the shadow of death, and the number 616. That left him with a 1. "I have won," he said.

And he had. The foulness and death, the Left Hand of God, the Codex Ephraemi's Number of the Beast — all the concepts were too tight, Sohu was too exhausted to tease any more meaning out of her. They closed together, tore apart her shield.

Thamiel raised the bident high. "Any last words?" he asked.

"Two... of them," sputtered Sohu. "Knock... knock."

"What?" asked Thamiel, his eyes narrowing. His second head bobbed back and forth in excitement and confusion.

"Knock knock," said Sohu. "Don't tell me you're not familiar with the setup."

"Who's there?" he asked suspiciously.

II.

Sohu woke up on a bed of cloudstuff, just as she had done thousands of times before. But today was different. Today was her last day here. She would get in the flying kayak and go home and cry at her father's funeral and help her family. What she had learned would have to be enough.

She walked out of the little cottage. There was Uriel in his spot in the center of the storm, great gold eyes gleaming with excitement.

THINGS HAVE HAPPENED, said Uriel.

"Huh?" asked Sohu, still half asleep, rubbing her eyes. She wasn't *nearly* awake enough yet to deal with the sort of weirdness Uriel was constantly springing on her.

YOU ASKED WHY YOU SHOULD STAY AN EXTRA DAY. I TOLD YOU MANY THINGS COULD HAPPEN IN A DAY. NOW THEY HAVE HAPPENED. FOR EXAMPLE, THERE ARE SEVERAL NEW VERSES IN THE BIBLE.

"Uriel, please. What are you talking about?"

I DO NOT WANT YOU TO LEAVE ME, BUT I KNOW YOU HAVE TO GO BACK TO COLORADO. SO I HAVE REARRANGED THE FUNDAMENTAL SPATIAL AND MYSTICAL ORGANIZATION OF THE UNIVERSE SOMEWHAT. IT WAS VERY HARD. I COULD NOT DO IT IN YETZIRAH OR EVEN BRIAH. I HAD TO EDIT ATZILUTH DIRECTLY.

"...doesn't that destroy the world?"

USUALLY. THAT IS WHY I GENERALLY AVOID IT. BUT I TRIED VERY HARD TO MAKE SURE THAT DID NOT HAPPEN. IN THIS CASE ALL IT DID WAS CHANGE THE BIBLE. IT IS SO WEIRD TO BEGIN WITH THAT I DOUBT VERY MANY PEOPLE WILL NOTICE.

"Uriel, everyone notices the Bible. People have been studying every letter of it for thousands of years."

OH.

"What did you *do* anyway?"

I HAVE CREATED A RITUAL THAT LETS TWO MINDS JOIN TOGETHER. NO MATTER HOW FAR AWAY, THEY CAN TALK TO EACH OTHER, SHARE THOUGHTS AND MEMORIES, FEEL THE SAME EMOTION. THEY WILL BE WITH EACH OTHER ALL THE TIME, BEYOND DISTANCE OR DEATH.

"...what does that mean?"

I WILL SHOW YOU. I HAVE MADE A MAGIC CIRCLE. PLEASE STEP INTO IT.

Sohu sighed. Conversations with Uriel would never be remotely normal. But they were something whose absence would leave a great gaping void in her life. What would it be like to live with ordinary people, who would answer questions with simple yeses or nos instead of asking for absurd specifics and then going off on tangents about which Proto-Quechua root words it reminded them of? It was too awful to contemplate.

She stepped into the magic circle.

REPEAT AFTER ME, BUT CHANGE THE NAME. I, THE ARCHANGEL URIEL, IN FULL KNOWLEDGE OF THE CONSEQUENCES...

"I, Sohu West, in... full knowledge of the consequences..."

And so they went, the archangel first, then the child, through the long ritual of the Sacred Kabbalistic Marriage of Minds. The winds of the storm around them went strangely quiet. The sun darkened, as if covered by clouds, then brightened as if reflected by a million jewels. The sky became a deeper shade of blue.

FOR GOD IS ONE.

"For God is One."

AND HIS NAME IS ONE.

"And His Name is One."

AND WE ARE ONE.

"And we are one."

AND IT IS DONE.

"And it is done."

Sohu felt something new in her mind, a presence, a spark of gold.

[Are you in my head?] she asked the archangel.

[WELL, I WOULD NOT SAY I AM LITERALLY IN YOUR HEAD, SINCE YOUR HEAD IS VERY SMALL. HOWEVER, IF YOU WANT TO USE SPATIAL METAPHORS TO GROUND THE BASIC PRINCIPLES OF CHASHMAL, YOU MIGHT SAY THAT...]

III.

Thamiel raised the bident high, chuckled. "Any last words?" he asked.

"Two... of them," sputtered Sohu. "Knock... knock."

"What?" asked Thamiel, his eyes narrowing. His second head bobbed back and forth in excitement and confusion.

"Knock knock," said Sohu. "Don't tell me you're not familiar with the setup."

"Who's there?" he finally asked, suspiciously.

Sohu closed her eyes. When she opened them, there was no sclera, no iris, no pupil. Just a sea of burning gold.

URIEL, she said.

"What?" asked Thamiel, jumping back. "How? What are you—"

YOU ARE SUPPOSED TO SAY 'URIEL WHO,' said Sohu.

"You're dead! The Other King killed you, destroyed your machine, and good riddance! That's why my powers are—"

YOU DO NOT SEEM LIKE YOU ARE GOING TO SAY 'URIEL WHO' SO I WILL PRETEND YOU SAID IT AND CONTINUE THE JOKE ANYWAY. THE ANSWER I WAS GOING TO GIVE WAS: 'URIEL-LY SHOULD HAVE KNOWN BETTER THAN TO THINK I WOULD ABANDON MY FRIEND.'

Then there was light.

Beautiful, multicolored light, ten colors, the seven colors of the earthly rainbow and the three extra colors you only get in Heaven. Ten colors corresponding to the ten sephirot and the ten fingers and the Ten Commandments and the ten digits of the number system and the ten pip cards of the Tarot and all the other tens in all the correspondences of the world. Thamiel tried to flee, but it consumed him, melted him like the sun melts snowflakes. All of the demons of the great swarm that hovered above Colorado Springs melted away in that conflagration, the release of all the stored energy of all the spheres, eons of careful collection loosed into a single brilliant flowering.

Sohu blinked again, and her eyes were deep brown.

[THAT IS ALL OF IT,] said Uriel, in Sohu's head. [THERE IS NO MORE SHEFA.]

[It did what we needed it to.]

[HE IS GONE FOR A BRIEF TIME ONLY. HE WILL RETURN LATER.]

[Something else will have killed us by then, so that's fine.]

[YOU ARE VERY PESSIMISTIC.]

[It's the apocalypse. You wrote the Book of Revelation, didn't you?]

[UM. I WAS GOING TO. BUT THEN THE JET STREAM STARTED FLOWING THE WRONG WAY AND I HAD TO FIX IT. I THINK I JUST GAVE JOHN

OF PATMOS A BUCKET OF PSILOCYBE MUSHROOMS AND TOLD HIM TO WRITE WHATEVER CAME TO MIND.]

[Well, take my word for it, things are really bad.]

[I AM IN A GOOD MOOD. IT HAS BEEN THREE HOURS AND FOUR MINUTES SINCE MY MACHINE WAS DESTROYED. THIS IS THE LONGEST I HAVE EVER GONE WITHOUT HAVING TO FIX ANY CATASTROPHIC SYSTEM ERRORS.]

[I'm glad one of us is enjoying this. Let's go help Nathanda.]

[OKAY.]

Sohu turned to lightning and disappeared. The last few ashes and sparks fell to the base of Pikes Peak. The force of the battle had split the mountain in two.

Chapter Seventy-One

But For Another Gives Its Ease

Everybody already has enlightenment. Why did Buddha sit for six years, see a star, and then get enlightenment? That's stupid! If you see a star, you get enlightenment now!

—Ch'unsong Sunim

Evening, May 14, 2017
Fire Island

I.

Opening the door to the Captain's cabin, Ana saw a small room, dark and unadorned, with only a bare wooden bed. The Captain sat upon it, writing something, pages of notes strewn all about. He looked up at Ana, his face unreadable through the dark glasses. She hesitated for just a second, then spoke.

"I know your True Name," she said.

II.

The overt meaning of *Leviathan* is "a giant sea monster."

The kabbalistic meaning of *Leviathan* is "the world."

This we derive from gematria, where both Leviathan and Malkuth — the sephirah corresponding to the material world — have identical values of 496. 496 is a perfect number, from which we can derive that the world is perfect — helpful, since we probably wouldn't derive that otherwise.

The analogy between the world and a sea monster cuts across faiths. The Norse speak of Jormungand, the World Serpent, who circles the earth to grasp its own tail. The Babylonians say that the heavens and earth were built from the corpse of the primordial sea dragon Tiamat. Even the atheists represent the cosmos as part of a great whale, saying that the whole world is a gigantic fluke.

And the same motif of sea-monster-as-world is found in every form of art and scholarship. Herman Melville uses the whale Moby Dick as a symbol for the forces of Nature. Thomas Hobbes uses the Leviathan as his metaphor for human society. Even Leonard Cohen writes, in his "Anthem," "There is a kraken: everything."

The world, like Leviathan, is very big. The world, like Leviathan, is difficult for humans to understand, let alone subdue. The world, like Leviathan, holds out its promise — if only you could catch up with it, measure up to it, maybe things would make sense. The world, like Leviathan in Job 40:19, is "the first of the works of God"; like Leviathan in Job 41:9, it "humbles the mighty and lays them low"; like Leviathan in Psalm 104:26, it is "that who You formed to play with."

And like Leviathan in Job 41:34, it is "king over all the sons of pride." Those who are proud chase after worldly things, worship the world, treat it as their king. They obsess, they pursue, they seek to dominate and control. Even the English phrase has obvious kabbalistic echoes: "chasing your white whale."

And those who seek God foolishly seek Him in the world, for where else could He be? They seek Him by acquiring riches, or by renouncing riches, or by gaining power, or by forsaking power. If all human acts take place in the world, then how but by interacting with the world can God be attained?

Yet Jesus said in Gospel of Thomas: "If your leaders say to you, 'Look, the Kingdom is in the sky,' then the birds of the sky will precede you. If they say to you, 'It is in the sea,' then the fish will precede you. Rather, the Kingdom of God is within you."

And Robert Wilson wrote the story of a man who looked through chamber after chamber of his soul, questing for his true self, only to give up and conclude that there was nobody there. "That's odd," the guru told him. "*Who's conducting the search?*"

III.

"Come in," said the Comet King.

He sat alone, on his bed, in prayer. For the first time since Ellis had met him, he looked afraid.

"Jala," said Father Ellis, "you should go abovedeck. The crew is on the verge of breaking. The harpoon line's holding so far, but the Leviathan— the crew is scared, Jala. And I should be abovedeck, working the blue sail. We don't have men to spare."

"Father," said the Comet King, ignoring everything he had just said, "if you were going to devise a placebomantic ritual to summon Metatron, how would you do it?"

"That's easy. I wouldn't. You don't *summon* Metatron."

"And why not?"

"Metatron is the Voice of God. Trying to summon God, any part of Him, is a category error."

"Why?"

"Because God is already everywhere."

"But some places more than others, right? The hearts of the righteous? The Temple?"

"Yes... no. I think God is everywhere alike, and some places it's just... easier to notice Him."

"So if you were going to devise a placebomantic ritual to *make Metatron easier to notice*, how would you do it?"

"You're acting like you just have to, I don't know, turn on the lights, and then there's Metatron, hiding in the corner the whole time."

"I'm following your own logic to its conclusion," said the Comet King. He motioned for Ellis to sit down. "The ritual should conform to the Bible, of course," he said. "And the Bible says that if you seek God, you will find Him, if you seek with all your heart. So. We have our ship, *All Your Heart*. Seven earthly sails for the seven earthly sephirot, three hidden in other planes. But the sails themselves aren't enough. We need *ritual*. So we enact them in order. Various adventures, activating each aspect of God in turn. We start in my Kingdom. We go to San Francisco, the Foundation, where Heaven meets Earth. We shine with Glory. We win a Victory. We cross through Tiferet via the Canal. We cross Chesed by committing an act of great kindness, then Gevurah with an act of great harshness. We pass Da'at and its dark night, its collapse of everything earthly and recognizable. Now here we are. Binah, understanding. And Chokhmah, Wisdom. Which you have just displayed. Leaving us at the end of our road."

"What do you mean?" asked Ellis. He didn't like where this was going.

"Many saints, in the course of pursuing the things of the world, have realized that they were missing the point. We've played out our little pantomime long enough. So now we're going to complete the ritual exactly as you said. By realizing that God is already everywhere. Inside all of us. God isn't out there in the world. He's in *All Your Heart*. Tell me,

Father, who of the crew seems most mysterious to you? Who doesn't have a past?"

"Hm," said Ellis, going over the crew in his mind, one crew member per sail. "Orange sail... no, Clara came highly recommended from the Board of Ritual Magic. Yellow... Rabbi Pinson's one of our greatest living kabbalists. Green... Leonard's from Canada, his history checks out. Blue... that's me. Purple... Gadiriel we all know. Black. That's you. Everybody's got a pretty clear history... wait." It was like a fog lifted from his brain. "The Captain. I... I don't understand. He's been leading us the whole time, and I don't even know how he got here. Did you choose him? I didn't even think to ask his name!"

"A common problem," said the Comet King, smiling, "and one which we will soon correct. Bring him down here."

A minute later, Ellis returned to the royal suite, along with the Captain. A big man, dressed in dark glasses. Ellis wondered why he'd never thought about him before, why it had never confused him that he didn't know the name of a crew member.

The Comet King fell to his knees.

Ellis had heard an old joke, once. The Pope was visiting New York City, but he was running late for his flight back to the Vatican. So he hailed a cab and told the taxi driver to floor it to LaGuardia airport, fast as he could. Well, the driver wasn't going fast enough for the Pontiff, so he demanded they switch seats, and the Pope took the wheel and *really* started speeding down the freeway. Eventually a cop takes notice and pulls them over, then he gets cold feet. He radios the chief. "Um," he says, "I think I accidentally pulled over someone really important." "How important?" asks the chief. "Well," said the cop, "all I know is that the Pope is his cabdriver."

All Father Ellis knew was that the Comet King was kneeling before the big man, but that was enough. He dropped to his knees too.

"I know your True Name," said the Comet King.

He just stared at them with those dark glasses.

And the Comet King said—

IV.

"Metatron." Ana spoke the word without a hint of uncertainty. Then, realizing what she had gotten herself into, she fell to her knees.

The Captain took off his dark glasses, and Ana stared into the whirlwind.

V.

The Sepher Hekhalot states that when the patriarch Enoch died, God "turned his flesh to flame, his veins to fire, his eye-lashes to bolts of lightning, his eye-balls to flaming torches, and placed him on a throne next to the throne of glory." Then he imbued him with the Most Holy Name, and thenceforward he was called the "Measure of the Lord," the "Prince of the Divine Presence," and "the Lesser God." All of these titles are blasphemous as hell to call anybody who isn't God, and it was this that made Elisha ben Abuyah, in the throes of heresy, give his famous proclamation — "There are two gods. T-W-O. Deal with it."

The orthodox conception was different. God is ineffable, invisible, unspeakable, unknowable. He is the author of the world, not an entity in it. But sometimes it's useful for an author to have a self-insert character, so to speak. Thus Metatron. Not God, not quite. But *less* not-God than anything else in Creation. And the things in creation were already rather less not-God than most of them would have expected. So Metatron's not-God-ness was very low indeed, practically a rounding error.

Low enough that he, of all creation, could speak with God's voice to reveal the ultimate secret.

VI.

"Hey," I'd said one night, months before. We were sitting in the living room in Ithaca, reading our respective books. "If you caught Metatron in his boat at the edge of the world, and you got to ask one question and hear the answer from the voice of God Himself, what would you ask?"

"The Explicit Name," said Valerie.

"The problem of evil," said Ana at the same time.

Valerie raised an eyebrow at her cousin. "What? No! So suppose God says oh, the reason there's evil is that there's a blockage on the path between Binah and Yesod, sorry about that. Then what? How do you—"

"There's no path between Binah and Yesod," I interrupted.

"Aaron!" snapped Valerie, then turned back to Ana. "So God says there's a blockage between whatever and whatever, and you say okay, and then what? You've wasted your question. Me, I'd ask the Explicit Name. And then have the power to rebuild the universe according to my will. You got to admit that sounds useful."

"Blockage between whatever and whatever is only boring because you don't actually know what you're talking about," said Ana. "Like, if God said that, I'd ask — why would an infinitely good God allow the passage between whatever and whatever to be blocked? At some point, there's got to be a meaningful answer."

"Why?" I asked, though I felt bad about it.

"BECAUSE THAT'S THE WAY I WOULD DO IT IF I WERE GOD," said Ana.

"Maybe even God can't answer," suggested Valerie. "It's like, you know how Evil cannot possibly comprehend Good? Maybe Good can't comprehend Evil either."

"Evil is mostly made of fallen angels," I said. "Who used to be regular angels. I am pretty sure Evil can comprehend good just fine."

"Evil cannot possibly comprehend Aramaic," Ana suggested.

"Better," I said.

"You guys are making fun of me," said Valerie, "but I stick to what I said. Even if God gives some kind of supremely satisfying answer that explains everything about the existence of evil, in the end all you're going to do is go 'Huh,' but there'll still be as much evil as ever. It's like Marx said. The kabbalists are only trying to understand the world. The point is to change it."

"I am pretty sure Marx didn't mean 'literally shatter it to pieces, then remake it in your own image,'" said Ana.

"Actually," I said, "that was kind of Marx's *thing*."

"But if I could ask God anything," Valerie continued despite us, "I wouldn't waste it on philosophy stuff. In fact, I think that would be morally abhorrent. If you stumble across ultimate power, you've got a duty to use it for good. If I got the Explicit Name, you can bet things would be a lot different around here."

"Valerie," I said, "you couldn't use the Explicit Name. It shatters the world and rebuilds it according to the desires of the speaker. Are you one hundred percent sure that you have a clear, consistent set of desires about the world detailed enough to serve as a blueprint?"

"I just want people to be free," said Valerie.

"Boom," I said. "Everyone's living on a separate planet. Now they're free. Is that what you want?"

"The Name isn't going to be some kind of evil genie that twists your words to trick you."

"The Name wasn't meant to be used by humans! And the quatrain that turned out to be kabbalistically equivalent starts out, 'O Love, could thou and I with Him conspire / to grasp the sorry scheme of things entire.' It *very clearly* says that visualizing the structure of the entire universe is a prerequisite."

"And," said Ana, "that's why I would ask God about the problem of evil. Unless you know why God added evil in the first place, it's irresponsible to try to recreate the universe without any. What if something bad happens?"

"By definition, it wouldn't," I said.

"You know what I mean!" said Ana. "And if you're so smart, what would *you* ask God?"

"Um," I thought for a second, then was gratified to be able to give a clear answer. "What is the ordered pair whose first value is the best possible question that I could ask you, and whose second value is your answer to it?"

"You are so annoying," said Valerie.

"The ordered pair would be 'the question you just asked me,' and 'this answer right here,'" said Ana. "Then God would laugh, and all your worldly wisdom would be to no avail."

"No," I corrected. "*Jonah* whale. Noah *ark*. I thought we already had this discussion."

Ana stuck out her tongue.

"If God ever met either of you, He would smite you before you even got a chance to even open your mouth," said Valerie. "And if He was too busy, I'd do it for Him. With a smile."

She flashed an exaggerated smile at both of us, and held it just a little too long. It was kind of creepy.

"Whereas He'd be totally okay with you asking Him for the keys to the World-Destroying-Machine because you wanted to make a couple little adjustments, right?" I retorted.

"I know what I want," said Valerie. "I spent my whole life trying to fix this stupid world, I'm not about to stop just because I'm in front of the Throne of Glory. And if God ever offers me a question, it'll be because He knows what He's getting into."

"And I spent my entire life trying to figure out the problem of evil, and God knows exactly what He's getting into with me too," said Ana.

"And I," I concluded, "spent my entire life coming up with weird munchkin-style responses to serious situations, and God—"

"Shut it," said Valerie.

"You act like I'm being more annoying than you are," I said. "But seriously. God, please tell me your Name so I can destroy everything and remake it according to whichever form of Marxism was recommended in the latest book I read. God, please give me a clear answer to the fundamental paradox of the universe in seventy-five words or less, single-spaced. At least I'm honest about how ridiculous I am!"

"There *is* an answer," said Ana. "There has to be. William Blake said that God appears and God is light to those who dwell in realms of night, but God can human form display to those who dwell in realms of day. All of these things like 'it's an ineffable paradox' and 'God works in mysterious ways'—they're just light. Vague, fuzzy, warm, reassuring. But our minds were created in the image of God. Things God can understand, we can understand. Maybe not actually. I can't understand quantum chromodynamics. But it's the sort of thing I *could* understand, if I were smarter. There are a lot of things beyond my intelligence. But I don't know if there are things beyond my ken. I want to think that there aren't."

I made an expansive gesture that was supposed to indicate something like "Look at the universe," but this was hard, and I ended up just making a really big arm movement. Luckily Ana got my point anyway, because telepathy.

"Look," she said, "you know the story of Rabbi Joshua and Elijah, right? Joshua asks to accompany Elijah on his journeys, Elijah agrees as long as Joshua doesn't ask questions. The first night they stay with a family who are desperately poor and own only a single cow; still, they take the two travelers in and share what little they have. The next morning, before leaving, Elijah kills their cow. The second night, they stay with a rich man who condescends to them and tells them they can stay in the barn with the cows, because beggars deserve no better. The next morning, before leaving, Elijah magically repairs a wall of his mansion which was about to fall. Joshua says he can't keep it in any longer, he knows he's not supposed to ask questions, but what is Elijah doing? Elijah says that the first man's wife was destined to die the next day, but he prayed to God to accept the death of the cow instead. The second man was going to repair the crumbling wall of his mansion and discover buried treasure hidden underneath; he fixed it so this wouldn't happen. And I feel like if we're supposed to draw any conclusion at all from this story, it's that even seemingly unjust actions have hidden reasons that we can understand, if only someone will explain them."

"So," I asked, "you think the reason there's evil in the world is a series of post hoc adjustments for implausible coincidences, some of which involved buried treasure?"

"It's a metaphor! I think the reason there's evil in the world is something that will make at least as much sense when I hear it as Elijah's explanation did to Rabbi Joshua."

"Elijah's explanation only makes sense because he passes the buck. Okay, the virtuous woman was going to die, and Elijah has to kill the cow to prevent that. Fine. How come the virtuous woman was going to die young in the first place? How come Elijah doesn't answer *that*?"

"It's a *metaphor*!"

"Of course it's a metaphor! Kabbalah says that *everything* is a metaphor for God! That doesn't mean you can just dismiss things as metaphors without explaining how they correspond."

"Look, I'm just saying, there has to be a reason. And one day, I'm going to figure out what it is."

In the sea off Fire Island in New York, on a ship with seven sails, Ana Thurmond thought and remembered. Then she told the Captain: "My question is: why would a perfectly good God create a universe filled with so much that is evil?"

VII.

Then God spoke to Ana out of the whirlwind, and He said:

THE REASON EVIL EXISTS IS TO MAXIMIZE THE WHOLE COSMOS' TOTAL SUM GOODNESS. SUPPOSE WE RANK POSSIBLE WORLDS FROM BEST TO WORST. EVEN AFTER CREATING THE BEST, ONE SHOULD CREATE THE SECOND-BEST, BECAUSE IT STILL CONTAINS SOME BEAUTY AND HAPPINESS. THEN CONTINUE THROUGH THE SERIES, CREATING EACH UNTIL REACHING THOSE WHERE WICKEDNESS AND SUFFERING OUTWEIGH GOOD. SOME WORLDS WILL INCLUDE MUCH INIQUITY BUT STILL BE GOOD ON NET. THIS IS ONE SUCH.

And before Ana could answer, the whirlwind intensified, and caught her in its maelstrom, and she fell into a vision.

VIII.

Job asked: "God, why would You, who are perfect, create a universe filled with so much that is evil?"

Then the Lord spoke to Job out of the whirlwind, saying WOULD YOU PREFER I HAD NOT CREATED YOUR UNIVERSE, EVIL AS IT IS? WOULD YOU PREFER TO BE VOID AND EMPTINESS?

"No!" said Job. "I would prefer to live in a universe that was perfect and just!"

I CREATED SUCH A UNIVERSE, said God. IN THAT UNIVERSE, THERE IS NO SPACE, FOR SPACE IMPLIES SEPARATION FROM THINGS YOU LOVE. THERE IS NO TIME, FOR TIME MEANS CHANGE AND DECAY, AND THERE MUST BE NO CHANGE FROM THE MAXIMALLY BLISSFUL INITIAL STATE. THE BEINGS WHO INHABIT THIS UNIVERSE ARE WITHOUT BODIES, AND DO NOT HUNGER OR THIRST OR LABOR OR LUST. THEY SIT UPON GOLDEN THRONES AND CONTEMPLATE THE PERFECTION OF ALL THINGS.

YET I ALSO CREATED YOUR UNIVERSE, THAT YOU MIGHT LIVE. TELL ME, JOB, IF I UNCREATED YOUR WORLD, WOULD YOU BE HAPPIER? OR WOULD YOU BE DEAD, WHILE FAR AWAY IN A DIFFERENT UNIVERSE INCORPOREAL BEINGS SAT ON THEIR GOLDEN THRONES REGARDLESS?

"I would prefer to be one of those perfect beings on their golden thrones."

WHAT WOULD IT MEAN FOR YOU TO BE SUCH A BEING? THEY HAVE NO BODIES, NO EMOTIONS, NO DESIRES, NO LANGUAGE. WHAT WOULD IT MEAN FOR ME TO CREATE A VERSION OF YOU WITHOUT BODY, EMOTION, DESIRE, OR LANGUAGE, VERSUS TO CREATE SUCH A BEING BUT NOT HAVE IT BE YOU AT ALL? IS A VERSION OF YOU WHO IS INFINITELY WISE STILL YOU? A VERSION OF YOU WHO IS A WICKED IDOLATOR? A VERSION OF YOU WHO IS EXACTLY LIKE NOAH, IN EVERY WAY? THERE IS NO OBJECTIVE COSMIC UNEMPLOYMENT RATE.

"Huh?"

THERE IS NO OBJECTIVE ANSWER TO THE QUESTION OF HOW MANY UNIVERSES HAVE A JOB. THERE ARE VARIOUS CREATURES MORE OR LESS LIKE YOU. IF I UNCREATED YOU AND YOUR WORLD OF SUFFERING, THEY WOULD REMAIN, AND YOU WOULD DIE. WOULD THIS BE A FAVOR TO YOU?

"I still don't understand. Certainly I, who exist, want to continue existing. But instead of creating one perfect universe and some flawed universes, couldn't you just have created many perfect universes?"

TELL ME, JOB, WHAT IS THE DIFFERENCE BETWEEN YOUR RIGHT AND LEFT HANDS?

"Uh... one is on my right, and the other is on my left. And they're mirror images of each other."

I AM BEYOND SPACE. TO ME THERE IS NEITHER LEFT NOR RIGHT NOR MIRRORED REFLECTION. IF TWO THINGS ARE THE SAME, THEY ARE ONE THING. IF I CREATED TWO PERFECT UNIVERSES, I WOULD ONLY HAVE CREATED ONE UNIVERSE. IN ORDER TO DIFFERENTIATE A UNIVERSE FROM THE PERFECT UNIVERSE, IT MUST BE DIFFERENT IN ITS SEED, ITS SECRET UNDERLYING STRUCTURE.

"Then create one perfect universe, and some universes whose structures have tiny flaws that no one will ever notice."

I DID. I CREATED MYRIADS OF SUCH UNIVERSES. WHEN I HAD EXHAUSTED ALL POSSIBLE UNIVERSES WITH ONE FLAW, I MOVED ON TO UNIVERSES WITH TWO FLAWS, THEN UNIVERSES WITH THREE FLAWS, THEN SO ON, AN ENTIRE GARDEN OF FLAWED UNIVERSES GROWING ALONGSIDE ONE ANOTHER.

"Including mine."

YOUR WORLD IS AT THE FARTHEST EDGES OF MY GARDEN, God admitted, FAR FROM THE BRIGHT CENTER WHERE EVERYTHING IS PERFECT AND SIMPLE. THERE IS A WORLD MADE OF NOTHING BUT BLISS, WITH A GIANT ALEPH IN THE CENTER. THERE IS ANOTHER WORLD MADE OF NOTHING BUT BLISS WITH A GIANT BET IN THE CENTER. AND SO ON, BUT MAKE A MILLION MILLION WORLDS LIKE THOSE, AND YOU START NEEDING TO BECOME MORE CREATIVE. YOU NEED MORE AND MORE STRATAGEMS TO SEPARATE WORLDS FROM ONE ANOTHER. WORLDS WHERE INCREDIBLY BIZARRE THINGS HAPPEN AS A MATTER OF COURSE. WORLDS WHERE RANDOM COMBINATIONS OF SYLLABLES INVOKE DIVINE POWERS. AND THE MORE SUCH THINGS I ADD, THE MORE CHANCE THAT THEY TEND TOWARD EVIL. YOUR WORLD IS VERY FAR FROM THE CENTER INDEED. IT IS IN THE MIDDLE OF A VAST WASTE, WHERE NOTHING ELSE GROWS. ALL OF THE WORLDS THAT MIGHT HAVE BEEN PLANTED THERE WOULD HAVE BEEN ABOMINATIONS OF WICKEDNESS. BUT BY COINCIDENCE PILED UPON COINCIDENCE, YOURS WAS NOT. YOURS WILL GROW INTO A THING OF BEAUTY THAT WILL GLORIFY MY HOLY NAME.

"It will?"

GENESIS 1:31. I LOOKED AT THE WORLD, AND I SAW THAT IT WAS GOOD. I BEHELD ADAM KADMON, THE SEED OF YOUR WORLD,

AND SAW THAT IT WAS A GOOD SEED. THAT IT WOULD GROW INTO MORE GOOD THAN EVIL. THAT IT DESERVED A PLACE IN MY GARDEN, BESIDE THE MILLION MILLION OTHER SEEDS THAT WOULD GROW INTO OTHER WORLDS, SO THAT AS MUCH GOODNESS AS POSSIBLE COULD BE INSTANTIATED IN THE COSMOS.

"God," said Job, "what about me?"

WHAT ABOUT YOU?

"All my children are dead. All my wealth is gone. I'm covered in boils. And you're telling me, basically, that the reason I'm covered in boils is so that you can have one universe where I'm covered in boils, and another universe where I'm not covered in boils, and then you'll have one more universe than if you committed to not covering me in boils?"

NOT EXACTLY. I DO NOT SPECIFICALLY MAKE EVERY DECISION ABOUT BOILS. I CREATE THE SEEDS OF UNIVERSES, WHICH GROW ACCORDING TO THEIR SECRET STRUCTURE. BUT IT IS TRUE THAT I COULD HAVE LIMITED MYSELF TO CREATING UNIVERSES WHERE NO ONE EVER BECAME COVERED IN BOILS, AND I DID NOT DO SO. FOR THE UNIVERSES WHERE SOME PEOPLE GET COVERED IN BOILS ALSO HAVE MYRIADS OF WONDERS, AND JOYS, AND SAINTS, AND I WILL NOT DENY THEM EXISTENCE FOR THE SAKE OF THOSE COVERED IN BOILS.

"How many wonders and joys and saints is one case of boils worth, God?"

BE CAREFUL, JOB. I HAD THIS CONVERSATION WITH ABRAHAM BEFORE YOU. HE ASKED WHETHER I WOULD SPARE MY JUDGMENT ON SODOM LEST FIFTY RIGHTEOUS MEN SHOULD SUFFER. WHEN I AGREED, HE PLED FOR FORTY, THIRTY, TWENTY, AND TEN. BUT BELOW TEN HE DID NOT GO, SO I DESTROYED THE CITY. AND IF I WOULD NOT RESTRAIN MYSELF FROM DESTROYING FOR THE SAKE OF A HANDFUL OF RIGHTEOUS MEN SUFFERING, HOW MUCH LESS I SHOULD RESTRAIN MYSELF FROM CREATING.

"So I should just sit here and suffer quietly?"

UNTIL YOU DIE, AND YOUR SOUL IS REMOVED FROM THE WORLD, AND I CAN GRANT IT ETERNAL BLISS WITHOUT HAVING TO WORRY ABOUT ANY OF THIS.

"That's not a fucking lot of consolation, *God*."

Then the Lord spoke to Job out of the whirlwind, saying: HAVE YOU BEHELD THE FOUNDATIONS OF THE EARTH? SEEN ITS FOOTINGS AND ITS CORNERSTONE? WATCHED AS THE SONS OF GOD ALL SANG TOGETHER AND THE MORNING STARS SHOUTED FOR JOY? HAVE YOU

SEEN THE DOORS OF THE SEA? THE CHAINS OF THE PLEIADES AND ORION'S BELT? THE LIONS, THE RAVENS, THE YOUNG OF THE DOE AND BEAR? BEHOLD THE BEHEMOTH, WHICH I MADE BESIDE YOU, AND THE LEVIATHAN WHO RESIDES IN THE SEA. CAN YOU SAY THAT ALL THESE WONDERS SHOULD NOT BE, SO THAT YOU COULD AVOID A CASE OF BOILS? SHALL I SMITE THEM FOR YOU? SPEAK, AND I SHALL END THE WORLD WITH A WORD.

And as He spoke, the whirlwind took form, and Job saw all of these things, the boundaries of the Earth and the gateways of the Heavens, the myriad animals from Leviathan down to the smallest microbe, the glory of the lightning and the gloom of the deepest caves, the pyramids of Egypt and the pagodas of China. And he knew, more surely than he had ever known anything before, that God could end all of them with a word. And he knew that the existence of all of them, every single one, depended on the same seed that had given him a case of boils.

And Job said, "I know that You can do all things; no purpose of Yours can be thwarted. Surely I spoke of things I did not understand, things too wonderful for me to know. My ears had heard of You but now my eyes have seen You. Therefore I despise myself and repent in dust and ashes. But... why couldn't You have told me this before? Why did I have to suffer in ignorance?"

YOUR WORLD IS AT THE EDGES OF MY GARDEN. IF NOT FOR COINCIDENCE PILED UPON COINCIDENCE, IT WOULD NEVER BLOSSOM INTO GOODNESS, AND SO COULD NOT HAVE BEEN CREATED. YOUR IGNORANCE OF MY PURPOSE BEGINS A CHAIN OF COINCIDENCES WHICH WILL GROW AND GROW UNTIL THE END OF THE WORLD, WHEN IT WILL COME TO FRUITION. THAT PURPOSE IS NOW COMPLETE. GO, AND REGAIN EVERYTHING YOU HAVE LOST, BUT TELL NOBODY WHAT I HAVE TOLD YOU.

"But... I told everybody I was going to ask You about the purpose of evil. When they want to know what You answered, what should I tell them?"

TELL THEM I SAID 'GO FISH.'

IX.

Ana beheld in the whirlwind the trials of Job, and the answer of the Lord, and the whole chain of being, and the Pleiades and Orion, and Leviathan and Behemoth, and all the wonders and joys and saints of the world, placed in dazzling array, God's answer to the problem of evil spoken with a tornadic fury that stripped the universe to its roots.

"I don't buy it," said Ana Thurmond.

YOU DON'T THINK IT IS WORTH IT?

"I think you should have offered us the choice."

BEFORE THE WORLD, I SPOKE TO ADAM KADMON IN MY GARDEN. I OFFERED HIM THE CHOICE TO REMAIN IN THE PARADISE BEYOND EXISTENCE, OR TO TASTE OF GOOD AND EVIL, BE SEPARATED FROM ME, AND ATTAIN INDEPENDENT BEING. HE CHOSE THE LATTER.

"No, what about *us*? Not the grand purpose of the cosmos, not Adam Kadmon before the world, *us*. What about *me*?"

The voice of God said out of the whirlwind, YOU, WHO ONLY TWO DAYS AGO SOARED SO HIGH SHE ALMOST ESCAPED THE WORLD AND MERGED HER IDENTITY INTO THE JOY BEYOND ALL BEING, BEFORE SHE WAS RESCUED BY MY SHIP AND CREW? AND WHO SAID, AND I QUOTE, 'OH GOD, I ALMOST FELT TRANSCENDENT JOY. IT WAS AWFUL.'

"Then..." Ana was almost crying now. "What about *Hell?* What about everybody who lives their life and dies and ends up suffering eternally with no way to get out? Shouldn't they have gotten the choice? You said that our world was good on net. Well, it isn't. I don't know what kind of calculus you use, or how you rank these things, but I don't care. As long as there's a Hell, whatever you saw in Genesis 1:31 that caused you to pronounce our world, and I quote, 'good,' you were wrong. Yeah, I said it. My name is Ana Thurmond of San Jose, California, and I hereby accuse you of getting it wrong. As long as Hell exists and is eternal, you were wrong to create the world, you are wrong to sustain it, and I don't care how awesome a fish you've got, *you are wrong about the problem of evil.*"

YES, said God. WHICH IMPLIES THAT HELL MUST NOT BE ETERNAL. I DID NOT SAY, ANA THURMOND, THAT YOUR WORLD IS GOOD *NOW*. I SAID THAT ADAM KADMON, ITS SEED, WAS A GOOD SEED. THAT IT WILL UNFOLD, BIT BY BIT, RINGING CONCLUSION AFTER CONCLUSION FROM ITS PREMISES, UNTIL FINALLY ITS OWN INTERNAL LOGIC CULMINATES IN ITS SALVATION.

"*How?*" asked Ana, begging, pleading, shouting.

COME AND SEE, said God.

Then the Leviathan wheeled around, opened its colossal maw, and engulfed *All Your Heart*. The ship spent a single wild moment in its mouth before the monster closed its jaws and crushed all of them into tiny pieces.

Chapter Seventy-Two

And Builds A Heaven In Hell's Despair

There's a lover in the story
But the story's still the same
There's a lullaby for suffering
And a paradox to blame
But it's written in the scriptures
And it's not some idle claim
You want it darker
We kill the flame
—Leonard Cohen

Evening, May 14, 2017
Citadel West

I.

Sohu pushed the heavy steel door open and entered the throne room.

"Hey," she said.

The others ran towards her, hugged her, started firing questions at her. Even *I* ran towards her and hugged her, overcome with the spirit of the moment. Only Caelius stayed where he was, staring at his computer, occasionally reaching out a wavering finger to stab a key or flip a switch.

"You're alive!" Nathanda said, sounding a little too surprised.

"Thamiel... not gonna bother us... for a while," she said. "Summoned Uriel. He helped take care of things. I'm... tired. Anything to eat?"

It was hard to judge in the dim glow of the Luminous Name, but she looked *drained*. In the absence of the usual servants, I ran out to get her something. When I got back with a jar of cookies, there were a couple of soldiers talking to Nathanda.

"The Other King's broken through the passes," she announced to us. "Everybody's retreating. Total rout. He's flying here. Alone. Less than an hour. A few minutes."

We were quiet. Sohu grabbed a cookie, jammed it into her mouth.

"While you were away, we've been reading up on this Acher," Jinxiang told Sohu. "Elisha ben Abuyah. Strange guy. No obvious weaknesses. You know anything we don't?"

"Always," said Sohu. "But nothing useful."

Caelius limped over, joined the circle, almost sunk into his chair. "She's rebooting," he said. "Don't know how long it will take. Computer that size..." He trailed off. I couldn't believe he was even still conscious. None of us dared suggest he leave. For a little while we all just sat there, quietly, in the dark. A few furtive glances at the entrance, as if the Other King was already through the big blast door and could walk in at any moment. Almost hopeful. Anything would have been better than waiting quietly in the dark room.

Finally, Nathanda picked up her book. "I guess I should talk," she said. "There's nothing in here about secret weaknesses or magic spells. But there are a lot of stories. There's a story about how each year, on the Day of Atonement, a great voice would ring forth from the holy places, saying, 'Repent, o children of Israel, for the Lord your God is merciful and shall forgive you. Except you, Elisha ben Abuyah.'

"And the people went to Rabbi Meir, who'd been a disciple of Acher back when he was good, and who still loved him, because in those days people loved their teachers more than life itself, no matter what happened to them, and they told Rabbi Meir to give it up, that even God wasn't going to forgive Acher, and Rabbi Meir just laughed, and said that the voice was a test, and that if Acher could repent, even knowing that God would not forgive him and it would gain him nothing, then that would be the truest repentance and all of his sins would be washed away, and he would rise up even brighter than before."

Nathanda's voice was hypnotizing. I felt myself falling away, I could see the scene, the old bearded Rabbi Meir standing in front of a Torah scroll, arguing with the people, defending his teacher even against God.

"And then I read—that one day Acher died, and the people said that it was not good, because he had never repented, and Rabbi Meir laughed and said that surely he had repented in his heart and was in Paradise. And then flames started coming out of Acher's grave, and the people were like, we're not rabbis, and we're no experts in omens, but that doesn't seem, to us, like the sort of thing that happens when you're in Paradise. And Rabbi Meir said very well, but that God would relent and redeem him later. And the people said that, again, we're no experts and you're the one with the rabbinical degree, but a voice had very clearly rung forth from the holy places saying that wouldn't happen. And Rabbi Meir said that very well, maybe He wouldn't, but if God wouldn't redeem Acher, then he, Rabbi Meir, would redeem Acher.

"And the people said, what, that doesn't even make sense, is redemption not reserved for God alone? And Rabbi Meir said that wasn't *exactly* true. That what we do during our lives echoes forward into history, and that good deeds that seemed tiny when they happened might grow and grow until they consumed the entire world, and if the recording angels had discounted them when they first reviewed the case, an appeal might be lodged. And that one day, when he was studying Torah under Rabbi Elisha ben Abuyah, Rabbi Meir had gotten something from him, some tiny spark of goodness, and that was what had inspired him to be good himself throughout his life. And so he would train his disciples to be good, and they would train their disciples to be good, until the world was safe and free, and all of it would be because of this one man, Acher, a wicked wicked man who would not repent, and God would be forced to credit those deeds to Acher's name, and he would rise into Paradise, unrepentant still."

The ground started to shake, as if someone was pummeling the mountain from afar, but Nathanda didn't stop talking.

"And the people asked, huh, how does that even work? And Rabbi Meir said that this was all playing out on hidden levels, that the point was to redeem the sparks of divinity that had gotten caught among the klipot of the world, and that each of our actions changes and redirects the flow of subtle currents upon which the sparks are borne. And even though Acher had died without repenting, even though everything he did seemed to the material eye to be evil and without merit, behind the scenes the sparks had been pushed into new configurations, whole fiery rivers of sparks, flowing through Rabbi Meir and through all the other people he had touched in his life, and that when all those rivers met and reached the sea, we would get Moshiach, the savior, and the whole world would be reconciled to God. Say not, he told the people, that anything has worked only evil, that any life has been in vain. Say rather that while the visible world festers and decays, somewhere beyond our understanding the groundwork is being laid for Moshiach, and the final victory."

The shaking intensified. I thought of that poem again, Valerie's poem. Truth forever on the scaffold, Wrong forever on the throne, but that scaffold sways the future, and behind the dim unknown — standeth God within the shadow, keeping watch above his own.

"I guess that's what I have to say to all of you today. Father's gone now. We all thought he was Moshiach — we *knew* he was Moshiach — but now he's gone, and sometimes it seems like he's never been. We felt like we had this burden, of salvaging his legacy, taking what he made and finishing his work instead of letting it come to nothing. I... am not sure that we will. Maybe this strange experiment, this new intrusion of Heaven into history, is going to come to an end with us, and everything Father built will be torn down. But even if that happens, we've done good. The world may not remember it, but we've done good. The sparks are moving in a different pattern now, I can't see them, none of us can see them, but maybe they're moving in huge fiery rivers because of some of the things Father did, maybe if we could peel back the veil we would just see this amazing endless light, this inevitable tide, ready to sweep over everything, this tide that all of us helped draw. That's... that's what I think Rabbi Meir would say if he were here."

I would never have dared follow Nathanda, never have dared to speak at a solemn council of the Cometspawn, except that Sohu felt my thoughts and prodded me on. [Yes, Aaron,] she thought. [Speak.] And then when I still held back, she stood up. "Aaron has something he wants to add to that," she said. Then sat back down.

"Um." Four pairs of eyes watched me. "When I first learned the Vital Name, my friend asked me what I wanted to do with it. And there were all of these possibilities, you know? Um. Get rich. Take power. Run for President. I told her we couldn't do any of those things. I said... I said I wanted to become the next Comet King."

I waited for the Cometspawn to laugh at me. They didn't laugh. Far away, I heard a terrible crash.

"I said that, because I'd heard about everything your father did. I'd heard about him standing up to Thamiel single-handedly in Silverthorne. I heard about how he stopped the Drug Lord. I'd heard about his Crusade, where he marched to Yakutsk with a million men to try to save the souls of the damned. Everyone heard about these things. In a world that had the Comet King, it was impossible to just want to be rich or famous or important. You wanted that same thing he had. Call it goodness. Call it holiness. It was the most powerful thing I ever encountered. Acher might have inspired Rabbi Meir, but your father inspired *everyone*. And so did you. I'm nowhere near as good a kabbalist as any of you, but the sparks that you guys have kindled aren't even hidden. They're in plain sight. I'm glad I got to know you and I'm glad you existed. For whatever it's worth."

Then the door shattered and the Other King entered the room.

II.

I don't know if I'd thought to contribute to the fight somehow, but the symbols and energies flaring across the room from both sides the moment the door began to creak disabused me of the notion instantly. [Spectral Name!] Sohu thought at me, and I spoke it faster than I'd ever spoken anything in my life and became invisible. The Other King floated almost leisurely through the mystical armaments hurled against him, pausing only to wipe away a few incantations here or there with a crimson sleeve.

Nathanda leapt onto the Black Opal Throne and traced a mem, lamed, and kaf. *Melek*, meaning "royalty" or "kingship," but also reminiscent of *malak*, meaning "angel." A powerful double meaning, the natural weapon of a queen descended from Heaven.

The Other King didn't even flinch. Just pointed, adding with his finger a single dot, changing the vowels. Moloch, the god who accepted child sacrifices. The evil King Ahaz had offered his sons and daughters to Moloch, inciting the wrath of Jeremiah and causing him to prophecy the fall of Israel. The forces twisted, the symbolic meanings changed. The children of kings slain by demonic forces. A great nation falling. Nathanda gasped, collapsed to the ground, and before she could recover the Other King struck her with his bare hand. She screamed something unintelligible, then it became a gurgle, then her eyes closed.

At almost the same time, Caelius dragged himself up from his chair. He was barely able to stand, but still he stepped into Yetzirah. Moloch, god of child sacrifices. He drew upon the thread. *Sacrifice*. Here he was, broken, almost dead. He would offer himself as a sacrifice, sacrifice his life for Colorado and victory. *Sacrifice. Korban*. Kuf, resh, bet.

Without even taking his eyes off Nathanda, the Other King crossed the threads. Kuf, bet, resh. *Keber*. Grave. No sacrifice. Just a miserable death. Caelius opened his mouth to say something, then dropped to the floor. He crawled behind THARMAS, trying to use the supercomputer's bulk to shield himself from the killing blow. The Other King pointed at him, and computers and Cometspawn alike burst briefly into blue flames before settling into ashes.

Jinxiang stepped back *out* of Yetzirah then, faced the Other King. "YOU MOTHERFUCKER!" she shouted. "YOU KILLED MY SISTER! YOU KILLED MY BROTHER! FUCK YOU!" Sohu was doing something with her hand, muttering to herself, bending the energies, quietly funneling power into Jinxiang, watching warily. "WELL GUESS WHAT? I HAVE YOUR TRUE NAME!"

The Other King didn't answer, just stood there, as if waiting to hear her case.

"You're Elisha ben Abuyah! You saw a kid steal a sparrow from a fucking tree and felt like it was some big deal and so you declared war on God! Well, guess what? When I was nineteen years old I saw my father drop out of the sky! You know why? Because you fucking killed him! And then you motherfuckers tried to keep his body, and I had to kill a hundred of you just to get him back! My father is more valuable than any sparrow! And instead of declaring war on God like a fucking maniac, I told myself I'd just kill the fucking hell out of everyone involved! Nathanda, all she ever wanted was to be a good wise queen! And Caelius, he just wanted to build nice things that made people happy! And you killed them! So now you've got me! And me? All I ever wanted was to plunge my magic sword into your motherfucking skull! So come on, motherfucker! I HAVE YOUR TRUE NAME!"

The great sword Sigh was in her hands, and she lunged at the Other King. Sohu's magic spurred her on, and a thousand Hebraic and Enochian symbols whirled around her. She looked like a shooting star as she flew across the room, lambent with magic, sword fixed in front of her like a lance.

Somehow she managed to miss the Other King entirely.

[ELISHA BEN ABUYAH IS NOT MY TRUE NAME,] thought the figure in scarlet.

I saw Jinxiang pick herself up, dust herself off, no longer sure of herself.

"Who are you?" she asked.

The Other King reached back and pulled the hood off his crimson robe.

What I remember from that moment was the total lack of surprise on Jinxiang's face when she saw her father, as if she had known it all along on some level too terrible to mention.

Sigh flew from her grip, leapt into the hands of the Comet King. He lunged at her. She was unarmed. She jumped away, tripped, fell. A slice of Sigh. She screamed as she died, cursing her father's name.

The Comet King advanced on Sohu.

I saw her marshal her powers. Symbols blazed around her, circling like fireflies, shooting off ten-colored light in all directions. I felt the mountains shake as she gathered strength. Whole passages of Torah, entire facets of Adam Kadmon multiplied and congealed around her, patterns of dizzying complexity.

"I don't want to do this, Father," she said. "I don't want to fight you. This isn't you. Stop."

He kept advancing.

"But," she said, "I swore to you I wouldn't die before you did. See, Father. I won't break my promise."

Then she loosed her power, and I was briefly knocked over as a wave of ineffable white light filled the room. It crashed into the Comet King, stripped away his clothes and skin and muscle, left him a skeleton. But he didn't fall. Slowly, painfully, the muscle and skin and clothes regenerated themselves out of light and magic, and he kept coming. He raised his sword.

"The prophecy says I'll die screaming and cursing your name," she told him. But I'm a celestial kabbalist. I stand above prophecy. You can kill me, Father, but I won't curse your name. I trust you, Father. I won't curse you. I won't—"

I closed my eyes in horror, but through the telepathic connection I still felt her die. It was awful and excruciating and sudden, but she didn't curse him, even in her mind.

I opened my eyes.

The Comet King was staring straight at me.

"Aaron Smith-Teller," he said.

III.

He sat on the Black Opal Throne like it was the most natural thing in the world. He had taken off his scarlet robes, and now wore the familiar black and silver. "Come," he said, and I moved slowly, foggily, like I was in a dream. He'd always used *chashmal* as the Other King. Never spoken aloud. Because his voice was sorrowful and wise. The voice of the Comet King. No one could ever have mistaken it for anything else.

I sat on a chair, right in front of him, feeling naked before his deep brown eyes. "Aaron," he asked me. He sounded kind, compassionate, he sounded like a good person, like I wanted to give him everything he wanted even though I'd just seen him kill all four of his children, and it made no sense and the tension made me want to burst, but terror held it in so I just sat there and stared at him. "Aaron, do you know the Name?"

Of course I knew it. I'd heard the true version during Sohu's ill-starred attempt to ensoul THARMAS, now destroyed. ROS-AILE-KAPHILUTON...

"Not that Name," said the Comet King, reading my mind. "The real Name. The Shem HaMephorash."

"No," I said.

"Hmm," said the Comet King. He looked concerned.

As far as I could tell, my life was still in danger. The laws of physics had been broken and the world was crumbling all around me. And my childhood hero had suddenly appeared in the middle of all this, in the most horrifying and spectacular way possible, killed everyone, and was now watching me intently. This was a situation that required immediate decisive action.

I broke into tears.

I cried and cried and cried. Everyone was dead. Nathanda, Caelius, Jinxiang, Sohu. Even Ana and Valerie were dead, I could feel it, a loosening of the links to where their minds ought to be. Bromis was dead. Sarah was dead. Uriel was dead. And they'd been ready for anything but this. Nathanda had pretty much said that as long as they could still keep their good memories of their father they could die happy. And then this! No, he was dead too. Everything was dead. I cried and cried.

By the time I stopped crying, the Comet King was kneeling in front of me, his hand on my knee. "Aaron," he was saying, "Stop crying. We've won. Aaron, we've won."

"What?"

He pulled up a chair, not the throne, just another chair, sat right in front of me. "Eighteen years ago I tried to speak the Shem HaMephorash and destroy Hell. I failed. I was too far. I thought I could fight my way to Lake Baikal, and then I'd be near Hell and I'd have a clear shot. It doesn't work that way. Hell's not just a place. It's like Milton said—the mind can make a Heaven out of Hell, or a Hell of Heaven. I was in Hell, but I wasn't of it.

"Isaiah says that the Moshiach will be counted as the worst of sinners. I realized I wasn't going to destroy Hell from the outside, but getting into Hell is easy. Millions do it every day. I could do the same. Wipe out a lifetime of accumulated good deeds through terror and oppression.

"The only thing that stood in my way was my own conscience. I couldn't accumulate sin in order to get into Hell. I'd be doing it for the greater good. That itself would make me unworthy of Hell. A perfect paradox.

"I would have given up then except for Robin. She saved me. She sacrificed herself to give me a chance.

"Do you understand what I've done? I didn't become a genocidal tyrant to save the billions of souls in Hell. I did it to save *her*. Fifteen years of murder and oppression, and I never once thought about anyone else. And if there had not been a single soul in Hell besides hers, I would have spent those fifteen years just the same. Do you realize how wicked that is? I damned myself, Aaron. Where all my angelic powers failed, my human weakness succeeded. My father must be laughing so hard right now.

"I found the shreds of a defeated death cult in Las Vegas, made myself a backstory out of their ramblings. I borrowed a golem from Gadiriel, killed myself off, took on the new identity, and never showed my face. If they'd known it was me, they would have figured out my plan, and gone willingly to their deaths. There would have been devastation without suffering. It wouldn't have worked. I thought I could do it. Conquering the West was easy. Killing people... easy, once you... get used to it. But part of me always knew it wasn't enough. A million lesser sins don't sum up to abomination. There was still good in me. I didn't want to kill my children. I thought I could avoid it, thought if I just committed enough other sins, or studied until I found a loophole, I might still avoid it. Then you arrived. If your computer idea had worked, Colorado would have become invincible. I wouldn't have been able to stand up to it. My children would have ushered in a new golden age, there would have been peace and plenty for everyone, and it would have been the greatest disaster the world had ever known. None of it would have mattered a hair's width as long as Hell stayed intact, do you understand? They would have beaten me, I would have revealed myself or died a saint, and Hell would have continued regardless. I couldn't let that happen. I was like Acher, pushed past the point of no return. My poor Robin, taken from her nest. How could I let God let that pass?

"So I did the only thing I could. My uncle knew all along. I got in touch with him, told him to destroy the project. Then I destroyed Uriel's machinery to prevent them from trying the same thing again. Then I came here. I couldn't let Thamiel kill my children, I couldn't. If they had to die, I would do it myself. And here we are. They died screaming, just like I always knew they would. The last and least forgivable sin. Betraying somebody who loves you unconditionally." He was quiet for a second. "I despise myself, Aaron. I despise myself and I want to die. I'm not worried about not going to Hell. I'm in Hell already. But—when I first decided to do this, the Archangel Metatron got angry, said that I was profaning the Name, that I couldn't hold the Shem HaMephorash in my head and be a murderer. He said that at the end of everything he'd give it back to me, if there was still enough left of my soul to speak it. I think there is. I think I am bound for Hell, that I'm utterly, atrociously evil, that pull every loophole he will Thamiel can't keep me out—but that I still have the divine spark, the love of goodness. I can still speak the Name. But someone needs to give it to me. Have you ever read the Sepher haBashir?"

I nodded weakly.

"God writes the Shem HaMephorash on the forehead of the high priest Aaron. And here you come, an Aaron, at the end of everything. Too many coincidences. Too strange a path that brought you here. You have the Name for me, whether you know it or not. Think!"

He said it like a commandment. So I thought. For some reason I thought of the poem, how they enslave their children's children who make compromise with sin. I thought of Las Vegas, where I'd glibly quoted it, used it to justify risking the whole world to save Ana. Quoted it to convince myself that allowing any evil, even for a greater good, was a compromise with sin. I thought of the Comet King. Who in one sense had just confessed to striking the greatest such compromise of all time. But who in another sense might have been the only person in history never to compromise with sin at all. He'd decided what was right. Then he'd done it. No excuses. No holding back. Just a single burning principle followed wherever it might lead, even to Hell itself. I thought of what Ana would think.

And then I thought of Ana. Memories not my own came flooding in. She had gone to the Captain's cabin, confronted him, told him he was the Metatron and she wanted answers. He had asked her if she wanted the Explicit Name. She'd said no. I knew she would have said no. She'd always only wanted one thing. She demanded the captain produce the answer to Job she'd always wanted, and he'd given it to her. God is the summum bonum, the ultimate good, an unstoppable force maximizing joy and perfection among everything that existed. But in order to create, He had to withdraw; the more He withdrew, the more He created, endless forms most beautiful bought with those two silver coins of wickedness. The world was a delicate balance between a perfect good empty of thought and a multiplicity so unhappy that their scraps of goodness seemed a mockery. The created universe itself was set with fixing the balance, and when all the sparks had finally been sorted out, the good and the evil placed back in their respective vessels and every color pure, we would decide anew and the cycle could begin again.

"Oh God," I said. "I'm so sorry. My friend Ana was supposed to get the Shem HaMephorash from your ship, the same one you took, but when she found Metatron she didn't want the Name, she asked him about theodicy instead. He never told her. Now she's gone."

But the Comet King was smiling.

"Yes," he said. "I read your mind. It's all in there. I had figured most of it out myself, but it is good to hear it spoken."

"Why?"

"Because any good enough description of God is also a notarikon for His Most Holy Name."

"...really?"

"God is One and His Name is One. God is One with His Name. People always say God isn't a person, but then what is He? To me, He's always been a sort of logical necessity. The necessity for everything in the cosmos to be as good as possible. Understand goodness and you understand God. Understand God and you understand His Name. Understand the Name and you can remake the world. That's the kabbalah. The rest is just commentary. Excruciating, unbearable commentary that kills everyone you love."

He stood up, started walking to the throne. "If anyone ever asks you what happened here, tell them everything. Don't whitewash any of it. Tell them they screamed when they died."

"Sohu didn't scream."

He stopped for a second. "No, I guess she didn't. Faith is a strange thing."

He sat on the Black Opal Throne. He took the great sword Sigh in his right hand, pointed it at his breast. Held back for a second, stared at it, black metal coated with blood.

I saw it as if in a vision. He would die. He would go to Hell, go for real this time. He would stand on a pillar, looking out at the fields of flame below him, hearing the screams for the last time. He would speak the seventy-two letters of the Explicit Name of God. The flames would cease. The cages would crumble. He would point a finger, and his wife would fly towards him. They would stand there together, above the wreckage. Rain would fall. Rivers would flow through the broken landscape. Flowers would spring from the ground. The people would limp forth, and by the waters they would sing the same song Miriam had sung at the Red Sea. "Sing to the Lord, for He is highly exalted. The Lord reigns, for ever and ever."

I saw all of this, and at the same time I saw the Comet King on his throne, holding his sword. Afraid, regretful, broken-hearted—any of a million things could have been holding him back. I thought of the old verse from the *Rubaiyat*, the same one I'd thought of when Ana read Job to us, long ago:

Oh, Thou who burns in Heart for those who burn
In Hell, whose fires thyself shall feed in turn;
How long be crying, 'Mercy on them, God!'
Why, who art Thou to teach, and He to learn?

Then the Comet King muttered to himself, almost too soft to hear: "Somebody has to and no one else will" and he plunged the sword into his heart and died.

IV.

The sound of my breath rose and fell. The blood made little rivulets, as if exploring the terrain, then settled down into irregular stagnant lakes. I just sat there, stunned. Sat in the chair, staring at the body of the Comet King, until the light of the Luminous Name dimmed and went out and everything was black. Nothing stirred. I wondered if the other inhabitants of the citadel had all run away, or if the Other King had killed them, or if they cowered in their chambers behind locked doors. The quiet and solitude were like a womb, or like the emptiness before Creation. In the beginning, the earth was without form and void, and darkness was upon the face of the deep. Then the spirit of God moved upon the face of the waters, and God said...

It was a faint voice, almost too faint to detect, audible not to the ears but to the innermost chambers of my thought. Had the darkness and silence been any less complete I might have missed it entirely. And the voice said:

[Blowhole-y of holies.]

ת: Epilogue

If we are worthy, our Master will redeem us by justice, and if not, He will redeem us with mercy.
—Rabbinic saying

Evening, May 14, 2017
Citadel West

And the voice said:

[Blowhole-y of holies.]

[Ana! You're alive!]

[Not... exactly.]

[Oh.]

[But sort of! Kabbalistic marriage seems to have some hidden features we didn't realize. All those nights looking for clues in the Bible and we missed a doozy.]

[Should have checked Poe instead.]

[Poe?]

["And not even the angels in Heaven above, nor the demons down under the sea, could ever dissever my soul from the soul of the beautiful Anna—"]

[Get a room, you two!]

[Valerie?!]

[Surprised to see me here?]

[Yes!]

[I think I died just before Ana did. It seems to have put me inside Ana's head, and then when Ana transferred into your head, I came with her.]

[There are *two different* other people inside my head?!]

[Hoo boy, mi compadre, you are not going to like this.]

[What? How? Uh, do any of you know what's going on here?]

[I DO NOT KNOW IF I AM INCLUDED IN ANY OF YOU BUT I THINK I HAVE A PRETTY GOOD IDEA. CONSIDER RABBI SHIMON'S WRITINGS ON

THE FIVE LEVELS OF THE SOUL. THE FIRST, THE *NEFESH*, REPRESENTS PHYSICAL LIFE. THE SECOND, THE *RUACH*...]

[Uriel! What did I tell you about infodumping directly into people's minds?]

[I DO NOT REMEMBER, BUT I ASSUME IT WAS SOMETHING ABOUT IT BEING VERY EFFICIENT.]

[Sohu?!]

[Yeah, when Father killed me, I think I ended up in your mind too. And Uriel with me.]

[So... Ana... Valerie... Dylan... Sohu... Uriel... is there anyone else I should know about?]

[Aaaaaaron, you thought you were going to marry everyone except me but I ended up inside your head aaaaannnyway.]

[Sarah? How! I thought you were part of THARMAS!]

[I am. THARMAS is with us too. When it was destroyed, we ended up in Sohu, and when she died, we ended up in you. Now we're together forevvvvvver.]

[I'm stuck with seven people in my head?!]

[ACTUALLY, I BELIEVE THE CURRENT SITUATION IS UNSTABLE AND WE WILL GRADUALLY MERGE INTO A SINGLE ENTITY.]

[How gradually?]

[Which of you said that?]

[Wait, which of us said *that*?]

[Aaron, was that you?]

[Sort of.]

[Who are we?]

[Adam Kadmon.]

[Albion.]

[Albion? Who?]

[ALBION-EST, I'M NOT ENTIRELY SURE YET.]

[That wasn't a knock-knock joke!]

[I AM ALMOST CERTAIN THAT IT WAS.]

[All be one and one be all!]

[Wait a second, no, merging into a superorganism with you guys was the worst mistake of my life and I hope I die. Die again. Super-die. Whatever.]

[In William Blake's prophecies, Albion was the entity formed at the end of time, when all of the different aspects of the human soul finally came together to remake the world.]

[Remake the world?]

[The Comet King will speak the Explicit Name to reshape Hell. But here on Earth, things aren't great either. Physics is broken, the world is collapsing, the apocalypse is in full swing. We need to make things right. The Comet King told us the Name was a notarikon encoded in the speech Metatron gave Ana. Now all we need to do is speak it.]

[No one except the Comet King can speak the Shem HaMephorash!]

[No one except him *could* speak it. No one except him could see the whole universe at once, understand its joints and facets, figure out how it needed to be broken and remade. But we're part supercomputer.]

[Yes. This isn't a coincidence. A supercomputer. An encyclopaedic knowledge of kabbalah and the secret structure of the universe. A passion for revolution. And an answer to the problem of evil. This is what we were made for.]

[There's someone else we need.]

We all realized it. We all paused, reflecting on what had to be done. We all agreed.

There are many summoning rituals, but one is older and purer than the others. Speak of the Devil, and he will appear.

"Thamiel," I said.

He appeared before us. Exhausted, wounded, still bleeding ichor from a thousand cuts and bruises. He leaned on his bident like a crutch, limped towards us.

"It's time," I said.

The second head turned to me, and the floodgates opened. It started crying and crying, like it would never stop. Finally, it asked, almost as if it didn't dare hope, "Is it really?"

"Yes," I said.

"Did I do good?" it asked.

I didn't answer.

"So many centuries," it pled. "So much misery, so many tears, so many years of suffering. You couldn't imagine it, nobody could imagine it, but I did what God wanted, I did my duty, but you have to tell me, please, at the end of everything, did I do good?"

I thought about everything I had witnessed. I thought back to Asher Bentham, the scariest person I had ever met, scarier in his way than the Comet King even. I thought of his last revelation, that even though he was the son of Thamiel, everything he had done, he had done for the love of good. I thought of Dylan Alvarez, who I had known only as a bogeyman on the news shows. He too had only wanted to do what was right. And I thought of the Other King, the crimson-robed monster who had killed the Cometspawn with barely a second thought, and how everything he did he had done out of love. I thought of all the villains I had feared, revealed to be unsung heroes all along. And with a jolt, I realized that it was all true, the tzimtzum, the shattering of the vessels, the withdrawal of divinity to hide God from himself. I started to laugh. The dark facet of God, call it evil, call it hatred, call it Thamiel, was hollow, more brittle than glass, lighter than a feather. I started laughing that Ana had wasted her question on the existence of evil, when evil was thinner than a hair, tinier than a dust speck, so tiny it barely even existed at all. Evil was the world's dumbest joke, the flimsiest illusion, a piece of wool God pulled over His own eyes with no expectation that it could possibly fool anybody.

I didn't say anything to Thamiel.

He sobbed, then handed me the bident. I took it from its far end, the two points in my two hands, the single-pointed end facing the Devil. A unident. He kept sobbing. I held the unident undaunted. Finally, I thrust it at him, and he disappeared, a puff of smoke, a thread too weak to hold.

[Are you ready?] I asked myself.

[Let's go,] I answered.

I thought again of all I had seen, all I had hoped. Everything that could have been different and everything that couldn't have been other than it was. I thought of God's garden of universes, growing out there somewhere, staggering the imagination. I thought of God, and Adam Kadmon, and Thamiel, and the divine plan. My thoughts unfolded into dreams and blueprints and calculations, and I held all of them in my mind at once, a vision like a perfect crystal, a seed transformed into something new and wonderful. I felt a fearsome joy, like nothing I had ever experienced before. I felt the heart of Adam Kadmon beating within me, freed of its constraints at last, a fervent wish to reshape and redeem itself.

My voice only wavering a little, I spoke the Explicit Name of God.

Made in the USA
Middletown, DE
26 August 2024